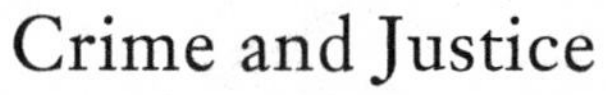

Crime and Justice

Crime and Justice
A Review of Research

Edited by Michael Tonry

VOLUME 44

The University of Chicago Press, Chicago and London

The University of Chicago Press, Chicago 60637
The University of Chicago Press, Ltd., London

Printed in the United States of America

ISSN: 0192-3234

ISBN: 978-0-226-33757-9

LCN: 80-642217

The paper used in this publication meets the minimum requirements of American National Standard for Information Sciences—Permanence of Paper for Printed Library Materials, ANSI Z39.48-1984. ♾

Contents

Preface

Upward of 400 essays have appeared in *Crime and Justice*. The aim has been to publish thoughtful, exhaustive analyses of the best work in a wide range of disciplines on crime and the criminal justice system. A plethora of subjects has been covered. Many have been revisited once, some several times, a few many times. This volume contains two first-timers, by Robert Crutchfield on race, crime, and social class and by Torbjørn Skardhamer and his colleagues on marriage and crime. Both are in part intellectual histories. Each casts new light and challenges conventional wisdom on subjects about which many believe there is little more to be learned.

The other essays to greater and lesser extents are sequels. By themselves they provide informed summaries and critiques of their subjects in our time. Together with their predecessors, they provide series of snapshots of knowledge and ways of thinking as they have evolved over time.

- Cassia Spohn's essay on racial injustice in the criminal justice system, the most comprehensive to appear in *Crime and Justice*, builds on earlier writings over four decades by Joan Petersilia, Robert J. Sampson and Janet Lauritsen, Richard Frase, and Matthew Melewski and me.
- John MacDonald's "Community Design and Crime" is a successor to writings by John Baldwin (vol. 1), Wesley Skogan, and David Kirk and John Laub and also many essays in volume 8, *Communities and Crime* (1986), which catalyzed revived interest in community crime studies.
- Brandon Welsh and David Farrington's examination of cost-benefit studies of crime prevention programs builds on their own 2000 essay and on a series of ground-breaking writings on developmental criminology by Farrington (vol. 1), Rolf Loeber, Marc Leblanc, Richard Tremblay, and their colleagues.

- Kathryn Monahan and her colleagues, building on the same landmarks, show how the steady accumulation of knowledge on brain science is changing ways of thinking about adolescent development and behavior.
- Beau Kilmer and his colleagues' essay on cross-national analyses of data on drug use, distribution, and law enforcement builds on earlier drug policy writings over 30 years by Peter Reuter, Mark Kleiman, and Jonathan Caulkins and parallels James Lynch's volume 34 essay on cross-national analyses of victimization data.
- Marianne van Ooyen-Houben and Edward Kleeman's essay on Dutch drug policy admirably brings up to date the story started in Eddy Leeuw's classic 1991 essay.
- Cheryl Jonson and Francis Cullen's examination of the effectiveness of prison reentry initiatives, community corrections programs in new garb, follows a long line of earlier analyses over 30 years by Cullen, Ken Pease, Joan Petersilia alone and with Susan Turner, and me.
- James Lynch and Lynn Addison's essay on victimization is in one sense part of a long series that Richard F. Sparks, the initiator of what became the British Crime Survey, started in volume 1. In another sense it is as new as today's newspaper. Janne Kivivuori's volume 43 article showed that declines in cultural acceptance of violence and disorder have caused victimization surveys to underestimate declines in crime rates. Lynch and Addison dig deep into US victimization data looking for similar evidence.
- Finally, last and most likely least, my federal sentencing policy history since 1984 follows comparable earlier accounts by Ronald Wright on North Carolina, Richard Frase on Minnesota, and Roxanne Lieb and David Boerner on Washington State.

Crime and Justice prefaces usually devote less space than this to detailing a volume's content. Readers are better advised to read what a writer has written than what someone else says about it, and in any case will decide for themselves whether the writing has merit. I distinguished novelty and continuity in subjects to help myself understand *Crime and Justice*'s distinctive past and possible future roles.

When the series' first editorial board meeting convened in 1977, meta-analyses were unheard of and systematic reviews of the sort associated in criminology with the Campbell Collaboration were not yet a glimmer in anyone's eye. The idea of a high-quality, closely vetted annual review of research made sense to the National Academy of Sciences panel that proposed it, the National Institute of Law Enforcement and Criminal Justice personnel who initiated and funded it, and the people who were asked to serve as editors and editorial board members. Other disciplines had influential annual reviews, and literatures in criminology and related disciplines were growing rapidly, so why not give it a shot? Norval Morris and I did: *Crime and Justice: An Annual Review of Research.* "Annual" was later dropped from the subtitle when the series undertook occasional publication of additional thematic volumes.

Crime and Justice has justified its creation. Many of its essays are widely read and have had long half-lives. Some published in 1979 and the 1980s, and many published in the 1990s, continue to be widely cited. Intermittently since the early 1990s, and most recently in 2010 and 2012, the series has topped impact lists in criminology citation analyses. *Crime and Justice* essays appear at or near the tops of lists of the most-cited articles of many major scholars of the past third of a century, including Alfred Blumstein, Philip J. Cook, Anthony N. Doob, Jeffrey A. Fagan, David P. Farrington, John Laub, Norval Morris, Daniel Nagin, Joan Petersilia, Alex Piquero, Peter Reuter, Julian Roberts, and Lawrence W. Sherman.

That is all good, and satisfying, but it speaks only to the past. Whatever the case may prove to be in the more electronically connected world of 2025 and later, this volume convinces me that the series has a role to play for the foreseeable future. It has not been made obsolete by meta-analyses and systematic reviews, which, like all scholarly writings, are of variable quality, uncertain influence, and divergent findings.

They suffer from two other shared problems. First, because they aim to exorcize the influence on outcomes of contextual and other unmeasured variations between studies by use of standardized selection criteria and quantitative modeling, they oversimplify. The resulting reports often have a cookie-cutter quality: specification of a narrow hypothesis to be tested, descriptions of selection criteria and a search strategy, tabular presentation of characteristics of the selected studies, tabular presentation of results, and usually brief discussions of findings and essential qualifications. The analyses are almost never replicated by others; they must be taken at face value and accepted as presented, which means that the scholarly world seldom gains more than a table of numbers.

The solution is to assure that meta-analyses and systematic reviews are carried out only by scholars of the first rank at the tops of their games and that they have time and space to reflect on the theoretical and practical plausibility of putative findings and on their real-world application. That is the second problem. Such analyses are, with important exceptions, not generally executed by top-flight scholars. When they are, journal publication conventions seldom allow time and space for thoughtful reflection and speculation.

Crime and Justice at its best does more. It attracts scholars of the first rank and allows them time and space to consider current knowledge, including from meta-analyses, systematic reviews, and others' narrative reviews, and to reflect on its implications and applications. Drafts are subjected to close scrutiny by paid referees who might themselves have been asked to write the papers being reviewed. Anyone who, in increasingly specialized scholarly worlds, has deep knowledge of the subjects of all the essays in this volume will recognize that eight or nine of them include among their authors the most distinguished active senior scholar of its subject, or one of the leading two or three. The others are by midcareer people who will in due course be widely acknowledged to fit that description.

The series has been fortunate throughout its existence to be able to attract writers of comparable accomplishment and promise. That partly explains why so many essays are cited so often and for so long. Throughout this preface I have mentioned essays published in earlier volumes, especially some published nearly four decades ago in volume 1. Taken alone, volume 44 writings provide rich cross-sectional impressions, still lifes, of their subjects; taken with their predecessors, they provide moving pictures. It could not have been done, or done well, without the painstaking and indefatigable talents of Su Smallen, to whom, as always, I am immensely grateful. Others will decide for themselves whether the result is useful to them.

Michael Tonry
Isola d'Elba, Italy, July 2015

Robert D. Crutchfield

From Slavery to Social Class to Disadvantage: An Intellectual History of the Use of Class to Explain Racial Differences in Criminal Involvement

ABSTRACT

Social class differences have been invoked to explain perceived racial differences in criminal involvement in the United States since the middle of the nineteenth century. Scholars have joined with the public and the media to make such arguments with mixed success. Despite criticism of the theories and research methods used and contradictory evidence, social class arguments have persisted. Among the most enduring are subculture of violence and subculture of poverty theories, which purportedly explain instrumental crimes such as property crime, drug sales, and robbery, but also violence including homicide and assault. Proponents argue that African Americans are carriers of pro-crime norms and values. Criminologists and sociologists have recently advanced more parsimonious theories that posit that structured social and economic disadvantage account for racial and ethnic patterns of crime. Good data and analysis provide compelling supporting evidence. Ethnographic evidence has compellingly shown that observable cultural differences are consequences of disadvantage and not causes of the conditions in which the impoverished poor live.

Electronically published July 28, 2015

Robert D. Crutchfield is professor of sociology, University of Washington.

0192-3234/2015/0044-0001$10.00

If you have thought about crime in the United States, you have thought about race and crime. To think about crime anywhere in the world is to think also about how and why some segments of the population have more criminal involvement and more victimization, or about differences in how states vary in responding to crimes by people of different groups (e.g., Tonry 1995; Wortley 2003; Crutchfield and Pettinicchio 2009; Crutchfield, Pettinicchio, and Robbins 2013). Where race is not the focus, differences in ethnicity, religion, immigration status, or some other marker of being "the other" are part of how we think about and talk about crime. In the United States and increasingly in other nations, higher levels of criminality among "others" are popularly attributed to one of two factors: inferiority or social class position. The "inferiority" explanations range from misplaced and antiquated biological conceptions of race to ethnocentric comparisons of cultures. A popular explanation of anti–Latin American immigration riots in Spain, for example, was that rioters were reacting to imported gang activity (Harter 2007). The French foreign minister at the time, and later president, Nicholas Sarkozy justified punitive police actions in Paris suburbs on the basis that the rioters were merely "thugs," who just happened to be North African and Muslim "immigrants." Notably, many participants have been residents of France for more than a generation, were French citizens, or both, but still were not considered to be French (Haddad and Balz 2006).

Efforts to explain racial and ethnic differences in criminality by explaining that "subordinated others" frequently are of the lower social and economic classes are common among both scholars and the general public, especially among those of a more liberal political persuasion. These explanations are the subject of this essay.

Some basic definitional clarifications are in order. Here in writing about race and ethnicity, I refer to basic understandings by educated Americans that are used by most scholars of race, crime, and ethnicity. The relevant groups in the United States are Asians, blacks, Latinos, Native Americans, and whites or, if one prefers, European Americans. These categories are socially constructed and meld scholarly understanding of the meaning of race and ethnicity. Within these groups there are important subdivisions. Within the category "black" are African Americans, a growing African immigrant population, and people whose families trace their lineage to the islands of the Caribbean. The Latino or "Hispanic" population is lumped together in government data collections but includes groups of people who have been in what is now the United States far longer than many who are generally referred to as "white." Hispanics include people from many different nations, people who are native to the United States, immigrants who have long lived in the United States, and more recent arrivals. The same is true of "Asians." Unfortunately, criminologists have only recently begun to explore this complexity. Most of the arguments and research discussed here use the black/white dichotomy that has long characterized the criminological literature. Since the 2010 census of the US population, Latinos have been the second-largest demographic group in the country, and criminologists have fortunately moved beyond the black/white dichotomy (Peterson, Krivo, and Hagan 2006). Where appropriate, I discuss some of that more recent literature, mostly concerning Latinos.

It is also important to define what is meant by "crime." My focus is on common crimes of property and violence, because that is where the literature on race and crime has focused. If we begin a conversation that asks "what racial group commits more crime, and why?" we come to very different answers if the focus is on common crimes, as has been true of most criminological literature on race, crime, and social class. If the focus is on white-collar crime, or even includes white-collar crime (or organized crime), we would be asking "why are white folks so crime-prone?" Unfortunately, criminologists have not frequently paid much attention to that issue and would likely say the reason is simply that whites are more frequently positioned to have opportunities for white-collar violations, so it is not very interesting. Some would disagree. Still others say that the lack of serious work on this topic says a great deal about American society and perhaps even more about American criminology. Nevertheless, my aim here is to examine the intellectual history of our collective use of conceptions of social class to explain why there are racial differences in common crime involvement.

Social class explanations for racial differences in criminality are popular because of two sets of observed correlations. First, more African Americans are involved in some types of crimes, especially the kinds of crimes likely to result in prison sentences, than are whites, and mostly people from the lower social classes serve time for these offenses. African Americans are overrepresented among lower socioeconomic classes. Second, neighborhoods, cities, and states with larger African American populations have higher crime rates, and those same places frequently also have higher poverty rates. No serious scholar should stumble into the ecological fallacy and interpret this second set of correlations in aggregate data as meaning that poor black people are the ones committing the crimes. Just that connection, however, perhaps because of the first set of correlations, is frequently made in the criminological literature, and it is certainly made in "polite company." In examining the intellectual history of use of social class to explain the correlation between race and crime, we should be careful to note that this explanation has been made at both individual and aggregate levels. Both levels have implications for our capacity to understand race and crime better by taking account of differences in racial distribution across social classes.

I use the notion of social class very broadly, unencumbered by the usual measurements of socioeconomic status or SES employed by social scientists. By social class I mean any and all distinctions in economic positioning or standing of individuals or groups. That ranges from aligning people on a linear social class hierarchy based on income and occupation to slave and free distinctions and variations between these poles such as those invented by Jim Crow, post–Civil War America. In this essay I trace efforts to explain that African Americans and increasingly Latinos engage in more crime because they disproportionately come from or live as lower social class people.

The intellectual history of this line of reasoning is rooted far back in American history. It predates the founding of the United States. Justifications for the slave trade included European conceptions of Africans as lazy and brutish and included assertions that they had only themselves to "blame" for the conditions in which they lived (conditions that were negatively and ethnocentrically evaluated by Eurocentric writers) and their enslavement (Daykin 2006; Rönnbäck 2014). Along the way, I consider arguments and evidence that contest the assertion that members of these groups are indeed more criminal, because much of that challenge is based on disputed conceptions of what social class means and how scholars have measured the critical concepts race and crime.

The first part of this essay briefly considers conceptions of Africans, slavery, and violations of law before the twentieth century. It should not be a surprise that conceptions were crude, but they set the stage for arguments that became popular in the last half of the twentieth century. The second section explores early answers to the question "why are more blacks arrested?" This became an important question as the United States became increasingly urbanized at the same time as large numbers of African Americans moved from the rural South to cities in the North, South, and West in what demographers call the Great Migration. Subcultural theories emerged to explain higher black crime rates that became evident when the federal government established the Uniform Crime Reports. A survey of theoretical and methodological debates follows. Finally, I discuss the reemergence of structural arguments that focus on social and economic disadvantage, and more nuanced versions of cultural considerations, that help provide good sociological-criminological explanations for why members of some communities of color have higher rates of crime.

I. The Early Years

We have no good measures to distinguish racial or ethnic differences in criminality before the middle of the twentieth century, and the measures developed then have been subjected to considerable criticism. The lack of measurement, though, did not stop people from asserting that blacks were more violent, more dangerous. The nineteenth-century southern writer and reformer, George W. Cable, describing the "sentiments" of white America that justified slavery wrote,

> First, then, what are these sentiments? Foremost among them stands the idea that he is of necessity an alien. He was brought to our shores a naked, brutish, unclean, captive, pagan savage,* to be and remain a kind of connecting link between man and the beasts of burden. The great changes to result from his contract with a superb race of masters were not taken into account. As a social factor he was intended to be as purely zero as the brute at the other end of his plow-line.
>
> *Sometimes he was not a mere savage but a trading, smithing, weaving, town-building, crop-raising barbarian. (Cable [1889] 1969, p. 6)

Where did these early conceptions of Africans come from? Thomson (2008) argues that there was not a coherent narrative about Africans to base the slave trade on until the abolition movement gained traction in Europe in the mid-eighteenth century. The abolitionists' narrative was countered by people who used "science" to justify slavery by arguing that Africans were a different sort of human, in need of the civilizing influence and religious enlightenment that Europeans could provide within the context of slavery. Scientific racism continued to be a basis for opposing equality for blacks in the United States well after emancipation (Smith 2007).

Perhaps ironically, in spite of the "brutish," "dangerous" nature of the African, very few were imprisoned in the slave-holding South before the Civil War. That region lagged behind the rest of the nation in penal reforms begun by Jeremy Bentham and others that led to the building of penitentiaries in the North. It made little economic sense to punish black law violators by locking them up and depriving their masters of their labor, so punishment, frequently harsh and "brutish," was left to the master.[1] After the war, after emancipation, when black southerners were no longer the property of slaveholders, when they were freedmen, the numbers of blacks held in captivity as convicts by states grew dramatically (Crutchfield and Finke 1983).

It is popularly believed that the convict lease system in the South after Reconstruction was a means of reinstating slavery. It is more accurate to portray it as part of a larger system to subjugate blacks and keep them subservient and available as cheap labor, shifting the economic or class position of blacks from being slaves to their new roles as sharecroppers and tenant farmers. The convict leasing system provided labor for dangerous and difficult jobs including mining and railroad construction and served as a threat to keep free black workers in line (Adamson 1983).

Cable's description of the lease system indicates how racialized it was. Cable, when studying southern prisons, found the published census numbers to be hiding something onerous, much as contemporary sociologists studying American prisons have done (Pettit and Western 2004; Pettit and Lyons 2009; Pettit 2012):

> The official testimony of the prisons themselves is before the world to establish the conjectures that spring from our reasoning. After the erroneous takings of the census of 1880 in South Carolina had been corrected the population was shown to consist of about twenty blacks to every thirteen whites. One would therefore look for a preponderance of blacks on the prison lists; and inasmuch as they are a people only twenty years ago released from servile captivity, one would not be surprised to see that preponderance large. Yet, when the actual

[1] US census reports for 1850 and 1860 show very few blacks held in prison, but by the 1870 census, even though this was during Reconstruction, their numbers increased considerably (Crutchfield and Finke 1983). For a description of slave punishments in the pre–American Revolutionary War period, see Aguirre (1999) or Paton (2001).

> numbers confront us, our speculations are stopped with a rude shock; for what is to account for the fact that in 1881 there were committed to the State prison in Columbia South Carolina, 406 colored persons and but 25 whites? The proportion of blacks sentenced to the whole black population was one into every 1488; that of the whites to the white population was but one in every 15,644. (Cable 1969, pp. 32–33)

The difference was that blacks were disproportionately held outside of what were, even by standards of the day, awful prison conditions in the South Carolina penitentiary, in the much worse lease systems, exploiting their labor, shortening their lives, and buttressing the post-Reconstruction racial and social hierarchy. Cable noted similar distributions in other states that used variations on the convict leasing systems.

We cannot credibly use racial distributions in nineteenth-century imprisonment to say anything meaningful about differences in criminal involvement, but at that time they were used for that purpose. This changed only marginally well into the twentieth century before the public, politicians, and even criminologists made the "enlightened" move toward using arrest statistics to demonstrate that blacks engaged in more crime than whites (e.g., von Hentig 1940; McKeown 1948). And, like the apologists for slavery noted by Cable, some attributed the higher number of blacks in confinement in the nineteenth century and higher levels of arrests in the twentieth century to the brutish nature of people of African blood. More liberal thinkers, like Cable himself, pointed to social conditions and notably blacks' economic positioning and social conditions.[2]

II. Why Are More Blacks Arrested?

When the FBI began collecting crime statistics for the Uniform Crime Reports in the early 1930s, arrest rates became available nationally, or nearly nationally. It became possible to make statements about characteristics of those taken into custody. Higher black arrest rates fit with the predominant belief that blacks were more involved in crime than whites. That led for many to the conclusion that blacks were more frequently arrested because they engage in more and more serious criminal

[2] At the turn of the twentieth century, African American intellectuals from different sides of the political spectrum argued that black law violations resulted from the conditions and circumstances of black day-to-day life (Du Bois 1899; Washington 1912).

behavior. This was a data source in which the more "liberal" explanation, the lower social class position occupied by nearly all black people, could not be tested.

While many assumed that social class differences explained racial differences, others took a different tack: blacks commit more crimes because they are embedded in a pro-crime subculture. That alternative is a hybrid of the two extremes I described above: either the brutish, in-born constitution of people of African descent makes them more criminal or continuous occupation of the lower rungs of the social class stratification ladder is responsible. This argument has the added benefit that it can explain their higher levels of both materially motivated property crime and violence. Underlying many low-SES-leads-to-high-crime arguments is an instrumental conception of crime motivation. With the exception of robbery and homicides resulting from robbery, however, additional conceptual work is required to explain why people from the lower social classes would be any more likely than other people to commit rapes or assaults or to kill without pecuniary motivation. That explanation was provided by those who argued that African Americans were affected by a subculture of violence or by subcultures of poverty values and beliefs.

A. Crime-Conducive Subcultures

African Americans who must live in lower-income places, which meant nearly all until late in the twentieth century, were exposed to and said to be more likely to internalize norms and values and patterns of behavior that made crime more likely. They became carriers of a crime-conducive subculture. Two variants of subculture theory link racial differences in crime to racial differences in social class: most prominently the subculture of violence thesis advanced by Wolfgang and Ferracuti (1967) and various theories of the subculture of poverty that have been prominent in sociology and criminology (e.g., Banfield 1970; Murray 1984).

The subculture of violence theory posited that high rates of violence in inner-city communities existed because residents carried pro-violence values and norms. The subculture of poverty thesis is that the values of the poor either directly cause crime, because people socialized into particular sets of values, norms, and beliefs engage in crime rather than patiently wait for legitimate opportunities, or indirectly cause crime because their values do not attach sufficient importance to such things as education and hard work. A fundamental thesis is that poverty subcultural values are a fundamental cause of poor peoples' continuing impoverished state. Central to both the subculture of violence and the subculture of poverty arguments are two tenets: first, that values, norms, beliefs, and patterns of behavior that are different from those of people in the cultural mainstream are fundamentally responsible for the criminal involvement of particular segments of the population (carriers of the subculture); and, second, that subcultures are passed down intergenerationally, primarily within families.

Wolfgang and Ferracuti did not limit the appearance of subcultures of violence to the lower classes but noted that there is fertile ground for the emergence of such values among those living in poor sections of cities. And, while they say that there are other generators of such subcultures, a great deal of their discussion is about its emergence in inner-city, poor, predominantly black neighborhoods. Their theory emerged from their study of homicide patterns in Philadelphia. They noticed higher rates in poorer neighborhoods and from that observation developed their version of the subculture of violence. Many of Philadelphia's black residents in the 1950s and 1960s lived in those poor places. So while their version of the theory is not expressly about race, they, and subsequently others, used it to explain why African Americans have higher rates of involvement in criminal violence than do native-born whites or most white immigrant groups. They specify that subcultures of violence emerge in lower-class, urban, nonwhite communities and are perpetuated by the social structure of the place, characteristics of the families that live there, the value system in place, and an emphasis on aggression. Poverty is central to their thesis, leading to more female-headed households with mothers who, more frequently than their white middle-class counterparts, act aggressively toward their partners and their children. This leads to higher levels of female homicide alongside high levels of male homicide, which result from street aggressions and gang activity. Childrearing (punishing) patterns help to transmit the subculture into subsequent generations.

Davis (1981, pp. 156–61) lumped the subculture of violence thesis together with differential association theory (Sutherland 1924) and other formulations that appeared in reaction to and rejection of consensus conceptions of society embraced by early disorganization theorists and functionalists (Park, Burgess, and McKenzie 1925; Davis 1937; Davis and Moore 1945). Her argument was that Wolfgang and Ferracuti acknowledged normative differences but would not take the political step to link the lot of the poor to their position in the social stratification system. Historian Roger Lane (1986), although he focused on an earlier period (1860–1900), studying many of the sections of Philadelphia that Wolfgang and Ferracuti wrote about, attributed black violence to "exclusion" (social and economic stratification, which Davis would likely consider more politically honest) rather than to cultural differences.

Another subculture of violence thesis, focusing on southern subculture, attributes pro-violence values that blacks purportedly carry to their southern roots (Gastil 1971; Butterfield 2008). Slavery, a harsh, violent, brutish system, was perpetuated by violence, as was the post-Reconstruction Jim Crow system. And lynching, used widely to keep blacks in their place, was a regular occurrence well into the twentieth century (Tolnay and Beck 1995). Gastil (1971) used the southern subculture of violence thesis to explain high rates of violent crime in the southern states and argued that blacks took it with them when they moved to the cities of the North and South. Butterfield (2008) traces high southern regional violence rates to the honor and manhood culture of the Scottish Highlands, brought to the American South by Scotch-Irish immigrants.

Subculture of poverty arguments have some elements in common with Wolfgang and Ferracuti's thesis. Two notable examples are Banfield's widely read *The Unheavenly City* (1970) and Murray's *Losing Ground* (1984). Murray's book was widely seen as providing the intellectual blueprint for federal welfare reform during the 1990s. Banfield, like Wolfgang and Ferrecuti, asserted that his was not a theory about race. Few who read it, however, would have thought of many other groups than blacks as he described how people of the lower classes, lacking middle-class values, such as capacity and willingness to defer gratification, were more likely to engage in behaviors, including crime, that caused urban problems. For Banfield, higher rates of crime among African Americans resulted from higher proportions of that population not having absorbed and not reflecting important middle-class values.

Banfield and Wolfgang and Ferracuti in their different ways link the emergence and perpetuation of subcultures to poverty and life in lower-class communities. They give a slight tip of the intellectual hat to the social forces that lead to people living in these circumstances. There is, especially for Banfield, an implication that these lower-class people, these black lower-class people, are there because of their own failings, because of their values and beliefs.

Lieberson's groundbreaking *A Piece of the Pie* (1981) was published a decade after Banfield's book. In it he contrasts the experiences of white European immigrants from southern, central, and eastern Europe and those of African Americans. He shows that blacks were substantially more disadvantaged by labor market discrimination and segregation than were any of those other groups. For post-Lieberson writers to fail to appreciate the very different experiences of black migrants from the American South compared with those of European immigrants is to paint an inaccurate picture and do real harm to people in public and political debates.

There are a number of things wrong with the subculture theories of crime. They tend toward tautology, because they tell us that people who engage in violence do so because they have pro-violence norms and values, and we know that because they have engaged in violence. Empirical support for subcultural arguments has been lacking; there have been notable critiques (see, e.g., Ryan 1971; Erlanger 1972; Ball-Rokeach 1973). Another, more fundamental problem, shared by other sweeping, aggregate theories of crime and delinquency, is that these perspectives grossly overpredict criminality. Most poor people, and for that matter most people who live in violent neighborhoods, do not engage in crime. Given the mechanisms that subculture theories describe, more of the people who live in those places should be criminals, and most are not. And, perhaps most importantly, poor and minority people in earlier times did not differ from people in the mainstream on basic norms and values (Ball-Rokeach 1973).

B. Social and Political Context of Theoretical and Methodological Shifts

The most relevant social, political, and methodological shifts precede 1975; they occurred in the turmoil of the 1960s and academics' responses to what was going on in the cities and on campuses. Nanette Davis (1981) argues that consideration of the social and political environment in which scholars were working as they developed explanations for crime and deviance offers a useful tool for understanding theoretical developments. Using her framework, it is not hard to understand why social constructionist and Marxist ideas became popular during a time when people marched and occasionally rioted in the streets, and campuses became centers of social and political activism ranging from nonviolence, to building takeovers, to bombings.

Both students and faculty were products of or saw themselves contributing to a new academic and political order. Labeling theory, Marxist theory, and conflict theories more generally provided intellectual explanation and justification for social movements they were supporting or watching. New (and old) left theorists did not look at subordinated racial or ethnic minorities, or the poor, and see in them or their lifestyles justification for their plight, but instead saw them as victims of oppressive states and systems. If these groups were more criminal, the reason was that they were made that way by inequitable social and political arrangements. They were more criminal because of the states' efforts to control and label them or because elites subjugated them and defined them that way. They were poor as a result of these same social arrangements, so any correlations between racial differences and crime and social class differences and crime were spurious and should not be taken seriously.

Both symbolic interactionist and Marxist arguments had been around since the earliest decades of the twentieth century (e.g., Bonger 1916; Tannenbaum 1938) but were not prominent in criminology until scholars and activists challenged the status quo. As a result, these old theoretical approaches became newly popular. Advocates vociferously challenged the status quo explanations of crime, and especially efforts to explain racial differences in crime, and they especially did not embrace subcultural explanations (e.g., Chambliss 1973). More importantly, they challenged the empirical bases for concluding that there were meaningful racial differences in criminality, except those created by the exercise of social control by the state. If there are racial differences, then they are caused by the behavior of state agents, and for that reason, racial distributions of crime observed in data on imprisonment and arrest that earlier theories sought to explain were suspect.

So, at about the same time that Wolfang and Ferracuti published *The Subculture of Violence* (1967) and Banfield *The Unheavenly City* (1970), critics had already been raising serious challenges to the uncritical use of official criminal justice statistics as a measure of group differences in crime (e.g., Chambliss and Nagasawa 1969; Quinney 1970). Loud critical voices were challenging the very basis for believing that African Americans were more criminal than white Americans.

For the purposes of this essay it is important that these same critics also challenged the proposition that there were real differences between social classes in criminality. Labeling theorists and Marxists held that the behavior of working people was distinguishable from that of elites only because of how laws were written and enforced. Even if there were racial differences in crime, they should not be explained by the preponderance of the African American population among working classes and poor people, but by the actions of elites that put them there through discrimination and by the creation and maintenance of social structures that oppressed and subjugated people of color, working people, and especially the poor.

Critics challenged the use of arrest statistics to describe the distribution of crime (Chambliss 1964, 1973; Quinney 1977). They argued that official data more accurately reflected the oppressive actions of the state than the behavior of those differentially subjugated by the state's power. Early self-reported crime studies (usually more accurately, self-reported juvenile delinquency studies) seemed to suggest that the critics were right. Using these data, which were not tainted by the actions of police, researchers initially concluded that if there were racial crime and delinquency differences, the differences were small (Schur 1973). Later work indicates that it is likely that arrest statistics exaggerate both racial and class differences in delinquency involvement but that differences do exist.[3]

The self-report studies also found that social class was unrelated to involvement in delinquency. Middle-class juveniles were as likely to report delinquency involvement as were working- or even lower-class youths. Tittle, Villimez, and Smith (1978) concluded from their meta-analysis of the literature on social class and criminality that if there ever was a relationship between the two variables, it was weak and no longer existed.

Using Davis's framework, one is left to wonder whether the continuing popularity of subculture explanations should be seen as a reactionary effort of the mainstream to assert that the racial differences that they were seeking to explain were real and that their particular theories explained those differences.

[3] Later, Elliot and Ageton (1980), studying race, social class, and delinquency in Denver, concluded that significant differences did exist, particularly for more serious violations. Piquero, MacIntosh, and Hickman (2002) concluded that the initial response categories in self-report studies were inadequate, and important differences could be observed when more careful methods were used.

I know of no previous argument that the continuing prominence of either the subculture of violence thesis or the subculture of poverty thesis was a part of the "culture wars" that now dominate much of what passes for public and political discourse in the United States. But that may be. A recurring theme among politicians of both major political parties and some media commentators is the importance of "personal responsibility" (see, e.g., Estrich 2012; Goldman 2013). This point of view has been especially popular among conservatives.[4] This same theme has been voiced by some academics (e.g., Sowell 1983; Steele 1991).

Subcultural theories, which minimize the effect of social forces and factors that influence behavior and are thus external to the person, are consistent with the "individual, personal responsibility" narrative. I cannot say if any of these commentators endorse subcultural explanations or not, but their popularity is consistent with both the subculture of poverty and the subculture of violence arguments. The rise and success of the welfare reform movement happened in this context. Both subcultural arguments are based on the belief that African Americans and the poor are more engaged in crime as shown by the numbers of both groups who are arrested or are in prison. Both explain how, using these measures, one would conclude that blacks are more engaged in crime than whites because they more heavily populate the lower classes. In light of theoretically based challenges to using official criminal justice statistics to draw conclusions about the distribution of crime, their continued popularity is curious.

The challenge to the use of official data to say anything meaningful about crime led criminologists to make wider use of self-reported and victimization data, information less tainted by the actions of criminal justice agents and the system they work for. Later and better self-report studies generally reported that African Americans engaged in more crime and delinquency than whites but that the gap is considerably narrower than is indicated by arrest statistics.

C. *The Resurgence of Subculture Arguments*

By 1975, critics were carrying a full-on attack on the views that people of color were more criminal and that this could be explained by social

[4] Both Mitt Romney (http://atlantablackstar.com/2012/09/17/romney-obama-supporters-dont-take-personal-responsibility-for-their-lives/) and Fox News' Bill O'Reilly (http://video.foxnews.com/v/2011766333001/america-and-personal-responsibility/?#sp=show-clips) have made strong statements about individual personal responsibility.

class differences. Nonetheless, the subculture explanations, initially articulated in the 1950s, were restated, repackaged, and revived. Although subculture explanations remained popular in public and political discourse, they appeared only inconsistently in the academic literature, frequently turning up when an aggregate analysis showed that the crime rate, especially the violent crime rate, increased as the nonwhite or poor percentage of a population increased. Curtis (1975) criticized some efforts to attribute crime and urban problems to a subculture of poverty:

> Because it contains more powerful directives of policy and has been more influential on decision makers, Banfied's *The Unheavenly City* is a much more unfortunate use of cultural determinism to reach the spurious conclusion that poor blacks have only themselves to blame for their situation. Although he is often factually inaccurate, not uncommonly misinterprets the works of others, and produces little empirical underpinning to justify what is authoritatively called the "Myth of Poverty," Banfield in effect concludes that the manifest and unheavenly matrix of urban America has one basic and latent function—the lower-class (read poor black) value system. "The lower-class forms of all problems are at bottom a single problem: the existence of an outlook and style of life which is radically present-oriented and which therefore attaches no value to work, sacrifice, self-improvement, or service to family, friend, or community." (Curtis 1975, p. 19)

Few things characterize the corporate and political elites of the United States more than "present-oriented" thinking. Wall Street indices dance up and down on the basis of quarterly earnings statements. Investment fund watchers, chief executive officers, and investors make million dollar decisions based on "what have you done for me lately" earnings reports. Members of Congress begin fund-raising for the next 2-year campaign before they are sworn in to their current seat. Curtis concludes his critique by asserting that Banfield failed to take seriously the structural circumstances in which poor, black, urban populations found themselves. "Thus the choice is not necessarily seen as one between immediate and deferred gratification, but probably more accurately as between immediate gratification and no gratification at all" (p. 19).

But Curtis's intent was not to bury subculture explanations, but to resurrect the arguments of his mentor, Marvin Wolfgang, and to breathe new life into this explanatory model using a multicity analysis of violent crime in 17 large American cities. He argued that subcultural norms and values are the intervening mechanisms between the stratification, discrimination, and disadvantage that urban blacks experience and higher rates of violent crime.

Unfortunately, though Curtis examined more cities than Wolfgang and Ferracuti's Philadelphia, he was still left positing that unmeasured forces, pro-violence norms and values, explain why aggregate African American arrest rates were high. His data gave him no better way than other proponents of the subcultural theses had tried to use to measure differences between those in the subculture and others on critical features of culture, norms, values, beliefs, and ways of behaving and those in the intergenerational transmission of these differences. In the absence of a capacity to measure these critical features of culture, one might think of such retreats to saying "it must be a subculture" as a black-box theory of criminology. Had the research focused on property crime, presumably subcultural values would have been unneeded in his explanations.

Unfortunately, Lieberson's work did not doom such subculture arguments. They kept reappearing. Murray (1984) came to a place similar to Banfield's but via a different route. Murray believed that the majority of poor Americans were hardworking and raised their children to value hard work in school and beyond and to avoid shortcuts like crime. However, that changed in the aftermath of establishment of the welfare state with New Deal programs such as Aid to Families with Dependent Children and Social Security and subsequent expansion of federal welfare programs in the 1960s and 1970s.[5] Welfare dependence, Murray argued, fostered an unhealthy dependence on the state, and as a result, recipients no longer conveyed messages about the value of hard work to succeeding generations. The welfare state no longer supported primarily a majority of poor recipients who believed in working hard and a very small minority content to let others care for them, but instead supported a new majority who were content to languish on the dole. As benefits improved, the size of this group, whose values not only were counter to education and hard work but were also criminogenic, grew larger. Essentially Mur-

[5] Many New Deal programs were instituted in a racialized way that excluded African Americans. Policy changes attempted, with mixed success, to address this (Lieberman 1995). Because a majority of African Americans lived in the South until after World War II, they disproportionately did not benefit from the welfare system because those states provided comparatively less welfare benefits and support (Wilson 1987).

ray argued that welfare made them do it. Like other subcultural theorists, Murray did not make race a central part of his thesis, but he acknowledged that the poor in America were disproportionately African American. It is hard to read *Losing Ground* and not think of black welfare dependents.

Lawrence Mead, also very influential in the 1980s and 1990s welfare reform debates, took a somewhat different tack. In *Beyond Entitlement* (1986) and subsequent books (1993, 2004, 2011), he argued that welfare should be used to develop and strengthen the work ethic among the poor, who he felt had been lulled into passively accepting that they were entitled to support. For Mead it is about jobs: if the poor learned the value of work, they would get good jobs and solve their own problems. Welfare programs should be used to compel poor people to take on employment so that they might come to value hard work. Mead's beginning point, like Murray's, was that the poor had a fundamental problem, undervaluing hard work.

Just as Ball-Rokeach (1973) reported earlier, contemporary scholars still find that the poor do not differ from other people, as most politicians and many in the public suppose, in their views of work and welfare (Harris 2002; Hays 2003).[6] Where they appear to differ, they usually do so because they adhere to dominant values in unexpected ways. Page (2013) found evidence of parents not discouraging their offspring from drug dealing when this entrepreneurial activity was all that was available. The parents were not pro-crime, they were pro–small business. In some struggling underclass communities, "the hot man" who sells stolen goods fills a supply vacuum that exists because there are few or no stores available.

For tracing the development of the idea that racial differences in criminality can be explained by racial differences in social class, subculture explanations are interesting in a number of ways. First, they drew direct attention to poverty and not just a linear conception of social class in trying to make sense of racial differences. This is particularly important because they did not have to explain noninstrumental crimes like violence. Most laypeople, and not a few social scientists, assume that a class-

[6] Harris (2002) found that views on issues such as the value of work and attitudes toward welfare reform varied not by demographic characteristics but by social location. To an extent that might surprise many, Hays (2003) found that women who received welfare payments also endorsed the "personal responsibility" ethic that social commentators and politicians frequently asserted had been lost.

crime connection exists because people steal to satisfy needs and wants. This may at times be true, but that does not help explain why African Americans have comparatively higher rates of homicide and other forms of criminal violence. In any case, it is far less clear that blacks have higher rates of property crime; studies that find such racial differences do not find them to be as large as the racial differences in involvement in violent crimes (Sampson and Lauritsen 1997).[7]

Second, the recurrence of and academic, political, and public embrace of subculture explanations are interesting in their timing. From the 1950s and 1960s, when notable criminological texts using subculture arguments appeared (Cohen 1955; Cloward and Ohlin 1960; Wolfgang and Ferracuti 1967), to the mid-1980s, when conservative arguments (Murray 1984; Mead 1986) were embraced by Republicans and Democrats alike during welfare reform debates, important theoretical and methodological changes were occurring in the scholarly literature, and universities, colleges, and cities were roiled by political conflict. Those conflicts led to the modern reemergence of symbolic interactionism, the labeling theory of deviance, and Marxist criminology. They were critical of mainstream criminology, including subculture perspectives, and the data sources mainstream scholars used.

A little later William Julius Wilson delivered a devastating critique of Murray's arguments, analyses, and policy recommendations in *The Truly Disadvantaged* (1987). Central to Murray's thesis is his contention that expanding welfare benefits in the early 1970s and stable benefits after the mid-1970s encouraged recipients to forsake work and subsist on benefits. In reality, Wilson points out, benefits fell substantially during that period.

Before I turn to the theoretical and methodological changes that defined the academic context in which subculture explanations inexplicably continued to flourish, a look at social and political occurrences in cities and on campuses that defined the social and political context is in order.

The continued popularity of subculture arguments into 1990 conversations about welfare reform, in light of academic criminology's near abandonment of these explanations of racial differences in crime, should be seen as a part of the American culture wars. Murray's *Losing Ground*

[7] Hindelang, Hirschi, and Weis (1979) found racial differences in property crime measured with arrest statistics to be smaller than were racial differences in arrest for violent crimes. Crutchfield (1994), examining data from the National Longitudinal Survey of Youth (NLSY), found no significant racial differences in property crime involvement.

(1984) should be seen as part of a wave of other books that developed similar ideas, including Wilson and Herrnstein's *Crime and Human Nature* (1985). That book sought to link sociobiology and behaviorism to create a grand theory explaining why criminals (not explicitly black and brown criminals, but . . .) were fundamentally and constitutionally different from the rest of us law-abiding citizens. Herrnstein and Murray's *The Bell Curve* (1995) argued that class differences, and racial differences too, were largely a consequence of inherited intelligence.

What these widely read, widely discussed books have in common is that they shift the focus of discussions from the structural economic, social, and criminal circumstances of the poor, the black, and the brown to the individuals themselves. This harkens back to the early-twentieth-century social Darwinists who advocated that individual poor people and families be helped to adjust to their inevitable straitened lots in life rather than attempt to alter the social arrangements in which they lived (Sumner 1952; Spencer 1961).

III. Individual Racial Differences in Criminal Involvement and Social Class

For a time, few researchers used arrest data in studies of race crime and justice in response to the leftist critiques of their use in mainstream criminology to measure the racial or social class differences in criminal involvement. That was short-lived.

Scholars began looking more closely at these data and concluded they were useful after all. Hindelang (1978) examined racial differences in commission of personal crimes using reports of victims in the National Crime Survey (NCS), later renamed the National Crime Victimization Survey (NCVS). Racial differences shown by victims' descriptions of their assailants in the NCS were not the same as those in Uniform Crime Reports arrest statistics, but they were much closer than self-report data indicated. African Americans were significantly more involved than whites in the more serious types of crime most likely to come to the attention of law enforcement.

Arrest data continue to be used in some bodies of research, notably studies of racial disproportionality in criminal justice case processing (Blumstein 1982, 1993; Langan 1985; Bridges and Crutchfield 1988; Crutchfield, Bridges, and Pitchford 1994; Travis, Western, and Redburn 2014; Spohn 2015). This is primarily a matter of convenience because no other national measures are widely available to investigate whether racial differences in the criminal justice system can be accounted for in part by criminal involvement differences. Langan (1985), like Hindelang earlier, used NCVS data to confirm that measuring aggregate variations by race in serious crimes was defensible. Blumstein (1982, 1993) concluded that racial arrest rate distributions are less error-laden when the focus is on the most serious crimes concerning which police use less discretion when deciding whether to make an arrest.

Scholars had used self-reports of crime and delinquency long before left-wing academics criticized mainstream criminology for using arrest records to study racial differences in offending (e.g., Glueck and Glueck 1940). Self-reports and then victimization studies became the preferred sources of data. Tittle, Villemez, and Smith (1978) published results of a meta-analysis of self-reported crime and delinquency studies and concluded that there was not a real association between crime and class. Researchers subsequently validated the use of well-designed self-report studies and concluded that there were racial differences in delinquency and crime but that they were much less than the stark differences shown in police data (Elliott and Ageton 1980; Morenoff 2005).

Hindelang, Hirschi, and Weis (1979, 1981) went further, arguing that there were important racial differences in commission of serious crimes, and there were likely also social class differences. After careful study of self-reported measures of delinquency and official records, they concluded that many of the earliest self-reported delinquency studies examined very minor forms of violation, some so minor that they might better be called "juvenile misbehavior" than delinquency. Scholars had focused too much on minor violations. More serious crimes are relatively rare, and younger and smaller school samples tended to undercount the most at-risk kids. As a consequence, the surveys frequently did not generate data that allowed for meaningful study.[8]

Hindelang, Hirschi, and Weis (1979, 1981) concluded that self-reports and official statistics did not differ so much because of errors in one, the other, or both, but because they measured different domains of crime and delinquency. Self-reports are good for examining variations in rel-

[8] That is, unless the survey has a very large sample. Both the NLSY and the National Longitudinal Study of Adolescent Health are sufficiently large. They have included self-reported crime and delinquency items, including some serious violations. Criminologists have used these data sources, but predictably the distributions on the crime variables are highly skewed.

atively minor forms of violation; for some topics, this is quite appropriate. But official records, they argued, provided better measures for more serious criminal activity. They did not dismiss the left's critique of these data. The authors acknowledge that, like nearly all data, official records contain errors, perhaps more errors than in many other data used by scientists, but they are the best widely available measures of serious crime and delinquency.

The NCVS has been used effectively to compare racial differences in criminal involvement, without distortions produced by police decision making and other problems that compromise arrest statistics. The NCVS and other victimization surveys, of course, have limitations. Most importantly, since race and perceptions of crime are intimately linked (Saperstein and Penner 2010; Drakulich 2013), victims of violent crimes, when asked about the characteristics of perpetrators, may guess at the race or ethnicity of the perpetrator and be more likely to guess a person of color if his or her appearance is ambiguous.

Victimization data afford important opportunities to get a better handle on the racial distribution of some serious crimes. Lauritsen and Heimer (2010) used NCVS data to examine racial differences in nonfatal violence and found that blacks and Latinos were the perpetrators of violence more frequently than whites, but this association is linked differentially to macroeconomic conditions.[9] This and other studies demonstrate the efficacy of using victimization surveys to get less biased views of racial distributions in offending, but most such studies do not help us understand to what extent differences can be accounted for by social class differences.

An interesting by-product is that we have learned that things are different than arrest data seemed to show. Police data suggest that African Americans and Latinos engage in more crime than do whites and that this does not appreciably vary by crime type. It is more complicated than that. The race/crime correlation for individuals is strongest for violent crime, weaker for property crime, and pretty much nonexistent for drug-related offenses (Felson, Glenn, and Armstrong 2008).

So, we should ask, what exactly are we trying to explain when using social class to make sense of racial differences in criminality? This is complicated by the weak social class and crime association. For instance,

[9] Lauritsen and Heimer found that nonfatal serious violent victimization was falling for Latino, African American, and white males; but while declines for whites are steady, those of men of color declined less during economic slowdowns.

notwithstanding higher minority conviction and imprisonment rates, there is no reason to believe that there are significant racial differences in drug use and drug sales (Tonry 2011). There is reason to believe that drugs of choice of users may vary by social class but that there are not significant differences in which groups use illegal substances (Mosher and Akins 2007). Among young people, substance use is equally distributed across racial and ethnic groups in the United States, and if any group is higher, it is, slightly, whites (Substance Abuse and Mental Health Services Administration 2015).

Violent crime is different. Victimization surveys (US Department of Justice 1994), public health system vital statistics (Reiss and Roth 1993; National Center for Health Statistics 1995), and even some self-report instruments that include serious offenses are consistent with arrest data in showing general racial differences in violent crime arrests data. Neither victimization studies nor vital statistics provide data on social class differences among perpetrators, but they do indicate that victims of violent crime are disproportionately from the lower classes, which is suggestive of the class of perpetrators. And, it is clear, no matter how scholars measure crime, for both class and race, crime most frequently occurs within groups (O'Brien 1987; Parker and McCall 1999).

These racial patterns have also been noted in studies that seek to examine racial differences in imprisonment. Blumstein (1982, 1993) and Tonry (1995, 2011) concluded that racial differences in arrest for violent crimes tracked well with racial differences in involvement, were unrelated to drug offenses, and have intermediate accuracy with property crimes. All of this leads me to conclude that efforts to disentangle racial differences in crime from racial differences in social class should focus primarily on violence.

IV. Aggregate Racial Differences in Criminal Involvement and Social Class

Some social scientists think that aggregate data are a poor substitute for measuring social reality when "better" individual data are not available. That is not the case. Some important questions are best answered using aggregate data. Simply adding up responses from a survey is not the same; to answer some questions doing so is fine, but for other issues it is not. A better example can hardly be found than the association of poverty rates with violence rates. The aggregate poverty rate is substantively different from individuals' status of being in poverty. The latter can be learned by asking survey respondents about their income and estimating local costs of living. If a person's or family's poverty status affects his or her lifestyle and life chances, warrants examination, and may provide partial explanation for the likelihood of criminal involvement.

But a group's level of poverty, and especially collective poverty of geographically isolated or segregated groups, has properties above and beyond the sum of the individual poor people in the group. This point has been made repeatedly by sociologists (Wilson 1987, 1996; Massey and Denton 1993). Its relevance for discussions of race and crime has also been prominently noted (Sampson and Wilson 1995; Peterson and Krivo 2009, 2010). And also, as Wikström and Loeber (2000) find, the effects of living in severely disadvantaged neighborhoods can overwhelm protective factors of good kids (good family, doing well in school, etc.), causing them to become involved in delinquency, even serious crime.

William Julius Wilson, in his widely cited books *The Truly Disadvantaged* (1987) and *When Work Disappears* (1996), identifies crime as one of the unhappy effects of the social and ecological isolation and concentration of the urban poor that resulted from deindustrialization of American manufacturing cities. When those books were published, the urban underclass was nearly completely black. Wilson hypothesized that these neighborhoods would have high levels of crime. It was not individuals' SES or poverty status that Wilson linked to higher levels of crime, but the group's. The context of concentrated social and economic disadvantage, social isolation, and living among large numbers of others in the same precarious circumstances, over a spatially extended area, was criminogenic. Because Wilson was writing about the urban poor, he was silent on the effects of low SES on people of whatever race living outside of underclass neighborhoods.

Massey and Denton's *American Apartheid* (1993) emphasized racial residential segregation, another feature of urban life that led to concentrated poverty and elevated criminality. A large proportion of the African American population has lived and continues to live in cities that Massey and Denton characterize as hypersegregated.[10] Their analyses

[10] Massey and Denton (1993) defined cities as hypersegregated when they display high segregation on four of five dimensions: unevenness, isolation, clustering, centralization, and concentration. Sixteen metropolitan areas were hypersegregated in 1980: Atlanta, Baltimore, Buffalo, Chicago, Cleveland, Dallas, Detroit, Gary, Indianapolis,

demonstrate that a high level of urban racial residential segregation concentrates and exacerbates social problems, including poverty and crime. Other scholars have reinforced aspects of Massey and Denton's thesis (Crowder, Pais, and South 2012; Quillian 2012).

Some social scientists have focused on how Wilson and Massey and Denton differ in the social structural forces they emphasize that make segments of urban America poorer and more dangerous. For my purpose their differences are not important. What is important is their focus on structural conditions—job losses for Wilson, residential racial segregation for Massey and Denton—that offer explanations for higher black crime rates and for how poverty contributes to that elevated rate. Neither specifies the mechanisms that produce crime in underclass, racially segregated places, but others have.

Sampson and Wilson (1995) explain the connection between underclass neighborhoods and high levels of violent crime. Using a contemporary version of social disorganization theory, they argue that disadvantaged, underclass black neighborhoods have more violence because their capacity to regulate what happens there is compromised by low levels of collective efficacy. They hypothesize that violence rates will be higher when collective efficacy is weak and populations living in underclass places face social and economic stresses. For them, SES composition, notably very high levels of poverty in the neighborhoods where many urban African Americans live, accounts for higher rates of violent crime.

Bursik and Grasmick (1993), writing about gang crime and violence and focusing on a different aspect of social organization, came to essentially the same conclusion. For them, it is the incapacity of deeply disadvantaged neighborhoods to get key institutions to work with them or on their behalf. Violence is a product of failures of law enforcement, other criminal justice factors, schools, city offices, and other important institutions to work with and on behalf of those neighborhoods as they do in economically better-off places, especially those populated by whites. Sampson and Wilson, and Bursik and Grasmick, while focusing on different aspects of social disorganization, both help explain how high

Kansas City, Los Angeles, Milwaukee, New York, Newark, Philadelphia, and St. Louis. Since then, racial residential segregation has diminished a bit, but it remains a major force in American social life.

violent crime rates are generated in black disadvantaged communities. A central feature for both is the social, economic, and political marginalization of very poor black neighborhoods.

An accumulating literature emphasizes structural consequences of class differences to explain racial differences in crime. Bruce (1999) found little support for cultural explanations of racial differences in criminal involvement but found that structural differences were linked to observed patterns. Wright, Entner, and Younts (2009) report that family disruption, lowered educational attainment, and living in disrupted communities are linked to higher crime rates in African American neighborhoods. Peterson and Krivo (2010) use both effects of social and economic disadvantage and racial residential segregation to examine the correlation between race and crime. Examining variations in census tract crime rates in 88 American cities of varying size, they conclude that segregation leads to differential access to the labor market and to social and economic disadvantage; both increase levels of crime and delinquency. Their study is distinctive because they looked at the association between crime and the concentration not only of black and white residents but also of Latinos. Latinos are not nearly as segregated as are African Americans but also suffer from residential segregation, exclusion from equal occupational opportunities, and resulting poverty. Peterson and Krivo conclude that segregation creates, perpetuates, and exacerbates disadvantage by walling off residents in isolated minority communities from social networks that connect people to job opportunities. They show how this causes crime in select neighborhoods:

> Neighborhoods that are highly disadvantaged have heightened crime rates for two broad reasons. First, processes that encourage criminal behavior are particularly prevalent in areas where disadvantage abounds. . . . Within a context of limited opportunities, theft and other property crimes may occur in an effort to secure resources, and luxuries that are not otherwise attainable. Activities such as prostitution, drug trafficking, shoplifting, theft and sale of stolen property, and other opportunistic crimes may become regular sources of "income" and a means of acquiring wanted goods and services. . . . Violence as "self-help" may also be used in these crimes, or in other social situations where conflict arises, as participants seek to protect themselves and their possessions rather than engage the police or other authorities. (Peterson and Krivo 2010, p. 33)

Parker (2008) focused on the uneven crime decline in the United States since 1991. African American violence rates have dropped precipitously, but less than they would have because of high levels of joblessness and inequality in inner-city black neighborhoods. Shihadeh (2009) notes that with decreases in racial residential segregation, modest though they may be, more prosperous African Americans have been able to move out of ghettos, leaving more disadvantaged portions of the black population living in more concentrated poverty. And this increases violent victimization in such places.

These scholars recognize that racial residential segregation was created and is maintained by decisions by governments, banks, the insurance industry, and individuals systematically to deprive African Americans of housing opportunities enjoyed, and likely taken for granted, by most white Americans. African American employment was more negatively affected by deindustrialization and the consequent job losses, and labor disadvantages continue because of exclusion from labor markets and housing opportunities and racialized inequalities in education.

The emphasis on continued racial oppression of very poor blacks distinguishes contemporary social disorganization arguments from early-twentieth-century conceptions of social disorganization theory. Those early Chicago School sociologists (see, e.g., Park, Burgess, and McKenzie 1925; Shaw and McKay 1942) did not much focus on the experience of black migrants from the rural South. Instead their efforts to understand the experiences of Poles, Italians, Irish, and other immigrants from Europe who moved into Chicago enclaves inspired them to adopt Durkheimian notions of social solidarity, community organization, and social disorganization. They noted that blacks moving to the city were constrained to live in the "Black Belt" on the South Side. When predicting that migrants from Europe over generations would be assimilated and move from ethnic enclaves into "better" communities, they did not explore the social forces that kept African Americans locked into a narrow, crowded, dense, impoverished strip of land.

Rigid residential segregation was maintained by landlords, rental agents, banks, and realtors who blocked blacks from moving into white areas (Lieberson 1981; Massey and Denton 1993). Many neighborhood associations and deed restrictions forbade new buyers to sell their properties to people of color, especially African Americans, members of some white ethnic groups, and Jews (Gotham 2000).

Federal fair housing law and judicial decisions striking down racial covenants have ameliorated racial bias in housing, but residential segregation in American cities continues. It remains a fact of urban life. The causes include people's preferences about where and with whom they want to live (South and Crowder 1998; Emerson, Chai, and Yancey 2001) and, to a lesser extent, social class (Adelman 2004). Early to mid-twentieth-century European immigrants did better economically in succeeding generations and moved to less disorganized, lower crime rate places.

By contrast, no other ethnic group has been more segregated and more restricted in where they live than African Americans (Massey and Denton 1993). Racial residential segregation and job discrimination kept a large percentage of African Americans in what Wilson would call underclass neighborhoods a half century later. Today, black, brown, and poor segments of the population are faced with gentrification, the movement of the middle and upper classes into the central city, displacing poor and minority residents (Zukin 1987).

Large American cities are increasingly likely to resemble large European cities, with poor and marginalized populations living in portions of the suburban ring but still in ghettoized communities. Those who argued that poor, black places had high levels of violence because of crime-conducive subcultures stepped into the intellectual space created by housing patterns and accompanying problems.

An appreciation of how macrostructural conditions explain racial differences in crime rates has emerged from research published in recent years. These explanations are fundamentally different from early, strain theory attempts to account for the observed patterns. Those early views were largely instrumental—people of color are disadvantaged, which led them more frequently to commit property and other crimes to satisfy wants and desires—and assumed that straightforward conceptions of social class helped explain crime: the working class committed more crimes than middle-class people, and the lower class committed even more, possibly even most street crime. This view was called into question by Tittle, Villemez, and Smith (1978) and disputed by Hindelang, Hirschi, and Weis (1981).

We need not resolve or even revive that debate. Linear notions of a monotonic relationship between SES and crime are weak at best. That connection does not aid understanding of racial differences in involvement in common crime, especially violent crime. But poverty as the focus, especially hyperpoverty, provides a better handle. And if that focus is narrowed more to the social and economic disadvantage of inner-city communities, where still too many black people, and a large number of Latinos, must live, we have an explanation for why people of color have higher crime rates, especially higher violent crime rates.

There remain, though, three very interesting issues: heterogeneity of Hispanics in the United States and the low rates of violence of some groups, particularly among immigrants; links between macro- and micro-level processes in understanding individual behavior in context; and the role of culture.

A. Confronting New Issues in Race, Class, and Crime Debates

A growing literature indicates that we should not readily link the Latino or Hispanic population and crime. That literature emphasizes that there is considerable complexity in the associations between Latino ethnicity and crime. Immigrants and nonimmigrants need to be distinguished, and there are different patterns for first and subsequent immigrant generations. National-origin groups have different experiences of immigration, assimilation, and crime. Most importantly for the subject of this essay, Hispanics are not a population segment that is necessarily predominantly lower SES. Martinez and Stowell (2012) find that increases in immigration from Latin America are linked to decreases in homicide, not the increases that xenophobes assume. Sampson (2008) reports that Latino communities have large immigrant populations and lower, not higher, rates of violence than other places. Some of these immigrant groups are among the lowest-SES, highest-poverty groups in the United States.

Complicating the picture more, Jennings et al. (2013) find that there are four distinct trajectories of crime involvement within the US Latino population, including a disproportionate number of low-rate offenders among early immigrants but others who, in varying patterns, offend at higher levels. Historically, Cubans had low levels of criminal involvement, but this changed recently, and they have also not been as economically disadvantaged as other Hispanics. More recently the criminal involvement of Cuban Americans, at least in acquaintance homicide, has increased (Martinez, Lee, and Nielsen 2001). Puerto Rican and perhaps Dominican communities tend to have economic and social experiences similar to those of African Americans, and their criminal involvement is more comparable (Felson, Deane, and Armstrong 2008; Tran 2012).

Two things are clear when examining the growing literature on Latino criminality and social class. First, it is neither simple nor monolithic. Second, both the immigration and the assimilation experiences of peoples and cultures play important roles, likely more than do social class positions. To the extent that social class matters, it seems to override culture in later generations when groups do not easily assimilate and thereby avoid the perils of living in long-term disadvantaged communities.

Sullivan's *Getting Paid* (1989) focused on labor markets, communities, race, and crime. The ethnographic study examines the effects of the distribution of job opportunities in three different, low-income communities in Brooklyn. Sullivan and his team found that young people's job opportunities were influenced by neighborhood characteristics: the work prospects in their immediate vicinities, the networks that were available to them, and the linkage between the employment of adults and where they worked. The Latino neighborhood, which he called La Barriada, was more isolated from the legitimate labor market than Hamilton Park, where white ethnic boys lived. This was a consequence of a lack of nearby job opportunities and the marginalization of La Barriada adults in the legitimate labor market. The African American juveniles living in "Projectville" came from even more impoverished households and were even more distant, both geographically and socially, from opportunities in the legitimate economy. The Latino boys, and especially the African American boys, were more involved in crime for longer periods than were the white boys. This study, though not focused on social class and crime, illustrates how the social structure of disadvantaged places connects, or fails to connect, individual outcomes to labor market organization and other macro processes.

Pager (2003, 2007) examined how incarceration influences employment and interacts with job aspirants' race and contributed to understanding of how class is linked to race. She found that African American men without criminal records were less successful in procuring interviews than whites with a record. Her findings suggest that racial job discrimination is alive and well in the American labor market. As long as this continues, blacks will disproportionately remain in the lower classes.

Juxtaposing Pager's findings with Sullivan's suggests that African American young men from underclass neighborhoods are handicapped by the continuing stigmata of race when they seek employment. This is not unlike the patterns reported by Kirschenman and Neckerman (1991) decades earlier. They found that employers in suburbs, where the jobs were, routinely elected not to hire blacks, using the logic that they were likely to be products of Chicago public schools, which were inferior to the suburban schools attended by white applicants.

Crutchfield (2014) linked macro, city, and community levels of labor market inequality, and long-term high levels of social and economic disadvantage in inner-city neighborhoods, to the labor market experience of individuals to explain why higher levels of crime persist in the places where poor black people live.

Lauritsen and Heimer (2010) using NCVS data studied the differential effects of economic downturns on victimization of white, African American, and Latino males. White men were not significantly affected, but Latino and African American victimization fluctuated with consumer sentiment; these men were more susceptible to negative fluctuations in the economy. This may be a by-product of both groups living closer to the margins. These groups suffered more job and housing losses in the recent Great Recession. Life on the economic margins may have caused them to experience more nonfatal violent victimization too.

B. Bringing Culture Back In

The earlier versions of theories about crime-conducive subcultures are often associated with Oscar Lewis's notions of "culture of poverty" or oppositional culture. Lewis (1959) saw these patterns as emerging from the social and economic circumstances in which the poor lived. For Lewis, oppositional culture arose because segments of the population were subjugated by social structure and social stratification, without opportunities and resources, and marginalized in their poverty. His initial work was in Mexico City. He came to believe that some segments of the poor developed the traits others later used to explain high inner-city crime rates, because of where they were in the class structure and because they were systematically marginalized in capitalist economies. For Lewis, these beliefs and behavior patterns emerged from the social positions the poor occupied. People were not poor because of their patterns of life; their patterns of life were adjustments and accommodations to the realities of their existence. Their social position was not the result of their beliefs.

In recent decades, ethnography has reemerged as an important tool for studying crime. A central theme has been the link between race and disadvantage. Small and his colleagues (Small and Newman 2001; Small, Harding, and Lamont 2011) have called for serious considerations of culture in scholarly discussions of poverty. What distinguishes recent ethnographies is their recognition of the critical roles of social structural factors as determinants of the patterns of life and behaviors of the poor. This is not unlike Curtis's (1975) view, but with a real effort to observe and chronicle the workings of culture in day-to-day life.

Too often conflict divides scholars who use quantitative methods and those using qualitative methodologies. This is not helpful to efforts to understand the role of economic forces in the relations between race and crime in the United States. Social structural explanations of the effects on crime of the emergence of underclass neighborhoods in the wake of deindustrialization, racial residential segregation, and labor market conditions tell only a portion of the story.

Left unexplained is the criminogenic culture that emerges in deeply socially and economically disadvantaged places. Ethnographers have studied and attempted to explain what happens in such places and how cultural patterns emerge that perpetuate disadvantage and encourage criminality.

What distinguishes these more recent ethnographies, in contrast to earlier subcultural theorists, is the central place they give to the structured inequality, segregation, and discrimination that have resulted in large numbers of African Americans and Latinos having to live in places where crime occurs all too frequently. They portray these social and economic forces as the creators of disadvantaged places and the crime-conducive belief systems, values, and norms that emerge as consequences of this structured disadvantage. For example, Anderson (1994, p. 81) writes, "Of all the problems besetting the poor inner-city black community, none is more pressing than that of interpersonal violence and aggression. It wreaks havoc daily with the lives of community residents and increasingly spills over into downtown and residential middle-class areas. . . . The inclination to violence springs from the circumstances of life among the ghetto poor—*the lack of jobs that pay a living wage, the stigma of race*, the fallout from rampant drug use and drug trafficking, and the resulting alienation and lack of hope for the future" (emphasis added). This acknowledgment that cultural adaptations emerge as a result of marginalization from good jobs and racial discrimination is critical. Here Anderson is not, using the phrasing of Ryan (1971), "blaming" the black poor for their circumstances by suggesting that they would not be where they are if not for their values. Instead, their structural circumstances create where they live, the plight in which they live, and the unfortunate crime and violence that plague their communities.[11]

In the past, some criminologists attributed racial patterns of criminality to subcultures, with no capacity, and too often with no effort, to measure or observe the values or beliefs that purportedly caused those patterns. Contemporary ethnographers, because they left their offices and libraries and went into the field, documented patterns of behavior from informers, interviews, and their own observations. They heard from people living in disadvantaged places and struggling to make it in a difficult, impoverished, challenging environment. They observed and measured the cultural patterns of which they write.

Anderson (1999) wrote of the code of the street that emerged in the context of street life in inner-city, disadvantaged, African American, Philadelphia neighborhoods. Central features of those places were the joblessness, hopelessness, and marginalization of many who lived there. The code of the streets is a response to crime and a cause of crime, but fundamentally this criminogenic cultural adaptation is a consequence of a deep, hyperpoverty of place.

Anderson's and Sullivan's analyses were not exclusively about males, but much of the focus was on boys and young men, who are most frequently the perpetrators and victims of inner-city criminality. Anderson's student, Nikki Jones (2010), focused on young African American women and their struggle to balance contradictory cultural expectations of them as women in the context of extreme social and economic dislocation. Miller's (2008) study of inner-city St. Louis examined the norms, values, and belief systems in communities and schools of girls and young women and the men and boys in their environment, and how all this contributed to the women's victimization. The social isolation and concentrated disadvantage resulting from long-term, collective economic marginalization and poverty are at the center of her narrative.

These studies focused on African Americans. Rios's (2011) examination of gang-involved kids in Oakland, California, included black and Latino boys. He too documents cultural patterns produced by structural

[11] Others have written about the importance and centrality of social structure as the basis for emergent belief systems (Miller 2008; Jones 2010; Rios 2011).

inequalities facing residents of inner-city neighborhoods. These and other studies describe processes that to the casual reader may seem to resemble earlier versions of subcultural theories that sought to explain why communities of color had higher levels of crime. What differentiates them is the evidence from in-depth ethnographies and the central role of social structure in the narratives they construct.

Three other ethnographies that focus on particular aspects of place are also relevant. Venkatesh (2000) and Rymond-Richmond (2007) write about how public policy, poverty, and gangs come together in Chicago housing projects to link race with crime. Patillo-McCoy's *Black Picket Fences* (1999) takes on what for some is a troubling question: "If it is about poverty and disadvantaged neighborhoods, why is crime also higher in a middle-class African American neighborhood?" Her answer is straightforward and illustrates the power of social and economic disadvantage. African American middle-class people generally do not live in communities like those occupied by whites of the same social standing (and generally black middle-class economic standing is not nearly as high). White middle-class communities are socially separated from places where poor people live, but they are also geographically separated.

This is not the case for middle-class blacks, who often live near distressed inner-city, sometimes underclass, neighborhoods. That was true of "Groveland," the site of Patillo-McCoy's ethnography. Negative influences spill over from underclass places to middle-class communities, and their children may go to the same schools and share the same parks as children who live in the ghetto. Crime is not higher in middle-class African American communities than in white communities because of some negative trait of the race of people who live there, but because of proximity to deeply poor, socially and economically disadvantaged sections of cities.

These three ethnographies bring the consideration of culture squarely back to the disadvantage and segregation that Sampson and Wilson and Peterson and Krivo conclude are the causes of higher crime rates among African Americans and to some extent of any observed higher criminal involvement among some segments of the Latino population.

C. Where Are We Now?

America in the second decade of the twenty-first century is not a postracial society. People of color are disproportionately arrested and incarcerated. Some of those differences can be attributed to higher rates of crime, but they cannot all be (Travis, Western, and Redburn 2014). There is now good evidence for believing that we should not uncritically accept police data when examining crime in black and brown communities (cf. Davies and Fagan 2012). There is reason to believe that African Americans are more involved in violent crime but even better evidence to believe that blacks and Hispanics are no more likely to use or sell drugs than are whites even though they are heavily overrepresented among those arrested and imprisoned for drug offenses. But what of the elevated rates of violence among African Americans and some Hispanic groups?

Mass incarceration is a social force of uniquely damaging proportions. Early in this essay I described how racial differences in imprisonment were long accepted as evidence of higher levels of criminal involvement among African Americans. The growth of American incarceration has been disproportionately experienced by communities of color (Tonry 2011; Travis, Western, and Redburn 2014). A sizable literature shows that some of those differences can be traced to higher levels of crime among African Americans and some segments of the Latino population, but all of the observed differences in police processing cannot be justified by this greater involvement. The increase in imprisonment after 1973 was in part due to the war on drugs. The disproportionate imprisonment of black and brown men and women for drug violations cannot be justified by higher levels of use or sale of drugs (Tonry and Melewski 2008).

A growing number of scholars have demonstrated that mass incarceration has major negative consequences for the political health of communities of color and the basic political rights of those locked up (Manza and Uggen 2006), increases and sustains economic inequality between blacks and whites (Pettit and Western 2004; Western 2006), damages the earning capability of former prisoners (Pettit and Lyons (2009), and harms long-term social and economic prospects for the convicted (Harris 2015). Pager (2003, 2007) has demonstrated that the experience of incarceration negatively affects men's ability to find employment and is especially damaging to African American and Latino former prisoners. Lack of success in the job market in turn increases the probabilities of returning to crime after release (Crutchfield 2014).

Rose and Clear (1998) and Clear (2007) have argued that the coerced mobility of mass incarceration, the population churning that occurs when large numbers of people, usually young men, are removed from communities and imprisoned and then returned to the same or similar communities, disrupts those places. They argue that it harms the collective efficacy of those sections of cities, making them even more criminogenic than they had been. Communities of color, and especially many African American neighborhoods, are the most disadvantaged by mass incarceration and are the hardest hit when black and brown men and women are disproportionately locked up.

Rose and Clear (1998) and Clear (2007) have provided empirical support for their argument, but the National Academy of Sciences Committee on the Causes and Consequences of High Rates of Incarceration could not validate it. There are too few highly disadvantaged white neighborhoods to be used for comparisons. But the committee did find evidence in ethnographic studies consistent with the coercive mobility argument (Travis, Western, and Redburn 2014, pp. 289–98).

It is likely that mass incarceration is criminogenic and increases black, brown, and white differences in criminal behavior. The agencies of the criminal justice system, charged with protecting society from crime, are now a major source of racial differences in criminal involvement. This happens because they disadvantage already heavily disadvantaged populations and communities.

People of color continue to face discrimination in the labor market, in housing, and in education. As a consequence, larger portions of the black and brown populations live in poverty and in socially and economically disadvantaged neighborhoods that spawn crime and violence.[12] Sampson and Lauritsen (1997) two decades ago called for researchers to examine macrostructural disadvantage to improve our understanding of crime differentials. Since then, Sampson and his colleagues have demonstrated that racial differences in violence can be explained by the greater frequency of African Americans living in underclass, disadvantaged neighborhoods (Morenoff, Sampson, and Raudenbush 2001; Sampson 2009). Racial differences in values or orientations, such as legal cynicism, are products of concentrated disadvantage (Sampson and Bartusch 1998). Ulmer, Casey, and Steffensmeier (2012), studying New York and California, report that racial differences in violent crimes among African Americans, whites, and Latinos can be accounted for by differential dis-

[12] See the Civil Rights Project (http://civilrightsproject.ucla.edu/research/k-12-education/school-discipline) for recent reports of continuing inequality in school discipline and suspension.

advantage. There remains some debate whether poverty or income inequality is the real force generating increased violence (Sampson 1985; Hipp 2007), but there is no disagreement that economic marginalization of African Americans is the source of high crime rates in black communities.

Racial differences in violence can be explained by social class differences when underclass neighborhoods and social and economic disadvantage are used as measures of social class. Unnever and Gabbidon (2011) argue that African Americans, in response to discrimination experienced by individuals and life in segregated places, develop a worldview that leads to higher levels of criminal involvement. They cite data consistent with this perspective. Their provocative micro-macro causal sequence will be challenging to test, but it is not inconsistent with a growing micro and macro literature on the causes of crime.

To make the case that higher African American criminal involvement results from structured economic and social disadvantage, we have to take seriously the things we teach students. Key concepts must be observable. The best data to be used are defined not by what we usually use or prefer to work with or is most convenient, but what is most appropriate for the questions to be answered. Research methods must flow from research questions. If we take these basic notions seriously, we cannot possibly posit that subcultural values carried by individuals living in particular neighborhoods and passed on intergenerationally account for racial differences in criminal violence. We should not retreat to the black-box theory and say or write, "It must be a subculture." As recently as the 2013 meetings of the American Society of Criminology, some scholars in prominently presented papers made just that retreat. By contrast, aggregate studies of neighborhood-level inequality and disadvantage have provided compelling evidence that these are the actual forces accounting for racial differences in violent crime.

If we allow for a more complex understanding of race/ethnicity, crime, and social class, we may make real headway in understanding the processes that shape the lives of criminals and noncriminals. Consider, for instance, Moffitt's (1993) distinction between adolescent limited and life course persistent delinquents. I imagine that a great many criminologists think only in terms of these categories distinguishing people with differential personality or other internal traits. But perhaps communities where generation after generation of people are marginalized from the labor market, quality schools, and decent housing, and feel subjugated by a social, political, and economic order that is not of their making or influence, are producing people who are at especially high risk of becoming life course persistent offenders.

Moving further away from traditional criminology, how might environmental insults that disproportionately affect disadvantaged places contribute to differential crime rates? Unnever and Gabbidon (2011) conclude that African Americans are far more likely to live in areas in which they are exposed to lead poisoning and other toxins. There is evidence that this is linked to higher levels of offending. An editor for *Chemical and Engineering News* has suggested, on the basis of work by social scientists (Stretsky and Lynch 2001; Nevin 2007) and medical researchers (Cecil et al. 2008), that banning leaded gasoline and lead in paint may be one cause of the crime decline (Wolf 2014). Lead has been linked to learning disabilities and reduced impulse control.

It is premature to endorse such ideas with the limited available evidence. We should, though, take seriously the observation that African Americans and to an extent Latinos engage in more violence because they live in disadvantaged neighborhoods. That would move us away from the lazy intellectual gymnastics involved in simply positing unobserved norms and values and take seriously the influence of circumstances outside of poor people's control.

Instead we should explore other mechanisms that connect race, disadvantage, and crime. Even in the most disadvantaged places, most children do not become delinquents and most adults are not criminals. Most African Americans and Hispanics are no more likely to engage in crime than are most white and Asian Americans.

Why, even in the face of discrimination and disadvantage, do not more people resort to crime and violence? Probably because most people who suffer those obstacles focus their energies on living their lives just as other people do, but with the added burden of overcoming the special difficulties that come with their position in the social structure.

Many parents in underclass neighborhoods work hard to shield their children from challenges and dangers on the streets. Anderson (1999) writes about these parents and labels them, using the vernacular of the ghetto, "decent families." They try to protect their children from the code of the street and other negative norms and values (Larzelere and Patterson 1990). Hirschi (1969) and others who have tested his version of control theory have reported that children who establish close bonds to their parents are less likely to become involved in delinquency (Gove and Crutchfield 1982; Leiber, Mack, and Featherstone 2009). Poverty, however, presents additional challenges for families, at times leading to family disruptions, inconsistent parenting, and low levels of supervision, which can lead in turn to more delinquency (Sampson and Laub 1994; Wadsworth 2000).

Perhaps it is the lack of collective efficacy in desperately poor places, or the lack of jobs for adults who live there, or the frustrations of their children, or unequal educations that limits their options, or the inevitably negative consequences of mass imprisonment. Scholars have observed value and normative differences. They have also observed that the structural conditions that generate such values are intergenerationally present. That is evidence that structural conditions, disadvantage, and isolation are the fundamental causes of continuing social and economic plight, including elevated crime rates. Distinctive values and behaviors are recreated in each new generation by the continuity of ongoing structural circumstances. Perhaps the progressives and Marxists of the 1960s and 1970s (and now) were correct when they asserted that people of color engage in more crime because of the actions of the state and elites.

Where might discussions of race, crime and social class go in the years ahead? I suggest three answers. First, the effects of mass incarceration will be brought increasingly into the discussion.

Second, income inequality is growing in the United States. This will likely increase the social distance between the poor and the wider society. If the socially and economically disadvantaged portion of the population grows appreciably, and it likely will, those who live in underclass neighborhoods will experience more marginalization and stress, which will affect crime patterns.

Third, though this prediction dismays me, publications will continue to appear and conference papers to be presented in which scholars advance traditional subculture of violence or subculture of poverty arguments. Those arguments resemble the zombies and vampires that populate books and movies popular among some young people. Like zombies and vampires, those arguments are already dead. Our disciplines have not yet found the crosses, silver bullets, or stakes to drive into the heart that will finally end the reappearances of the "undead" traditional subculture arguments.

REFERENCES

Adamson, Christopher R. 1983. "Punishment after Slavery: Southern State Penal Systems, 1865–1890." *Social Problems* 50(5):555–69.

Adelman, Robert M. 2004. "Neighborhood Opportunities, Race, and Class: The Black Middle Class and Residential Segregation." *City and Community* 3 (1):43–63.

Aguirre, Adalberto, Jr. 1999. "Slave Executions in the United States: A Descriptive Analysis of Social and Historical Factors." *Social Science Journal* 36(1):1–31.

Anderson, Elijah. 1994. "The Code of the Streets." *Atlantic Monthly* 273(5):81–94.

———. 1999. *Code of the Street: Decency, Violence, and the Moral Life of the Inner City*. New York: Norton.

Ball-Rokeach, Sandra J. 1973. "Values and Violence: A Test of the Subculture of Violence Thesis." *American Sociological Review* 38:736–49.

Banfield, Edward C. 1970. *The Unheavenly City*. Boston: Little, Brown.

Blumstein, Albert. 1982. "On the Racial Disproportionality of the US States' Prison Population." *Journal of Criminal Law and Criminology* 73(3):1259–81.

———. 1993. "Racial Disproportionality of US Prison Populations Revisited." *University of Colorado Law Review* 64:743–60.

Bonger, Willem. 1916. *Criminality and Economic Conditions*. Boston: Little, Brown.

Bridges, George S., and Robert D. Crutchfield. 1988. "Law, Social Standing and Racial Disparities in Imprisonment." *Social Forces* 66:699–724.

Bruce, Marino A. 1999. "Inequality and Delinquency: Sorting Out Some Class and Race Effects." *Race and Society* 2(2):133–48.

Bursik, Robert J., and Harold G. Grasmick. 1993. *Neighborhoods and Crime: The Dimensions of Effective Community Control*. New York: Lexington.

Butterfield, Fox. 2008. *All God's Children: The Bosket Family and the American Tradition of Violence*. New York: Vintage.

Cable, George W. 1969. *The Silent South*. Montclair, NJ: Patterson Smith. (Originally published 1889. New York: Scribner's.)

Cecil, Kim M., Christopher J. Brubaker, Caleb M. Adler, Kim N. Dietrich, Mekibib Altaye, John C. Egelhoff, Stephanie Wessel, Ilayaraja Elangovan, Richard Hornung, Kelly Jarvis, and Bruce P. Lanphear. 2008. "Decreased Brain Volume in Adults with Childhood Lead Exposure." *Public Library of Science Medicine* 5(5):e112. http://www.plosmedicine.org/article/info:doi/10.1371/journal.pmed.0050112.

Chambliss, William J. 1964. "A Sociological Analysis of the Law of Vagrancy." *Social Problems* 12(1):67–77.

———. 1973. "Race, Sex, and Gangs: The Saints and the Roughnecks." *Trans-Action* 11(1):24–31.

Chambliss, William J., and R. H. Nagasawa. 1969. "On the Validity of Official Statistics: A Comparative Study of White, Black, and Japanese High-School Boys." *Journal of Research in Crime and Delinquency* 6:71–77.

Clear, Todd R. 2007. *Imprisoning Communities: How Mass Incarceration Makes Disadvantaged Neighborhoods Worse*. New York: Oxford University Press.
Cloward, Richard A., and Lloyd E. Ohlin. 1960. *Delinquency and Opportunity: A Theory of Delinquent Gangs*. Glencoe, IL: Free Press.
Cohen, Albert K. 1955. *Delinquent Boys: The Culture of the Gang*. Glencoe, IL: Free Press.
Crowder, Kyle, Jeremy Pais, and Scott J. South. 2012. "Neighborhood Diversity, Metropolitan Constraints, and Household Migration." *American Sociological Review* 77(3):325–53.
Crutchfield, Robert D. 1994. "Ethnicity, Labor Markets, and Crime." In *Ethnicity, Race, and Crime Perspectives across Time and Place*, edited by Darnell F. Hawkins. Albany: State University of New York Press.
———. 2014. *Get a Job: Labor Markets, Economic Opportunity and Crime*. New York: New York University Press.
Crutchfield, Robert D., George S. Bridges, and Susan R. Pitchford. 1994. "Analytical and Aggregation Biases in Analyses of Imprisonment: Reconciling Discrepancies in Studies of Racial Disparity." *Journal of Research in Crime and Delinquency* 31(2):166–82.
Crutchfield, Robert D., and R. Finke. 1983. "Convict Lease Systems: The Political Economy of Post–Civil War Development." Paper presented at the 1983 meetings of the American Society of Criminology, Denver.
Crutchfield, Robert D., and David Pettinicchio. 2009. "'Cultures of Inequality': Ethnicity, Immigration, Social Welfare, and Imprisonment." *Annals of the American Academy of Political and Social Science* 623:134–47.
Crutchfield, Robert D., David Pettinicchio, and Blaine Robbins. 2013. "Cultures of Inequality and Threat: National Values and Minority Imprisonment." In *Proceedings of Colloque International: Déviance/s*. Bordeaux: Université Michel de Montaigne Bordeaux 3.
Curtis, Lynn A. 1975. *Violence, Race, and Culture*. Lexington, MA: Lexington.
Davies, Garth, and Jeffrey Fagan. 2012. "Crime and Enforcement in Immigrant Neighborhoods: Evidence from New York City." *Annals of the American Academy of Political and Social Science* 641(1):99–124.
Davis, Kingsley. 1937. "The Sociology of Prostitution." *American Sociological Review* 2(5):744–55.
Davis, Kingsley, and Wilbert E. Moore. 1945. "Some Principles of Stratification." *American Sociological Review* 10:242–49.
Davis, Nanette J. 1981. *Sociological Constructions of Deviance: Perspectives and Issues in the Field*. 2nd ed. Dubuque, IA: William C. Brown.
Daykin, Jeffer B. 2006. "'They Themselves Contribute to Their Misery by Their Sloth': The Justification of Slavery in Eighteenth-Century French Travel Narratives." *European Legacy* 11(6):623–32.
Drakulich, Kevin M. 2013. "Perceptions of the Local Danger Posed by Crime: Race, Disorder, Informal Control, and the Police." *Social Science Research* 42 (3):611–32.
Du Bois, W. E. B. 1899. *The Philadelphia Negro*. Philadelphia: University of Pennsylvania Press.

Elliot, Delbert, and Suzanne Ageton. 1980. "Reconciling Race and Class Differences in Self-Reported and Official Estimates of Delinquency." *American Sociological Review* 45:95–110.

Emerson, Michael O., Karen J. Chai, and George Yancey. 2001. "Does Race Matter in Residential Segregation? Exploring the Preferences of White Americans." *American Sociological Review* 66(6):922–35.

Erlanger, Howard. 1972. "An Empirical Critique of Theories of Interpersonal Violence." In *The American Sociological Association 1972 Annual Proceedings*. Washington, DC: American Sociological Association.

Estrich, Susan. 2012. "Politics and Personal Responsibility." Yahoo News. http://news.yahoo.com/politics-personal-responsibility-080000029.html.

Felson, Richard B., Glenn Deane, and David P. Armstrong. 2008. "Do Theories of Crime or Violence Explain Race Differences in Delinquency?" *Social Science Research* 37(2):624–41.

Gastil, Raymond D. 1971. "Homicide and a Regional Culture of Violence." *American Sociological Review* 36(3):412–27.

Glueck, Sheldon, and Eleanor Glueck. 1940. *Juvenile Delinquents Grown Up*. New York: Commonwealth Fund.

Goldman, Samuel. 2013. "Responsibility, Personal and Individual (or, How to Do Political Theory by Watching 'Girls')." American Conservative. http://www.theamericanconservative.com/responsibility-personal-and-individual-or-how-to-do-political-theory-by-watching-girls/.

Gotham, Kevin Fox. 2000. "Urban Space, Restrictive Covenants and the Origins of Racial Residential Segregation in a US City, 1900–50." *International Journal of Urban and Regional Research* 24(3):616–33.

Gove, Walter R., and Robert D. Crutchfield. 1982. "The Family and Delinquency: An Old Issue Revisited." *Sociological Quarterly* 23(2):301–19.

Haddad, Yvonne Yazbeck, and Michael J. Balz. 2006. "The October Riots in France: A Failed Immigration Policy or the Empire Strikes Back?" *International Migration* 44:23–34.

Harris, Alexes. 2015. *A Pound of Flesh: Monetary Sanctions as a Permanent Punishment for Poor People*. New York: Sage.

Harris, Cherise A. 2002. "Who Supports Welfare Reform and Why?" *Race, Gender and Class* 9(1):96–121.

Harter, Paséale. 2007. "Madrid Clashes over Latin Gangs." BBC News, January 22. http://news.bbc.co.ukZ2/hi/europe/6286977.stm.

Hays, Sharon. 2003. *Flat Broke with Children: Women in the Age of Welfare Reform*. New York: Oxford University Press.

Herrnstein, Richard J., and Charles Murray. 1995. *The Bell Curve: Intelligence and Class Structure in American Life*. New York: Free Press.

Hindelang, Michael J. 1978. "Race and Involvement in Common Law Personal Crimes." *American Sociological Review* 43(1):93–109.

Hindelang, Michael J., Travis Hirschi, and Joseph G. Weis. 1979. "Correlates of Delinquency: The Illusion of Discrepancy between Self-Report and Official Data." *American Sociological Review* 44:995–1014.

———. 1981. *Measuring Delinquency*. Beverly Hills, CA: Sage.

Hipp, John R. 2007. "Income Inequality, Race, and Place: Does the Distribution of Race and Class within Neighborhoods Affect Crime Rates?" *Criminology* 45(3):665–97.

Hirschi, Travis. 1969. *Causes of Delinquency*: Berkeley: University of California Press.

Jennings, Wesley G., Kristen M. Zgoba, Alex R. Piquero, and Jennifer M. Reingle. 2013. "Offending Trajectories among Native-Born and Foreign-Born Hispanics to Late Middle Age." *Sociological Inquiry* 83(4):622–47.

Jones, Nikki. 2010. *Between Good and Ghetto: African American Girls and Inner-City Violence*. New Brunswick, NJ: Rutgers University Press.

Kirschenman, Joleen, and Kathryn M. Neckerman. 1991. "'We'd Love to Hire Them, but . . .': The Meaning of Race for Employers." In *The Urban Underclass*, edited by Christopher Jencks and Paul E. Peterson. Washington, DC: Brookings Institution.

Lane, Roger. 1986. *Roots of Violence in Black Philadelphia*. Cambridge, MA: Harvard University Press.

Langan, Patrick. 1985. "Racism on Trial: New Evidence to Explain the Racial Composition of Prisons in the United States." *Journal of Criminal Law and Criminology* 76:666–83.

Larzelere, Robert E., and Gerald R. Patterson. 1990. "Parental Management: Mediator of the Effect of Socioeconomic State on Early Delinquency." *Criminology* 28(2):301–24.

Lauritsen, Janet L., and Karen Heimer. 2010. "Violent Victimization among Males and Economic Conditions." *Criminology and Public Policy* 9(4):665–92.

Leiber, Michael J., Kristin Y. Mack, and Richard A. Featherstone. 2009. "Family Structure, Family Processes, Economic Factors, and Delinquency: Similarities and Difference by Race and Ethnicity." *Youth Violence and Juvenile Justice* 7(2):79–99.

Lewis, Oscar. 1959. *Five Families: Mexican Case Studies in the Culture of Poverty*. New York: Basic Books.

Lieberman, Robert C. 1995. "Race, Institutions, and the Administration of Social Policy." *Social Science History* 19(4):511–42.

Lieberson, Stanley. 1981. *A Piece of the Pie: Blacks and White Immigrants since 1880*. Berkeley: University of California Press.

Manza, Jeff, and Christopher Uggen. 2006. *Locked Out: Felon Disenfranchisement and American Democracy*. New York: Oxford University Press.

Martinez, Ramiro, Jr., Matthew T. Lee, and Amie L. Nielsen. 2001. "Revisiting the Scarface Legacy: The Victim/Offender Relationship and Mariel Homicides in Miami." *Journal of Behavioral Sciences* 23(1):37–56.

Martinez, Ramiro, Jr., and Jacob Stowell. 2012. "Extending Immigration and Crime Studies: National Implications and Local Settings." *Annals of the American Academy of Political and Social Science* 641:174–91.

Massey, Douglas S., and Nancy A. Denton. 1993. *American Apartheid: Segregation and the Making of the Underclass*. Cambridge, MA: Harvard University Press.

McKeown, James Edward. 1948. "Poverty, Race and Crime." *Journal of Criminal Law and Criminology* 39:480–84.

Mead, Lawrence M. 1986. *Beyond Entitlement: The Social Obligations of Citizenship*. New York: Free Press.

———. 1993. *The New Politics of Poverty: The Nonworking Poor in America*. New York: Basic Books.

———. 2004. *Government Matters: Welfare Reform in Wisconsin*. Princeton, NJ: Princeton University Press.

———. 2011. *Expanding Work Programs for Poor Men*. Washington, DC: AEI Press.

Miller, Jody. 2008. *Getting Played: African American Girls, Urban Inequality and Gendered Violence*. New York: New York University Press.

Moffitt, Terrie E. 1993. "Adolescence-Limited and Life-Course-Persistent Antisocial Behavior: A Developmental Taxonomy." *Psychological Review* 100 (4):674–701.

Morenoff, Jeffrey D. 2005. "Racial and Ethnic Disparities in Crime and Delinquency in the United States." In *Ethnicity and Causal Mechanisms*, edited by Jeffrey D. Morenoff. Cambridge: Cambridge University Press.

Morenoff, Jeffrey D., Robert J. Sampson, and Steven W. Raudenbush. 2001. "Neighborhood Inequality, Collective Efficacy, and the Spatial Dynamics of Urban Violence." *Criminology* 39(3):517–60.

Mosher, Clayton J., and Scott Akins. 2007. *Drugs and Drug Policy: The Control of Consciousness Alteration*. Thousand Oaks, CA: Sage.

Murray, Charles. 1984. *Losing Ground: American Social Policy, 1950–1980*. New York: Basic Books.

National Center for Health Statistics. 1995. "Advance Report of Final Mortality Statistics, 1992." *Monthly Vital Statistics Report* 43(6).

Nevin, Rick. 2007. "Understanding International Crime Trends: The Legacy of Preschool Lead Exposure." *Environmental Research* 104(3):315–36.

O'Brien, Robert M. 1987. "The Interracial Nature of Violent Crimes: A Reexamination." *American Journal of Sociology* 92(4):817–35.

Page, Joshua. 2013. "On the Edge: Juvenile Former Prisoners and the Struggle to Make It in Urban America." Paper presented to the European Society of Criminology, Working Group on Offender Supervision, Liverpool Hope University, April 25.

Pager, Devah. 2003. "The Mark of a Criminal Record." *American Journal of Sociology* 108:937–75.

———. 2007. *Marked: Race, Crime, and Finding Work in an Era of Mass Incarceration*. Chicago: University of Chicago Press.

Park, Robert E., Ernst W. Burgess, and Roderick D. McKenzie. 1925. *The City*. Chicago: University of Chicago Press.

Parker, Karen F. 2008. *Unequal Crime Decline: Theorizing Race, Urban Inequality, and Criminal Violence*. New York: New York University Press.

Parker, Karen F., and Patricia McCall. 1999. "Structural Conditions and Racial Homicide Patterns: A Look at the Multiple Disadvantages in Urban Areas." *Criminology* 37(3):447–77.

Paton, Diana. 2001. "Punishment, Crime, and the Bodies of Slaves in Eighteenth Century Jamaica." *Journal of Social History* 34(4):923–54.

Pattillo-McCoy, Mary. 1999. *Black Picket Fences: Privilege and Peril among the Black Middle Class*. Chicago: University of Chicago Press.

Peterson, Ruth D., and Lauren J. Krivo. 2009. "Segregated Spatial Locations, Race-Ethnic Composition, and Neighborhood Violent Crime." *Annals of the American Academy of Political and Social Science* 623(1):93–107.

———. 2010. *Divergent Social Worlds: Neighborhood Crime and the Racial-Spatial Divide*. New York: Russell Sage Foundation.

Peterson, Ruth D., Lauren J. Krivo, and John Hagan. 2006. *The Many Colors of Crime: Inequalities of Race, Ethnicity, and Crime in America*. New York: New York University Press.

Pettit, Becky. 2012. *Invisible Men: Mass Incarceration and the Myth of Black Progress*. New York: Russell Sage Foundation.

Pettit, Becky, and Christopher Lyons. 2009. "Incarceration and Legitimate Labor Market: Examining Age-Graded Effects on Employment and Wages." *Law and Society Review* 43(4):725–56.

Pettit, Becky, and Bruce Western. 2004. "Mass Imprisonment and the Life Course: Race and Class Inequality in US Incarceration." *American Sociological Review* 69(2):151–69.

Piquero, Alex R., Randall MacIntosh, and Matthew Hickman. 2002. "The Validity of a Self-Reported Delinquency Scale: Comparisons across Gender, Age, Race, and Place of Residence." *Sociological Methods and Research* 30(4):492–529.

Quillian, Lincoln. 2012. "Segregation and Poverty Concentration: The Role of Three Segregations." *American Sociological Review* 77(3):354–79.

Quinney, Richard. 1970. *The Social Reality of Crime*. Boston: Little, Brown.

———. 1977. *Class, State and Crime: On the Theory and Practice of Criminal Justice*. New York: David McKay.

Reiss, Albert J., and Jeffrey Roth, eds. 1993. *Understanding and Preventing Violence*. Washington, DC: National Academy Press.

Rios, Victor M. 2011. *Punished: Policing the Lives of Black and Latino Boys*. New York: New York University Press.

Rönnbäck, Klas. 2014. "The Idle and the Industrious—European Ideas about the African Work Ethic in Precolonial West Africa." *History in Africa: A Journal of Method* 41:117–45.

Rose, Dina R., and Todd R. Clear. 1998. "Incarceration, Social Capital and Crime: Examining the Unintended Consequences of Incarceration." *Criminology* 36(3):441–79.

Ryan, William. 1971. *Blaming the Victim*. New York: Pantheon.

Rymond-Richmond, Wenona. 2007. "The Habitus of Habitat: Mapping the History, Redevelopment, and Crime in Public Housing." PhD dissertation, Northwestern University, Department of Sociology.

Sampson, Robert J. 1985. "Structural Sources of Variation in Race-Age-Specific Rates of Offending across Major US Cities." *Criminology* 23(4):647–74.

———. 2008. "Rethinking Crime and Immigration." *Contexts* 7:28–33.

———. 2009. "Racial Stratification and the Durable Tangle of Neighborhood Inequality." *Annals of the American Academy of Political and Social Science* 621 (1):260–80.

Sampson, Robert J., and Dawn Jeglum Bartusch. 1998. "Legal Cynicism and (Subcultural?) Tolerance of Deviance: The Neighborhood Context of Racial Differences." *Law and Society Review* 32(4):777–804.

Sampson, Robert J., and John H. Laub. 1994. "Urban Poverty and the Family Context of Delinquency: A New Look at Structure and Process in a Classic Study." *Child Development* 65(2):523–40.

Sampson, Robert J., and Janet L. Lauritsen. 1997. "Racial and Ethnic Disparities in Crime and Criminal Justice in the United States." In *Ethnicity, Crime, and Immigration: Comparative and Cross-National Perspectives*, edited by Michael Tonry. Vol. 21 of *Crime and Justice: A Review of Research*, edited by Michael Tonry. Chicago: University of Chicago Press.

Sampson, Robert J., and William Julius Wilson. 1995. "Toward a Theory of Race, Crime, and Urban Inequality." In *Crime and Inequality*, edited by John Hagan and Ruth D. Peterson. Stanford, CA: Stanford University Press.

Saperstein, Aliya, and Andrew M. Penner. 2010. "The Race of a Criminal Record: How Incarceration Colors Racial Perceptions." *Social Problems* 57(1):92–113.

Schur, Edwin. 1973. *Radical Non-intervention*. Englewood Cliffs, NJ: Prentice-Hall.

Shaw, Clifford R., and Henry McKay. 1942. *Juvenile Delinquency and Urban Areas*. Chicago: University of Chicago Press.

Shihadeh, Edward S. 2009. "Race, Class, and Crime: Reconsidering the Spatial Effects of Social Isolation on Rates of Urban Offending." *Deviant Behavior* 30 (4):349–78.

Small, Mario Luis, David Harding, and Michele Lamont. 2011. "Reconsidering Culture and Poverty." *Sociologia and Antropologia* 1(2):91–118.

Small, Mario Luis, and Katherine Newman. 2001. "Urban Poverty after the Truly Disadvantaged: The Rediscovery of the Family, the Neighborhood, and Culture." *Annual Review of Sociology* 27:23–45.

Smith, Thomas E. 2007. "The Discourse of Violence: Transatlantic Narratives of Lynching during High Imperialism." *Journal of Colonialism and Colonial History* 8(2):15. doi:10.1353/cch.2007.0040.

South, Scott J., and Kyle D. Crowder. 1998. "Housing Discrimination and Residential Mobility: Impacts for Black and Whites." *Population Research and Policy Review* 17(4):369–87.

Sowell, Thomas. 1983. *The Economics and Politics of Race*. New York: Morrow.

Spencer, Herbert. 1961. "The Nature of Society." In *Theories of Society*, edited by Talcott Parsons, E. Shils, K. Naegele, and J. E. Pitts. New York: Free Press.

Spohn, Cassia. 2015. "Race, Crime, and Punishment in the Twentieth and Twenty-First Centuries." In *Crime and Justice: A Review of Research*, vol. 44, edited by Michael Tonry. Chicago: University of Chicago Press.

Steele, Shelby. 1991. *The Content of Our Character: A New Vision of Race in America*. New York: Harper.

Stretsky, Paul B., and Michael J. Lynch. 2001. "The Relationship between Lead Exposure and Homicide." *Archives of Pediatric and Adolescent Medicine* 155 (5):579–82.

Substance Abuse and Mental Health Services Administration. 2015. *Behavioral Health Barometer: United States, 2014*. HHS Publication no. SMA-15-4895. Rockville, MD: Substance Abuse and Mental Health Services Administration.

Sullivan, Mercer L. 1989. *Getting Paid: Youth Crime and Work in the Inner City*. Ithaca, NY: Cornell University Press.

Sumner, William G. 1952. *What Social Classes Owe to Each Other*. Caldwell, ID: Caxton.

Sutherland, Edwin. 1924. *Criminology*. Philadelphia: Lippincott.

Tannenbaum, Frank. 1938. *Crime and the Community*. Boston: Ginn.

Thomson, Ann. 2008. "Abolitionism and the Question of Race." *Revue Française de Civilisation Britannique* 15(1):175–86.

Tittle, Charles R., Wayne J. Villemez, and Douglas A. Smith. 1978. "The Myth of Social Class and Criminality: An Empirical Assessment of the Empirical Evidence." *American Sociological Review* 43:643–56.

Tolnay, Stewart E., and E. M. Beck. 1995. *A Festival of Violence: An Analysis of Southern Lynching*. Champaign-Urbana: University of Illinois Press.

Tonry, Michael. 1995. *Malign Neglect: Race, Crime, and Punishment in America*. New York: Oxford University Press.

———. 2011. *Punishing Race: A Continuing American Dilemma*. New York: Oxford University Press.

Tonry, Michael, and Matthew Melewski. 2008. "The Malign Effects of Drug and Crime Control Policies on Black Americans." In *Crime and Justice: A Review of Research*, vol. 37, edited by Michael Tonry. Chicago: University of Chicago Press.

Tran, Van Chi. 2012. "How Neighborhoods Matter, and for Whom: Disadvantaged Context, Ethnic Cultural Repertoires and Second-Generation Social Mobility in Young Adulthood." PhD dissertation, Harvard University, Department of Sociology.

Travis, Jeremy, Bruce Western, and Stevens Redburn, eds. 2014. *The Growth of Incarceration in the United States: Exploring Causes and Consequences*. Washington, DC: National Academies Press.

Ulmer, Jeffery T., Casey T. Harris, and Darrell Steffensmeier. 2012. "Racial and Ethnic Disparities in Structural Disadvantage and Crime: White, Black, and Hispanic Comparisons." *Social Science Quarterly* 93(3):799–819.

Unnever, James D., and Shaun L. Gabbidon. 2011. *A Theory of African American Offending: Race, Racism, and Crime*. New York: Routledge.

US Department of Justice. 1994. *Criminal Victimization in the United States, 1973–1992 Trends*. Washington, DC: US Government Printing Office.

Venkatesh, Sudhir Alladi. 2000. *American Project: The Rise and Fall of a Modern Ghetto*. Cambridge, MA: Harvard University Press.

von Hentig, Hans. 1940. "The Criminality of the Negro." *Journal of Criminal Law and Criminology* 30:662–80.

Wadsworth, Tim. 2000. "Labor Markets, Delinquency, and Social Control Theory: An Empirical Assessment of the Mediating Process." *Social Forces* 78(3):1041–66.

Washington, Booker T. 1912. "Negro Crime and Strong Drink." *Journal of the American Institute of Criminal Law and Criminology* 3:384–92.

Western, Bruce. 2006. *Punishment and Inequality in America*. New York: Russell Sage Foundation.

Wikström, Per-Olof H., and Rolf Loeber. 2000. "Do Disadvantaged Neighborhoods Cause Well-Adjusted Children to Become Adolescent Delinquents? A Study of Male Juvenile Serious Offending, Individual Risk and Protective Factors, and Neighborhood Context." *Criminology* 38(4):1109–42.

Wilson, James Q., and Richard J. Herrnstein. 1985. *Crime and Human Nature: The Definitive Study of the Causes of Crime*. New York: Simon & Schuster.

Wilson, William Julius. 1987. *The Truly Disadvantaged: The Inner City, the Underclass, and Public Policy*. Chicago: University of Chicago Press.

———. 1996. *When Work Disappears: The World of the Urban Poor*. New York: Knopf.

Wolf, Lauren. 2014. "The Crimes of Lead." *Chemical and Engineering News* 92 (5):27–29.

Wolfgang, Marvin, and Franco Ferracuti. 1967. *The Subculture of Violence: Towards an Integrated Theory in Criminology*. London: Tavistock.

Wortley, Scot. 2003. "Hidden Intersections: Research on Race, Crime, and Criminal Justice in Canada." *Canadian Ethnic Studies/Etudes Ethniques au Canada* 35(3):99–117.

Wright, Bradley, R. Entner, and C. Wesley Younts. 2009. "Reconsidering the Relationship between Race and Crime: Positive and Negative Predictors of Crime among African American Youth." *Journal of Research in Crime and Delinquency* 46(3):327–52.

Zukin, Sharon. 1987. "Gentrification: Culture and Capital in the Urban Core." *Annual Review of Sociology* 13:129–47.

Cassia Spohn

Race, Crime, and Punishment in the Twentieth and Twenty-First Centuries

ABSTRACT

Flagrant and widespread racism that characterized the criminal justice system during the early part of the twentieth century has largely been eliminated, but racial disparities persist. Whether because of overt racism, implicit bias, or laws and practices that have racially disparate effects, black (and Hispanic) men and women make up a disproportionate number of people in American prisons and on death row. Researchers have conducted dozens of studies designed to untangle the complex relationships between race and punishment to determine the causes of racial disparities. Findings vary somewhat, but most conclude that the share of racial disproportionality in imprisonment that can be explained by differential involvement in crime has declined over time; attribute the continuing—possibly worsening—disparity to policies pursued during the war on drugs and officials' race-linked stereotypes of culpability, dangerousness, and likelihood of reoffending; and contend that race affects the capital sentencing process. Remedying this will require reducing the size of the prison population, reforming the sentencing process so that many more offenders convicted of nonserious crimes receive alternatives to incarceration, and abolishing or severely restricting use of the death penalty.

In the late 1930s, Gunnar Myrdal, an economics professor at the University of Stockholm, was invited by the Carnegie Corporation of New York to undertake a "comprehensive study of the Negro in the United

Electronically published August 6, 2015

Cassia Spohn is foundation professor and director of the School of Criminology and Criminal Justice at Arizona State University.

0192-3234/2015/0044-0002$10.00

States" (1944, p. ix). Myrdal's examination of "courts, sentences and prisons," which relied primarily on anecdotal accounts of differential treatment of blacks and whites in southern court systems, documented widespread racial discrimination in court processing and sentencing. Myrdal noted that southern courts failed to provide black defendants with competent lawyers to represent them, imposed prohibitively high bail on black defendants, and engaged in quasi-legal machinations to preserve the all-white jury. He also observed that black defendants were handled informally and with a lack of dignity and observed that convictions often were obtained with less-than-convincing evidence.

Myrdal reserved his harshest criticism for the differences in punishment imposed on similarly situated black and white defendants. He noted that grand juries routinely refused to indict whites for crimes—even very serious crimes—against blacks, that whites who were indicted for crimes against blacks were rarely convicted, and that those who were convicted received only the mildest punishments. He also pointed out that crimes by blacks against other blacks were not regarded as serious and, as a result, also were unlikely to result in indictment, conviction, or severe punishment. By contrast, blacks convicted, or even suspected, of crimes against whites were subject to the harshest treatment. According to Myrdal, if the crime was serious and there was threat of a lynching, "the court makes no pretense at justice; the Negro must be condemned, and usually condemned to death, before the crowd gets him" (1944, p. 553). He concluded that "the whole judicial system of courts, sentences, and prisons in the South is overripe for fundamental reforms" (p. 555).

Several highly publicized cases confirm the validity of Myrdal's accusations. Perhaps the most infamous involved the "Scottsboro Boys." In March 1931, nine black teenage boys were accused of raping two white girls on a slow-moving freight train traveling through Alabama. They were arrested and taken to Scottsboro, Alabama, where they were indicted for rape, a capital offense. Within a short time, all were tried and convicted by all-white juries, and eight of the nine were sentenced to death. In 1932, the US Supreme Court overturned their convictions on the grounds that they had been denied the right to counsel at trial (*Powell v. Alabama*, 287 U.S. 45 [1932]). The Scottsboro Boys were quickly retried, reconvicted, and resentenced to death, even though one of the alleged victims had recanted and questions were raised about the other victim's credibility. In 1935, the Supreme Court again reversed their convictions, this time ruling that the exclusion of blacks from jury service deprived black defendants of their right to equal protection of the laws guaranteed by the Fourteenth Amendment (*Norris v. Alabama*, 294 U.S. 587 [1935]). Less than 8 months later, a grand jury composed of 13 whites and one black returned new indictments against the nine defendants. The state eventually dropped charges against four of them and allowed a fifth to plead to a lesser charge, but the other four defendants were convicted of rape a third time. One was sentenced to death, one was sentenced to 99 years in prison, and the remaining two were sentenced to 75 years in prison. Collectively, the nine Scottsboro Boys served 104 years in prison for a crime that many believe was "almost certainly a hoax" (Kennedy 1997, p. 104).

Another example is the case of Ed Johnson, a black man accused of raping a white woman in Chattanooga, Tennessee, in 1906 (Curriden and Phillips 1999). There was no evidence other than the word of a paid informant to connect Johnson to the crime, and more than a dozen witnesses testified that Johnson, who steadfastly maintained his innocence, was working at a local tavern when the crime occurred. The attorneys prosecuting the case described Johnson's alibi witnesses, most of them black, as "thugs, thieves and sots—the offscourings of hell" and urged the jurors to "send that black brute to the gallows" (pp. 117–18). Seventeen days after the crime had been committed, the jurors convicted Johnson of rape, which under Tennessee law at that time resulted in an automatic death sentence. His execution, which was scheduled for 5 weeks later, never took place. After the US Supreme Court issued an order staying the execution pending Johnson's appeal to the federal courts, a white lynch mob snatched him from the Hamilton County jail, marched him through town, and hanged him from a bridge spanning the Tennessee River. Fifty-three days after he was arrested for rape, Johnson, whose last words were "God bless you all, I am innocent," was dead (p. 213). A grand jury was convened to investigate the lynching, but none of the witnesses who were called to testify could (or would) identify any of the members of the lynch mob. The grand jury issued no indictments.[1]

[1] The case, however, did not end there. The US Department of Justice filed contempt of court charges against 26 individuals believed to be responsible for Johnson's lynching. For the first and only time in history, the justices of the US Supreme Court, outraged that Chattanooga officials defied their court order and did nothing to stop the lynching, conducted a criminal trial. Six individuals, including the sheriff and one of the

Those two cases illustrate overt discrimination directed against black criminal defendants. However, these events took place in the early part of the twentieth century, and much has changed since then. Legislative reforms and Supreme Court decisions protecting the rights of criminal defendants, coupled with changing attitudes toward race and race relations, have made it less likely that criminal justice officials treat defendants of different races differently. Black defendants are no longer routinely denied bail, tried by all-white juries without attorneys, or convicted on scanty evidence. The level of opprobrium assigned to crimes and the severity of punishment imposed on those convicted of crimes no longer reflect overt discrimination based on the races of the defendant and the victim. Thus, whites who commit crimes against blacks are not beyond the reach of the criminal justice system, blacks who victimize other blacks are not immune from punishment, and blacks suspected of crimes against whites do not receive "justice" at the hands of white lynch mobs. As the twenty-first century unfolds, there is little evidence of widespread and systematic overt racial discrimination in punishment.

Although most commentators would agree that the flagrant racism described in *An American Dilemma* and documented by the Scottsboro Boys and Ed Johnson cases has been eliminated, most also would agree that significant inequities persist. Whether because of explicit discrimination, implicit bias, or the implementation of laws and practices that have racially disparate effects, the punishment imposed on black offenders is often more severe than that imposed on similarly situated white offenders. These inequities are particularly pronounced for drug offenses and, in the case of the death penalty, for offenses involving blacks convicted of crimes against whites. As a result, black (and Hispanic) men and women make up a highly disproportionate number of those locked up in our nation's prisons and on death row.

Criminologists and legal scholars use three complementary perspectives to explain the persistence of racial disparities. Critical race theorists (Crenshaw et al. 1995; Delgado and Stefancic 2001) contend that racism (as well as sexism) is ubiquitous and deeply embedded in laws and criminal justice policies and that the criminal justice system re-

---

jailers, were found guilty of contempt of the Supreme Court. Three of the six were sentenced to serve 90 days in jail; the other three received sentences of 60 days (Curriden and Phillips 1999).

inforces hierarchies in society based on race, class, gender, and other sociodemographic characteristics. These theorists further contend that the substance and procedures of American law are structured to maintain the privilege of whites (white males in particular) to the detriment of people of color. Similarly, conflict theorists (Turk 1969; Quinney 1970; Chambliss and Seidman 1971) emphasize the salience of race and class in explanations of social control. They argue that society is made up of groups with competing norms and values and maintain that the authority of the state is used to protect the interests of those in power. Central to conflict theory is the premise that the law is applied to maintain the power of the dominant group to control the behavior of those who threaten that power; thus, criminal justice agencies wield their considerable power to control and subjugate those—especially racial minorities—who threaten the political and economic elite.

In contrast to critical race theory and conflict theory—both of which focus on systemic factors and macro-level processes—attribution theory posits that race-linked perceptions and stereotypes shape decisions. This theory also focuses on the micro-level processes through which decision makers assess and evaluate offenders and their crimes. A number of scholars, for example, argue that the decisions made by judges, probation officers, and other criminal justice officials reflect race- (and gender- and class-) linked beliefs about an offender's dangerousness, threat, and potential for rehabilitation (Hawkins 1980; Albonetti 1991; Bridges and Steen 1998; Steffensmeier, Ulmer, and Kramer 1998). According to this perspective, criminal justice officials typically do not have the information needed to make accurate assessments of an offender's culpability, dangerousness, and likelihood of reoffending; as a result, they develop a "perceptual shorthand" (Hawkins 1980) based on stereotypes and attributions that are themselves linked to offender characteristics such as race, ethnicity, gender, and age. Thus, race, age, and gender interact to influence criminal justice outcomes "because of images or attributions relating these statuses to membership in social groups thought to be dangerous and crime prone" (Steffensmeier, Ulmer, and Kramer 1998, p. 768).

These complementary theoretical perspectives provide a cogent and convincing explanation of the persistence of racial disparity in punishment. Although it may no longer be true, as W. E. B. Du Bois (1903) asserted more than 100 years ago, that the central problem facing the United States is "the problem of the color line," race nonetheless remains a salient feature of American society. Criminal justice officials—whether consciously or unconsciously, overtly or implicitly—use race "as a proxy for an increased likelihood of criminal misconduct" (Kennedy 1997, p. 137), with the result that blacks and Hispanics are subject to more formal social control than whites. Viewed in this way, racial profiling, whether on the streets or in the courtroom, is an institutionalized practice firmly embedded in the agencies of the criminal justice system and is widely regarded as a legitimate and effective weapon in the war on crime.

This essay is organized as follows. Section I provides historical and contemporary evidence regarding race and punishment in the United States, with a focus on disparity in imprisonment and the use of the death penalty. Section II summarizes the results of research designed to determine whether the overrepresentation of racial minorities in our nation's prisons reflects differential involvement in crime or differential treatment by the criminal justice system. In this section, I also explore the possibility that the continuing racial disproportionality in imprisonment can be attributed to the policies pursued during the war on drugs. Section III summarizes the evolution of research examining the relationship between race and sentencing. This is followed in Section IV by a discussion of race and the application of the death penalty; I examine the constitutional issues and summarize the results of empirical research. Section V discusses policy changes that have the potential to reduce racial disparity in punishment and calls for research designed to identify more precisely the ways in which race affects criminal case outcomes and punishment severity.

I. Race and Punishment: Historical and Contemporary Evidence of Disparity

In 1918, the Bureau of the Census published a report on the *Negro Population*. It observed that blacks made up only 11 percent of the population but constituted 22 percent of the inmates of prisons, jails, reform schools, and workhouses. The report then posed a question that sparked debate and generated controversy throughout the twentieth century: "While these figures ... will probably be generally accepted as indicating that there is more criminality and law-breaking among Negroes than among whites and while that conclusion is probably justified by the facts . . . it is a question whether the difference . . . may not be to some extent the result of discrimination in the treatment of white and Negro offenders on the part of the community and the courts" (US Department of Commerce, Bureau of the Census 1918, p. 438). This question—whether the disproportionate number of racial minorities incarcerated in state and federal prisons might be "to some extent the result of discrimination"—is still being asked today. The reason is that the racial disparity in imprisonment documented by the Bureau of the Census has worsened over time. The proportion of blacks locked up in state and federal prisons, which was 22 percent in 1918, increased steadily over the next half century, reaching 33 percent by 1960 and just under 40 percent by 1970. By the mid-1990s more than half of all state and federal prisoners were black. Eighty years after the Census Bureau issued its report and posed its question about discrimination in punishment, the percentage of prisoners who were black had more than doubled.[2] Data on the race of those admitted to state and federal prisons confirm this trend. As shown in figure 1, blacks constituted 21 percent of prison admissions in 1926; they made up 30 percent in 1950, 39 percent in 1970, 41 percent in 1980, and 44 percent in 1986. By 1990, blacks constituted more than half of all persons admitted to state and federal prisons. According to Garland (2001, p. 2), these statistics suggest the "systematic imprisonment of whole groups of the population."

There also are substantial racial and ethnic differences in the lifetime likelihood of imprisonment, with black males having the highest likelihood of incarceration and experiencing the most rapid increase in that likelihood since 1974. In 2001, the chances of ever going to prison were highest among black males (32.2 percent) and Hispanic males (17.2 percent); by contrast, the odds of lifetime imprisonment were 5.9 percent for white males, 5.6 percent for black females, 2.2 percent for Hispanic females, and 0.9 percent for white females (Bureau of Justice Statistics 2003). For black men, the lifetime chances of going to prison increased from 13.2 percent in 1974 to 32.2 percent in 2001, compared to an increase from 2.2 percent to 5.9 percent for white males. Among black men born in the late 1960s who dropped out of high school, the cumulative risk of imprisonment was an astonishing 58.9 percent; by contrast,

[2] Calculation of trends over time is complicated by the decision of the Bureau of Justice Statistics in the 1990s to report separate figures for whites, blacks, and Hispanics. Before that time, Hispanics were included within the white and black racial categories.

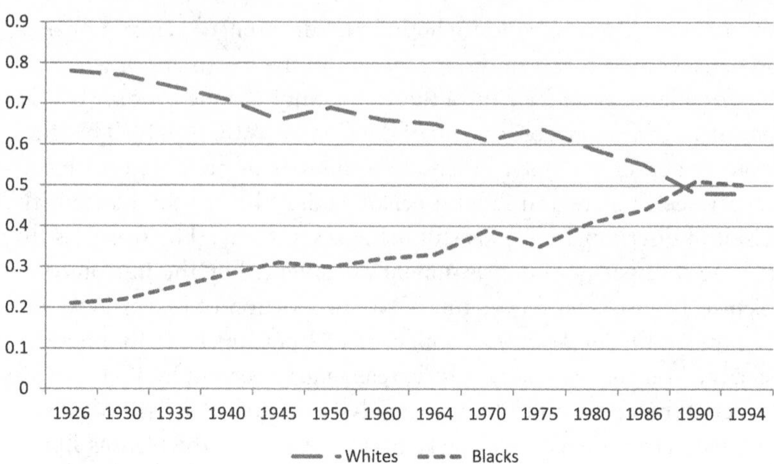

FIG. 1.—Race of persons admitted to state and federal prisons, 1926–86. Source: US Department of Justice, Bureau of Justice Statistics (1991, 1992, 1994).

it was 11.2 percent for white male high school dropouts (Western 2006, p. 26). According to Western, "The criminal justice system has become so pervasive that we should count prisons and jails among the key institutions that shape the life course of recent birth cohorts of African American men" (p. 31).

There is also clear and convincing evidence of racial disparity in the application of the death penalty. Although blacks make up only 13 percent of the US population, they have been a much larger proportion of offenders sentenced to death and executed, both historically and in more recent years. Of the 1,338 prisoners executed from 1977 through 2013, 56 percent were white, 35 percent were black, 8 percent were Hispanic, and 2 percent were Native American or Asian. There is compelling evidence that those who murder whites, and particularly blacks who murder whites, are sentenced to death and executed at disproportionately high rates. From 1977 through 2013, 52 percent of the persons executed were whites convicted of killing other whites, 20 percent were blacks convicted of killing whites, 11 percent were blacks convicted of killing other blacks, and only 1.5 percent were whites convicted of killing blacks (NAACP Legal Defense and Educational Fund 2013). These disparities were particularly pronounced for rape (use of the death penalty for rape was ruled unconstitutional in 1977 in *Coker v. Georgia* [486 U.S. 584]). Among those executed for rape from 1930 through 1972, 89 percent (405 of the 455 who were executed) were black men (US Department of Justice, Bureau of Justice Statistics 1992, p. 8). During this time period, Louisiana, Mississippi, Oklahoma, Virginia, West Virginia, and the District of Columbia executed 66 black men, but not a single white man, for rape (Wolfgang and Riedel 1973).

There is other evidence that blacks—and increasingly Hispanics—who find themselves in the arms of the law pay a punishment penalty. Consider the following statistics:

- In 2012, the rate of incarceration (per 100,000 citizens) was 2,841 for black males, 1,158 for Hispanic males, and 463 for white males. For females, the rates ranged from 49 (whites) to 64 (Hispanics) to 115 (blacks). Among males, in other words, the incarceration rate for blacks was more than six times the rate for whites and the incarceration rate for Hispanics was nearly three times the rate for whites. Although the numbers are much smaller, the pattern for females was similar (US Department of Justice, Bureau of Justice Statistics, n.d.).
- The Pew Center on the States reported that as of January 1, 2008, one of every 100 adults was behind bars. The figures were one of every 106 white men, one of every 36 Hispanic men, and one of every 15 black men; among black men aged 20–34, one of every nine was incarcerated. The Pew Center concluded that "for Hispanic men and black men . . . imprisonment is a far more prevalent reality than it is for white men" (2008, pp. 5–6).
- A Sentencing Project (2013) report on life sentences revealed that blacks made up 47.2 percent of those serving life sentences and 58 percent of those serving life sentences with no possibility of parole in state and federal prisons in 2012. The proportion of blacks among those serving life sentences was even higher in states such as Maryland (77.4 percent), Georgia (72 percent), and Mississippi (62.3 percent). In seven states, at least two-thirds of those serving life without parole sentences were black.
- In 2013, there were 3,095 prisoners under sentence of death in the United States. Of these, 1,334 (43.1 percent) were white, 1,291 (41.7 percent) were black, and 391 (12.6 percent) were Hispanic (NAACP Legal Defense and Education Fund 2013, p. 3).

The statistics presented above provide compelling historical and contemporary evidence of racial disparity in punishment. They indicate that the sentences imposed on black (and Hispanic) offenders have been and continue to be harsher than the sentences imposed on white offenders. These statistics, however, do not tell us why this occurs. They do not tell us whether the racial disparities in imprisonment and use of the death penalty reflect racial discrimination and, if so, whether that discrimination is institutional or contextual, overt or implicit.

Explanations for the disproportionate number of blacks and Hispanics under the control of the criminal justice system are complex. A number of studies have concluded that a large portion of the racial disparity in incarceration rates can be attributed to racial differences in offending patterns and criminal histories. As the National Research Council's Panel on Sentencing Research concluded in 1983, "Factors other than racial discrimination in the sentencing process account for most of the disproportionate representation of black males in US prisons" (Blumstein et al. 1983, p. 92). Although there is recent evidence that the proportion of the racial disparity in incarceration unexplained by racial differences in arrest rates is increasing (Western 2006; Tonry and Melewski 2008; Baumer 2013), most scholars would contend that this conclusion is still valid today.

Not all of the racial disparity, however, can be explained away in this fashion. Critics contend that at least some of the overincarceration of racial minorities is a result of the pursuit of criminal justice policies and practices with racially disparate effects (Wacquant 2002*a*, 2002*b*; Tonry and Melewski 2008; Alexander 2010). As one commentator noted, "A conclusion that black overrepresentation among prisoners is not primarily the result of racial bias does not mean that there is no racism in the system" (Tonry 1995, p. 49). Alexander's (2010) critique is even more pointed. As she put it, "The fact that more than half of the young black men in any large American city are currently under the control of the criminal justice system (or saddled with criminal records) is not—as many argue—just a symptom of poverty or poor choices, but rather evidence of a new racial caste system at work" (p. 16).

Researchers have conducted dozens of studies to untangle the complex relationship between race and punishment and to determine if racial disparities result "to some extent" from overt or unconscious racial bias or the implementation of policies and practices with racially disparate effects. This issue has been a major focus of research since at least the

1970s. The studies that have been conducted vary enormously in theoretical and methodological sophistication. They range from simple bivariate comparisons of incarceration and death penalty rates for whites and racial minorities, to methodologically more rigorous multivariate analyses designed to identify direct race effects, to sophisticated designs incorporating tests for indirect race effects and for interaction between race and other predictors of sentence severity. The findings generated by these studies and the conclusions drawn by their authors vary.

II. Research on Racial Disparities in Imprisonment

There is irrefutable evidence that blacks make up a disproportionate share of the US prison population. There also is evidence that the disparity in black/white incarceration rates has worsened over time. Research conducted over the past three decades has attempted to determine whether and to what extent this disparity reflects differential involvement in crime or differential treatment by the criminal justice system. The most frequently cited work compares the racial disparity in arrest rates for serious crimes with the racial disparity in incarceration rates for these crimes. According to Blumstein (1982), if there were no discrimination following arrest, then "one would expect to find the racial distribution of prisoners who were sentenced for any particular crime type to be the same as the racial distribution of persons arrested for that crime" (p. 1264).

To determine the overall portion of the racial disproportionality in prison populations that could be attributed to differential involvement in crime, Blumstein calculated the proportion of the prison population that, on the basis of arrest rates, was expected to be black for 12 separate violent, property, and drug offenses. He then compared these expected rates with the actual rates of incarceration for blacks. Using 1979 data, he found that 80 percent of the racial disproportionality in incarceration rates could be attributed to racial differences in arrest rates (Blumstein 1982, p. 1267). He reached a similar conclusion when he replicated the analysis using 1991 data: 76 percent of the racial disproportionality in incarceration rates was accounted for by racial differences in arrest rates (Blumstein 1993, p. 751). Blumstein stressed that these results did not mean that there was no racial discrimination in the criminal justice system. Rather, his findings implied that "the bulk of the racial disproportionality in prison is attributable to differential involvement in arrest, and probably in crime, in those most serious offenses that tend to lead to imprisonment" (p. 750).[3]

Blumstein's estimates that 80 and 76 percent of the racial disproportionality in imprisonment could be explained by racial differentials in arrest rates did not apply to each of the crimes he examined. For some crimes, arrest explained more than 80 percent of the disparity, but for others, arrest accounted for substantially less than 80 percent. In both 1979 and 1991, there was a fairly close match between the racial distribution in prison and the racial distributions at arrest for homicide, robbery, and (to a lesser extent) burglary. For drug offenses, however, blacks were overrepresented in prison by nearly 50 percent. Racial differences in arrest rates for drug offenses, in other words, could explain only half of the racial disproportionality in imprisonment for drug offenses.

A. Critiques of the "Blumstein Approach"

Blumstein's oft-cited conclusions have not gone unchallenged (Hawkins and Hardy 1987; Sabol 1989; Crutchfield, Bridges, and Pitchford 1994; Tonry 1995; Mauer 2006; Western 2006; Tonry and Melewski 2008). More recent analyses suggest, first, that the percentage of the imprisonment disparity that is unexplained by arrest disparities is substantially larger than 20 percent and, second, that results vary significantly by jurisdiction. Tonry and Melewski (2008) replicated Blumstein's approach at the national level using arrest and prison population data for 2004, finding that 38.9 percent of the imprisonment disparity was unexplained by arrest. The "unexplained disparity" in 2004 was 38.4 percent for violent crimes, 38.3 percent for property crimes, and 57.4 percent for drug offenses. According to Tonry and Melewski, "such large unexplained variation creates a strong presumption of racial bias" (p. 18). Research conducted following the publication of Blumstein's landmark study also has revealed considerable interstate (Hawkins and Hardy 1987; Sabol 1989; Crutchfield, Bridges, and Pitchford 1994) and regional (Sorensen, Hope, and Stemen 2003) variability. Hawkins and Hardy's (1987) analysis of state-by-state data found that the percentage of racial

[3] Blumstein's conclusions were confirmed by Langan (1985), who argued that it was more appropriate to use prison admissions and victimization data on the perceived race of the offender. Using data from 1973, 1979, and 1982 on five different offense types, he concluded that only about 20 percent of the racial disparity in prison admissions was unexplained by the (perceived) race of the offender.

disproportionality in imprisonment that could be explained by arrest ranged from 22 percent in New Mexico to 96 percent in Indiana and Missouri. In nine states, arrest accounted for 40 percent or less of the disproportionality in imprisonment; in six states, arrest accounted for more than 80 percent of the variation. Thus, according to Hawkins and Hardy, "Blumstein's figure of 80 percent would not seem to be a good approximation for all states" (p. 79). Sorensen, Hope, and Stemen (2003) documented similar variations across regions in the United States.

Blumstein's work also has been criticized for assuming that arrests are good measures of criminal involvement and that the number of arrests for serious violent crimes is the primary determinant of the number of persons incarcerated. Tonry and Melewski (2008, p. 18), for example, pointed out that the proportions of blacks among those arrested for violent crimes declined over time. Forty-nine percent of those arrested for rape in 1982–86 were black, compared to 33 percent in 2002–6. For robbery, the figures were 63.2 percent (1982–86) and 54.9 percent (2002–6); for aggravated assault, they were 39.7 percent (1982–86) and 33.7 percent. If Blumstein's assumption about the relationship between arrest rates for serious violent crimes and incarceration rates were correct, we would have expected that the proportion of blacks among those imprisoned would have declined. This is not what happened. Instead, the percentage of blacks incarcerated in state and federal prisons increased from about 45 percent in 1986 to 50 percent in 1990, where it has remained, with only minor fluctuations ever since. That the percentage of blacks among those arrested for violent crimes declined over time while the percentage of blacks among those incarcerated increased, in other words, raises questions about one of Blumstein's key underlying assumptions.

B. *Explaining the Continuing Racial Disproportionality in Imprisonment: The War on Drugs*

If, as recent research concludes, the proportion of the racial disproportionality in imprisonment that can be explained by differential involvement in crime (as measured by arrest rates) has decreased over time, why over the past three decades has the black incarceration rate been six to seven times higher than the white rate? Many commentators attribute the continuing—some would say worsening—racial disproportionality to policies pursued during the war on drugs, which have swept increasing numbers of young black (and Hispanic) men into the arms of the law and into prison. In fact, Blumstein (1993) himself raised this issue. He noted that the percentage of drug offenders in the prison population increased almost fourfold from 1979 (5.7 percent) to 1991 (21.5 percent). Blumstein also noted that "arrests for drug offenses are far less likely to be a good proxy for offending patterns than they are for aggravated assault, murder, and robbery" and that the black arrest rate for drug offenses had "grown dramatically in the late 1980s." He concluded that his findings regarding drug offenses "raise serious questions about the degree to which the policy associated with the drug war has significantly exacerbated the racial disproportionality in prison" (pp. 752–54).

Other critics countered that the evidence examined by Blumstein did more than simply "raise questions" about the policies pursued during the war on drugs. Miller (1996, p. 80), who characterized the war on drugs as a "disaster-in-waiting for African Americans from the day of its conception," argued that "from the first shot fired in the drug war African-Americans were targeted, arrested, and imprisoned in wildly disproportionate numbers." Tonry (1995) was even more blunt. He charged that officials in the Reagan and Bush administrations knew that the war on drugs would be waged primarily in poor minority communities and that these officials knew, or should have known, that the outcome of the war would be a worsening of racial disparities in imprisonment. He also argued that the architects of the drug war knew, or, again, should have known, that imprisonment would not deter drug use or drug-related crime; both drug abuse education and substance abuse treatment were more effective policy choices; and the choice of punishment rather than education or treatment would destroy the lives of countless young blacks. According to Tonry, "The architects of the War on Drugs should be held morally accountable for the havoc they have wrought among disadvantaged members of minority groups" (p. 104).

There is clear and convincing evidence that the assertions of these critics of the war on drugs are correct. As shown in figures 2 and 3, the arrest rate for blacks is—and has been since 1980—substantially higher than the rate for whites, for both drug possession or use and drug manufacture or sale. The data show that for both whites and blacks, arrest rates for using or possessing drugs are several times higher than rates for manufacturing or selling drugs; over time, they are two to three

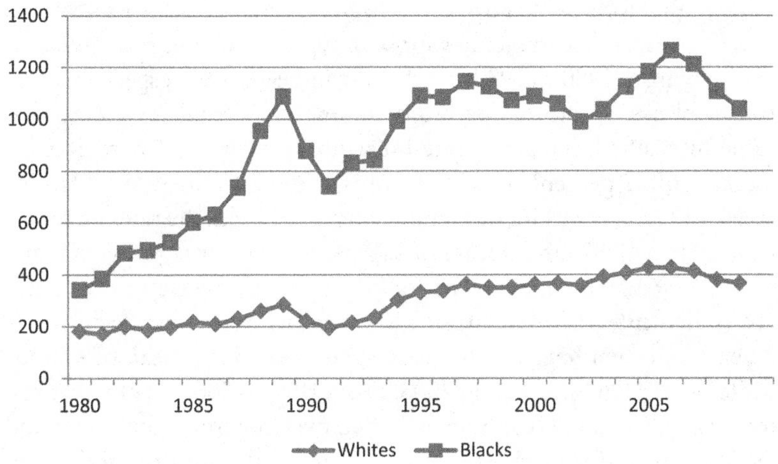

FIG. 2.—Arrest rates for drug possession/use, by race: 1980–2009. Source: US Department of Justice, Bureau of Justice Statistics (2011, fig. 40).

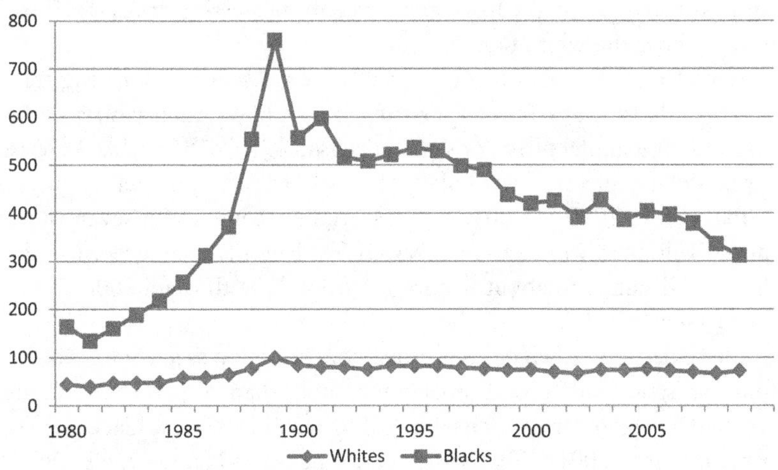

FIG. 3.—Arrest rates for drug manufacture/sale, by race: 1980–2009. Source: US Department of Justice, Bureau of Justice Statistics (2011, fig. 44).

times higher for blacks and are four to five times higher for whites. The data also reveal that arrest rates for both types of offenses increased dramatically from 1980 to 1989 and that the increases were especially notable for blacks. As the war on drugs and the moral panic over crack cocaine intensified, the arrest rate for whites went from 182 to 285 (an increase of 57 percent) for drug possession and from 44 to 99 (an increase of 125 percent) for drug trafficking. For blacks, the rates increased from 341 to 1,087 (an increase of 218 percent) for drug possession and from 164 to 759 (an increase of 363 percent) for drug trafficking. After 1989, the white and black arrest rates for drug possession declined for 2 years and then began to increase again, reaching a peak of 428 for whites and 1,266 for blacks in 2006. From 1980 to 2006, in other words, the drug possession arrest rate increased by 135 percent for whites and by 271 percent for blacks. By contrast, arrest rates for drug trafficking fell precipitously for blacks and gradually for whites. For blacks the rate declined from 759 in 1989 to 312 in 2009 (a decrease of 59 percent), and for whites the rate declined from 99 to 72 (a decrease of 27 percent).

These data also demonstrate that racial disparity in the arrest rates for both types of offenses increased over time. In the case of drug possession/use, in 1980 the rate for blacks was about twice the rate for whites. By 1989, the rate for blacks was nearly four times the rate for whites; for the next two decades, the black arrest rate for possessing drugs was three to four times the white rate.

The black/white disparity was even more pronounced for drug trafficking. Blacks were about four times more likely than whites to be arrested for manufacturing or selling drugs in 1980; by 1989, blacks were seven and a half times more likely than whites to be arrested for these crimes. From 1990 to 2003, blacks were between six and seven times more likely than whites to be arrested for drug manufacture/sales; the disparity declined to about five to one from 2004 through 2008 and to four to one in 2009.

These disparities, which reflect data for the nation as a whole, are also found in states and cities. For example, more than 80 percent of adults arrested for felony drug offenses in California in 1989 were black or Hispanic (Mosher 2001). That same year, Operation Hammer, a policing strategy employed by the Los Angeles Police Department, resulted in the arrest of more than 1,000 persons for drug offenses over the course of one weekend; all were black or Hispanic (Walker, Spohn, and DeLone 2012). A similar policing strategy in New York City—Operation Pressure Point—led to dramatic increases in arrests of street dealers, almost all of whom were nonwhite (Belenko, Fagan, and Chin 1991). Also in New York City, the implementation of quality-of-life policing resulted in both a dramatic increase in arrests for possession of marijuana in public (arrests increased from fewer than 1,000 in 1990 to 51,000 in 2000) and racial disparity in arrests; in 2000, blacks made up less than one-quarter of the population of New York City but constituted 52 percent of arrests for use of marijuana in public (Golub, Johnson, and Dunlap 2007). And in Seattle, where blacks constituted only 8.4 percent of the population in 2000, they made up 36.4 percent of arrestees for possession of marijuana, 22.6 percent of arrestees for possession of powder cocaine, and 63.1 percent of arrestees for possession of crack cocaine; they also made up 79 percent of arrestees for delivery of crack cocaine (Beckett et al. 2005; Beckett, Nyrop, and Pfingst 2006).

C. *Why Are Blacks Arrested for Drug Offenses at Higher Rates than Whites?*

Why are blacks so much more likely than whites to be arrested for drug offenses? There are three possible answers: blacks use drugs at higher rates than whites, blacks sell drugs at higher rates than whites, and police arrest blacks for drug offenses in numbers disproportionate to their involvement in using and selling drugs.

Regarding the first explanation, there is persuasive evidence that blacks do not use or sell drugs at substantially higher rates than whites. Figure 4 presents longitudinal data from the National Survey on Drug Use and Health (formerly the National Household Survey on Drug Abuse) on illicit drug use in the past month by persons aged 12 and older. Over time, relatively small percentages of blacks and whites report using any illicit drug, and the rates for blacks, which are higher than the rates for whites in some years, do not vary by more than 2 percentage points from the rates for whites over the time period. Moreover, when the data are disaggregated by age and by type of drug, different patterns appear. The higher rates of use found for blacks than for whites shown in figure 4 are primarily due to higher rates for blacks among respondents aged 25 and older. Among high school seniors, by contrast, rates of illicit drug use are lower for blacks than for whites (Johnston et al. 2005, table D-3). Moreover, the higher rates for blacks than for whites shown in figure 4 are primarily due to higher rates of marijuana use among blacks. As shown in figure 5, the rate of using any illicit drugs other than marijuana in the past year among twelfth graders was substantially

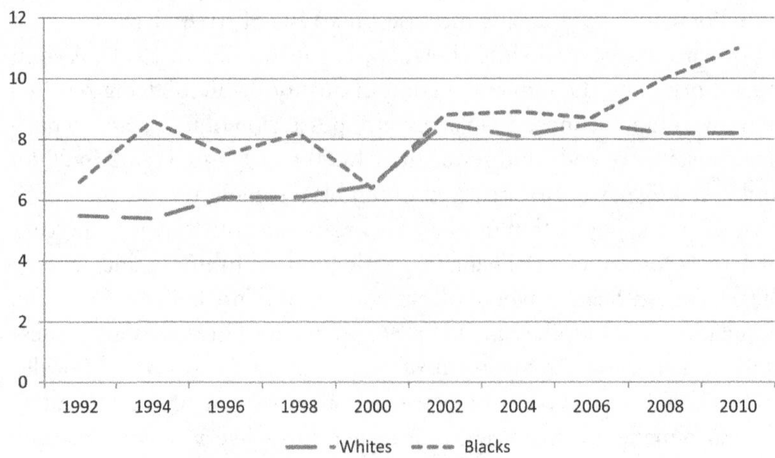

Fig. 4.—Any illicit drug use in the past month, persons 12 and older, by race. Source: US Department of Health and Human Services, Substance Abuse and Mental Health Services Administration, Center for Behavioral Health Statistics and Quality, National Survey of Drug Use and Health (formerly National Survey of Drug Abuse), various years (https://nsduhweb.rti.org/).

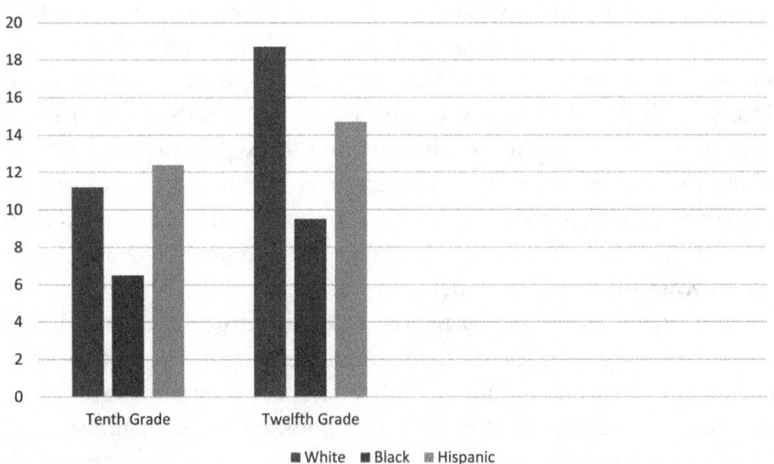

Fig. 5.—Use of any illicit drug other than marijuana in the past year, by race and Hispanic origin, 2012–13. Source: Johnston et al. (2014, tables 5, 6).

higher for whites than for either blacks or Hispanics; among tenth graders, both whites and Hispanics had higher rates than blacks (Johnson et al. 2014, table 6).

These data also demonstrate that blacks are more likely than whites to be arrested for selling or trafficking in drugs. Like the explanation proffered to explain racial disparity in arrest rates for drug use, this difference could reflect differences in the rates at which blacks and whites sell drugs. However, data from a variety of sources suggest that blacks do not sell drugs at a higher rate than whites. For example, data from the National Longitudinal Survey of Youth, which involves annual interviews with a nationally representative sample of youths who were aged 12–17 at the end of 1996, revealed that blacks were less likely than either whites or Hispanics to report selling drugs; 17 percent of whites, 16 percent of Hispanics, and 13 percent of blacks reported that they sold drugs at least once by the time they were 17 (Snyder and Sickmund 2008). According to a 2006 national survey of drug abuse conducted by the Substance Abuse and Mental Health Services Administration, 1.6 percent of white adults and 2.8 percent of black adults reported selling drugs in the past 12 months (Fellner 2009). As this report pointed out, although the proportion of sellers was higher among blacks than among whites, in absolute numbers, far more whites (2,461,797) than blacks (712,044) reported selling in the previous year (p. 268). Similarly, a study conducted in Seattle revealed that a majority of the heroin, methamphetamine, and ecstasy drug delivery transactions and a plurality of the powder cocaine transactions involved a white drug dealer (Beckett, Nyrop, and Pfingst 2006).

As these data make clear, blacks are not arrested more often than whites for drug offenses because blacks are more likely than whites to use or sell illegal drugs. Similarly, the typical drug seller is white, not black. Thus, the racial disparities in arrest rates for using or possessing drugs and for selling drugs cannot be explained away by racial disparities in rates of drug offending. This leaves the third explanation, that is, that high black arrest rates for drug offenses primarily reflect racial differences in drug law enforcement. According to Tonry, "Black arrest rates for drug crimes are high for two reasons. First, police invest more energy and effort in arresting people in inner cities and on the streets, circumstances that disproportionately target drug transactions among blacks. Second, racial profiling in police stops of citizens identifies disproportionate numbers of black people possessing drugs who can be arrested" (2011, p. 70). Alexander's (2010, pp. 101–2) critique is similar. Noting that "the ubiquity of illegal drug activity, combined with its consensual nature, requires a far more proactive approach by law enforcement," she contends that law enforcement agencies decided to use their discretion to fight the war on drugs in black communities.

There is evidence in support of the argument that high arrest rates for blacks reflect police concentration on arresting people in inner cities and on the streets, where using and selling drugs are more conspicuous and where it is therefore easier to make arrests. A number of surveys reveal that blacks are more likely to buy drugs from someone they do not know and that these transactions are much more likely to occur outdoors in public settings than in private homes or college dormitories. This is particularly true of those who buy and use crack cocaine. According to the Office of National Drug Control Policy, which summarized the results of a survey of people arrested for serious crimes in 10 US cities, crack is "often exchanged in an open air or more public market; in 9 of 10 sites at least 40 percent of arrestees report that their crack purchases were made in outdoor settings and in some sites (Atlanta, Washington, D.C., New York, and Chicago), that proportion is even higher (63–87 percent report outdoor sales)" (2009, p. viii).

Convincing evidence of the degree to which disproportionately high black arrest rates for drug offenses reflect police enforcement strategies that focus on inner-city drug markets, particularly for crack cocaine, also is found in two methodologically rigorous studies conducted in Seattle. Katherine Beckett and her colleagues examined racial disparities in drug possession arrests (Beckett et al. 2005) and drug delivery arrests (Beckett, Nyrop, and Pfingst 2006) using data on drug use obtained from three sources: a needle exchange survey, in which those who arrived to exchange needles were asked to report their race/ethnicity, the drugs present in the needles just exchanged, whether they obtained the drugs in Seattle or elsewhere, and the race/ethnicity of the person from whom they obtained the drugs; public drug treatment admissions data, which included the race/ethnicity of those admitted to treatment; and ethnographic observations of two open-air drug markets, one in downtown Seattle and one in a neighborhood (Capitol Hill) known for drug activity. Information on the race/ethnicity of those arrested for drug possession or drug delivery was obtained from Seattle Police Department Incident Reports.

Turning first to drug possession arrests, the authors compared the drug-using and drug-arrested populations, finding that blacks were significantly overrepresented among marijuana, methamphetamine, and crack arrestees; that Hispanics were overrepresented among heroin and crack arrestees; and that whites were underrepresented among crack arrestees. For example, according to the needle exchange survey, blacks made up 6.2 percent and whites made up 84.6 percent of marijuana users; however, blacks constituted 36.4 percent and whites 50.8 percent of those arrested for marijuana possession. Similarly, whereas blacks made up 15.6 percent of crack cocaine users but 63.1 percent of those arrested for use of crack cocaine, whites made up 68.8 percent of crack users but only 26.3 percent of arrestees for crack possession. The authors also concluded that blacks were overrepresented among those arrested for drug possession largely because "possession arrests were far more likely to involve crack offenders than any other type of drug user" (Beckett et al. 2005, p. 429). From January 1999 to April 2001, the Seattle Police Department made 3,058 arrests for possession of crack but only 384 arrests for possession of methamphetamine, ecstasy, and powder cocaine combined. The authors noted, "the focus on crack is the primary cause of the racial disparity in drug possession arrests" (p. 429).

Similar results were found in the study of drug delivery arrests in Seattle (Beckett, Nyrop, and Pfingst 2006). As part of the needle exchange survey, exchangers were asked to identify the race/ethnicity of the person who provided them with each of the drugs they used. The authors found that racial and ethnic patterns of involvement in drug delivery varied by type of drug. The majority of those who delivered methamphetamine (81.9 percent), heroin (55.1 percent), and ecstasy (83.3 percent) were white; relatively equal percentages of whites, blacks, and Hispanics were identified as deliverers of powder cocaine; and whites (40.6 percent) and blacks (46.9 percent) were about equally likely to deliver crack cocaine. Because the authors believed that the responses for crack cocaine probably underestimated black involvement as dealers, they concluded that it was "reasonable to assume that a majority of crack transactions involve a black crack dealer" (p. 118). From the data on arrests for drug delivery, blacks constituted 64.2 percent of those arrested for drug delivery; 17.4 percent of those arrested were white and 14.1 percent were Hispanic. Among those arrested for delivering crack cocaine, 79 percent were black. As with drug possession arrests, the Seattle Police Department made 2,018 arrests for delivering crack cocaine but only 138 for ecstasy, methamphetamine, and powder cocaine combined. The conclusion: "although a majority of drug transactions involving the five serious drugs under consideration here involve a white drug dealer, 64 percent of those arrested for drug delivery . . . were black" (p. 121).

Both of the studies revealed that the Seattle Police Department focused on arresting those who used and sold crack cocaine: they made eight times as many arrests for possession of crack cocaine as for possession of the other drugs combined, and they made almost 15 times as many arrests for delivery of crack cocaine as for delivery of other drugs. To explain this focus, Beckett and her colleagues considered the possibility that crack is purchased more frequently and is more likely to be purchased outdoors than are other drugs. They found that only one-third of all outdoor drug transactions, but 75.2 percent of all outdoor drug possession arrests, involved crack. Similarly, 25 percent of all indoor drug transactions, but 69.6 percent of all indoor arrests for drug possession, involved crack. Beckett et al. concluded, "In short, the available evidence indicates that neither the prevalence of crack use in the Seattle area nor the frequency with which it is acquired explains the preponderance of crack users among arrestees" (2005, p. 433).

Beckett et al. also considered, and rejected, arguments that the focus was on crack cocaine because the crack cocaine market was associated with a higher level of violence or of the concentration of crack transactions in outdoor, public spaces. These findings led them to conclude that "it appears that both the focus on crack and the overrepresentation of blacks and Latinos among those arrested for crack and other drugs reflect a racialized conception of 'the drug problem'" (Beckett et al. 2005, p. 436).

The validity of these findings and conclusions was called into question by a recent study of drug arrests in Seattle (Engel, Smith, and Cullen 2012). The authors argued that Beckett et al.'s original study underestimated the role played by police deployment strategies (i.e., the saturation of police patrols in high-crime areas), that citizen calls for service (CFS) about drug activity were a "more appropriate benchmark available for comparisons to Seattle Police Department (SPD) drug arrests" (p. 665), and that it was important to examine racial disparities in arrest rates in smaller geographic areas (city blocks) than were used by Beckett and her colleagues (census tracts).

Using data from January 2004 through September 2007 on drug-related arrests, Engel, Smith, and Cullen found that blacks constituted 53.3 percent of all arrests citywide, whites 33.6 percent, and Hispanics 4.4 percent. They also examined 911 calls regarding drug-related activity, which included the location of the incident and a description, including race/ethnicity, of the person(s) about whom the caller was complaining. When they compared drug arrests to drug-related calls for service in the two areas examined by Beckett et al. (i.e., Downtown and Capitol Hill), they found that the race/ethnicity of the individuals identified by those who called 911 was very similar to the race/ethnicity of those arrested. In the downtown area, for example, 26.5 percent of the CFS and 24.9 percent of the arrests involved whites, 63.9 percent of the CFS and 65.4 percent of the arrests involved blacks, and 6.5 percent of the CFS and 3.5 percent of the arrests involved Hispanics (Engel, Smith, and Cullen 2012, fig. 1). Their findings indicated that "Blacks and Hispanics are not overrepresented among drug arrestees in the city of Seattle when compared with CFS data" (p. 619).

The differences in the findings of these methodologically sophisticated studies, which Engel, Smith, and Cullen acknowledge are most likely due to differences in their research designs and, particularly, their indicators of drug-related activity, suggest that there are no definitive answers to questions regarding the meaning of racial disparities in arrests for drug offenses. However, regardless of the way in which one interprets the substantially higher black than white arrest rates for drug offenses, that they are higher has important implications for explaining racial disproportionality in imprisonment. The reason is that mandatory minimum sentences for drug offenses, which were enacted in every state and by the federal government by the mid-1990s, have made it increasingly likely that those convicted of drug offenses are sentenced to prison and that those incarcerated receive long prison terms. Assuming that racial disparities in arrest rates for drug offenses are paralleled in conviction rates for drug offenses, blacks will be significantly more likely than whites to be sentenced to prison for drug offenses, and the severe punishments mandated will exacerbate racial disparities.

D. Racial Disproportionality in Imprisonment

Research conducted during the past several decades suggests that an answer to the question posed by the Bureau of the Census in 1918 remains elusive. The studies conducted by Blumstein and others who replicated and refined his approach indicate that some portion of racial disproportionality in prison can be attributed to higher black than white arrest rates for serious violent crimes. It is true that we do not know with any confidence whether the percentage that can be explained away in this fashion is 80 percent, 76 percent, or something substantially less. However, even those who criticize Blumstein's approach acknowledge that the higher black arrest rate for violent crimes is a primary reason why blacks, particularly young males, are locked up at dramatically higher rates than whites. As Randall Kennedy observed, "That relative to their percentage of the population, blacks commit more street crime than do whites is a fact and not a figment of a Negrophobe's imagination" (1997, p. 22).

It is also true, however, that the black-white disparity in incarceration rates has worsened since the Bureau of the Census published its report in 1918 and results "to some extent" from racial bias in the criminal justice process and from implementation of policing and sentencing policies with racially disparate effects. We do not know how much disparity results from conscious or unconscious bias or how much from policies and practices that punish more severely crimes for which blacks are more likely than whites to be arrested, prosecuted, and convicted. Blumstein conceded that at least some of the "other 20 percent" might reflect "a residual effect that is explainable only as racial discrimination" (1982, p. 1230).

That the proportion of blacks arrested for serious violent crime has declined but the proportion of blacks arrested for drug offenses has skyrocketed, and that increasingly large proportions of prisoners are incarcerated for drug offenses, suggests that racial differences in arrests for serious violent crimes account for a declining share of racial disparity in imprisonment. It also suggests that the war on drugs and the belief that incarceration is the appropriate penalty for drug offenses are major causes.

III. Race and Sentencing: Five Waves of Research

Social scientists and legal scholars have been examining the complex relationship between race and sentencing for more than eight decades. The questions asked became more theoretically sophisticated and the methodologies used to answer them became more analytically rigorous. The answers to these questions also changed over time.

A. *The Early Research—Waves 1 and 2*

Studies conducted from the 1930s through the 1960s often concluded that racial disparities in sentencing reflected racial discrimination and that "equality before the law is a social fiction" (Sellin 1935, p. 217). Reviews of these early studies, however, found that most were methodologically flawed (Hagan 1974; Kleck 1981). Many employed inadequate or no controls for crime seriousness and prior criminal record, and most used inappropriate statistical techniques to isolate the effect of race. Kleck's evaluation of 40 noncapital sentencing studies revealed that many found no evidence that race affected sentence outcomes and that most that found such evidence either did not control for prior record or used a crude measure that simply distinguished between offenders with some type of criminal history and those with none. "The more adequate the control for prior record, the less likely it is that a study will produce findings supporting a discrimination hypothesis" (p. 792).

Hagan's and Kleck's conclusions, coupled with the findings of its own review of sentencing research (Hagan and Bumiller 1983), led the National Research Council's Panel on Sentencing Research to conclude that the sentencing process, although not racially neutral, was not characterized by systematic and widespread racial discrimination. Rather, "some pockets of discrimination are found for particular judges, particular crime types, and in particular settings" (Blumstein et al. 1983, p. 93). The panel echoed Hagan's and Kleck's concerns about the paucity of controls for prior criminal record in many early studies. The panel also noted that more recent, methodologically rigorous studies published in the late 1970s and early 1980s suffered from measurement error and sample selection problems that threatened "serious biases in the estimates of discrimination effects" (Blumstein et al. 1983, p. 109). It concluded that the disproportionate number of black males locked up in US prisons was due primarily to factors other than racial discrimination in sentencing.

Marjorie Zatz reached a somewhat different conclusion. Although she acknowledged that "it would be misleading to suggest that race/ethnicity is *the* major determinant of sanctioning," she nonetheless asserted that "race/ethnicity is *a* determinant of sanctioning, and a potent one at that" (1987, p. 87). Zatz reviewed and evaluated four waves of research on race and sentencing. The studies published during the first wave (1930s through the mid-1960s), which generally found evidence of racial bias, were methodologically flawed. The studies of the second wave, which began in the late 1960s and continued through the 1970s, were more methodologically sophisticated and typically uncovered little, if any, direct racial discrimination. Some researchers argued that racially discriminatory practices of earlier years had been eliminated in the wake of the civil rights movement or that race effects largely disappeared once crime seriousness and prior criminal record were controlled for adequately. Such findings led many scholars to embrace the so-called no-discrimination thesis and conclude, with the National Research Council panel, that there was no evidence of widespread or systematic discrimination in sentencing (Kleck 1981).

B. *The Third Wave*

What Zatz called the third-wave studies suggested that these conclusions were premature. Research in the 1970s and 1980s challenged the no-discrimination thesis and suggested that racial disparities had not declined or disappeared but had become more subtle and difficult to detect. They contended that testing only for direct race effects was insufficient and asserted that disentangling the effects of race and other predictors of sentence severity required tests for indirect race effects and the use of both interactive and additive models. Methodological refinements and availability of more complete data enabled third-wave researchers to test hypotheses about indirect and interactive effects. Some researchers uncovered evidence of direct racial bias. Others demonstrated that race affected sentence severity indirectly through its effect on variables such as pretrial status or type of attorney, or that race interacted with other variables to produce harsher sentences for racial minorities for some types of crimes (e.g., less serious crimes), in some types of settings (e.g., the South), or for some types of offenders (e.g., the unemployed). Third-wave research also showed that blacks who victimized whites were sentenced much more harshly than were blacks who victimized other blacks or whites who victimized blacks. The third-wave studies persuaded Zatz "that overt and more subtle forms of bias against minority defendants *did* occur, at least in some social contexts" (1987, p. 70).

C. *The Fourth Wave*

Zatz (1987) reviewed work from the fourth wave just as it was beginning. Researchers began to investigate the effects of race on sentencing severity using data from jurisdictions—including federal courts—with determinate sentencing and sentencing guidelines. Research conducted during this era, published from the mid-1980s through the mid-2000s, improved on earlier work in a number of important ways. Individual studies varied in analytical rigor, but most did not suffer from the serious methodological deficiencies that characterized the early research. A few studies combined sentence type and sentence length decisions into a single measure of sentence severity or analyzed only one of those decisions, but most analyzed each separately and some analyzed other outcomes as well. The studies conducted during this era used appropriate multivariate statistical techniques and controlled for relevant legal and extralegal variables. Most also included a wide variety of offenses rather than only one or two types of offenses. Many tested interactive and additive models. Finally, many, particularly those conducted using federal data, examined the effects of ethnicity as well as race.

There are several comprehensive reviews of fourth-wave research (Chiricos and Crawford 1995; Spohn 2000; Mitchell 2005). Chiricos and Crawford (1995) reviewed 38 noncapital sentencing studies published between 1979 and 1991, finding that there was substantial evidence that race directly affected the decision to incarcerate or not but had little effect on the length of the sentence once the effects of crime seriousness and prior record were controlled. They also considered whether the effect of race varied depending on structural or contextual conditions; black offenders faced significantly greater odds of incarceration in the South, in places where blacks made up a larger percentage of the population, and in places where the unemployment rate was high.

Spohn's (2000) review of studies using data from the 1980s and 1990s highlighted the importance of attempting to identify "the structural and contextual conditions that are most likely to result in racial discrimination" (Hagan and Bumiller 1983, p. 21). Spohn (2000) reported that many of the 40 studies she examined found a direct race effect (see also Mitchell 2005). At both the state and federal levels, blacks and Hispanics were more likely than whites to be sentenced to prison; at the federal level, there also was evidence that blacks received longer sentences. Noting that "evidence concerning direct racial effects . . . provides few clues to the circumstances under which race matters," Spohn (2000, p. 458) also evaluated research on indirect or contextual discrimination. Studies revealed four themes or patterns of contextual effects: the combination of race and ethnicity and other legally irrelevant offender characteristics (e.g., age, sex, education, and employment status) produced greater sentence disparity than race or ethnicity alone; process-related factors such as being detained before trial, pleading guilty, hiring an attorney, and providing evidence or testimony in other cases moderated the effect of race and ethnicity on sentence severity; the severity of punishment was contingent on the races of both victims and offenders; and the effects of race and ethnicity were conditioned by the nature of the crime. Spohn concluded that the sentencing reforms implemented during the last quarter of the twentieth century had not achieved their goal of eliminating racial disparity and discrimination in sentencing (p. 478).

D. *The Fifth Wave*

The studies conducted during Zatz's (1987) fourth wave improved on earlier work in a number of important ways. Nonetheless, as Baumer (2013) argued recently, even the fourth wave left important questions unanswered (see also Piehl and Bushway 2007; Ulmer 2012). Of particular importance is that the typical race and sentencing study from this era, using what Baumer refers to as "the modal approach" involving regression-based analysis of the final sentencing outcome, could not identify the mechanisms that led to racially disparate sentencing. Even these more theoretically and methodologically sophisticated studies were unable to explain why racial minorities were sentenced more harshly than whites, whether disparate treatment was found only at sentencing or accumulated as cases moved through the court process, or whether disparities resulted from decisions made by prosecutors as well as by judges. These criticisms are not new. Forty years ago, Hagan (1974, p. 379) called for studies that better captured "transit through the criminal justice system" especially as it operates "cumulatively to the disadvantage of minority group defendants." Baumer reiterated this concern, arguing that "it would be highly beneficial if the next generation of scholars delved deeper into the various ways that 'race'" matters "across multiple stages of the criminal justice process" (2013, p. 240).

Researchers are just beginning to address these issues. During this fifth wave, the focus has begun to shift from the final sentencing outcome to the life course of a criminal case and the ways in which disparities accumulate through the criminal process. Arguing that a key limitation of extant research is its failure to consider the conditioning effects of consequential case processing decisions that precede the final punishment decision, wave 5 scholars point out that focusing on a single decision-making stage (i.e., sentencing) may mask disparities originating at other discretionary stages. Some studies demonstrate that early charging decisions affect final sentencing outcomes (Wright and Engen 2006; Piehl and Bushway 2007; Shermer and Johnson 2010; Starr and Rehavi 2013). So do intermediate bail and pretrial detention decisions (Spohn 2009; Wooldredge et al. 2011). However, only four studies address the issue of cumulative disparity. Each used different statistical techniques and reached somewhat different conclusions. Three used county-level data from the State Court Processing Statistics series (Schlesinger 2007; Stolzenberg, D'Alessio, and Eitle 2013; Sutton 2013; Kutateladze et al. 2014).

One used data on men charged with felony drug offenses to examine decisions regarding bail, pretrial detention, felony adjudication, and sentencing (Schlesinger 2007). The results revealed that blacks and Latinos were treated more severely than whites at several stages and, more importantly, that racial/ethnic disparities in these earlier decisions increased disparities in sentencing outcomes. By contrast, Stolzenberg, D'Alessio, and Eitle (2013) used data on all felony defendants and a meta-analysis procedure to examine the effect of race and ethnicity on eight decision points, finding a significant overall effect for blacks but not for Hispanics.

A third approach was employed by Sutton (2013), who used data on male defendants sampled in 2000 to estimate the direct and indirect effects of race and ethnicity on pretrial detention, guilty pleas, and sentence severity. He found that blacks and Latinos were substantially more likely than whites to be detained prior to trial; that pretrial detention had differential effects on the likelihood of a guilty plea for whites, blacks, and Latinos; and that both pretrial detention and guilty pleas affected sentence outcomes. However, the patterns of results were somewhat different for each racial group. Sutton calculated conditional probabilities of sentence outcomes for defendants who were detained or released and who pled guilty or went to trial. He found that "once prior events are fully taken into account, Latinos and blacks experience about the same rather large cumulative disadvantage," but that the mechanisms that produced this cumulative disadvantage varied for the two racial groups (p. 1217). He concluded with a call for research that "plumb[s] the murky depths of the prosecutor's office" (p. 1219).

Kutateladze et al. (2014) answered this call. Using data on a large sample of white, black, Latino, and Asian defendants charged with misdemeanors and felonies in New York City, they investigated racial and ethnic disparity across multiple prosecutorial and judicial decisions. Their analysis revealed strong evidence of disparity in pretrial detention, plea offers, and use of incarceration: for each, blacks and Latinos were treated more harshly and Asians more leniently than whites. Pretrial detention had a large and statistically significant effect on subsequent outcomes. Blacks, and to a lesser extent Latinos, were more likely than whites to suffer from cumulative disadvantage; for both felonies and misdemeanors, the most disadvantaged combination of outcomes (pretrial detention, case not dismissed, custodial plea offer [misdemeanors only], and incarceration) was most likely for blacks and Latinos and least likely for Asians. Noting that research on the justice system traditionally has been divided into studies of policing, courts, or corrections, Kutateladze et al. concluded that "it may be time to begin examining the broader nexus among different domains of the system—for the pursuit of racial justice ultimately will require thoughtful examination of the many diverse and interrelated discretionary components of the entirety of the formal criminal punishment process" (2014, p. 54).

Research examining the relationship between race and sentencing has evolved both theoretically and methodologically. Of particular importance is that the questions asked have changed dramatically. Most researchers now acknowledge that it is overly simplistic to ask whether race and ethnicity matter at sentencing. The more interesting questions—and those whose answers will help us understand the harsher punishments imposed on blacks and Hispanics—revolve around contexts in which and circumstances under which race and ethnicity influence sentencing and the ways in which disparities accumulate throughout the life course of a criminal case.

Statistical techniques also have changed. Researchers have moved from bivariate comparisons of outcomes for members of different racial groups, to multivariate and multilevel models incorporating relevant control variables, to propensity score matching methods designed to ensure that offenders in each racial group are equivalent, and to structural equation models that identify direct, indirect, and total racial effects and techniques that allow the calculation of cumulative effects. As the fifth wave of research unfolds, more definitive answers to questions regarding racial disparity and racial discrimination in punishment should be forthcoming.

IV. Race and the Death Penalty: Constitutional Issues and Empirical Research

In January 2003, Illinois Governor George Ryan ignited national debate by announcing that he had commuted the sentences of all of the state's 167 death row inmates to life in prison. He justified his unprecedented and highly controversial decision, which came after a 3-year moratorium he announced earlier, on the basis that "our capital system is haunted by the demon of error: error in determining guilt and error in determining who among the guilty deserves to die" (Flock 2003). Governor Ryan, who left office 2 days after the announcement, also expressed concern about the effects of race and poverty on death penalty decisions. He acknowledged that his decision would be unpopular but said he felt he had no choice but to strike a blow in "what is shaping up to be one of the great civil rights struggles of our time."

Similar views were expressed a decade earlier by Supreme Court Justice Harry A. Blackmun, who announced in February 1994 that he would "no longer tinker with the machinery of death" (*Callins v. Collins*, 510 U.S. 1141 [1994], at 1145). In an opinion dissenting from the Court's order denying review in a Texas death penalty case, Blackmun charged the Court with coming "perilously close to murder" and announced that he would vote to oppose all future death sentences, and he observed that the death penalty was applied in an arbitrary and racially discriminatory manner. "Rather than continue to coddle the Court's delusion that the desired level of fairness has been achieved and the need for regulation eviscerated," Blackmun wrote, "I feel morally and intellectually obligated simply to concede that the death penalty experiment has failed."

Governor Ryan and Justice Blackmun are not alone. Legal scholars, civil libertarians, and state and federal policy makers also have questioned the fairness of the process by which a small proportion of convicted murderers are sentenced to death and an even smaller proportion are eventually executed (Sarat 1998*b*). They contend that skin color and socioeconomic status have much to do with who gets sentenced to death and executed. Some allege that "the most profound expression of racial discrimination in sentencing occurs in the use of capital punishment" (Murphy 1988, p. 172).

As these comments demonstrate, controversy swirls around the use of the death penalty. Although issues other than race and class animate this controversy, these issues clearly are central. The questions asked and the positions taken on each side mimic to some extent the issues that dominate discussions of noncapital sentencing. Supporters of capital punishment contend that the death penalty is administered evenhandedly on those who commit the most heinous murders. They also argue that restrictions contained in death penalty statutes and procedural safeguards preclude arbitrary and discriminatory decision making. Opponents contend that the process involves a series of highly discretionary charging, convicting, and sentencing decisions and is fraught with race- and class-based discrimination. They also argue that the appellate process is unlikely to uncover, much less remedy, these abuses.

There is substantial evidence of racial disparity in the use of the death penalty. Despite constituting only 12–13 percent of the US population, blacks make up a much larger proportion of persons sentenced to death and executed, both historically and recently. There is compelling evidence that those who murder whites, and particularly blacks who murder whites, are sentenced to death and executed at disproportionately high rates and that the death penalty for rape was largely reserved for black men convicted of raping white women. Although these differences might reflect racial discrimination in decision making, they also might result from legitimate legal factors—the heinousness of the crime or the prior criminal record of the offender, for example—that prosecutors, judges, and juries consider in deciding whether an offender should be charged with and convicted of a capital offense and, if so, sentenced to death and executed. Appellate court judges, social scientists, and legal scholars have grappled with this issue for more than half a century. In the sections that follow, I review the constitutional issues and the results of empirical research on the influence of race and ethnicity on death penalty decisions.

A. Race and the Death Penalty: Constitutional Issues

Empirical evidence of racial discrimination has been used to mount constitutional challenges to the imposition of the death penalty. Black defendants—and especially blacks convicted of raping or murdering whites—have claimed that the death penalty is applied in a racially discriminatory manner in violation of the Equal Protection Clause of the Fourteenth Amendment and the Cruel and Unusual Punishment Clause of the Eighth Amendment. These claims have been consistently rejected by state and federal appellate courts. The Martinsville Seven case, in which seven black men were sentenced to death in 1949 for the gang rape of a white woman, was the first in which defendants explicitly argued that the death penalty was administered in a racially discriminatory manner (Rise 1995). It was also the first in which lawyers presented statistical evidence to prove systematic racial discrimination. Despite evidence showing that 45 blacks, but not a single white, had been executed for rape in Virginia since 1908, the defendants' contention that the Virginia rape statute had "been applied and administered with an evil eye and an unequal hand" (p. 122) was repeatedly rejected by Virginia appellate courts.

The issue has been addressed repeatedly in federal court, with very similar results. The US Courts of Appeals for the Fourth, Fifth, and Eighth Circuits ruled that the empirical studies used to document systematic racial discrimination did not take into account every variable related to capital sentencing and that the evidence did not demonstrate that the appellant's own sentence was the product of discrimination.[4] For example, in *Maxwell v. Bishop*, F. 2d 138 (8th Cir. 1968), the Court of Appeals for the Eighth Circuit rejected William L. Maxwell's claim in Arkansas. The lawyers for Maxwell, a 22-year-old black man sentenced to death for rape of a white woman, introduced results of an empirical study demonstrating that blacks convicted of raping whites were disproportionately sentenced to death and that no other variables could account for the disparate results. The court observed that few cases in the study came from the county in which Maxwell was tried and convicted and ruled that the evidence was not "sufficiently broad, accurate, or precise as to establish satisfactorily that Arkansas juries in general practice unconstitutional racial discrimination in rape cases involving Negro men and white women."

Racial discrimination was not at issue in *Furman v. Georgia*, 408 U.S. 238 (1972), the case in which the US Supreme Court struck down the death penalty as it was then being administered, but the subject was raised by three of the five justices in the majority. Justices Douglas and Marshall cited evidence of discrimination against defendants who were poor, powerless, and black. Marshall argued that giving juries "untrammeled discretion" to impose a sentence of death was "an open invitation to discrimination" (*Furman* at 257, concurring). Douglas stated that the procedures used in administering the death penalty were "preg-

[4] See, e.g., *Spinkellink v. Wainwright*, 578 F. 2d 582 (5th Cir. 1978); *Shaw v. Martin*, 733 F. 2d 304 (4th Cir. 1984); and *Prejean v. Blackburn*, 743 F. 2d 1091 (5th Cir. 1984).

nant with discrimination" (at 257). Justice Stewart noted that "racial discrimination has not been proved" but nonetheless stated that Douglas and Marshall had "demonstrated that, if any basis can be discerned for the selection of these few to be sentenced to die, it is the constitutionally impermissible basis of race" (at 210).

In *Gregg v. Georgia*, 428 U.S. 153 (1976), the Supreme Court upheld the guided discretion statutes enacted in the wake of *Furman*, noting that procedural safeguards in these statutes narrowed the jury's discretion and reduced the likelihood that the jury would impose arbitrary or discriminatory sentences.[5] The majority concluded that these safeguards meant that a jury could no longer "wantonly and freakishly impose the death sentence" and stated that the concerns that motivated their decision in *Furman* were "not present to any significant degree in the (revised) Georgia procedure" (*Gregg* at 206–7).

The Supreme Court directly addressed the issue of racial discrimination in application of the death penalty in *McCleskey v. Kemp*, 481 U.S. 279 (1987). Warren McCleskey, a black man, was convicted and sentenced to death in Georgia for killing a white police officer during an armed robbery. Lawyers for McCleskey claimed that the Georgia capital sentencing process was administered in a racially discriminatory manner. He offered the results of a sophisticated empirical study that concluded that blacks in Georgia convicted of murdering whites had a significantly greater likelihood than other defendants of being sentenced to death (Baldus, Woodworth, and Pulaski 1985).

The Supreme Court rejected McCleskey's Fourteenth and Eighth Amendment claims. The majority accepted the validity of the Baldus study but refused to accept its implication that the disparities documented were adequate evidence of unconstitutional racial discrimination. That the Baldus study was statistically valid, Justice Powell, writing for the majority, observed, did not prove "that racial considerations actually enter into any sentencing decisions in Georgia" (*McCleskey* at 1766, n. 7, 1775). The disparities were "unexplained," Powell wrote, and the Court would not "assume that what is unexplained is invidious." He concluded that "at most, the Baldus study indicates a discrepancy that appears to correlate with race" (at 1775). The Baldus study was

[5] The Court also upheld guided-discretion statutes enacted in Florida (*Proffitt v. Florida*, 428 U.S. 242 [1976]) and Texas (*Jurek v. Texas*, 428 U.S. 262 [1976]).

"clearly insufficient to support an inference that any of the decision makers in McCleskey's case acted with discriminatory purpose" (at 1769).

The four dissenting justices were outraged. Justice Brennan, joined in dissent by Justices Blackmun, Marshall, and Stevens, wrote, "The Court today holds that Warren McCleskey's sentence was constitutionally imposed. It finds no fault with a system in which lawyers must tell their clients that race casts a large shadow on the capital sentencing process." Brennan characterized the majority's concern that upholding McCleskey's claim would encourage other groups—"even women"—to challenge the criminal sentencing process "as a fear of too much justice" and "a complete abdication of our judicial role" (*McCleskey* at 339).

The decisions in *Furman*, *Gregg*, and *McCleskey* were guided by a number of assumptions about discretion and discrimination in the capital sentencing process. In *Furman*, the court struck down the death penalty statutes being challenged on the basis of an assumption that the absence of guidelines and procedural safeguards opened the door to arbitrary, capricious, and discriminatory decisions. In *Gregg*, the Court affirmed the validity of the guided-discretion statutes and assumed that the presence of guidelines and procedural safeguards would eliminate the problems condemned in *Furman*. And in *McCleskey*, the Court assumed that the Baldus study was statistically valid but argued that the evidence of victim-based racial discrimination was insufficient to prove intentional discrimination in McCleskey's case.

In the next section, I discuss the results of empirical research investigating the relationship between race and the administration of the death penalty. My purpose is to assess the validity of the assumptions on which *Furman*, *Gregg*, and *McCleskey* rest: that race may have played a role in death penalty decisions prior to *Furman*, that the guided-discretion statutes enacted since 1976 have removed arbitrariness and discrimination from the capital sentencing process, and that the Baldus study merely identified a disparity that seems to correlate with race.

B. Empirical Research on Race and the Death Penalty

In *Furman v. Georgia*, three of the five justices in the majority mentioned the problem of racial discrimination in the application of the death penalty. Two of the dissenting justices—Chief Justice Burger and Justice Powell—acknowledged historical evidence of discrimination against black defendants. Justice Powell also stated, "If a Negro defendant, for instance, could demonstrate that members of his race were being singled out for more severe punishment than others charged with the same offense, a constitutional violation might be established" (*Furman v. Georgia* at 449).

Substantial evidence documents that blacks, particularly those convicted of murdering or raping whites, were sentenced to death and executed at disproportionately high rates during the pre-*Furman* time period. The most persuasive evidence is found in studies examining the use of the death penalty for rape, which revealed that capital punishment was primarily used for black men convicted of raping white women (Florida Civil Liberties Union 1964; Wolfgang and Reidel 1973).[6] Evidence of differential treatment is also found in pre-*Furman* studies of use of the death penalty for murder (Mangum 1940; Johnson 1941; Garfinkel 1949). Most of these studies were conducted in the South, and many uncovered evidence of both victim-based and defendant-based discrimination. For example, Garfinkel's (1949) study of capital sentencing in North Carolina in the 1930s revealed that only 5 percent of those who killed blacks were sentenced to death, compared with 24 percent of those who killed whites. Garfinkel also found that blacks who killed whites faced the highest odds of being indicted for, charged with, and convicted of first-degree murder, which carried a mandatory death sentence.

Early research examining the relationship between race and the death penalty was criticized on many of the same grounds as early research on noncapital sentencing. Kleck's (1981) analysis of 17 studies of capital sentencing showed that only one included a control for prior record, most did not differentiate between felony and nonfelony murder, and none controlled for the defendant's social class. He also noted that "every single study consistently indicating discrimination towards blacks was based on older data from Southern states" (p. 788). He acknowledged that studies of use of the death penalty for rape revealed strong evidence of direct discrimination against black offenders (particularly

[6] The Supreme Court in *Coker v. Georgia*, 486 U.S. 584 (1977), declared use of the death penalty for rape to be unconstitutional. The defendants did not raise the equal protection issue of racially discriminatory decision making in violation of the Fourteenth Amendment. Seven years earlier, in *Maxwell v. Bishop*, 398 U.S. 262 (1970), the defendant raised the issue of racial discrimination in use of capital punishment for rape. The Court vacated the judgment on other grounds but refused even to hear arguments on equal protection (Rise 1995).

those who assaulted whites) but concluded that "the evidence as a whole indicates no racial discrimination in the use of the death penalty for murder outside the South, and even for the South empirical support for the discrimination thesis is weak" (p. 788).

Two methodologically sophisticated studies subsequently published found that racial differences in use of the death penalty before 1972 did not disappear once offense seriousness, prior record, and other legally relevant factors were taken into consideration (Baldus, Woodworth, and Pulaski 1990; Ralph, Sorensen, and Marquart 1992). Baldus, Woodworth, and Pulaski (1990) found that the death penalty was imposed more often in Georgia on blacks and on those convicted of murdering whites than on other equally culpable defendants. A methodologically rigorous study of death penalty decisions in Texas similarly found that those who killed whites were significantly more likely to be sentenced to death than those who killed blacks (Ralph, Sorensen, and Marquart 1992).

The US Supreme Court in *Gregg v. Georgia* noted that concerns about arbitrariness and discrimination that prompted their earlier decision in *Furman* were not "present to any significant degree" under the revised Georgia process (*Gregg* at 206–7), observing that the newly required restrictions on discretion and procedural safeguards would address those problems. Critics were less optimistic (Wolfgang and Reidel 1975; Bowers and Pierce 1980). They argued that the guided-discretion statutes restricted but did not eliminate discretion and that the new statutes would likely shift discretion from judges and juries at sentencing to prosecutors at charging.

The critics were correct. Studies conducted in the post-*Gregg* era document substantial defendant-based and victim-based discrimination under guided-discretion statutes in the early post-*Gregg* period. The US General Accounting Office (GAO) reviewed 28 post-*Gregg* studies and noted that the race of the victim had a significant effect in all but five. Those who murdered whites were more likely to be charged with capital murder and to be sentenced to death than those who murdered blacks. Moreover, these differences could not be attributed to differences in the defendant's prior criminal record, the seriousness of the crime, or other legally relevant factors. The GAO noted that evidence regarding the significance of the race of the defendant was "equivocal" but that half of the studies found that blacks were more likely than whites to be charged with capital crimes and sentenced to death. The overall conclusion was that there was "a pattern of evidence indicating racial disparities in the charging, sentencing, and imposition of the death penalty after the *Furman* decision" (US General Accounting Office 1990, p. 5).

The strongest evidence in support of the GAO conclusion came from a detailed study of capital sentencing in Georgia (see also Gross and Mauro's [1989] analysis of death penalty decisions in eight states). Baldus, Woodworth, and Pulaski (1990) analyzed the effect of race on the outcomes of more than 600 homicide cases from 1973 through 1979. This study, widely regarded as the most comprehensive and methodologically sophisticated study of death penalty decisions to date, controlled for more than 200 variables that might explain racial disparities. These included detailed information on the defendant's background and prior criminal record, information concerning the circumstances and heinousness of the crime, and measures of the strength of evidence against the defendant. They analyzed both the prosecutor's decision to seek the death penalty and the jury's decision to sentence the offender to death, finding substantial race-of-victim effects and more modest race-of-defendant effects for both decisions. Noting that "the race-of-victim effects are about the same or stronger in the post-*Gregg* period," they concluded that their findings "are squarely at odds with the Supreme Court's assumption in *Gregg v. Georgia* that the only factors that would influence decisions in post-*Gregg* Georgia were the culpability of the offender and the strength of the evidence" (Baldus, Woodworth, and Pulaski 1990, pp. 185–86).

The Baldus study provides compelling evidence of victim-based racial discrimination in the use of the death penalty in the years immediately following the *Gregg* decision. Recent research in Maryland (Paternoster and Brame 2008), North Carolina (Unah and Boger 2001), Virginia (American Civil Liberties Union 2003), Ohio (Welsh-Huggins 2005), Texas (Texas Civil Rights Project 2000), and California (Pierce and Radelet 2005) provides equally persuasive evidence of racial disparities in the capital sentencing process in those states during the 1990s and 2000s. There also is evidence of racial disparity in federal capital sentencing (US Department of Justice 2000, 2001); that blacks, and to a lesser extent, Hispanics, who kill whites are executed a higher rates than other death-sentenced offenders (Jacobs et al. 2007); and that those who kill white females face higher odds of a death sentence than other offenders (Williams, Demuth, and Holcomb 2007).

The findings are consistent over several decades: race influences decisions regarding who will be sentenced to death and executed. Although the methodological problems in the earliest studies give reasons to be cautious in drawing conclusions, the weight of the evidence confirms that the Supreme Court was correct in assuming that race infected the capital sentencing process in the pre-*Furman* era. There is irrefutable evidence that the penalty for rape was reserved primarily for black men who raped white women. The evidence regarding homicide, although somewhat less consistent, indicates that blacks, particularly those who murder whites, are sentenced to death and executed at disproportionately high rates. Thus, "on the issue of racial discrimination, the system pre-*Furman* was as bad as the majority justices in *Furman v. Georgia* feared it to be" (Baldus, Woodworth, and Pulaski 1990, p. 185).

The court's assumption that the guided-discretion statutes enacted in the wake of *Furman* would eliminate these abuses was incorrect. Carefully designed and methodologically rigorous research documents the persistence of racial discrimination in capital sentencing. Evidence of victim-based discrimination is found in both the prosecutor's decision to seek the death penalty and the jury's decision to impose the death penalty. It is found in nonsouthern and southern states. Most studies find that blacks accused of murdering whites are substantially more likely than any other race-of-defendant/race-of-victim category to be charged with a capital crime and sentenced to death.

Most commentators assumed that the Supreme Court's opinion in *McCleskey* was a fatal blow to attempts to strike down the death penalty. Recent publicity about race and class inequities in capital sentencing, coupled with calls for death penalty moratoriums at state and federal levels, suggests that the issue has not been laid to rest.

V. Race, Crime, and Punishment in the Twenty-First Century

In 2004, the United States celebrated the fiftieth anniversary of *Brown v. Board of Education*, 347 U.S. 483 (1954), the landmark decision that declared segregated public schools to be unconstitutional on equal protection grounds. The Sentencing Project in 2004 issued a report entitled "Schools and Prisons: Fifty Years after *Brown v. Board of Education*" that noted that many institutions in American society had become more diverse and more responsive to the needs of people of color in the wake of

Brown; the American criminal justice system had taken "a giant step backward" (2004, p. 5). The report pointed out that in 2004 there were nine times as many blacks in prison or jail as on the day *Brown* was handed down, rising from 98,000 to 884,500, and that one of every three black males and one of every 18 black females born at the turn of the century could expect to be imprisoned during his or her lifetime. The report asserted, "such an outcome should be shocking to all Americans" (p. 5).

The situation has not improved appreciably in the past 10 years. Blacks, especially young men, continue to be locked up in numbers wildly disproportionate to their representation in the US population. Blacks—particularly those convicted of murdering whites—continue to be sentenced to death and executed at disproportionately high rates. Racial disparities in imprisonment and the death penalty result primarily from racial differences in crime seriousness, prior record, and other legally relevant factors, but most studies conclude that they result "to some extent" from discrimination in the criminal justice system.

A. Remedying the Situation

What can be done to ensure that imprisonment will no longer be a "common life event" for young black men (Western 2006, p. 31)? The most obvious solution—decarceration—may also be the most politically unpalatable, as releasing large numbers of offenders before they complete their sentences or reducing the incarceration rate will inevitably trigger charges that those who advocate these solutions are "soft on crime." Nonetheless, as Tonry and Melewski (2008) convincingly demonstrate, it is the only solution that will significantly reduce the prison population and, in so doing, reduce the number of imprisoned black Americans. Although reducing racial bias and discrimination in the criminal justice system is important and should continue to be a goal of policy efforts, doing so will not appreciably affect the number of blacks behind bars. By contrast, if imprisonment rates were returned to 1980 levels, the black incarceration rate would fall from 2,661 to 827 per 100,000 and there would be 702,400 fewer black Americans locked up (Tonry and Melewski 2008, p. 36). They observe, "To attempt to limit damage done to people now entangled in the arms of the criminal justice system, devices need to be created for reducing the lengths of current prison sentences and releasing hundreds of thousands of people from prison" (p. 37).

A number of policy changes would reduce the likelihood that those convicted of crimes go to prison and reduce the severity of sentences they receive. They include the elimination of mandatory minimum sentences, restrictions on the use of life without parole sentences, and the repeal or modification of three strikes and truth-in-sentencing laws. Each of these sentencing "reforms," which proliferated over the past several decades, played a role in the imprisonment boom that ensnared disproportionately large numbers of racial minorities. Modifying or repealing them will reduce the punitive bite of conviction for nonserious crimes, help bring the US incarceration rate more in line with the rates of other Western democracies, and reduce disparities that result from racially biased implementation of these policies.

A final area of reform concerns the death penalty. Following *McCleskey v. Kemp*, the US House of Representatives added the Racial Justice Act to the Omnibus Crime Bill of 1994. A slim majority of the House voted for it. It would have allowed condemned offenders to challenge their death sentences using statistical evidence showing a pattern of racial discrimination in the capital sentencing process in their jurisdictions. The offender would not have had to show that criminal justice officials acted with discriminatory purpose in his or her case. Opponents argued that it would effectively abolish the death penalty in the United States, and the provision eventually was eliminated from the crime bill. Although racial justice acts were enacted in Kentucky in 1998 and in North Carolina in 2009, the North Carolina legislature repealed its act in 2013. No other states have enacted racial justice acts.

The most effective remedy for racial bias in capital sentencing is abolition of the death penalty. Advocates for reforming the process contend that capital sentencing can be fixed through enactment of measures (e.g., access to postconviction DNA testing, funding to pay for DNA tests for indigent offenders, better funding for capital defense services, and more rigorous standards on qualifications and experience for defense attorneys in capital cases) designed to ensure that innocent persons are not convicted and sentenced to death. By contrast, those who advocate abolishing the death penalty contend that the system is fatally flawed. The "new abolitionists" cite mounting evidence of wrongful convictions of those on death row and the evidence on arbitrary and racially discriminatory administration of the death penalty (Sarat 1998*a*).

Advocates of abolition also contend that new procedural rules cannot solve the inherent problems in the application of the death penalty and eliminate racial disparities. The American Bar Association (1997) has called for a moratorium on executions based in part on evidence that race influences death penalty decisions and for development of "effective mechanisms" to eliminate racial discrimination. Similarly, the national Death Penalty Moratorium Act (2001), introduced unsuccessfully in both houses of Congress in 2001, would have set up a National Commission on the Death Penalty. The commission would have been charged with "establishing guidelines and procedures which . . . ensure that the death penalty is not administered in a racially discriminatory manner." However, it is not at all clear that any such mechanisms, guidelines, or procedures exist or, even if they existed, would be effective. According to Sarat, "Participants in the legal system—whether white or black—demonize young black males, seeing them as more deserving of death as a punishment because of their perceived danger. These cultural effects are not remediable in the near term" (1998*b*, p. 256).

A number of states have gone down the road to abolition. In 2007, New Jersey became the first state in the nation to abolish the death penalty since the use of capital punishment was reinstated by *Gregg v. Georgia* in 1976. Since then the death penalty has been abolished in five states, either by legislation (New Mexico, Connecticut, Maryland, Illinois) or by an appellate court ruling (New York). The governors of Colorado, Oregon, and Washington placed a moratorium on executions while they were in office.

Reducing the racial disproportionality in prison and eliminating racial bias in noncapital and capital sentencing should be high-priority goals of policy makers and politicians. The mass imprisonment of young black (and Hispanic) men has altered their life course trajectories, which, in turn, has had dire consequences for their families, children, and communities. Evidence that race infects the sentencing process undermines respect for the law and casts doubt on the ability of the criminal justice system to ensure due process and equal protection for all. The policy changes needed to accomplish these goals and to erase the legacy of several decades of insensitivity to the plight of racial minorities are straightforward. Policy makers must significantly reduce, through decarceration, the number of men and women locked up in our nation's prisons and must modify or repeal sentencing laws and practices that make imprisonment for decades the rule rather than the exception and that lead to racially tainted death sentences and execution.

B. A Research Agenda for the Twenty-First Century

These policy changes should be informed by the results of research designed to identify more precisely the ways in which race affects criminal case outcomes and sentence severity. Researchers have moved beyond asking "does race matter?" to attempting to identify the circumstances and contexts in which race matters, but we still do not fully understand the mechanisms by which race affects case outcomes, or why blacks are sentenced more harshly than whites. We must understand how racial disparities are produced and whether they result primarily from judges' sentencing decisions or from some combination of decisions made by prosecutors, judges, and other criminal justice officials. Researchers should continue to focus on the ways racial disparities accumulate over the course of a criminal case. They should develop more analytically rigorous methods for calculating cumulative disparity and for documenting the degree to which racial disparities result from decisions regarding bail, pretrial detention, charging, plea bargaining, and sentencing.

There also is a need for qualitative research designed to identify the factors that motivate prosecutors and judges to treat blacks and Hispanics, especially young men, more harshly than whites. The focal concerns perspective, the most common theoretical perspective used by contemporary sentencing researchers, suggests that harsher treatment results from stereotypes of racial minorities as more dangerous, more culpable, and less amenable to rehabilitation (Steffensmeier, Ulmer, and Kramer 1998). Many studies purport to test the focal concerns perspective, but all rely on indirect evidence showing that factors linked to dangerousness, threat, and culpability influence sentencing outcomes. What is needed is qualitative research designed to document how prosecutors and judges view certain types of defendants and how these perceptions influence their decisions.

Research on noncapital sentencing must focus on the role played by the race of the victim and the racial makeup of the offender/victim pair. Researchers examining death penalty decisions have shown that those who murder (and, prior to 1977, rape) whites are substantially more likely to be sentenced to death; many studies also find that blacks who victimize whites are treated most harshly. Some research addressed these subjects in the context of sexual assault, but the studies are limited and dated. We need to understand better how the race of the victim—alone and in interaction with the race of the offender—influences decisions by judges and prosecutors and whether race-of-victim effects accumulate over the life of the case.

Theoretically informed and methodologically rigorous research identifying the racial effects of charging and sentencing policies and practices is critically important to efforts to reform the system and reduce racial disparities and disproportionality. We know that disparities in incarceration result "to some extent" from racially discriminatory decision making in the criminal justice system and "to some extent" from policies and practices that have racially disparate effects. We need to be able to pinpoint where in the system they occur and to identify the policies and practices that produce them.

REFERENCES

Albonetti, Celesta. 1991. "Integration of Theories to Explain Judicial Discretion." *Social Problems* 38:247–66.

Alexander, Michelle. 2010. *The New Jim Crow: Incarceration in the Age of Colorblindness*. New York: New Press.

American Bar Association. 1997. "Whatever You Think about the Death Penalty, a System That Will Take Life Must First Give Justice." *Human Rights* 24(1):22–24.

American Civil Liberties Union. 2003. "Broken Justice: The Death Penalty in Virginia." http://www.aclu.org/files/FilesPDFs/broken_justice.pdf.

Baldus, David C., George G. Woodworth, and Charles A. Pulaski Jr. 1985. "Monitoring and Evaluating Contemporary Death Penalty Systems: Lessons from Georgia." *University of California at Davis Law Review* 18:1375–1407.

———. 1990. *Equal Justice and the Death Penalty: A Legal and Empirical Analysis*. Boston: Northeastern University Press.

Baumer, Eric P. 2013. "Reassessing and Redirecting Research on Race and Sentencing." *Justice Quarterly* 30:231–61.

Beckett, Katharine, Kris Nyrop, and Lori Pfingst. 2006. "Race, Drugs, and Policing: Understanding Disparities in Drug Delivery Arrests." *Criminology* 44:105–37.

Beckett, Katharine, Kris Nyrop, Lori Pfingst, and Melissa Bowen. 2005. "Drug Use, Drug Possession Arrests, and the Question of Race: Lessons from Seattle." *Social Problems* 52:419–41.

Belenko, Steven, Jeffery Fagan, and K.-L. Chin. 1991. "Criminal Justice System Responses to Crack." *Journal of Research in Crime and Delinquency* 28:55–74.

Blumstein, Alfred. 1982. "On the Racial Disproportionality of United States' Prison Populations." *Journal of Criminal Law and Criminology* 73:1259–81.

———. 1993. "Racial Disproportionality of US Prison Populations Revisited." *University of Colorado Law Review* 64:743–60.

Blumstein, Alfred, Jacqueline Cohen, Susan E. Martin, and Michael H. Tonry, eds. 1983. *Research on Sentencing: The Search for Reform*. Vol. 1. Washington, DC: National Academy Press.

Bowers, William, and Glenn L. Pierce. 1980. "Arbitrariness and Discrimination under Post-*Furman* Capital Statutes." *Crime and Delinquency* 26:563–75.

Bridges, George S., and Sara Steen. 1998. "Racial Disparities in Official Assessments of Juvenile Offending: Attributional Stereotypes as Mediating Mechanisms." *American Sociological Review* 65:554–70.

Bureau of Justice Statistics. 2003. *Prevalence of Imprisonment in the US Population, 1974–2001*. Washington, DC: Bureau of Justice Statistics.

Chambliss, William J., and R. B. Seidman. 1971. *Law, Order and Power*. Reading, MA: Addison-Wesley.

Chiricos, Theodore G., and Charles Crawford. 1995. "Race and Imprisonment: A Contextual Assessment of the Evidence." In *Ethnicity, Race, and Crime*, edited by Darnell Hawkins. Albany: State University of New York Press.

Crenshaw, Kimberle, Neil Gotanda, Gary Peller, and Kendall Thomas. 1995. *Critical Race Theory: The Key Writings That Formed the Movement*. New York: New Press.

Crutchfield, Robert D., George S. Bridges, and Susan R. Pitchford. 1994. "Analytical and Aggregation Biases in Analyses of Imprisonment: Reconciling Discrepancies in Studies of Racial Disparity." *Journal of Research in Crime and Delinquency* 31:166–82.

Curriden, Mark, and Leroy Phillips Jr. 1999. *Contempt of Court: The Turn-of-the-Century Lynching That Launched 100 Years of Federalism*. New York: Faber & Faber.

Delgado, Richard, and Jean Stefancic. 2001. *Critical Race Theory: An Introduction*. New York: New York University Press.

Du Bois, W. E. B. 1903. *The Souls of Black Folk*. Chicago: McClurg.

Engel, Robin S., Michael E. Smith, and Francis T. Cullen. 2012. "Race, Place, and Drug Enforcement." *Criminology and Public Policy* 11:603–35.

Fellner, Jamie. 2009. "Race, Drugs, and Law Enforcement in the United States." *Stanford Law and Policy Review* 20:257–92.

Flock, Jeff. 2003. "'Blanket Commutation' Empties Illinois Death Row." CNN, January 13. http://www.cnn.com/2003/LAW/01/11/illinois.death.row/index.html.

Florida Civil Liberties Union. 1964. *Rape: Selective Electrocution Based on Race*. Miami: Florida Civil Liberties Union.

Garfinkel, Harold. 1949. "Research Note on Inter- and Intra-racial Homicides." *Social Forces* 27:369–81.

Garland, David. 2001. "Introduction: The Meaning of Mass Imprisonment." *Punishment and Society* 3:5–7.

Golub, Andrew, Bruce D. Johnson, and Eloise Dunlap. 2007. "The Race/Ethnicity Disparity in Misdemeanor Marijuana Arrests in New York City." *Criminology and Public Policy* 6:131–64.

Gross, Samuel, and Robert Mauro. 1989. *Death and Discrimination: Racial Disparities in Capital Sentencing*. Boston: Northeastern University Press.

Hagan, John. 1974. "Extra-legal Attributes and Criminal Sentencing: An Assessment of a Sociological Viewpoint." *Law and Society Review* 8:357–83.

Hagan, John, and Kristin Bumiller. 1983. "Making Sense of Sentencing: A Review and Critique of Sentencing Research." In *Research on Sentencing: The Search for Reform*, vol. 1., edited by Alfred Blumstein, Jacqueline Cohen, Susan E. Martin, and Michael H. Tonry. Washington, DC: National Academy Press.

Hawkins, Darnell. 1980. "Perceptions of Punishment for Crime." *Deviant Behavior* 1:193–215.

Hawkins, Darnell, and Kenneth A. Hardy. 1987. "Black-White Imprisonment Rates: A State-by-State Analysis." *Social Justice* 16:75–94.

Jacobs, David, Jason T. Carmichael, Zhenchao Qian, and Stephanie I. Kent. 2007. "Who Survives on Death Row: An Individual and Contextual Analysis." *American Sociological Review* 72:610–32.

Johnson, Guy. 1941. "The Negro and Crime." *Annals of the American Academy* 217:93–104.

Johnston, Lloyd D., Patrick M. O'Malley, Jerald G. Bachman, and J. E. Schulenberg. 2005. *Demographic Subgroup Trends for Various Licit and Illicit Drugs, 1975–2004*. Monitoring the Future Occasional Paper no. 61. Ann Arbor, MI: Institute for Social Research. http://monitoringthefuture.org/.

Johnston, Lloyd D., Patrick M. O'Malley, Jerald G. Bachman, J. E. Schulenberg, and R. A. Miech. 2014. *Demographic Subgroup Trends among Adolescents in the Use of Various Licit and Illicit Drugs: 1975–2013*. Monitoring the Future Occasional Paper no. 81. Ann Arbor, MI: Institute for Social Research.

Kennedy, Randall. 1997. *Race, Crime, and the Law*. New York: Vintage Books.

Kleck, Gary. 1981. "Racial Discrimination in Sentencing: A Critical Evaluation of the Evidence with Additional Evidence on the Death Penalty." *American Sociological Review* 43:783–805.

Kutateladze, Besiki, Nancy Andiloro, Brian Johnson, and Cassia Spohn. 2014. "Cumulative Disparity: Examining Racial and Ethnic Disparity in Prosecution and Sentencing." *Criminology* 52(3):514–51.

Langan, Patrick. 1985. "Racism on Trial: New Evidence to Explain the Racial Composition of Prisons in the United States." *Journal of Criminal Law and Criminology* 76(3):666–83.

Mangum, Charles S., Jr. 1940. *The Legal Status of the Negro*. Chapel Hill: University of North Carolina Press.

Mauer, Marc. 2006. *Race to Incarcerate*. 2nd ed. New York: New Press.

Miller, Jerome. 1996. *Search and Destroy: African-American Males in the Criminal Justice System*. New York: Cambridge University Press.

Mitchell, Ojmarrh. 2005. "A Meta-Analysis of Race and Sentencing Research: Explaining the Inconsistencies." *Journal of Quantitative Criminology* 21:439–66.

Mosher, Clayton. 2001. "Predicting Drug Arrest Rates: Conflict and Social Disorganization Perspectives." *Crime and Delinquency* 47:84–104.

Murphy, Clyde E. 1988. "Racial Discrimination in the Criminal Justice System." *North Carolina Central Law Journal* 17:171–90.

Myrdal, Gunnar. 1944. *An American Dilemma: The Negro Problem and American Democracy*. New York: Harper & Row.

NAACP Legal Defense and Educational Fund. 2013. *Death Row USA*. Washington, DC: NAACP Legal Defense and Educational Fund.

Office of National Drug Control Policy. 2009. *ADAM II: 2008 Annual Report*. Washington, DC: Executive Office of the President.

Paternoster, Raymond, and Robert Brame. 2008. "Reassessing Race Disparities in Maryland Capital Cases." *Criminology* 46:971–1008.

Pew Center on the States. 2008. *One in 100: Behind Bars in America, 2008*. Washington, DC: Pew Charitable Trust.

Piehl, Anne Morrison, and Shawn D. Bushway. 2007. "Measuring and Explaining Charge Bargaining." *Journal of Quantitative Criminology* 23:105–25.

Pierce, Glenn L., and Michael Radelet. 2005. "The Impact of Legally Inappropriate Factors on Death Sentencing for California Homicides, 1990–1999." *Santa Clara Law Review* 46:1–47.

Quinney, Richard. 1970. *The Society Reality of Crime*. Boston: Little, Brown.

Ralph, Paige H., Jonathan R. Sorensen, and James W. Marquart. 1992. "A Comparison of Death-Sentenced and Incarcerated Murderers in Pre-*Furman* Texas." *Justice Quarterly* 9:185–209.

Rise, Eric W. 1995. *The Martinsville Seven: Race, Rape, and Capital Punishment*. Charlottesville: University Press of Virginia.

Sabol, William J. 1989. "Racially Disproportionate Prison Populations in the United States: An Overview of Historical Patterns and Review of Contemporary Issues." *Contemporary Crises* 13:405–32.

Sarat, Austin. 1998*a*. "Recapturing the Spirit of Furman: The American Bar Association and the New Abolitionist Politics." *Law and Contemporary Problems* 61:5–28.

———. 1998*b*. *When the State Kills: Capital Punishment and the American Condition*. Princeton, NJ: Princeton University Press.

Schlesinger, Traci. 2007. "Racial and Ethnic Disparity in Pretrial Criminal Processing." *Justice Quarterly* 22:170–92.

Sellin, Thorsten. 1935. "Race Prejudice in the Administration of Justice." *American Journal of Sociology* 41:212–17.

Sentencing Project. 2004. "Schools and Prisons: Fifty Years after *Brown v. Board of Education*." http://www.sentencingproject.org/doc/publications/rd_brownvboard.pdf.

———. 2013. *Life Goes On: The Historic Rise in Life Sentences in America*. Washington, DC: Sentencing Project.

Shermer, Lauren O'Neill, and Brian D. Johnson. 2010. "Criminal Prosecutions: Examining Prosecutorial Discretion and Charge Reductions in US Federal District Courts." *Justice Quarterly* 27:394–430.

Snyder, Howard, and Melissa Sickmund. 2008. *Juvenile Offenders and Victims: 2006 National Report*. Pittsburgh: National Center for Juvenile Justice.

Sorensen, Jon, Robert Hope, and Don Stemen. 2003. "Racial Disproportionality in State Prison Admissions: Can Regional Variation Be Explained by Differential Arrest Rates?" *Journal of Criminal Justice* 31:73–84.

Spohn, Cassia. 2000. "Thirty Years of Sentencing Reform: The Quest for a Racially Neutral Sentencing Process." In *Criminal Justice 2000: Policies, Process, and Decisions of the Criminal Justice System*. Washington, DC: US Department of Justice.

———. 2009. "Race, Sex, and Pretrial Detention in Federal Court: Indirect Effects and Cumulative Disadvantage." *University of Kansas Law Review* 57: 879–902.

Starr, Sonia, and M. M. Rehavi. 2013. "Mandatory Sentencing and Racial Disparity: Assessing the Role of Prosecutors and the Effects of *Booker*." *Yale Law Journal* 123:2–80.

Steffensmeier, Darrell, Jeffery Ulmer, and John Kramer. 1998. "Interaction of Race, Gender, and Age in Criminal Sentencing: The Punishment Cost of Being Young, Black, and Male." *Criminology* 36:763–97.

Stolzenberg, Lisa, Stewart J. D'Alessio, and David Eitle. 2013. "Race and Cumulative Discrimination in the Prosecution of Criminal Defendants." *Race and Justice* 3:275–99.

Sutton, John R. 2013. "Structural Bias in the Sentencing of Felony Defendants." *Social Science Research* 42:1207–21.

Texas Civil Rights Project. 2000. *The Death Penalty in Texas: Due Process and Equal Justice or Rush to Execution?* Austin: Texas Civil Rights Project.

Tonry, Michael. 1995. *Malign Neglect: Race, Crime, and Punishment in America*. New York: Oxford University Press.

———. 2011. *Punishing Race: A Continuing American Dilemma*. New York: Oxford University Press.

Tonry, Michael, and Matthew Melewski. 2008. "The Malign Effects of Drug and Crime Control Policies on Black Americans." In *Crime and Justice: A Review of Research*, vol. 37, edited by Michael Tonry. Chicago: University of Chicago Press.

Turk, Austin. 1969. *Criminality and Legal Order*. Chicago: Rand McNally.

Ulmer, Jeffery T. 2012. "Recent Developments and New Directions in Sentencing Research." *Justice Quarterly* 29:1–40.

Unah, Isaac, and Jack Boger. 2001. "Race and the Death Penalty in North Carolina: An Empirical Analysis: 1993–1997." http://www.deathpenaltyinfo.org.

US Department of Commerce, Bureau of the Census. 1918. *Negro Population: 1700–1915*. Washington, DC: US Government Printing Office.

US Department of Justice. 2000. *The Federal Death Penalty System: A Statistical Survey (1988–2000)*. Washington, DC: US Department of Justice.

———. 2001. *The Federal Death Penalty System: Supplemental Data, Analysis, and Revised Protocols for Capital Case Review*. Washington, DC: US Department of Justice.

US Department of Justice, Bureau of Justice Statistics. n.d. *Imprisonment Rate of Sentenced State and Federal Prisoners per 100,000 Residents, by Sex, Race, Hispanic Origin, and Age, December 31, 2012*. Generated using the Corrections Statistical Analysis Tool at http://www.bjs.gov.

———. 1991. *Race of Prisoners Admitted to State and Federal Institutions, 1926–1986*. Washington, DC: US Department of Justice, Bureau of Justice Statistics.

———. 1992. *Correctional Populations in the United States, 1990*. Washington, DC: US Department of Justice, Bureau of Justice Statistics.

———. 1994. *Correctional Populations in the United States, 1994*. Washington, DC: US Department of Justice, Bureau of Justice Statistics.

———. 2011. *Arrest in the United States, 1980–2009*. Washington, DC: US Department of Justice, Bureau of Justice Statistics.

US General Accounting Office. 1990. *Death Penalty Sentencing: Research Indicates Pattern of Racial Disparities*. Washington, DC: US General Accounting Office.

Wacquant, Loic. 2002*a*. "Deadly Symbiosis: Rethinking Race and Imprisonment in Twenty-First Century America." *Boston Review* (April/May).

———. 2002*b*. "From Slavery to Mass Incarceration." *New Left Review* 13:41–60.

Walker, Samuel, Cassia Spohn, and Miriam DeLone. 2012. *The Color of Justice: Race, Ethnicity and Crime in America*. 5th ed. Belmont, CA: Wadsworth.

Welsh-Huggins, Andrew. 2005. "Death Penalty Unequal." Associated Press, May 7.

Western, Bruce. 2006. *Punishment and Inequality in America*. New York: Sage.

Williams, Marian R., Stephen Demuth, and Jefferson E. Holcomb. 2007. "Understanding the Influence of Victim Gender in Death Penalty Cases: The Importance of Victim Race, Sex-Related Victimization, and Jury Decision Making." *Criminology* 45:865–91.

Wolfgang, Marvin E., and Marc Riedel. 1973. "Race, Judicial Discretion and the Death Penalty." *Annals of the American Academy of Political and Social Science* 407:119–33.

———. 1975. "Rape, Race, and the Death Penalty in Georgia." *American Journal of Orthopsychiatry* 45:658–68.

Wooldredge, John, Timothy Griffin, Amy Thistlethwaite, and Fritz Rauschenberg. 2011. "Victim-Based Effects on Racially Disparate Sentencing in Ohio." *Journal of Empirical Legal Studies* 8:85–117.

Wright, Ronald, and Rodney Engen. 2006. "The Effects of Depth and Distance in a Criminal Code on Charging, Sentencing, and Prosecutor Power." *North Carolina Law Review* 84(6):1935–82.

Zatz, Marjorie. 1987. "The Changing Forms of Racial/Ethnic Biases in Sentencing." *Journal of Research in Crime and Delinquency* 25:69–92.

Michael Tonry

Federal Sentencing "Reform" since 1984: The Awful as Enemy of the Good

ABSTRACT

The federal sentencing system was conceived in one era and delivered in another. When the first bills that culminated in passage of the Sentencing Reform Act of 1984 were introduced, they aimed at reducing the worst excesses of indeterminate sentencing and achieving greater fairness, consistency, equality, accountability, and transparency in sentencing federal offenders. The overriding goal was reduction of unwarranted racial and other disparities. In the different political climate of the mid-1980s the federal sentencing commission instead sought to achieve greater rigidity and severity and to respond to the law-and-order, policy preferences of the Reagan administration and the Republican-controlled US Senate. Probation, formerly the sentence of half of convicted federal offenders, was nearly eliminated as a stand-alone punishment. Lengths of prison sentences increased enormously. After the federal guidelines took effect, buttressed by a plethora of mandatory minimum sentence laws, the growth of the federal prison population far outpaced that of the states, and the federal system became the extreme example nationally and internationally of the dangers of politicization of crime policy. The political climate may be changing and the federal system may change with it. Only time will tell.

"Wrong time, wrong place" would be a fitting epitaph for the US Sentencing Commission and its guidelines. The initiative was conceived in a kinder, gentler time, as the first President George Bush might have put

Electronically published July 30, 2015

Michael Tonry is professor of law and public policy, University of Minnesota.

0192-3234/2015/0044-0005$10.00

it, before sentencing policy became highly politicized and when the principal aims of sentencing reform were fair procedures, just punishments, and reduced disparities.

Senate Bill 2699, the first proposal to establish a federal sentencing commission, was introduced by Senator Edward Kennedy in 1975. It was ahead of its time. It was the first legislative proposal anywhere for a sentencing commission: the same year as enactment of the first modern determinate sentencing law in Maine, 3 years before enactment of the first state sentencing commission legislation in Minnesota and Pennsylvania, and 9 years before the US Congress enacted the Sentencing Reform Act of 1984.

The legislation was enacted, the commission was appointed, and the guidelines took effect, however, just as the tough on crime period hit its stride. The archetypal symbol is the federal Anti–Drug Abuse Act of 1986, which contained a host of lengthy mandatory minimum sentence laws including the 100-to-1 crack cocaine provisions. The act was passed between the appointment in 1985 of the initial commissioners and the implementation in 1987 of the federal guidelines.

What began as a modest, technocratic reform proposal, which by 1984 had been adopted and was working well in several states, resulted in the most radical, controversial, and disliked sentencing system in American history. The initial guidelines were criticized on normative grounds (because they were too harsh), on fairness grounds (because they forbade consideration of offender characteristics most judges believe to be important), on outcome grounds (because they would not reduce sentencing disparities), on technocratic grounds (because they were too complex), on practical grounds (because their complexity made calculation errors inevitable), on policy grounds (because they narrowed judicial discretion and increased prosecutorial power), and on process grounds (because they foreseeably led practitioners to circumvent them) (Stith and Cabranes 1998).

Although all these problems were apparent by the late 1980s, successive commissions have refused to address them, generally digging in their heels instead. Gradually, beginning in the mid-1990s and culminating in 2005, the US Supreme Court loosened the guidelines and reined in the commission. Before that happened, though, the quality of justice in federal courts suffered grievously. Tens of thousands of people received sentences much more severe than could be justified in terms of the crimes they committed or of any imaginable salutary effects of their punishments. The federal example became a major impediment to reform of state sentencing. The drafters of the American Bar Association's 1993 *Standards for Sentencing* explained that their work used the clumsy phrase "sentencing structures" instead of the more familiar "sentencing guidelines" because of the federal guidelines' fearsome reputation. Mere mention of guidelines proposals in the states led to knee-jerk hostility and opposition (Reitz and Reitz 1993).

Recent incarnations of the federal commission have in some ways tried to make the guidelines more rational and less severe, especially in relation to mandatory minimum sentences and crack cocaine, and have regularly sought advice from outsiders. The commission has become slightly bolder and in 2014 proposed lowering guideline ranges for many drug offenses with retroactive application to potentially more than 46,000 federal inmates (US Sentencing Commission 2014*c*). The Congress accepted the proposal (US Sentencing Commission 2014*a*).

The commission has, however, consistently failed to propose or make major changes to the guidelines' most controversial features. Those include their complexity, their rigidity, their severity, their aversion to use of community-based punishments, and their "relevant conduct" provision that directs judges to increase sentences on the basis of alleged crimes for which the defendant was not charged or convicted, and even of which he or she was acquitted. The only full-blown commission-related proposal for a major overhaul came from former commission chairman Federal District Court Judge William K. Sessions III (2011). The envisioned reformed guidelines would remain largely mandatory, judges would not be allowed to take offenders' personal background and characteristics into account, and, save for acquittals, the relevant conduct rule would endure. Those proposals would have retained all the worst features, including complexity and severity, of the failed mandatory guidelines (Baron-Evans and Stith 2012).

The current commission chair, Federal District Court Judge Patti B. Saris (2011, 2013), has repeatedly decried what she describes as growing disparities in application of the guidelines and urged Congress to enact legislation to reinvigorate them. She does not acknowledge that most practitioners and outside observers believe federal sentencing is more just under the advisory guidelines. A 2010 survey of federal district court judges demonstrates how far out of step the commission is. Only 3 percent of the judges thought the "mandatory" guidelines in effect in 2005 before they were made "advisory" by the US Supreme Court "best achieve the purposes of sentencing" and 75 percent said the then-current advisory guidelines did. Seventy-six percent of judges said that commission policies on individualization of sentences did not provide appropriate grounds for departures, and 65 percent said the departure policies were "too restrictive" (US Sentencing Commission 2010, tables 14, 17). Those figures are striking because the vast majority of federal judges were appointed after the guidelines took effect. They have known nothing else and could have been expected to be socialized into the values of the system as it existed when they took office. The vast majority of district court judges in 1990 held similar views (Federal Court Study Committee 1990).

This essay tells that story. It is an important story. The federal sentencing guidelines' notoriety significantly set back constructive sentencing policy change in the states. American political culture may, however, soon be as receptive to fundamental rethinking of sentencing as it was 40 years ago. Presumptive guidelines of the sort Federal District Court Judge Marvin Frankel first proposed are the best means Americans have identified for establishing sentencing systems that are reasonably fair, just, and consistent (Frankel 1972, 1973; Frase 2013).

The problems of the federal guidelines were not inevitable. They resulted from the tough on crime politics of the 1980s and the personalities and political ambitions of the original members of the US Sentencing Commission. Even now the guidelines could be reformulated in ways that offer reasonable prospects for achieving their original aims. At the end of this essay, I describe how that can be done.

Two not unimportant questions are whether federal sentencing is more or less just than before the guidelines took effect on October 1, 1987, and whether "unwarranted" disparities are more or less common. Federal sentencing for sure is less just. For many offenses, sentences are much too severe both absolutely and compared with lesser punishments commonly received for more serious crimes. Judges are forbidden to take into account circumstances of offenders' lives that would justify less harsh punishment. Judges are strongly discouraged from imposing community punishments in cases in which that is the most appropriate thing to do. The relevant conduct policy is fundamentally unfair. It is unimaginable in the legal system of any other Western democracy.[1]

[1] The list could go on. Reduced punishments are authorized, e.g., for offenders who give "substantial assistance" to the prosecution of other people. High-level drug and organized-

Federal sentencing disparities are undoubtedly worse than they were before October 1, 1987, and are worse than they would have been in the counterfactual world in which the Sentencing Reform Act of 1984 was not enacted. There are two reasons to be confident this is true. The first is that nearly half of convicted federal offenders received community punishments in 1985, compared with fewer than 10 percent in 2014; by definition many fewer people were at risk of disparities in prison sentences. Unwarranted disparities in community penalties are, of course, also undesirable. As a practical matter, however, the stakes are much higher when prison is involved. Disparities in who is sent there and for how long are what really matter. The mere fact of conviction is stigmatizing and has detrimental effects on offenders' employment prospects, reputations, and community standing. A community punishment is seldom likely to worsen those effects. Prison sentences, however, ruin lives, break up families, and damage offenders' children in ways that community punishments do not (Murray et al. 2014; Jacobs 2015).

The second is that the Federal Parole Commission's guidelines for release from prison were impressively successful at reducing disparities in prison sentences (Gottfredson, Wilkins, and Hoffman 1978; Arthur D. Little, Inc. and Goldfarb and Singer, Esqs. 1981). The Sentencing Reform Act eliminated parole release and replaced it with "truth in sentencing" that requires prisoners to serve at least 85 percent of their sentences. Federal sentencing was fairer in 1985 for those who were sent to prison and for those who were not.

It is impossible to know what federal sentencing would have looked like had the guidelines not been adopted. Had the 1984 indeterminate system continued without major changes, disparities would have been less. Had another guidelines commission been established later, it is reasonable to believe that it would not have made the radical policy decisions made by the original commission. No other sentencing commission before (Minnesota, Pennsylvania, Washington), contemporaneous with (Oregon), or after the federal commission (North Carolina, Ohio, Kansas) established a system of comparable severity, rigidity, and complexity.

---

crime offenders, who have information to share, often receive less severe punishments than low-level offenders. Prosecutors have unilateral authority to decide to charge or insist on guilty pleas to offenses subject to lengthy mandatory minimum sentences; all else equal, targeted defendants receive dramatically longer sentences (US Sentencing Commission 2004; Shermer and Johnson 2009; Hofer 2012).

It is plausible to suppose that another later commission would have followed the paths pioneered by the states.

I say a bit more about those answers in the conclusion. First, I tell the federal story in more detail. Section I provides a capsule history of the conception, design, implementation, and ultimate emasculation of the federal guidelines. In Section II, I sketch what the federal sentencing system looked like in the years immediately before the guidelines took effect and compare that to the years since.

Section III then describes critical decisions made by the initial commission in the development of the guidelines and their implications. This is not only of historical interest and importance. Many critical decisions were not required by the Sentencing Reform Act. Some statutory provisions, for example, those creating a presumption that nonviolent first offenders should normally not be sentenced to imprisonment and directing that the guidelines not generate prison populations larger than existing and planned facilities could accommodate within their design capacity, were flatly ignored. Much that the initial commission did could have been, and still could be, done differently under the terms of the enabling legislation.

Section IV describes the guidelines development process and why the guidelines took the shape they did. Former commission member and now Supreme Court Associate Justice Stephen Breyer at the time painted a picture of earnest, hardworking commissioners struggling against overwhelming complexities and making difficult technocratic decisions in order to devise a workable system that would reduce disparities. Critics did not understand this, Justice Breyer wrote, and made the best the enemy of the good. The true story is of a poorly managed agency that made fateful but fundamental early mistakes, many politically motivated, compounded by arrogance and an unwillingness to reconsider.

Section V sets out what needs to be done to create a system of federal sentencing that does less harm and more good. The Supreme Court's decision in *Blakely v. Washington*, 542 U.S. 296 (2004), points the way forward.

I. The Rise and Fall of the Federal Sentencing Guidelines

The federal commission and guidelines can be traced directly to Judge Frankel's proposal in the *University of Cincinnati Law Review* (1972) for creation of specialized administrative agencies charged to develop rational sentencing policies. Frankel elaborated the proposal in *Criminal Sentences—Law without Order* (1973).[2] He argued that American sentencing was "lawless" because, uniquely in American law, no standards governed judges' sentencing decisions or provided criteria for appellate courts to apply in reviewing them. Presumptive sentencing rules developed by an independent, expert, politically semi-insulated administrative agency could, he wrote, provide those standards.

Frankel's ideas were explored in a series of workshops run by Daniel J. Freed at Yale Law School. Participants drafted model enabling legislation (O'Donnell, Curtis, and Churgin 1977).[3] Senate Bill 2699, based on the Yale model, was introduced by Edward Kennedy in 1975.

A. The Sentencing Reform Act of 1984

Senator Kennedy reintroduced successive versions of Senate Bill 2699 in every succeeding congress until it passed, both while he was chair of the Senate Judiciary Committee and later when Republican Senator Strom Thurmond replaced him. After a few iterations as a stand-alone, the sentencing proposals were merged into omnibus bills to enact a federal criminal code based on the recommendations of the National Commission on Reform of Federal Criminal Law (1971). The code bills, designated as Senate Bill 1 in several congresses as a symbol of the importance congressional leaders attached to them, were eventually abandoned in the face of mostly conservative opposition to expansion of federal authority in criminal justice matters, traditionally a state and local sphere.[4] Finally, once again a stand-alone measure, supported by Sen-

[2] According to Google Scholar, Frankel's book is by far the most frequently cited book or article on sentencing. As of June 23, 2015, it had been cited 1,310 times, far ahead of the 827 and 688 of the next-most-cited works.

[3] The late Norval Morris and I, with others including Judge Frankel, Deputy Attorney General Harold Tyler, Bureau of Prisons director Norman Carlson, US Parole Commission research director Peter B. Hoffman, and the US Department of Justice's criminal code specialist Ronald Gainer, in 1977 created a simulated commission that attempted to develop model guidelines (Tonry 2009). Personal (e.g., clashing egos, eccentric personalities), political (e.g., larger ambitions), and policy (e.g., control of prosecutorial discretion) problems that bedeviled the federal commission arose in the simulation.

[4] That is a tad ironic. Republican senators and congressmen in the 1980s and 1990s were the principal proponents of a wide range of laws that federalized criminal law. This was notably true of drug crimes, carjacking, child pornography, firearms offenses, domestic violence, sex offender registration and notification laws, and truth-in-sentencing laws.

ators Kennedy and Thurmond, the Sentencing Reform Act of 1984 became law.

In retrospect, too much time had passed. Washington, DC, had become the wrong place for an overhaul of sentencing policy. Part of the problem was that the proposals had become encrusted with provisions added at different times, reflecting diverse ideological and political beliefs, and sometimes pointing in different policy directions. Some reflected the essentially liberal and proceduralist values of the sentencing reform period in which Frankel's ideas took shape. They expressed the influence and attitudes of Judge Frankel, Senator Kennedy, and those around them:

- *Diversion of nonviolent first offenders*. Section 994(j) reflected the premises of the "National Moratorium on Prison Construction" and "alternatives to imprisonment" movements of the 1970s and early 1980s that imprisonment is harmful, should be used only as a last resort, and should seldom be used for first offenders (Platt and Takagi 1977, p. 11; Austin and Krisberg 1982). The commission was directed "to *insure* that the guidelines reflect the *general appropriateness* of imposing a sentence other than imprisonment in cases in which the defendant is a first offender who has not been convicted of a crime of violence *or an otherwise serious offense*" (emphasis added for reasons explained below).
- *Tailoring guidelines to prison capacity*. Section 994(g) drew on the Minnesota Sentencing Commission's successful use of a "capacity constraint" policy to prevent prison overcrowding. That commission assumed for humanitarian and operational reasons that the number of inmates in a prison should never exceed 95 percent of its design capacity. If the projected numbers were larger, the legislature could authorize and fund construction of additional capacity or the commission could revise the guidelines to reduce the numbers (Parent 1988). Accordingly, section 994(g) provided, the "sentencing guidelines prescribed under this chapter shall be formulated to minimize the likelihood that the Federal prison population will exceed the capacity of the Federal prisons."
- *Coercive rehabilitation programs*. Section 994(k) reflected contemporaneous skepticism about the ethical justifications and effectiveness of rehabilitative programs associated with the "Nothing Works" movement that took shape in the mid-1970s (Martinson 1974; Morris

1974; Cullen 2013). It specified that the guidelines should "reflect the inappropriateness of imposing a sentence to a term of imprisonment for the purpose of rehabilitating the defendant or providing the defendant with needed . . . correctional treatment."

However, other provisions reflected the essentially conservative and punitive values of the tough on crime period and expressed the influence and attitudes of Senator Thurmond, Attorney General Ed Meese, and those around them:

- *Three strikes*. Section 994(h), anticipating the three-strikes laws enacted in many states and by the Congress in 1993–96, charged the commission to "assure that the guidelines specify a sentence to a term of imprisonment at or near the maximum term authorized for categories of defendants" convicted of a violent or drug offense and having two prior violent or drug felony convictions.
- *Career criminals*. Section 994(i) directed the commission to "assure that the guidelines specify a sentence to a substantial term of imprisonment for categories of defendants" who had two or more prior felony convictions; derived substantial income from crime; committed the offense in furtherance of certain conspiracies; committed a violent felony while on release pending trial, sentence, or appeal; or committed certain drug felonies.
- *Serious injury*. Section 994(j) directed the commission "to *insure* that the guidelines reflect . . . the *general appropriateness* of imposing a term of imprisonment on a person convicted of a crime of violence that results in *serious* bodily injury" (emphasis added).

Senators Kennedy and Thurmond reconciled their differences in cosponsoring the legislation. The commission could likewise easily have reconciled the "liberal" and "conservative" directives. Guidelines could have been drafted that prescribed community punishments for most nonviolent first offenders, specified significant prison terms for people convicted of unusually violent crimes or who had serious and extensive criminal records, and set presumptive sentence lengths so that projected numbers of prisoners could have been accommodated in available and planned prison capacity. Minnesota had shown that these things are doable, including making explicit policy trade-offs by reducing sentences for some offenses in order to increase them for others. This was done both in designing the initial Minnesota guidelines and in revising them over time (Knapp 1984). Washington, Oregon, and North Carolina later also demonstrated the effectiveness and rationality of guidelines that included prison capacity constraints (Frase 2013; Tonry 2013).

The optimal federal strategy would have been to increase punishments for people convicted of violent crimes and decrease them for the much larger number of people convicted of nonviolent and drug crimes. Then and now known as "bifurcation," that is how most countries' governments responded to the trebling of crime rates throughout the Western world in the 1970s and 1980s (Bottoms 1977; Tonry 2007). New prosecutorial diversion and community sanction programs proliferated in other Western countries, and prison space was increasingly reserved for violent offenders (Albrecht 2001; Tonry 2001). In the United States, North Carolina's sentencing commission in the early 1990s, also in the heat of the tough on crime period, received enormous attention, including a public-sector innovation award from Harvard's Kennedy School of Government, for doing exactly that. New guidelines made prison sentences for serious crimes harsher than those previously served but also vastly increased the proportion of people convicted of lesser crimes who received community punishments (Wright 2002).

The founding members of the US Sentencing Commission, however, vigorously carried out only the "conservative" statutory directives. Politics and political ideology were the explanation. Republicans were hammering away at law and order and welfare fraud as "wedge issues" meant to separate working-class voters from their traditional Democratic leanings (Edsall and Edsall 1991). The Reagan administration was in power. The commission's seven members were appointed by President Ronald Reagan, three of them judges proposed by Supreme Court Chief Justice Warren Burger. Six of the seven members were openly identified as conservatives, and the seventh, Stephen Breyer, then a federal circuit court judge, was well known as a pragmatist who as a legislative assistant to Senator Kennedy had shown he could work with conservative Republicans. One indication is that he was nominated for appointment to the Federal First Circuit Court of Appeals in the fall of 1980, after Republicans had made it clear that they would block President Jimmy Carter's judicial nominees pending the presidential election. Breyer was nonetheless confirmed before the election, a man conservatives believed they could trust.

The federal commission ignored the "liberal" directives in the 1984 act, followed the conservative directives, and developed guidelines that together with California's three-strikes law and the federal 100-to-1 crack cocaine law became the emblems of the excesses of the tough on crime period (Travis, Western, and Redburn 2014, chap. 3). Below, I describe the major junctions at which the commission repeatedly made right turns when the statute would have permitted, and sometimes prescribed, policy moves in other directions. One I describe here as illustrative and discuss in more detail below involves the commission's interpretation of section 994(j)'s directive calling for diversion from imprisonment of nonviolent first offenders.

In quoting from the statute, I twice italicized the word "insure." The reason is that the Congress directed the commission "to insure" two things: that the guidelines reflect the general appropriateness, first, "of imposing a sentence other than imprisonment in cases in which the defendant is a first offender who has not been convicted of a crime of violence or an otherwise serious offense," and, second, "of imposing a term of imprisonment on a person convicted of a crime of violence that results in serious bodily injury." No informed person would disagree that the commission did the second. As to the first, the commission ignored the symmetrical phrasing "violence or an otherwise serious offense" and defined "otherwise serious" to include almost all federal offenses. Before the guidelines took effect, the commission's own data showed, nearly half of sentenced offenders were sentenced to a fine or probation, without prison time; afterward, the commission projected that many fewer would receive straight probation. The percentages were projected to decline from 60 to 33 percent for property offenders, from 64 to 43 percent for burglars, from 21 to 5 percent for drug offenders, and from 31 to 15 percent for violent offenders (US Sentencing Commission 1987*c*, p. 68).

The results of that single low-visibility choice to nullify a clear congressional directive contributed significantly to the ensuing rapid increase in federal imprisonment rates and to the guidelines' intense unpopularity among federal practitioners. The presumption against imprisonment of most nonviolent first offenders disappeared. Judges were directed to send to prison many people whose later lives would be fundamentally damaged. Below, I discuss a considerable number of comparable low-visibility choices that made federal sentencing more inflexible, mechanical, and severe. First, though, I discuss the guidelines' reception in their early years.

B. Early Reactions to Federal Sentencing Guidelines

The federal guidelines were not foreordained to have much influence. Many changes in sentencing laws and policies have relatively little impact. Evaluations of "voluntary" (or now "advisory") sentencing guidelines in the 1970s and early 1980s, for example, concluded that they had little or no effect on sentencing patterns (Blumstein et al. 1983). Evaluations of mandatory minimum sentence laws over a half century concluded that, depending on the prevailing policy climate, they are always or often circumvented (Tonry 2009; Travis, Western, and Redburn 2014, chap. 3). Evaluations showed that intermediate sanctions programs established in the 1980s to serve as alternatives to imprisonment were typically used instead as alternatives to probation (Morris and Tonry 1990).

The federal guidelines potentially faced two major challenges. The first was that practitioners would nullify them. They could simply ignore the guidelines, as happened with the early voluntary sentencing guidelines (Rich et al. 1982; Carrow et al. 1985). Or, practitioners could change how cases were processed in order to circumvent the guidelines and continue doing business as usual, as happened with many mandatory minimum sentence laws (Joint Committee on New York Drug Law Evaluation 1978; Heumann and Loftin 1979).

The commission attempted to compel judicial compliance in a variety of ways. One, not based on the enabling statute, which describes a system of presumptive guidelines akin to Minnesota's or Washington's, was to describe the federal guidelines as "mandatory" (e.g., 1991*b*). The aim was presumably to give the guidelines greater psychological or moral force. Judges might be expected to be more uncomfortable disregarding a "mandatory" than a "presumptive" guideline.

Another was to draft guidelines and policy statements in exceedingly close detail. Drug offenses, for example, were defined in terms of quantities and property offenses in terms of amounts in much greater detail than did federal statutes. Separate guideline ranges were provided for robbery on the basis of the amount; whether a weapon was present, brandished, or used; what type of weapon; whether injury resulted, and if so of what type and degree. Most state guidelines systems by contrast recognize two or three main categories of major offenses; judges take account of other factors in deciding whether to depart from them.

Still another effort to force compliance was to forbid or disapprove many offender characteristics that most judges believe to be appropriate and ethically relevant as bases for departures from otherwise applicable guidelines ranges.[5] Section 3553(b) authorized departures concerning factors "not adequately taken into consideration" by the commission. In order to minimize successful appeals, the commission sought to show that it had adequately considered all factors that judges commonly consider important. It forbade many things most people would consider obviously appropriate considerations in many cases. Declared "not ordinarily relevant" were age, physical condition, drug or alcohol dependence or abuse, education, vocational skills, employment record, and family ties and responsibilities. Lack of guidance as a youth and a disadvantaged childhood were later declared to be "not relevant" and civic, charitable, or public service or a record of prior good works to be "not ordinarily relevant."

The second major challenge, especially acute because many commission decisions alienated judges, was that the courts would declare them unconstitutional. Most who considered the matter did: "more than 200 district judges invalidated the guidelines and all or part of the Sentencing Reform Act" (US Sentencing Commission 1990*a*, p. 11).[6] Those decisions were explained in constitutional terms, but the number of cases and their vehemence suggested that the underlying problem was antipathy to the guidelines.

The US Supreme Court, in a decision many of its members likely later regretted, upheld the commission's, the guidelines', and the Sentencing Reform Act's constitutionality.[7] *Mistretta v. United States*, 488 U.S.

[5] The commission has recently preferred that the term "departure" be reserved for decisions expressly permitted under guidelines policy statements and that other sentences not consistent with guidelines be referred to as "variances" (Saris 2011, p. 58). "Departure" has long been used in most settings to refer to sentences not within applicable guidelines ranges, including by state sentencing commissions. I use the term "departure" in that broader, conventional way.

[6] That was more than a third of the 541 sitting district court judges in 1990 (United States Courts 2014, table 1.1).

[7] *U.S. v. Booker*, 543 U.S. 220 (2005), the culmination of a series of Supreme Court decisions that progressively undermined the guidelines and restored discretion to district court judges, made the guidelines "advisory."

361 (1989), rejected constitutional arguments that district and appellate court judges had accepted. One was that Congress delegated excessively broad rule-making authority to the commission. The second was that separation-of-powers doctrines were violated when the commission, a rule-making administrative agency typically part of the executive branch of government, was placed in the judicial branch. A third argument, on which the Court did not rule, was that the guidelines violated defendants' constitutional due process rights to individualized consideration of offense and offender characteristics.

The federal dice were cast, but the controversies did not go away. The Federal Courts Study Committee, appointed by Chief Justice William Rehnquist to assess the guidelines' early operation, observed, "It became obvious from our earliest requests for comment and information from federal judges and others who work daily in the system . . . that there is a pervasive concern that the Commission's guidelines are producing fundamental and deleterious changes in the way federal courts process criminal cases" (1990, p. 135).

The Study Committee received testimony from 270 people, including judges, probation officers, prosecutors, defense lawyers, representatives of organized groups such as the American Bar Association, and members of the US Sentencing Commission. Only three commission members and Attorney General Richard Thornburgh spoke in favor of the guidelines. No other witness opposed the following proposal: "Congress should amend the Sentencing Reform Act to state clearly that the guidelines promulgated by the Sentencing Commission are general standards regarding the appropriate sentence in the typical case, not compulsory rules. Although the guidelines should identify the presumptive sentence, the trial judge should have general authority to select a sentence outside the range prescribed by the guidelines, subject to appellate review for abuse of discretion. The exercise of this discretion may be based upon factors such as an appropriate plea bargain or the defendant's personal history" (Federal Courts Study Committee 1990, p. 142). The Study Committee proposed not the abandonment of guidelines but replacement of the "mandatory" federal guidelines with presumptive guidelines like those in Minnesota, Washington, and Oregon. All by 1990 had proven effective at reducing disparities while permitting judges flexibility to take account of the distinctive circumstances of individual offenses and offenders (Tonry 1996).

The committee noted a series of practical problems. Sentencing proceedings had become much more time-consuming. The guidelines were inflexible and arbitrary. They disrupted plea bargaining, threatened to increase demands for trials, and distorted the role of the probation officer. Most disturbingly to judges, "the rigidity of the guidelines is causing a massive, though unintended, transfer of discretion and authority from the court to the prosecutor. . . . The result, it appears, is that some prosecutors (and some defense counsel) have evaded and manipulated the guidelines" (Federal Courts Study Committee 1990, p. 138).

A short time later, Judge William W. Schwartzer, director of the Federal Judicial Center (FJC), the research and training agency of the federal courts, wrote, "We are paying a high price for the present sentencing system, and not only in dollars. It is a high price in terms of the integrity of the criminal justice process, in terms of human life and the moral capital of the system. The elimination of unwarranted disparities is a worthy objective but it has not been achieved. Instead a system conducive to producing arbitrary results has been created" (1991, p. 341).

Schwartzer took a risk saying that. Earlier, under pressure from commission chairman William Wilkins, the FJC embargoed a research report by staffer Paul Hofer (1990) that documented manipulation and evasion of the guidelines by prosecutors and judges.[8] The research, based on interviews and analyses of case files in six districts, had been approved for publication by the FJC's board. It was the first time in the FJC's history that an approved report was later withdrawn.[9]

[8] The project "Sentencing Procedures under the 1984 Sentencing Reform Act" was one of two on sentencing announced in the center's 1989 annual report: "This study [Hofer 1990], based on field research in six districts, will analyze the operation of different procedures adopted by courts to accommodate the demands of guideline sentencing. It will address procedures that seem to work well and, of the procedures that have been tried, those that seem not to" (Federal Judicial Center 1989, p. 21). The other project is described in the 1990 annual report as completed. The field study is never again mentioned in an annual report.

[9] Two commission-sponsored studies of the guidelines' early implementation reached the same results (Schulhofer and Nagel 1989; Nagel and Schulhofer 1992). So did the commission's congressionally mandated self-evaluation (US Sentencing Commission 1991*a*). Hofer (1990), despite Judge Wilkins's displeasure, was made available to the Federal Courts Study Committee and was relied on (Beale 1989, pp. 14–15): "Both the FJC Study and the Schulhofer and Nagel Study found that the Guidelines are being manipulated and evaded on a widespread basis."

Judge Gerald W. Heaney, a senior judge of the Eighth Circuit Court of Appeals, in one of the first empirical evaluations of the guidelines' operation, examined experiences in four district courts. Here are his main conclusions: "The roles of the prosecutor and the probation officer in the sentencing process have been enhanced and that of the district judge diminished. While district judges are required to devote more time to sentencing, their discretion has been severely limited. . . . There is little evidence to suggest that the congressional objective of reducing unwarranted sentencing disparity has been achieved. . . . Voluminous anecdotal evidence and case law show the unfairness of the guidelines and the disparities created through their application" (Heaney 1991, pp. 163–64, 167).

The federal guidelines' reputation was set. At the founding meeting of the National Association of Sentencing Commissions in Boulder, Colorado, in 1993, directors of state sentencing commissions emphasized that the federal example created huge problems: "No state commission representative, in more than three hours of conversation, mentioned the federal sentencing guidelines except to emphasize that their state had taken pains to avoid association with the federal model" (Orland and Reitz 1993, p. 838). Kay A. Knapp, the first executive director of the federal commission, ruefully later observed, "No matter how misguided otherwise, no state commission has been so foolish as to adopt the highly complex and mechanistic federal sentencing policy that has so incurred the wrath of the legal community" (1993, pp. 678–80). Knapp and the federal commission's first general counsel, Denis J. Hauptly, had earlier described the federal guidelines' failures in detail and advised states how to avoid them (Knapp and Hauptly 1992).

The federal guidelines' reputation presented serious challenges for the committee drafting the American Bar Association's 1993 *Standards for Sentencing*. The principal draftsmen, father and son Curtis and Kevin Reitz, observed that "the widespread unpopularity of the federal guidelines" was "a major stumbling block." The *Standards* refer to "sentencing structures" to make its proposals: the word "guidelines," they wrote, "was excised from the standards to avoid any appearance of approval of federal law." They elaborated, "At every stage of the drafting process, detailed presentations were made to explain the ways in which the proposed standards were substantially different than the federal system, and were borrowed instead from more promising state innovations" (Reitz and Reitz 1993, pp. 170–71).

Except as a model to be repudiated, the federal guidelines have had no significant influence on subsequent development of American sentencing policy. This can be seen in the reports issued to date from the American Law Institute's ongoing effort to develop a *Model Penal Code—Sentencing* to serve as a resource for state and federal policy makers. The federal commission and guidelines are mentioned only a handful of times, usually as a bibliographical reference (American Law Institute 2007, 2011). This is the only textual mention: "The revised Code discourages commissions from following the early practice of the United States Sentencing Commission, which has been much-criticized for its failure in its early years to borrow from the experiences of preexisting state commissions and, indeed, for its failure adequately to investigate those experiences" (2007, p. 58).

C. *The Commission since* Mistretta

From their inception until 2005 when the US Supreme Court in *U.S. v. Booker*, 543 U.S. 220, converted them from "mandatory" to "advisory," the federal guidelines were widely disliked and resented by judges and other practitioners. The commission paid little attention to complaints, but eventually the US Supreme Court did. In *Koons v. United States*, 518 U.S. 81 (1996), the court broadened judges' discretion to depart. In *Booker*, the court decided that the guidelines suffered from fundamental constitutional problems and that the only way to preserve them was to make them advisory. In *Gall v. United States*, 522 U.S. 38 (2007), the court directed appellate courts to use a deferential "abuse of discretion" standard when assessing the adequacy of reasons given by sentencing judges for departing from the guidelines. A series of cases, including *Kimbrough v. United States*, 552 U.S. 85 (2007), and *Spears v. United States*, 555 U.S. 261 (2009), authorized judges to depart from guidelines when they disagreed with commission policy decisions. This ended the obligatory effects of the commission's effort to declare particular considerations "not relevant" or "not ordinarily relevant." The commission nonetheless continues to insist that trial judges' decisions should be governed by those provisions (Saris 2011, 2013; US Sentencing Commission 2012*b*).

U.S. v. Booker also nullified much of the 2003 Feeney Amendment, which attempted to make the guidelines even more rigid. In Justice Breyer's words, the amendment was thereafter "not relevant." The Feeney Amendment sought to limit sentencing judges' discretion to depart downward from the guidelines, provided tighter standards for appellate sentence review, and directed the commission to amend the guidelines in particular ways and "ensure that the incidence of downward departures are [sic] substantially reduced." Part of the Prosecutorial Remedies and Tools against the Exploitation of Children Today (PROTECT) Act of 2003 (Pub. L. no. 108-21, 117 Stat. 650 [2003]), it was motivated by Republican Representative Tom Feeney's real or feigned belief that federal judges too often departed downward to impose "lenient" sentences. Its provisions on judicial discretion were in effect only a bit more than a year, but caused a furor (e.g., Bibas 2004; Mason 2004). The Feeney Amendment is primarily only of historical interest, but while it lasted it substantially affected federal sentencing, reducing downward departures by 5 percent and increasing average prison sentences by 2 months (Freeborn and Hartmann 2010).

The commission never seriously considered making fundamental changes to the guidelines during the 18 years before *Booker* was decided. It devoted much of its energy to trying to make the guidelines more prescriptive. In the period since the appointment in 1994 of Judge Richard P. Conaboy as the commission's second chair, however, it has sometimes done or tried to do admirable things aiming to make federal sentencing somewhat more just in relation to mandatory minimums and drug crimes. In 1991 and repeatedly subsequently, the commission has shown the injustice and distorting effects of mandatory minimum sentence laws and urged their repeal or modification (e.g., US Sentencing Commission 1991*b*, 2011; Saris 2013).[10] In 1995, and repeatedly thereafter, the commission urged the Congress to revise or repeal the 100-to-1 crack cocaine sentencing law (1995*d*, 1997*b*, 2002, 2007). In 2007, the commission amended the guidelines to correct one of its most egregious earlier errors. The guidelines ceased directing judges to impose prison sentences on drug offenders that were longer than were required by applicable mandatory minimum sentence laws.

The commission several times examined its policies on the use of nonincarcerative punishments but never made any significant changes to its policy of limiting their use to a tiny percentage of sentenced offenders. Table 1 summarizes commission policy statements on permitted, dis-

[10] In this and the following paragraphs, citations showing only dates refer to US Sentencing Commission publications.

couraged, and forbidden reasons to depart from the guidelines. The changes are few and modest. An effort led by commissioner Helen Corrothers, whose earlier career involved correctional work, proposed that the commission broaden use of intermediate sanctions (US Sentencing Commission 1990*b*). A simplification project launched by commission chairman Richard Conaboy in 1995–96 included a working group on alternatives (US Sentencing Commission 1996*e*). A recent examination of intermediate punishments in the federal system noted their important potential roles but recommended no meaningful policy changes

TABLE 1

Departure Provisions, Federal Sentencing Guidelines, 1987, 2014

Section	Subject	1987	2014
5H1.1	Age	NOT ordinarily relevant	MAY be relevant*
5H1.2	Education and vocational skills	NOT ordinarily relevant	NOT ordinarily relevant
5H1.3	Mental and emotional conditions	NOT ordinarily relevant	MAY be relevant*
5H1.4	Physical condition or appearance	NOT ordinarily relevant	MAY be relevant*
5H1.4	Drug or alcohol dependence or abuse	NOT a reason for downward departure	ORDINARILY NOT a basis for downward departure
5H1.4	Gambling addiction	[no provision]	NOT a basis for downward departure
5H1.5	Employment record	NOT ordinarily relevant	NOT ordinarily relevant
5H1.6	Family ties and responsibilities	NOT ordinarily relevant	NOT ordinarily relevant
5H1.11	Military service	[no provision]	MAY be relevant*
5H1.11	Civic, charitable, and public service, etc.	[no provision]	NOT ordinarily relevant
5H1.12	Lack of guidance as a youth	[no provision]	NOT relevant in determining whether to depart
5H1.12	Disadvantaged upbringing	[no provision]	NOT relevant in determining whether to depart

Source.—US Sentencing Commission 1987*a*, 2014*b*, secs. 5H1.1–5H1.12. Explanations for changes are set out in app. C to the 2014 manual (amendments 386, 466, 475, 569, 649, 651, 674, 739).

* "[If] present to an unusual degree and distinguish[es] the case from the typical case covered by the guidelines." This wording varies slightly between provisions but is substantively similar in all.

(US Sentencing Commission 2009). None of these undertakings resulted in significant changes.

Table 2 shows the issues given primary emphasis in the commission's annual reports to Congress since 1991. Mandatory minimums and sentencing for cocaine offenses recur. Other subjects come and go, usually in response to new legislation or to heightened congressional attention to particular offenses. For a short time in the mid-1990s, "simplification" was a prominent issue, though it never happened (US Sentencing Commission 1996*d*). In recent years, the commission has been preoccupied with the effects of *Booker* and efforts to reinvigorate the guidelines in its aftermath.

The commission has submitted reports to Congress on many other subjects urging guideline and statutory changes. Proposals never involved changes to the guidelines' basic structures or features. Topics include campaign finance (2003*a*), computer crime (1996*b*, 2003*b*), disaster relief (2008), money laundering (1997*a*), sexual offenses (1995*b*, 1995*c*, 1996*c*, 2012*a*), and corporate crime (1995*a*, 1998, 2003*c*). Not surprisingly, the reports correspond to the changing emphases shown in table 2.[11]

In some minor ways, the commission over time slightly humanized the guidelines. The original version provided that age, education and vocational skills, mental and emotional conditions, physical condition including drug dependence and alcohol abuse, employment records, family ties and responsibilities, and community ties are "not ordinarily relevant in determining whether a sentence should be outside the applicable guideline range" (US Sentencing Commission 1987*a*, part H, §§5H1.1–5H1.6). To this the commission later added that "lack of guidance as a youth and similar circumstances indicating a disadvantaged upbringing" are "not relevant" and that "civic, charitable, or public service . . . and similar prior good works" are not ordinarily relevant. Those latter changes aimed to undo the effects of federal appellate court decisions that had approved judges' departures from the guidelines for reasons of extraordinary disadvantage or public service.

Many of the offender characteristics the commission ruled out of bounds concern subjects that most judges and other practitioners (and

[11] Each annual report of course also discusses amendments proposed for congressional consideration.

TABLE 2

US Sentencing Commission, Priority Topics, 1990–2014

Year	Business	Drugs	Mandatories	Other	Sex	Simplification
1990				Plea negotiation, alternatives		
1991			Mandatories			
1992		Quantity guidelines				
1993	Computer	100:1		Corruption		
1994						
1995	Elder fraud	100:1			Rape, HIV	Simplification
1996	Computer				Child victims	Simplification
1997	Money laundering	100:1				
1998	Telemarketing					
1999	Fraud	Methamphetamine				
2000		Drugs	Mandatories			
2001	Money laundering	Ecstasy, methamphetamine				
2002		100:1		Native Americans		
2003	Cyber crime, fraud			Departures, campaign finance		
2004				Departures, recidivism, *Blakely*		
2005	Antitrust			*Booker*, recidivism		
2006		Steroids		*Booker*		
2007		Cocaine				
2008	Disaster fraud	100:1		*Gall*, *Kimbrough*		
2009			Mandatories			
2010			Mandatories	Alternatives		
2011	Iran sanctions	100:1	Mandatories			
2012			Mandatories	*Booker*	Child pornography	
2013	Economic crimes			*Booker*	Child pornography	
2014	Fraud		Mandatories			

SOURCE.—US Sentencing Commission, annual reports—various years; US Sentencing Commission (2014*b*).

most people) believe are often germane to deciding what a just and appropriate sentence might be. In more recent years the commission has allowed judges somewhat greater authority. Education and vocational skills, employment record, and family ties and responsibilities in 2013 continued to be "not ordinarily relevant." However, age and mental, emotional, and physical conditions have been shifted into a "may be relevant" category; this is less of a change than appears from the words used.[12] Drug and alcohol abuse shifted from "not" to "not ordinarily" relevant. Moving in the other direction, the commission has declared that gambling addiction is not a valid reason for mitigating a sentence. Anyone familiar with criminal courts knows that alcoholism, drug dependence, and gambling addiction are often primary causes of offending (US Sentencing Commission 2014*b*).

In 2015, despite commission proposals for legislation to reinvigorate its authority, the guidelines limped along (US Sentencing Commission 2012*b*). Judges are still expected under a "three-step" process to calculate sentences according to guideline provisions, consult the Guidelines Manual concerning commission policies and determine whether they authorize a "departure," and then to consider whether a "variance" is appropriate notwithstanding that a departure is not authorized (Saris 2011, pp. 57–58).[13] In principle, departure decisions are subject to appeal by the aggrieved party under the criteria set out in the Sentencing Reform Act of 1984, as amended, but as a practical matter, recent Supreme Court decisions give judges broad discretion. An "abuse of discretion" review standard effectively requires appellate judges to rule that no reasonable judge would have imposed a challenged sentence. That is not often likely to happen. Not surprisingly, rates of downward departures have steadily increased since *Booker* was decided.

Table 3 shows patterns of compliance for selected years since 1996. The overwhelming picture is of judges and prosecutors increasingly mitigating the guidelines' severity, with short-lived hiccups in 2004 while the Feeney Amendment was in effect. Striking patterns appear for

[12] Baron-Evans and Stith (2012, p. 1723) point out that despite the changes of a few characteristics from "not ordinarily relevant" to "may be relevant," commission policy statements specify that they must be "present to an unusual degree and distinguish the case from the typical cases covered by the guidelines." This, they observe, is essentially the same standard for characteristics deemed "not ordinarily relevant."

[13] Departure and variance are in quotation marks to signify the commission's distinctive use of those terms.

TABLE 3

Within-Guidelines Sentences and Departures, Federal Courts, Selected Years 1996–2013, Percentages

Disposition	1996	2000	2004[a]	2004[b]	2006[c]	2008	2010	2012	2013
A. Within range	69.6	64.5	72.2	71.8	61.7	59.4	55.0	52.4	51.2
B. Departure down	10.3	17.0	11.6	13.2	12.0	13.4	17.8	17.8	18.7
C. Government requests, of which	19.2	17.9	15.5	14.4	24.6	25.6	25.4	27.8	27.9
Substantial assistance	19.2	17.9	15.5	14.4	13.4	13.3	11.6	11.7	11.7
Early disposition					7.4	7.9	9.9	11.2	10.6
Other					2.8	2.4	3.9	4.9	5.2

SOURCE.—US Sentencing Commission, annual reports, various years.

[a] Pre-*Blakely* (October 1, 2003–June 24, 2004).

[b] Post-*Blakely* (June 25–September 30, 2004). Data for 2004 are divided to take account of *Blakely v. Washington*, 542 U.S. 296 (2004), a decision concerning the Washington State guidelines that raised doubts about the federal guidelines' constitutionality. Many federal judges construed *Blakely* to apply in principle to federal sentencing and altered their practices accordingly. Departure rates rose immediately.

[c] Beginning in 2006, "government requests" includes "early dispositions" and "other" government-sponsored downward departures.

sentences imposed from within applicable guideline ranges, downward departures, and departures requested by prosecutors. The percentage of within-guideline sentences fell almost continuously from 70 percent to a bit more than half. The latter rate, however, is attributable more to the effects of mandatory minimum sentence laws than to discretionary judicial decisions to comply with the guidelines. The percentage of downward departures nearly doubled in absolute terms, but by more than that for cases in which the judge took the initiative without a prosecutorial request. Prosecutors also increasingly requested mitigated sentences, some for defendants who provided substantial assistance to the government in other cases and some under a 2003 law that authorized reductions, mostly in immigration cases, for defendants who agreed to fast-track dispositions that involve simplified court procedures.

The federal guidelines were controversial and were disliked mostly because of critical decisions the commission made. Although a few of the resulting policies have been tinkered with, most remain fully or largely in effect. Only if most of them are eventually changed is there much chance that federal guidelines will someday work as Judge Frankel hoped and expected they would. In Sections III and V, I discuss those critical choices and the changes that need to be made. The stage needs first to be set, though, by describing the federal sentencing system before the guidelines took effect and shortly afterward.

II. Federal Sentencing Before and Under Guidelines

The federal sentencing system in the mid-1980s was, along with the guidelines systems in Minnesota and Washington, among the best run and least unjust of any in the United States. There were two reasons why that was so. First, the US Parole Commission had been successfully operating and continuously refining and revalidating its prison release guidelines for more than a decade (Hoffman 1976, 1983, 1995). It incorporated evidence-based policy decisions about prediction of reoffending and reduction of disparities in prison terms (Gottfredson, Wilkins, and Hoffman 1978). Presumptive sentencing guidelines in Minnesota and Washington were reducing disparities in sentence lengths in those states. The federal system was the one other jurisdiction that was doing that effectively.

Second, federal judges had discretion for many offenses and offenders to fine-tune sentences to individual offenders' circumstances. If imprisonment seemed unwarranted, it need not be imposed. Only 50.3 percent of federal sentences in 1985 were to imprisonment, including split sentences (Bureau of Justice Statistics 1990, table 4.1, p. 47). Thirty-seven percent were "straight" probation. Eleven percent were stand-alone fines. By 1990, still a turbulent year because *Mistretta* had just been decided, 60.4 percent of sentences were to imprisonment and 37.5 percent were to straight probation (McDonald and Carlson 1992, tables 1, 5).

In 1995, however, after *Mistretta*, 78.7 percent of sentences were to imprisonment and only 13.6 percent were to straight probation (US Sentencing Commission 1996*a*, table 18). In 2013, only 7.1 percent of sentenced offenders received straight probation; 5.4 percent received split sentences including some confinement. The remaining 87.6 percent were sentenced solely to prison (US Sentencing Commission 2013, fig. D).

The reduction in use of straight probation was the result of an explicit commission policy choice. It required prison sentences for many cases that previously in the federal system and typically in state systems resulted in community punishments. The reason is that the federal guidelines apply to all federal convictions, including both felonies and misdemeanors. In Minnesota, by contrast, the sentencing guidelines apply only to felonies, which are less than half of all convictions. The guidelines create a presumption in favor of a prison sentence only for about 20 percent of felonies. Minnesota judges then had and now have complete discretion over the vast majority of cases they sentence.

There was another important contextual consideration when the US Sentencing Commission set to work. America in the late 1980s, like America today, was socially, economically, and politically diverse. This is manifested within individual states in substantially different sentencing norms in different areas. The classic pattern is that sentences are most severe in rural areas and least in large cities, with suburbs and towns falling in between. Effective guidelines can ameliorate those differences, but only a little. Attitudes and beliefs about crime and punishment vary geographically. Judges and prosecutors almost inevitably are influenced by the prevailing views in the communities of which they are a part. Many prosecutors passionately believe that as elected officials in a democratic society they should take account of and reflect local beliefs (Boerner 2012; Wright 2012).

What is true of a single state in the nature of things is even truer in a large, federal country characterized by major regional differences in cultural traditions and political beliefs. It would be astonishing if attitudes toward crime and punishment were the same in California, Louisiana, Maine, and Texas or in "Red" and "Blue" states generally. Table 4 shows familiar data on differences in state imprisonment rates in 1987 and 2011. There were distinctive state and regional patterns in 1987. They were much the same in 2011. The US Sentencing Commission, in its research on past sentencing practices, like every other sentencing commission, learned that there were major differences in sentencing patterns in different district courts and either naively or in willful denial acted as if guidelines can substantially alleviate them.

The continuities over a quarter century shown in table 4 are stunning. The average ranking in the Northeast, the lowest, was 38 in 1987 and 41 in 2011. The Midwest was 31 and 30, the West 24 and 27, and the South 16 and 13. Five states, Louisiana, Alabama, Oklahoma, Georgia, and Arizona, ranked in the top 10 in both years. Eight states were among the 10 lowest ranked in both years (Minnesota, North Dakota, Maine, Massachusetts, New Hampshire, Rhode Island, Vermont, and Utah). Some states changed relative rankings significantly, but most only slightly. Minnesota was forty-ninth in both years and New Hampshire was forty-seventh. Louisiana was ranked second in 1987 and first in 2011.

Federal judicial districts are organized within states. States with small populations constitute a single district. Populous states are divided into several. Judges and US Attorneys mostly are selected from within the states in which courts are located. Many assistant US attorneys, defense lawyers, and probation staff also come from the states where they work. Those who do not are quickly socialized into prevailing local norms and practices. It would be remarkable if their work in federal courts were not powerfully influenced by local standards. Sentencing standards will inevitably be resisted and circumvented if they vary substantially from beliefs about just punishments of people who must apply them.

No system of sentencing guidelines can substantially reduce disparities across an entire continent, as table 5 illustrates. It shows patterns of compliance with the federal guidelines in six federal district courts in 1991, 2000, and 2010. Two of the districts were selected because they had especially low departure rates in 1991, two because they had especially high departure rates, and two because their departure rates reflected national means. Reflecting the guidelines' increasing flexibility over time, the percentages of sentences imposed from within applicable guideline ranges fell continuously in five of the six districts. The continuities, however, are much more striking. Each district has its own distinctive pattern. Virginia and Oklahoma judges most often sentenced from within guideline ranges and Arizona and Pennsylvania judges least often. North Carolina and Maryland judges fell in between. The differences are robust over two decades.

Patterns are shown for the three most common dispositions: within-range sentences, downward departures following prosecutorial "substantial assistance" motions, and other discretionary downward departures. The latter two are shown separately and combined.

There were dramatic differences in formal guidelines compliance in 1991 in terms of percentages of cases falling within guidelines ranges: above 95 percent in Oklahoma and Virginia, around 80 percent in Maryland and North Carolina, and about 55 percent in Arizona and Pennsylvania. In 2010, the rankings were the same. Oklahoma and Virginia judges were nearly twice as likely as Arizona and Pennsylvania judges to impose sentences within applicable guideline ranges. North Carolina and Maryland judges again fell in between.

There were also major differences between districts in the kinds of departures judges made and how often they made them:

- In Virginia, substantial assistance departures were at all times rare, ranging between 3 and 7 percent of cases. In Pennsylvania, they were at all times common, ranging between 32 and 41 percent.
- In North Carolina, discretionary downward departures were at all times rare, ranging between 3 and 13 percent of cases. In Arizona, they were at all times common, ranging between 32 and 64 percent.
- In Virginia and North Carolina, downward departures of either kind were comparatively rare, never exceeding 25 percent combined, and were usually much less frequent. In Arizona and Pennsylvania, downward departures were the norm, ranging between 43 and 71 percent of cases.

Each of the six districts is in recognizably the same place in post-*Mistretta* 1991, post-*Koons* 2000, and post-*Booker* 2010 relative to the others and carries on its own distinctive practices. No system of federal guidelines could have produced similar sentencing patterns in those six districts or in Louisiana, Maine, and California. It was foolhardy for

TABLE 4

Imprisonment Rates per 100,000 Population and National Rank, by Region and State, 1987 and 2011

	1987	2011
	Northeast	
Northeast total	169	296*
Connecticut[a]	144 (35)	350 (34)
Maine	106 (42)	147 (50)
Massachusetts[b]	106 (43)	206 (45)
New Hampshire	81 (47)	198 (47)
New Jersey[c]	177 (26)	270 (40)
New York	229 (18)	283 (39)
Pennsylvania	136 (37)	402 (23)
Rhode Island[a,d]	100 (45)	196 (48)
Vermont[a]	91 (46)	255 (42)
Average region rank	37.7	40.9
	Midwest	
Midwest total	185	389*
Illinois[c]	171 (27)	376 (28)
Indiana	192 (25)	442 (17)
Iowa	101 (44)	295 (37)
Kansas	237 (15)	324 (36)
Michigan	259 (12)	434 (20)
Minnesota	60 (49)	183 (49)
Missouri	222 (21)	512 (10)
Nebraska	123 (40)	244 (43)
North Dakota	57 (50)	206 (46)
Ohio[f]	224 (20)	441 (18)
South Dakota	154 (30)	426 (22)
Wisconsin	124 (39)	359 (33)
Average region rank	31	29.9
	South	
South total	254	552*
Alabama	307 (6)	650 (3)
Arkansas	227 (19)	544 (8)
Delaware[a,e]	327 (5)	440 (19)
Florida	265 (11)	538 (9)
Georgia	274 (10)	547 (7)
Kentucky	147 (32)	478 (12)
Louisiana	346 (2)	865 (1)
Maryland	282 (9)	380 (27)
Mississippi	254 (13)	690 (2)
North Carolina	250 (14)	362 (32)
Oklahoma	296 (8)	631 (5)
South Carolina	344 (3)	473 (13)

TABLE 4 (*Continued*)

	1987	2011
	South	
Tennessee	156 (29)	443 (16)
Texas	231 (17)	632 (4)
Virginia[c]	217 (22)	469 (14)
West Virginia	77 (48)	366 (31)
Average region rank	15.5	12.7
	West	
West total	214	418*
Alaska[a]	339 (4)	400 (24)
Arizona[e]	307 (7)	589 (6)
California	231 (16)	394 (25)
Colorado[f]	145 (34)	427 (21)
Hawaii[a,d]	141 (36)	283 (38)
Idaho	149 (31)	486 (11)
Montana	147 (33)	367 (30)
Nevada	432 (1)	463 (15)
New Mexico	169 (28)	328 (35)
Oregon	200 (23)	372 (29)
Utah	111 (41)	242 (44)
Washington[c]	134 (38)	259 (41)
Wyoming	195 (24)	383 (26)
Average region rank	24.3	26.5

SOURCE.—1987 data, Greenfeld 1988; 2011 data, Carson and Sabol 2012; 2010 regional rates, Guerino, Harrison, and Sabol 2011.

NOTE.—2011 counts are based on prisoners, sentences more than 1 year, under jurisdiction of correctional officials. Imprisonment rate is number of prisoners with a sentence of more than 1 year per 100,000 US residents. Resident population estimates are for January 1 of the following year. Jurisdiction counts include inmates held in nonsecure privately operated community corrections facilities and juveniles held in contract facilities.

[a] 2011 prisons and jails form one integrated system. Data include total jail and prison populations.

[b] The 2010–11 imprisonment rates include prisoners sentenced to more than 1 year but held in local jails or houses of correction in Massachusetts.

[c] 2011 includes some prisoners sentenced to 1 year.

[d] 2011 counts include dual jurisdiction cases in which the inmate is currently housed in another jurisdiction's facilities.

[e] 2011 prison jurisdiction population is based on custody counts.

[f] 2011 includes some prisoners sentenced to 1 year or less.

* Regional rates shown are for 2010.

TABLE 5

Compliance with Federal Sentencing Guidelines, Six Districts, 1991, 2000, 2010

	Within Range			Substantial Assistance			Downward			All Down		
District	1991	2000	2010	1991	2000	2010	1991	2000	2010	1991	2000	2010
OK, East	96.8	67.7	63.7	0	3.1	22.1	3.2	29.2	13.3	3.2	32.3	35.4
VA, East	94.5	89.0	73.7	3.1	7.4	4.1	1.3	3.5	20.3	4.4	10.9	24.4
MD	80.6	57.7	46.2	14.3	28.2	22.3	4.2	13.3	27.3	18.5	41.5	49.6
NC, Midwest	80.3	81.2	73.2	15.8	13.9	10.2	2.9	3.0	13.0	18.7	16.9	25.2
AZ	55.7	28.6	43.5	10.9	7.2	2.8	32.0	63.5	52.3	42.9	70.7	55.1
PA, East	54.0	52.2	37.3	41.0	36.6	32.0	4.0	10.2	29.8	45.0	46.8	61.8

SOURCE.—US Sentencing Commission, 2010 Datafile, OPAFY10.

anyone ever to think that rigid, detailed guidelines, covering all felonies and misdemeanors, would be applied in the same way across a vast continent.

III. The Critical Choices

The commission, for reasons no outsider will presumably ever fully understand, promulgated a system of detailed, mechanistic guidelines. Justice Breyer twice offered unpersuasive behind-the-scenes accounts that emphasize technocratic problems to be solved and an idealistic commitment to reducing sentencing disparities while insisting that ideological and political considerations had little influence (Breyer 1988, 1999). Former commissioner Ilene Nagel (1990) offered a similar though less closely argued apologia. The introduction to the Guidelines Manual attributes the guidelines' main features to a determination to reduce the prevalence of unwarranted disparities. There was, however, never any convincing evidence that the initial guidelines reduced disparities compared with sentencing or imprisonment patterns before the guidelines took effect, despite a congressionally mandated commission self-evaluation that declared victory (US Sentencing Commission 1991*a*).

Most sentencing specialists found the commission evaluation so flawed methodologically and conceptually that no conclusions could be reached (Rhodes 1992; Tonry 1992*a*; Weisburd 1992; Doob 1995). The US General Accounting Office in an independent, congressionally mandated evaluation concluded that it is "impossible to determine how effective the sentencing guidelines have been in reducing overall sentencing disparity" (1992, p. 10).

A commission assessment of the guidelines' first 15 years concluded that, relative to the guidelines' offense severity and criminal history categories, an important limitation, disparities significantly declined under the guidelines in comparison with earlier periods (US Sentencing Commission 2004). However, Paul Hofer, long-time special projects director of the US Sentencing Commission and lead author of its 15-year self-evaluation, more recently observed:

> While reduction of disparity was the most important goal of sentencing reform, there is little doubt that total unwarranted disparity was greater under the mandatory guidelines than it was prior to their implementation. Unwarranted disparity must be defined in relation to the purposes of sentencing and assessed in the system as a whole and

> not merely at one stage or decision. By this measure, disparity from other sources increased even as disparities among judges due to philosophical differences were modestly reduced. Disparities were created by prosecutors' charging and plea-bargaining decisions. (Hofer 2011, p. 680)

In other words, analyses of cases as they appear in court suggested that disparities decreased. Analyses of cases as prosecutors received them would have shown increased disparities. The guidelines increased prosecutors' capacity to influence sentences through charging and dismissal decisions, especially for offenses potentially subject to mandatory minimums. Neither the commission report nor Hofer attempted to compare disparities before and under guidelines relative to the broader, but more appropriate, criteria of offense characteristics, criminal history, and morally relevant offender characteristics. Nor to my knowledge has anyone else. There the matter rests.[14]

The federal guidelines cover all federal crimes. These include many federal regulatory and "white-collar" crimes, but also drug crimes, common law crimes coming within federal jurisdiction, and, in recent years,

[14] Commission staff and outside researchers have continued empirical investigations of sentencing disparity. There are two types of studies. One attempts to model sentencing to determine the respective influence of interjudge (or interdistrict) differences, guideline offense severity levels, and criminal history scores (e.g., Scott 2010). Interjudge and interdistrict differences are always found, but they are usually less significant than offense severity and criminal history variables. This is not surprising given the guidelines' rigidity and their vigorous enforcement for many years by appellate courts. Selection bias is the Achilles' heel of these studies. They use offense level and criminal history scores as they appear in the court record and cannot take account of presentencing variations between cases in charges and dismissals or offense characteristics (and, sometimes, criminal history) that the prosecution chose not to mention or assistant US attorneys and defense counsel jointly chose not to include in an agreed stipulation of facts (Hofer 2011).

The other develops models for a sample of recent cases and a sample of cases in the commission's original preguidelines database and assesses comparative "consistency." They typically show reduced disparities under guidelines. They suffer from a larger selection bias problem since it is impossible to control for presentencing differences in case processing in the two periods. There are two other insurmountable problems. First, apples and oranges: preguidelines prison sentences were premised on parole release eligibility and cannot be directly compared with guidelines prison sentences (and estimated times served before parole release are too crude to be credible). Second, the analyses measure consistency in relation to guidelines' offense severity and criminal history variables. This was long ago shown to be premised on a non sequitur (Doob 1995). It would be astonishing if consistency with variables used in the guidelines were not greater after the guidelines amid vigorous commission and appellate court efforts to enforce them than in a period when they did not exist as formal criteria. Doob pointed out, hypothetically, that preguidelines sentencing could have been perfectly consistent, but according to a set of criteria different from those the commission chose. Using guidelines criteria as the measure of consistency would completely miss the prior pattern.

large numbers of immigration offenses. Discretionary parole release was abolished. The sentence announced, less mechanically determined 15 percent time off for good behavior, is the sentence that is served.

Judges in setting sentences are supposed first to consult a schedule for the particular offense of conviction that specifies a "base offense level." Then, on the basis of various offense characteristics, the offense level is adjusted upward or downward (almost always upward). Next, the judge is directed to determine the offender's criminal history score. Finally, the judge is to consult a two-dimensional grid to determine the prescribed sentence.

To this point, the federal guidelines differ from state systems in Minnesota, Washington, Oregon, North Carolina, and Kansas only in their ornateness. The federal guidelines divide offenses into 43 categories rather than, at that time, 10 (Minnesota), 11 (Oregon), or 14 (Washington) and are considerably more detailed in differentiating offenses. These might be described as differences in degree rather than in kind, but there are other, much more fundamental, differences.

Many features of the federal guidelines that judges found most objectionable resulted not from the requirements of the Sentencing Reform Act of 1984, but from the commission's policy choices. This section discusses nine critical choices that could have been made otherwise:

- first, nullifying the statutory directive (sec. 994[j]) against imprisonment of first offenders "not convicted of a crime of violence or an otherwise serious offense" by defining as "serious" many offenses that typically received probation before the guidelines took effect;
- second, ignoring section 994(g)'s directive that the guidelines "shall be formulated to minimize the likelihood that the Federal prison population will exceed the capacity of the Federal prisons";
- third, treating sentences to probation as "zero months imprisonment" and thereby triggering statutory section 994(b)(2)'s provision that "if a sentence specified by the guidelines includes a term of imprisonment," the top of the guideline range may not exceed the bottom by the greater of 25 percent or 6 months; the effect was to reduce the use of probation as a stand-alone punishment in the federal courts by 80 percent;
- fourth, interpreting a statutory directive to consider the relevance to sentencing of a list of personal characteristics in such a way as to declare that almost all were either "not relevant" or "not ordinarily relevant," thereby depriving sentencing judges of authority to take ac-

count of characteristics in individual cases that many believed to be highly germane;

- fifth, giving the prosecutor sole discretion to decide when defendants are eligible for sentence reductions for providing substantial assistance to the government;
- sixth, adopting "relevant conduct" rather than the offense of conviction as the basis for applying guidelines;
- seventh, providing guidelines only for imprisonment and, to a much lesser extent than before the guidelines took effect, probation; there are no guidelines for fines as stand-alone sanctions for individual offenders or for any other nonincarcerative punishments;
- eighth, raising sentencing severity generally, in order to incorporate mandatory penalty provisions into the grid, rather than having the mandatories operate as trumps; and
- ninth, adopting a 43-level sentencing grid that is and looks arbitrary, impersonal, and mechanical and reduces the credibility of the guidelines in the eyes of judges and others.

None of these decisions was required by the Sentencing Reform Act of 1984. They all could have been made otherwise. The first five involve statutory interpretations; the rest involve commission policy decisions about guidelines architecture.

A. Nullifying the Directive to Divert Nonviolent First Offenders from Imprisonment

The commission largely overrode the statutory directive in section 994(j) to "insure" that nonviolent first offenders should ordinarily receive nonincarcerative sentences. Confronted by its own empirical research showing that many first offenders were sentenced to probation before the guidelines took effect, the commission devised its own broad definition of "serious" (US Sentencing Commission 1987*b*).

Here is how the commission described what it did: "The Commission's solution to this problem has been to write guidelines that classify as serious many offenses for which probation previously was given and provide for at least a short period of imprisonment in such cases" (US Sentencing Commission 1987*b*, sec. 4[c]). The rationale was that the courts had in the past ordered probation for "inappropriately high percentages" of white-collar offenders, including such crimes as "theft, tax evasion, antitrust offenses, insider trading, fraud, and embezzlement."

White-collar crimes such as antitrust, insider trading, and tax evasion represent only a tiny percentage of offenders who received probation before the guidelines took effect.[15] The people who were swept into the commission's "white-collar" net were mostly not investment bankers, business executives, and wealthy tax evaders but ordinary people convicted of immigration offenses, minor postal thefts, drug offenses, and property crimes and low-level bank teller embezzlers. As I noted above, 37 percent of sentenced offenders in 1985 received straight probation and only 7.1 percent in 2013. Most of the difference involves minor offenders. For nondrug offenses, the commission claimed that it set prison sentence lengths largely on the basis of research on past practice (Breyer 1999). Had it done the same for community penalties, the guidelines would have required imprisonment of many fewer minor offenders and fostered less prosecutorial evasion and judicial agonizing.

B. Ignoring the Prison Population Constraint Directive

Section 994(g)'s statutory directive to formulate guidelines that "minimize the likelihood that the Federal prison population will exceed the capacity of the Federal prisons" is straightforward. Minnesota's experience since 1980 had demonstrated that a population constraint policy could be effective. Complying required only that the commission make adjustments concerning use of prison sentences for particular categories of offenders and sentence lengths for offenders on whom imprisonment should be imposed.

The commission ignored the directive.[16] The clearest example was its nullification of the presumption that many first offenders not be sentenced to prison. That inevitably increased the prison population.

[15] Justice Breyer likewise disingenuously referred to "white-collar offenders, including tax, insider-trading, and antitrust offenders who previously would have likely only received probation" as the group affected. The justification for disregarding the congressional "insure" was that the "Commission considered present sentencing practices, where white-collar criminals receive probation more often than other offenders who committed crimes of comparable severity, to be unfair" (Breyer 1988, p. 22). Concerning sec. 994(j)'s parallel directive to "insure" long sentences for repeat offenders, Breyer indicated that the commission felt obliged to obey. "In this area, where the Commission had little legal room to set sentences, prison sentences will increase" (p. 25).

[16] Justice Breyer snidely observed, "Minnesotans may agree, for example, that building new prisons is undesirable or impractical; they may be willing to tailor prison sentences to create a total prison population of roughly constant size. There is no such consensus, however, throughout the nation as a whole" (1988, p. 4). That, however, is precisely what sec. 994(g) directed the commission to do.

A second policy decision that affected prison populations concerned sentence lengths. The commission "analyzed data drawn from 10,000 presentence investigations, crimes as distinguished in substantive criminal statutes, the United States Parole Commission's guidelines and resulting statistics, and data from other relevant sources." The commission indicated that while it did not consider itself "bound by existing sentencing practice, it has not tried to develop an entirely new system of sentencing on the basis of theory alone. Guideline sentences in many instances will approximate existing practice" (US Sentencing Commission 1987*a*, pp. 1–4, 10–11).

Justice Breyer's explanation of the commission's policy choices was more explicit: "It decided to base the guidelines primarily upon typical, or average, actual past practice. The distinctions that the guidelines make in terms of punishment are primarily those which past practice has shown were actually important factors in pre-guideline sentencing. The numbers used and the punishments imposed would come fairly close to replicating the average pre-guidelines sentence handed down to particular categories of criminals" (Breyer 1988, p. 17). The commission, following Minnesota's example, could have shortened prison terms relative to practices before the guidelines took effect in order to offset the decision largely to eliminate use of probation as a stand-alone punishment.[17] It declined to do so.

A third policy decision concerning mandatory minimum sentences, discussed in subsection H below, also defied the prison population constraint directive. The Anti–Drug Abuse Act of 1986, creating a series of mandatory minimum sentences for drug crimes, was enacted after the commission was appointed and before it submitted draft guidelines to

[17] In combination with the near elimination of probation, for mathematical reasons this inevitably caused a substantial increase in prison numbers. For many minor offenses, only small percentages of convicted offenders received prison sentences before the guidelines took effect. By definition, those sent to prison on average committed relatively more serious versions of those offenses. The mean average prison sentence length thus represented exceptional cases but under the guidelines was prescribed for all cases. Here is an example. In 1985, the year used as the basis of projections, only 24 percent of low-level ($1,500) embezzlers received prison time. The original guidelines specified a prison sentence of 2–8 months. The commission assumed an average of 5 months under the guidelines. Because so few minor embezzlers received prison sentences, the commission observed, "The average time served by all first-time embezzlers convicted at trial of stealing $1500 is actually about one month (rather than 2–8 months)" (US Sentencing Commission 1987*c*, p. 24). The commission could have calculated past sentence lengths for all cases by counting as 0 months those that previously received probation. The effect would have been to reduce sentence lengths under the guidelines and respected the prison capacity constraint.

Congress. It pegged minimum sentences for powder cocaine and heroin offenses to quantities, often 500 (5 years) and 5,000 grams (10). Thus any offense involving 500–4,999 grams triggered a minimum 5-year sentence. Rather than build that into the guidelines, the commission chose to establish longer sentences for intermediate quantities. Congress did not mandate those sentence lengths. They substantially exacerbated federal prison population growth. In reporting to Congress on projected prison population growth under the guidelines, the commission claimed its policies would cause only modest growth but that the mandatories would cause substantial growth. The commission disingenuously attributed growth resulting from its gratuitous higher sentences for intermediate drug quantities not to its own policy choices, but to the mandatory minimum sentence laws (US Sentencing Commission 1987*b*, 1987*c*).[18]

C. *Probation as a Form of Imprisonment*

A critical low-visibility choice with major consequences concerned the almost metaphysical question of whether probation is a generically distinct punishment or a term of "0 months' imprisonment." The commission took the second position and thereby nearly eliminated probation as a stand-alone sentence. In so doing, the commission also greatly reduced scope for the use of other community punishments because they are authorized only as conditions of straight probation or the probation component of a split sentence. This obscure conceptual point was made important by statute section 994(b)(2), which provided that "if a sentence specified by the guidelines includes a term of imprisonment, the maximum of the range established for such a term shall not exceed the minimum of that range by more than the greater of 25 percent or six months."

If probation had been treated as a stand-alone punishment, section 994(b)(2) would have been irrelevant. A guideline for a specific offense/

[18] Justice Breyer, likewise ignoring prison population increases attributable to the commission's handling of mandatory minimums, made the same claim: "Accordingly, the Commission propounded guidelines that, by themselves, do not deviate enormously from average prior practice. . . . [The commission] predicts that the effect of the guidelines on prison population is somewhere between −2 percent and 10 percent in comparison to what would have occurred had they not been put into effect" (1988, p. 24). Paul Hofer (2012) has observed that the current commission in its 2011 report on mandatory minimum sentences continues to attribute the effects of its incremental drug quantity steps to the mandatory sentence laws without acknowledging the effects of its own discretionary decisions.

criminal history combination could have specified sentences that included probation or, in the alternative, a range of prison sentences that satisfied the 25 percent/6 months requirement (e.g., probation or a sentence of 12–18 months). Several states do something similar. Minnesota's guidelines grid contains many cells in which the presumptive sentence is not to a prison term, but in which a range of sentence lengths is prescribed for cases in which judges reject the presumption against imposition of a state prison sentence. When, however, the federal commission defined probation as 0 months' imprisonment, section 994(b)(2) applied and a maximum range of 0–6 months was the result.

Before the federal guidelines took effect, probation sentences were ordered for 64 percent of burglars, 60 percent of property offenders, 59 percent of fraud offenders, and 57 percent of income tax offenders in the sample of cases used to project the guidelines' effects. The corresponding figures under the guidelines were projected, respectively, to be 43 percent, 33 percent, 24 percent, and 3 percent (US Sentencing Commission 1987*c*, table 2).

Little can be said in favor of the commission's decision. It required a tortured interpretation of words whose common language meaning is clear. Probation is and has always been a distinct form of punishment, an alternative to imprisonment and not ordinarily a supplement. Split sentences that combine a prison term with probation have always been a hybrid that combined the two different punishments.

The commission's interpretation is conceptually muddled. The guidelines authorize fines as stand-alone punishments for individuals on the same basis as straight probation. In effect, the commission also characterized fines as 0 months' incarceration and limited their use to cases potentially subject otherwise to not more than 6 months' imprisonment.

Prison in most jurisdictions serves as a backup for both fines and probation, to be used sometimes when offenders fail to meet their obligations. When obligations are met, offenders are entitled to absolute discharges. The commission's decision to define probation as a form of imprisonment was a major part of its near nullification of the first-offender nonimprisonment presumption.

D. *Departures*

Booker and its progeny provided much broader latitude within which sentencing judges may operate than the commission was initially prepared to allow. The original guidelines and, with some minor modifications, the guidelines in effect in 2015 aggressively sought to limit departures. The statute allowed but did not require the commission to do this. Section 994(d) directed the commission in classifying offenders to consider the relevance of a number of factors: (1) age; (2) education; (3) vocational skills; (4) mental and emotional condition to the extent that such condition mitigates the defendant's culpability or to the extent that such condition is otherwise plainly relevant; (5) physical condition, including drug dependence; (6) previous employment record; (7) family ties and responsibilities; (8) community ties; (9) role in the offense; (10) criminal history; and (11) degree of dependence on criminal activity for a livelihood.

The commission decided that numbers 9–11 were relevant, principally as bases for increasing sentence severity. Numbers 1–8 were determined to be "not ordinarily relevant in determining whether a sentence should be outside the applicable guideline range" (US Sentencing Commission 1987*a*, part H, §§5H1.1–5H1.6).

Section 3553(b), as initially enacted, describing the sentencing judge's considerations at sentencing, is deferential to the commission's discretionary choices. It directed the court to "impose a sentence of the kind, and within the range" indicated by the applicable guideline and policy statements, unless it "finds that there exists an aggravating or mitigating circumstance of a kind, or to a degree, not adequately taken into consideration by the Sentencing Commission in formulating the guidelines that should result in a sentence different from that described." Those provisions mesh and meant that sentencing judges had very little authority to depart from the guidelines. Before *Booker* was decided, it was not easy to convince appellate courts that the sentencing commission had not "adequately" considered particular offender circumstances.

The commission claimed that its policies concerning offenders' personal characteristics were rooted in concern to prevent preferment of privileged white-collar offenders. In practice, those policies mostly damaged poor and minority offenders. Kate Stith and Steve Yoh (1993) long ago observed that "denying judges the opportunity to mitigate sentences on the basis of social disadvantage has worked *against* poor and minority defendants" (p. 287; emphasis in original). Except for white-collar and regulatory offense defendants, most criminal defendants in federal courts, as in state courts, come from socially and economically disadvantaged backgrounds. Such considerations as education, employment record, family ties, and severe childhood adversity do not ordinarily distinguish privileged defendants from others but differentiate among unprivileged defendants.

That this is so can be seen in two instances in which the commission closed "loopholes" that appellate courts opened. In *U.S. v. Big Crow*, 898 F. 2d 1326 (1990), the Eighth Circuit Court of Appeals approved a downward departure for a Native American defendant who overcame severe childhood adversity and achieved an exemplary work record. In response, the commission forbade mitigated sentences for "contributions related to employment and similar prior good works." When the Ninth Circuit in *U.S. v. Lopez*, 945 F. 2d 1096 (1991), approved a sentence reduction because of a defendant's troubled childhood and lack of guidance as a youth, the commission responded by forbidding reductions for "lack of guidance as a youth and similar circumstances indicating a disadvantaged upbringing."

E. Substantial Assistance Motions

Much the most common basis for open reduction of sentences below guideline ranges has been that the defendant provided "substantial assistance to the government." The prosecution must request the reduction before the judge may grant it. If the motion is made, the judge may impose sentences less severe than is otherwise specified in guidelines.

The commission, not the Congress, conditioned sentence reductions for assistance to the government on prosecutorial motions. Statute section 994(n) directed the commission to "assure that the guidelines reflect the general appropriateness [of sentence reductions] to take into account a defendant's substantial assistance in the investigation or prosecution of another person who has committed an offense." The statute says nothing to suggest that the prosecutor should have sole authority to decide when and whether substantial assistance has been provided. The commission, however, in guidelines section 5K1.1 provided, "upon motion of the government stating that the defendant has provided substantial assistance . . . the court may depart from the guidelines." The appellate courts upheld the commission's decision. Had they not, trial judges would have been able to exercise much greater control.

From the outset this has been a gaping hole in the guidelines and undermines the claim that the commission was primarily motivated to reduce disparities, for two reasons. It is anything goes once the motion is made. Judges have discretion to impose any sentence they believe warranted. The rule inevitably created vast disparities between serious offenders, especially in drug and organized-crime settings, who had information prosecutors wanted or needed, and as a result benefited, and small fry who had little or nothing to offer and seldom benefited. Kind-hearted prosecutors have long gotten around this by making the motion on the basis of disingenuous claims of assistance. In its 1991 self-evaluation, the commission excluded departures following substantial assistance motions from its analysis: those disparities in its judgment did not count.

F. Sentencing "Relevant Conduct"

The single feature of the federal sentencing guidelines that American state officials, and judges, officials, and academics outside the United States, find most astonishing is the commission's decision to base guideline application on the defendant's "relevant conduct," including conduct alleged in charges that were not filed, that were dismissed, or that resulted in acquittals. More than once I have been accused outside the United States of misreporting or exaggerating when describing the relevant conduct policy.

There is no statutory basis for relevant conduct sentencing. The commission invented it. Many state sentencing commissions considered, usually briefly and dismissively, whether to adopt a "relevant conduct" or "real offense" policy. Each rejected the proposal out of hand. To most people, the idea that offenders can be sentenced for crimes with which they were not charged or of which they were acquitted is inherently distasteful and obviously unjust (Tonry 1981; Reitz 1993).

The commission offered three major justifications, all demonstrably mistaken or misconceived. The first, that relevant conduct offense sentencing would prevent a shift of power to the prosecutor by breaking the link between charges and punishments, has been discredited since the earliest days (e.g., Federal Courts Study Committee 1990).

The second is that *Williams v. New York*, 337 U.S. 241 (1949), long ago held that judges have authority to look beyond the conviction offense and have always done so. The problem with this argument is that *Williams* was decided in the heyday of indeterminate sentencing when judges were expected to individualize sentences in every case and in which parole boards decided the lengths of nominal prison sentences (nominal because the parole board set release dates). The pre-*Booker* guidelines were premised on the commission's view that judges' discretion should be vastly more narrowly constrained than under indeterminate sentencing. The rationale of *Williams* has little relevance to modern determinate sentencing. *Williams* in any case held that judges in sentencing *may* take account of nonconviction behavior and uncharged or unproven behavior. The guidelines indicate that they *must*.

The third is that the federal criminal law is incomparably more complex than state criminal laws and that many federal offenses in their labels and elements provide no meaningful basis for measuring culpability. Mail and wire fraud and Racketeer-Influenced Corrupt Organizations offenses are examples. If a majority of federal offenders were convicted of mail fraud, the commission's point might have been arguable. In practice, however, drug and immigration crimes make up a large proportion of the federal criminal docket. In 1993, for example, drug offenders constituted 18,352 of 41,838 convictions reported to the commission (US Sentencing Commission 1994, table 22). In 2013, drug offenders constituted 31.2 percent of sentenced offenders and immigration offenders another 31.2 percent; another 10.1 percent were firearms offenders (US Sentencing Commission 2013, table 3).

Many of the rest are convicted of common law crimes such as theft, robbery, and embezzlement. Most federal crimes are conceptually uncomplicated: drugs, immigration, firearms, and common property offenses. In 2013, only 13 percent of sentenced offenders were arguably white-collar criminals (fraud, embezzlement, bribery, tax, forgery, and antitrust; and many of those, especially embezzlement, were minor offenses). Thus, except for immigration offenses, most modern federal criminal cases look much like state cases.

The commission's argument also understated the complexity of state criminal codes. Many offenders are convicted of inchoate offenses, including conspiracy. Many state codes were based on the *Model Penal Code*, which defined felonies broadly and classified them into only three classes, on the indeterminate sentencing rationale that sentencing should be based primarily on the offender's personal characteristics. States wrestled with these problems and solved them without adopting relevant conduct sentencing. Knapp (1984) and Parent (1988), the founding executive and research directors of Minnesota's commission, described how that state did it. There was no more need for relevant conduct sentencing in the federal system than in the states.

G. Prohibiting Community Punishments

The only freestanding sentences authorized by the guidelines are imprisonment and, for cases not otherwise subject to 6-month or longer prison terms, probation and fines. They allow no independent role for community punishments such as house arrest, intensively supervised probation, restitution, or community service. They also allow no significant space within which mediation or restorative justice programs can operate.

Fines, in many Western countries the most commonly imposed sanction, are conspicuously underdeveloped. Although the Congress in section 994(a)(1) charged the commission to promulgate "guidelines for use by the court in determining the sentence to be imposed . . . including (A) a determination whether to impose a sentence to probation, a fine, or a term of imprisonment," fines are not authorized as a sole sentence for individuals except for trifling cases. Instead, guidelines section 5E1.2 (a) provides that "the court shall impose a fine in all cases, except [when the defendant lacks ability to pay]." Thus fines are effectively available only as add-ons to prison or probation sentences or in lieu of probation.

The guidelines do not permit use of other nonincarcerative sanctions as independent sentences. Guidelines sections 5F1.1–3 authorize use of community confinement, home detention, and community service, but only "as a condition of probation or supervised release." In 1993, only 14.8 percent of convicted offenders received straight probation (i.e., without confinement conditions), and thus in less than one-sixth of federal convictions was it possible for a judge to sentence a defendant to an intermediate sanction (US Sentencing Commission 1994, p. 67). By 2013, that one-sixth had fallen to one-fourteenth; only 7.1 percent of offenders received straight probation.

There is much experience in the United States and western Europe with use of intermediate sanctions that the commission could have drawn on. Sentencing commissions in North Carolina, Oregon, Pennsylvania, and Washington explicitly incorporated intermediate sanctions into their guidelines as independent sanctions (Morris and Tonry 1990). A commission task force headed by then-Commissioner Helen Carrothers offered concrete proposals for building intermediate punishments into the guidelines (US Sentencing Commission Alternatives to Imprisonment Project 1990). The commission took no action.

H. Integrating Mandatory Minimum Sentence Laws

Mandatory minimum legislation enacted in the 1980s required prison terms that were longer than most prisoners sentenced before that would have served (US Sentencing Commission 1987*b*) and longer than a sentencing commission aiming to proportion sentences to offense severity would prescribe. The commission dealt with this by prescribing sentences even longer than the laws required. There were two ways the mandatory minimums could have been handled.

The first was to develop a comprehensive set of guidelines for all offenses based on knowledge of past practices and conscious policy decisions to make changes. If mandatory minimum sentence laws required longer sentences than resulted from that process, policy statements could instruct that the statute took precedence and trumped the guidelines. An asterisked note for affected offenses would have said, "The provisions of an applicable mandatory minimum sentence law setting a lengthier minimum sentence shall take precedence over the guidelines."

The other approach was to integrate the sentences mandated by statutes into the guidelines and scale other penalties around them. This necessarily would increase the severity of guideline sentences generally.

A metaphor makes the options more vivid. Imagine a sentencing guidelines grid as a lattice. Under the mandatories-as-trumps option, long minimum sentences for specific crimes would poke through the lattice and tower above it. Under the commission's integrative approach, the entire lattice was lifted, as if the mandatory minimums were posts, and the sentences for many other crimes were lifted also.

This can be illustrated by an example from typical state mandatory minimum laws. In Arizona in the early 1990s, a majority of felony defendants were charged with offenses subject to mandatory minimums, but many fewer were sentenced under such statutes. The reason is that the mandatories typically applied only to completed offenses; attempts and conspiracies were not covered. Defendants who agreed to plead guilty to attempted robbery, or conspiracy to commit robbery, were not subject to the minimum (Knapp 1991).

The commission decided to raise sentences for many drug crimes, including inchoate offenses, even more than was required by the mandatory penalty provisions. In the federal law as it existed in 1987, minimums for many drug crimes were pegged for offenses involving 500 and 5,000 grams. For powder cocaine, 500 grams triggered a minimum 5-year sentence and 5,000 grams a minimum 10 years. The commission could easily have provided that offenses involving 500–4,999 grams receive 5 years and those of 5,000 or more grams receive 10. Instead, it established intermediate quantity levels with sentences scaled between 5 and 10 years: 2,000 and 3,500 grams, respectively, were made subject to 78- and 97-month minimum guideline sentences, thereby specifying even harsher sentences than were required by the statute (US Sentencing Commission 1997*b*). The same approach was taken under the 100-to-1 rule for crack cocaine sentences, which meant that a minor sale of 5 grams elicited a 5-year sentence and still tiny sales of 7 or 10 grams meant even longer prison terms.

The commission gratuitously raised sentences for drug offenders in three other ways. First, under the relevant conduct policy, sentences increased substantially for defendants who were not convicted under statutory sections subject to the mandatory minimums, but whose offenses involved the triggering quantities. Second, the commission decided that sentences for people convicted of drug-related conspiracies and attempts—offenses, as in my Arizona example, not then subject to mandatory minimums—should be calculated by reference to penalties for completed offenses involving the same amount. This raised sentences for inchoate offenses substantially. Third, the commission chose to base drug quantity calculations on the combined weight of the drug and the medium in which it was conveyed, baking soda for crack or blotter paper for LSD, rather than the weight of the pure drug itself. Paul Hofer observed:

> This has proven a recipe for arbitrary variation, and an invitation to probation officers to increase penalties based on water weight, baking soda, and other inert ingredients. The Parole Commission guidelines were based on *pure* drug amounts, and laboratory analyses included in presentence reports today routinely provide pure amounts. But the Commission followed the Anti–Drug Abuse Act and based punishment on total weight, which caused such outrageous outcomes that the approach was dropped for guideline calculations involving LSD and marijuana plants (but remains in force for determining the applicability of a statutory minimum). For other drugs, the approach per-

versely increases punishments for offenders *lower* in the distribution chain, where drugs are cut for retail distribution. (2012, p. 201)

The commission was aware of how controversial its guidelines were, and why. Carrying out a congressional mandate, the commission in its early years completed an ambitious and sophisticated analysis of the effects of mandatory sentencing laws on federal sentencing. It concluded that mandatory penalties are unwise and unsound because they remove incentives to plead guilty and thereby increase trial rates, case processing times, and workloads; they foster prosecutorial manipulation in charging and plea bargaining; they often result in imposition of sentences that are unduly harsh; and they do not permit judges to take into account special circumstances concerning the defendant that might justify some other sentence. These are, of course, the same charges that critics lay against the federal guidelines. Capturing this point precisely, in what may initially have been a Freudian slip, the commission, on the first page of its mandatory sentencing report, refers to its own "mandatory" guidelines (US Sentencing Commission 1991*b*). From that day until *Booker* was decided, implicitly conceding the point, the commission generally described its guidelines as mandatory.

I. The Sentencing Machine

The 43-level sentencing grid was one of the commission's worst blunders.[19] It confirmed skeptics' worst stereotypes of arbitrary sentencing by numbers. There were two major problems, both foreseeable. First, the guidelines were not facially credible. The effectiveness of a guidelines system depends on the willingness of officials to accept and apply them. If their logic and plausibility are not immediately apparent, if they look mechanical and arbitrary, judges and others will be alienated.

[19] It resulted in part from the federal commission's lack of understanding of state guidelines and even of the logic of guidelines. Judge Breyer and Judge Jon Newman, then chief judge of the Second Circuit Court of Appeals and an active and influential commission advisor, argued that the guidelines must prescribe sentences for the entire range authorized by statutory maximums. The commission decided to fill the range between 0 and 30 years. The state systems, by contrast, created guideline ranges for particular offenses, e.g., 22–30 months, and permitted judges to impose longer sentences ultimately to the statutory maximum as upward departures, subject to appellate sentence review. This accords with the original logic of sentencing (and parole) guidelines. The recommended or presumptive ranges in guidelines were meant for ordinary cases; extraordinary cases should be handled differently (Gottfredson, Wilkins, and Hoffman 1978).

The best illustration for that proposition is that more than 200 federal district court judges declared the guidelines unconstitutional.

At the time, this was commonly referred to as the problem of the "sentencing machine" (Blumstein et al. 1983, p. 159). Judges and lawyers believe that their function in sentencing is to impose fair, deserved, and appropriate punishments. Sentencing by use of a process akin to a bank's calculation of a credit risk score is antithetical to that. Judges and others who are alienated by what appears to be a mechanical and arbitrary set of standards are unlikely to invest much effort in preventing efforts by lawyers to circumvent it. That is what has happened since the guidelines' earliest days (e.g., Nagel and Schulhofer 1992).

The problem of the sentencing machine was well known. It is one reason why state guidelines systems have relatively few offense-severity levels. Minnesota's in 1987 had 10 and in 2013 had 11. Pennsylvania's guidelines, which also cover misdemeanors, in 1995 had 13 and in 2013 had 14. Washington State considered adopting a 26-level grid but rejected it in favor of 14. The rhetorical question was asked, "Could we plausibly explain to a judge why a level 16 crime is more serious than a level 15?" When the Washington commission realized that it could not persuasively answer that question, it realized it had a sentencing machine problem.

The contemporaneous Canadian Sentencing Commission unequivocally rejected the idea of a sentencing machine setting "mandatory" guidelines: "As a result of their rigidity, any of these options would meet with extreme resistance from judges as well as from most professionals involved in the administration of the criminal law. Their reservations would be justified" (1987, p. 294).

The second problem with a complicated sentencing machine is that there will foreseeably be high rates of miscalculation. A major evaluation of four parole guideline grid systems showed that even simple grids produce significant levels of inaccurate calculations (Arthur D. Little, Inc., and Goldfarb and Singer, Esqs. 1981). Complicated grids produce higher error rates. That this is true of the federal guidelines was shown long ago by an FJC study. Forty-seven experienced federal probation officers were asked to calculate "base offense levels" for hypothetical defendants described in sample cases used for discussion at a 1992 sentencing institute for federal judges from the Second and Eighth Circuits. There were enormous differences (Lawrence and Hofer 1992). In a 1996 survey, less than 20 percent of federal probation officers indicated that they believed guidelines' calculations were accurate in most cases they had seen; 40 percent indicated they believed that calculations were more likely than not to be incorrect (Probation Officers Advisory Group 1996).

IV. The Stories behind the Stories

The guidelines' shortcomings are inseparable from those of the initial US Sentencing Commission. It was badly managed, highly politicized, and riven by factionalism. Two original commissioners, Paul Robinson (in 1987) and Michael Block (in 1989), and one ex-officio member, Ronald L. Gainer, the attorney general's initial designee and for a decade the US Department of Justice's sentencing policy specialist, resigned on principle over the commission's failings.[20] In the mid-1990s, two remaining initial commissioners, Judge William Wilkins and Ilene Nagel, and an early replacement, Michael Gelacek, holding over after their terms expired until successors were appointed, engaged in open media warfare (Bendavid 1993, 1994*a*, 1994*b*).

No one factor can explain why the federal commission and guidelines were so much less successful than those in the states. Some observers argued that the failure was in imagination. With seven full-time commissioners, 70 staff members, and 2 years to develop guidelines, a better-managed commission would have consulted widely and learned from the state experiences.[21] That did not happen. Kay Knapp, the first staff director, had first been research director and then staff director of the Minnesota Sentencing Guidelines Commission; internal politics forced her out within a year. Otherwise, no senior commission staffer was hired during the development period from the Minnesota, Pennsylvania, and Washington commissions that had established guidelines systems. Nor, I know from talking with the senior staff and chairmen of the state commissions at the time, were any of them asked to serve as consultants or advisors.

The federal commission failed to draw on the intellectual capital amassed in the states and to learn from the mistakes, successes, and policy processes of its predecessors. All of the policy and practice issues the

[20] Robinson (1987, p. 1), in his dissent, reported that Gainer informed the commission that "if he were a voting commissioner, as a personal matter, he would not have voted to support the guidelines in their current form."

[21] State commissions typically have part-time members and five to 10 staff.

US commission faced had already been addressed. Many of its most serious mistakes—including the "relevant conduct" policy, the guidelines' alienating detail and unnecessary complexity, the daunting 43-level grid—could have been avoided by learning from the state experience.

The problem may partly have been that the initial commissioners lacked personal knowledge of sentencing. Judge Frankel (1973) envisioned sentencing commissions as specialist agencies that would draw on expert knowledge. None of the initial commissioners, however, had any prior experience or expertise with sentencing guidelines or sentencing policy. Only two, federal district court Judge William W. Wilkins Jr. and retired court of appeals Judge George MacKinnon, had ever practiced criminal law, and only Wilkins had sentenced a convicted offender. Judge Wilkins had been a federal trial judge only since 1981. Judge MacKinnon was appointed directly to the US Court of Appeals for the DC Circuit in 1969 and had never served as a state or federal trial judge. Judge Stephen Breyer was appointed to the First Circuit Court of Appeals in 1980 directly from the staff of the US Senate and had no prior judicial experience. Two of the other original commissioners, Michael Block and Ilene Nagel, were social scientists without legal training. Helen Corrothers had worked with parole boards. Paul H. Robinson was a law professor.

Some observers, more conspiracy minded, note that three initial members were former congressional aides, some with well-known political ambitions: Breyer (Senator Edward Kennedy), Wilkins (Senator Strom Thurmond), and Robinson (Senator John McClellan). All had good reasons to want to maintain good relations with conservative Republicans who then controlled the Senate. Everyone involved with the commission (for a short time I was a consultant) recognized that Wilkins and Breyer were the most powerful commissioners. Both were widely known to be aspirants for higher office. Both made it. Wilkins was unsuccessful in an effort to be appointed FBI director but was appointed in 1986 to the US Court of Appeals for the Fourth Circuit. Breyer was appointed to the US Supreme Court.

Almost all outside observers agree that the commission was badly managed in its early years. The US General Accounting Office (GAO), when asked by the Congress to assess the commission's management and operations in its early years, described an agency in disarray. Much of the critique concerned individual commissioners who created a volatile and unpleasant working environment (1990, pp. 3, 12–15):

> The extensive involvement of individual commissioners in what would normally be staff activities . . . contributes to the organizational disarray we found.
>
> Commissioner involvement in research . . . raises another concern . . . the potential for the research to reflect the perspectives and interests of the commissioner conducting the project.
>
> According to former staff directors, it was difficult to manage in an environment where they could not maintain authority over the staff because of commissioner involvement.
>
> Part of the problem has been finding qualified candidates who would be willing to take the [research director's] position, given perceptions that the working environment is complicated by commissioner involvement in research and other matters. (Pp. 14–15)

"Out-of-control internal politics" is one way to characterize the problems described in the GAO report. "Failure of management" is another. Good managers know how to recruit and motivate capable staff, develop and carry out a work plan, create and maintain a congenial working environment, work with and accommodate important constituencies, and control obstreperous appointees.

None of those attributes characterized the commission. In 4 years it had four staff directors. General counsel came and went at the same rate. The commission lacked a research director for several years during the development and implementation phases when empirical analyses were fundamentally important to its work (US General Accounting Office 1990, p. 14). William C. Rhodes (1992), one early research director, wrote a devastating critique of the competence of the commission's congressionally mandated 1991 self-evaluation. Joel Garner, a nationally prominent researcher who long had worked for the National Institute of Justice, joined the commission as research director in 1990–91 in the face of warnings from friends; he explained that he had many years of experience working in a politically contentious government agency, things had gotten so bad that they were bound to improve, and he would start work as the commission rebounded. He quickly quit.[22] Qualified

[22] "'When I worked there, some of the staff called the commission an information-free environment,' says Joel Garner, the commission's research director in 1990 and 1991. 'It was worse than that. It was an evil place. . . . I've been a bureaucrat for almost two decades, and I've served in lots of different administrations, but this was remarkable'" (Bendavid 1993, p. 18).

research directors proved elusive, and the position was abolished for a time.

The process by which the guidelines were developed illustrates the commission's management problems. Except for the GAO study, articles by commissioners Breyer and Nagel, and a few newspaper articles, there is almost no literature on internal commission processes. This account accordingly draws on extensive discussions with former commissioners and commission staff and my experience as a member of the commission's first research advisory board and as an occasional paid consultant.

The commission had no overall strategy for developing guidelines. Separate teams under the leadership of professor/commissioners worked on incompatible guideline drafts. One team, led by commissioner Paul Robinson, worked on "just deserts guidelines" that would calibrate sentences to detailed assessments of offenders' culpability. The logic came from criminal law "elements analysis," in which crimes are deconstructed into their mental and physical components. Mental states include purpose, knowledge, recklessness, negligence, and inadvertence. Physical elements include such things as the amount of property loss, the degree of harm, and the circumstances. Both mental and physical elements can be scaled for seriousness. All physical elements equal, a purposeful crime can be said to be more serious than a negligent crime. A theft involving $500 is more serious than a theft involving $50. An armed robbery is more serious than an unarmed one. Because most definitions of crimes include four or more physical elements, separate mental elements can be specified for each.

The insurmountable problem of the proposed just deserts guidelines lay in their complexity. Guidelines for robbery, for example, had to distinguish not only between attempted and completed robberies, but also on the basis of whether a weapon was involved and what kind (handgun, other gun, knife, blunt instrument), how the weapon was used (carried, shown, pointed, discharged, or otherwise used), whether injuries or death were caused and if so how serious, and how much property was involved or lost.

To deal with that complexity, a system of "punishment units" was created, into which any element could be translated. Injuries might be valued at 0 to 1,000 points, the nature of any weapon at 0 to 500, the manner of weapon use at 0 to 500, property loss at 0 to 1,000. The sentence would be determined by summing the points associated with each physical and mental element. Some elements, such as property loss, are hard to accommodate in such a scheme. If a $500 theft equals 50 units and that leads to 90 days in jail, what sentences should corporate fraudsters receive for billion-dollar crimes? To deal with such problems the scheme called on judges to calculate the square and cube roots of property values above thresholds and to plug the answers into the sentencing calculation. Not surprisingly, judges and other outsiders who were shown confidential drafts were bewildered. After many months the proposal was abandoned.

Unfortunately, the other guidelines drafting team by that time had given up its effort. Led by economist Michael Block and sociologist Ilene Nagel, the goal was to devise crime-control guidelines based on research on deterrence and incapacitation. Penalties would be set that had optimal deterrent effects or that would cost-effectively incapacitate those at highest risk for future crimes. The effort soon was stymied on the insuperable difficulty that existing crime-control research gave no adequate answers to such questions as "What is the optimal deterrent sentence for a $5,000 theft?" or "Who among 3,000 robbery defendants has a 40 percent likelihood of committing a serious violent crime within the next 5 years?" Then and now, research on deterrence and incapacitation is utterly incapable of answering such questions (Apel and Nagin 2011; Nagin 2013; Travis, Western, and Redburn 2014, chap. 5).

Andrew von Hirsch, on the basis of extensive discussion with commission members and senior staffers, provided a similar, but less detailed, account:

> Shortly after the commissioners were appointed, however, problems began to be apparent. A first draft of the guidelines was written in the spring of 1986 by one of the commissioners [Robinson], and then jettisoned. The next two drafts emanated from the Chairman's office, were circulated for public comment, and then abandoned after an unfavorable response. It was only in the winter of 1986 that other commissioners were drawn actively into the process. The final draft was written at a late date in some haste to meet the submission deadline. (1988, p. 2)

Many of the guidelines' most fundamental problems derive from the aborted Robinson "just deserts" draft. Because to that point the only drafting had been the doomed efforts headed by academics, there was nothing else to build on. The Robinson draft's legacies include the guidelines' daunting complexity, the enormous guidelines grid, and "relevant conduct sentencing." Within the logic of the Robinson draft, those features made sense. If every mental and physical element of every crime had to be translated into a punishment unit score, the guidelines had to specify which elements were material and how they were to be scored. Complexity was conceptually essential. If punishment unit totals for a robbery could range from 200 to 3,000 units, the guidelines had to be complex and to contain many gradations of offense seriousness. Closely scaling punishment severity to offense seriousness was also conceptually essential. Finally, in a system in which plea bargaining is ubiquitous, "real offense sentencing" made sense. Otherwise, plea-bargaining lawyers could manipulate the sentencing system at will by agreeing which offense elements would be admitted and thereby precisely determine sentences.

An initial official set of draft guidelines was scheduled for release for public comment early in the fall of 1986. When, therefore, the commission finally started work on what became its official proposal, there was nothing to do but adapt the Robinson draft. The concept of punishment units disappeared. So did the square and cube roots. However, the enormous guidelines grid, the complexity, and real offense sentencing survived in the first guidelines draft that was publicly released. In later drafts, in response to adverse comment, real offense sentencing became "relevant conduct" sentencing. This meant that calculations began with the offense of which the defendant was convicted. Increments were to be added on a "real offense basis." The guidelines that took effect and that survive to this day reject the premises and logic of the Robinson draft, but contain much of its apparatus.

The process by which the federal guidelines were devised thus explains many of their most disliked features. It does not explain, however, why they are so harsh, why the commission so narrowly limited the use of probation and precluded use of other community punishments as stand-alone sentences, or why sentences for many drug offenses were made even longer than statutes mandated.

The explanations for those policy choices lie elsewhere. Part of it was bad management. Part of it was the commissioners' lack of sentencing experience and knowledge of sentencing guidelines. Part was hubris. The largest part was that the crime-control policies of the Reagan administration were oriented more toward toughness than fairness. The commissioners Reagan appointed sought to show that they too were tough on crime and had little sympathy for "lenient" judges. Judge Frankel's sentencing commission proposal to the contrary was predicated on the notion of an expert nonpartisan administrative agency, the ideal that sentencing should be just, and the aspiration that detailed sentencing policy should be insulated from politics. The individuals who dominated the commission's work in its early years did not share those beliefs.

V. What Next?

Federal sentencing is less just and less fair in 2015 than it was in 1985. In the earlier year, more than one-third of convicted offenders received straight probation and 14 percent received split sentences of probation and a few weeks or months of confinement. For them, unwarranted disparities in prison sentences were not much of an issue. For the half of convicted offenders sentenced to imprisonment, the US Parole Commission's guidelines evened out the worst disparities.

By contrast, the 87.3 percent of convicted federal offenders who received straight prison sentences in 2013 had little recourse against disparately severe punishments. Parole release no longer existed. Appeals of sentences to higher courts were possible, but under the deferential "abuse of discretion" standard of review set by the Supreme Court in *Gall v. United States*, 522 U.S. 38 (2007), few succeed.

Reasonable people can differ about the merits, and justice, of basing release decisions on the parole commission's Salient Factor Score, with its predictive premises. Surely it is better, though, that there be some defensible, systematic set of criteria than no criteria at all as in many determinate sentencing systems or the rigid provisions of mechanistic federal guidelines.

Federal sentencing in 2015 is more unjust and unfair than it need have been for three reasons. First, commission policy decisions made sentencing much more severe. A large part of the increased severity occurs because that is what the commission wanted; it aimed to increase punishments for many crimes. Partly it results from tight limitations on sentences to probation and other community punishments. Partly it results from many discretionary decisions made by the commission to make sentencing more severe than the 1984 act required or directed. Partly it results from the abolition of parole release and its replacement by the "truth in sentencing" requirement that prisoners serve at least 85 percent of the sentence imposed.

Second, federal legislation enacted between 1984 and 1996 mandated minimum 5-, 10-, and 20-year, and longer, prison sentences for drug and violent offenders; these were much longer than had been served for those offenses under the prior regime. Commission decisions concerning sentences for drug crimes exacerbated the effects of mandatories. Paul Hofer, the leading authority on federal sentencing data, recently observed, "Average prison time served by federal offenders more than doubled after introduction of the guidelines, and this was due in large part to the [commission's] linkage of the guidelines with the mandatory minimum penalties" (2012, p. 185).

Third, the combination of detailed, mechanistic guidelines, the relevant conduct policy, and mandatory minimum sentence laws gave federal prosecutors unprecedented power to offer plea bargains that are too good to be turned down, not because the sentences offered are mild, but because the sentences threatened are enormous. As a practical matter the prosecutor, not the judge, determines which defendants, if any, warrant special consideration and which will serve lengthy prison sentences. Federal Court of Appeals Judge Gerald Lynch observed,

> The prosecutor, rather than a judge or jury, is the central adjudicator of facts (as well as replacing the judge as arbiter of most legal issues and of the appropriate sentence to be imposed). Potential defenses are presented by the defendant and his counsel not in a court, but to a prosecutor, who assesses their factual accuracy and likely persuasiveness to a hypothetical judge or jury, and then decides the charge of which the defendant should be adjudged guilty. Mitigating information, similarly, is argued not to the judge, but to the prosecutor, who decides what sentence the defendant should be given in exchange for his plea. (Lynch 2003, pp. 1403–4)

A. *Attributing Blame*

Not all the problems in federal sentencing can fairly be attributed to the commission and its guidelines, but a large majority can. The commission made many low-visibility but important policy decisions that exacerbated the effects of other punitive changes in federal law.

The Congress enacted the 100-to-1 crack cocaine sentencing law, but the commission made it, and other mandatory minimum sentence laws, even harsher by setting higher guidelines sentences for many crimes than the laws required. The Congress enacted the 85 percent time-to-be-served truth-in-sentencing law, but the commission in three ways made the sentences to which the law applies longer or harsher than they need have been. It made the relevant conduct policy mandatory, which meant that judges were directed to increase sentence lengths to take account of prior alleged crimes of which defendants had not been convicted and other aggravating factors set out in the guidelines. It forbade judges to mitigate sentences on the basis of most commonsensical offender characteristics. By severely limiting imposition of straight probation sentences, it assured that many more people were sentenced to imprisonment and thereby affected by the 85 percent rule.

Some might say that the commission had no choice to do otherwise given the political climate of Washington, DC, in the 1980s. That cannot be right. Many of the commission's decisions were both radically severe and so low-profile that few recognized their import at the time (Tonry 1992*b*). The commission did not have to nullify the presumption that most first offenders should be diverted from prison. It did not have to define probation as 0 months' imprisonment. It did not have to narrowly limit use of fines as free-standing punishments. It did not have to ignore the explicit statutory "capacity constraint" directive to tailor the guidelines to fit available prison capacity. It did not have to adopt the relevant conduct standard or give prosecutors exclusive control over sentence reductions for "substantial assistance."

That all these things are so can be seen by comparing the experiences of the federal and North Carolina sentencing commissions. Tough-on-crime attitudes were at their harshest during the early 1990s when the North Carolina Sentencing Commission did its work. This is the period when every state enacted Megan's laws and more than half enacted truth-in-sentencing or three-strikes laws or both (Travis, Western, and Redburn 2014, chap. 3). North Carolina is a conservative, southern state, and its commission observed the politics and the rhetoric of the day by creating "mandatory" imprisonment guidelines for serious violent and high-level drug offenses. However, it also provided for diversion of most people convicted of lesser crimes to community penalties and created capacity constraint guidelines that made North Carolina the most successful state in the country at managing the size of its prison population (Wright 2002).

The difference was not in the political climate, but in the quality of members and leaders of the two commissions. North Carolina chairman Judge Thomas Ross made good-faith efforts to develop principled, fair guidelines. Federal chairman Judge William Wilkins, despite statutory directives that the federal guidelines do the same, did not. The federal commission adopted a bunker mentality and rejected the experience and technical knowledge accumulated in the states. The North Carolina commission made serious efforts to learn from experiences elsewhere, including the unfortunate federal experiences, and hired and retained Robin Lubitz, deputy director of the Pennsylvania Commission on Sentencing, as its executive director. The federal commission had no plausible management plan for developing guidelines; no reasonable person would have expected competing academics' proposals for "just deserts" and "crime control" guidelines to produce something viable and realistic. They did not. The failure to have a fallback locked the federal guidelines into a structure and an approach from which they never recovered.

In the end, though, the federal guidelines had enormous—albeit negative—influence. As the American Bar Association's *Standards for Sentencing* and the American Law Institute's *Model Penal Code—Sentencing* stories demonstrate, the federal experience became a serious impediment to guidelines efforts in the United States. Negatives cannot be proven, but it is likely that the federal experience killed what otherwise might have been a march of progress toward development of effective presumptive sentencing guidelines systems throughout the United States.

B. Reinventing Federal Sentencing

The federal sentencing guidelines need not have failed so dismally. Reviving them as an instrument of justice is not impossible. The best way to do that would be for the Congress to enact new enabling legislation for creation of presumptive sentencing guidelines of the sort that operate successfully in Minnesota, North Carolina, and Washington. The book on the current federal commission could be closed, and it could be given residual authority over cases sentenced under its guidelines as was done with the US Parole Commission when parole release was prospectively abolished under the Sentencing Reform Act of 1984.

A new commission developing presumptive guidelines of the sort Judge Frankel envisioned would, ironically, be working in a more hospitable legal environment than did any of the early guidelines commissions. Under *Blakely v. Washington*, 542 U.S. 296 (2004), judges in a presumptive system may not impose sentences in excess of the upper boundary of applicable guidelines a judge or a jury finds beyond a reasonable doubt that facts have been proven that justify the harsher punishment. This means that the greatest injustices in sentencing, disproportionately severe punishments, cannot happen casually.

When *Blakely* was decided, many people assumed that it meant the end of presumptive guidelines because judges and prosecutors would not tolerate a system that so limited their powers. For that reason, Ohio made its presumptive guidelines advisory. Commissions in Kansas, Minnesota, North Carolina, and Washington made minor adjustments and retained their presumptive guidelines (Frase 2013). As a matter of procedural fairness, those systems were improved. Facts justifying harsher punishments must be charged and proven. That has always been the legal requirement in other common law legal systems. Only behavior that is charged and proven beyond a reasonable doubt, or admitted, may be taken into account at sentencing (e.g., Australia: Freiberg 2001, 2014; England and Wales: Ashworth 2001, 2010).

On the basis of the experiences of state sentencing commissions, and 30 years of unhappy federal experience, a new federal commission would be highly unlikely to adopt relevant conduct sentencing, to disregard directives about diversion of first offenders from imprisonment or to take account of correctional resources, to forbid judges to take account of offender characteristics that most believe are germane to imposition of just and appropriate sentences, to discourage use of community punishments, or gratuitously to exacerbate the punitive effects of mandatory minimum sentence and similar laws.

The US Congress is unlikely to enact legislation to create a new sentencing commission. The next best thing would be for the current commission to revive the aborted effort initiated in the mid-1990s by commission chair Richard P. Conaboy to revise and simplify the guidelines. Even Justice Breyer (1999), for many years the guidelines' most outspoken apologist, long ago called for simplification. The agenda should be the same as Judge Conaboy's: to reconsider and substantially address the policy subjects described in the preceding paragraph. The commission undoubtedly has the authority to do so and, one faint 1984 echo of Judge Frankel's call for a politically removed commission, the changes would automatically take effect 6 months later unless the Congress voted to reject them. Leadership and vision are all that is needed.

REFERENCES

Albrecht, Hans-Jörg. 2001. "Post-adjudication Dispositions in Comparative Perspective." In *Sentencing and Sanctions in Western Countries*, edited by Michael Tonry and Richard S. Frase. New York: Oxford University Press.

American Law Institute. 2007. *Model Penal Code—Sentencing*. Tentative Draft no. 1. Philadelphia: American Law Institute.

———. 2011. *Model Penal Code—Sentencing*. Tentative Draft no. 2. Philadelphia: American Law Institute.

Apel, Robert, and Daniel Nagin. 2011. "General Deterrence: A Review of Recent Evidence." In *The Oxford Handbook of Crime and Criminal Justice*, edited by Michael Tonry. New York: Oxford University Press.

Arthur D. Little, Inc., and Goldfarb and Singer, Esqs. 1981. *An Evaluation of Parole Guidelines in Four Jurisdictions*. Washington, DC: National Institute of Corrections.

Ashworth, Andrew. 2001. "The Decline of English Sentencing and Other Stories." In *Sentencing and Sanctions in Western Countries*, edited by Michael Tonry and Richard S. Frase. New York: Oxford University Press.

———. 2010. *Sentencing and Criminal Justice*. 5th ed. Cambridge: Cambridge University Press.

Austin, James, and Barry Krisberg. 1982. "The Unmet Promise of Alternatives to Incarceration." *Crime and Delinquency* 28:374–409.

Baron-Evans, Amy, and Kate Stith. 2012. "Booker Rules." *University of Pennsylvania Law Review* 160:1631–1743.

Beale, Sara Sun. 1989. "Sentencing Guidelines." Staff memorandum prepared for the Federal Court Study Committee. Federal Courts Study Committee—Working Papers. Washington, DC: Federal Judicial Center. https://www.yumpu.com/en/document/view/20990701/federal-courts-study-committee-working-papers-and-/895.

Bendavid, Naftali. 1993. "Sentencing Panel's Political Firestorm: As New Era Dawns, US Commission Rocked by Jostling over Leadership, Goals." *Legal Times* 16(September 13):10–18.

———. 1994*a*. "Sentencing Commission at the Brink: Plagued by Vacancies, Panel's Expiration Looms." *Legal Times* 17(August 17):10–17.

———. 1994*b*. "Who's Minding the Sentencing Store?" *Legal Times* 16(April 4): 4–9.

Bibas, Stephanos. 2004. "The Feeney Amendment and the Continuing Rise of Prosecutorial Power to Plea Bargain." *Journal of Criminal Law and Criminology* 94(2):295–308.

Block, Michael K. 1989. "Emerging Problems in the Sentencing Commission's Approach to Guidelines Amendments." *Federal Sentencing Reporter* 1: 451–55.

Blumstein, Alfred, Jacqueline Cohen, Susan E. Martin, and Michael Tonry, eds. 1983. *Research on Sentencing: The Search for Reform*. 2 vols. Washington, DC: National Academy Press.

Boerner, David. 2012. "Prosecution in Washington State." In *Prosecutors and Politics: A Comparative Perspective*, edited by Michael Tonry. Vol. 41 of *Crime and Justice: A Review of Research*, edited by Michael Tonry. Chicago: University of Chicago Press.

Bottoms, Anthony E. 1977. "Reflections on the Renaissance of Dangerousness." *Howard Journal of Criminal Justice* 16(2):70–96.

Breyer, Stephen. 1988. "The Federal Sentencing Guidelines and the Key Compromises upon Which They Rest." *Hofstra Law Review* 17:1–50.

———. 1999. "Federal Sentencing Guidelines Revisited." *Federal Sentencing Reporter* 11:180–86.

Bureau of Justice Statistics. 1990. *Compendium of Federal Justice Statistics—1985*. Washington, DC: US Department of Justice, Bureau of Justice Statistics.

Canadian Sentencing Commission. 1987. *Sentencing Reform: A Canadian Approach*. Ottawa: Canadian Government Publishing Centre.

Carrow, Deborah M., Judith Feins, Beverly N. W. Lee, and Lois Olinger. 1985. *Guidelines without Force: An Evaluation of the Multi-jurisdictional Sentencing Guidelines Field Test*. Report to the National Institute of Justice. Cambridge, MA: Abt Associates.

Carson, E. Ann, and William J. Sabol. 2012. *Prisoners in 2011*. Washington, DC: US Department of Justice, Bureau of Justice Statistics.

Cullen, Francis. 2013. "Rehabilitation: Beyond Nothing Works." In *Crime and Justice in America, 1975–2025*, edited by Michael Tonry. Vol. 42 of *Crime and Justice: A Review of Research*, edited by Michael Tonry. Chicago: University of Chicago Press.

Doob, Anthony N. 1995. "The United States Sentencing Commission Guidelines: If You Don't Know Where You Are, You Might Not Get There." In *The Politics of Sentencing Reform*, edited by Christ Clarkson and Rod Morgan. Oxford: Clarendon.

Edsall, Thomas, and Mary Edsall. 1991. *Chain Reaction: The Impact of Race, Rights, and Taxes on American Politics*. New York: Norton.

Federal Courts Study Committee. 1990. *Report*. Washington, DC: Administrative Office of the US Courts.

Federal Judicial Center. 1989. *Annual Report 1989*. Washington, DC: Federal Judicial Center.

Frankel, Marvin. 1972. "Lawlessness in Sentencing." *Cincinnati Law Review* 41 (1):1–54.

———. 1973. *Criminal Sentences—Law without Order*. New York: Hill & Wang.

Frase, Richard. 2013. *Just Sentencing: Principles and Procedures for a Workable System*. New York: Oxford University Press.

Freeborn, Beth A., and Monica E. Hartmann. 2010. "Judicial Discretion and Sentencing Behavior: Did the Feeney Amendment Rein In District Judges?" *Journal of Empirical Legal Studies* 7(2):355–78.

Freiberg, Arie. 2001. "Three Strikes and You're Out—It's Not Cricket: Colonization and Resistance in Australian Sentencing." In *Sentencing and Sanctions in Western Countries*, edited by Michael Tonry and Richard S. Frase. New York: Oxford University Press.

———. 2014. *Fox and Freiberg's Sentencing—State and Federal Law in Victoria*. 3rd ed. Melbourne: Lawbook.

Gottfredson, Don M., Leslie T. Wilkins, and Peter B. Hoffman. 1978. *Guidelines for Parole and Sentencing*. Lanham, MD: Lexington.

Greenfield, Lawrence. 1988. *Prisoners in 1987*. Washington, DC: US Department of Justice, Bureau of Justice Statistics.

Guerino, Paul, Paige M. Harrison, and William J. Sabol. 2011. *Prisoners in 2010*. Washington, DC: US Department of Justice, Bureau of Justice Statistics.

Heaney, Gerald W. 1991. "The Reality of Guidelines Sentencing: No End to Disparity." *American Criminal Law Review* 28:161–233.

Heumann, Milton, and Colin Loftin. 1979. "Mandatory Sentencing and the Abolition of Plea Bargaining: The Michigan Felony Firearms Statute." *Law and Society Review* 13:393–430.

Hofer, Paul J. 1990. "Sentencing Procedures and the Federal Guidelines." Draft research report. Washington, DC: Federal Judicial Center.

———. 2011. "Beyond the 'Heartland': Sentencing under the Advisory Federal Guidelines." *Duquesne Law Review* 49:675–705.

———. 2012. "Review of the US Sentencing Commission's Report to Congress: Mandatory Minimum Penalties in the Federal Criminal Justice System." *Federal Sentencing Reporter* 24(3):193–213.

Hoffman, Peter B. 1976. "Salient Factor Score Validation: A 1972 Release Cohort." *Journal of Criminal Justice* 6:69–76.

———. 1983. "Screening for Risk: A Revised Salient Factor Score (SFS 81)." *Journal of Criminal Justice* 11(6):539–47.

———. 1995. "20 Years of Operational Use of a Risk Prediction Instrument: The United States Parole Commission's Salient Factor Score." *Journal of Criminal Justice* 22(6):477–94.

Jacobs, James B. 2015. *The Eternal Criminal Record*. Cambridge, MA: Harvard University Press.

Joint Committee on New York Drug Law Evaluation. 1978. *The Nation's Toughest Drug Law: Evaluating the New York Experience*. Project of the Association of the Bar of the City of New York and the Drug Abuse Council. Washington, DC: US Government Printing Office.

Knapp, Kay A. 1984. *The Impact of the Minnesota Sentencing Guidelines: Three-Year Evaluation*. St. Paul: Minnesota Sentencing Guidelines Commission.

———. 1991. "Arizona: Unprincipled Sentencing, Mandatory Minimums, and Prison Crowding." *Overcrowded Times* 2(5):10–12.

———. 1993. "Allocation of Discretion and Accountability within Sentencing Structures." *University of Colorado Law Review* 64:679–706.

Knapp, Kay A., and Denis J. Hauptly. 1992. "State and Federal Sentencing Guidelines: Apples and Oranges." *University of California at Davis Law Review* 25:679–94.

Lawrence, Pamela B., and Paul J. Hofer. 1992. *An Empirical Study of the Application of Relevant Conduct Guidelines*. Washington, DC: Federal Judicial Center.

Lynch, Gerard E. 2003. "Screening versus Plea Bargaining: Exactly What Are We Trading Off?" *Stanford Law Review* 55:1399–1408.

Martinson, Robert. 1974. "What Works?—Questions and Answers about Prison Reform." *Public Interest* 35(2):22–54.

Mason, David P. 2004. "Barking Up the Wrong Tree: The Misplaced Furor over the Feeney Amendment as a Threat to Judicial Independence." *William and Mary Law Review* 46:731–85.

McDonald, Douglas C., and Kenneth E. Carlson. 1992. *Federal Sentencing in Transition, 1986–90.* Washington, DC: US Department of Justice, Bureau of Justice Statistics.

Morris, Norval. 1974. *The Future of Imprisonment.* Chicago: University of Chicago Press.

Morris, Norval, and Michael Tonry. 1990. *Between Prison and Probation: Intermediate Punishments in a Rational Sentencing System.* New York: Oxford University Press.

Murray, Joseph, David P. Farrington, Catrien C. J. H. Bijleveld, and Rolf Loeber. 2014. *Effects of Parental Incarceration on Children: Cross-National Comparative Studies.* Washington, DC: American Psychological Association.

Nagel, Ilene H. 1990. "Foreword: Structuring Sentencing Discretion: The New Federal Sentencing Guidelines." *Journal of Criminal Law and Criminology* 80 (4):883–943.

Nagel, Ilene H., and Stephen J. Schulhofer. 1992. "A Tale of Three Cities: An Empirical Study of Charging and Bargaining Practices under the Federal Sentencing Guidelines." *Southern California Law Review* 66:501–66.

Nagin, Daniel. 2013. "Deterrence in the Twenty-First Century." In *Crime and Justice in America, 1975–2025*, edited by Michael Tonry. Vol. 42 of *Crime and Justice: A Review of Research*, edited by Michael Tonry. Chicago: University of Chicago Press.

National Commission on Reform of Federal Criminal Law. 1971. *Report.* Washington, DC: US Government Printing Office.

O'Donnell, Pierce, Dennis Curtis, and Michael Churgin. 1977. *Toward a Just and Effective Sentencing System.* New York: Praeger.

Orland, Leonard, and Kevin R. Reitz. 1993. "Epilogue: A Gathering of State Sentencing Commissions." *Colorado Law Review* 64:837–45.

Parent, Dale G. 1988. *Structuring Criminal Sentences: The Evolution of Minnesota's Sentencing Guidelines.* New York: LEXIS Law Publications.

Platt, Tony, and Paul Takagi. 1977. "Intellectuals for Law and Order: A Critique of the New 'Realists.'" *Crime and Social Justice* 8:1–24.

Probation Officers Advisory Group. 1996. "Survey." *Federal Sentencing Reporter* 8:303–6.

Reitz, Kevin. 1993. "Sentencing Facts: Travesties of Real-Offense Sentencing." *Stanford Law Review* 45:523–73.

Reitz, Kevin, and Curtis R. Reitz. 1993. "The American Bar Association's New Sentencing Standards." *Federal Sentencing Reporter* 11(3):169–73.

Rhodes, William. 1992. "Sentence Disparity, Use of Incarceration, and Plea Bargaining: The Post-Guideline View from the Commission." *Federal Sentencing Reporter* 5:153–55.

Rich, William D., L. Paul Sutton, Todd D. Clear, and Michael J. Saks. 1982. *Sentencing by Mathematics: An Evaluation of the Early Attempts to Develop Sentencing Guidelines*. Williamsburg, VA: National Center for State Courts.

Robinson, Paul. 1987. *Dissenting View of Commissioner Paul H. Robinson on the Promulgation of Sentencing Guidelines by the United States Sentencing Commission*. Washington, DC: US Government Printing Office.

Saris, Patti B. 2011. Prepared Testimony of Judge Patti B. Saris, Chair, US Sentencing Commission, before the Subcommittee on Crime, Terrorism, and Homeland Security, Committee on the Judiciary, US House of Representatives, October 12. Washington, DC: US Sentencing Commission.

———. 2013. Prepared Statement by Judge Patti B. Saris, Chair, US Sentencing Commission, for the Hearing on "Reevaluating the Effectiveness of Federal Mandatory Minimum Sentences" before the Committee on the Judiciary, US Senate, September 18. Washington, DC: US Sentencing Commission.

Schulhofer, Stephen J., and Ilene Nagel. 1989. "Negotiated Pleas under the Federal Sentencing Guidelines: The First Fifteen Months." *American Criminal Law Review* 27:231–88.

Schwartzer, William W. 1991. "Judicial Discretion in Sentencing." *Federal Sentencing Reporter* 4:339–41.

Scott, Ryan W. 2010. "Inter-judge Sentencing Disparity after Booker: A First Look." *Stanford Law Review* 63:1–66.

Sessions, William K., III. 2011. "At the Crossroads of the Three Branches: The US Sentencing Commission's Attempts to Achieve Sentencing Reform in the Midst of Inter-branch Power Struggles." *Journal of Law and Politics* 26: 305–57.

Shermer, Lauren O'Neill, and Brian D. Johnson. 2009. "Criminal Prosecutions: Examining Prosecutorial Discretion and Charge Reductions in U.S. Federal District Courts." *Justice Quarterly* 27(3):394–430.

Stith, Kate, and José Cabranes. 1998. *Fear of Judging: Sentencing Guidelines in the Federal Courts*. Chicago: University of Chicago Press.

Stith, Kate, and Steve Yoh. 1993. "The Politics of Sentencing Reform: The Legislative History of the Federal Sentencing Guidelines." *Wake Forest Law Review* 28:233–90.

Tonry, Michael. 1981. "Real Offense Sentencing—the Model Sentencing and Corrections Act." *Journal of Criminal Law and Criminology* 72:1550–96.

———. 1992*a*. "GAO Report Confirms Failure of US Sentencing Commission's Guidelines." *Federal Sentencing Reporter* 5:144–48.

———. 1992*b*. "Salvaging the Sentencing Guidelines in Seven Easy Steps." *Federal Sentencing Reporter* 4:355–59.

———. 1996. *Sentencing Matters*. New York: Oxford University Press.

———. 2001. "Punishment Policies and Patterns in Western Countries." In *Sentencing and Sanctions in Western Countries*, edited by Michael Tonry and Richard S. Frase. New York: Oxford University Press.

———. 2007. "Determinants of Penal Policies." In *Crime, Punishment, and Politics in Comparative Perspective*, edited by Michael Tonry. Vol. 35 of *Crime and*

Justice: A Review of Research, edited by Michael Tonry. Chicago: University of Chicago Press.

———. 2009. "The Untold Story of America's First Sentencing Commission." *Federal Sentencing Reporter* 21(4):265–70.

———. 2013. "Sentencing in America, 1975–2025." In *Crime and Justice in America, 1975–2025*, edited by Michael Tonry. Vol. 42 of *Crime and Justice: A Review of Research*, edited by Michael Tonry. Chicago: University of Chicago Press.

Travis, Jeremy, Bruce Western, and Stephens Redburn, eds. 2014. *The Causes and Consequences of High Incarceration Rates in the United States*. Washington, DC: National Academies Press.

US Courts. 2014. *Judicial Facts and Figures—2012*. http://www.uscourts.gov/uscourts/Statistics/JudicialFactsAndFigures/2012/Table101.pdf.

US General Accounting Office. 1990. *US Sentencing Commission: Changes Needed to Improve Effectiveness*. Washington, DC: US General Accounting Office.

———. 1992. *Sentencing Guidelines: Central Questions Remain Unanswered*. Washington, DC: US General Accounting Office.

US Sentencing Commission. 1987*a*. *Sentencing Commission Guidelines Manual*. Washington, DC: US Sentencing Commission.

———. 1987*b*. *Sentencing Guidelines and Policy Statements, April 13, 1987*. Washington, DC: US Government Printing Office.

———. 1987*c*. *Supplemental Report on the Initial Sentencing Guidelines and Policy Statements, June 18, 1987*. Washington, DC: US Government Printing Office.

———. 1990*a*. *Annual Report, 1989*. Washington, DC: US Sentencing Commission.

———. 1990*b*. *The Federal Offender: A Program of Intermediate Punishments*. Report from the Alternatives to Imprisonment Project. Washington, DC: US Sentencing Commission.

———. 1991*a*. *The Federal Sentencing Guidelines: A Report on the Operation of the Guidelines System and Short-Term Impacts on Disparity in Sentencing, Use of Incarceration, and Prosecutorial Discretion and Plea Bargaining*. Washington, DC: US Sentencing Commission.

———. 1991*b*. *Special Report to the Congress: Mandatory Minimum Penalties in the Federal Criminal Justice System*. Washington, DC: US Sentencing Commission.

———. 1994. *Annual Report, 1993*. Washington, DC: US Sentencing Commission.

———. 1995*a*. *Report to Congress: Adequacy of Penalties for Fraud Offenses Involving Elderly Victims*. Washington, DC: US Sentencing Commission.

———. 1995*b*. *Report to Congress: Adequacy of Penalties for the Intentional Exposure of Others, through Sexual Activity, to Human Immunodeficiency Virus*. Washington, DC: US Sentencing Commission.

———. 1995*c*. *Report to Congress: Analysis of Penalties for Federal Rape Cases*. Washington, DC: US Sentencing Commission.

———. 1995*d*. *Special Report to Congress: Cocaine and Federal Sentencing Policy*. Washington, DC: US Sentencing Commission.

———. 1996*a*. *Annual Report—Fiscal Year 1995*. Washington, DC: US Sentencing Commission.

———. 1996*b*. *Report to the Congress: Adequacy of Federal Sentencing Guideline Penalties for Computer Fraud and Vandalism Offenses*. Washington, DC: US Sentencing Commission.

———. 1996*c*. *Report to the Congress: Sex Crimes against Children*. Washington, DC: US Sentencing Commission.

———. 1996*d*. *Simplification Draft Paper*. Working Group on Guideline Simplification. Washington, DC: US Sentencing Commission.

———. 1996*e*. *Staff Discussion Paper: Sentencing Options under the Guidelines*. Washington, DC: US Sentencing Commission.

———. 1997*a*. *Sentencing Policy for Money Laundering Offenses, Including Comments on Department of Justice Report*. Washington, DC: US Sentencing Commission.

———. 1997*b*. *Special Report to Congress: Cocaine and Federal Sentencing Policy*. Washington, DC: US Sentencing Commission.

———. 1998. *Report to the Congress: Telemarketing Fraud Offenses—Explanation of Recent Guideline Amendments*. Washington, DC: US Sentencing Commission.

———. 2002. *Special Report to Congress: Cocaine and Federal Sentencing Policy*. Washington, DC: US Sentencing Commission.

———. 2003*a*. *Report to the Congress: Increased Penalties for Campaign Finance Offenses and Legislative Recommendations*. Washington, DC: US Sentencing Commission.

———. 2003*b*. *Report to the Congress: Increased Penalties for Cyber Security Offenses*. Washington, DC: US Sentencing Commission.

———. 2003*c*. *Report to the Congress: Increased Penalties under the Sarbanes Oxley Act of 2002*. Washington, DC: US Sentencing Commission.

———. 2004. *15 Years of Guidelines Sentencing: An Assessment of How Well the Federal Criminal Justice System Is Achieving the Goals of Sentencing Reform*. Washington, DC: US Sentencing Commission.

———. 2007. *Special Report to Congress: Federal Cocaine Sentencing Policy*. Washington, DC: US Sentencing Commission.

———. 2008. *Report to the Congress: Amendments to the Federal Sentencing Guidelines in Response to the Emergency Disaster Assistance Fraud Penalty Enhancement Act of 2007*. Washington, DC: US Sentencing Commission.

———. 2009. *The Federal Offender: A Program of Intermediate Punishments*. Washington, DC: US Sentencing Commission.

———. 2010. *Results of Survey of United States District Judges—January 2010 through March 2010*. Washington, DC: US Sentencing Commission.

———. 2011. *Report to the Congress: Mandatory Minimum Penalties in the Federal Criminal Justice System*. Washington, DC: US Sentencing Commission.

———. 2012*a*. *Report to the Congress: Federal Child Pornography Offenses*. Washington, DC: US Sentencing Commission.

———. 2012*b*. *Report to the Congress: Report on the Continuing Impact of United States v. Booker on Federal Sentencing*. Washington, DC: US Sentencing Commission.

———. 2013. *2013 Sourcebook of Federal Sentencing Statistics*. Washington, DC: US Sentencing Commission.

———. 2014*a*. "Comment of Honorable Patti B. Saris, Chair, US Sentencing Commission, on Amendment Reducing Drug Guidelines becoming Effective Tomorrow." News release, October 31.

———. 2014*b*. *Sentencing Commission Guidelines Manual*. Washington, DC: US Sentencing Commission.

———. 2014*c*. "Summary of Key Data Regarding Retroactive Application of the 2014 Drug Guidelines Amendment." Office of Research and Data Memorandum, July 25. Washington, DC: US Sentencing Commission.

———. 2014*d*. "US Sentencing Commission Selects Policy Priorities for 2014–2015 Guidelines Amendment Cycle—Continued Work on Mandatory Minimum Penalties, Review of Fraud Guidelines on List of Priorities." News release, August 14.

US Sentencing Commission Alternatives to Imprisonment Project. 1990. *The Federal Offender: A Program of Intermediate Punishments: Executive Summary*. Washington, DC: US Sentencing Commission.

von Hirsch, Andrew. 1988. "Federal Sentencing Guidelines: The United States and Canadian Schemes Compared." Occasional Papers from the Center for Research in Crime and Justice, no. 4. New York: New York University Law School.

Weisburd, David. 1992. "Sentencing Disparity and the Guidelines: Taking a Closer Look." *Federal Sentencing Reporter* 5:149–52.

Wright, Ronald. 2002. "Counting the Cost of Sentencing in North Carolina, 1980–2000." In *Crime and Justice: A Review of Research*, vol. 29, edited by Michael Tonry. Chicago: University of Chicago Press.

———. 2012. "Persistent Localism in the Prosecutor Services of North Carolina." In *Prosecutors and Politics: A Comparative Perspective*, edited by Michael Tonry. Vol. 41 of *Crime and Justice: A Review of Research*, edited by Michael Tonry. Chicago: University of Chicago Press.

Marianne van Ooyen-Houben and Edward Kleemans

Drug Policy: The "Dutch Model"

ABSTRACT

Dutch drug policy, once considered pragmatic and lenient and rooted in a generally tolerant attitude toward drug use, has slowly but surely shifted from a primarily public health focus to an increasing focus on law enforcement. The "coffee shop" policy and the policy toward MDMA/ecstasy are illustrations. Both were initiated from a public health perspective but were attacked because of unintended side effects relating to supply markets, crime, and nuisance. Coffee shops became the subject of increasing restrictions and MDMA/ecstasy production became the target of a comprehensive enforcement program. It took some time before the tougher strategies were applied. The health-oriented approach and the conviction that drug problems can be contained, but not eradicated, are deeply rooted. This led to acknowledgment of the adverse consequences of increased law enforcement and tempered its application. Research showed effectiveness in some regards but also unintended consequences. The expansion of illegal cannabis consumer markets after restrictions on coffee shops is one example. The use of alternative chemical ingredients for ecstasy production is another. Changes in drug policy have an effect on supply markets, but drug use seems largely unaffected.

Dutch "tolerance" was the driving force in the emergence of the much-debated "alternative" Dutch drug policy of the 1970s. Ed Leuw in a classic *Crime and Justice* essay characterized Dutch drug policy as normalizing, pragmatic, and nonmoralistic: "It accepts the existence of the use of

Electronically published July 30, 2015

Marianne van Ooyen-Houben is a research manager with the Research and Documentation Centre (WODC), Ministry of Security and Justice, Netherlands. Edward Kleemans is full professor at the VU School of Criminology, Faculty of Law, VU University Amsterdam.

0192-3234/2015/0044-0003$10.00

illegal drugs as inevitable in modern society. Official reactions are directed at a reduction of social and personal harm. . . . It focuses law enforcement efforts on the higher levels of the supply system. Retail trade is tolerated in numerous 'coffee shops.' The use of hard drugs is primarily considered a public health problem" (1991, p. 229). Leuw observed that drug policy was based on the central notion that the drug problem is primarily a public health and welfare issue and that risk reduction is its core concept (pp. 248, 258).

The Dutch drug tolerance policy was implemented in 1976, when the Opium Act was revised. A basic principle was that marginalization and criminalization of drug users should be avoided. The Opium Act as a result did not define use of drugs as an offense. Possession of small amounts for personal use is an offense, but the "expediency principle" allows the public prosecutor to refrain from prosecution if this is in the general interest. In practice, this means that drugs are seized, but possession of small amounts for personal use is not actively investigated and in principle does not lead to arrest or prosecution (Staatscourant 2015).

A two-schedule distinction was made in the Opium Act, on the basis of drugs' risks to the user's health. Schedule I deals with drugs with "unacceptable risks." These are the so-called hard drugs, of which in 1976 heroin stood out as most problematic. Schedule II deals with "soft drugs" considered less harmful. The main drug in this schedule is cannabis. Law enforcement concerning hard drug offenses was more vigorous than for soft drug offenses.

The distinction between cannabis and other illegal drugs should be viewed within the historical context of the sudden increase in the 1970s of the problematic use of heroin, with very high health risks but concentrated in marginalized groups, versus the much broader use of less addictive and less harmful cannabis by young people from a variety of backgrounds. The distinction between hard and soft drugs served a purpose, as the substances and target populations were quite distinct. By introducing separate schedules, a less strict enforcement regime for cannabis could be maintained while a stricter one for hard drugs could be implemented.

After reviewing the situation in 1991, Leuw concluded: "Dutch experience with de-escalation of risks and rewards of drug problems indicates that a pragmatic approach may be a viable alternative to approaches that rely mainly on law-enforcement strategies" (1991, pp. 271–72).

A lot has happened, however, since 1991. Dutch drug policy became more focused on controlling crime and drug-related disorder, usually referred to as "nuisance." The Dutch cannabis policy came under attack. An expectation that other countries would soon follow the "rational" Dutch approach did not materialize in the short run. New drugs, such as MDMA/ecstasy, of which the Netherlands became a major producer, came on the scene in the 1990s. Unintended consequences and international criticism led to a more stringent approach. There was a shift in perspective from containment and risk reduction to the control of nuisance and crime as a goal in itself. This control element plays a role in contemporary drug policy almost equal to the health element (Blom 2006; van der Stel 2006; van Laar and van Ooyen-Houben 2009). The shift occurred gradually and in a subtle way and can be illustrated by comparing official definitions of drug policy goals over time, as table 1 shows.

The drug situation has changed since Leuw wrote his 1991 essay. Below we summarize major topics regarding drug use, coffee shops, drug-related organized crime, cannabis cultivation, the emergence of new synthetic drugs, and nuisance and crime caused by hard drug users that have emerged since then. The main issues are summarized in table 2. These issues gave rise to discussions and debates and—finally—a shift

TABLE 1

Official Definitions of Drug Policy Goals in the Netherlands

Year	Definition	Source
1976	Prevention and reduction of societal and individual risks caused by the use of drugs	Tweede Kamer* 1975, p. 5†
1985	The drug policy has three aims: protection of (public) health, public order, and the health and welfare of drug users	ISAD 1985, p. 12†
1995	Prevention and containment of the societal and individual risks that result from the use of drugs	Tweede Kamer 1995, p. 4
2007	The primary aims of the Dutch drug policy are: protection of (public) health, counteracting of nuisance and the control of (drug-related) crime	Tweede Kamer 2007, p. 3919†
2011	The Dutch drug policy has two pillars: one for the protection of public health on the one hand and the control of nuisance and crime on the other	Tweede Kamer 2011*a*, p. 1

* The Lower House of Parliament.

† Cited in van der Stel, Everhardt, and van Laar (2009), p. 66.

TABLE 2

Important Developments Concerning Drug Policy

Early 1990s	Mid-1990s	2010–14
Drug use:		
Use of "traditional" drugs (heroin, cocaine, amphetamines, cannabis) and MDMA/ecstasy	Increase in use and production of MDMA/ecstasy; increase in drug use in general	MDMA/ecstasy still on the market and popular among users; trends in use among youths stable or decreasing
Coffee shops:		
Increased share of retail market by coffee shops; commercialization of coffee shops; coffee shops sell mainly hashish from abroad	High number of coffee shops (estimate: 1,100–1,500); emergence of large-scale coffee shops; increasing complaints of nuisance around coffee shops; increasing "drug tourism" related to coffee shops; Nederwiet on the rise	Decreasing number of coffee shops (614 in 2013); less drug tourism since 2012; closure of some large-scale coffee shops in border regions; Nederwiet most popular product sold in coffee shops, high levels of THC
Drug-related organized crime:		
The Netherlands is a major transit point in international drug trade, crossroads for hashish (smuggled by organized Dutch networks), heroin, cocaine, production of amphetamines	Increase of drug-related organized crime, international drug trade, production of Nederwiet, amphetamines, ecstasy	Organized crime still involved in international drug trade and production of Nederwiet, amphetamines, ecstasy
Supply of cannabis:		
Import of hashish from abroad, Nederwiet in development	Growth of indoor cultivation of Nederwiet; Nederwiet and hashish from abroad both cover about half of the domestic cannabis market; first signs of export of Nederwiet	Nederwiet cultivation is widespread and professional, and there exists a mature cannabis cultivation industry; high levels of export; Nederwiet dominates hashish on domestic market
Problematic users of opiates and cocaine:		
Nuisance and crime caused by problematic users of opiates and cocaine; start of (lenient) quasi-compulsory treatment for hard drug users with high rates of	Continuing nuisance and crime by problematic hard drug users; local programs against nuisance; broadening of quasi-compulsory treatment in judicial system; increase of harm-	Signs of decreasing nuisance and crime by hard drug users; more compulsive quasi-compulsory treatment; structural embeddedness of harm-reduction approaches; de-

TABLE 2 (*Continued*)

Early 1990s	Mid-1990s	2010–14
crime; harm-reduction approaches; ±28,000 problematic hard drug users (estimate)*	reduction approaches; stabilization of numbers (estimate 25,000–29,000)*	creasing numbers (17,700; range 17,300–18,100)*

* Van Laar et al. (2002, 2013).

in focus toward law enforcement, while at the same time the health perspective remained important.

There was a major shift in the direction of law enforcement:

- More law enforcement tools were introduced to combat drug-related crime and nuisance (van Ooyen-Houben, Bieleman, et al. 2009; van Ooyen-Houben, Meijer, et al. 2009; Centrum voor Criminaliteitspreventie en Veiligheid 2014).
- Some municipalities introduced "blowing bans" in public places and schools (Centrum voor Criminaliteitspreventie en Veiligheid 2014). A "zero-tolerance" policy for drug possession has been applied at large dance events and festivals, implying that partygoers who carry drugs with them may be arrested (Nabben 2010; Tweede Kamer 2014*a*).
- Sanctions for Opium Act offenses were raised (van Ooyen-Houben, Meijer, et al. 2009).
- High enforcement priority is given to combat organized crime in relation to drugs (Tweede Kamer 2008, 2013*a*). The share of police investigations of "more serious forms of organized crime" that concern drugs increased from 53 percent in 2000 to more than 70 percent since 2005 (fig. 1). There appears to have been a substantial increase in cases related to soft drugs (mainly cannabis).

Another important change is that investigations and dismantlements of indoor cannabis cultivation sites were intensified (Tweede Kamer 2004). In 1993 and 1994, 237 and 323 (mainly indoor) cultivation sites were dismantled (Tweede Kamer 1995). During 2004–13, between 5,000 and 6,000 sites were dismantled each year (van Laar et al. 2014). The dismantling process is well structured and organized (Wouters,

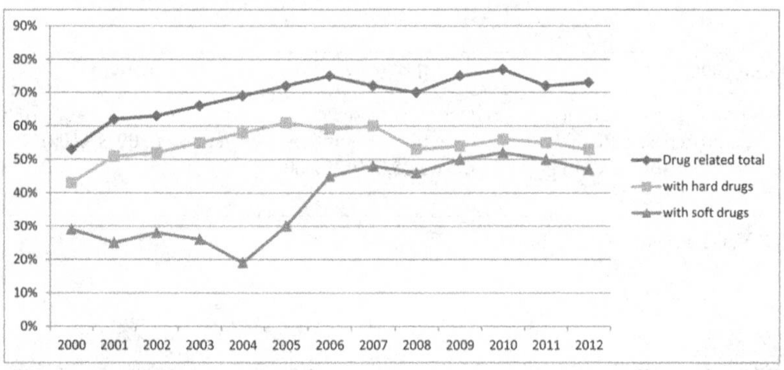

FIG. 1.—Criminal investigations into more serious forms of organized crime, 2000–2012. Between 2002 and 2003, 2004 and 2005, 2005 and 2006, and 2011 and 2012 changes were made in recording. Figures for 2005 cover January–November. Source: National police, unit of national information organization; reported in van Ooyen-Houben, Meijer, et al. (2009); van Laar et al. (2013). Figures for 2012 are based on manual calculations of national police data.

Korf, and Kroeske 2007; Tweede Kamer 2014*g*).[1] Yet another change is that entrance into coffee shops was increasingly restricted, and criteria concerning tolerance of them became more restrictive (van Laar, van Ooyen-Houben, and Monshouwer 2009; van Ooyen-Houben, Bieleman, and Korf 2014).

The shift toward law enforcement can also be illustrated by the increasing number of police arrests for Opium Act offenses, for both hard and soft drugs (fig. 2). Since 1996, Opium Act offenses form 5–8 percent of all criminal offenses, with an increasing trend since 2009 (van Ooyen-Houben, Meijer, et al. 2009; van Laar et al. 2014). The high number in 2004 can be attributed to increased arrests of cocaine ball swallowers and body packers at Schiphol Airport. In 2013, they comprised 8.3 percent. Figures on prosecutions and sentencing show similar trends.

The shift is also evident in estimated public expenditures for Opium Act offenses (fig. 3), rising from €275 million in 1995 to €717 million in 2007 (prices 2007). The percentage of all public expenditures related to crime rose from 7 percent in 1995 to 10 percent in 2002–7. Moolenaar et al. (2014) report different calculations for 2005–12 (not comparable

[1] Figures on seizures of drugs are not reported because they are incomplete and cannot be compared over time (van Ooyen-Houben, Meijer, et al. 2009; van Laar et al. 2014).

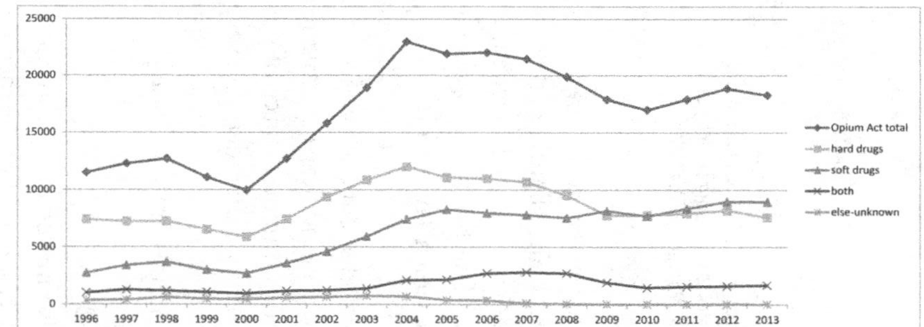

FIG. 2.—Suspects of Opium Act offenses arrested by the police, 1996–2013. Source: National police registration of suspects; reported in van Ooyen-Houben, Meijer, et al. (2009) and van Laar et al. (2014).

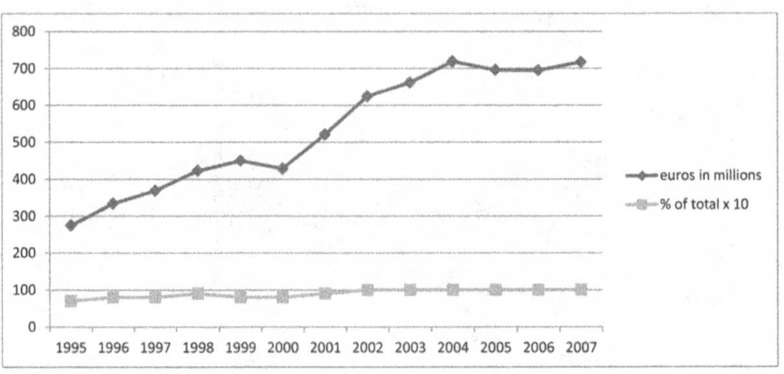

FIG. 3.—Estimated annual public expenditure for Opium Act offenses, national government, 1995–2007, in millions of euros (prices 2007). Source: Research and Documentation Centre 2009; reported in van Ooyen-Houben, Meijer, et al. (2009).

with fig. 3) and show that there was an increase until 2009 and a decrease in 2010–12, with 2012 being slightly higher than 2006.

Finally, there was a shift toward law enforcement in relation to hard drug users. Leuw observed: "The hard-drug problem . . . is treated as a public health problem in which law enforcement plays a restricted and secondary role" (1991, p. 230). Over time, the hard drug problem increasingly involved criminal elements, which led to an increased role for law enforcement. Hard drug addicts committed numerous thefts and burglaries and became a continuous source of public nuisance.

The approach toward hard drug offenders, however, retains an important element of harm reduction. Methadone substitution programs and heroin prescription programs are official approaches in addiction health care. Police and prosecutors formally tolerate consumption rooms for hard drug users.

However, policies have also moved in the direction of intensified use of pressure and compelled treatment. The Netherlands has used treatment as an alternative to imprisonment for many years, since the beginning of the 1990s. Quasi-compulsory treatment is used in response to offenses of addicts, mainly users of heroin and cocaine (Stevens et al. 2005; van Ooyen-Houben 2013). The idea is that addicts need treatment and that imprisonment is not effective in reducing the crime and addiction problems. Many addicts who are arrested, prosecuted, or detained can choose to participate in treatment outside prison in place of imprisonment or as part of their sanction (van Ooyen-Houben et al. 2008; Eerste Kamer 2014).[2] Treatment is not officially compulsory, but there is judicial pressure: if participants do not adhere to the conditions or drop out of the treatment, they will be imprisoned.

Court-ordered treatment of drug-dependent offenders (Strafrechtelijke Opvang Verslaafden, or SOV) was introduced in 2001. In 2004, SOV was replaced by court-ordered placement in an institution for recurring offenders (Inrichting voor Stelselmatige Daders, or ISD; Staatsblad van het Koninkrijk der Nederlanden 2001, 2004). These measures—which retain treatment as a crucial element (van Ooyen-Houben and Goderie 2009)—were a break from the earlier softer approaches; they can be applied for up to 2 years and have a "three strikes and you're out" character (for ISD the criterion is arrests for more than 10 offenses in 5 years with at least one in the last year).

Underneath the more repressive streams of law enforcement, there is, however, an important continuity: the drug problem continues primarily to be dealt with from a health perspective. The Drug Policy Letter of 2011 confirms this: "The cabinet continues to approach the drug problem from a health perspective" (Tweede Kamer 2011*a*, p. 6).[3]

This means that there have been no fundamental changes in basic principles since the 1970s. These basic principles, however, do not receive much attention in the 2011 policy letter. It addresses problems such as the increased use of drugs and alcohol among youths and the growth of coffee shops and drug-related organized crime, and it describes practical responses to them. This is a stark departure from the Drug Policy Letter of 1995, which formulated broader perspectives and deliberated on continuities and changes (Tweede Kamer 2011*a*).

The health perspective remains important. Drug use is approached primarily from a noncriminal viewpoint. Drug users are not criminalized. The harm that drug use can cause is controlled primarily through social and medical approaches, although repressive administrative and criminal law measures are increasingly applied. Harm reduction thus still plays an important role. Croes and van Gageldonk (2009), in a re-

[2] Eerste Kamer is the Upper House of the Parliament.

[3] The cabinet adds in the same sentence that it "wants to focus attention more decidedly on the youth." The Policy Letter of 2011 is signed by the minister of health, welfare, and sports and the minister of security and justice. Unless otherwise noted, all translations are ours.

view of the Dutch literature on harm reduction, describe it as a typical characteristic of the Dutch drug policy. Some people elsewhere and in the Netherlands sometimes find this controversial, but it is a long-standing tradition. Harm-reduction policies started in the 1980s with methadone programs, low-threshold shelter facilities, needle exchange programs, and condom distribution (Croes and van Gageldonk 2009). In the 1990s special rooms for problematic hard drug addicts were added to the existing facilities: "user rooms" in which addicts can use drugs in a safe and clean environment and without causing nuisance on the streets. Professionals are present. The sale of drugs is forbidden. These user rooms are formally tolerated by the public prosecutor, as long as they adhere to restrictions and rules (Staatscourant 2015).

Other examples of the health perspective concern pill testing, medical heroin prescription, medical marijuana, and the coffee shop system. Pill testing relates to the testing facilities at large-scale dance parties and is meant for recreational users of synthetic drugs such as ecstasy. Pills can be presented on the spot for an expert opinion and a test of their safety. This testing facility was meant as prevention against unexpected and dangerous ingredients. Testing on the spot was officially abandoned, but partygoers can still have pills tested at a "test service," for instance, at an addiction care organization.

In 1998, an experiment started with medical heroin prescriptions, carefully monitored by expert committees and researchers (e.g., van den Brink, Hendriks, and van Ree 1999; Hendriks et al. 2000). The program was expanded in 2004, with a structural anchoring in the Opium Act in 2009 (Staatsblad van het Koninkrijk der Nederlanden 2009; van der Stel 2010). Since 2001, cannabis can be obtained in pharmacies on a doctor's prescription. Cultivation for this use is regulated by the state (Tweede Kamer 2000). Last but not least, the coffee shop system continues, with the objective of reducing harm to cannabis users.

An important continuity concerns the Opium Act of 1976. Its original structure remains basically the same. It still has two schedules: one for "hard drugs" and one for "soft drugs."[4] Possession of small quantities

[4] The two-schedule structure was discussed in Parliament in 2010. An advisory committee was established to review the evidence and judge the adequacy of the two schedules. The committee saw no point in creating more schedules or having only one. According to the committee, the two-schedule system is specific enough to distinguish between more dangerous and less dangerous drugs. The committee proposed splitting cannabis into soft and hard forms, that with a THC concentration of 15 percent or more being considered a

for private use is not actively investigated by the police and does, in principle, not lead to a criminal justice reaction (in the case of possession of 5 grams or less of cannabis) or only prosecution for the sake of treatment (in the case of possession of one consumption unit of a hard drug; Staatscourant 2015).[5] The same is true for the small-scale noncommercial cultivation for private use of up to five cannabis plants. In principle, drug users in the Netherlands can possess up to 5 grams of cannabis, a half gram of a hard drug such as heroin or cocaine, or one tablet of a synthetic drug, without fear of arrest or prosecution. If the drug is discovered, however, it will be confiscated.

Important developments in drug markets and drug-related crime have occurred in recent decades, and there were major changes in the direction of law enforcement. The changes mainly concern reduction of supply and nuisance. Supply reduction has always been a priority, initially with a focus on the combat of commercial drug trafficking (see Leuw 1991).

Yet public health remains the primary focus, and the Ministry of Health remains the leading player. The notion that the drug problem is primarily a health problem and that reduction of the harm caused by drug use is a central aim of drug policy is deeply rooted. This basic continuity is as important as the changes, although these were substantial.

In Section I of this essay, we observe that drug-related nuisance, organized crime, and the high prevalence of use among youths were increasingly perceived as serious problems. This led to more vigorous approaches, more law enforcement, and less tolerance. We illustrate the changes and the continuities by looking closely at developments concerning the coffee shops and the synthetic drug ecstasy.

As it is difficult to measure drug markets in a straightforward way, we combine available evidence about prevalence of use, problematic use, purity, prices, seizures, and nuisance. We use findings from evaluation studies, monitoring studies, and reviews. There are a substantial number of studies available, mostly monitoring studies with repeated assessments but without (quasi-)experimental designs. These studies provide good in-

---

hard drug (Expertcommissie Lijstensystematiek Opiumwet 2011). The government observed this suggestion in its November 2012 plans (Tweede Kamer 2012). Preparation of this amendment is ongoing at the time of writing (Tweede Kamer 2014*b*, 2014*c*, 2014*d*).

[5] See the directive "Aanwijzing Opiumwet" at https://www.om.nl/beleidsregels/algemeen/Aanwijzing Opiumwet (2015A003).

sight into developments and changes, but it is difficult to draw conclusions about effectiveness.

In Section II we describe the origin of the coffee shop system and present facts and figures on developments since the 1990s. The coffee shops play a valuable role as tolerated outlets of cannabis for users, but problems with nuisance and drug tourism have long existed. The system seems to separate markets for hard and soft drugs effectively. The prevalence of cannabis use, however, is high among young people (15–16 years old), especially among vulnerable young people, and there have been unexpected adverse side effects regarding supply, crime, and nuisance.

In Section III we describe the emergence of the synthetic drug MDMA/ecstasy (XTC) as a popular drug and the development during the 1990s of the Netherlands as a worldwide major producer. Ecstasy can give a sense of intimacy and diminish anxiety; it can induce euphoria and mild psychedelic effects. Ecstasy was initially considered to carry low risks, which is why policy makers focused on harm reduction. International pressure was the primary reason for more intensive efforts against production and trafficking. Intensified law enforcement led neither to total eradication of production nor to total eradication of use. Producers adapted their methods, and use has continued, albeit at a lower level.

In Section IV we conclude that policies change over time and react to shifting constellations of problem definitions, possible solutions, and political support. Policy changes are "path dependent." It is difficult to make radical changes. Past choices limit future options. In the early 1970s, a policy window opened for a different approach to cannabis use. In contrast to the sudden increase of the problematic use of heroin, with very high risks, the much broader use of the less addictive and less harmful cannabis by young people from a variety of backgrounds provided backing for the idea of the "separation of markets" and a tolerant approach. Public health concerns became the major objective. The changes over time came about slowly and rather erratically, as a response to problems that had been around for a longer time.

I. Changes in Drug Policy

Dutch drug policy has been debated, embraced, and criticized by scientists, policy makers, politicians, and lobbying groups for many years.

Behind the debates, however, major developments took place and drug-related crime and nuisance became important public concerns.

The national government in 1995 published a comprehensive statement on drug policy entitled "Drug Policy in the Netherlands: Continuity and Change." It described "complications" in drug policy: "Despite the fact that in international terms the situation as regards public health is not unfavorable, the use of drugs and everything that is related to it constitutes an acute, major social and administrative problem in the Netherlands as elsewhere. In tackling this problem three complications arise" (Tweede Kamer 1995, p. 9).

There were several complications: nuisance and crime caused by hard drug addicts; the nuisance from coffee shops caused by large numbers of customers, many from abroad; an increase in organized crime involvement in supply and trafficking of drugs; and fierce criticisms from foreign governments and international organizations. The International Narcotics Control Board in 1995 observed:

> At the same time, however, the Board expresses its continued concern at the persistence of certain practices, only slightly altered, which call into question the Government of the Netherlands' fidelity to its treaty obligations. This includes continuing the failed policy of "separation of markets," tolerating the continued cultivation of nederwiet provided that it is of lower THC content, permitting the operation of so-called coffee shops, many of which have fallen under the control of criminal elements, and continuing to stockpile narcotic drugs for non-medical purposes. . . . [We] will continue to observe closely the progress made by the Government of the Netherlands in fulfilling its treaty obligations. (INCB 1996, p. 58)

Since 1995, control of nuisance and crime has evolved. This is reflected in administrative and criminal laws and amendments to the Opium Act aiming at improvement and facilitation of the investigation and prosecution of drug offenses (van der Stel, Everhardt, and van Laar 2009; van Ooyen-Houben, Meijer, et al. 2009). To mention a few:

- Specifications for "professionalism" of cannabis cultivation in the Opium Act in 1999, with more severe sanctions for professional cultivation, and increased maximum sanctions for large-scale production and trafficking of drugs, with special emphasis on large-scale cultivation.

- Enabling mayors to close drug-dealing premises in a municipality; an article was added to the Opium Act in 1999 and broadened in scope in 2007.
- The "Bibob" Act in 2003 empowered mayors to check criminal antecedents of applicants for licenses. This law is applied increasingly often to coffee shop owners (van Laar et al. 2013).
- An article was added to the Opium Act in 2014 criminalizing preparation or facilitation of cannabis cultivation (Staatsblad 2014).

These changes went hand in hand with increased law enforcement priority concerning drug trafficking and production. The 1995 policy letter introduced more intensive law enforcement concerning the "complications." In 2001, a comprehensive program entitled "A combined effort against ecstasy" was launched (Tweede Kamer 2001). In 2004, an intensified control of professional cannabis cultivation was announced, aimed in particular at indoor cultivation of "Nederwiet" (Tweede Kamer 2004). Since 2008, organized crime in relation to drugs has been a high priority, particularly concerning heroin, cocaine, cannabis, and synthetic drugs (Tweede Kamer 2008, 2011*a*, 2013*a*).

A review of the research evidence in 2009 concluded that policy developments since 1995 had positive and negative effects (van Laar and van Ooyen-Houben 2009). They achieved objectives of harm reduction for users. The prevalence of use of highly addictive drugs such as heroin, crack, amphetamines, and methamphetamines remained low. Infectious diseases like HIV and hepatitis C among injecting hard drug users remained limited, and death rates were low.

However, too many youths, especially vulnerable youths who dropped out of education or lived in institutions, used drugs, including cannabis and alcohol. The prevalence of Dutch use of cannabis and ecstasy remains high in international comparisons. Van Laar and van Ooyen-Houben report that more cannabis users turned to addiction care because of inability to control their cannabis use. Another negative aspect was that coffee shops, especially in border regions, caused a lot of nuisance because of the large number of foreign visitors they attract. They observed that the Netherlands is intensively involved in drug crime throughout Europe.

These findings were confirmed by an expert advisory committee (Adviescommissie Drugsbeleid 2009). It concluded that in some areas the policy was in "urgent need of change" and that the use of drugs and alcohol by minors should be tackled far more rigorously. Coffee shops should return to their original purpose of selling small amounts to local consumers, especially in areas along the border. The illegal drug markets and organized crime must be tackled more vigorously.

The government acted on this advice with a policy letter:[6] "The Dutch drug policy needs a new impulse" and should initiate a "decisive approach against nuisance and (organized) crime" (Tweede Kamer 2011*a*, p. 2). It announced a more restrictive policy toward coffee shops. More intense and integrated efforts to control organized crime were advocated involving cooperation between public and private parties at a regional level and administrative, fiscal, and criminal law authorities. Extra efforts have been made to seize criminal proceeds. Legislation was enacted to increase and harmonize sanctions on large-scale cannabis cultivation. Finally, drug policy toward use among youths was to focus on prevention, addiction care, and cure (Tweede Kamer 2011*b*). School prevention programs were stimulated and e-health was promoted, including a special interactive online program to help young people develop protective skills in relation to drug use and addiction.

II. Coffee Shops

Coffee shops operate under national and local regulations. The system is a regulatory regime for adults (MacCoun, Reuter, and Schelling 1996). The sale of cannabis is tolerated in order to prevent consumers from entering the more criminal and dangerous illegal drugs market and to reduce exposure to hard drugs. Separation of the cannabis and hard drug consumer markets is the cornerstone of the coffee shop system. Coffee shops also offer a safer environment to buy and consume drugs. Revenues from coffee shops do not play a role in the policy (as they do elsewhere; Fijnaut 2014).

United Nations conventions define cannabis as a dangerous drug and contemplate prohibitive, repressive, and multilayer controls. Under these conventions, the Netherlands has applied its own policies concerning cannabis, including the coffee shop system. Its origins date back to 1976, when the enabling amendment in the Opium Act was imple-

[6] In 2009 and 2010 there were also policy letters in reaction to the advice of the committee, but these were conceived by a cabinet under resignation (Tweede Kamer 2009, 2010).

mented. Since then, cannabis has been listed on Schedule II for soft drugs. Small-scale sale of cannabis in coffee shops developed in the slipstream of the system, and the commercialization that resulted was unintended.

Both criminal and administrative law apply to coffee shops. Guidelines for investigation and prosecution of Opium Act offenses by the public prosecutor, described in table 3, set out criteria for nonprosecution of coffee shops. The first specifications of these criteria date to 1991. Since then, the criteria were sharpened and expanded.

Apart from these criteria, a coffee shop is not allowed to sell alcohol. If a coffee shop fails to comply with one of these criteria, the mayor can apply administrative measures, varying from a fine to closure of the shop for a definite or indefinite period. The public prosecutor can prosecute the coffee shop owner and staff. The severity of the sanction depends on the violation. The presence of hard drugs and youths is punished more severely than advertising violations, as are repeated violations (de Bruin, Dijkstra, and Breeksema 2008). Local criteria, for instance, banning terraces outside the coffee shop or limiting opening hours, can be applied after consultation of the mayor with the public prosecutor and the police.

TABLE 3

National Criteria Governing Coffee Shops, 2014

	Description
No advertising	No advertising, apart from a minor reference (on the shop)
No hard drugs	It is forbidden to have or sell hard drugs in the shop
No nuisance	Nuisance may consist of parking problems around coffee shops, noise, litter, or customers who loiter in front of or in the neighborhood of the coffee shop
No young people	No selling to and no access by young people under age 18; strict enforcement focuses on customers younger than 18 years
No large quantities	No selling of large quantities per transaction, which means quantities larger than suitable for personal use (5 grams); a transaction comprises all buying and selling in one coffee shop on the same day by one same customer; furthermore, the maximum selling stock is 500 grams
No nonresidents	Access to residents of the Netherlands only*

Source.—Staatscourant (2015), Directive Opium Act 2015.

* This criterion has been applied since May 2012 in the southern Netherlands and was extended in a revised version to the whole country in 2013. Enforcement is a local matter.

Compliance is checked periodically by municipalities, local police, and other agencies such as tax authorities. Customer IDs and the stock of cannabis on the premises are checked. The mayor, the public prosecutor, and the police agree on enforcement actions. Bieleman et al. (2013) in 2012 surveyed all 671 coffee shops in municipalities that permit them. Fifty-six violations were recorded (compared with 51 in 2011), mainly for the maximum stock criterion (13 municipalities), the youth criterion (seven municipalities), and the residence criterion (seven municipalities).

These regulations concern the "front door" policy relating to the sale of cannabis. The "back door" problem is that there are no regulations to establish an official authorized system for coffee shops to obtain cannabis. The police turn a blind eye to its purchase, as long as this is done discreetly and in small quantities. This makes the system vulnerable. Tijhuis (2006) points out that coffee shops are in a complicated interface position between the illegal production market and the tolerated sale of cannabis to consumers. Mayors call this a "balancing act" and demand further regulation (Gemeente Utrecht 2014). The minister of security and justice, however, has consistently refused (e.g., Tweede Kamer 2013*c*, 2013*e*, 2013*f*, 2014*f*):

> *Member of Parliament of the Socialist Party*: We can sell weed. Why does the Minister not choose to make an exception concerning the cultivation of weed?[7]
>
> *Minister*: No, for one thing I am unable to do it and besides that I don't want to do it. I can't put it more clearly or concise than that. (Tweede Kamer 2013, p. 29)

Governmental regulation of cannabis cultivation is incompatible with international treaties (T. M. C. Asser Instituut 2005; van Kempen and Fedorova 2014). Van Kempen and Fedorova (2014, p. 242) conclude that "legalization, decriminalization, policy-based tolerance and/or other forms of regulating cannabis cultivation for the recreational user market

[7] The Netherlands imposed a limitation concerning art. 3, subsec. 6, of the UN Illicit Traffic Convention of 1988. This limitation is a basis for toleration of coffee shops (e.g., Brouwer and Schilder 2012; van Kempen and Fedorova 2014).

is not permissible under the UN Narcotic Drugs Conventions or European Law."

The Dutch government has also concluded that formal regulation of cannabis cultivation would violate international treaties and would not solve existing problems; most Dutch-cultivated cannabis is exported (Jansen 2012; Tweede Kamer 2013*c*, 2014*e*, 2014*f*, 2014*h*; van der Giessen, Moolenaar, and van Ooyen-Houben 2014). Twenty-five mayors, however, developed a "Manifest Joint Regulation" in 2013 that pleaded for regulation of cannabis cultivation for supply of coffee shops. The city of Utrecht announced a noncommercial "social cannabis club" in 2013. The Ministry of Health, Welfare, and Sports and the Ministry of Security and Justice both forbade this initiative.

Coffee shops need a license from the mayor to sell coffee and other legal products but also to sell cannabis. The decision to tolerate coffee shops is made at a municipal level, by the mayor in consultation with the public prosecutor and the police and with approval by the city council.

Seventy-six percent of municipalities (312 of 415) in 2012 did not permit coffee shops. The number has remained more or less the same over the years (Bieleman et al. 2013). Shops are scattered throughout the country but concentrated in the most populated regions and in medium-sized cities. Amsterdam had the highest number in 2012 (208) and the highest concentration: one per 3,513 inhabitants. Rotterdam had 41 coffee shops, and The Hague, 37.

Developments concerning coffee shops and cannabis use are closely monitored:

- Since 1997 the National Prevalence Study, a periodic survey of use of all drugs, not only cannabis, has been conducted every 4 years among a sample of the population age 15–64 (e.g., van Rooij, Schoenmakers, and van de Mheen 2011).
- Since 1988 a school survey of use of all drugs has been conducted every 4 years among 12–18-year-olds in regular secondary education (e.g., Verdurmen et al. 2012).
- Since 1999, the number of coffee shops, violations of tolerance criteria, and coffee shop policies at a local level have been regularly monitored (e.g., Bieleman et al. 2013).
- Since 2000, the THC content and prices of cannabis sold by coffee shops have been regularly monitored by buying samples of cannabis, which are then chemically analyzed (e.g., Rigter and Niesink 2014).

- Since 1986, addiction care agencies have continuously monitored and reported annually on treatment demand (e.g., Wisselink, Kuijpers, and Mol 2013).
- Health incidents in relation to drugs are monitored and reported annually (e.g., Vogels and Croes 2013).
- Finally, tens of reports on new measures are released at national and local levels.

The annual National Drug Monitor contains a comprehensive chapter on cannabis (e.g., van Laar et al. 2013, 2014). The monitor is sent to Parliament with an accompanying letter from the secretary of state of health, welfare, and sports (Tweede Kamer 2013*d*).

A. Coffee Shops: Facts and Figures

Most users buy their cannabis in a coffee shop: 70 percent according to Korf et al. (2005); 56–67 percent according to van Laar, van Ooyen-Houben, and Monshouwer (2009); 82–94 percent according to Korf, Benschop, and Wouters (2013, 2014; in municipalities with coffee shops). According to van der Giessen, Moolenaar, and van Ooyen-Houben (2014) the market share of coffee shops is an estimated 62–85 percent. Table 4 shows data from Korf, Benschop, and Wouters (2013). They are based on a March–April 2012 street survey of 942 cannabis users in 14 municipalities with coffee shops. Results distinguish between users in the southern provinces and elsewhere. This was before more restrictive measures came into force in the southern provinces (see below).[8] Those surveyed were between ages 18 and 66; the mean was 24.3 years. Most users (94.4 percent in both groups) bought their cannabis in the past 3 months mostly in a coffee shop. In 2013, this proportion was somewhat lower as a consequence of more restrictive measures adopted in May 2012 (Korf et al. 2014). Korf et al. (2013) identified other sources: mobile phone dealers, self-growers, home dealers, street dealers, under-the-counter dealers, and other dealers. Some users cultivated cannabis themselves.

[8] Figures from March to April 2012 provide the best approximation. The percentages decreased after adoption of restrictions on coffee shops in the three southern provinces in May 2012 (Korf et al. 2013) but increased when restrictions were loosened in 2013 (van Ooyen-Houben, Bieleman, and Korf 2014). In 2013, the situation was not stable yet.

TABLE 4

Sources of Cannabis, Last 3 Months, Numbers and Percentages, March–April 2012

	Southern Provinces		Other Provinces	
	Number	Percent	Number	Percent
Where did users obtain their cannabis:				
Bought in a coffee shop	403	94.4	486	94.4
Bought from a mobile phone dealer	35	8.2	25	4.9
Bought from a self-grower	22	5.2	34	6.6
Bought from a home dealer	34	8.0	44	8.6
Bought from a street dealer	42	9.9	25	4.9
Bought from an under-the-counter dealer	5	1.2	5	1.0
Bought from a home dealer at a usual meeting place	3	.7	4	.8
Bought elsewhere	2	.5	5	1.0
Bought from friends who live in the Netherlands	35	8.2	26	5.1
Self-cultivated	21	4.9	19	3.7
Provided free of charge	84	19.7	121	23.5
N	427		515	

SOURCE.—Korf, Benschop, and Wouters (2013).

Nijkamp and Bieleman (2013) and Nijkamp, Mennes, and Bieleman (2014) asked 1,045 and 720 visitors to coffee shops, respectively, how easy it was to buy cannabis in the Netherlands. Perceived availability was high: 9.0–9.3 in 2012 on a 1–10 scale and 9.0–9.2 in 2013.

Rigter and Niesink (2014) monitored raw prices and percentages of THC in cannabis bought from coffee shops. As figure 4 shows, prices of the most popular Dutch cannabis ("Netherweed" or "Nederwiet") steadily increased. Without controlling for inflation, prices rose from a mean of €5.85 in 2000 to €9.50–€9.60 in 2013–14, roughly 64 percent. Between 2000 and 2004, the percentage of THC doubled from 9 to 20 percent and then fell until 2009. Between 2010 and 2013, the average concentration decreased again from 17.8 to 13.5 percent. In 2014 it was 15 percent.

The absence of sharp troughs in the percentage of THC (the "retail purity") in combination with the absence of fluctuations in raw prices may indicate that there were no robust market disruptions in supply of Nederwiet to coffee shops after 2000 (at least until 2013). So suggested

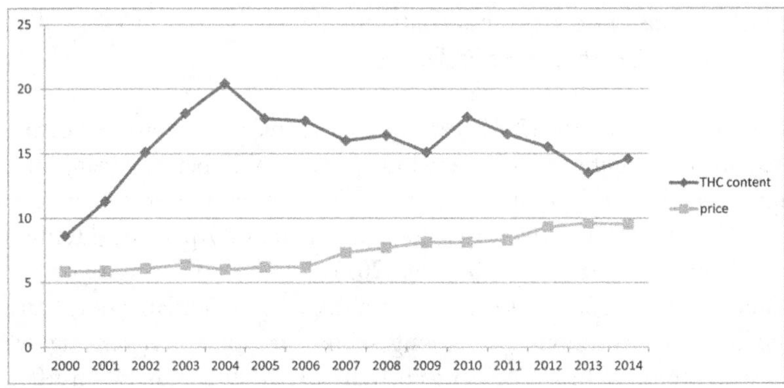

FIG. 4.—Percentage THC content and mean price per gram, most popular Nederwiet in coffee shops, 2000–2014. Source: THC-monitor Trimbos Institute; Rigter and Niesink (2014).

Caulkins, Rajderkar, and Vasudev (2010) in an analysis of purity-adjusted prices.

Characteristics of coffee shop customers have often been studied (Surmont 2005, 2007; Bieleman and Naayer 2007; Korf, Doekhie, and Wouters 2011; Nijkamp and Bieleman 2013):

- Over 80 percent are male with a mean age of 24–32 years.
- The majority are students or employed.
- Many take cannabis with them for use at home. Around half do not smoke cannabis on the premises.
- The majority use cannabis daily or several times a week. In one study, 64 percent were daily users and 20 percent used two to three times a week.
- Visits reflect the amounts used.
- Coffee shops have a substantial proportion of regular customers.
- The quality and reliability of the cannabis is important; if cannabis in a shop is good and of constant quality, customers will continue to purchase there.
- Friendly attitudes of staff, a "cozy" atmosphere, and the presence of friends and acquaintances play important roles.
- Price and accessibility (close to home or en route to school or work) play less important roles.

- About one-third of respondents bought in more than one coffee shop per day; they traveled farther.

Trends in use among 12–18-year-olds in regular secondary education are shown in figure 5. Use peaked in 1996, with 22 percent being lifetime users (lifetime prevalence) and 11 percent current users (last month prevalence), and later decreased to approximately 17 percent (lifetime) and 8 percent (current) in 2007 and 2011. Numbers have more or less stabilized since 2003. Use among youths in (residential) youth care and judicial institutions and among school dropouts is much higher, ranging from 29 to 65 percent current use in studies between 2006 and 2009 (van Laar et al. 2013, 2014).

The lifetime prevalence of cannabis use among the general population age 15–64 in 1997 was around 19 percent; in 2005, 23 percent. Recent use (last year prevalence) was around 5 percent and current use around 3 percent (van Rooij, Schoenmakers, and van de Mheen 2011). The prevalence figures were stable during 1997–2005. In 2009 they were higher: 26 percent lifetime use, 7 percent recent use, and 4 percent current use. There is, however, a problem with comparability of data since 2009 due to a change in data collection methods (van Rooij, Schoenmakers, and van de Mheen 2011).[9]

Making international comparisons is difficult because of differences in method and years of assessment. Also, the validity of self-reported use is not known. Van Laar et al. (2013, 2014) report international comparisons concerning cannabis in the general population age 15–64 for European Union countries and Norway. The Netherlands level is near the average. Romania, Malta, Lithuania, Hungary, Estonia, Bulgaria, Sweden, and Greece rank lowest (1 percent or less current use). Spain and the United States rank highest (7 percent current use). The Netherlands figure is 4 percent (van Laar et al. 2013, 2014; see also EMCDDA 2012).

Better international comparisons are possible for 15–16-year-olds who attend regular secondary schools (because the studies use comparable methods).[10] Current use was highest in France (24 percent) and the United States (18 percent) in 2011 and lowest in Norway, Sweden,

[9] In 2009 respondents filled out the questionnaire themselves. More anonymous and privacy-protecting methods, such as in 2009, appear to produce higher prevalence figures (van Laar et al. 2013, p. 60).

[10] See the European School Survey Project on Alcohol and Other Drugs (ESPAD).

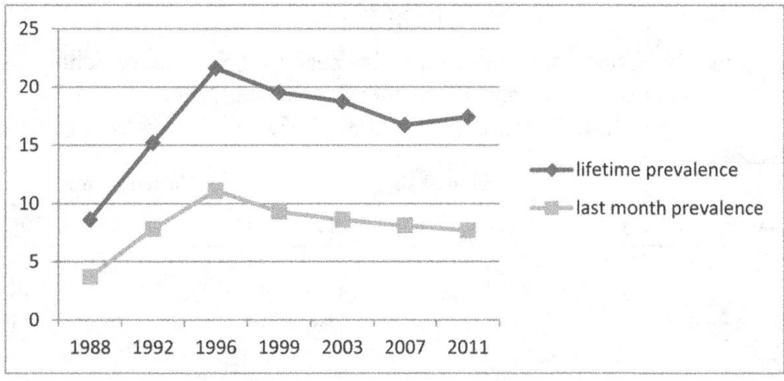

FIG. 5.—Cannabis use prevalence among 12–18-year-olds in regular secondary education. Source: Peilstationsonderzoek, Trimbos Institute; Verdurmen et al. (2012).

and Finland (2–3 percent).[11] Dutch adolescents ranked fourth highest (14 percent; van Laar et al. 2013, 2014; see table 5).

B. Does the Coffee Shop System Work?

1. *Separating Soft and Hard Drugs Markets.* Coffee shops dominate the consumer market for cannabis, thereby keeping users—for the most part—away from illegal drug markets (van Laar, van Ooyen-Houben, and Monshouwer 2009). Research indicates that consumer markets for cannabis and for hard drugs like heroin, crack, cocaine, and amphetamines are more separate in the Netherlands than in other European countries and the United States. It would appear that the coffee shop system contributes to separation of the markets and weakens links to hard drug markets (MacCoun and Reuter 2001). From a health perspective, this is a good result. Pertinent research findings are as follows.

- Coffee shops are the most important direct or indirect source for the purchase of cannabis. The likelihood of finding hard drugs in a coffee shop is low (Korf et al. 2005; de Bruin, Dijkstra, and Breeksema 2008; van Laar, van Ooyen-Houben, and Monshouwer 2009; Monshouwer, van Laar, and Vollebergh 2011; Bieleman et al. 2013; Korf et al. 2013).

[11] The surveys in the United States are comparable to ESPAD.

TABLE 5

Cannabis Consumption, 15- and 16-Year-Old Secondary School Students: European Union Member States, Norway, and the United States, 1999, 2003, 2007, and 2011 (%)

	Lifetime Use				Current Use			
Country	1999	2003	2007	2011	1999	2003	2007	2011
France	35	38	31	39	22	22	15	24
United States*	41	36	31	35	19	17	14	18
Netherlands	28	28	28	27	14	13	15	14
Spain†	. . .	36	36	26	. . .	22	20	15
Belgium‡	. . .	32	24	24	. . .	17	12	11
Italy	25	27	23	21	14	15	13	12
Germany§	. . .	27	20	19	. . .	12	7	7
Ireland	32	39	20	18	15	17	9	7
Denmark†	24	23	25	18	8	8	10	6
Portugal	8	15	13	16	5	8	6	9
Finland	10	11	8	11	2	3	2	3
Sweden	8	7	7	9	2	1	2	3
Greece	9	6	6	8	4	2	3	4
Norway	12	9	6	5	4	3	2	2
Switzerland	. . .	40	33	. . .	. . .	20	15	. . .
United Kingdom‖	35	38	29	. . .	16	20	11	. . .
Austria	. . .	21	17	. . .	. . .	10	6	. . .

SOURCE.—European School Survey Project on Alcohol and Other Drugs (ESPAD), reported in van Laar et al. (2014).

* The United States did not participate in ESPAD but conducted comparable surveys.

† Data are less representative.

‡ In 2007 and 2011, only Flanders.

§ In 2007 for six and in 2011 for five of the 16 states.

‖ No data for 2011 because of too low response rate (only six of the schools).

- Away from coffee shops there is a lively trade in cannabis and other (party) drugs (Korf et al. 2005; Blokker et al. 2011; Snippe and Bieleman 2012). The risk of mixing hard drugs and soft drugs is higher (Korf et al. 2005; van Laar, van Ooyen-Houben, and Monshouwer 2009; Monshouwer, van Laar, and Vollebergh 2011).
- The higher the coffee shop density in an area, the lower the likelihood that users buy cannabis outside the coffee shop system (Wouters 2012).
- Separation of markets seems to have decreased the correlation between cannabis use and use of cocaine and amphetamines (MacCoun

2011). Separating soft and hard drugs markets may have reduced the "gateway" to hard drug use (MacCoun 2010).

- Dutch cannabis users use relatively little heroin or crack but relatively more ecstasy (van Laar, van Ooyen-Houben, and Monshouwer 2009; Monshouwer, van Laar, and Vollebergh 2011).

2. *The Commercialization Hypothesis.* A "commercialization hypothesis" has been the subject of debate. MacCoun and Reuter (1997) examined the effects of the Dutch cannabis policy since 1976. They analyzed the prevalence of use in the Netherlands and observed that commercial promotion and sales by coffee shops between 1984 and 1992 paralleled an increase in use by youths in the Netherlands that was not observed in other nations. They argued that the rapid proliferation of commercial retail cannabis outlets is a plausible explanation for the increase in prevalence of use.

What does the evidence show?

- Korf (1995) also observed a correlation in the 1980s between prevalence of cannabis use and the rising number of coffee shops. He compared trends in Amsterdam with trends in Hamburg. He concluded that the increase in use is attributable to increased availability of cannabis associated with the coffee shops.
- De Zwart and van Laar (2001) observed that causal conclusions cannot be based on correlations and that MacCoun and Reuter's comparisons of prevalence rates were unconvincing because of differences in samples and methods. The increase in cannabis use seemed to have taken place much earlier in the United States than in Europe. De Zwart and van Laar rejected the commercialization hypothesis and argued that trends in drug use result from a complex interplay of factors.
- Van Laar, van Ooyen-Houben, and Monshouwer (2009) and Monshouwer, van Laar, and Vollebergh (2011) observed trends in the use of cannabis and found that they paralleled the number of coffee shops. There was a clear increase in the 1980s and the first half of the 1990s in both, followed by stabilization in use and then a decrease when the number of coffee shops decreased. They observed, however, that the increase in cannabis use was not an isolated phenomenon but also occurred in other countries without coffee shops. It seemed therefore not plausible to attribute the Netherlands increase

to the coffee shops. Besides, the prevalence of cannabis use in the Netherlands did not show excessive trends upward when compared to other countries, whereas the age of onset of cannabis use is relatively low in the Netherlands.

- Palali and van Ours (2013) conducted exploratory analysis on the age of onset of cannabis use, using data from a 2008 survey with a retrospective question on the age of onset. They report indications that youngsters who live more than 20 kilometers from a municipality with a coffee shop have a lower starting rate of cannabis use, and youngsters living closer to coffee shops are more likely to start using cannabis earlier on. The overall welfare effect, however, also depends on how the closeness of coffee shops affects the intensity of use, total cannabis consumption, and the uptake of other drugs.
- MacCoun (2011) correlated trends in use with trends in the number of coffee shops over a longer period. Like others, he compared use patterns in the general population and coffee shops numbers and concluded there was only a modest correlation. He also concluded that the coffee shops did not appear to encourage escalation into heavier use or lengthier using careers, although cannabis treatment rates are higher than elsewhere in Europe. MacCoun observed that Netherlands use patterns are typical for Europe but that Dutch youths report higher-than-average availability of cannabis. He calculated that cannabis use is lower than would be expected in a free market and concluded that the coffee shops did not cause an escalation in heavy cannabis use. MacCoun (2010) observed that the increase in cannabis use in the 1980s and early 1990s occurred in a hybrid system, in which high-level enforcement probably kept prices higher than they would have been in a fully legalized scheme.
- Cannabis users find other suppliers in illegal retail markets when there are no coffee shops or when the entrance to coffee shops is restricted (Korf et al. 2005; Korf, Benschop, and Wouters 2013; Nijkamp and Bieleman 2013; Korf et al. 2014; Nijkamp, Mennes, and Bieleman 2014). Displacement to illegal retail markets after the introduction of restrictions on coffee shops was confirmed by local experts (van Ooyen-Houben and van der Giessen 2013).

It seems that coffee shops and the decriminalization policy thus contributed at most modestly to an increase in cannabis use, despite the possible influence of proximity of coffee shops on age of onset of use. Van 't

Loo et al. (2003) conclude that the evidence does not support a strong connection between the coffee shop policy and the prevalence of cannabis use. Nor does it disprove a connection. The deciding factor for changes in cannabis use in the Netherlands is not depenalization but the form it takes (van 't Loo et al. 2003, p. 39). Other factors, such as the perceived benefits or harmfulness of cannabis, availability and price, severity of sanctions, chances of getting caught, and characteristics of the youth culture, seem to play major roles (e.g., Korf 1995; de Zwart and van Laar 2001; van 't Loo et al. 2003; Monshouwer 2008; Monshouwer, van Laar, and Vollebergh 2011; Wouters 2012). These factors are probably influenced by the policy and the presence of coffee shops, but they also seem to play a role independently from the presence of coffee shops.

The commercialization hypothesis may have been valid in the 1980s, when there was an exponential growth of coffee shops (Korf 1995; Korf et al. 2001). For later periods, the story is more complicated. Our alternative hypothesis is that neither depenalization nor the coffee shop model is decisive and that other factors, partly mediated by the coffee shop system, play more prominent roles. This would explain why the prevalence of cannabis use is high in countries without coffee shops and even higher in the United States, Spain, and France. It also explains why restrictions on coffee shops have not substantially influenced cannabis use. Enough cannabis is available on the domestic market, and it can be obtained through other channels (van Ooyen-Houben, Bieleman, and Korf 2014).

That the coffee shops operate in a regulated system may also play a role. Commercialization was limited after the early 1990s (at least within a certain range) by restrictive criteria for toleration (see table 3; de Zwart and van Laar 2001). The license system and the local constraints on the number of coffee shops led to a controlled number of coffee shops. Local authorities have effective instruments to control the coffee shop situation (van Ooyen-Houben, Bieleman, and Korf 2014).

Pessimistic assessments, however, have been offered. Van Laar, van Ooyen-Houben, and Monshouwer (2009) and van Laar et al. (2013, 2014) report that the prevalence of cannabis use among Dutch adolescents in regular secondary schools is relatively high compared with other countries. Young people perceive cannabis as easily available and the associated risks to be lower than do young people in other countries. The high level of use was identified as a problem by experts and policy makers (Adviescommissie Drugsbeleid 2009; Tweede Kamer 2011*a*). Van Laar, van Ooyen-Houben, and Monshouwer (2009) report that users of cannabis use more hard drugs than do nonusers. Use is higher among vulnerable young people and young people who suffer from aggression, problems at school, and psychological problems (van Laar et al. 2013). For some users, cannabis can trigger psychotic symptoms or addiction (e.g., van den Brink 2006; de Graaf et al. 2012; van der Pol 2014). Van der Pol (2014) assessed a group of frequent users—coffee shop customers, mean age at first assessment 22 years—over a 3-year period. Thirty-seven percent showed the first symptoms of cannabis dependence during the 3 years.

Cannabis seems not to be as harmless for all users as was first thought in the 1970s. The number of admissions to addiction care facilities for cannabis-related problems has increased (van Laar et al. 2013). The relatively high levels of THC in Dutch cannabis make homegrown Nederwiet potentially more harmful (according to the Expertcommissie Lijstensystematiek Opiumwet 2011; see also fig. 4). However, cannabis was ranked as a low-risk drug by the Coordination Point for the Assessment and Monitoring of Drugs in 2009 (van Amsterdam et al. 2009).

3. *Unintended Side Effects.* The lenient policy toward cannabis produced several unwanted side effects. They were to a large extent unforeseen and were not taken into account by policy makers in the early 1970s.

Van de Bunt (2006) reviewed policy documents preceding the changes in the Opium Law (1976) and highlights the one-sided focus on users and risks to users. Important arguments for changes were that the state should not interfere with the individual choices of citizens, that risks to users were much less than from heroin, and that a "separation of markets" would insulate cannabis users from hard drug consumption. This one-sided focus on health risks for users was paralleled by a general neglect of the processes associated with tolerated use of soft drugs and a naive view of the commercial attractiveness of soft drugs markets (van de Bunt 2006). The dominant ideas for the influential Hulsman Committee were that youths would buy soft drugs from reliable "home dealers" in a youth activity center, that "trade" was not an issue, and that the Netherlands was too small and uninteresting to attract international organized drug traders. Van de Bunt (2006, p. 15) quotes the committee's proposition that in the Netherlands "not many people will get 'rich' from the cannabis trade." These blind spots, he suggests, explain why the emergence and exponential growth of coffee shops after the 1980s—in the mid-1990s there were an estimated 1,100–1,500 (Tweede Kamer 1995; Korf 2011)—came as such a surprise. That is also true of other unintended side effects.

One involved "drug tourism." The Netherlands is close to Germany, Belgium, and France, which makes coffee shops easily accessible. In some cities 70–90 percent of coffee shop customers were from abroad (Surmont 2005, 2007; Rovers and Fijnaut 2011; Snippe, Nijkamp, and Bieleman 2012; Mein and van Ooyen 2013). There were at times thousands of visitors per day, adding up to a few million a year. In Maastricht, close to the German and Belgian borders, the annual number of foreign visitors was estimated at 2–3 million (COT Instituut voor Veiligheids- en Crisismanagement 2011). Some coffee shops became large commercial enterprises. One called Checkpoint in Terneuzen, a border city close to Belgium, in 2006 attracted 2,000–2,500 foreign customers per day, 200 per hour, mostly Belgians and French (Surmont 2005, 2007).

Citizens complained about nuisances. This involved double parking, youths hanging around, noise and music from cars, loud talking, smoking joints in porches, the smell of cannabis, traffic, and parking problems (van Ooyen-Houben, Bieleman, et al. 2009).[12]

Other unintended consequences included the emergence of major cannabis trafficking by organized crime groups and indoor cultivation in the Netherlands (e.g., de Kort 1995; Fijnaut et al. 1998; Bovenkerk and Hogewind 2003; Korf et al. 2006; Kleemans 2007; Spapens, van de Bunt, and Rastovac 2007; Decorte et al. 2011).

In both political and practical terms, it is impossible to combine tolerance of cannabis supply in coffee shops with strict enforcement of laws forbidding sales to coffee shops (which are illegal). As a result, the illegal supply of coffee shops was for long a very low law enforcement priority. Cross-border trafficking of hard drugs, particularly heroin and cocaine, was a much higher priority and involved much higher sentences than cannabis trafficking. The trafficking of cannabis flourished under the low enforcement priority (de Kort 1995). Fijnaut et al. (1998) describe how Dutch seamen, engaged in the early 1970s in hydraulic engineering

[12] Recent research has shown that in 2011 and 2012 nuisances experienced by people in the direct vicinity of coffee shops were not that serious in many places (De Hoog et al. 2012) and restricted to a some municipalities in border regions (van Ooyen-Houben, Bieleman, and Korf 2013, 2014).

projects near Dubai, came into contact with Pakistani hashish exporters. Dutch criminal entrepreneurs funded large shipments of hashish from Pakistan to the Netherlands and to other European countries and North America (Fijnaut et al. 1998, p. 74). Access to the condoned Dutch retail market and lenient law enforcement facilitated the growth of these criminal networks. The presence of a substantial Moroccan immigrant population also facilitated import of cannabis from Morocco in later years. In recent decades, the cultivation of homegrown indoor Dutch cannabis has made an appearance. Dutch cannabis has largely replaced imported cannabis (Korf et al. 2006). Bovenkerk and Hogewind (2003) analyzed police files and found that cultivation was widespread. They suggested that criminal networks were involved that compelled people to join cannabis cultivation networks. This prompted a government "cannabis letter" that included a range of measures aimed at curbing professional cannabis cultivation (Tweede Kamer 2004).

Spapens, van de Bunt, and Rastovac (2007) analyzed 19 closed large-scale criminal investigations and interviewed 16 professional cannabis growers. They describe the production process and the organization of cannabis cultivation and paint a different picture than did Bovenkerk and Hogewind. They deny the existence of substantial coercion and describe a logistic process that is strongly "democratized." Many people have the necessary knowledge and skills, and most of the required materials are widely used and could easily be acquired at so-called grow-shops: "They usually supply all the necessary legal cultivation equipment and they also give advice to growers. None of these activities are currently punishable by law.[13] However, there are also a number of mala fide grow shops that will refer prospective cannabis growers to sellers of cuttings, wholesale cannabis buyers and service providers such as electricians or 'grow room builders.' They also collect hemp waste from cannabis growers" (Spapens, van de Bunt, and Rastovac 2007, pp. 143–44).

Criminal groups are involved in cannabis cultivation but are part of a wider landscape involving four categories. Small-scale independent growers, operating at their own risk and using their own financial resources, typically grow 100–1,000 plants on their own premises. Large-scale independent growers, operating plantations in (rented) commercial

[13] Since 2014, these activities are punishable.

properties, grow 1,000 or more plants. Smallest-scale operators install five to 10 plants in other people's houses (mostly acquaintances). Criminal groups, the fourth category,

> are involved in buying, processing and selling cannabis products on a large scale and, in addition, often run their own sizeable plantations. They have one or more grow shops at their disposal, or a less visible address where independent growers or operators can deliver their harvests. . . . A turnover of 100 to 200 kilos per week is not unusual. . . . Criminal cooperatives play an important role in the world behind the cultivation of cannabis, not because they force people into installing plantations in their homes, but because they provide an assured market to independent growers and operators. They offer growers and operators an opportunity to cultivate cannabis in the knowledge that they will have no difficulty selling their harvest. (Spapens, van de Bunt, and Rastovac 2007, pp. 144–45)

Negative aspects of indoor cannabis cultivation relate to criminal involvement, criminal revenues, and its assumed export orientation. Recent estimates by the national police of the rate of export range from 48 to 97 percent, with 85 percent being the most plausible (Jansen 2012). A new study was conducted (van der Giessen, Moolenaar, and van Ooyen-Houben 2014), which reports its most plausible estimate of the Netherlands export as 78–91 percent of the domestic production when consumption by nonresidents is defined as "domestic consumption" and 86–95 percent when consumption by nonresidents is defined as "export." Apart from this, indoor cultivation uses large amounts of electricity and water that are often illegally obtained (e.g., by diverting electricity) and present dangers to neighbors and premises (Gemeente Utrecht 2014).

C. *Coffee Shops under Attack*

The 1995 policy letter already touched on most of these problems. It announced measures but maintained a strong focus on the primarily health-oriented strategy (Tweede Kamer 1995). In 2009, the Advisory Committee Drug Policy characterized the situation with coffee shops as "urgent" (Adviescommissie Drugsbeleid 2009). They have since become a recurring subject of debate in municipalities and in Parliament. Several policy changes have been implemented at national and local levels. The system has become more restrictive.

The first coffee shops opened in the beginning of the 1980s, after which the number rose sharply. The 1995 policy letter observed that "the in themselves valuable coffee shops did, however, increase in number and burden" (Tweede Kamer 1995, p. 37). It was estimated that there were then 1,100–1,200 coffee shops (1,500 according to Korf [2011]). The policy letter supported local initiatives to "rationalize" the coffee shop policy and decrease their number. As figure 6 shows, the number fell 27 percent from 846 in 1999 to 614 in April 2013.

The reduction has several causes, among which is the implementation of municipal policies aimed at the "eradication" of coffee shops, implying that no new ones will be authorized once an existing shop closes or violates regulations. In some cases, local ordinances forbidding coffee shops within a certain distance from schools led to the closure of several. The city of Rotterdam, for example, in 2009 closed 16 coffee shops located within 250 meters from schools (Bieleman, Nijkamp, and Sijtstra 2011; Nijkamp and Bieleman 2012).

D. Constraints on Criteria for Tolerance at a National Level

The national criteria for toleration of coffee shops, described in the Directive Opium Act for the public prosecutor in 1991, have been subject to restrictions and specifications since 1995:

- The maximum transaction per customer per day was reduced from 30 to 5 grams (Staatscourant 1996).
- Access was restricted to persons over age 18 (Staatscourant 1996).
- The maximum amount of cannabis in stock was limited to 500 grams (Staatscourant 1996).
- Coffee shops are required to be alcohol-free premises (Staatscourant 1996).
- Limits on advertising were established in 2006.

In 2011, further restrictions were announced:

- Coffee shops had to become private clubs with access limited to Netherlands residents in 2012 (Staatscourant 2011).
- In 2013 no coffee shop could be located within 350 meters from schools for secondary education and secondary vocational education (Tweede Kamer 2011*a*).

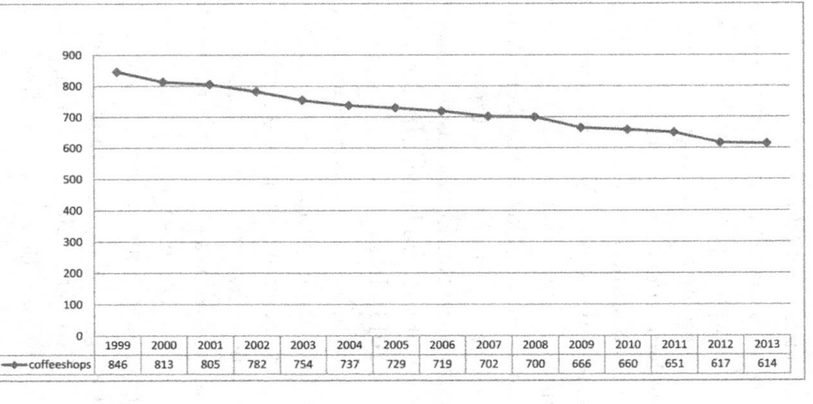

FIG. 6.—Coffee shops, the Netherlands, 1999–April 2013. Source: Bieleman et al. (2013)

- The government initiated the procedure to transfer cannabis with a THC level of 15 percent or more to Schedule I of the Opium Act (Tweede Kamer 2012, 2014*b*, 2014*c*, 2014*d*). Coffee shops will only be allowed to sell cannabis with a THC level lower than 15 percent.[14]

The introduction of the private club requirement and the rule denying entrance to persons living outside the Netherlands are substantial changes. Enforcement started as a pilot in May 2012 in three provinces where the problems of nuisance and drug tourism were most urgent. The remaining provinces were supposed to follow in January 2013.

The introduction of these measures was evaluated in 14 municipalities, seven in the southern provinces where they were implemented and seven in other provinces where they were not. The researchers assessed nuisances around coffee shops, the number of coffee shop visits, characteristics of visitors, and developments on the illegal market. They also assessed implementation (van Ooyen-Houben, Bieleman, and Korf 2013). There were three assessments: a baseline, one after 6 months, and another after 18 months. One conclusion was that drug tourists stayed away after introduction of the residence criterion (Korf et al. 2013; Nijkamp and Bieleman 2013). In this respect, it was successful.

The private club criterion, however, was not successful. It had a number of adverse side effects. Some former customers, Netherlands residents, turned away from the coffee shops and started buying cannabis on the illegal market, thus fostering nuisance from street dealers. These people did not want to register as a club member (van Ooyen-Houben, Bieleman, and Korf 2013).[15] There was a substantial increase in the illegal cannabis consumer market. Young customers age 18–24 in particular turned away. The growing illegal market attracted young dealers with a vulnerable background (Korf et al. 2014; Nijkamp, Mennes, and Bieleman 2014; van Ooyen-Houben, Bieleman, and Korf 2014).

Instances of nuisance in the vicinities of the coffee shops were not significantly reduced but changed in nature. Initially, neighbors were

[14] This procedure was underway at the time of writing. There was opposition from some parties in the Lower House. Most political parties support the measure, so it will probably be approved. If so, some observers anticipate risks of displacement to illegal markets and issues concerning the control of the THC level by coffee shops and police.

[15] Registration was controlled by the police and the local authorities. Coffee shops often themselves use a "pass" system to control the 5 grams per person limit, but this is not controlled by official authorities.

bothered by nuisances associated with the coffee shop. After the new measures were implemented, neighbors were bothered by illegal street dealers (Snippe and Bieleman 2013). The new criteria had no influence on the use of cannabis among Netherlands residents (Korf et al. 2013).

The government rescinded the private club criterion in November 2012. The planned national distance criterion of 350 meters was also rescinded. The residence criterion remained in force but was adapted: local authorities can decide whether to enforce it (Tweede Kamer 2012).

After the removal of the private club criterion, residents returned to the coffee shops, but not all. The illegal market decreased but remained bigger than it had been before the policy change.

Drug tourism decreased. However, 10 of the 15 municipalities in the study sample did not enforce the residence criterion. This makes it less effective but nonetheless reduces the role of the illegal markets to which users turned.

The radical entry restrictions were only partly successful. They were also responsible for a number of serious unintended consequences in relation to fundamental policy goals, notably separation of cannabis and hard drug consumer markets and creation of safe places to buy and use cannabis. Too many Dutch customers turned to the illegal market to avoid registration and police control of coffee shop membership. The negative side effects especially affected youths, who turned to the illegal market and were attracted to it as dealers.

E. Constraints on Criteria at a Local Level

Regulations for coffee shops were also tightened at the local level. Municipal criteria for coffee shops became more numerous and restrictive (Bieleman et al. 2013). One municipality limited the maximum amount per transaction to 2 grams. Others restricted opening hours or forbade coffee shops to use a terrace. Some obligated coffee shops to introduce a pass system for their customers or to hire staff to help reduce noise and litter.

Coffee shops in general adhere to all these criteria (de Bruin, Dijkstra, and Breeksema 2008; van Ooyen-Houben and van der Giessen 2013). The number of violations is low (Bieleman et al. 2013). One explanation is that coffee shops are lucrative businesses that their owners do not want to compromise (van Ooyen-Houben and van der Giessen 2013).

F. Relocation and Dispersion of Coffee Shops

Relocating a coffee shop in case of nuisance is difficult (Bootsma 2012). The new location must be selected with care. Residents can initiate judicial procedures and request compensation for expected losses. Some municipalities, such as Rotterdam, refuse to permit relocations. Others, such as Amsterdam, will consider relocation only if the coffee shop can demonstrate that it has done all it could to prevent nuisance at its old location.

One municipality that managed successfully to relocate coffee shops is Venlo, a city close to the German border. It has had to deal with large numbers of German drug tourists since the 1980s (Snippe et al. 2005). By the end of the 1980s, there were 39 coffee shops. In 1995, there were only five. Problems with drug tourists, street dealing, drug runners, and drug-dealing premises led to the decline of the city center at the end of the 1990s. In response, Project Hektor was implemented in 2001. One aim was relocation of two coffee shops away from the city center and toward the German border. It occurred in 2004, in combination with intensive police enforcement against related nuisances and a program to regenerate the city center.

The initiative was a success. Cases of nuisance in the inner city decreased, and German customers found their way to the new location. Thanks to police efforts and active cooperation from the coffee shop, instances of nuisance at the new location stayed within limits. Displacement to other locations was not observed (Snippe, Nijkamp, and Bieleman 2012).

In 2012 and 2013, the situation changed because the two coffee shops near the German border closed. This was at the initiative of the shops themselves but was influenced by the introduction of the residence criterion. After May 2012, drug-related nuisances increased because German customers started buying cannabis from street dealers and friends more often. Local youths became involved in street dealing (Snippe, Nijkamp, and Bieleman 2013). As a consequence, Venlo in 2013 tolerated small numbers of German customers in its coffee shops despite the residence criterion (Snippe, Nijkamp, and Bieleman 2013; van Ooyen-Houben and van der Giessen 2013). The drug-related nuisance decreased but was higher than before.

The municipality of Maastricht also considered relocating coffee shops from the city center to the periphery. However, there was opposition from municipalities, businesses, and individuals in the envisaged new locations. In August 2013, an administrative court (Raad van State) ruled that relocation of coffee shops is a legal option (ECLI: NL:RVS:2013:696). It is unclear what will happen. For coffee shop owners, relocation closer to the border is no longer an attractive option since the residence criterion is enforced.

The city of Terneuzen, located close to the Belgian border, also considered relocation in 2006. Agreement, however, could not be reached. The public prosecutor declared that he could not be held responsible for relocation to the border region. The mayor saw relocation as a solution for the city's nuisance problems (Mein and van Ooyen 2013).

G. Closure of Coffee Shops

Closure is another option. Municipalities are wary, however, as they fear that former customers will turn to the illegal market, thus increasing nuisances by street dealers. Even so, coffee shops have been closed by the mayor. The most prominent example occurred in Bergen op Zoom and Roosendaal, near the Belgian border.

Thousands of Belgian and French drug tourists visited these cities each week, resulting in parking problems, noise, litter, and citizens' complaints. In 2008–9 the mayor, in consultation with the public prosecutor and the local police chief, decided to close all eight coffee shops. The closures in 2009 were a component of a broader project entitled "Courage." It included intensive reinforcement, a targeted communication campaign aimed at drug tourists, and swift responses to nuisance complaints by citizens. Evaluations showed that drug tourism and nuisance were reduced substantially and that there were only limited visible displacement effects on Breda, a neighboring town (Berghuis and de Waard 2010, 2011; van der Torre, Lagendijk, and Bervoets 2010; van der Torre et al. 2013).[16]

The city of Terneuzen, near the Belgian border, provides a second example of coffee shop closure. Terneuzen had a very large coffee shop (Checkpoint) and a smaller one (Miami). Checkpoint attracted many foreign visitors; it was well organized and successful. The constant

[16] See Braga (2007), Bowers et al. (2011), and Braga, Papachristos, and Hureau (2012) for systematic reviews of research on displacement, which confirms the findings reported here.

stream of customers, however, caused incidents of nuisance. Relocation was not an option. The municipality tried to regulate the traffic and parking problems, but this did not stop drug tourism.

In 2007, the police raided Checkpoint. It was suspected of violating the coffee shop criteria. The police discovered much too much stock, 96 kilos (500 grams is the maximum allowed). In another raid in 2008, 130 kilos were confiscated. The owner and some staff were prosecuted. The violations were reason enough to close the coffee shop, initially for 6 months and later permanently. The closure did not result in increased incidents of nuisance in the streets as was expected; the municipality had always feared that street dealing would occur and nuisances would increase. This was why the municipality had long been lenient. The city had even facilitated the growth of the coffee shop, by regulating traffic flow from abroad and providing Checkpoint opportunity to expand. Nuisance associated with the closure was managed by intensive law enforcement (Mein and van Ooyen 2013). Displacement occurred in nearby towns such as Bergen op Zoom and Roosendaal but was limited (Bieleman, Nijkamp, and Buit-Minnema 2009).

Rotterdam, which is not a border city, closed 16 coffee shops on the basis of a new local ordinance that forbade coffee shops to be located within 250 meters from secondary schools. Here also, there were no substantial side effects. The situation was easily managed (Nijkamp and Bieleman 2012).

H. Restrictions and Interventions within an Accepted System

Despite the increased restrictions on running coffee shops, the system as such is not under attack. Local authorities want to maintain coffee shops so as to prevent users turning to illegal markets. As a result, the system is treated with care. Rotterdam wanted to decrease the number of coffee shops but decided to do this slowly and gradually, in order to prevent customers turning to the illegal market (Gemeente Rotterdam 2013). Lelystad, a provincial town, opened a new coffee shop in 2013, to offer its citizens an alternative to the illegal market and to coffee shops farther away (Korf et al. 2013). The mayor of Maastricht sanctioned 13 of the 14 coffee shops in the city with temporary closures for rule violations but did so in phases to ensure that enough coffee shops remained open at any time (van Ooyen-Houben, Bieleman, and Korf 2014).

I. Controlling Cannabis Cultivation

Large-scale professional cultivation of cannabis in the Netherlands has been subject to intensified law enforcement since 2004 (Tweede Kamer 2004). The problem was addressed in the 1995 policy letter but was placed high on the policy agenda only after a study by Bovenkerk and Hogewind (2003), who examined case files and observed police raids of cultivation sites. They concluded that indoor cannabis cultivation was widespread and that criminal networks forced people to become involved. They observed that investigation and prosecution of cannabis cultivation were not law enforcement priorities. This was later confirmed by the Court of Audit (Algemene Rekenkamer), which described a lack in law enforcement (Tweede Kamer 2005). Bovenkerk and Hogewind raised the alarm for policy makers (Tweede Kamer 2003*b*).

Cultivation has been tackled since 2004 by a combination of administrative and financial measures and criminal law. A special task force was created, which resulted in annual dismantling of 5,000–6,000 cultivation sites (van Laar et al. 2013, 2014). Little is known about the scale of cultivation and whether intensified law enforcement reduced it. Some researchers, such as Wouters, Korf, and Kroeske (2007), observed displacement to other less detectable locations, increases in cultivation, and improvements in technology. Police researchers observed a transition to professional commercial cultivators and criminal networks (Korps Landelijke Politiediensten 2008) and to locations abroad (Korps Landelijke Politiediensten 2008; Jansen 2012). As it is difficult to measure cannabis cultivation, these findings are merely observations and indications.

J. Conclusion

Coffee shops function as reliable and safe places for the sale of cannabis to Dutch adults. The system contributes to the separation of consumer markets for cannabis and hard drugs and therefore to achievement of the health and harm-reduction goals of drug policy. Adult users do not have to turn to illegal markets. The system, however, struggled with persistent nuisance and drug tourism problems and flourishing cultivation. Only in 2004 was this tackled by intensified law enforcement. In addition, coffee shops became large-scale, lucrative enterprises.

Authorities reacted through enforcement of rules and criteria in the 1990s. When the problems persisted, more radical policies were adopted, including relocations, closures, introduction of the private club system, and exclusion of nonresidents.

Some of these policies had considerable consequences. The private club criterion led many Dutch customers to turn to the illegal retail market. The residence criterion resulted in an enormous reduction of drug tourism in the south of the country. Relocation of coffee shops has resulted in large reductions in the number of nuisance cases. Complete closures of coffee shops can result in substantial reductions in the number of drug tourists and in nuisances they cause. However, to achieve these goals intensive police involvement is needed. Targeted communication toward drug tourists about closures is also helpful.

These measures influenced only the supply side. The effects of law enforcement efforts on cannabis use prevalence are negligible: there is a continuing demand. After the introduction of the private club criterion, 17 percent of 79 current users in a random street survey cohort stopped their (current) use (Korf, Benschop, and Wouters 2013). However, the decrease also occurred in a comparison group that was interviewed in municipalities where the new policy did not apply. The same trend was visible in the cross-sectional street survey (n = 907). The amount of use did not change. Korf, Benschop, and Wouters conclude that the policy had no influence on the prevalence of cannabis use.

The case of the coffee shops illustrates the shift toward law enforcement and repression over time. The problems have long existed and measures have been taken, but this happened gradually. Important measures were implemented, only in reaction to the urgency of the problems. The shift was tempered by fear of side effects and the policy focus on public health.

III. Ecstasy

The synthetic drug ecstasy, or XTC, is a special case. The Netherlands became a major worldwide producer during the 1990s. Ecstasy can give a sense of intimacy and diminish anxiety; it can induce euphoria and mild psychedelic effects. It is called a "hug drug" (Spapens 2006). Policy concerning ecstasy has had a strong international dimension (Spapens 2006; Neve et al. 2007). It fueled international criticisms of Dutch drug policy, particularly by the United States (Neve et al. 2007).

A. The Rise of Ecstasy

The Netherlands classified ecstasy as a hard drug in 1988. It took some time to decide to do so. Experts could not agree. The main reasons for hard drug classification were signs that preparations for large-scale production and export were occurring (Tweede Kamer 1994). The classification allowed tough enforcement and sanctioning. At the time, however, there were no significant problems with the use or abuse of ecstasy.

The Netherlands was relatively late in criminalizing ecstasy. The United Nations placed it on its drug list in 1986. This delay may partly explain why large-scale production occurred. Producers had more time to settle in than in other countries. Criminal network infrastructure was already in place in the southern Netherlands, which had a tradition of smuggling liquors and amphetamines to Scandinavian countries (Spapens 2006). Chemicals were readily available, thanks to the chemical industries and the harbors of Rotterdam and Antwerp (Spapens 2006).[17] Criminal entrepreneurs in the Netherlands are said to be used to operating in networks, and new groups can easily enter the market (Neve et al. 2007).

In the late 1980s and early 1990s, ecstasy use was mainly incidental and risks were considered low. Korf, Blanken, and Nabben (1991) conducted the first study of use and users. Users appeared to be a heterogeneous group of well-integrated people who attended school or were employed. There were few indications of abuse or adverse consequences.

During the 1990s, use increased, especially among young people at large-scale parties and dance events. Nabben (2010) conducted long-term ethnographic research in the Amsterdam party scene. He describes the sudden emergence of electronic dance music, also known as "house," "techno," "trance," and other terms connected to specific electronic music styles, and how it coincided with large-scale parties and dance events that lasted into the early hours. Ecstasy became increasingly popular as a "party drug," gaining the reputation of a "love drug" because of its affection-stimulating effects. In 1992, 3.4 percent of young people age 12–18 had used ecstasy, and 1 percent had taken it within the last month. As figure 7 shows, these numbers rose in the early 1990s.

The first policy document was formulated by the minister of welfare, health and culture in 1994 (Tweede Kamer 1994). It mainly concerned

[17] Belgium was also an important producer of ecstacy (Neve et al. 2007).

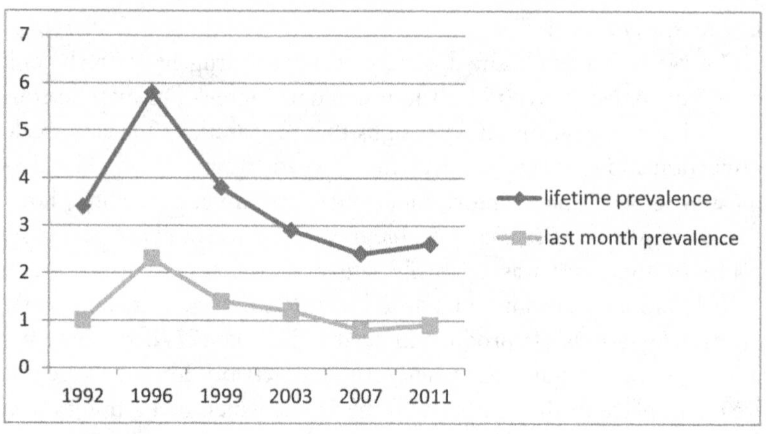

FIG. 7.—Ecstasy use prevalence (in percentages), 12–18-year-old secondary school students. Source: Peilstationsonderzoek, Trimbos Institute; Verdurmen et al. (2012).

prevention of possible health problems. The risks were considered low. Policy makers were reluctant to introduce law enforcement approaches, as it was assumed this would lead to the production of a lower quality of the drug and create greater health risks for users. This assumption was based on evidence from research on users (Korf, Doekhie, and Wouters 2011). This reaction comported with the main objective of Dutch drug policy: prevention and management of risks to individuals and society. A decision was made to monitor the purity and composition of tablets on the consumer market by the Drug Information and Monitoring System. Pill testing at large-scale dance parties became a common occurrence. Other harm-reduction measures were also encouraged, such as providing sufficient supplies of water and areas where people could cool down (Ministerie van Volksgezondheid, Welzijn en Sport 1995).

Production of synthetic drugs flourished in the 1990s. The police published a report on large-scale production as early as 1993 (Korps Landelijke Politiediensten 1993). It was mainly about amphetamines but mentioned ecstasy. There were signals from Belgium and Germany that the Netherlands was becoming a production country (Spapens 2006). Until the mid-1990s, however, ecstasy production did not receive special priority.

In 1995, policy makers acknowledged that the Netherlands had become an important production country, announced a strengthening of law enforcement on production and trafficking, and established a national police squad to control synthetic drugs (Tweede Kamer 1995). They also used new legislation that facilitated prevention of the abuse of chemicals (such as precursor chemicals, the basic chemical ingredients for the production of synthetic drugs) and confiscation of criminal proceeds. There was no sense of urgency in the 1995 policy paper (Spapens 2006). Existing efforts seemed sufficient. Officials hoped that production could be reduced and that this would counteract international criticism.

Spapens (2006) describes how all this changed in 1996. It became clear that ecstasy tablets produced in the Netherlands found their way into neighboring countries (Interregionaal Rechercheteam 1996). Dutch organizations appeared to play a key role in smuggling. Neighboring countries such as France and Germany urged the Netherlands to adopt new policies. The government's initial reaction was one of reluctance. It responded by saying that labs had already been dismantled and that the police were actively pursuing the situation. Spapens quotes the minister of justice: "I think that this in itself is enough for the moment and that we should not also install a flying brigade, as this would focus too much on ecstasy, while there are other matters to focus on" (Tweede Kamer 1996, p. 82).

On the basis of research, it was feared that imposing repressive measures would lead to the production of contaminated or poor-quality tablets, which would increase health risks for users. Dutch policy makers, however, soon decided to opt for a stronger focus on law enforcement. External pressure played a decisive role.

B. Vigorous Law Enforcement and Decline of Ecstasy Production

In 1997, a special police squad was established. The Unit Synthetic Drugs aimed to fight synthetic drugs and precursor chemicals.[18] It became operational in 1998 and developed into a center of expertise. It gathered and coordinated information and cooperated with agencies abroad and in national and international investigations. Production facilities were dismantled, and there were many seizures: 1.16 million tablets, 54.3 kilograms of MDMA powder, and 60 liters of base in 1998 and 3.66 million tablets, 406 kilograms of MDMA powder, and 40 liters of base in 1999.

[18] The name in 2004 became the Expertise Centre Synthetic Drugs and Precursor Chemicals.

The efforts seemed to pay off. Ecstasy use appeared to wane: the prevalence of use declined and it became less popular among partygoers (see fig. 7). The Drug Monitoring and Information System, installed in 1992 at the Trimbos Institute to monitor recreational drugs on the consumer market, observed a disruption of the ecstasy market in 1997 and 1998 (van der Gouwe 2013). Tablets sold to consumers as "ecstasy" contained less MDMA, sometimes none at all. The fight began to focus on interception of precursor chemicals and tableting machines for production (Spapens 2006; Neve et al. 2007).

The optimism was short-lived. The ecstasy problem was "globalizing." The trafficking of ecstasy pills to other countries continued. Seizures in the Netherlands in 2000 included 5.5 million tablets and 632 kilograms of MDMA powder. Even more tablets, linked to the Netherlands, were seized abroad, one-third in the United States. Dutch policy makers came under increasing pressure to intensify the fight. The United States threatened to place the Netherlands on the "Majors Drug Transit List," a digest of countries involved in drug trafficking into the United States (Spapens 2006).

The Dutch government launched a comprehensive program in 2001: "a combined effort against ecstasy" (Tweede Kamer 2001). Ninety million euros, from the Dutch perspective a considerable sum, were made available. The program aimed primarily to reduce production and trafficking, although prevention of use also received attention. The Unit Synthetic Drugs continued and intensified its cooperation with other agencies and with law enforcement agencies abroad. The approach focused on all aspects of the production chain, from the fight on PMK, the precursor chemical, and hardware (e.g., glass instruments and pressure vessels), to consumer sale and use.

This approach seemed to work. Several indications pointed to a reduction in production. Neve et al. (2007) conducted an evaluation of the "combined efforts against ecstasy." The number of exposed production sites decreased, as did the number of warehouses for chemicals and hardware. This is confirmed by Spapens (2006) and was reported to Parliament (Tweede Kamer 2003*a*). The dumping of waste materials also decreased. Figure 8 presents some figures concerning synthetic drugs in general; ecstasy is not shown separately.[19] These figures are a result

[19] The figures appear in Expertise Centre on Synthetic Drugs and Precursor Chemicals annual reports. They may be incomplete. It is not mandatory for regional police forces to

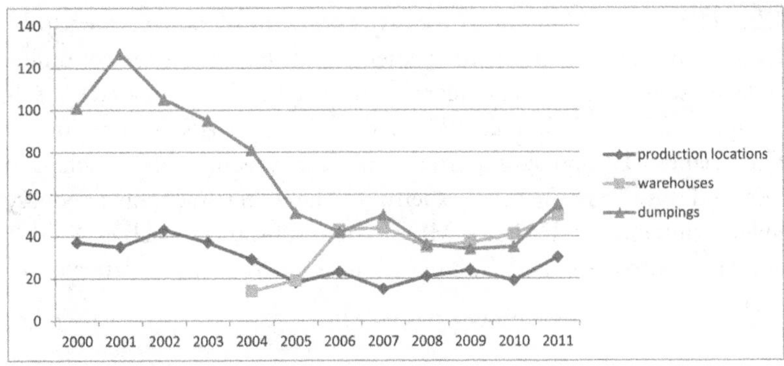

FIG. 8.—Dismantled production locations and warehouses and registered chemical waste-dumping sites for production of synthetic drugs, 2000–2011. Source: Expertise Centre on Synthetic Drugs and Precursor Chemicals annual reports, 2010 and 2012.

of the combined law enforcement efforts and the presence of production locations, warehouses, and dumping sites but provide some indication of the results of the intensified efforts. The number of dismantled production sites abroad where Dutch criminal groups were involved seemed to have dropped. There was also a drop in the number of arrests of ecstasy couriers (Neve et al. 2007).

The drop in production and dismantlements was good news. Actions continued despite a slackening of efforts in 2004, due to a decrease in capacity as a consequence of a police reorganization (Spapens 2006; Neve et al. 2007). Since 2006, the fight on synthetic drugs has been a well-functioning focal area of the national police. It has been a priority for law enforcement since 2008 (Tweede Kamer 2013*a*, 2013*b*).

Production of synthetic drugs, however, has not ceased. Neve et al. (2007) observed indications of continued production. During the first half of 2006, the quantity of ecstasy seized in the Netherlands equaled that seized in 2004. The number of waste-dumping sites remained small but increased in size. Very large production sites were discovered. Prices for tablets remained relatively low, and purity remained relatively high. Ecstasy was still readily available. Spapens (2006) concluded that the organization and methods of ecstasy producers had not changed.

---

report to the center. The figures are probably relatively valid because of the center's close involvement in cases with synthetic drugs.

In 2008 and 2009, however, ecstasy production finally seemed to be falling. The number of dismantlements and dumping sites continued to decrease (see fig. 8). The quantity of seized PMK decreased considerably. In 2008, 2010, and 2011 there were no PMK seizures in the Netherlands. The police reported that PMK was difficult to obtain in 2008 and was becoming more expensive. The total percentage of ecstasy tablets containing MDMA or MDMA-like substances, such as MDEA and MDA also decreased (van der Gouwe 2013). It was relatively low in 2009.

C. Resilience

Ecstasy production, however, only appeared to have been contained. Vijlbrief (2012) reviewed the actions of the Dutch authorities with regard to precursor chemicals such as PMK (for ecstasy production) and BMK (for amphetamines). He concluded that, from 2008 onward, "It was observed that the same perpetrators who dominated the production and trade of ecstacy and amphetamine in the Netherlands were trying to obtain other precursor chemicals in order to produce the necessary PMK and BMK themselves" (p. 207).

Instead of smuggling precursor chemicals from China and elsewhere, criminal groups started producing them in the Netherlands, using chemicals such as safrole (for PMK) and APAAN (for BMK). In theory, blocking access to precursor chemicals was a viable prevention option, but displacement effects were observed: "The first conversion lab was discovered in 2009, with a further two in 2010; by 2011, however, the number of conversion laboratories dismantled had already increased to eight" (Vijlbrief 2012, p. 208). Producers had hardware for the conversion process at their disposal. Another pre-precursor chemical, used since 2009, is PMK-glycidate. It is not under international control at the time of writing.

The national police conclude that production of ecstasy (MDMA) recovered in 2011. There no longer seemed to be a shortage of precursor chemicals (Korps Landelijke Politiediensten 2012). There was increased dismantling of production locations, as figure 8 shows. The police report more seizures of pre-precursors, more dumping of chemicals, and more dismantlements of production laboratories in 2012, 2013, and the first half of 2014 (van Rijn 2014).

The Drug Information and Monitoring System reported that the percentage of ecstasy tablets containing genuine MDMA or an MDMA-like substance decreased in 2008 and 2009 but increased in 2012 and 2013 (van der Gouwe 2013; van Laar et al. 2014). As figure 9 shows, the average concentration of MDMA in tablets sold as ecstasy (containing at least 1 milligram MDMA) also increased. In 2012, it was 107 milligrams, and in 2013 it was 111 milligrams.[20] The median consumer price for a tablet of ecstasy decreased in 2012 to €2; it had been €3 (van Laar et al. 2013). Trends suggest that MDMA and the necessary production chemicals are readily available after a decrease in 2009 (van Laar et al. 2014). Production processes seem to have adapted, and production seems to be increasing (van Rijn 2014). This indicates that there has been a strong recovery of the ecstasy market.

D. Conclusion

The reaction to the emergence of ecstasy in 1994 was primarily health oriented and focused on harm reduction. Health risks were believed to be low. Law enforcement efforts were expected to be expensive and possibly endanger the health of users. This led to initial reluctance among policy makers to adopt a law enforcement approach. International pressure was the prime reason later on for intensive law enforcement efforts directed at production and trafficking. This was initially successful but did not lead to the eradication of production or use of ecstasy. Producers have adapted their methods and use has continued, albeit at a lower level than in the 1990s.

IV. Drug Policy as a Balancing Act

Policies change over time and react to shifting constellations of problem definition, contemplated solutions, and political support (e.g., Kingdon 1995). In the early 1970s, a "policy window" emerged for a different approach to cannabis use in the Netherlands. In contrast to a sudden increase in problematic use of heroin, with very high risks, widespread use of a less addictive and harmful drug by young people from a variety of backgrounds precipitated backing for "separation of markets" and a tolerant approach toward cannabis use. Public health concerns became the major objective. It was generally expected that many countries would soon follow the alternative Dutch drug policy, which was perceived as

[20] The average concentration of MDMA in 2000–2004 was 70–80 milligrams.

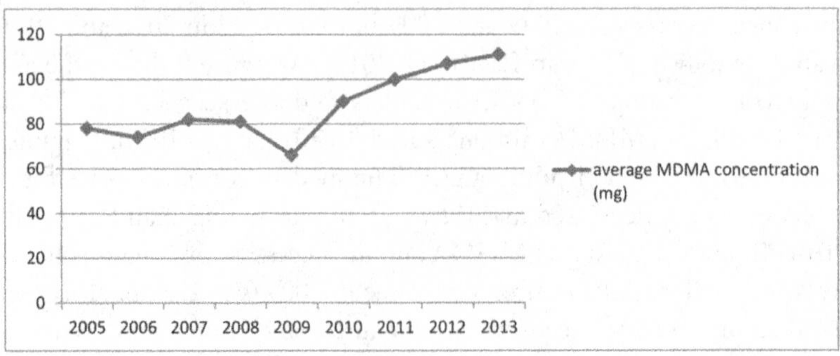

FIG. 9.—Tablets sold as ecstasy, average MDMA concentration. Tablets analyzed in the laboratory containing at least 1 milligram MDMA. Source: Drug Information and Monitoring System (van der Gouwe 2013; van Laar et al. 2014).

normalizing, pragmatic, and nonmoralistic (Leuw 1991). Primary concern with public health and harm reduction was also evident when ecstasy emerged in the 1990s.

Policy changes are "path dependent." It is difficult to make radical changes. Choices made in the past shape future options. A primarily public health focus and a diversified approach to hard and soft drugs are basic elements of Dutch drug policy. Unanticipated side effects generated new policy discussions concerning the coffee shops: drug tourism, cannabis trafficking and cultivation, and crime and nuisance. These side effects evolved in a context of established patterns of consumption without risk of arrest and—over time—an established system of retail supply in the case of cannabis.

It is not easy to explain why a health-oriented and harm-reduction-focused approach has characterized Dutch drug policies. Boekhout van Solinge (2004) suggests that the academic and pragmatic attitudes of a trading nation explain it. The Netherlands, he wrote, being a delta country with lots of rivers, situated near the sea, needed an attitude of accommodation in its enduring fight against the sea. He notes that the Netherlands has also always had to deal with large minority groups, which produced a problem-solving culture of deliberation and negotiation. It lacks a strong centralized state; cities and harbors always were powerful (de Kort 1995; Boekhout van Solinge 2004). Korf (1995) mentions "profound skepticism" in the Netherlands about the efficacy of repressive measures. Leuw (1991) and Boekhout van Solinge (2004) stress the importance of individual freedom, which has long been a core value and gave rise to "a high tide of moral pluralism" in the 1970s (Leuw 1991, p. 245). This is illustrated by the conditional and regulated decriminalization of abortion, prostitution, and euthanasia. Homosexuality has been widely accepted, and same-sex marriages have been possible since 2001.

Dutch drug policy has changed since Leuw wrote his 1991 essay. Its focus shifted more toward law enforcement. This was a reaction to perceived persistence in drug-related nuisances and crime. The shift occurred slowly and, as it turned out, rather erratically as a reaction to urgent problems that had been around for a longer time. It was tempered by deliberations about adverse health consequences and harmful side effects of vigorous law enforcement. This appears to reflect a continuing primarily health and harm-reduction perspective. It also reflects modest Dutch drug policy aims to "contain" rather than "solve" or "eradicate" the problem. Those perspectives are deeply rooted. The health-oriented focus may have inhibited recognition of the lucrative supply side of the market. De Kort (1995) suggests that drug policy is such a complex and controversial issue, and so much surrounded by insecurities and ideologies, that this might slow down decision making.

The delayed decision to implement more vigorous law enforcement approaches suggests that supply controls were applied relatively late in the drug use cycle. Caulkins (2007), who modeled drug use as an epidemic, describes how new drugs spread rapidly via positive feedback loops generated by current users, who introduce the drugs to nonusing friends. This may have happened with cannabis and ecstasy. They were well suited to the youth cultures of the 1960s and 1990s. According to Caulkins, use at some point reaches critical levels, and markets supplying that use "shift" toward more efficient and resilient forms. They achieve economies of scale that result in reduced prices, which stimulate greater initiation and use.

This seems to fit the pattern observed regarding cannabis and ecstasy use in the Netherlands. The supply sides of both had ample opportunities to develop a solid base. Caulkins's model predicts that increased numbers of longer-term users may over time lead to an association of the drug with problems of chronic users. This can stifle initiation and lead to a negative feedback loop that can curb an epidemic. Caulkins's model implies that supply control may be most effective during the explosive early growth stage of a drug epidemic. Treatment and other measures to mitigate consequences of dependence and aggressive drug markets may have comparative advantages later on. From this viewpoint, the more intensive supply control of cannabis and particularly ecstasy in the Netherlands came a bit late and had to deal with well-established and resilient markets of use and supply.

Cultural and political factors apart from unintended and persistent drug-related problems may have influenced the shift toward law enforcement approaches. There was a general increase in arrests and prosecutions after the mid-1990s, not only for drug offenses. Bruin (2011) suggests that local authorities became more important in cannabis policy. This may correlate with an increasing focus on nuisance and, according to Boekhout van Solinge (2000), more pragmatic approaches to problems. Local authorities tend to "role up their sleeves." Fijnaut (2014) observes that within the European Union, especially since the introduction of open borders, it is difficult for countries to apply policies by themselves because of the risk of cross-border organized crime (see also Spapens, Müller, and van de Bunt 2015). This could lead to more consensus between member states and to adaptations in Dutch drug policy. Boekhout van Solinge (2010) argues that the policy shift is attributable to critics from abroad and to right-wing governments of recent years. The general societal climate in the Netherlands also changed, as in other Western countries (Garland 2001), putting risk prevention and safety high on political agendas. Brain research showed that use of cannabis and ecstasy, long considered relatively harmless, is not without danger. This may have laid a foundation for greater repression and less tolerance. In the case of the Dutch drug policy, not only may crime have changed, but society as well.

Law enforcement has had effects on supply markets, but they have reacted flexibly. Sales of cannabis in coffee shops shifted to illegal sources when restrictions hindered access to the coffee shops. When access to the main precursor chemical for ecstasy was blocked, producers found substitutes. This is also evident on an international level (EMCDDA 2013). The cannabis market particularly is characterized by pervasiveness and resilience (EMCDDA 2013).

None of the interventions in supply markets had any noticeable effect on the use of drugs. Demand continued, and the specific drugs did not disappear from the market. Cannabis and ecstasy remain the most popular illegal drugs in the Netherlands (see van Laar et al. 2014).

Dutch drug policy has had successes in relation to the health of users, but it has also had to deal with unintended and unforeseen negative side effects. The Netherlands chose a different approach to drug policy in the 1970s and found itself on the edge of what is legally possible within the context of international treaties. Recently, other countries and states have gone further. Colorado and Washington state since 2012 have allowed adults age 21 and older to possess up to 1 ounce of cannabis and to cultivate up to six plants.[21] Uruguay legalized cannabis production, distribution, and possession of amounts for personal use in 2013. In the Netherlands there have been vivid debates about regulation of the supply to coffee shops, without a change in policy.

The story of the evolution of drug policy in the Netherlands shows that the ideas behind innovative policy initiatives can be reasonable and well intentioned but that unintended consequences can occur. It also shows that policy changes take time and a "policy window" to be effectuated. Past choices often limit future options, as suppliers and users adapt to new circumstances. Caulkins, together with the Dutch Advisory Committee for drug policy in 2009, advocate a dynamic and flexible drug policy as the best response to drug problems in fluid and fast-moving markets. Ideological preferences for particular policy options are strong and fiercely debated. It is important to maintain an open mind to allow for field experiments accompanied by research in order to find the best possible solutions.

REFERENCES

Adviescommissie Drugsbeleid. 2009. *Geen deuren maar daden: Nieuwe accenten in het Nederlandse drugsbeleid.* The Hague: Wetenschappelijke Raad voor het Regeringsbeleid.

Berghuis, B., and J. de Waard. 2010. *Drugsmarkt effectief verplaatst.* Feitenflits 1. The Hague: Ministerie van Veiligheid en Justitie.

———. 2011. "Sluiting coffeeshops voor buitenlanders kan drugsproblematiek 'terugduwen.'" *Secondant* 3–4:46–49.

[21] This is described in more detail in Kilmer et al. (2013). Commercial retail stores opened in Colorado and Washington in 2014.

Bieleman, B., and H. Naayer. 2007. *Onderzoek coffeeshops Terneuzen*. Rotterdam: Bureau Intraval.

Bieleman, B., R. Nijkamp, and A. Buit-Minnema. 2009. *Coffeeshopbezoekers Terneuzen najaar 2009*. Rotterdam: Bureau Intraval.

Bieleman, B., R. Nijkamp, J. Reimer, and M. Haaijer. 2013. *Coffeeshops in Nederland 2012: Aantallen coffeeshops en gemeentelijk beleid 1999–2012*. Rotterdam: Bureau Intraval.

Bieleman, B., R. Nijkamp, and M. Sijtstra. 2011. *Monitor Rotterdamse coffeeshopbeleid, 0-, 1- en 2-meting*. Rotterdam: Bureau Intraval.

Blokker, N., S. van Dijken, C. Meulenbroek, and J. Snippe. 2011. *Rapportage onderzoek alcohol- en drugsgebruik en handel in drugs in de gemeente Noordoostpolder*. Noordoostpolder: GGD Flevoland and Intraval.

Blom, T. 2006. "Coffeeshops, gedoogbeleid en Europa." *Justitiële Verkenningen* 1(6):146–56.

Boekhout van Solinge, Tim. 2000. *De besluitvorming rond drugs in de Europese Unie*. Amsterdam: Cedro/Mets en Schilt.

———. 2004. *Dealing with Drugs in Europe: An Investigation of European Drug Control Experiences; France, the Netherlands and Sweden*. Utrecht: Utrecht University.

———. 2010. "Het Nederlandse drugsbeleid en de wet van de remmende voorsprong." *Nederlands Juristen Blad* 85:2579–636.

Bootsma, J. 2012. "Wenselijkheden en mogelijkheden van verplaatsen van coffeeshops vanuit juridisch perspectief." In *Verkenning verplaatsingsmogelijkheden coffeeshops in de gemeente Rotterdam*. Rotterdam: Gemeente Rotterdam.

Bovenkerk, F., and W. I. M. Hogewind. 2003. *Hennepteelt in Nederland: Het probleem van de criminaliteit en haar bestrijding*. Zeist: Uitgeverij Kerckebosch.

Bowers, K., S. Johnson, R. Guerette, L. Summers, and S. Poynton. 2011. "Spatial Displacement and Diffusion of Benefits among Geographically Focused Policing Initiatives." *Campbell Systematic Reviews* 2011:3.

Braga, A. A. 2007. "The Effects of Hot Spots Policing on Crime." *Campbell Systematic Reviews* 2007:1.

Braga, A. A, A. Papachristos, and D. Hureau. 2012. "Hot Spots Policing Effects on Crime." *Campbell Systematic Reviews* 2012:8.

Brouwer, J., and J. Schilder. 2012. "Over de grenzen van het gedogen: Het failliet van de B en de I in het coffeeshopbeleid." *Nederlands Juristenblad* 44–45:3082–89.

Bruin, Deborah. 2011. *Onkruid vergaat niet: Ontwikkeling van het Nederlandse coffeeshopbeleid en de samenwerking tussen strafrecht en bestuursrecht*. Rotterdam: Erasmus University Rotterdam, Erasmus School of Law.

Caulkins, J. P. 2007. "The Need for a Dynamic Drug Policy." *Addiction* 102 (1):4–7.

Caulkins, J. P., S. Rajderkar, and S. Vasudev. 2010. "Creating Price Series without Data: Harnessing the Power of Forensic Data." In *Understanding Illicit Drug Markets, Supply-Reduction Efforts, and Drug-Related Crime in the European Union*, edited by B. Kilmer and S. Hoorens. Santa Monica, CA: Rand.

Centrum voor Criminaliteitspreventie en Veiligheid. 2014. *Instrumentarium drugsoverlast*. Vers. 1.1. Utrecht: Centrum voor Criminaliteitspreventie en Veiligheid.

COT Instituut voor Veiligheids- en Crisismanagement. 2011. *Ervaren coffeeshopgerelateerde overlast in Maastricht and coffeeshopbezoek in Maastricht, Heerlen, Kerkrade en Sittard-Geleen: Gebundelde resultaten nulmeting 2011*. The Hague: COT Instituut voor Veiligheids- en Crisismanagement.

Croes, E., and A. van Gageldonk. 2009. "Preventie en harm reduction." In *Evaluatie van het Nederlandse drugsbeleid*, edited by M. van Laar and M. van Ooyen-Houben. Utrecht: Trimbos-instituut/WODC.

de Bruin, D., R. Dijkstra, and J. Breeksema. 2008. *Coffeeshops in Nederland 2007: Naleving en handhaving van coffeeshopregels*. Utrecht: CVO.

Decorte, Tom, Gary R. Potter, and Martin Bouchard, eds. 2011. *World Wide Weed: Global Trends in Cannabis Cultivation and Its Control*. Aldershot, UK: Ashgate.

de Graaf, R., M. ten Have, M. Tuithof, and S. van Dorsselaer. 2012. *Incidentie van psychische aandoeningen: Opzet en eerste resultaten van de tweede meting van de studie Nemesis-2*. Utrecht: Trimbos-instituut.

de Hoog, D., E. van den Brink, L. van der Varst, M. Wensveen, and E. Verberne. 2012. *Overlastbeperkende maatregelen rondom coffeeshops: Lessen voor lokale partners*. The Hague: COT, Institute for Safety- and Crisismanagement.

de Kort, M. 1995. *Tussen patiënt en delinquent: Geschiedenis van het Nederlandse drugsbeleid*. Hilversum: Verloren.

de Zwart, W., and M. van Laar. 2001. "Cannabis Regimes." *British Journal of Psychiatry* 178:574–75.

Eerste Kamer. 2014. *Vaststelling van een Wet forensische zorg en daarmee verband houdende wijzigingen in diverse andere wetten (Wet forensische zorg): Eindverslag van de vaste commissie voor veiligheid en justitie*. Files of the House of Representatives 2013–2014, no. 32398, nr. J. The Hague: Sdu Uitgevers.

EMCDDA (European Monitoring Centre for Drugs and Drug Addiction). 2012. *2012 Annual Report on the State of the Drugs Problem in Europe*. Lisbon: EMCDDA.

———. 2013. *EU Drug Markets Report: A Strategic Analysis*. Lisbon: EMCDDA.

Expertcommissie Lijstensystematiek Opiumwet. 2011. *Drugs in lijsten*. The Hague: VijfkeerBlauw.

Fijnaut, C. 2014. "Legislation of Cannabis in Some American States: A Challenge for the European Union and Its Member States?" *European Journal of Crime, Criminal Law and Criminal Justice* 22:207–17.

Fijnaut, C., F. Bovenkerk, G. Bruinsma, and H. van de Bunt. 1998. *Organized Crime in the Netherlands*. Boston: Kluwer Law International.

Garland, David. 2001. *The Culture of Control: Crime and Social Order in Contemporary Society*. Chicago: University of Chicago Press.

Gemeente Rotterdam. 2013. *Het Rotterdamse coffeeshopbeleid 2013*. Rotterdam: Gemeente Rotterdam.

Gemeente Utrecht. 2014. "Manifest: Joint Regulation." Utrecht: Gemeente Utrecht.

Hendriks, V. M., W. van den Brink, P. Blanken, and J. M. van Ree. 2000. "Onderzoek naar heroïne op medisch voorschrift." *Epidemiologisch Bulletin* 35(1):13–19.

INCB (International Narcotics Control Board). 1996. *Report of the International Narcotics Control Board for 1995*. New York: United Nations.

Interregionaal Rechercheteam. 1996. *Fenomeenonderzoek Synthetische Drugs, "een eerste verkenning."* Veldhoven: Interregionaal Rechercheteam Zuid-Nederland.

ISAD (Interdepartementale Stuurgroep Alcohol- en Drugbeleid). 1985. *Drugbeleid in beweging: Naar een normalisering van de drugproblematiek*. Rijswijk: Ministerie van WVC.

Jansen, F. 2012. *Georganiseerde hennepteelt: Criminaliteitsbeeldanalyse 2012*. Zoetermeer: Korps Landelijke Politiediensten.

Kilmer, B., K. Kruithof, M. Pardal, J. P. Caulkins, and J. Rubin. 2013. *Multinational Overview of Cannabis Production Regimes*. Cambridge: Rand Europe.

Kingdon, J. W. 1995. *Agendas, Alternatives, and Public Policies*. New York: Harper Collins.

Kleemans, E. R. 2007. "Organised Crime, Transit Crime, and Racketeering." In *Crime and Justice in the Netherlands*, edited by Michael Tonry and Catrien J. C. Bijleveld. Vol. 35 of *Crime and Justice: A Review of Research*, edited by Michael Tonry. Chicago: University of Chicago Press.

Korf, D. J. 1995. *Dutch Treat: Formal Control and Illicit Drug Use in the Netherlands*. Amsterdam: University of Amsterdam.

———. 2011. "Marihuana Behind and Beyond Coffeeshops." In *World Wide Weed: Global Trends in Cannabis Cultivation and Its Control*, edited by Tom Decorte, Gary R. Potter, and Martin Bouchard. Aldershot, UK: Ashgate.

Korf, D. J., A. Benschop, T. Nabben, and M. Wouters. 2013. *Coffeeshop, overlast en illegale markt: De gevolgen van de komst van een coffeeshop in Lelystad*. Amsterdam: Rozenberg.

———. 2014. "De illegale gebruikersmarkt." In *Coffeeshops, toeristen en locale markt: Evaluatie van het Besloten Club- en het Ingezetenencriterium voor coffeeshops; Eindrapport*, edited by M. van Ooyen-Houben, B. Bieleman, and D. J. Korf. The Hague: WODC.

Korf, D. J., A. Benschop, and M. Wouters. 2013. "De illegale gebruikersmarkt van cannabis." In *Het Besloten club- en het Ingezetenencriterium voor coffeeshops: Evaluatie van de implementatie en de uitkomsten in de periode mei-november 2012*, edited by M. van Ooyen-Houben, B. Bieleman, and D. J. Korf. Tussenrapportage, Cahier 2013–2. The Hague: WODC.

Korf, D. J., P. Blanken, and T. Nabben. 1991. *Een nieuwe wonderpil? Verspreiding, effecten en risico's van ecstasygebruik in Amsterdam*. Amsterdam: Jellinek Centrum.

Korf, D. J., J. Doekhie, and M. Wouters. 2011. *Amsterdamse coffeeshops en hun bezoekers*. Amsterdam: Rozenberg.

Korf, D. J., E. Kleemans, T. Decorte, and T. Boekhout van Solinge. 2006. "Drugs en drugshandel in Nederland en België." *Tijdschrift voor Criminologie* 48(2):115–30.

Korf, D. J., M. van der Woude, A. Benschop, and T. Nabben. 2001. *Coffeeshops, jeugd and toerisme*. Amsterdam: Rozenberg.

Korf, D. J., M. Wouters, T. Nabben, and P. van Ginkel. 2005. *Cannabis zonder coffeeshop: Niet-gedoogde cannabisverkoop in tien Nederlandse gemeenten*. Amsterdam: Rozenberg.

Korps Landelijke Politiediensten. 1993. *Synthetische drugs*. Driebergen: Korps Landelijke Politiediensten.

———. 2008. *Het groene goud: Verslag van een onderzoek naar de cannabissector voor het Nationaal dreigingsbeeld 2008*. Zoetermeer: Korps Landelijke Politiediensten.

———. 2012. *Synthetische drugs en precursoren 2012: Criminaliteitsbeeldanalyse 2012*. Driebergen: Korps Landelijke Politiediensten.

Leuw, Ed. 1991. "Drugs and Drug Policy in the Netherlands." In *Crime and Justice: A Review of Research*, vol. 14, edited by Michael Tonry. Chicago: University of Chicago Press.

MacCoun, R. J. 2010. "What Can We Learn from the Dutch Cannabis Coffeeshop Experience?" Working Paper WR-768-RC. Rand Drug Policy Research Centre. http://www.rand.org/content/dam/rand/pubs/working_papers/2010/RAND_WR768.pdf.

———. 2011. "What Can We Learn from the Dutch Cannabis Coffee Shop System?" *Addiction* 106(11):1899–1910.

MacCoun, R. J., and P. Reuter. 1997. "Interpreting Dutch Cannabis Policy: Reasoning by Analogy in the Legalization Debate." *Science* 278(5335):47–52.

———. 2001. "Cannabis Regimes: A Response." *British Journal of Psychiatry* 179:369–70.

MacCoun, R. J., P. Reuter, and T. Schelling. 1996. "Assessing Alternative Drug Control Regimes." *Journal of Policy Analysis* 15(3):330–52.

Mein, A., and M. van Ooyen. 2013. *Bestuurlijke rapportage checkpoint*. Utrecht: Verwey-Jonker Instituut/EUR.

Ministerie van Volksgezondheid, Welzijn en Sport. 1995. *Stadhuis en house: Handreikingen voor gemeentelijk beleid inzake grootschalige manifestaties en uitgaansdrugs*. Rijswijk: Ministerie van Volksgezondheid, Welzijn en Sport.

Monshouwer, K. 2008. *Welcome to the House of Fun: Epidemiological Findings on Alcohol and Cannabis Use among Dutch Adolescents*. Utrecht: University of Utrecht.

Monshouwer, K., M. van Laar, and W. A. Vollebergh. 2011. "Buying Cannabis in 'Coffee Shops.'" *Drug and Alcohol Review* 30(2):148–56.

Moolenaar, D. E. G., M. M. van Rosmalen, M. Vlemmings, and F. P. van Tulder. 2014. "Kosten van criminaliteit." In *Criminaliteit en Rechtshandhaving 2013: Ontwikkelingen en samenhangen*, edited by N. E. de Heer-de Lange and S. N. Kalidien. The Hague: WPDC, CBS, Raad voor de Rechtspraak.

Nabben, A. 2010. *High Amsterdam*. Amsterdam: Rosenberg.

Neve, R., M. van Ooyen-Houben, J. Snippe, B. Bieleman, A. Kruize, and R. Bijl. 2007. *Samenspannen tegen XTC: Eindevaluatie van de XTC-nota*. Cahier 2007-2. The Hague: WODC/Intraval.

Nijkamp, R., and B. Bieleman. 2012. *Coffeeshopbezoek Rotterdam voorjaar 2012*. Rotterdam: Bureau Intraval.

———. 2013. "Coffeeshopbezoek." In *Het Besloten club- en het Ingezetenencriterium voor coffeeshops: Evaluatie van de implementatie en de uitkomsten in de periode mei-november 2012*, edited by M. van Ooyen-Houben, B. Bieleman, and D. J. Korf. Tussenrapportage, Cahier 2013-02. The Hague: WODC.

Nijkamp, R., R. Mennes, and B. Bieleman. 2014. "Coffeeshopbezoek." In *Coffeeshops, toeristen en locale markt: Evaluatie van het Besloten Club- en het Ingezetenencriterium voor coffeeshops; Eindrapport*, edited by M. van Ooyen-Houben, B. Bieleman, and D. J. Korf. The Hague: WODC.

Palali, A., and J. van Ours. 2013. "Distance to Cannabis-Shops and Age of Onset of Cannabis Use." Center Paper 2013-048. Tilburg: Tilburg University.

Rigter, S., and R. Niesink. 2014. *THC-concentraties in wiet, nederwiet en hasj in Nederlandse coffeeshops (2013–2014)*. Utrecht: Trimbos-instituut.

Rovers, B., and C. Fijnaut. 2011. *De drugsoverlast in Maastricht en omliggende gemeenten: Een schets van de problemen en het effect van tegenmaatregelen*. Tilburg: Universiteit van Tilburg.

Snippe, J. M., and B. Bieleman. 2012. *Onderzoek invoering wietpas Dordrecht*. Rotterdam: Bureau Intraval.

———. 2013. "Omwonenden van coffeeshops." In *Het Besloten club- en het Ingezetenencriterium voor coffeeshops: Evaluatie van de implementatie en de uitkomsten in de periode mei-november 2012*, edited by M. van Ooyen-Houben, B. Bieleman, and D. J. Korf. Tussenrapportage, Cahier 2013-02. The Hague: WODC.

Snippe, J. M., B. Bieleman, A. Kruize, H. Naayer, and P. Goeree. 2005. *Hektor in Venlo: Eindevaluatie; Inspanningen, proces en resultaten 2001–2004*. Groningen: Intraval.

Snippe, J. M., R. Nijkamp, and B. Bieleman. 2012. *Hektor 2010 en 2011: Evaluatie aanpak drugsoverlast Venlo*. Rotterdam: Bureau Intraval.

———. 2013. *Onderzoek drugsbeleid Venlo 2012–2013*. Rotterdam: Bureau Intraval.

Spapens, A. 2006. *Interactie tussen criminaliteit en opsporing: De gevolgen van opsporingsactiviteiten voor de organisatie en afscherming van XTC-productie en -handel in Nederland*. Antwerpen: Intersentia.

Spapens, A. C. M., H. G. van de Bunt, and L. Rastovac. 2007. *De wereld achter de wietteelt*. Den Haag: Boom Juridische Uitgevers.

Spapens, T., T. Müller, and H. van de Bunt. 2015. "The Dutch Drug Policy from a Regulatory Perspective." *European Journal of Criminal Policy Research* 21(1):191–205.

Staatsblad van het Koninkrijk der Nederlanden. 2001. *Wet van 21 december 2000 tot wijziging van het Wetboek van Strafrecht, het Wetboek van Strafvordering, de wet op de rechterlijke organisatie en de Penitentiaire Beginselenwet (strafrechtelijke opvang verslaafden)*. Staatsblad van het Koninkrijk der Nederlanden. Jaargang 2001, no. 28. The Hague: Sdu Uitgevers.

———. 2004. *Wet van 9 juli 2004 tot wijziging van het Wetboek van Strafrecht, het Wetboek van Strafvordering en de Penitentiaire Beginselenwet (plaatsing in een inrichting voor stelselmatige daders)*. Staatsblad van het Koninkrijk der Nederlanden. Jaargang 2004, no. 351. The Hague: Sdu Uitgevers.

———. 2009. *Besluit van 18 juli 2009, houdende wijziging van het Opiumwetbesluit in verband met de opname van het geneesmiddel heroïne cq diamorfine in de bijlage bij dat besluit*. Staatsblad van het Koninkrijk der Nederlanden. Jaargang 2009, no. 348. The Hague: Sdu Uitgevers.

———. 2014. *Wet van 12 november 2014 tot wijziging van de Opiumwet in verband met de strafbaarstelling van handelingen ter voorbereiding of vergemakkelijking van illegale hennepteelt*. Staatsblad van het Koninkrijk der Nederlanden. Jaargang 2014, no. 444. The Hague: Sdu Uitgevers.

Staatscourant. 1996. *Richtlijnen opsporings- en strafvorderingsbeleid strafbare feiten Opiumwet*. Staatscourant September 27, nr. 187. The Hague: Sdu Uitgevers.

———. 2011. *Aanwijzing Opiumwet 2011A021*. Staatscourant December 27, nr. 22936. The Hague: Sdu Uitgevers.

———. 2015. *Aanwijzing Opiumwet 2015A003*. Staatscourant February 27, nr. 5391. The Hague: Sdu Uitgevers.

Stevens, Alex, Daniele Berto, Wolfgang Heckmann, Viktoria Kerschl, Kerralie Oeuvray, Marianne van Ooyen, Elfriede Steffan, and Ambros Uchtenhagen. 2005. "Quasi-Compulsory Treatment of Drug Dependent Offenders: An International Literature Review." *Addiction* 40(3): 269–83.

Surmont, T. 2005. *De afzetmarkt van grenscoffeeshops in Zeeuws-Vlaanderen: Het profiel van de coffeeshopbezoeker en beleidsmatige reacties*. Gent: Universiteit Gent.

———. 2007. "Het profiel van de coffeeshopbezoekers in Terneuzen." In *Grensoverschrijdend drugstoerisme: Nieuwe uitdagingen voor de Euregio's*, edited by B. De Ruyver and T. Surmont. Antwerpen: Maklu.

Tijhuis, A. J. G. 2006. *Transnational Crime and the Interface between Legal and Illegal Actors: The Case of Illicit Art and Antiquities Trade*. Leiden: Netherlands Institute for the Study of Crime and Law Enforcement.

T. M. C. Asser Instituut. 2005. *Experimenteren met het gedogen van de teelt van cannabis ten behoeve van de bevoorrading van coffeeshops: Internationaal rechtelijke en Europees rechtelijke aspecten*. The Hague: T. M. C. Asser Instituut.

Tweede Kamer. 1975. *Achtergronden en risico's van druggebruik: Memorie van antwoord*. Files of the House of Representatives 1974–75, no. 11742, nr. 8. The Hague: Sdu Uitgevers.

———. 1994. *Notitie over het beleid inzake XTC*. Files of the House of Representatives 1993–94, no. 23760, nr. 1. The Hague: Sdu Uitgevers.

———. 1995. *Het Nederlandse drugsbeleid, continuïteit en Verandering*. Files of the House of Representatives 1994–95, no. 24077, nr. 3. The Hague: Sdu Uitgevers.

———. 1996. *Drugbeleid: Verslag van een nota-overleg*. Files of the House of Representatives 1995–96, no. 24077, nr. 35. The Hague: Sdu Uitgevers.

———. 2000. *Vaststelling van de begroting van de uitgaven en de ontvangsten van het Ministerie van Volksgezondheid, Welzijn en Sport (XVI) voor het jaar 2001*. Files of the House of Representatives 2000–2001, no. 27400, nr. 60. The Hague: Sdu Uitgevers.

———. 2001. *Samenspannen tegen XTC: Een plan van aanpak ter intensivering van het Nederlandse beleid inzake synthetische drugs*. Files of the House of Representatives 2000–2001, no. 23760, nr. 14. The Hague: Sdu Uitgevers.

———. 2003*a*. *Beleid inzake XTC*. Files of the House of Representatives 2002–3, no. 23760, nr. 16. The Hague: Sdu Uitgevers.

———. 2003*b*. *Drugbeleid: Brief van de minister van Justitie aan de Voorzitter van de Tweede Kamer der Staten-Generaal*. Files of the House of Representatives 2002–3, no. 24077, nr. 120. The Hague: Sdu Uitgevers.

———. 2004. *Drugbeleid: Brief van de ministers van Volksgezondheid, Welzijn en Sport, van Justitie en van Binnenlandse Zaken en Koninkrijksrelaties aan de Voorzitter van de Tweede Kamer der Staten-Generaal*. Files of the House of Representatives 2003–4, no. 24077, nr. 125. The Hague: Sdu Uitgevers.

———. 2005. *Handhaven en gedogen: Rapport*. Files of the House of Representatives 2004–5, no. 30050, nr. 2. The Hague: Sdu Uitgevers.

———. 2007. *Aanhangsel van de Handelingen: Vragen gesteld door de leden der Kamer, met de daarop door de regering gegeven antwoorden*. Files of the House of Representatives 2006–7, Aanhangsel no. 2060712390, nr. 1854. The Hague: Sdu Uitgevers.

———. 2008. *Bestrijding georganiseerde criminaliteit: Brief van de ministers van Justitie, en van Binnenlandse Zaken en Koninkrijksrelaties aan de Voorzitter van de Tweede Kamer der Staten-Generaal*. Files of the House of Representatives 2008–9, no. 29911, nr. 17. The Hague: Sdu Uitgevers.

———. 2009. *Drugbeleid: Brief ministers over de implicaties van het rapport van de Adviescommissie voor het huidige drugsbeleid*. Files of the House of Representatives 2009–10, no. 24077, nr. 239. The Hague: Sdu Uitgevers.

———. 2010. *Drugbeleid: Brief van de minister van Volksgezondheid, Welzijn en Sport aan de Voorzitter van de Tweede Kamer der Staten-Generaal*. Files of the House of Representatives 2009–10, no. 24077, nr. 253. The Hague: Sdu Uitgevers.

———. 2011*a*. *Drugbeleid: Brief ministers over het drugsbeleid aan de Voorzitter van de Tweede Kamer der Staten-Generaal*. Files of the House of Representatives 2010–11, no. 24077, nr. 259. The Hague: Sdu Uitgevers.

———. 2011*b*. *Preventief gezondheidsbeleid: Brief van de Minister van Volksgezondheid, Welzijn en Sport aan de Voorzitter van de Tweede Kamer der Staten-Generaal*. Files of the House of Representatives 2010–11, no. 32793, nr. 2. The Hague: Sdu Uitgevers.

———. 2012. *Drugbeleid: Brief van de minister van Veiligheid en Justitie aan de Voorzitter van de Tweede Kamer der Staten-Generaal*. Files of the House of Representatives 2012–13, no. 24077, nr. 293. The Hague: Sdu Uitgevers.

———. 2013*a*. *Bestrijding georganiseerde criminaliteit: Brief regering; Nationaal Dreigingsbeeld Georganiseerde Criminaliteit 2012 en Vierde rapportage op basis van de Monitor Georganiseerde Criminaliteit*. Files of the House of Representatives 2012–13, no. 29911, nr. 79. The Hague: Sdu Uitgevers.

———. 2013*b*. *Bestrijding georganiseerde criminaliteit: Brief regering; Resultaten bestrijding georganiseerde criminaliteit*. Files of the House of Representatives 2013–14, no. 29911, nr. 84. The Hague: Sdu Uitgevers.

———. 2013*c*. *Drugbeleid: Brief van de minister van Veiligheid en Justitie aan de Voorzitter van de Tweede Kamer der Staten-Generaal*. Files of the House of Representatives 2013–14, no. 24077, nr. 314. The Hague: Sdu Uitgevers.

———. 2013*d*. *Drugbeleid: Brief van de staatssecretaris van Volksgezondheid, Welzijn en Sport aan de Voorzitter van de Tweede Kamer der Staten-Generaal*. Files of the House of Representatives 2013–14, no. 24077, nr. 313. The Hague: Sdu Uitgevers.

———. 2013*e*. *Drugbeleid: Verslag van een Algemeen Overleg*. Files of the House of Representatives 2012–13, no. 24077, nr. 307. The Hague: Sdu Uitgevers.

———. 2013*f*. *Drugbeleid: Verslag van een Algemeen Overleg*. Files of the House of Representatives 2012–13, no. 24077, nr. 312. The Hague: Sdu Uitgevers.

———. 2014*a*. *Aanhangsel van de Handelingen: Vragen gesteld door de leden der Kamer, met de daarop door de regering gegeven antwoorden*. Files of the House of Representatives 2014–15, nr. 295 and nr. 296. The Hague: Sdu Uitgevers.

———. 2014*b*. *Besluit, houdende wijziging van lijst I, behorende bij de Opiumwet, in verband met plaatsing op deze lijst van hasjiesj en hennep met een gehalte aan tetrahydrocannabinol (THC) van 15 procent of meer: Verslag van een rondetafelgesprek*. Files of the House of Representatives 2013–14, no. 33593, nr. 4. The Hague: Sdu Uitgevers.

———. 2014*c*. *Besluit, houdende wijziging van lijst I, behorende bij de Opiumwet, in verband met plaatsing op deze lijst van hasjiesj en hennep met een gehalte aan tetrahydrocannabinol (THC) van 15 procent of meer: Verslag van een schiftelijk overleg*. Files of the House of Representatives 2013–14, no. 33593, nr. 2. The Hague: Sdu Uitgevers.

———. 2014*d*. *Besluit, houdende wijziging van lijst I, behorende bij de Opiumwet, in verband met plaatsing op deze lijst van hasjiesj en hennep met een gehalte aan tetrahydrocannabinol (THC) van 15 procent of meer: Verslag van een schiftelijk overleg*. Files of the House of Representatives 2013–14, no. 33593, nr. 3. The Hague: Sdu Uitgevers.

———. 2014*e*. *Drugbeleid: Brief van de minister van Veiligheid en Justitie aan de Voorzitter van de Tweede Kamer der Staten-Generaal*. Files of the House of Representatives 2013–14, no. 24077, nr. 315. The Hague: Sdu Uitgevers.

———. 2014*f*. *Drugbeleid: Brief van de minister van Veiligheid en Justitie aan de Voorzitter van de Tweede Kamer der Staten-Generaal*. Files of the House of Representatives 2013–14, no. 24077, nr. 316. The Hague: Sdu Uitgevers.

———. 2014*g*. *Drugbeleid: Brief van de minister van Veiligheid en Justitie aan de Voorzitter van de Tweede Kamer der Staten-Generaal*. Files of the House of Representatives 2013–14, no. 24077, nr. 321. The Hague: Sdu Uitgevers.

———. 2014*h*. *Drugbeleid: Verslag van een algemeen overleg*. Files of the House of Representatives 2013–14, no. 24077, nr. 317. The Hague: Sdu Uitgevers.

van Amsterdam, J. G. C., A. Opperhuizen, M. W. J. Koeter, L. A. G. J. M. van Aerts, and W. van den Brink. 2009. *Ranking van drugs: Een vergelijking van de schadelijkheid van drugs*. Bilthoven: RIVM.

van de Bunt, H. G. 2006. "Hoe stevig zijn de fundamenten van het cannabisbeleid?" *Justitiële Verkenningen* 32(1):10–23.

van den Brink, W. 2006. "Hoe schadelijk zijn softdrugs?" *Justitiële Verkenningen* 1(6):72–87.

van den Brink, W., V. M. Hendriks, and J. M. van Ree. 1999. "Medical Co-prescription of Heroin to Chronic, Treatment-Resistant Methadone Patients in the Netherlands." *Journal of Drug Issues* 29:587–608.

van der Giessen, M., D. Moolenaar, and M. van Ooyen-Houben. 2014. *De export van in Nederland geteelde cannabis, een omvangsschatting en een bespreking van de mogelijkheden en beperkingen*. The Hague: WODC.

van der Gouwe, D. 2013. *Drugs Informatie en Monitoring Systeem: Jaarbericht; Update 2012*. Utrecht: Trimbos Institute.

van der Pol, P. 2014. *The Dynamics of Cannabis Use and Dependence*. Amsterdam: University of Amsterdam.

van der Stel, J. 2006. "De rust is weergekeerd: 25 jaar drugs, drugsbeleid en drugsgebruikers." *Tijdschrift voor Criminologie* 48(2):131–43.

———. 2010. *Heroïne op medisch voorschrift: De geschiedenis van een geneesmiddel in Nederland*. Utrecht: Centrale Commissie Behandeling Heroïneverslaafden.

van der Stel, J., V. Everhardt, and M. van Laar. 2009. "Ontwikkeling van het Nederlandse drugsbeleid." In *Evaluatie van het Nederlandse drugsbeleid*, edited by M. van Laar and M. van Ooyen-Houben. Utrecht: Trimbos-instituut/WODC.

van der Torre, E. J., B. Beke, E. Bervoets, M. Gieling, D. Keijzer, J. Bik, and L. Schaap. 2013. *Drugsmonitor midden en west Brabant and Zeeland*. S.L.: Politieacademie/LokaleZaken/Beke Advies.

van der Torre, E. J., E. Lagendijk, and E. Bervoets. 2010. *Drugstoeristen in Roosendaal and Bergen op Zoom: Tellingen na de valreep*. Report. Roosendaal/Rotterdam.

van Kempen, P. H. P. H. M. C., and M. I. Fedorova. 2014. *Internationaal recht en cannabis: Een beoordeling op basis van VN-drugsverdragen en EU-drugsregelgeving van gemeentelijke en buitenlandse opvattingen pro regulering van cannabisteelt voor recreatief gebruik*. Deventer: Kluwer.

van Laar, M., A. Cruts, H. Rigter, J. Verdurmen, R. Meijer, and M. van Ooyen. 2002. *Nationale Drug Monitor, Jaarbericht 2002*. Utrecht: Trimbos-instituut.

van Laar, M., A. Cruts, M. van Ooyen-Houben, R. Meijer, E. Croes, A. Ketelaars, J. Verdurmen, and T. Brunt. 2013. *Nationale Drug Monitor, Jaarbericht 2012*. Utrecht: Trimbos-instituut/WODC.

van Laar, M., and M. van Ooyen-Houben. 2009. *Evaluatie van het Nederlandse drugsbeleid*. Utrecht: Trimbos-instituut/WODC.

van Laar, M., M. van Ooyen-Houben, G. Cruts, R. Meijer, E. Croes, A. Ketelaars, and P. van der Pol. 2014. *Nationale Drug Monitor, Jaarbericht 2013*. Utrecht: Trimbos-instituut/WODC.

van Laar, M., M. van Ooyen-Houben, and K. Monshouwer. 2009. "Scheiding der markten en beleid ten aanzien van coffeeshops." In *Evaluatie van het Nederlandse drugsbeleid*, edited by M. van Laar and M. van Ooyen-Houben. Utrecht: Trimbos-instituut/WODC.

van Ooyen-Houben, M. 2013. "Zorg als alternatief voor detentie: De toepassing van drang bij drugsverslaafde justitiabelen." In *Handboek forensische verslavingszorg*, edited by E. Blaauw and H. Roozen. Houten: Bohn Stafleu van Loghum.

van Ooyen-Houben, M., B. Bieleman, S. Biesma, J. Snippe, W. van der Wagen, and A. Beelen. 2009. "Drugsgerelateerde overlast." In *Evaluatie van het Nederlandse drugsbeleid*, edited by M. van Laar and M. van Ooyen-Houben. Utrecht: Trimbos-instituut/WODC.

van Ooyen-Houben, M., B. Bieleman, and D. J. Korf, eds. 2013. *Het Besloten club- en het Ingezetenencriterium voor coffeeshops: Evaluatie van de implementatie en de uitkomsten in de periode mei-november 2012*. Tussenrapportage, Cahier 2013-2. The Hague: WODC.

———. 2014. "Coffeeshops, Tourists and the Local Market: Evaluation of the Private Club and the Residence Criterion for Dutch Coffeeshops." In *Coffeeshops, toeristen en locale markt: Evaluatie van het Besloten Club- en het Ingezetenencriterium voor coffeeshops; Eindrapport*, edited by M. van Ooyen-Houben, B. Bieleman, and D. J. Korf. Final report: summary and conclusions. The Hague: WODC.

van Ooyen-Houben, M., and M. Goderie. 2009. "Veelplegers terug bij af? De ISD in retrospectief." *Justitiële Verkenningen* 35(2):10–30.

van Ooyen-Houben, M., R. Meijer, H. Kaal, and M. Galloway. 2009. "Drugswetcriminaliteit." In *Evaluatie van het Nederlandse drugsbeleid*, edited by M. van Laar and M. van Ooyen-Houben. Utrecht: Trimbos-instituut/WODC.

van Ooyen-Houben, M., D. Roeg, C. H. De Kogel, and M. Koeter. 2008. "Zorg onder dwang en drang: Een verkenning van mogelijkheden en grenzen." *Justitiële Verkenningen* 34(3):11–41.

van Ooyen-Houben, M., and M. van der Giessen. 2013. "De implementatie van de B- en I-criteria volgens de betrokken actoren: Resultaten van de procesevaluatie." In *Het Besloten club- en het Ingezetenencriterium voor coffeeshops: Evaluatie van de implementatie en de uitkomsten in de periode mei-november 2012*, edited by M. van Ooyen-Houben, B. Bieleman, and D. J. Korf. Tussenrapportage, Cahier 2013-02. The Hague: WODC.

van Rijn, A. J. 2014. *LFO: Voortgangsrapportage 1-1-2013 t/m 30-6-2014*. Amsterdam: Nationale Politie.

van Rooij, A. J., T. M. Schoenmakers, and D. van de Mheen. 2011. *Nationaal prevalentie onderzoek middelengebruik 2009: Kerncijfers 2009*. Rotterdam: IVO.

van 't Loo, M., S. Hoorens, C. van 't Hof, and J. Kahan. 2003. *Cannabis Policy, Implementation and Outcomes*. Leiden: Rand Europe.

Verdurmen, J., K. Monshouwer, S. van Dorsselaer, E. Vermeulen, S. Lokman, and W. Vollebergh. 2012. *Jeugd en riskant gedrag 2011: Kerngegevens uit het Peilstationsonderzoek scholieren; roken, drinken: Drugsgebruik en gokken onder scholieren vanaf 10 jaar*. Utrecht: Trimbos-instituut.

Vijlbrief, M. F. J. 2012. "Looking for Displacement Effects: Exploring the Case of Ecstasy and Amphetamine in the Netherlands." *Trends in Organized Crime* 15(2–3):198–214.

Vogels, N., and E. Croes. 2013. *Monitor drugsincidenten: Factsheet 2012*. Utrecht: Trimbos-instituut.

Wisselink, D. J., W. G. T. Kuijpers, and A. Mol. 2013. *Kerncijfers verslavingszorg 2012: Landelijk Alcohol en Drugs Informatie Systeem (LADIS)*. Houten: Stichting Informatie Voorziening Zorg.

Wouters, M. 2012. *Cannabis Control: Consequences for Consumption and Cultivation*. Amsterdam: Rozenberg.

Wouters, M., D. J. Korf, and B. Kroeske. 2007. *Harde aanpak, hete zomer? Een onderzoek naar de ontmanteling van hennepkwekerijen in Nederland*. Amsterdam: Rozenberg.

Beau Kilmer, Peter Reuter, and Luca Giommoni

What Can Be Learned from Cross-National Comparisons of Data on Illegal Drugs?

ABSTRACT

There has been relatively little effort at cross-national analysis of data concerning drug policy, though there is growing variation in how nations deal with illegal drugs. Systematic accounts of barriers to, and opportunities for, making comparisons are scarce. Comparisons of drug use prevalence, the focus of most cross-national studies, are undermined by fundamental and unacknowledged methodological differences. Prevalence is a poor measure of drug problems, but more appropriate indicators, such as drug-related crime and morality, are generated by institutional and legal systems that differ across countries, making them even more difficult to compare. The same is true of intensity of enforcement; besides problems of creating comparable arrest, conviction, and incarceration data, there is difficulty in generating an appropriate denominator of offenses. Collaboration among national data collection programs can help somewhat, but substantial progress will depend on harmonization of basic measurement systems, such as arrests and incarceration and on more subtle measures such as the prevalence of problem drug use.

Cross-national analysis is part of the twenty-first-century zeitgeist. Nations anxiously compare themselves with their peers to see how they are doing. Even the insular United States has been dragged in, at least selectively.

Electronically published August 6, 2015

Beau Kilmer is a senior policy researcher at the RAND Corporation, where he co-directs the RAND Drug Policy Research Center. Peter Reuter is a professor in the School of Public Policy and the Department of Criminology at the University of Maryland. Luca Giommoni is a lecturer at the Cardiff School of Social Sciences, Cardiff University. The authors thank Jonathan Caulkins for unusually detailed and helpful comments. Two other anonymous reviewers provided additional helpful comments.

0192-3234/2015/0044-0004$10.00

While the success or failure of health insurance schemes in other nations was often a forbidden topic in the debate about the Affordable Care Act,[1] debates on education policy now routinely refer to results of the international league tables generated by PISA, the Program for International Student Assessment (http://www.oecd.org/pisa/), and envious mention of the great success of innovations in countries such as Finland and Singapore. Discussions of Social Security reform, when they are active, are now likely to include mention of the experiences of nations such as Chile and Sweden that have been leaders in reform of public old-age pensions (e.g., Government Accounting Office 2005). Globally there seems to be more interest in comparisons of at least crime, if not criminal justice, as evidenced by the prominence of the UN Office on Drugs and Crime (UNODC) and the World Health Organization (WHO) *Global Study on Homicide* (2011). A recent *Crime and Justice* volume has just examined cross-country comparability of crime and victimization figures and what can be learned from such comparisons (e.g., Tonry 2014).

As illicit drug use and problems related to drugs have become perennial concerns throughout the Western world, there has been understandable interest in trying to learn from cross-national comparisons. The British Home Office in late 2014 released a study entitled *Drugs: International Comparators* that examined a number of innovations in other countries and attempted to assess their relevance to Great Britain. Having made sharp judgments about the applicability of innovations such as drug consumption rooms and heroin-assisted therapy to Britain, when it confronted decriminalization of drug use, the report suddenly discovered methodological qualms: "It would be inappropriate to compare the success of drug policies in different countries based solely on trends which are subject to differences in data collection, and are affected by various cultural, social and political factors besides legislation, policing and sentencing" (2014, p. 51).

Most of the few scholarly analyses to date have focused on highly visible policy changes in other countries; how well have they worked? In particular, the creation of the coffee shop regime in the Netherlands in the 1980s and the removal of criminal penalties for possession of small

[1] One Obama health advisor during the 2008 campaign recalls being told on a conference call that no one should mention foreign experiences because that would bring the cry of "socialism" (personal communication).

amounts of psychoactive drugs in Portugal in 2001 have both generated evaluation literatures using cross-national data.

Another small literature has had a primarily descriptive focus: How much do drug use and related problems differ across countries (e.g., Maxwell 2001; Zobel and Götz 2011)? A few papers have attempted to detect the influence of policy through analysis of such variation (e.g., Reuband 1995; Solinge 2004) but without much success. There are too many factors that have to be controlled for and the samples are small.

Thus few insights about illicit drug policy have been obtained so far from formal cross-national comparisons. Our intent is to provide a systematic examination of indicators in different countries and assess the extent to which they might be used to inform an understanding of variation in drug problems and policies. The policy emphasis is on drug enforcement rather than on treatment or prevention, reflecting the primary interests of *Crime and Justice* readers. Moreover, there are more consistent and richer measures for health-oriented interventions; see Babor et al. (2010) for a review.

In this essay we examine the adequacy and comparability of indicators across countries of drug use in the general population, the prevalence of frequent use of hard drugs, and drug enforcement stringency. The choice of countries discussed is driven by data availability. In addition to the United States, about which there is a voluminous literature on both measures and the methodology of measurement, we chose countries that have relatively highly developed data systems. The European Monitoring Center on Drugs and Drug Addiction (EMCDDA) gives us a starting point on some major indicators for EU members and Norway (Decorte et al. 2009). Australia and Canada also do a relatively good job of measuring at least some aspects of their drug problems. Few countries besides the United States have much of a methodological literature (cf. Pudney et al. 2006). Nor in most countries is there opportunity to analyze population surveys since few have the tradition of requiring the creation of public use data sets.[2] The important consequences of restricting comparisons to statistics published in the survey reports, and not permitting reanalysis to improve standardization, are discussed below.

[2] The European Commission is attempting to make such data readily available. "The Digital Agenda for Europe set out an ambitious 'open data' policy covering the full range of information that public bodies across the European Union produce, collect or pay for. The EU's Innovation Union flagship also explicitly backs Open Access as an essential element in real-

Our findings are readily summarized. At present it would be hazardous to make comparisons with respect to almost any major indicator of drug problems or policy across countries, even those with the most sophisticated measurement systems. Population surveys, which are more fundamental to the field than to other parts of criminal justice research, have well-known weaknesses, particularly nonresponse among high-using groups and underreporting of sensitive behaviors. The problem of comparisons is greatly worsened by variation across countries in many basic features of the surveys, most importantly in the mode of data collection (face-to-face vs. phone or mail) but also by varying age coverage (e.g., 16–59 in England and Wales vs. 18–64 in Germany vs. 12+ in the United States). Moreover, nations often change their modalities and age coverage without making any effort to estimate how much that might contribute to changes in reported prevalence. This further complicates comparison of trends over time within countries let alone across countries. The small literature that makes comparisons almost entirely ignores these critical methodological problems.

The prevalence of drug use is the measure that dominates policy discussions (EMCDDA 2013*b*; UNODC 2013; Home Office 2014). Thus, we devote a great deal of attention to problems associated with comparisons. However, a nation's drug problem, the consequences for crime and health, is better captured by measures of the extent of more intensive use, particularly of more expensive and dangerous drugs, rather than population prevalence. For these purposes, it is necessary to supplement, possibly even replace, the traditional general population surveys. Recent years have seen a surge in estimates of the extent of intensive use, for example, of problematic drug use in EU member states. Unfortunately, there are again fundamental differences in methodology and administrative definitions that sharply limit comparability across countries.

We also assess the possibility of comparing enforcement efforts. In principle, indicators of drug law enforcement can be used to understand the expected sanctions facing users and dealers, a reasonable measure for enforcement intensity. However, measures that are readily available, such as arrests and seizures, have well-known problems. For example, it is well established in the cross-national criminology literature that arrests have different meanings in different countries, and this is more

---

ising the European Research Area (ERA)" (http://europa.eu/rapid/press-release_IP-12-790_en.htm).

pronounced with drug offenses where countries have different thresholds for determining arrests for possession or use compared with trafficking. Even seizures, conceptually more straightforward, present comparability problems because of corruption (resulting in fraudulent figures) and unmeasured purity variation. Price and purity are also discussed as potential indicators of policy performance.

It is possible to improve the situation at least modestly. Our agenda includes creation of an accessible compilation of surveys that allows use of individual-level data from population surveys and use of more common questions and methodologies in the surveys themselves. There also needs to be more effort in general population surveys (GPS) to gather details about use intensity. However, the major needed developments are in data outside of GPSs. The Arrestee Drug Abuse Monitoring program in the United States provided an important model of how data might be collected from those most involved in consumption of expensive and harmful drugs. Purity data are already being collected in many countries for law enforcement purposes and could be used with price data to improve understanding of how well enforcement is working. However, we do not claim to offer a complete agenda for solving the problem of making cross-national problems and policies.

The essay is structured as follows. Section I is primarily conceptual: What are the ideal measures for comparing drug problems and policies across countries; how do existing measures relate to them? Section II presents a brief discussion of the few existing efforts at cross-country comparisons, noting that the literature rarely pays attention to the major methodological differences in these indicators. The following three sections then consider the problems of comparisons confronted for each of the three classes of indicators: prevalence of use, problematic use, and drug enforcement. Section VI summarizes and offers suggestions for the path forward.

I. Conceptual Issues

Simple prevalence of use is the measure that dominates the literature. That is probably regarded by the general public as the best indicator of how well a nation is doing in controlling drugs. It may be, for reasons offered below, a poor measure, yet it is so intuitively appealing that analyses ignoring this figure are unlikely to be compelling. That raises the question, though, of which prevalence figure is most relevant: lifetime use, past year, or past month? Lifetime is of little value for policy purposes, whatever its epidemiologic significance. If there was an epidemic of drug use 20 years ago that ended before the current year, there may be many who report ever having used but very few who are current users. Past-year use includes many users who are at low risk of suffering harms, so that past-month use is the preferred prevalence method. That measure is generally available in surveys that are focused on drug use and problems, but often is not included in surveys for which the drug questions are secondary, such as the first wave of the World Mental Health Survey.

What aspects of drug problems are most useful to compare across countries? Since the goals of policy certainly include the reduction of total net harms caused by drugs, it seems reasonable to suggest that the focus should be on measures of those harms, primarily in the domains of population health and crime.[3]

Three numbers seem particularly useful for comparative purposes. First, the number of frequent or heavy users is a better measure of the threat to population health than simple prevalence, since most of the health problems are associated with those who are dependent or who abuse these drugs. The number is also correlated with another important harm, namely, addiction itself. Second is the quantity (weight) consumed because risks for users are a rising function of how often and how much they consume, which is summed in that total. Third, total expenditure provides a measure of the criminal harms resulting from drugs in two senses: the revenues give resources to criminals and perhaps organized crime, and the expenditures, at least for cocaine, heroin, and methamphetamine, provide incentives for property crimes by heavy users (Goldstein 1985). All three numbers can be estimated—albeit with large error bands—with existing US data sets; see ONDCP (2014*b*) for an instance of this kind of estimation.

Even these three measures are mostly indirect proxies for the extent of a nation's drug problems. For health, more direct indicators would be emergency room visits or hospitalizations, disease spread by intravenous drug use, or deaths arising from drug use. Reliable mortality figures have proven difficult to generate in many countries, simply because of how death certificates are generated. The US Drug Abuse Warning Network system, explicitly set up to count deaths related to substance use, has not managed to develop national estimates; instead it represents estimates

[3] For a concise survey of the state of the art in measurement of drug problems from a public health perspective, see Degenhardt and Hall (2012).

only for some major metropolitan areas and specific regions. Instead, analysts have had to rely on a less comprehensive measure of "poisonings" based on International Classification of Diseases (ICD) codes for various drugs (Warner et al. 2011). Moreover, death certificates record only proximate rather than fundamental causes. For example, a long-term heroin user who dies of kidney failure may not have his heroin dependence listed as one of the causes. The EMCDDA has made sustained efforts to create comparable measures of drug deaths across EU member states but acknowledges limited progress, noting that "progress has been considerable but variable and not constant across all countries" (personal communication with Paul Griffiths, May 2015).[4]

HIV is well enough studied and measured that comparisons can be made across countries in the number of cases and new infections associated with intravenous drug use, more specifically, with the use of infected needles (Joint UN Program on HIV/AIDS 2006). Drugs and drug policies can also influence mortality in other ways that do not get captured by ICD codes, even with the inclusion of drug-related HIV/AIDS. For example, a drug dealer who has been killed by a competitor will simply be recorded as the victim of a bullet or knife, without any reference to the reason for the killing. In all of the nations considered in this essay, that is a small omission, but if one were considering drug-related mortality in Mexico since 2006, homicides would be the dominant source.

Efforts to develop a measure of the extent to which illegal drugs contribute to crime continue (e.g., Pacula et al. 2013). Australia and the United States have conducted regular arrestee surveys that provide at least a measure of what share of arrestees are regular users of specific drugs (Stafford and Burns 2013; ONDCP 2014*a*). However, Stevens (2011) accurately notes that this is a conceptually controversial measure of drug-related crime since not every crime committed by a regular drug user is caused by drug use.

[4] "The appropriate implementation of the component on deaths directly caused by drugs requires the existence of quality information sources: general mortality registries, and/or special mortality registries. An EMCDDA protocol establishes common criteria and procedures to extract and report cases from existing registries. . . . Considerable progress has been obtained in this indicator over the last 12 years, and in many European Union countries both General and Special Mortality Registries exist, and cohort studies have been or are being conducted. However, considerable work still has to be done in some countries to improve quality and completeness of drug-related mortality information. This improvement has to be seen in general in the context of improvement of the quality of information on external causes of death and youth mortality" (EMCDDA 2009*b*, p. 1).

Drug prices, the subject of a recent *Crime and Justice* essay (Caulkins and Reuter 2010), might be seen as an indicator of policy success; after all, enforcement aims to make drugs expensive and hard to get. Unfortunately, not only are purity-adjusted price measures available for just a handful of countries, but it turns out that they provide an ambiguous measure. Prices may be high because of high demand (policy failure) or because of high risks for suppliers (policy success). The more complex set of indicators needed to sort this out are not available for any country.

In summary, there is no single criterion for judgment of the success of drug policies. Indeed, there is not even an agreed-on set of indicators. However, there are a few that have a good conceptual basis and that can serve to inform discussions about whether innovations have been successful and which nations have particularly severe problems.

II. How Have Cross-National Data Been Used?

Comparisons of drug policy and problems across countries are relatively rare. We examine here the small, peer-reviewed, and gray literatures on this topic. Most of the analyses making comparisons across countries on drug-related issues utilize estimates from GPSs, which are more attractive for comparative purposes than administrative data because the latter (e.g., drug-related deaths or hospital admissions) are clearly generated by nationally idiosyncratic methods (Hofer 2000). However, as already noted and discussed much more extensively in Section III, the appearance of consistency across surveys is partly illusion, primarily because different survey modes (e.g., phone vs. mail) can produce strikingly different estimates of drug use in the same population. A critical failing, relevant to our own analysis, is the almost deafening silence on the major methodological differences in the indicators in different countries.

To identify studies to be examined, we used electronic databases and search engine methods from three universities.[5] We also examined the most-cited scientific journals for the categories substance abuse and criminology and penology. Particular attention was given to articles analyzing the effect of the Dutch coffee shop system and the Portuguese decriminalization. EMCDDA and the UNODC provided an anchor point. Only English-language studies were retrieved. However, this limitation has

[5] In particular, we used the WorldCat (2014), a network of libraries providing access to library content around the world, as well as the search engines provided by the University of Maryland, Università Cattolica del Sacro Cuore of Milan, and University of Trento.

been somewhat mitigated since for each EU country the EMCDDA national report published in English is based on native-language surveys and research.

Comparative data on drug prevalence are used for two main purposes: analysis of common patterns in trends and consumption across countries and drug policy analysis and recommendations.

A. Comparing Prevalence and Problems

The EMCDDA is the organization most involved in producing comparable data across nations; indeed, that is probably the most important element of its mission. Yet the organization has been extremely cautious in its interpretation of data. For example, EMCDDA (2012) presents the first-ever estimates of the prevalence of daily cannabis use across EU member countries and Norway. The estimates for each of the 20 countries come from analysis of the 37 GPSs that have been conducted in those countries between 2005 and 2010. The study uses the data almost solely for the purpose of producing a European-wide estimate of daily marijuana use, with no analysis of either the sources or consequences of the national differences.

Other EMCDDA analyses have been similarly cautious. Klempova and Zobel (2010) and Zobel and Götz (2011) present national differences on a variety of indicators, mostly GPS and the European School survey, but do no more than group countries together by broad commonality of problems; the same can be said of a paper derivative from EMCDDA (Ravera and de Gier 2008).

Descriptive comparisons outside of Europe are very rare. Maxwell (2001, 2003, 2008) compares findings from the Australian National Drug Survey (ANDS) and the US National Survey on Drug Use and Health (NSDUH). Facilitated by open access to data, Maxwell appropriately adjusted prevalence estimates for the same age range and avoided comparisons of questions that were subject to changes in wording. However, there is no reference to survey modality differences; the US survey employs audio computer-assisted self-interviews, whereas the ANDS uses a mix of methods including phone and mail surveys that are likely to generate lower estimates of prevalence in a given population.

The most ambitious comparative study comes from a relatively new WHO survey, the World Mental Health Survey, which is to be conducted roughly every 4 years (Degenhardt et al. 2008). Data were collected through a uniform methodology across 17 countries, asking questions on lifetime and first substance use. A particular strong point of this survey is its sensitivity to potential differences in self-reported drug use across countries due to cultural factors. Several efforts were made to enhance the candor of respondents including pilot tests to understand the best way to describe the survey, involvement of local leaders, training of the interviewers in the use of nondirective probing, and use of self-report formats for sensitive questions.[6]

The data collected for cannabis and cocaine, the only illegal drugs included in the questionnaire, covered whether the respondent had ever used the drug and, if so, the age of first use. These items were employed to show differences across nations among different birth cohorts and offered more detail for respondents aged 22–29, notably the percentage who used the drug by age 15 and by age 21. The findings are broadly consistent with data from other sources; for example, the US cocaine lifetime figure for cocaine use at age 21 is almost three times the next highest (Germany), and the drug is almost unknown in Asian populations. Passing comment is made about policy implications,[7] but the emphasis is on population differences and on correlates of use in different countries.

The European School Survey Project on Alcohol and Other Drugs (ESPAD) produces more descriptive analyses of national differences in drug use but is limited by the age range, 15–16-year-olds. With a common methodology for a large number of countries, it has been used in a number of studies (e.g., Kokkevi, Gabhainn, and Spyropoulou 2006; Kokkevi, Arapaki, et al. 2007; Kokkevi, Richardson, et al. 2007; Bjarnason, Steriu, and Kokkevi 2010; ter Bogt et al. 2014). They eschew policy conclusions and are more often used to identify socioeconomic correlates of adolescent drug use (Kokkevi, Arapaki, et al. 2007; Kokkevi, Richardson, et al. 2007; ter Bogt et al. 2014) or to examine early initiation of drug use with other risk behaviors (Kokkevi, Gabhainn, and Spyropoulou 2006).

B. Dutch Coffee Shops

In the last 40 years, numerous countries changed their regulation on cannabis. Since 1976 in the Netherlands, the possession of small amounts

[6] The authors suggest the possible use of bioassay in future cross-national surveys (Degenhardt et al. 2008, p. 1063).

[7] At the end of a single paragraph comparing the United States (punitive) and the Netherlands (less punitive), the authors conclude, "Clearly, by itself, a punitive policy to-

of cannabis, although formally illegal, is not subject to any penalties. In addition, licensed coffee shops can sell small amounts, though production and trafficking remain illegal and subject to aggressive enforcement. The exact regime governing the coffee shops has changed a number of times over the last 30 years (van Ooyen-Houben and Kleemans 2015).

This change has triggered a stream of analyses, mostly comparing the Netherlands with other nations. For example, MacCoun and Reuter (1997, 2001*a*, 2001*b*) compared cannabis use data from the Netherlands with data from other countries producing 15 matching surveys (many at the city level) in their 1997 paper and 28 in their 2001*a* and 2001*b* papers. They argue that "meaningful cross-sectional comparisons of drug use should be matched for survey year, measure of prevalence . . . , and age groups covered in the estimate" (2001*b*, p. 124). However, they do not consider the consequence of differences in modality of survey. MacCoun and Reuter emphasize that the Netherlands has a cannabis prevalence rate comparable to that of other European countries, but they conclude that the shift from more controlled distribution to the commercial coffee shop system increased cannabis use prevalence. Abraham, Cohen, and Beukenhorst (2001) criticized MacCoun and Reuter's "commercialization hypothesis." They fault the analysis for the matching between Amsterdam and the whole United States and for "creating a series of 'absolute' differences between Dutch and other data, and averaging them" (p. 176).

MacCoun (2011), writing 10 years later and taking advantage of the ESPAD data and data on both prices and treatment, reaffirmed the two conclusions from the earlier analysis, though with more nuance than was possible with the sparser data of the 1980s and 1990s. For example, he noted that cannabis treatment demand in the Netherlands was higher than in other European nations.

C. Portugal's Decriminalization

In 2001, Portugal removed criminal penalties for the possession of small amounts of drugs. Instead, those arrested by the police would be referred to three-person commissions that would choose an option for the individual most appropriate to his or her circumstances. Jail was not one of the options. This has led to a series of studies using cross-country analysis that

---

wards possession and use accounts for limited variation in nation-level rates of illegal drug use" (Degenhardt et al. 2008, p. 1062).

have concluded that it has been a "resounding success" (Greenwald 2009) or a "disastrous failure" (Coelho 2010). Besides several indicators used to assess changes before and after decriminalization, Greenwald (2009) compared data on lifetime drug consumption prevalence gathered from national GPSs. As Hughes and Stevens (2012) note, lifetime prevalence is a weak indicator for assessing postdecriminalization changes.

Hughes and Stevens (2010) conducted a more comprehensive analysis using data from 2001–7 for Italy, Spain, and Portugal. Like Greenwald (2009), they used a large set of indicators (seizures, prices, etc.) including drug consumption. Since most of their comparative analysis is focused on change over time for the three countries rather than absolute levels, the work is less sensitive to cross-national differences in methodologies.[8] Also like Greenwald, they concluded that compared to Spain and Italy, Portugal is similar or performing better for most indicators. Greenwald (2009) and Hughes and Stevens (2010) have been harshly criticized by Coelho (2010), according to whom Portugal performed poorly compared to other European countries. For instance, he noted that "behind Luxembourg, Portugal has the highest rate of consistent drug users" (p. 6). Hughes and Stevens in a subsequent article concluded that "post-reform Portugal is performing—*longitudinally*—similarly or slightly better than most European countries" (2012, p. 109; emphasis added).

D. *Other Policy Analyses*

A few other papers have used data on prevalence across countries to assess whether consumption is related to drug policy. However, most made use of surveys limited in scope or coverage in order to skirt the comparability issue of national GPSs. Cohen and Kaal (2001) used the results from in-depth interviews of samples of individuals in Amsterdam, San Francisco, and Bremen who had used cannabis more than 25 times during their lifetimes. Overall the sample was composed of 216 (Amsterdam), 266 (San Francisco), and 59 (Bremen) interviews. The results, confirmed in other publications using the same data, concluded that "policy is not a key determining factor when it comes to the usage patterns of experienced users" (p. 107); see also Reinarman, Cohen, and Kaal (2004) and Reinarman (2009). Reuband (1998), relying exclusively on the limited GPSs

[8] However, in discussing the changes in past-year prevalence, they did not note a surprising increase in the Italian cannabis prevalence. Given that the covered age range of the survey shifted from 15–44 in 2001 to 15–64 in 2007, a substantial decrease would have been expected; the age group 45–64 in Italy would have a very low rate of current use.

available in Europe in the mid-1990s, also concluded that policy had no observable consequence.

Solinge (2004) compares drug policy with prevalence considering three countries (France, the Netherlands, and Sweden) that, he reports, "cover the European drug policy continuum under drug prohibition" (p. 25). He concludes that "no logical relationship can be found between the extent of use and the policy response" (p. 26). All of these studies have weak designs, small samples of countries, and no meaningful controls for the many other factors that might affect prevalence.

Few studies compare indicators other than prevalence. Stevens (2011) compares rates of problem drug users across several countries, although the outcomes are estimated from different methods and data. Kraus et al. (2003) recommend using estimates of heavy users for cross-country comparability purposes with caution, a matter we take up in detail below.

A few studies compare rates of drug arrests. MacCoun and Reuter (2001*a*) collect and compare data on drug arrests for several countries as do Kilmer (2002) and Room et al. (2008) for cannabis offenses. Methodological problems that might limit comparability are mentioned but not dealt with.

There have also been some studies of differences in the quantity of drugs seized, often considered as a proxy of drug supply (Farrell, Mansur, and Tullis 1996; MacCoun and Reuter 2001*a*; Kopp 2004; Legget 2006). Seizures unfortunately reflect three distinct factors: the flow of drugs, the care dealers exercise, and the level of the enforcement. There is at present no means or data for separating the three factors (further discussed in Sec. V).[9]

E. *Summary*

The scholarly community has had minimal interest in making rigorous comparisons of drug problems and policies across countries. This may reflect a lack of curiosity or a healthy concern about whether the data can support meaningful comparison or both. The one truly bold effort at comparison is the recent Home Office (2014) study, which has many indications of political rather than analytic purpose.[10] Thus our analysis

[9] As this essay went to press, Laqueur (2014) published her insightful and appropriately titled article "Uses and Abuses of Drug Decriminalization in Portugal." This should be required reading for those participating in discussions about Portuguese drug policy.

[10] The report's release was accompanied by a firestorm about political interference. See, e.g., http://news.yahoo.com/uk-mps-debate-drugs-policy-study-backs-decriminalisation

of methodological issues is concerned not so much with critiques of studies past but to provide the basis for future studies.

III. Prevalence of Drug Use

The most common metric for assessing and comparing drug policies is the prevalence of drug use. Most developed countries and many developing countries track this information via self-report surveys of students and the general population. In some countries these national surveys are conducted annually (e.g., Britain and the United States), while in most they are less frequent (e.g., roughly every 2–3 years in Australia). Differences across national surveys limit cross-sectional comparisons and survey changes over time hamper trend analyses. Fortunately, a growing number of international self-report surveys ask the same questions to all participants (albeit in different languages), sometimes on a regular basis. Some of these surveys inquire about the number of days a substance was used in the past month, but most do not collect information about the amount of the drug consumed during a typical use day. This makes it difficult to measure total or per capita consumption of these substances. To this end, there is a growing interest in analyzing wastewater (sewage) to determine the amount of consumption at the local level.

This section largely focuses on the issues surrounding the use of national self-report surveys (e.g., accuracy of self-report, differences in modality). The limits and opportunities surrounding the international surveys and attempts to use wastewater analyses are also discussed.

A. The Accuracy of Self-Reports

General population surveys involving self-reported drug use have well-known limits (Harrison and Hughes 1997; Fendrich et al. 2004; Turner et al. 2005). The most severe are nonresponse by those who frequently use expensive drugs, misreporting of frequency by those who do report use, and unwillingness by many users to report. For expensive drugs (such as cocaine or heroin), nonresponse is probably the most serious of the three problems. For marijuana, it may be underreporting of frequency by current users. A brief discussion of these limitations is necessary to understand the accuracy of the current indicators.

-114259699.html. It is also interesting that the report has no authors listed, contrary to usual Home Office practice.

1. *Nonresponse.* Nonresponse has multiple sources: exclusion of groups from the sampling frame, failure to reach the respondent in the designated number of attempts, and refusal to participate (Fowler 2013).[11] For example, the exclusion of jails and prisons from the US sampling frame for the NSDUH ensures that many individuals with serious drug problems are excluded from the survey. This may not be a problem for estimating current prevalence (e.g., the percentage of the population that used a drug in the past year) since drug use in US prisons appears to be modest.[12] However, if the focus is to use the survey to gain insight into the need for treatment, this exclusion can be important, since prisons are rich in inmates with drug problems (Sevigny, Pollack, and Reuter 2013).

The problem of homelessness or at least unstable housing may be a comparable problem. A Swedish study found that, of the problematic drug users in Stockholm in contact with the legal or treatment system, only 46 percent had a fixed living space (Olsson, Adamsson Wahren, and Byqvist 2001; cited in Rehm et al. 2005). In the United States, studies of the homeless population report extremely high rates of drug use (Kipke, Montgomery, and MacKenzie 1993; Rosenthal et al. 2008; Wenzel et al. 2010; US Department of Housing and Urban Development 2011), and the NSDUH now includes shelters in the sampling frame. For expensive drugs such as cocaine, heroin, and methamphetamine, those who are unstably housed and avoid shelters may account for a nontrivial share of the total consumption.

2. *Misreporting of Frequency.* Even if users admit to consuming an illegal drug, misreporting can occur with respect to the reported number of days used in the past month or year. This may be due to deception or the very real possibility that respondents do not remember the exact number of days they consumed in the past month; the error could be in either direction. This information is especially important for under-

[11] Refusal rates are rising for many surveys in the United States; in some major surveys they now account for a large share of nonresponse rates (National Research Council 2013). For example, the refusal rate for the National Health Interview Survey, which captures health information from US households, rose from 2.7 percent in 1990 to 10.8 percent in 2009. For the NSDUH, the refusal rate in 2012 was 19.6 percent, up from 15.9 percent in 2002. Rising nonresponse is also a problem in other countries such as the United Kingdom (Steeh et al. 2001). We do not know whether this trend will continue or how this has influenced prevalence estimates.

[12] A recent jail scandal that has attracted national attention throws this into sharp relief. The Baltimore city jail was dominated by a national gang, which had worked out cooperative relations with the correctional officers, many of them female. Drugs were available but at extraordinarily high prices, and few inmates could afford them (Toobin 2014).

standing total consumption and expenditures as quantities consumed during a use day tend to be larger for more frequent users (e.g., Caulkins, Kilmer, and Graf 2013). Unfortunately, a recent report found that there is essentially no scientific literature on underreporting of the frequency of illegal drug use (Kilmer et al. 2013, app. B).

A related issue is whether those admitting consumption are honest about the consequences associated with their use. Since GPSs are often used to measure dependence and assess treatment gaps, one has to be concerned that some users will downplay problems surrounding their use. Indeed, one of the hallmarks of addiction is denial of problems.[13]

3. *Unwillingness to Report Drug Use.* A number of studies have examined unwillingness to report by comparing self-report information with information from a drug test, usually urinalysis. Much of this research has occurred in North America. Here we highlight a large US study examining concordance for almost 4,000 individuals aged 12–25 who participated in the 2000/2001 National Household Survey on Drug Abuse (Harrison et al. 2007).[14]

Table 1 presents the share of those testing positive who reported using the substance in the previous 30 days (this is known as sensitivity of the test).[15] While these tests are not 100 percent accurate (e.g., there are false positives), they provide useful insight into the honesty of those reporting information about drug consumption in surveys.[16] The sensitivity of the test is inversely related to the stigma (and legal penalties) associated with the substance. These results suggest that nearly 80 percent of tobacco users in the household population were honest about their use; the comparable figures for cannabis and cocaine were close to 60 percent and 20 percent, respectively.

However, additional analyses of these data suggest that the share of respondents admitting past-month use of marijuana is fairly close to the share testing positive (12.7 percent and 11.3 percent, respectively; Kilmer et al. 2013). This is partly attributable to there being some respondents

[13] We thank Jonathan Caulkins for this particular insight.

[14] Other notable studies include Hser, Maglione, and Boyle (1999) and Fendrich et al. (2004). See also the edited volume by Harrison and Hughes (1997).

[15] There were not enough heroin users in the sample to make comparisons, and the study was unable to distinguish between legal, illegal, and over-the-counter amphetamines.

[16] For a discussion of false positives in the Harrison et al. (2007) study, see Kilmer et al. (2013, app. B).

TABLE 1

Share of Those Testing Positive Who Self-Report Use in Previous 30 Days in the United States

	Household Survey Respondents Aged 12–25 in 2000/2001 (%) (*N* = ~4,000)	Male arrestees in 2003 (%) (*N* = 9,000)
Tobacco	80	NA
Cannabis	61	82
Cocaine	21	56

SOURCE.—Harrison et al. (2007, pp. 30, 61, 84); authors' analysis of ADAM (US Department of Justice 2004).

who admitted use but did not test positive; however, underreporting tends to be a much bigger issue in these surveys than overreporting.[17]

Table 1 also presents the sensitivity rates for a large sample of arrestees in the Arrestee Drug Abuse Monitoring (ADAM) program. While there are several differences between these two populations (e.g., arrestee rates are based only on men, arrestees are older, the same time periods are not covered), the magnitude of the difference is still striking. It appears that arrestees were more honest about their drug use than was the household population, which is consistent with other studies (e.g., Hser, Maglione, and Boyle 1999). Whether this pattern holds outside of the United States is an empirical question.

B. Marijuana versus Other Drugs

Throughout the Western world, marijuana is much more widely used than any other illicit drug. For example, in France the last-year prevalence for marijuana is reported at 8 percent, while that for cocaine, the highest among other drugs, is just 0.8 percent. While GPSs can be useful for tracking frequent users of popular intoxicants such as alcohol and marijuana, they are ill suited for capturing frequent users of hard drugs. Not only are hard drug users more likely to lie about their use (Harrison et al. 2007; ONDCP 2014*a*), but they are also more likely to be excluded from the sampling frame. For instance, Caulkins et al. (2015) note that estimates from NSDUH suggest that roughly 60,000 individuals used heroin on a daily or near-daily basis; however, their analysis for ONDCP

[17] This is also the case for alcohol (cf. Stockwell et al. 2008).

based on survey data from arrestees with biological validity tests (ADAM) suggests that the actual figure was closer to 1 million.

C. The Consequences of Modality Choice

A major problem in making cross-country comparisons is that the data on prevalence are often collected through different modalities of surveys. What are seen as major differences in drug use levels may reflect primarily the use of different survey techniques.

Three different methods are used to collect information: face-to-face, telephone surveys, and mail surveys. Each has important subvariants. For example, face-to-face can use traditional paper and pencil interviews (PAPI), computer-assisted personal interviews (CAPI), computer-assisted self-interviews (CASI), or audio computer-assisted self-interviews (ACASI).[18] Telephone surveys can be conducted through an audio computer-assisted self-interview (T-ACASI) or rely on a human interviewer (CATI). Mail surveys may include drop and collect (D and C) as well as mailed questionnaires that go through the postal service. For the former, the interviewer collects questionnaires from the mailbox, while the latter includes just those mailed back. Internet surveys are also used to generate information about prevalence and consumption, but this method is in its infancy (e.g., van Laar et al. 2013).[19]

These modes of data collection differ in many ways; each has strengths and drawbacks. Most importantly, the different modes have a strong influence on response rates, respondents' willingness to report sensitive information, coverage sampling, and costs of the survey (Bowling 2005; Decorte et al. 2009). Table 2 reports a summary of the principal strengths and weaknesses of each mode of interview for drugs.

Given the sensitivity of the topic, respondents are more willing to report stigmatized behavior when their anonymity is protected. Therefore, CASI and ACASI show a higher level of reporting for sensitive topics (drug consumption, sexual behavior, health) than the traditional self-administered paper and pencil (Tourangeau and Smith 1996; Turner

[18] PAPI can be self-completed or administered by an interviewer. In CAPI, the interviewer enters the questions into a laptop computer. In CASI, the respondent enters answers directly into the laptop. In ACASI, the respondent receives audio prompts from the computer.

[19] For a detailed analysis of the opportunities and problems presented by web-based surveys, as well as an assessment of their role in EU member state drug surveys, see Skarupova (2014).

TABLE 2

Differences by Mode of Questioning

	Sampling Coverage	Response Rate	Willingness to Report Information	Costs
Face-to-face (P and P, CAPI)	High	High	Low	Medium-high
Self-administered P and P	High	High	Medium-high	Medium
Self-administered (CASI, ACASI)	High	High	High	High
Telephone interview (T-ACASI)	Low	Medium	Medium	Low
Telephone interview (CATI)	Low	Medium	Low	Medium
Mail	High	Low	High	Low
Internet survey	Low	Low	High	Low

SOURCE.—Authors' judgments.

et al. 1998; Johnson et al. 2001; Decorte et al. 2009).[20] Telephone interview respondents are more likely to report drug use when interviewed through a T-ACASI instead of a human interviewer (Turner et al. 2005). Likewise, self-administered questionnaires (P and P) and mail surveys are more likely to report a higher incidence of drug consumption than telephone interviews (Aquilino 1992, 1994; Beebe et al. 2005). Pencil and paper surveys in the context of classrooms, where anonymity is truly guaranteed, may yield still higher rates; Monitoring the Future, a high school survey in the United States, consistently reports higher rates than the NSDUH for the relevant age groups (Gfroerer, Lessler, and Parsley 1997).

One of the main issues for telephone and mail surveys is the generalizability of the survey given the low response rate and the possible differences in terms of prevalence between respondents and nonrespondents. Studies in the United States showed that nonrespondents do not necessarily have a higher drug prevalence rate (Gfroerer, Lessler, and Parsley 1997;

[20] Respondents, as in everyday life, try to avoid circumstances that can embarrass them or may bring repercussions as a result of what they reported (Tourangeau and Yan 2007). Hence the willingness to report sensitive behaviors depends on two main factors: the stigma associated with that behavior and the instrument of the interview. For instance, Turner et al. (1998), comparing self-administered P and P with ACASI, found no difference in the estimate of the incidence of male to female sexual intercourse. However, respondents were 3.6 times as likely to report sexual contact with a prostitute and four times as likely to report male-male sex in the ACASI mode compared with the self-administered questionnaire (SAQ).

McColl et al. 2001); further, the screening and recruitment procedures for this GPS have improved over time (see, e.g., Chen et al. 2011). Some countries (i.e., the Netherlands and Germany) employ web surveys together with other methods, but results showed a low response rate for web surveys (Decorte et al. 2009). Little is known about the characteristics of nonresponse in web surveys.

The choice of the mode of questionnaire administration thus can have dramatic consequences in terms of recorded drug use prevalence. For example, in a comparative analysis of data from CAPI and CASI, Dutch authorities found that last-month prevalence of cannabis use was registered at 6.5 percent for the former and 12 percent for the latter (van Laar et al. 2012). Table 3, reporting US data from Turner et al. (1998), shows that the differences in revealed drug consumption prevalence can be even bigger whether measured with a self-administered paper and pencil (SA-P and P) questionnaire or with ACASI.[21] Similarly, remarkable differences are shown for telephone interviews when the questionnaire is applied by a human interviewer rather than by a programmed device. Table 4, again reporting US data, shows the large differences for two types of telephone interviews; for example, the cocaine prevalence is three times higher for T-ACASI than for an interviewer-administered telephone interview (CATI).

For many countries, cost is the main criterion for the choice of the mode of questioning (Decorte et al. 2009). For this reason, despite their higher level of data quality, CASI and ACASI have only recently been adopted by Britain (England and Wales) and the United States. For the same reason, regardless of their low response rate, mail surveys are used by Italy, Germany, and Australia. National authorities justify their decision to use mail surveys by claiming that respondents are more willing to report information in mail surveys than to an interviewer (Decorte et al. 2009).

The response rate is over 70 percent for the United States and England and Wales. In order to increase the response rate, since 2002 the Substance Abuse and Mental Health Services Administration (SAMHSA)

[21] Turner et al.'s (1998) study was carried out within the context of the 1995 National Survey of Adolescent Males to test the use of the ACASI mode of interview in the measurement of sensitive behaviors. The sample was built with a multistage probability sample of the male population aged 15–19. Initially all respondents completed a self-administered interview concerning sensitive questions. To assess the effect of the ACATI mode, respondents were randomly assigned to a group for which questions were administered with ACASI and the other group with SAQ.

TABLE 3

Estimates of Drug Prevalence Use, Different Method of Questioning.

Measurement	Prevalence of Drug Use (%)	
	Self-Administered P and P	ACASI
Ever taken street drugs using a needle	1.4	5.2
Injected drug within last year	0	.8
Ever shared needle	.1	1.1
Smoked marijuana daily during last year	4.1	6.7
Used crack/cocaine within last year	3.3	6.0
Ever smoked marijuana	41.2	43.0

SOURCE.—Turner et al. (1998).

has provided an incentive of $30 for completing the interview. France, Germany, and the Netherlands, despite the modes of interview typically associated with much lower response rates, have achieved a response rate of 50–60 percent. Among the countries in our analysis, Italy and Australia have the lowest response rate calculated; however, the Australian results are based on a different denominator.[22] The response rate for the 2010 Italian General Population Survey is an abysmal 15 percent. Given the low response rate, the results of this survey were not published by the EMCDDA.

D. *Coverage*

The population coverage for surveys in different countries varies; we focus here on age, but there are other relevant dimensions, such as institutional exclusions. Moreover, the same exclusion can have very different effects across countries. Since the United States has an incarcerated population rate almost seven times that of western Europe, the exclusion of prisons from the US sampling frame has potentially a larger effect on some drug use measures, especially those involving harder drugs.[23]

For many surveys, the most prominent figure in the official report is prevalence for the population in a broad age range. The British Crime

[22] The response rate for the Australian survey is calculated very conservatively, including all households not contacted in the denominator, as suggested by the Australian Institute of Health and Welfare (2011).

[23] According to the International Centre for Prison Studies, in the United States, there are 707 inmates per every 100,000 inhabitants, while in 2011, the average European prison

TABLE 4

Estimates of Drug Prevalence Use, Different Method of Questioning.

	Prevalence of Drug Use (%)	
Measurement	T-ACASI	CATI
Marijuana use in last 30 days	10	5.7
Cocaine use in last 30 days	2.1	.7
Drug injection in the last year	1.3	.1

SOURCE.—Turner et al. (2005).

Survey, which also serves as the general population survey of drug use, has always covered ages 16–59.[24] Other nations use different age ranges, such as 15–64 in Italy and 12–75 in France. The consequences of these differences are potentially profound. Drug use is low in the age ranges 12–14 and 64+; thus we would expect Italy to have a higher prevalence than France on age coverage grounds alone. However, it would take examination of the specific prevalence rates for these age ranges in the French data to estimate how much difference it makes. To give a sense of how large the difference might be, we used 2012 NSDUH data to compare the prevalence for 12+ with that for 15–64; the results are given in table 5. For both past-month and past-year prevalence, the narrower age range resulted in a figure 20 percent higher.

Table 6 shows that in the last 10 years, all countries considered in our analysis except England and Wales and France, have made major changes in their survey methods. Germany, the Netherlands, Italy, and Australia have changed the mode of questioning. For example, the 2000 German survey was purely a mail survey; by 2010 this was supplemented by both CATI and web interviews.

France, Germany, the Netherlands, and Italy have changed sample coverage across the years. For example, France covered ages 12–75 in 2005 but shifted to 15–85 in 2010. In 2002 the American survey on general population underwent significant changes (e.g., the new survey provides an incentive—$30 for completing the interview) and modified its name from Na-

population rate, including eastern and central Europe, is 154 inmates per 100,000 inhabitants (Aebi and Delgrande 2013; International Centre for Prison Studies 2014).

[24] The survey was renamed the Crime Survey for England and Wales in 2013.

TABLE 5

Prevalence of Marijuana Use in 2012 NSDUH: Ages 12+ versus 15–64

Age	Past 30 Days (%)	Past Year (%)
12+	7.3	12.2
15–64	8.9	14.9

SOURCE.—Authors' calculations.

tional Household Survey on Drug Abuse to the current National Survey on Drug Use and Health, which may have increased willingness to report.

Despite the variation across years, few countries acknowledge that there are limitations on trend measurement. One exception is that the SAMSHA specifically states that "methodological differences affect the comparability of the 2002 to 2012 estimates with estimates from prior surveys" (2013, p. 8). The estimated annual prevalence of marijuana use, which was stable for the years before and following 2002, increased from 9.3 to 11.1 percent and from 1.9 percent to 2.5 for cocaine.[25] That stability provides strong evidence that the 2001–2 increase was the result of methodological rather than population changes. Other national reports fail to deal with this kind of issue.

E. *Reported Prevalence*

We consider now observed differences in reported prevalence. Table 7 provides data for seven Western countries that have regular, if in some cases infrequent, GPSs. The emphasis is on the possible substantive effects of methodological characteristics as shown in the data.

Begin by noting the behavior of prevalence figures in the two surveys that have been consistent over the most years, namely, the United Kingdom and the United States. The changes in marijuana prevalence form a fairly smooth curve in both cases. The United States experienced a gradual and very slight decline from 2002 to 2007, reversing then to a figure in 2010 that was 14 percent higher than at the nadir of 2007. For the United Kingdom, the curve is exactly the opposite, rising modestly from

[25] In addition to the new name and the respondent payment, the survey increased the number of interviews, which required the hiring of many new interviewers. Quite unexpectedly, experienced interviewers generated lower prevalence than inexperienced interviewers. The reasons for this have not been determined, but this made it impossible to splice the two series.

TABLE 6

Characteristics of Survey by Country by Year, 2000–2010

	England and Wales*	France	Germany	Netherlands	Italy	United States†	Australia
2000:							
Modality	CAPI and CASI	CATI	Mail			ACASI	
Sample size	14,364	13,685	8,139			71,764	
Response rate	74%	70.8%	51%			73.9%	
Age range	16–59	12–75	18–59			12+	
2001:							
Modality	CASI			CAPI/P and P	Mail	ACASI	FTF, D and C, CATI
Sample size	23,935			2,312	6,032	68,929	26,744
Response rate	73%			48.7%	48.2%	73.3%	NA
Age range	16–59			12+	15–44	12+	14+
2002:							
Modality	CASI	CATI				ACASI	
Sample size	26,973	1,744				68,126	
Response rate	74%	NA				78.5%	
Age range	16–59	15–75				12+	
2003:							
Modality	CASI		Mail		Mail	ACASI	
Sample size	28,448		8,061		11,869	67,784	
Response rate	75%		55%		34.4%	77.4%	
Age range	16–59		18–59		15–54	12+	

2004:							
Modality	CASI					ACASI	D and C, CATI
Sample size	33,840					67,760	29,445
Response rate	75%					77%	33%[‡]
Age range	16–59					12+	14+
2005:							
Modality	CASI	CATI		CAPI	Mail	ACASI	
Sample size	35,847	30,514		4,516	27,995	68,308	
Response rate	75%	63.1%		62.7	33%	76.2	
Age range	16–59	12–75		15–64	15–64	12+	
2006:							
Modality	CASI		Mail, CATI			ACASI	
Sample size	35,402		7,912			67,802	
Response rate	75%		45%			74.2%	
Age range	16–59		18–64			12+	
2007:							
Modality	CASI					ACASI	D and P, FTF
Sample size	35,707					67,870	23,356
Response rate	76%					74%	34%[‡]
Age range	16–59					12+	14+
2008:							
Modality	CASI				Mail	ACASI	
Sample size	35,177				10,940	68,736	
Response rate	76%				32%	74.4%	
Age range	16–59				15–64	12+	
2009:							
Modality	CASI		Mail, CATI	CASI		ACASI	
Sample size	33,925		7,912	5,769		68,700	
Response rate	76%		45%	63%		75.7%	
Age range	16–59		18–64	15–64		12+	

TABLE 6 (*Continued*)

	England and Wales*	France	Germany	Netherlands	Italy	United States†	Australia
2010:							
Modality	CASI	CATI			Mail, CATI	ACASI	D and C
Sample size	35,533	27,700			15,332	67,804	26,648
Response rate	76%	NA			15%	74.6%	33.7%‡
Age range	16–59	15–85			15–64	12+	14+

SOURCE.—Decorte et al. (2009) and EMCDDA; supplemented by authors.

NOTE.—CASI: computer-assisted self interviewing; CAPI: computer-assisted personal interviewing; ACASI: audio computer-assisted self-interviewing.

* Data on sample size and response rate for England and Wales refer to the whole survey and not to the specific section on drug use.

† Results of 2002–10 survey are not comparable with results from previous surveys because of methodological changes.

‡ The response rate for the Australian survey is calculated very conservatively, including all households not contacted in the denominator, as suggested by Australian Institute of Health and Welfare (2011).

2000 to 2002 and then declining steadily by almost 40 percent over the next 8 years. In contrast, other countries show large changes in successive surveys, associated with methodological and age range changes. The German cannabis prevalence falls from 6.9 percent in 2003 to 4.7 percent in 2006, a decline of almost one-third in 3 years; however, some of the decline might reflect the change in age range (18–65 in 2006 as compared to 18–59 in 2003) and the addition of some CATI interviews to the purely mail survey in 2003. The dramatic decline in the Italian cannabis prevalence from 2008 to 2010 was surely associated with changes in procedures that halved the response rate from 32 percent to 15 percent.

Our interest is more in comparability across countries than across time, though many of the most policy-relevant analyses are precisely of changes over time across countries. Assume for the moment, though, that one did want to compare prevalence of drug use across countries in 2009/10, a 2-year period in which each of the seven countries conducted a survey. As arrayed by cannabis prevalence, the United States would appear to have the highest rate (11.6 percent) and Germany the lowest (4.8 percent). Yet if one notes that Germany's age range excludes some high-prevalence ages (15–17) and some low-prevalence ages (above 64) and uses methods known to have low reporting rates, in particular mail, the difference is certainly sharply diminished. Similar observations can be said about differences for the other three drugs reported in table 7.

F. *International Surveys*

To help address these comparability issues, international surveys have been created that employ similar methods and ask the same questions, albeit in the native language of each country. For substance use, the most notable international survey is the European School Survey Project on Alcohol and Other Drugs (ESPAD), which surveys a nationally representative sample of 15–16-year-old students in the classroom every 4 years. In 1995, more than 25 European countries participated, and by 2011 the number was almost 40.[26] To promote cross-Atlantic comparability, many of the ESPAD questions are modeled on the Monitoring the Future survey conducted with students in the United States.

[26] Before 2007, participating countries could choose whether they wanted to submit their data to a central ESPAD database, but now it is mandatory. Researchers interested in using the international database must submit a request to the ESPAD Database Application Committee, although the newest version of the database is restricted to ESPAD-affiliated researchers.

TABLE 7

Past-Year Prevalence of Drug Use (Cannabis, Cocaine, Amphetamines, and Ecstasy) in the General Population for England and Wales, France, Germany, Netherlands, Italy, United States, and Australia

	Past Year										
Country and Drug	2000	2001	2002	2003	2004	2005	2006	2007	2008	2009	2010
England and Wales:											
Cannabis	10.5	10.6	10.9	10.8	9.7	8.7	8.2	7.6	7.9	6.6	6.8
Cocaine	2.0	2.0	2.1	2.5	2.0	2.4	2.6	2.4	3.0	2.5	2.2
Amphetamines	2.1	1.6	1.6	1.5	1.4	1.3	1.3	1	1.2	1.0	1.0
Ecstasy	1.8	2.2	2.0	2.0	1.8	1.6	1.8	1.5	1.8	1.6	1.4
France:											
Cannabis	8.4					8.6					8.0
Cocaine	.2					.6					.9
Amphetamines	.2					.1					.2
Ecstasy	.2					.4					.3
Germany:											
Cannabis	6.0			6.9			4.7			4.8	
Cocaine	.9			1			.6			.8	
Amphetamines	.6			.9			.5			.7	
Ecstasy	.7			.8			.4			.4	
Netherlands:											
Cannabis		5.5				5.4				7.0	
Cocaine		.7				.6				1.2	
Amphetamines		.4				.3				.4	
Ecstasy		1.1				1.2				1.4	

Italy:										
Cannabis	6.2		7.1		11.2			14.3		5.2
Cocaine	1.1		1.2		2.2			2.06		.9
Amphetamines	.1		.2		.4			.7		.18
Ecstasy*	.2		.4		.5			.4		.16
United States:†										
Cannabis	9.3	11.0	10.8	10.7	10.5	10.3	10.2	10.3	11.4	11.6
Cocaine	1.9	2.5	2.5	2.4	2.2	2.5	2.3	2.1	2	1.8
Stimulants	1.1	1.4	1.2	1.2	1.2	1.3	1.1	1.1	1.1	1.1
Australia:										
Cannabis	12.9			11.3			9.1			10.3
Cocaine	1.3			1.0			1.6			2.1
Amphetamines	3.4			3.2			2.3			2.1
Ecstasy	2.9			3.4			3.5			3.0

SOURCE.—General population surveys of various countries.

NOTE.—Data for France and Netherlands refer to the population 15–64 years old.

* Included "designer drugs" before 2004.

† Results of the 2002–10 survey are not comparable with results from previous surveys because of methodological changes. Data for stimulants should not be compared with estimates before 2007 because of changes in the questionnaire.

There are other international surveys of adolescents and young adults that inquire about substance use. The International Self-Reported Delinquency Study was conducted in 13 European countries in 1994/95 and in 31 countries in 2006: 25 European and six American (Enzmann et al. 2010). And since 1985/86, the WHO's Survey of Health Behavior among School-Aged Children has been conducted every 4 years in now more than 40 countries and includes questions about alcohol and cannabis use (http://www.hbsc.org/).

Aside from instrument comparability, a clear advantage of these international efforts is to make sure the surveys cover the same age range. This is especially important for obtaining information about initiation to substance use; this is an important policy goal, especially for prevention efforts. Many GPSs have different minimum ages (e.g., 12, 15, or 18 years), which hampers cross-national efforts to compare initiation rates. Of course, the downside to efforts that target adolescents and teenagers is that they do not provide much information about initiation and prevalence of harder drugs (e.g., cocaine, heroin, methamphetamine), whose use typically starts in the late teens or early 20s.

While the use of similar survey methodologies should reduce the problems associated with using different techniques, these international surveys are still vulnerable to cross-national differences in honest reporting. The 2003 ESPAD asked respondents, "If you had ever used marijuana or hashish, do you think you would have said so in this questionnaire?" A similar question was asked about heroin. Figure 1 displays the share of respondents who reported that they would "definitely not" report use of these drugs if they had used them. Given that heroin is more stigmatized than marijuana, it is not surprising that the rate is higher for heroin in the vast majority of countries. The take-away message from this chart is that there is great variation across countries in the propensity to honestly report use among students. Whether or not the variation is similar for older populations is unknown.

Fewer international surveys focused on illegal drug use have been conducted with adult populations, with the most notable being WHO's World Mental Health Survey, discussed above. In addition to providing information about initiation, prevalence, dependence, and treatment need, these data have subsequently been used to explore other important issues about substance use, such as those surrounding the gateway effect (Degenhardt et al. 2010). Van Laar et al. (2013) conducted a web survey in seven European countries with different instruments for those using

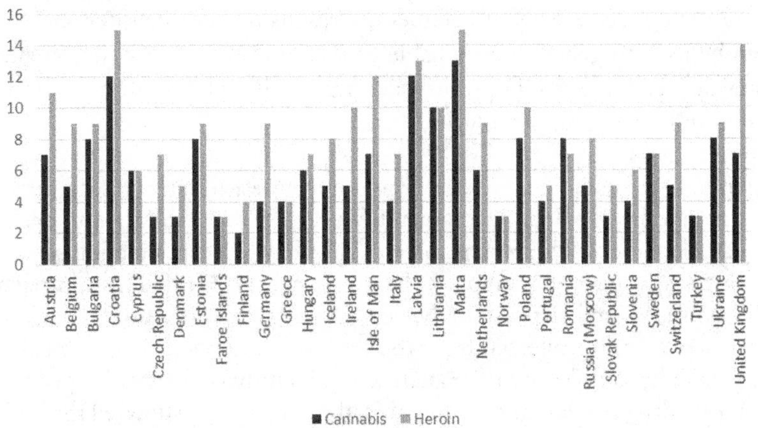

FIG. 1.—Percentage of 2003 ESPAD respondents who would "definitely not" report cannabis or cocaine use if they had used, by country. Source: Hibell et al. (2004, table G).

cannabis, amphetamine, ecstasy, or cocaine. While these web surveys were not based on a random sample of users, they demonstrate the feasibility of using this method simultaneously to collect data about substance use, consumption, and expenditures from users in multiple countries.

G. *Wastewater Analysis*

Wastewater analysis is an innovative approach for collecting information about drug use that does not require questioning users. Since illegal drugs and their metabolites are excreted in the urine of users, scientists can take samples of wastewater and estimate the level of drug use in a particular community (Zuccato et al. 2008). This approach yields estimates of quantity consumed, not prevalence. While there have been attempts to use this approach in North America (see, e.g., Banta-Green and Field, 2011; Burgard, Banta-Green, and Field 2014), most research has been conducted in Europe (van Nuijs et al. 2011; EMCDDA 2013*c*, 2014*c*). Researchers in 42 cities across 21 European countries collected wastewater over the same week in 2013, searching for amphetamine, methamphetamine, and methyline dimethamphetamine (i.e., MDMA, ecstasy) and metabolites for cocaine (benzoylecgonine) and cannabis (THC-COOH) (Ort et al. 2014). The spatial differences observed in wastewater analyses were largely in agreement with more traditional surveillance data, with the biggest difference being for cocaine.

Questions remain about whether the results from wastewater analysis can be used to generate reasonable estimates of total consumption and prevalence. The EMCDDA provides a good description of the calculations and uncertainty involved:

> In order to estimate levels of drug use from wastewater, researchers attempt first to identify and quantify drug residues, and then to back-calculate the amount of the illicit drugs used by the population served by the sewage treatment plants [Castiglioni et al. 2013]. This approach involves several steps. Initially, composite samples of untreated wastewater are collected from the sewers in a defined geographical area. The samples are then analyzed to identify concentrations of the target drug residues. Following this, the drug use is estimated through back-calculation by multiplying the concentration of each target drug residue with the corresponding flow of sewage. A correction factor for each drug is taken into account as part of the calculation. In a last step, the result is divided by the population served by the wastewater treatment plant, which shows the amount of a substance consumed per day per 1,000 inhabitants. Population estimates can be calculated using different biological parameters, census data, number of house connections, or the design capacity, but the overall variability of different estimates is generally very high. (2014*c*, p. 4)

But we should not be scared by this uncertainty. As Burgard, Banta-Green, and Field (2014) note in their nice summary of the wastewater research, many of the national drug use survey estimates have small error terms even though the validity is highly suspect. They sensibly observe that "it is preferable to have a larger error term around a valid estimate than a small error term around an invalid estimate" (p. 1366).

IV. Frequent Drug Users

Tracking the prevalence and initiation of substance use is necessary but insufficient for informing drug policy. For example, estimates of the number of frequent drug users are required for decisions about treatment funding levels. Estimates of frequent users are also central for calculating the total amount spent on drugs and how much is consumed.[27] Recent re-

[27] It is also possible, for some drugs, to generate consumption and expenditure estimates using information from production and seizure statistics. For more information, see ONDCP (2012).

search from the United States finds that daily and near-daily users account for the bulk of spending for illegal drugs; for marijuana and heroin the figure is roughly 80 percent, and for cocaine and methamphetamine it is closer to 50 percent (Kilmer et al. 2014; ONDCP 2014*b*).[28]

Unfortunately, GPSs are not credible sources of data for these estimates. We observed in Section III that the US NSDUH generates an estimate of just 60,000 daily and near-daily heroin users, whereas ADAM-based estimates provide a much more credible estimate of 1 million.

A. *Approaches for Counting Frequent Drug Users and Their Limits*

Just as there is variation in how countries implement GPSs, there is variation in how countries develop estimates of frequent users that are underrepresented in GPSs. For example, the EMCDDA has made "problem drug users" (PDU) a priority measure since the mid-1990s, with PDU defined as "injecting drug use or long duration or regular use of opioids, cocaine and/or amphetamines. This definition specifically includes regular or long-term use of prescribed opioids such as methadone but does not include their rare or irregular use nor the use of ecstasy or cannabis" (2014*b*). A series of guidelines have been produced by the EMCDDA to help with these efforts (e.g., EMCDDA and Centre for Drug Misuse Research 1999; EMCDDA 2004; Scalia Tomba et al. 2008).

In the United States, efforts to quantify the number of frequent users have mostly focused on the number of individuals who used a specific substance four or more times in the past month (e.g., ONDCP 2012); these individuals have been referred to as "chronic" users and others were referred to as "occasional." Recent estimates have disaggregated these "chronic" users into three subgroups: 4–10 days' use in the past month, 11–20, and 21+ (ONDCP 2014*b*). While the GPS has been used to generate estimates of users who meet clinical criteria for a substance use disorder (e.g., Office of Applied Studies 2002), these figures deserve great skepticism since many frequent hard drug users are not included in the GPS.

A first-order concern when comparing numbers of frequent users across countries is making sure that similar populations are being measured. Some focus their efforts on injection drug users, which may serve

[28] Cook (2007) calculates that the top quintile of alcohol users account for 80 percent of consumption.

as a proxy for problem opioid users, but the injection of stimulants and other substances in some countries cannot be ignored.[29] In addition, some frequent heroin users inhale instead of inject.

A variety of approaches exist for generating estimates of frequent hard drug users, including capture-recapture, multiplier methods (e.g., dividing the treatment population by an estimate of the share of frequent users who use treatment), and extrapolation via multiple indicators. But even if countries focus on similar methods, differences in administrative definitions can complicate comparisons. Kraus et al. (2003, p. 472) note that "even using equivalent methods, differences with respect to national data collection procedures, case definitions and availability of these data can still jeopardize comparability. Differences in data collection procedures in EU member states are well recognized. Even the apparently simple task of recording drug-related deaths or treatment admission is confounded by national definitions, state laws and country-specific reporting regulations." While definitional differences can be problematic, some researchers take refuge in looking at how the same measures change over time within countries. Unfortunately, this is not a viable option for most countries, simply because of the infrequency of PDU estimates (EMCDDA 2014*a*).

B. *Example: Comparing Frequent Opioid Users*

To highlight some of the opportunities and challenges associated with making these comparisons, table 8 provides the best information possible about frequent opioid users for six countries circa 2010.

Germany has three entries in table 8. For 2010, the German focal point submitted low and high estimates of problem opioid users to the EMCDDA based on three different methods. The first is a mortality multiplier that combines mortality data with information about the share of heroin outpatient clients who died during treatment. The second estimate is an "extrapolation based on suspects registered as users of hard drugs by the police." The two approaches yield fairly similar ranges for

[29] The terms opioids and opiates are sometimes used interchangeably. They should not be. Opiates are derived from the opium plant. Opioids are "defined simply as those compounds that have agonist or partial agonist activity at the opioid receptor and may or may not have structural similarity to the principle opium alkaloids. Opiates can also be classified as opioids, but not all opioids are classified as opiates" (National Laboratory Certification Program 2011).

TABLE 8

Measures of Heavy Opioid Users Circa 2010

Country	Year (1)	Method (2)	Drug (3)	Measure (4)	Central Estimate (5)	Lower Bound (6)	Upper Bound (7)	Upper/ Lower (8)	Central per 1,000 (15–64) (9)
France	2011	Treatment multiplier	Opioid and stimulant	Problem	222,000	176,000	267,000	1.52	5.5
Germany	2010	Mortality multiplier	Opioid	Problem	NA	82,467	137,444	1.67	4.1*
Germany	2010	Police multiplier	Opioid	Problem	NA	81,493	116,628	1.43	3.7*
Germany	2010	Treatment multiplier	Opioid	Problem	NA	156,164	185,445	1.19	6.3*
Italy	2010	Treatment multiplier	Opioid	Problem	218,423	197,285	231,106	1.17	5.5
Netherlands	2008	Treatment multiplier	Opioid	"Problem opiate users who are socially marginalized"	17,700	17,300	18,100	1.05	1.6
United Kingdom	2004–10	Cap-recap, combined	Opioid	Problem	335,496	327,659	351,438	1.07	8.2
United States	2010	Multivariate indicator	Heroin	>3 days in past month	1,500,000	800,000	2,600,000	3.25	7.2
United States	2010	Multivariate indicator	Heroin	>20 days in past month	1,000,000	NA	NA	NA	4.8

SOURCE.—Data for Australia are not reported since they were last estimated in 2002 soon after their heroin shortage (Weatherburn et al. 2003; Degenhardt et al. 2005). Data for the five European countries come from the EMCDDA's table PDU-102: Prevalence of Problem Drug Use at National Level. European figures are from http://www.emcdda.europa.eu/stats11/pdutab102a. Data about heroin users in the United States come from the recently published update to ONDCP's "What America's Users Spend on Illegal Drugs" series (ONDCP 2014*b*).

* Central figures are not reported for Germany; they are based on the midpoint of lower and upper bounds.

2010 (82,467–137,444 and 81,493–116,628, respectively). The third approach, based on a treatment multiplier, produces considerably larger figures (156,164–185,445). This illustrates how different methods can produce different estimates even within the same jurisdiction.

Also noteworthy are the figures for France and the Netherlands, which are both based on treatment multipliers but likely are biased in different directions. While the French figures do not distinguish between heroin and cocaine users (thus making it a high estimate for heroin users), the Dutch figures include only "problem opiate users who are socially marginalized due to criminal activities, a psychiatric disorder, a lifestyle causing public nuisance or an instable housing situation" (http://www.emcdda.europa.eu/stats12/pdutab102a). Perhaps not surprising, the French per capita figure is larger (5.5 per 1,000 population aged 15–64 in 2011) than that for the Netherlands (1.6 in 2008).

The US figures capture the number of heroin users by their frequency of use; there is no judgment or assessment made whether this use is problematic. While many of the European PDU estimates are rooted in treatment data, the US figures for hard drugs have traditionally been based on criminal justice sources, namely, the ADAM program. ADAM interviewed arrestees in booking facilities about their substance use patterns and expenditures (over 40,000 arrestees per year at its peak), and subjects were also asked to take a voluntary confirmatory drug test. The vast majority complied with the latter request. This partly mitigates the misreporting problem that plagues most self-report studies but does not solve it completely since use days could still be misreported (ONDCP 2014*b*). Extrapolating national estimates from arrestee data requires statistical models, many assumptions, and data from many other sources (ONDCP 2014*a*; Caulkins et al. 2015).

Table 8 reports US estimates for the number of heroin users who used on more than 3 days in the past month (1.5 million) and those who used on more than 20 days in the past month (daily or near-daily; 1 million). The number of daily and near-daily users per 1,000 population aged 15–64 in the United States (4.8) is close to the problem opioid rate for Italy (5.5) and France (5.5, which is combined with cocaine). While the reason could be that the Italian and French estimates are based on more than frequency of use, it suggests that the United States has an opioid problem on par with some major European countries. This is significant since these US estimates do not include the misuse of prescription opioids, which has become a significant public health problem over the past decade (Centers for Disease Control and Prevention 2011) but is not so severe in Europe or Australia.

Attention must also be paid to the uncertainty surrounding these figures. Column 9 in table 8 presents the ratio of the high estimate to the low estimate for each of the countries; larger numbers denote greater levels of uncertainty. The figure for the United States exceeds three, while the French estimates and two from Germany hover around 1.5.[30] The size of the United States in terms of land and population combined with minimal treatment funding makes it harder to locate heroin users, so this is not unexpected. Furthermore, the US range is based only on uncertainty surrounding one of the many calculations and should not be thought of as extreme bounds. The estimates for the other countries (as well as the German estimate based on a treatment multiplier) range from 1.05 to 1.19, suggesting a surprising and implausible amount of precision.[31] In comparison, estimates of alcohol abuse, which are based on stronger data, typically show broader confidence intervals. For example, a Danish estimate of "harmful alcohol use" in 2005 showed a 95 percent confidence interval of 439,000–945,000 (Hansen et al. 2011), suggesting a high-to-low ratio greater than two.

C. Summary

Since frequent users of hard drugs such as heroin, cocaine, and methamphetamine are not well represented in general population surveys, researchers must use more complex statistical methods on data from multiple sources to generate these estimates. The uncertainty surrounding these figures along with differences in definitions and data systems increases the difficulty of making meaningful cross-national comparisons.

Important progress has been made in the European Union, with most member states producing national estimates of problem drug use by 2010 (EMCDDA 2014*a*; http://www.emcdda.europa.eu/stats11/pdu/methods). The United States appears to be heading in the opposite direction with respect to hard drugs. While the legalization of marijuana in Alaska, Colorado, Oregon, Washington, and the District of Columbia is expected to

[30] For reference, dividing the top of the 95 percent confidence interval by the bottom for past-month marijuana users in the United States via the NSDUH is 1.07 (2011/12: 7.37/6.91; http://www.samhsa.gov/data/NSDUH/2k12State/Tables/NSDUHsaeTables2012.pdf).

[31] More work should be done to understand how these confidence intervals were generated and how the approaches to generating them vary across countries.

improve knowledge about the heavy users who drive these markets, the situation for cocaine, heroin, and methamphetamine is dismal. As of this writing, the federal government has eliminated funding for the ADAM program that serves as the central data source for estimating frequency of hard drug use in the United States (Kilmer and Caulkins 2014).[32] Without these data it will be difficult to generate future estimates of frequent users, expenditures, and consumption.

V. Drug Law Enforcement

Nations differ in their approaches to illegal drugs. Some are, by international reputation, tough enforcers of prohibition. The United States stands out in that respect, having close to a half million individuals locked up for violations of drug laws in 2010 (Reuter 2013). But broad generalizations about national drug policies can be misleading. Some countries have very different approaches to marijuana versus other drugs, and some places can be both lax about possession or use offenses and punitive when it comes to drug traffickers. There can be substantial variation in drug law enforcement intensity within a country.

For purposes of learning about the effectiveness of drug enforcement in cross-national studies, it is critical to standardize the measures used. We propose to do that with relatively simple ratios that have a strong conceptual base in terms of the risks and prices model of drug enforcement (Reuter and Kleiman 1986; Caulkins and Reuter 2010). Though the indicators involve measures that are not uniformly available across countries, they are well within reach.

This section assesses the expected sanctions associated with using, possessing, or distributing drugs.[33] These are a function of the probability of being arrested conditional on offending, of being convicted given arrest, and of the level of penalty conditional on conviction. Seizure of drugs is an additional penalty, primarily (though not exclusively) aimed at drug

[32] In the early 2000s, 35+ counties participated in ADAM and the number was expected to be expanded to 75. Instead, the program was discontinued after 2003. ONDCP resurrected a smaller version in 2007 with 10 counties, but funding constraints led to a reduction to five counties and eventually none after 2013.

[33] This section does not consider how drug law enforcement affects nongovernmental sanctions for illegal drug use within a country. For example, many employers in the United States conduct preemployment drug tests and random testing for those in certain types of positions; fear of losing one's job can be a powerful deterrent to using drugs.

producers and distributors. We consider all three areas of drug law enforcement: arrests, adjudication and sentencing, and seizures.[34] Since an important goal of drug enforcement is to inflate the prices of these substances, we discuss the quality and comparability of the available information about drug prices, purity, and purity-adjusted prices.

A. Arrests for Drug Offenses

What gets reported as an arrest for drug law offenses can differ across, and within, countries. For example, the EMCDDA (2013*a*) notes that "data on drug law offences might be recorded at an initial stage when a first report is made by law enforcement agencies, or after investigation by the Judicial Police, or even following a decision for a charge to be issued by the Prosecutor." Switzerland objects to the term "arrest" being used when a police officer charges a cannabis user with violation of the law, even though the fine levied can be larger than what is imposed for some possession arrests in the United States (see Killias 2009). There are also general issues surrounding whether someone arrested for multiple different charges at the same time enters the official arrest statistics once or more (Aebi et al. 2010). There are at least three additional complications specific to comparing drug offenses across jurisdictions: arrests for drugs are sometimes combined into broad categories, making it hard to develop estimates for a specific substance; different jurisdictions (even within countries) use different weight thresholds to determine what constitutes a drug sales arrest versus simple possession/use or possession with the intent to distribute; and some individuals who are sanctioned for drug use are caught by a probation or parole officer (possibly because of a positive urine test), not by the police. This last category, though not formally an arrest, is the equivalent in terms of detection and punishment.

The *European Sourcebook of Crime and Criminal Justice Statistics* (ESB) is produced by a group of European crime experts and is a rich resource for tracking how various offenses, including drug offenses, are processed at the national level.[35] The ESB includes data as well as "information on the statistical rules and the definitions behind these figures." With re-

[34] Data on asset seizures, typically through money laundering investigations, are so scarce that these are omitted here (Levi and Reuter 2006).

[35] For a systematic analysis of the strengths and weaknesses in the ESB, see Harrendorf (2012).

spect to drugs, total drug offenses and total drug trafficking offenses are reported as is information about drug convictions and sentencing for some countries. While there are notable differences across countries with respect to offense definitions, research by Harrendorf (2012) gives the ESB high marks for total drug offenses in particular.[36]

That said, assessing European trends in drug law offenses can be difficult. Many countries submit drug offense data to both the EMCDDA and Eurostat; the latter often pulls figures from the ESB. The organizations make the data available on their webpages. These organizations should be lauded for highlighting potential limitations to direct comparisons, but unexplained discrepancies persist. What is especially troubling is that drug trafficking arrest data reported to these international agencies by the same country can show very different trends (Kilmer et al. 2010). After comparing Eurostat and EMCDDA drug trafficking offense data from 2001 to 2007, Kilmer et al. noted major inconsistencies at almost every level of analysis.

There are noticeable differences between the EMCDDA and Eurostat estimates, and they are not consistent across countries. In fact, there is only one country for which the figures are identical: Germany, 2002–7. There are major, systematic differences in the estimates for Poland and Greece, and it is not as if one data system is always larger. For 2007, the EMCDDA figure is 432 percent larger for Poland and the Eurostat figure is 118 percent larger for Greece. The size of the difference has also changed for some countries over time. For example, in 2001 the EMCDDA estimates for France were 34 percent larger, and by 2007 the size of the difference had increased to 70 percent. There are also instances in which the two data series show differing trends. The EMCDDA series shows a generally upward trend for Portugal from 2001 to 2007, whereas Eurostat shows a generally downward trend after 2002 (Kilmer et al. 2010, p. 75).

Figure 2 displays the number of drug trafficking arrests reported to the EMCDDA and Eurostat for five European countries from 2003 to 2010. The data for the EMCDDA capture "drug law offences related to drug supply" and the Eurostat data represent "drug offences reported by the

[36] "Altogether, definitions in the ESB seem to be well-defined and thus show high conformity levels throughout Europe. This is true for both overall and item conformity, and equally applies to the police and convictions levels. The definitions that work best according to all checks executed here are robbery, theft total and drug offences total" (Harrendorf 2012, p. 52).

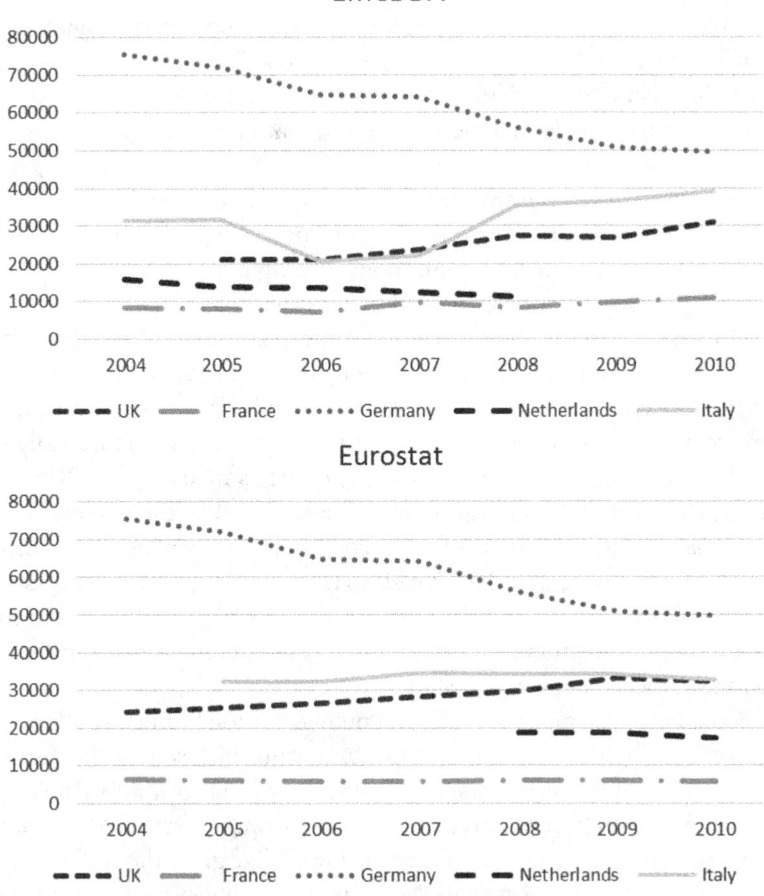

FIG. 2.—Drug trafficking offenses reported to EMCDDA and Eurostat. Based on our analysis of data published by EMCDDA and Eurostat. EMCDDA: http://www.emcdda.europa.eu/stats09/dlo/methods. Source: National Focal Points. Eurostat: http://epp.eurostat.ec.europa.eu/cache/ITY_SDDS/en/crim_esms.htm.

police for drug trafficking." Germany reported identical information to both organizations. For the Netherlands, the EMCDDA data stop at 2008 and the Eurostat data note a break in the series in 2007. There is virtually no overlap, and the Eurostat figures are roughly 50 percent larger.

Other differences in figure 2 are even harder to reconcile. The 2005 figures for Italy are similar for EMCDDA and Eurostat (both close to

32,000), but they display very different trends through 2010. The Eurostat figures suggest stability through 2010, with a very slight decline after 2007. The EMCDDA figures show great volatility: a decline of about one-third between 2005 and 2006 and then a 50 percent increase from 2007 to 2008. The French figures are also puzzling: Eurostat suggests a 4 percent decline from 2008 to 2010, while EMCDDA shows a 31 percent increase in drug trafficking offenses. While this could be attributable to differences in reporting protocols for the departments that submit information to these organizations, it is nonetheless frustrating for analysts seeking to make cross-national comparisons.

Anyone seeking to draw insights from arrest information must also make a decision about the appropriate denominator. While it is easy to use per capita measures since population and subpopulation (e.g., by age and sex) totals are routinely used and are readily available, a more analytically useful measure comes from dividing arrests by users (e.g., Kilmer 2002; Room et al. 2008; Nguyen and Reuter 2012).[37] Table 9 presents cannabis arrests as fractions of users and population for four European countries, Australia, and the United States. Given the caveats discussed previously about GPS and drug offense data, extreme caution needs to be exercised in attempting to make comparisons. Our main goal is to demonstrate why denominators matter.

Column 5 of table 9 presents the number of total cannabis offenses normalized by the number of past-month cannabis users in the country.[38] While differences in survey methods, age ranges, arrest definitions, and years covered preclude drawing strong inferences, it is not surprising that the Netherlands has the lowest rate given the coffee shop regime and the official policy of not enforcing the laws against small-scale transactions (Ministry of Foreign Affairs et al. 1995). The Dutch figure (13.2 offenses per 1,000 past-month users), however, is not zero since arrests are still made for producing and distributing cannabis. The country with the second-lowest arrest rate is the United States (41.9) and the country with the highest is Germany (75.5). The low figure for

[37] Another useful denominator would be total use days, but these data are not readily available for most countries. For a detailed analysis of cannabis use day information in the United States, see Burns et al. (2013).

[38] Nguyen and Reuter (2012) use past-year rather than past-month figures. This is conceptually easier to justify, but since past-month users account for almost 90 percent of total use days, past-month users as a denominator is a more realistic representation of risk.

TABLE 9

Cannabis Arrest Rates with Different Denominators Circa 2011, by Country (Unadjusted for Differences in Ages Covered by GPS or Misreporting)

	Cannabis Arrests in 2011 (1)	GPS Year (2)	GPS Age Range (3)	Past-Month Cannabis Users (4)	Arrests per 1,000 Past-Month Users (5)	Country Population in 2011 (6)	Offenses per 1,000 Population (7)
Australia	61,011	2011	14+	1,050,172	58.1	22,340,024	2.7
France	137,741	2010	15–64	2,845,829	48.4	64,994,907	2.1
Germany	131,951	2009	18–64	1,748,240	75.5	81,751,602	1.6
Italy	37,118	2012	18–64	777,538	47.7	60,626,442	.6
Netherlands	9,236	2009	15–64	698,728	13.2	16,655,799	.6
United States	757,969	2011	12+	18,071,000	41.9	311,591,917	2.4

NOTE.—Differences in survey methods, age ranges, arrest definitions, and years covered preclude drawing strong inferences.

the United States will come as a surprise to many readers given the publicity that has been given to the rise in marijuana possession arrests over the last 20 years, but it is a reminder that the United States has a high rate of cannabis use.

Column 7 changes the denominator from past-month users to the entire population. Once again the Netherlands is at the bottom of the list; however, it is not alone. It is virtually tied with Italy for the lowest rate of per capita arrests (~0.6 cannabis offense per 1,000 population). This is very different from column 5, where the Italian rate was more than three times the Dutch rate. The United States had the second-lowest offense rate in terms of users but the second-highest in terms of total population (2.4).

Conceptually, arrests per 1,000 past-month users seem much more compelling than the per capita rate as a measure of the toughness of the regime. A nation with a larger cannabis problem will be expected to make more arrests per capita for cannabis offenses, ceteris paribus. A better denominator would use a measure of consumption such as use days or grams consumed; these estimates are just beginning to be developed in the United States (e.g., Humphreys 2015) and have not been calculated for any other country.

Another factor to consider in comparing drug arrest statistics is that not all drug-involved arrests are classified as such. In addition to the hierarchy rules, in the United States, offenders under community supervision (e.g., probation or parole) who are caught with drugs may simply be arrested for a violation of supervision since it typically does not require filing new charges (and in some places involves a lower burden of proof). In addition, drug offenders who missed a court appointment and have been issued a bench warrant may be brought in by police and booked only for the warrant. It is unknown how often this happens.

We conclude this section by highlighting a critical question that remains largely unanswered: What is the expected sanction of a drug law offense conditional on being detected by law enforcement officials?

B. Adjudication and Sentencing

What happens after an individual is apprehended by law enforcement for an alleged drug offense varies across and within countries and by substance. Unfortunately, detailed data on adjudication and sentencing of drug offenses, especially for possession or use, are hard to locate and harder to compare.

Many countries track information about drug arrests and convictions, but the information reported to international bodies varies. The EMCDDA does not ask member states to report drug conviction data regularly, while the fifth edition of the *European Sourcebook on Criminal Justice Statistics* (Aebi et al. 2010) collects conviction information for all drug offenses and drug trafficking.[39] As with arrests, caution is required if attempting to use these *Sourcebook* conviction data for cross-national comparisons. One example from the chapter endnotes: "In the Netherlands many cases are dealt with by the prosecution imposing a fine (a 'transactie'). The case is not brought before a court and, technically, the offender does not admit guilt, so these cases are excluded from the tables in Chapter 3 [which focuses on convictions]" (p. 194). Since many drug possession offenses are dealt with via fines, this is a notable caveat.

There are striking inconsistencies in data reported for countries. For example, table 10 presents per capita drug trafficking conviction figures for England and Wales, Northern Ireland, and Scotland from the *European Sourcebook*. It is difficult to believe that Scotland, admittedly with a somewhat more serious drug problem than England and Wales, is nonetheless convicting 15 times as many drug traffickers per 1,000 population. The most likely explanation for this extraordinary difference is to be found in the definitions of offenses of conviction.[40]

It is possible to get information about the number of days sentenced to incarceration for some offenses in some jurisdictions, but this information provides an incomplete picture.[41] Most obviously, days sentenced is not the same as days served, and in some places, prison sentences are immediately

[39] Comprehensive comparisons should also consider the extent to which drug convictions are expunged from criminal records. Is it possible, and if so, does it happen automatically after a certain period of time, or does the offender have to initiate the process?

[40] For analysts interested in conviction trends, the outlook is mixed. Using data from the first three *Sourcebook* versions, Aebi and Linde (2012) argue that for western European countries from 1990 to 2006, "changes in legal definitions had only punctual effects that, in general, did not alter the overall trend observed on convictions for each type of offence" (p. 114). However, after the breakup of the USSR, there were major changes to criminal law in eastern and central Europe: "such changes should have a minor impact on very serious offences such as homicide, [but] they surely had some effect on the trends in convictions for other offences" (p. 114).

[41] Ideally we need case- and individual-level data including criminal history and information about other charges associated with the arrest. In countries with plea negotiations, preeminently the United States, it would also be useful to know whether the defendant was offered a plea agreement and was ultimately convicted of a lesser charge. If analysts are unable to condition sentences for other factors (e.g., a prior conviction for violence), it can complicate inferences about how strict the country is about drug policy.

TABLE 10

Persons Convicted per 100,000 Population in the United Kingdom, Drug Offenses: Drug Trafficking

	2003	2004	2005	2006	2007
England and Wales	2.0	1.9	2.0	1.6	1.5
Northern Ireland	7.0	10.6	8.6	9.1	. . .
Scotland	32.0	35.5	33.5	. . .	. . .

SOURCE.—Aebi et al. (2010).

suspended (see fig. 3). Second, many of those sentenced to community supervision or a fine may eventually serve time in confinement for not complying with conditions or not paying. Finally, some arrested for a drug offense may spend time behind bars before they are convicted.

The EMCDDA asked member states to report information about the outcomes of drug law offenses for one of its "Selected Issues" reports. While the resulting document does not include information for specific drugs (as some countries do not collect data at this level), it does provide useful insights to those seeking to learn from cross-national comparisons (EMCDDA 2009*a*).[42] Many countries collect separate sentencing data for "drug use and personal possession offenses" and "drug supply offenses." Figure 3 provides information on sentences ordered for persons convicted for drug use and personal possession in 14 countries.

Figure 3 displays substantial cross-national variation, with fines, suspended prison sentences, and "other" outcomes being the most common sanctions reported for drug use and personal possession offenses. These data combine information for first-time and repeat offenders; this could account for some of the variation. The Netherlands has the highest incarceration rate conditional on conviction, which might be thought surprising since the Netherlands is known for being fairly lax about possessing small amounts of illegal drugs. It is unclear what is driving this. The numbers are comparatively small (3,190 in 2012) compared with Denmark, which had a population only a third as large but sentenced 12,500.[43] It might be the case that the Dutch do not keep statistics on most possession

[42] Detailed information is published at http://www.emcdda.europa.eu/attachements.cfm/att_92889_EN_onlineannex_SIsentencing.pdf.

[43] We owe this observation to Melvin Soudijn.

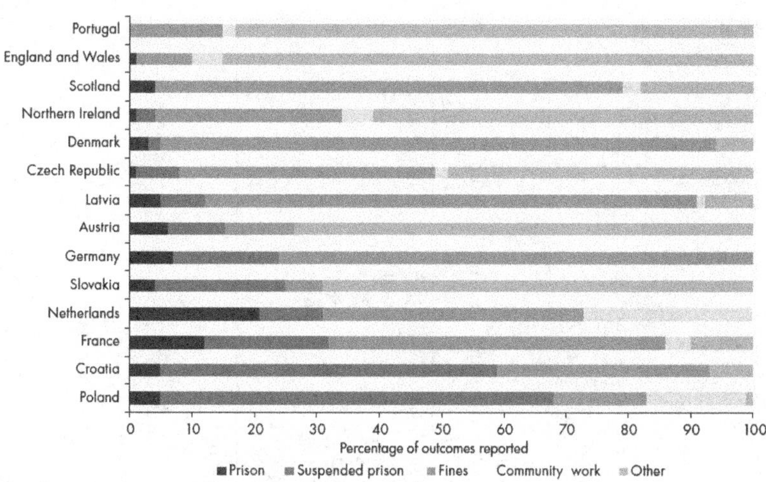

FIG. 3.—Outcomes for persons convicted of drug use and personal possession offenses, ca. 2006. Source: Reproduced from EMCDDA (2009*b*).

violations, and those that do lead to a recorded arrest are aggressively punished. It may also be the case that some of these individuals were in fact traffickers.

The EMCDDA notes that a similar chart focused on sentences for drug supply offenses was more uniform, with prison and suspended prison sentences accounting for the vast majority of sentences. It is unclear what conditions must be met to keep the prison sentence suspended and how many eventually turn into time behind bars. In some cases it is likely that offenders with substance use problems will be required to attend self-help meetings or participate in a drug treatment program.

The number of prison admissions in the United States has steadily declined since 2006, but it continues to have the highest incarceration rate in the world. At the end of 2011, 16.6 percent of inmates in state prisons were incarcerated for drug offenses; the number would exceed 20 percent if convicted offenders in federal and county facilities were included. This is not greatly higher than the 14 percent share of prisoners in a number of European countries convicted of drug trafficking shown in table 11, including the Netherlands. The outlier is Italy.

Even if good cross-national comparisons could be made of arrest, conviction, and incarceration probabilities, there remain other consequences that go beyond the criminal justice system and vary between countries.

TABLE 11

Prisoners Sentenced for Drug Trafficking

Country	Prison Population Sentenced for Drug Trafficking	Total Prison Population Sentenced	% Sentenced for Drug Trafficking	Total Number of Inmates (including Pretrial Detainees)	Imprisonment Rate: Sentenced*	Imprisonment Rate: Total Inmates*
England and Wales	10,688	73,562	14.5	86,048	130.0	152.1
France	8,269	59,492	13.9	76,407	91.1	117.0
Germany	8,125	57,607	14.1	69,268	70.4	84.6
Netherlands	793	5,658	14.0	11,324	33.8	67.7
Italy	15,080	38,906	38.8	66,271	65.5	111.6
Australia	3,633	30,768	11.8			
United States, state and federal	237,000	1,362,028	17.4			

SOURCE.—Carson and Sabol (2012); Aebi and Delgrande (2014); Australian Bureau of Statistics (2014).

* Rate per 100,000 inhabitants.

The United States may be unique in the range of consequences outside the justice system that follow convictions for drug offenses. These can include loss or suspension of professional licenses and loss of food assistance, access to public housing, and federal financial aid for postsecondary education.

C. Seizures

Levels of drug seizures are a function of several factors including the quantity shipped, the relative skill of the interdictors, the care taken by smugglers, and whether the jurisdiction is a known transshipment point (Reuter 1995). Changes in any of these factors can lead to changes in seizures, and there is rarely any basis for distinguishing the source of an increase or decrease in observed quantities. In addition, seizure data must be placed in the context of whether the country is primarily a producer, a transit country, or a consumer of illegal drugs. For example, much of the cocaine entering Europe comes through Spain or the Netherlands (UNODC 2011), so it would be incorrect to assume that total amounts of cocaine seized are correlated with domestic consumption.

Most European countries report information about the total number of seizures and the total weight to the EMCDDA. Some also report seizure-specific data of "significant" quantities to the UNODC on a biannual basis (Kilmer et al. 2010, table 4.2).[44] Australia and the United States do not contribute to this database. These publicly available UNODC data include the raw quantity seized, the place of seizure, and for some seizures, the mode of transportation and the departure and destination countries, which allows the mapping of routes of drug smuggling. The data do not include information about the purity of what is seized, though there is evidence that even very large shipments can be of quite modest purity (ca. 60 percent), contrary to what one might expect of rational smugglers (Paoli, Greenfield, and Reuter 2009).[45]

[44] The information is presented per seizure case and contains details, as reported, on the type of drug, place and date of seizure, quantity seized, origin and destination of drug seized, means of transportation, and the number and nationality of traffickers. An analysis of these data is included in the regional drug trafficking trend reports and other statistical documents prepared by UNODC. Information is reported only for seizures above these thresholds: opium, cannabis herb, cannabis resin, and cannabis plants: 1 kilogram and above; heroin, morphine, and cocaine: 100 grams and above; psychotropic substances: 100 grams and above; and seizures referring to trafficking by mail: all quantities.

[45] See also http://www.unodc.org/documents/data-and-analysis/statistics/Drugs/Seizure_Cases_Guidance_Note_English.pdf.

Total weights seized and numbers of seizures often tell different stories for a country. A few abnormally large seizures can have a noticeable effect on annual statistics. Figure 4 presents heroin seizures by number and total weight for the United Kingdom and Germany. For the United Kingdom, the number of seizures from 2003 to 2010 was fairly stable, fluctuating around 13,000 each year. However, the total weight of heroin seized during this period plummeted from 2,700 kilograms to less than 900. The number of seizures in Germany was very stable at 6,000–7,000 per year, but the total weight seized fluctuated greatly. There was a 70 percent rise from 2003 to 2007 followed by a 55 percent decrease through 2010.

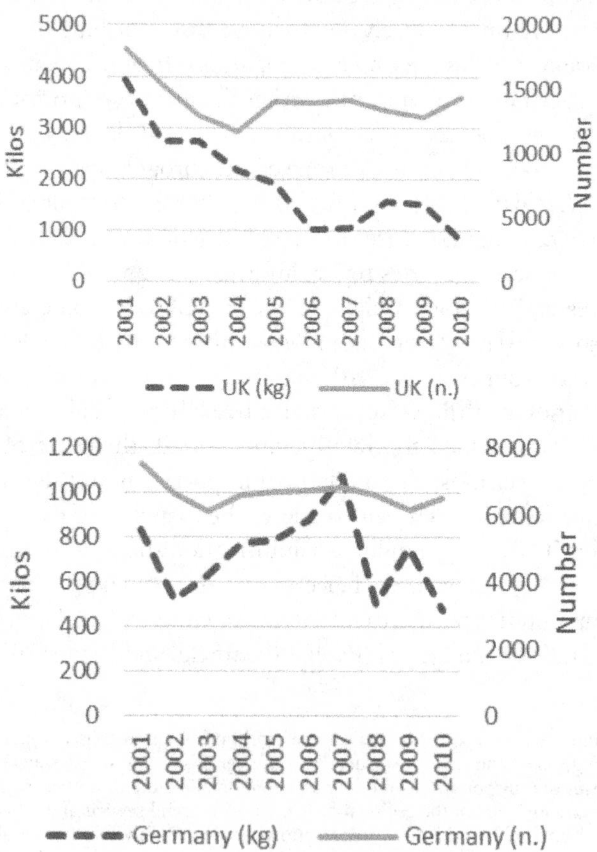

FIG. 4.—Heroin seizures, number, and total weight, United Kingdom and Germany. Source: EMCDDA.

There is clearly room for improvement in the collection and analysis of seizure data. Reviewing the data available about seizures, Kilmer et al. (2010) recommended that information about the total number, total weight, and median weight (and purity if possible) was reported for transactions at different levels of the market. While the "weight bins" that capture the retail, midlevel, and wholesale transactions will likely differ by country and drug, reporting data for these bins can allow law enforcement officials to learn more about whether certain activities are influencing the market.[46]

D. Prices, Purity, and Potency

Price plays an important, albeit ambiguous, role in drug policy. Lower prices tend to lead to higher consumption and many of the consequences associated with greater use. Higher prices, though lowering consumption, will generate higher revenues for drug sellers and criminal organizations, assuming that the demand is inelastic as most studies show (Gallet 2014). Rises in price are regularly offered by police forces as evidence of success in drug enforcement, even though they can inflate criminal earnings.

The price paid for illegal drugs in an individual transaction is determined by many factors. These include distance between production and purchase locations, the amount being purchased, the purity or potency, the buyer-seller relationship, and policy interventions that aim to create risks for selling and transporting drugs. These risks are a function of the expected legal sanction (i.e., the probability of detection and the severity of punishment if convicted). Separate from this are threats of robbery and violence from other participants, which may also raise prices. The main goal of drug law enforcement is to increase the expected sanction for supplying drugs, which, in theory, should increase the retail price as sellers need to be compensated for their risk of arrest and incarceration (Reuter and Kleiman 1986).[47] Since drug users are price sensitive (see, e.g., Gallet 2014), the increase in retail prices should reduce consumption.

[46] The EMCDDA is now attempting to do this, but it is unclear how many countries will be able to report seizure information in this format (personal communication with Paul Griffiths, May 2015).

[47] Prohibition inflates retail prices since there are structural costs of product illegality (Caulkins and Reuter 1998). Caulkins and Lee (2012) provide a revealing example: "The precautions required to evade detection make the production of drugs very labor intensive. Grocery-store cashiers, for instance, are more than 100 times as productive as re-

Unfortunately, price does not represent a straightforward variable. Cocaine, heroin, and methamphetamine vary in their purity. Marijuana varies in its THC content, best thought of as potency. Thus to measure the true price, it is necessary to measure purity and produce a "purity-adjusted price." Most observed variation in street-level drug prices comes from changes in purity rather than nominal price (Caulkins 1994; Caulkins, Rajderkar, and Vasudev 2010). A dime bag typically costs $10, but what is inside fluctuates over time and location.

Extensive analyses of purity-adjusted prices have been conducted in the United States, largely reliant on the Drug Enforcement Administration's System to Retrieve Information from Drug Evidence (STRIDE). STRIDE includes purity data from police seizures and from transactions involving money (e.g., from undercover buys). Elaborate algorithms have been produced to convert information from this administrative data system into national and subnational price series (Arkes et al. 2004; Fries et al. 2008). This information has been used to evaluate various drug law enforcement efforts (e.g., Kuziemko and Levitt 2004; Dobkin and Nicosia 2009).[48]

Very few countries have a STRIDE equivalent, and in some places undercover purchases are illegal. The United Kingdom's Project ENDORSE is a notable exception, which has many of the same attributes as STRIDE (Serious Organised Crime Agency 2011). Australia uses an annual survey of drug users to estimate purity-adjusted prices (Stafford and Burns 2013).

The EMCDDA undertook a feasibility study in 2009 to collect wholesale-level purity-adjusted prices, and as a result, "10 countries revised or have set plans to revise their internal law enforcement practices, to comply with this data price collecting framework" (Costa Storti 2011, p. 9). RAND conducted a survey of the European Network of Forensic Science Institutes and found that a majority of respondents had

tail drug sellers in terms of items sold per labor hour. Similarly, hired hands working for crack dealers can fill about 100 vials per hour, whereas even older-model sugar-packing machines can fill between 500 and 1,000 sugar packets per 'minute.' This labor intensity of drug production, combined with the high wages demanded for that labor, are what drive up the costs of drugs; by comparison, materials and supplies—glassine bags, gram balances, and even guns—are relatively cheap."

48. STRIDE does not collect information about the potency of marijuana seizures and transactions. However, a different database maintained by the University of Mississippi collects THC, CBD, and other cannabinoid levels for thousands of law enforcement samples sent to Drug Enforcement Administration labs. See Sevigny, Pacula, and Heaton (2014) for a recent policy analysis involving these data.

computer databases with drug purity information; half went back to the year 2000 or earlier. The survey also revealed that "the vast majority of respondents would in fact be willing to share this information with researchers under certain conditions" (Pacula, Kilmer, and Hunt 2010, p. 42). It would be helpful if these purity observations could be linked back to specific transactions. However, Caulkins, Rajderkar, and Vasudev (2010) have demonstrated that with enough high-frequency forensic data, it is possible to create a purity-adjusted price series without price data.

While most analyses involving purity-adjusted prices assess within-country variation, these data can be useful for understanding the downstream effects of drug law enforcement efforts on prices in other countries (Chandra, Barkell, and Stefan 2011; Chandra and Barkell 2012). As countries significantly vary the intensity of drug law enforcement efforts or experiment with new legal regimes, information about purity- or THC-adjusted prices will be critical for understanding these efforts' effects on wholesale and retail drug markets.

E. *Summary*

Focusing on drug law enforcement is much more important for cross-national drug policy comparisons than focusing on drug laws, but it is also much more difficult. National law enforcement data are seldom directly comparable with information from other countries. Further, countries sometimes report conflicting figures to different international agencies for similar measures. Inferences from cross-national comparisons may vary depending on how data are denominated (e.g., by population size or number of drug users).

Expected sanctions associated with using or possessing illegal drugs appear to be quite low in most developed countries. Even if information about arrests and sentences were comparable across countries, uncertainty about the fractions of drug offenses that lead to an arrest or formal caution make it hard to capture the true expected sanction for breaking a drug law.

Even if two countries had identical expected sanctions for possessing or selling a particular drug, that would not necessarily mean that the countries have similar approaches to being "tough" on drugs. If one country gives 50 percent of sellers a 1-month prison sentence and the other gives 1 percent of sellers a 50-month sentence, they would both have the same expected sanction. Their approaches to policing, adjudicating, and sentencing sellers would be quite different.

VI. Concluding Comments

Over the past 40 years a number of developed countries have changed their approaches to illegal drugs. Some have formally reduced the penalties for possessing small amounts of all illegal drugs. Others have addressed cannabis supply by tolerating home production or explicitly not enforcing the law against small-scale transactions (Room et al. 2008). What is currently happening with legal, large-scale marijuana production in Colorado and Washington is unprecedented in the modern era (Kilmer et al. 2013). It is likely that other jurisdictions will experiment with alternatives to marijuana prohibition in the coming years. Voters in Alaska, Oregon, and the District of Columbia approved marijuana legalization in 2014. Whether there will be widespread change remains to be seen; much will likely depend on what happens with these early adopters.

Will the marijuana reform efforts spill over to other illegal drugs such as cocaine and heroin? That seems unlikely in the short run, but experts' predictions should be taken with heaps of salt. We are aware of no one in the drug policy analysis community in 2005 who predicted that marijuana would be legalized in multiple states and an entire country within 10 years. Note, however, that there is little sign of reductions in punitiveness in some other regions of the world, notably Asia and parts of Africa.

It is not just laws that are changing. In the Western world, there has also been a shift in programmatic approaches. Broadly speaking, there has been increasing emphasis on punishing dealers along with the provision of more treatment for users and more prevention services (Reuter and Trautmann 2009).[49]

There is much to learn from the growing differences in drug policies and drug problems. Unfortunately, existing data systems make it difficult to exploit this heterogeneity to improve our knowledge of what works best to improve social welfare. To this end, after briefly describing current barriers, we offer some ideas for a path forward.

We emphasize the problems of comparisons in general population surveys not because this measure is a particularly useful indicator of drug

[49] The United States in the last few years has been an exception to the statement about increased punitiveness toward dealers (see Kilmer, Midgette, and Saloga 2015). As part of a broad effort to reduce state prison populations, there has been a reduction in incarceration of those convicted of drug offenses. At the federal level, the Attorney General has directed prosecutors to lower charges for many drug dealers.

policy outcomes but because it has such a firm grip on popular and political views of the drug problem. No analysis will be credible for policy purposes if it does not take account of the prevalence of use. Superficially there appears to be a great deal of comparable prevalence data from general population surveys in many countries. However, as we showed, fundamental differences in methodology make national estimates, even if corrected for age range differences, simply not comparable for many countries. Poorly documented changes in methods over time for individual countries make the problem worse.

If GPSs must be used, there should be more focus on computing total use days, especially for marijuana-related analyses. Focusing on prevalence alone can mask potentially important changes across and within countries. For example, Burns et al. (2013) show that the share of past-year marijuana users in the United States increased by roughly 15 percent from 2007 to 2011, but the number of marijuana use days increased by more than 30 percent. The increase was driven by an increase in the number of marijuana users reporting daily or near-daily use. Use day figures could be useful for improving measures of enforcement risk.

Moving to our preferred indicators, prevalence of problem use, consumption, and expenditures, there has been progress only on the first. The EMCDDA has encouraged member states to develop occasional estimates of PDU, but the results often demonstrate false precision and so many inconsistencies as to have limited credibility in some European countries. Estimates of hard drug consumption and expenditure have not received systematic attention outside the United States.

Turning to the question of comparing policies, we have focused on enforcement. Measures of enforcement intensity should use market size as the denominator. Even when that is attempted, familiar conceptual and administrative problems bedevil cross-national comparisons. A few are specific to drugs, including how to distinguish possession and distribution offenses and how to measure seizures and prices. The last is an intermediate outcome of separate interest.

Can the situation be improved? Of course. We offer proposals intended to be practical, to build on what exists and not imagine a new world.

First, there should be an international repository for GPS respondent-level data collected by developed countries. Despite well-charted limitations in these data, additional insights can be gained by making them readily available to researchers around the globe, for example, to allow for comparisons for similar age groups. The host would be responsible for collecting these data, translating variable names, creating codebooks, granting permissions to researchers, and possibly facilitating online analysis. Since there are obvious privacy concerns even with de-identified data and some countries may not allow foreigners to analyze their data, an intermediate solution may be to make select variables from these surveys available to international researchers. Over the last two decades a variety of arrangements have been developed, reflecting new technologies, to allow access to data for analysis while preserving privacy protections.[50]

Second, there is need to generate standardized information from GPSs across countries. It is unrealistic to think that all countries could or would want to commit to converting their GPS to a universal survey instrument, but periodically supplementing existing surveys with a global module would provide important new information. This would include the same questions, modality, age range, and relative incentives (e.g., five times the price of a Big Mac in the capital city) and would greatly increase long-term understanding of differences among nations in the use of popular intoxicants.[51] Even more useful would be to include biological validity checks. There is substantial variation in valid reporting across subpopulations within the United States. There is no reason to believe that rates of honesty are constant across countries.

The International Crime Victims Survey, though not without its limits, presents a useful model. It has not supplanted individual national victimization surveys where those are well established. For those countries, it provides a supplement. In other nations it provides the sole source of victimization data. As Lynch (2006) notes, comparability comes at a cost; the budgets are inevitably small and samples are too small for all but the broadest comparisons. If an international drug use survey is developed, there may be small national samples. Given that use of most expensive drugs is a rare behavior, comparisons for all but the most popular intoxicants will be crude.

[50] It is now possible for researchers to access the NSDUH with state- and substate-level indicators. Researchers must submit an application: "For approved projects, a researcher downloads software onto their computer that allows them to access servers where the confidential data reside" (http://www.icpsr.umich.edu/icpsrweb/SAMHDA/support/faqs/2012/02/is-state-level-data-available-for-nsduh). Researchers cannot store data on their own computers, and their access can be gained only "through approved computer location(s) and IP address(es) at the researcher's organization" (http://www.icpsr.umich.edu/icpsrweb/content/SAMHDA/dp-call.html).

[51] The EMCDDA has made significant progress on this front with the European Model Questionnaire (http://www.emcdda.europa.eu/html.cfm/index19541EN.html).

However, even the best GPSs are weak as the source of estimates of the number of frequent users of expensive drugs. The US estimates of frequent users perhaps are a reasonable proxy for PDU but build on a data set, the Arrestee Drug Abuse Monitoring, which did not attract much international interest and was recently abandoned. Developing comparable estimates of these numbers requires further investigation of the techniques that the EMCDDA uses in Europe. We are agnostic as to whether these can be developed so as to provide comparable estimates across a broader set of nations. We encourage discussions of the utility and possibility of reviving the international ADAM (I-ADAM) program (Taylor 2002) or creating something similar (e.g., an international survey of probationers).

Finally, to compare drug law enforcement across countries and over time, more effort should be placed on estimating the time offenders spend behind bars for drug offenses and denominating for specific substances by past-month use days or the number of problem users. This measure is not without problems, but incarceration days per heavy user may serve as a better proxy for the punitiveness of drug policies than per capita arrests. One possibility is to build on existing jail and prison censuses to determine how many individuals are behind bars for drug offenses, including those who are incarcerated before conviction.[52] Efforts could be made to conduct them on the same day across countries (e.g., March 31, every 5 years).

We have focused on aspects of drug problems that are easier to measure, so it may be useful to highlight important indicators for which cross-nationally consistent systems seem unattainable. Figures on nonfatal drug overdoses require special data collection that is hard to justify in countries with modest drug problems. Fatal overdoses, to the extent that they are not well captured by public health systems of recording causes of death, are difficult to collect on a consistent basis. Compara-

[52] A European Commission–funded prison census of "Mentally Disordered Persons in European Prison Systems" is conducted in a number of European countries on December 31 or March 31 of each year (Salize, Dreßing, and Kief 2007). Some countries collect more than just a total number. The report for Finland notes, "On census day (31.12.2004), the prison population was distributed as follows: prisoners serving a sentence, 2,953; fine defaulters, 35; prisoners held in preventive detention for dangerous recidivists, 24; juvenile prisoners, 62; remand prisoners, 461. . . . The most common principal offences of the prisoners serving their sentence in 1 May 2004 were homicide (18.1%), narcotics offense (17.9%) and other violent offence (17.2%)" (p. 138). It is unclear how many countries collect this level of information or can disaggregate narcotics offenses by substance.

ble measures of the contributions of drugs to nations' crime problems also seem unattainable for conceptual and institutional reasons.

The complexities surrounding data collection on sensitive topics and the difficulties of trying to standardize data collection across multiple jurisdictions are daunting. That said, improving the comparability of measures of drug problems and drug policies is worth the effort.[53] Learning from other nations is an increasingly acceptable avenue for gaining policy insights. There is enough similarity across developed countries in the fundamental nature of their drug problems for this to be a fruitful path forward.

REFERENCES

Abraham, M. D., P. D. A. Cohen, and D. J. Beukenhorst. 2001. "Comparative Cannabis Use Data." *British Journal of Psychiatry* 179(2):175–77.

Aebi, Marcelo F., Bruno Aubusson de Cavarlay, Gordon Barclay, Beata Gruszczynska, Stefan Harrendorf, Markku Heiskanen, Vasilika Hysi, Véronique Jaquier, Jörg-Martin Jehle, Martin Killias, Olena Shostko, Paul Smit, and Ranneveig Borisdottir. 2010. *European Sourcebook of Crime and Criminal Justice—2010*. https://english.wodc.nl/images/ob285_full%20text_tcm45-294766.pdf.

Aebi, Marcelo F., and Natalia Delgrande. 2013. *Council of Europe Annual Penal Statistics. SPACE I. Survey 2011*. Strasbourg: Council of Europe.

———. 2014. *Council of Europe Annual Penal Statistics. SPACE I. Survey 2012*. Strasbourg: Council of Europe.

Aebi, Marcelo F., and Antonia Linde. 2012. "Conviction Statistics as an Indicator of Crime Trends in Europe from 1990 to 2006." *European Journal on Criminal Policy and Research* 18(1):103–44. doi:10.1007/s10610-011-9166-7.

Aquilino, William S. 1992. "Telephone versus Face-to-Face Interviewing for Household Drug Use Surveys." *International Journal of the Addictions* 27(1):71–91.

———. 1994. "Interview Mode Effects in Surveys of Drug and Alcohol Use: A Field Experiment." *Public Opinion Quarterly* 58(2):210–40. doi:10.1086/269419.

Arkes, Jeremy, Rosalie L. Pacula, Susan Paddock, Jonathan P. Caulkins, and Peter Reuter. 2004. *Technical Report for the Price and Purity of Illicit Drugs: 1982 through the Second Quarter of 2003*. Washington, DC: RAND, Drug Policy Research Center. https://www.ncjrs.gov/ondcppubs/publications/pdf/price_purity_tech_rpt.pdf.

[53] An anonymous reviewer correctly notes, "Improvements in comparative data quality would cost a tiny fraction of the amounts that are currently invested in drug policies."

Australian Bureau of Statistics. 2014. "2011 Census QuickStats: Australia." http://www.censusdata.abs.gov.au/census_services/getproduct/census/2011/quickstat/0.

Australian Institute of Health and Welfare. 2011. "2010 National Drug Strategy Household Survey Report." Drug Statistics Series. Canberra: Australian Institute of Health and Welfare. http://www.aihw.gov.au/WorkArea/DownloadAsset.aspx?id=10737421314.

Babor, Thomas F., Jonathan P. Caulkins, Griffith Edwards, Benedikt Fischer, David R. Foxcroft, Keith Humphreys, Isidore S. Obot, Jürgen Rehm, and Peter Reuter. 2010. *Drug Policy and the Public Good.* New York: Oxford University Press.

Banta-Green, Caleb, and Jennifer Field. 2011. "City-Wide Drug Testing Using Municipal Wastewater." *Significance* 8(2):70–74.

Beebe, Timothy J., James A. McRae Jr., Patricia A. Harrison, Michael E. Davern, and Kathryn B. Quinlan. 2005. "Mail Surveys Resulted in More Reports of Substance Use than Telephone Surveys." *Journal of Clinical Epidemiology* 58(4):421–24. doi:10.1016/j.jclinepi.2004.10.007.

Bjarnason, Thoroddur, Andreea Steriu, and Anna Kokkevi. 2010. "Cannabis Supply and Demand Reduction: Evidence from the ESPAD Study of Adolescents in 31 European Countries." *Drugs: Education, Prevention, and Policy* 17 (2):123–34. doi:10.3109/09687630802419155.

Bowling, Ann. 2005. "Mode of Questionnaire Administration Can Have Serious Effects on Data Quality." *Journal of Public Health* 27(3):281–91.

Burgard, Daniel A., Caleb Banta-Green, and Jennifer A. Field. 2014. "Working Upstream: How Far Can You Go with Sewage-Based Drug Epidemiology?" *Environmental Science and Technology* 48(3):1362–68.

Burns, Rachel M., Jonathan P. Caulkins, Susan S. Everingham, and Beau Kilmer. 2013. "Statistics on Cannabis Users Skew Perceptions of Cannabis Use." *Frontiers in Psychiatry* 4:138.

Carson, Ann, and William J. Sabol. 2012. *Prisoners in 2011.* Washington, DC: US Department of Justice, Bureau of Justice Statistics.

Castiglioni, Sara, Kevin V. Thomas, Barbara Kasprzyk-Hordern, Liesbeth Vandam, and Paul Griffiths. 2013. "Testing Wastewater to Detect Illicit Drugs: State of the Art, Potential and Research Needs." *Science of the Total Environment* 487(July):613–20.

Caulkins, Jonathan P. 1994 *Developing a Price Series for Cocaine.* Santa Monica, CA: RAND Corporation.

Caulkins, Jonathan P., Beau Kilmer, and Marlon Graf. 2013. "Estimating the Size of the EU Cannabis Market." In *Further Insights into Aspects of the Illicit EU Drugs Market*, edited by Franz Trautmann, Beau Kilmer, and Paul Turnbull. Luxembourg: Publications Office of the European Union. http://ec.europa.eu/justice/anti-drugs/files/eu_market_full.pdf.

Caulkins, Jonathan P., Beau Kilmer, Peter H. Reuter, and Greg Midgette. 2015. "Cocaine's Fall and Marijuana's Rise: Questions and Insights Based on New Estimates of Consumption and Expenditures in US Drug Markets." *Addiction* 110(5):728–36. doi:10.1111/add.12628.

Caulkins, Jonathan P., and Michael A. C. Lee. 2012. "The Drug-Policy Roulette." *National Affairs*. http://www.nationalaffairs.com/publications/detail/the-drug-policy-roulette.

Caulkins, Jonathan P., Sudha S. Rajderkar, and Shruti Vasudev. 2010. "Appendix A. Creating Price Series without Data: Harnessing the Power of Forensic Data." In *Understanding Illicit Drug Markets, Supply Reduction Efforts, and Drug-Related Crime in the European Union*, edited by Beau Kilmer and Stijn Hoorens. Cambridge: RAND.

Caulkins, Jonathan P., and Peter H. Reuter. 1998. "What Price Data Tell Us about Drug Markets." *Journal of Drug Issues* 28(3):593–613.

———. 2010. "How Drug Enforcement Affects Drug Prices." In *Crime and Justice: A Review of Research*, vol. 39, edited by Michael Tonry. Chicago: University of Chicago Press.

Centers for Disease Control and Prevention. 2011. "Vital Signs: Overdoses of Prescription Opioid Pain Relievers—United States, 1999–2008." *Morbidity and Mortality Weekly Report* 60(43):1487–92. http://www.cdc.gov/mmwr/preview/mmwrhtml/mm6043a4.htm.

Chandra, Siddharth, and Matthew Barkell. 2012. "What the Price Data Tell Us about Heroin Flows across Europe." *International Journal of Comparative and Applied Criminal Justice* 37(1):1–13.

Chandra, Siddharth, Matthew Barkell, and Kelly Steffen. 2011. "Inferring Cocaine Flows across Europe: Evidence from Price Data?" *Journal of Drug Policy Analysis* 4(1).

Chen, Patrick, Devon Cribb, Lanting Dai, Harper Gordek, Jeff Laufenberg, Neeraja Sathe, and Matthew Westlake. 2011. *2009 National Survey on Drug Use and Health: Person-Level Sampling Weight Calibration*. Rockville, MD: Substance Abuse and Mental Health Services Administration.

Coelho, Pinto M. 2010. *The "Resounding Success" of Portuguese Drug Policy: The Power of an Attractive Fallacy*. Lisbon: Associação para Uma Portugal Livre de Drogas. http://www.drugfree.org.au/fileadmin/library/Policies__Legislation_and_law/ThePortugueseDrugFallacyReport.pdf.

Cohen, Peter D. A., and Hendrien L. Kaal. 2001. *The Irrelevance of Drug Policy: Patterns and Careers of Experienced Cannabis Use in the Populations of Amsterdam, San Francisco and Bremen*. Amsterdam: CEDRO. http://www.cedro-uva.org/lib/cohen.3cities.html.

Cook, Philip J. 2007 *Paying the Tab: The Costs and Benefits of Alcohol Control*. Princeton, NJ: Princeton University Press.

Costa Storti, Cláudia. 2011. *Pilot Study on Wholesale Drug Prices in Europe*. Lisbon: European Monitoring Centre for Drugs and Drug Addiction. http://www.emcdda.europa.eu/attachements.cfm/att_143083_EN_PilotStudy_WDP%20in%20Europe.pdf.

Decorte, Tom, Dimitri Mortelmans, Julie Tieberghien, and Sabrine De Moore. 2009. "Drug Use: An Overview of General Population Surveys in Europe." Lisbon: European Monitoring Centre for Drugs and Drug Addiction. http://www.emcdda.europa.eu/publications/thematic-papers/gps.

Degenhardt, Louisa, Wai-Tat Chiu, Nancy Sampson, Ronald C. Kessler, James C. Anthony, Matthias Angermeyer, Ronny Bruffaerts, et al. 2008. "Toward a Global View of Alcohol, Tobacco, Cannabis, and Cocaine Use: Findings from the WHO World Mental Health Surveys." *PLoS Med* 5(7):e141. doi:10.1371/journal.pmed.0050141.

———. 2010. "Evaluating the Drug Use 'Gateway' Theory Using Cross-National Data: Consistency and Associations of the Order of Initiation of Drug Use among Participants in the WHO World Mental Health Surveys." *Drug and Alcohol Dependence* 108(1–2):84–97.

Degenhardt, Louisa, and Wayne Hall. 2012 "Extent of Illicit Drug Use and Its Contribution to the Global Burden of Disease." *Lancet* 379:55–66.

Degenhardt, Louisa, Peter Reuter, Linette Collins, and Wayne Hall. 2005. "Evaluating Explanations of the Australian 'Heroin Shortage.'" *Addiction* 100(4):459–69.

Dobkin, Carlos, and Nancy Nicosia. 2009. "The War on Drugs: Methamphetamine, Public Health, and Crime." *American Economic Review* 99(1):324–49.

EMCDDA (European Monitoring Centre for Drugs and Drug Addiction). 2004. *EMCDDA Recommended Draft Technical Tools and Guidelines. Key Epidemiological Indicator: Prevalence of Problem Drug Use*. Lisbon: European Monitoring Centre for Drugs and Drug Addiction. http://www.emcdda.europa.eu/html.cfm/index65519EN.html.

———. 2009*a*. "Drug Offences: Sentencing and Other Outcomes." Lisbon: European Monitoring Centre for Drugs and Drug Addiction. http://www.emcdda.europa.eu/publications/selected-issues/sentencing-statistics.

———. 2009*b*. *An Overview of the Drug-Related Deaths and Mortality among Drug Users (DRD) Key Indicator*. Lisbon: European Monitoring Centre for Drugs and Drug Addiction.

———. 2012. "Prevalence of Daily Cannabis Use in the European Union and Norway." Luxembourg: Publications Office of the European Union. http://www.emcdda.europa.eu/attachements.cfm/att_191926_EN_emcdda-daily-cannabis-use-2012.pdf.

———. 2013*a*. "Drug Law Offences—an Overview of the Methods and Definitions Used." Lisbon: European Monitoring Centre for Drugs and Drug Addiction. http://www.emcdda.europa.eu/stats13#dlo:displayMethods.

———. 2013*b*. "European Drug Report." Lisbon: European Monitoring Centre for Drugs and Drug Addiction. http://www.emcdda.europa.eu/edr2013.

———. 2013*c*. "Wastewater Analysis." Lisbon: European Monitoring Centre for Drugs and Drug Addiction. http://www.emcdda.europa.eu/wastewater-analysis.

———. 2014*a*. "EMCDDA—Methods and Definitions." Lisbon: European Monitoring Centre for Drugs and Drug Addiction. http://www.emcdda.europa.eu/stats07/PDU/methods.

———. 2014*b*. "Studies of the Problematic Drug Use Population." Lisbon: European Monitoring Centre for Drugs and Drug Addiction. http://stats05.emcdda.europa.eu/en/page014-en.html.

———. 2014*c*. *Wastewater Analysis and Drugs: A European Multi-city Study*. Lisbon: European Monitoring Centre for Drugs and Drug Addiction.

EMCDDA and Centre for Drug Misuse Research. 1999. "Methodological Guidelines to Estimate the Prevalence of Problem Drug Use on the Local Level." Lisbon: European Monitoring Centre for Drugs and Drug Addiction.

Enzmann, Dirk, Ineke Haen Marshall, Martin Killias, Josine Junger-Tas, Majone Steketee, and Beata Gruszczynska. 2010. "Self-Reported Youth Delinquency in Europe and Beyond: First Results of the Second International Self-Report Delinquency Study in the Context of Police and Victimization Data." *European Journal of Criminology* 7(2):159–83.

Farrell, Graham, Kashfia Mansur, and Melissa Tullis. 1996. "Cocaine and Heroin in Europe: 1983–93: A Cross-National Comparison of Trafficking and Prices." *British Journal of Criminology* 36(2):255–81.

Fendrich, Michael, Timothy P. Johnson, Joseph S. Wislar, Amy Hubbell, and Vina Spiehler. 2004. "The Utility of Drug Testing in Epidemiological Research: Results from a General Population Survey." *Addiction* 99(2):197–208. doi:10.1111/j.1360-0443.2003.00632.x.

Fowler, Floyd J. 2013. *Survey Research Methods*. 5th ed. Los Angeles: Sage.

Fries, Arthur, Robert W. Anthony, Andrew J. Cseko, Carl C. Gaither, and Eric Schulman. 2008. *Technical Report for the Price and Purity of Illicit Drugs: 1981–2007*. Alexandria, VA: Institute for Defense Analysis. http://www.whitehouse.gov/sites/default/files/ondcp/policy-and-research/price_purity_tech_rpt07.pdf.

Gallet, Craig A. 2014. "Can Price Get the Monkey Off Our Back? A Meta-Analysis of Illicit Drug Demand." *Health Economics* 23(1):55–68.

Gfroerer, Joseph, Judith Lessler, and Teresa Parsley. 1997. "Studies of Nonresponse and Measurement Error in the National Household Survey on Drug Abuse." In *The Validity of Self-Reported Drug Use: Improving the Accuracy of Survey Estimates*, edited by Lana H. Harrison and Arthur Hughes. Research Monograph 167. Rockville, MD: National Institute on Drug Abuse.

Goldstein, Paul J. 1985. "The Drugs/Violence Nexus: A Tripartite Conceptual Framework." *Journal of Drug Issues* 39:143–74.

Government Accounting Office. 2005. *Social Security Reform: Other Countries' Experiences Provide Lessons for the United States*. Report to Congressional Requesters. Washington, DC: Government Accounting Office.

Greenwald, Glenn. 2009. "Drug Decriminalization in Portugal: Lessons for Creating Fair and Successful Drug Policies." Washington, DC: Cato Institute. http://www.cato.org/sites/cato.org/files/pubs/pdf/greenwald_whitepaper.pdf.

Hansen, Anders B. Gottlieb, Ulla Arthur Hvidtfeldt, Morten Grønbæk, Ulrik Becker, Annette Søgaard Nielsen, and Janne Schurmann Tolstrup. 2011. "The Number of Persons with Alcohol Problems in the Danish Population." *Scandinavian Journal of Public Health* 39:128–36.

Harrendorf, Stefan. 2012. "Offence Definitions in the European Sourcebook of Crime and Criminal Justice Statistics and Their Influence on Data Quality and Comparability." *European Journal on Criminal Policy and Research* 18(1): 23–53.

Harrison, Lana H., and Arthur Hughes, eds. 1997. *The Validity of Self-Reported Drug Use: Improving the Accuracy of Survey Estimates*. Research Monograph 167. Rockville, MD: US Department of Health and Human Services, National Institute on Drug Abuse. http://rzbl04.biblio.etc.tu-bs.de:8080/docportal/servlets/MCRFileNodeServlet/DocPortal_derivate_00001893/Monograph167.pdf.

Harrison, Lana H., Steve S. Martin, Tihomir Enev, and Deborah Harrington. 2007. "Comparing Drug Testing and Self-Report of Drug Use among Youths and Young Adults in the General Population." Rockville, MD: Substance Abuse and Mental Health Services Administration, Office of Applied Studies.

Hibell, Björn, Barbro Andersson, Thoroddur Bjarnason, Salme Ahström, Olga Balakireva, Anna Kokkevi, and Mark Morgan. 2004. *The ESPAD Report 2003: Alcohol and Other Drug Use among Students in 35 European Countries*. Stockholm: Swedish Council for Information on Alcohol and Other Drugs, CAN Council of Europe, Co-operation Group to Combat Drug Abuse and Illicit Trafficking in Drugs (Pompidou Group). http://www.espad.org/Uploads/ESPAD_reports/2003/The_2003_ESPAD_report.pdf.

Hofer, Hanns von. 2000. "Crime Statistics as Constructs: The Case of Swedish Rape Statistics." *European Journal on Criminal Policy and Research* 8(1):77–89. doi:10.1023/A:1008713631586.

Home Office. 2014. *Drugs: International Comparators*. London: Home Office.

Hser, Yih-Ing, Margaret Maglione, and Kathleen Boyle. 1999. "Validity of Self-Report of Drug Use among STD Patients, ER Patients, and Arrestees." *American Journal of Drug and Alcohol Abuse* 25(1):81–91.

Hughes, Caitlin Elizabeth, and Alex Stevens. 2010. "What Can We Learn from the Portuguese Decriminalization of Illicit Drugs?" *British Journal of Criminology* 50(6):999–1022.

———. 2012. "A Resounding Success or a Disastrous Failure: Re-examining the Interpretation of Evidence on the Portuguese Decriminalisation of Illicit Drugs." *Drug and Alcohol Review* 31(1):101–13.

Humphreys, Keith. 2015. "Even as Marijuana Use Rises, Arrests Are Falling." *Washington Post*, Wonkblog, February 11. http://www.washingtonpost.com/blogs/wonkblog/wp/2015/02/11/even-as-marijuana-use-rises-arrests-are-falling/.

International Centre for Prison Studies. 2014. "World Prison Brief—United States of America." Colchester: International Centre for Prison Studies. http://www.prisonstudies.org/country/united-states-america.

Johnson, Anne M., Andrew J. Copas, Bob Erens, Sundhiya Mandalia, Kevin Fenton, Christos Korovessis, Kaye Wellings, and Julia Field. 2001. "Effect of Computer-Assisted Self-Interviews on Reporting of Sexual HIV Risk Behaviours in a General Population Sample: A Methodological Experiment." *AIDS* 15(1):111–15.

Joint UN Program on HIV/AIDS. 2006. *2006 Report on Global AIDS Epidemic*. Geneva: Joint UN Program on HIV/AIDS.

Killias, Martin. 2009. "Comments on Peter Reuter/Dominic Schnoz Assessing Drug Problems and Policies in Switzerland, 1998–2007." http://www.bag.admin.ch/themen/drogen/00042/00624/06044/07683/index.html?lang=en.

Kilmer, Beau. 2002. "Do Cannabis Possession Laws Influence Cannabis Use?" Cannabis 2002 Report. Brussels: Ministers of Public Health of Belgium,

France, Germany, the Netherlands, and Switzerland. http://www.cpha.ca/uploads/portals/substance/cannabis_report_2002.pdf.

Kilmer, Beau, and Jonathan Caulkins. 2014. "Hard Drugs Demand Solid Understanding: Column." *USA Today*, March 8. http://www.usatoday.com/story/opinion/2014/03/08/heroin-abuse-hoffman-research-column/6134337/.

Kilmer, Beau, Jonathan P. Caulkins, Gregory Midgette, Linden Dahlkemper, Robert J. MacCoun, and Rosalie Liccardo Pacula. 2013. "Before the Grand Opening: Measuring Washington State's Marijuana Market in the Last Year before Legalized Commercial Sales." Santa Barbara, CA: RAND Corporation. http://www.rand.org/pubs/research_reports/RR466.html.

Kilmer, Beau, Susan S. Everingham, Jonathan P. Caulkins, Gregory Midgette, Rosalie Liccardo Pacula, Peter Reuter, Rachel M. Burns, Bing Han, and Russell Lundberg. 2014. "How Big Is the U.S. Market for Illegal Drugs?" Rand Research Brief 9770. Santa Monica, CA: RAND Corporation. http://www.rand.org/pubs/research_briefs/RB9770.html.

Kilmer, Beau, Greg Midgette, and Clinton Saloga. 2015. *Back in the National Spotlight: An Assessment of Recent Changes in Drug Use and Drug Policies in the United States*. Washington, DC: Brookings.

Kilmer, Beau, Rosalie L. Pacula, Priscillia Hunt, and Lila Rabinovich. 2010. "Indicators for Understanding Supply-Reduction Efforts." In *Understanding Illicit Drug Markets, Supply Reduction Efforts, and Drug-Related Crime in the European Union*, edited by Beau Kilmer and Stijn Hoorens. Cambridge: RAND Europe.

Kipke, Michele D., Susanne Montgomery, and Richard G. MacKenzie. 1993. "Substance Use among Youth Seen at a Community-Based Health Clinic." *Journal of Adolescent Health* 14(4):289–94. doi:10.1016/1054-139X(93)90176-P.

Klempova, Danica, and Frank Zobel. 2010. "Insights into Shared and Specific Features of Intensive Drug Use in Europe." *Nordic Studies on Alcohol and Drugs* 27:95–100.

Kokkevi, Anna E., Angeliki A. Arapaki, Clive Richardson, Silvia Florescu, Marina Kuzman, and Eva Stergar. 2007. "Further Investigation of Psychological and Environmental Correlates of Substance Use in Adolescence in Six European Countries." *Drug and Alcohol Dependence* 88(2–3):308–12. doi:10.1016/j.drugalcdep.2006.10.004.

Kokkevi, Anna E., Saoirse Nic Gabhainn, and Maria Spyropoulou. 2006. "Early Initiation of Cannabis Use: A Cross-National European Perspective." *Journal of Adolescent Health* 39(5):712–19. doi:10.1016/j.jadohealth.2006.05.009.

Kokkevi, Anna E., Clive Richardson, Silvia Florescu, Marina Kuzman, and Eva Stergar. 2007. "Psychosocial Correlates of Substance Use in Adolescence: A Cross-National Study in Six European Countries." *Drug and Alcohol Dependence* 86(1):67–74. doi:10.1016/j.drugalcdep.2006.05.018.

Kopp, Pierre. 2004. *Political Economy of Illegal Drugs*. London: Routledge.

Kraus, Ludwig, Rita Augustin, Martin Frischer, Petra Kümmler, Alfred Uhl, and Lucas Wiessing. 2003. "Estimating Prevalence of Problem Drug Use at National Level in Countries of the European Union and Norway." *Addiction* 98(4):471–85. doi:10.1046/j.1360-0443.2003.00326.x.

Kuziemko, Ilyana, and Steven D. Levitt. 2004. "An Empirical Analysis of Imprisoning Drug Offenders." *Journal of Public Economics* 88(9–10):2043–66.

Laqueur, Hannah. 2014. "Uses and Abuses of Drug Decriminalization in Portugal." *Law and Social Inquiry*. Electronically published December 11.

Legget, T. 2006. "Bulletin on Narcotics: Review of the World Cannabis Situation." New York: UN Department of Social Affairs; UN Division of Narcotic Drugs; UN International Drug Control Program. http://www.unodc.org/documents/data-and-analysis/bulletin/2008/Bulletin2008_web.pdf.

Levi, Michael, and Peter Reuter. 2006. "Money Laundering." In *Crime and Justice: A Review of Research*, vol. 34, edited by Michael Tonry. Chicago: University of Chicago Press.

Lynch, James P. 2006. "Problems and Promise of Victimization Surveys for Cross-National Research." In *Crime and Justice: A Review of Research*, vol. 34, edited by Michael Tonry. Chicago: University of Chicago Press.

MacCoun, Robert J. 2011. "What Can We Learn from the Dutch Cannabis Coffeeshop System?" *Addiction* 106(11):1899–1910.

MacCoun, Robert J., and Peter Reuter. 1997. "Interpreting Dutch Cannabis Policy: Reasoning by Analogy in the Legalization Debate." *Science* 278(5335):47–52.

———. 2001*a*. *Drug War Heresies: Learning from Other Vices, Times, and Places*. New York: Cambridge University Press.

———. 2001*b*. "Evaluating Alternative Cannabis Regimes." *British Journal of Psychiatry: Journal of Mental Science* 178(February):123–28.

Maxwell, Jane Carlisle. 2001. "Changes in Drug Use in Australia and the United States: Results from the 1995 and 1998 National Household Surveys." *Drug and Alcohol Review* 20(1):37–48. doi:10.1080/09595230123805.

———. 2003. "Update: Comparison of Drug Use in Australia and the United States as Seen in the 2001 National Household Surveys." *Drug and Alcohol Review* 22(3):347–57. doi:10.1080/0959523031000154490.

———. 2008. "Are We Becoming More Alike? Comparison of Substance Use in Australia and the United States as Seen in the 1995, 1998, 2001 and 2004 National Household Surveys." *Drug and Alcohol Review* 27(5):473–81. doi:10.1080/09595230802090055.

McColl, Elanie, A. Jacoby, Lois Thomas, J. Soutter, Claire H. Bamford, Nick Steen, Rosemann Thomas, E. Harvey, A. Garratt, and J. Bond. 2001. "Design and Use of Questionnaires: A Review of Best Practice Applicable to Surveys of Health Service Staff and Patients." *Health Technology Assessment* 5(31):1–256.

Ministry of Foreign Affairs, Ministry of Health, Welfare, and Sport, Ministry of Justice, and Ministry of the Interior. 1995. *Drugs Policy in the Netherlands: Continuity and Change*. Rijswijk: VWS.

National Laboratory Certification Program. 2011. "Opiates History and Chemical Structures." Drug Testing Matters. Washington, DC: National Laboratory Certification Program. http://datia.org/eNews/2011/NLCP_DTM_Bourland_Opiates_Part1_12Dec2011.pdf.

National Research Council. 2013. "Nonresponse in Social Science Surveys: A Research Agenda." Washington, DC.: National Research Council. http://www.nap.edu/catalog.php?record_id=18293.

Nguyen, Holly, and Peter Reuter. 2012. "How Risky Is Marijuana Possession? Considering the Role of Age, Race, and Gender." *Crime and Delinquency* 58 (6):879–910. doi:10.1177/0011128712461122.

Office of Applied Studies. 2002. "National and State Estimates of the Drug Abuse Treatment Gap: 2000 National Household Survey on Drug Abuse." Rockville, MD: Substance Abuse and Mental Health Services Administration. https://www.ncjrs.gov/App/publications/abstract.aspx?ID=197713.

Olsson, Börje, Caroline Adamsson Wahren, and Siv Byqvist. 2001. *Det tunga narkotikamissbrukets omfattning i Sverige 1998*. Rapport, vol. 61. Stockholm: CAN.

ONDCP (Office of National Drug Control Policy). 2012. "What America's Users Spend on Illegal Drugs." Prepared by W. Rhodes, C. Dyous, D. Hunt, J. Luallen, M. Callahan, and R. Subramanian. Washington, DC: Executive Office of the President, Office of National Drug Control Policy. http://www.rand.org/pubs/research_reports/RR534.html.

———. 2014*a*. *2013 Annual Report, Arrestee Drug Abuse Monitoring Program II*. Washington, DC: Executive Office of the President, Office of National Drug Control Policy.

———. 2014*b*. "What America's Users Spend on Illegal Drugs." Prepared by B. Kilmer, S. Everingham, J. Caulkins, G. Midgette, R. Pacula, P. Reuter, R. Burns, B. Han, and R. Lundberg. Washington, DC: Executive Office of the President, Office of National Drug Control Policy. http://www.rand.org/pubs/research_reports/RR534.html.

Ort, Christoph, Alexander L. N. van Nuijs, Jean-Daniel Berset, Lubertus Bijlsma, Sara Castigioni, Adrian Covaci, Pim de Voogt, et al. 2014. "Spatial Differences and Temporal Changes in Illicit Drug Use in Europe Quantified by Wastewater Analysis." *Addiction* 109(8):1338–52.

Pacula, Rosalie Liccardo, Beau Kilmer, and Priscillia Hunt. 2010. "A Framework for Thinking about Drug Markets." In *Understanding Illicit Drug Markets, Supply Reduction Efforts, and Drug-Related Crime in the European Union*, edited by Beau Kilmer and Stijn Hoorens. Cambridge: RAND.

Pacula, Rosalie Liccardo, R. Lundberg, J. Caulkins, B. Kilmer, S. Greathouse, T. Fain, and P. Steinberg. 2013. *Improving the Measurement of Drug-Related Crime*. Washington, DC: Executive Office of the President, Office of National Drug Control Policy.

Paoli, Letizia, Victoria A. Greenfield, and Peter Reuter. 2009. *The World Heroin Market: Can Supply Be Cut?* Oxford: Oxford University Press.

Pudney, Stephen, Celia Badillo, Mark Bryan, Jon Burton, Gabriella Conti, and Maria Iacovou. 2006. "Estimating the Size of the UK Illicit Drug Market." In *Measuring Different Aspects of Problem Drug Use: Methodological Developments*. London: Home Office.

Ravera, Silvia, and Johan J. de Gier. 2008. *Prevalence of Psychoactive Substances in the General Population*. Project cofunded by the European Commission within the Sixth Framework Programme. Groningen: Department of Pharmacotherapy and Pharmaceutical Care.

Rehm, Jurgen, Robin Room, Wim van den Brink, and Ludwig Kraus. 2005. "Problematic Drug Use and Drug Use Disorders in EU Countries and Norway: An Overview of the Epidemiology." *European Neuropsychopharmacology* 15:389–97.

Reinarman, Craig. 2009. "Cannabis Policies and User Practices: Market Separation, Price, Potency, and Accessibility in Amsterdam and San Francisco." *International Journal of Drug Policy* 20(1):28–37.

Reinarman, Craig, Peter D. A. Cohen, and Hendrien L. Kaal. 2004. "The Limited Relevance of Drug Policy: Cannabis in Amsterdam and in San Francisco." *American Journal of Public Health* 94(5):836–42.

Reuband, Karl-Heinz. 1995. "Drug Use and Drug Policy in Western Europe." *European Addiction Research* 1(1–2):32–41.

———. 1998. "Drug Policies and Drug Prevalence: The Role of Demand and Supply." *European Journal on Criminal Policy and Research* 6(3):321–36.

Reuter, Peter. 1995. "Seizure of Drugs." In *Encyclopedia of Drugs and Alcohol.* New York: Macmillan.

———. 2013. "Why Has US Drug Policy Changed So Little over 30 Years?" In *Crime and Justice in America, 1975–2025*, edited by Michael Tonry. Vol. 42 of *Crime and Justice: A Review of Research*, edited by Michael Tonry. Chicago: University of Chicago Press.

Reuter, Peter, and Mark A. R. Kleiman. 1986. "Risks and Prices: An Economic Analysis of Drug Enforcement." In *Crime and Justice: An Annual Review of Research*, vol. 7, edited by Michael Tonry and Norval Morris. Chicago: University of Chicago Press.

Reuter, Peter, and F. Trautmann, eds. 2009. *Assessing the Operations of the Global Illicit Drug Markets, 1998–2007*. Report for the European Commission. http://ec.europa.eu/justice_home/doc_centre/drugs/studies/doc_drugs_studies_en.htm.

Room, Robin, Benedikt Fischer, Wayne Hall, and Peter Reuter. 2008. *Cannabis Policy: Moving beyond Stalemate* Oxford: Oxford University Press.

Rosenthal, Doreen, Shelley Mallett, Norweeta Milburn, and Mary Jane Rotheram-Borus. 2008. "Drug Use among Homeless Young People in Los Angeles and Melbourne." *Journal of Adolescent Health* 43(3):296–305.

Salize, Hans Joachim, Harald Dreßing, and Christine Kief. 2007. *Mentally Disordered Persons in European Prison Systems—Needs, Programmes and Outcome (EUPRIS)*. Mannheim: Central Institute of Mental Health. http://www.antoniocasella.eu/archipsy/Salize_EU_psy-prisons_31oct2007.pdf.

Scalia Tomba, Carla Rossi Giampaolo, C. Taylor, D. Klempova, and Lucas Wiessing. 2008. "Guidelines for Estimating the Incidence of Problem Drug Use." Lisbon: European Monitoring Centre for Drugs and Drug Addiction. http://www.emcdda.europa.eu/html.cfm/index65345EN.html.

Serious Organised Crime Agency. 2011. *The United Kingdom Threat Assessment of Serious Organised Crime: 2010/11*. London: Serious Organised Crime Agency.

Sevigny, Eric L., Rosalie Liccardo Pacula, and Paul Heaton. 2014. "The Effects of Medical Marijuana Laws on Potency." *International Journal of Drug Policy* 25(2):308–19.

Sevigny, Eric L., Harold A. Pollack, and Peter Reuter. 2013. "Can Drug Courts Help to Reduce Prison and Jail Populations?" *Annals of the American Academy of Political and Social Science* 647(1):190–212.

Skarupova, Katerina. 2014. *Computer-Assisted and Online Data Collection in General Population Surveys*. Lisbon: European Monitoring Center on Drugs and Drug Abuse.

Solinge, Tim Boekhout van. 2004. *Dealing with Drugs in Europe: An Investigation of European Drug Control Experiences? France, the Netherlands and Sweden*. The Hague: Willem Pompe Institute for Criminal Law and Criminology.

Stafford, Jennifer, and Lucy Burns. 2013. *Australian Drug Trends 2012: Findings from the Illicit Drug Reporting System*. Australian Drug Trend Series no. 91. Sydney: National Drug and Alcohol Research Centre, University of New South Wales. https://ndarc.med.unsw.edu.au/sites/default/files/ndarc/resources/National%20IDRS%20report%202012.pdf.

Steeh, Charlotte, Nicola Kirgis, Brian Cannon, and Jeff DeWitt. 2001. "Are They Really as Bad as They Seem? Nonresponse Rates at the End of the Twentieth Century." *Journal of Official Statistics* 17(2):27–47.

Stevens, Alex. 2011. *Drugs, Crime and Public Health: The Political Economy of Drug Policy*. London: Routledge-Cavendish.

Stockwell, Tim, Jinhui Zhao, Tanya Chikritzhs, and Tom K. Greenfield. 2008. "What Did You Drink Yesterday? Public Health Relevance of a Recent Recall Method Used in the 2004 Australian National Drug Strategy Household Survey." *Addiction* 103(6):919–28.

Substance Abuse and Mental Health Services Administration. 2013. "Results from the 2012 National Survey on Drug Use and Health: Summary of National Findings." NSDUH Series H-46. HHS Publication no. (SMA) 13-4795. Rockville, MD: Substance Abuse and Mental Health Services Administration. http://www.samhsa.gov/data/NSDUH/2012SummNatFindDetTables/index.aspx.

Taylor, Bruce G. 2002. *I-ADAM in Eight Countries: Approaches and Challenges*. Washington, DC: US Department of Justice, Office of Justice Programs, National Institute of Justice.

ter Bogt, Tom F. M., Margreet de Looze, Michal Molcho, Emmanuelle Godeau, Anne Hublet, Anna Kokkevi, Emmanuel Kuntsche, et al. 2014. "Do Societal Wealth, Family Affluence and Gender Account for Trends in Adolescent Cannabis Use? A 30 Country Cross-National Study." *Addiction* 109(2):273–83. doi:10.1111/add.12373.

Tonry, Michael. 2014. "Why Crime Rates Are Falling throughout the Western World." In *Why Crime Rates Fall and Why They Don't*, edited by Michael Tonry. Vol. 43 of *Crime and Justice: A Review of Research*, edited by Michael Tonry. Chicago: University of Chicago Press.

Toobin, Jeffrey. 2014. "This Is My Jail." *New Yorker*, April 14. http://www.newyorker.com/reporting/2014/04/14/140414fa_fact_toobin.

Tourangeau, Roger, and Tom W. Smith. 1996. "Asking Sensitive Questions: The Impact of Data Collection Mode, Question Format, and Question Context." *Public Opinion Quarterly* 60(2):275–304.

Tourangeau, Roger, and Ting Yan. 2007. "Sensitive Questions in Surveys." *Psychological Bulletin* 133(5):859–83.

Turner, Charles F., Leighton Ku, Susan M. Rogers, Laura D. Lindberg, Joseph H. Pleck, and Freya L. Sonenstein. 1998. "Adolescent Sexual Behavior, Drug Use, and Violence: Increased Reporting with Computer Survey Technology." *Science* 280(5365):867–73.

Turner, Charles F., Maria A. Villarroel, Susan M. Rogers, Elizabeth Eggleston, Laxminarayana Ganapathi, Anthony M. Roman, and Alia Al-Tayyib. 2005. "Reducing Bias in Telephone Survey Estimates of the Prevalence of Drug Use: A Randomized Trial of Telephone Audio-CASI." *Addiction* 100(10):1432–44. doi:10.1111/j.1360-0443.2005.01196.x.

US Department of Housing and Urban Development. 2011. "The 2010 Annual Homeless Assessment Report to Congress." Washington, DC: US Department of Housing and Urban Development, Office of Community Planning and Development.

US Department of Justice, Office of Justice Programs. 2004. *National Institute of Justice: Arrestee Drug Abuse Monitoring (ADAM) Program in the United States, 2003*. Ann Arbor, MI: Inter-University Consortium for Political and Social Research.

UNODC (UN Office on Drugs and Crime). 2011. *Global Study on Homicide: Trends, Contexts and Data*. Vienna: UN Office on Drugs and Crime.

———. 2013. *World Drug Report 2013*. Vienna: UN Office on Drugs and Crime. http://www.unodc.org/unodc/secured/wdr/wdr2013/World_Drug_Report_2013.pdf.

van Laar, Margriet, Guus Cruts, Marianne van Ooyen-Houben, André van Gageldonk, Esther Croes, Ronald Meijer, and Toinne Ketelaars. 2012. "Report to the EMCDDA by the Reitox National Focal Point: The Netherlands Drug Situation." Lisbon: European Monitoring Centre for Drugs and Drug Addiction. http://www.emcdda.europa.eu/html.cfm/index191640EN.html.

van Laar, Margriet, Tom Frijns, Franz Trautmann, and Linda Lombi. 2013. "Cannabis Market: User Types, Availability and Consumption Estimates." In *Further Insights into Aspects of the EU Illicit Drugs Market*, edited by Franz Trautmann, Beau Kilmer, and Paul Turnbull. Luxembourg: Publications Office of the European Union. http://ec.europa.eu/justice/anti-drugs/files/eu_market_full.pdf.

van Nuijs, Alexander L. N., Sara Castiglioni, Isabela Tarcomnicu, Cristina Postigo, Miren Lopez de Alda, Hugo Neels, Ettore Zuccato, Damia Barcelo, and Adrian Covaci. 2011. "Illicit Drug Consumption Estimations Derived from Wastewater Analysis: A Critical Review." *Science of the Total Environment* 409(19):3564–77.

van Ooyen-Houben, Marianne, and Edward Kleemans. 2015. "Drug Policy: The 'Dutch Model.'" In *Crime and Justice: A Review of Research*, vol. 44, edited by Michael Tonry. Chicago: University of Chicago Press.

Warner, Margaret, Li Hui Chen, Diane M. Makuc, Robert N. Anderson, and Arialdi M. Miniño. 2011. "Drug Poisoning Deaths in the United States, 1980–2008." Washington, DC: US Department of Health and Human Services, Centers for Disease Control and Prevention. http://www.cdc.gov/nchs/data/databriefs/db81.htm.

Weatherburn, Don, Craig Jones, Karen Freeman, and Toni Makkai. 2003. "Supply Control and Harm Reduction: Lessons from the Australian Heroin 'Drought.'" *Addiction* 98(1):83–91.

Wenzel, Suzanne L., Joan S. Tucker, Daniela Golinelli, Harold D. Green Jr., and Annie Zhou. 2010. "Personal Network Correlates of Alcohol, Cigarette, and Marijuana Use among Homeless Youth." *Drug and Alcohol Dependence* 112(1):140–49.

Zobel, Frank, and Wolfgang Götz. 2011. "Drug Use in Europe: Specific National Characteristics or Shared Models?" In *Drugs and Culture: Knowledge, Consumption and Policy*, edited by Geoffrey Hunt and Henri Bergeron. Farnham, UK: Ashgate.

Zuccato, Ettore, Chiara Chiabrando, Sara Castiglioni, Renzo Bagnati, and Roberto Fanelli. 2008. "Estimating Community Drug Abuse by Wastewater Analysis." *Environmental Health Perspectives* 116(8):1027–32.

James P. Lynch and Lynn A. Addington

Crime Trends and the Elasticity of Evil: Has a Broadening View of Violence Affected Our Statistical Indicators?

ABSTRACT

Macro-social theories posit that societies become more civil as they modernize. An open question is whether these changes affect major social indicators of crime. To produce level and change estimates, national data collection systems employ safeguards to promote stability. Cultural changes, though, might affect these systems in more subtle ways by affecting what citizens view as criminal violence and how these behaviors are recounted in crime surveys and reported to police. Three subclasses of violence appear most susceptible: rape and sexual assault, domestic violence, and lesser forms of violence such as verbal threats. Findings are strongest that changing cultural definitions have affected official statistics for domestic violence. Rape and sexual assault also have shown changes in the willingness of victims to report to the police. Evidence does not indicate that the cultural definition of lesser violence has changed in a way that has affected trends in official statistics. Estimating change over time is a key reason statistical systems employ safeguards to remove shifting views of violence. These safeguards may limit an accurate view of victimization risk and exposure. Balancing the need for stability with a desire to capture emerging crimes and risks requires developing careful systematic processes for reviewing and updating national crime statistics.

Electronically published July 28, 2015

James P. Lynch is professor and chair of the Department of Criminology and Criminal Justice, University of Maryland. Lynn A. Addington is associate professor in the Department of Justice, Law, and Criminology, American University.

0192-3234/2015/0044-0008$10.00

Systems of crime statistics in the United States and elsewhere have matured and improved over the last 40 years. This evolution has resulted in data that give greater context and a much richer understanding of the crime problem than was previously possible. While crime data based on police administrative records have been collected at the national level in the United States since the 1930s, these statistics continue to improve in scope, detail, and accuracy as police have grown increasingly attuned to the operational and management uses of these data and as technological advancements permit more sophisticated collection (Poggio et al. 1985). Prior to the 1960s, policy makers and officials viewed with suspicion the accuracy of data collected through surveys of victimization and offending. Self-report victimization surveys now constitute an official indicator of crime in the United States and other nations (van Dijk, van Kesteren, and Smit 2007; Chaplin, Farley, and Smith 2011; Langton, Planty, and Truman 2013). Self-report offending survey data similarly have developed into a staple of criminological research (Roe and Ashe 2008; Thornberry and Krohn 2011).

With the maturation of these systems, we have the benefit of decades of data with which to assess the effects of macro-social changes on the rate and distribution of crime (Heimer, Lauritsen, and Lynch 2009; Lauritsen, Heimer, and Lynch 2009; Baumer and Lauritsen 2010). These long time series, though, may be vulnerable to concurrent changes in the definition of crime, which could make trends difficult to readily interpret. Of specific concern are the legal and cultural changes affecting the definition of criminal violence (Tonry 2014).

Several macro-social theories suggest that societies become more civil over time as they modernize (Eisner 2003). As civility increases, the cultural and legal definitions of criminal violence expand. Relatively minor incivilities not previously defined as violent are considered so, and violence that did not rise to illegal behavior becomes classified as criminal. While these theories are based on changes over centuries, more recent history suggests a similar pattern. The case of bullying illustrates this point. Until fairly recently, bullying was often dismissed as a normal part of growing up. Now it is considered a serious social problem affecting both children at school and adults in work environments. In many jurisdictions, bullying has been codified as criminal behavior (Faris and Felmlee 2012; Kowalski, Limber, and Agatston 2012; Robers et al. 2014). Stalking is another example of threatening behavior that has elevated from being viewed as a nuisance to constituting a violent crime (Catalano

2012). Societies need to adopt laws and policies to reflect changes in public views of crime and violence. An unintended consequence is that these changes in the definition of violence could produce increases (or smaller decreases) in official crime statistics that reflect an expanded scope rather than capturing an actual change in behaviors traditionally defined as violent crime.

An open question is whether this broadening definition of violence has affected our major social indicators of crime. A strong argument can be made that these changes would have little effect as a result of safeguards designed to minimize such external influences. Official crime statistics in the United States—as with other developed nations—come from two sources: police administrative records and victimization survey data. In the United States, the Federal Bureau of Investigation collects police data as part of its Uniform Crime Reporting Program (UCR), and the Bureau of Justice Statistics gathers victimization data in its National Crime Victimization Survey (NCVS).[1] In addition to generating annual-level estimates, US national crime data collections produce change estimates and trends. As a practical matter, neither format can collect data on every crime, and both are limited to a specific subset of crimes.[2]

To effectively estimate change, the UCR and NCVS use definitions and procedures to promote stability in the measurement of those crimes that both data collections cover. For example, while changes in the law might now include stalking as a crime and a victim might call the police to report it, this incident would not be reflected in the official violent crime rate because the UCR excludes stalking in the crimes it covers. Similarly, a respondent to the NCVS might report an instance of bullying, but the attributes of the incident must rise to those of a crime included in the survey such as a threatened assault. If not, this incident will not be classified as a crime in the NCVS. It is important to note that these definitions and procedures themselves are subject to updating that can be motivated

[1] More detailed discussions of the UCR and NCVS are referred to in sources such as Lynch and Addington (2007).

[2] These crimes primarily encompass street-level offenses. The UCR list is rooted in decisions made in the 1920s and has changed little since that time. The offenses included in Part I (formerly known as index) crimes include homicide, rape, robbery, aggravated assault, burglary, motor vehicle theft, larceny-theft, and arson. The NCVS originated in part as a check on the UCR system. The crimes it includes are largely tethered to the UCR. Its list includes rape and sexual assault, robbery, aggravated assault, simple assault, burglary, motor vehicle theft, and theft. Other countries have included different types of crimes. All systems have limits on the number of crimes that can be included.

by culturally changing views of violence and crime. The sponsoring agencies can opt to officially expand the statistical series to include lesser forms of violence. These changes can be implemented to minimize the effect on the continuity of the data and preserve the time series. While these "self-conscious" revisions are possible, they are not common in US crime data. We address this method of formal change in our concluding comments. Our focus is on the more subtle and unintentional effects of cultural changes in violence on American crime statistics.

Alternatively, an equally strong argument can be made that these changes affect our crime data, but in a more subtle way. Procedural safeguards limit what crimes are captured in the UCR and NCVS by prescribing the attributes and definitions of the incidents that can be counted. Cultural changes affect what people view as criminal violence, which influences their recall of events to surveys and reporting of incidents to the police. The idea here is that by having an increased scope of what constitutes criminal violence, citizens would increase their reporting of victimization incidents. Some of these incidents will be filtered out of the official crime statistics by procedural safeguards. Others will not, and since more incidents are being reported overall, it is possible that a greater number of incidents will be captured by the statistical systems and in turn included in official crime counts. These changes are most likely to affect the "grayer" or more loosely defined crimes included in the UCR and NCVS rather than traditional crime types. The broadening view of violence is also likely to influence crime statistics as a result of changes in perceptions of the social context of violent events that make them criminal or not.

"Gray area events" involve violence that is not clearly criminal. Cultural changes could affect how victims perceive these events as violent and then recount these to a survey and report them to police. For example, "weapon use" is an attribute of assaults and a key element that distinguishes the more serious crime of aggravated assault from simple assault. What constitutes a weapon is likely to remain fairly constant, as is a victim's identification of an incident involving a weapon as a crime. Conversely, an attribute like "threatened harm" allows more room for judgment and expanding perceptions of violence. This change could affect the UCR and NCVS crimes of threatened assault, which include verbal threats that do not involve weapons and rely heavily on the victim's view that the offender intended harm. As these examples illustrate, the effects of cultural changes in the definition of violence are likely to be observed in—and affect the measure of—the most flexible crimes collected by statistics series such as the UCR and NCVS since these crimes will be sensitive to an elastic view of violent crime.

Another area in which an evolving cultural definition of violence could affect statistical systems concerns the social context of a crime event, specifically, changes in the statuses of persons who were less likely to be considered crime victims previously but are now included. The case of domestic violence presents one example. Historically, these behaviors were considered private matters rather than crimes not only by the perpetrators but also by victims, police, and the criminal justice system. Now these incidents are considered criminal violence. To the extent that this changed view of violence has occurred, it is likely to have increased the number of violent incidents committed by intimates that are reported to the NCVS as well as the UCR. Specifically, this argument is that the change is not attributable to the underlying number of incidents but rather to what is captured by official statistics. An increased willingness to report by victims who now view violence by an intimate as a crime will, in turn, lead to increases in official statistics. Since the underlying actions, that is, assaults, are crimes included in the UCR and NCVS, self-protective filters and practices are less effective in mitigating the effect of elasticity related to statuses and relationships.

In this essay, we examine change in the social definition of criminal violence in the United States and explore whether this change affected trends in official statistics. To do so, we focus on changes in crime classes that are more likely to be affected by cultural change and are more likely to pass the filters in major statistical systems. Specifically, we focus on crimes affected by changing statuses (violence against women—particularly rape and sexual assault as well as domestic violence) and more loosely defined crimes (threats and lesser forms of assaultive violence). To explore these issues, we emphasize the NCVS for a few reasons.

Compared with other data sources such as the UCR, the NCVS is better documented in its design and allows more in-depth analyses based on the manner in which the data are collected and disseminated. The NCVS provides detailed incident information as well as specific crime type coding. Unlike the NCVS, the UCR relies primarily on aggregate counts of crime data collected at the police jurisdiction level.[3] This

[3] We use national-level statistics provided by the UCR's traditional summary system, which it uses for its annual *Crime in the United States*. The UCR is changing its data col-

format does not allow extensive disaggregation of these crime classes into events with greater or lesser violence. Our analysis requires a more refined identification of crimes than is possible with UCR data. For example, aggravated assault can include completed, attempted, and threatened aggravated assaults. Identifying these variations is important to exploration of a broadening definition of violence. The UCR data, though, collect information only on completed and attempted aggravated assaults and do not distinguish between these two types. In addition, the UCR aggravated assault data do not provide any information on the characteristics of victims or offenders, so incidents of domestic violence cannot be identified. In contrast, the NCVS distinguishes completed, attempted, and threatened aggravated assaults and identifies incident details such as victim-offender relationships.

In Section I, we explore how we interpret changes in the cultural definition of violence and present evidence of these changes. We approach this examination in two primary ways. First, we identify forms of violence that have been the object of intense advocacy to define them as crimes and provide greater attention for victims. This targeted attention is hypothesized to affect societal views of violence regarding these classes of behavior. Second, we examine whether lesser violence in general is becoming more central to the general concept of violence over time. To do so, we use the cuing structure of the screening interview in the NCVS to see if lesser forms of violence are mentioned in response to global violence cues over time. After identifying these examples of broadening views of violence, in Section II, we explore whether we can ascertain changes over time, specifically, changes that may have affected our national statistical systems. We link the previously identified examples of a broadening definition of violence with possible effects on trends in official statistics. Here we compare trends for crime classes affected by cultural changes to those less likely to be affected. In addition, we examine changes in reporting to the police for these crimes as providing another indicator of broadening definitions of criminal violence. In Section III, we conclude by discussing the results and raise the issue of whether statistical systems such as the UCR and NCVS should self-consciously change to keep attuned with broadening societal views of

---

lection to an incident-based one that includes more crimes and more details about them. The change to the National Incident-Based Reporting System has been slow, and it currently lacks national coverage.

violence and the challenges of implementing such revisions without also introducing error into the long-standing time series of data.

When we examine changes in responses to cues in the NCVS screener, we find the strongest support for a change in criminal violence affecting the popular definition of domestic violence as a crime, with less support for sexual violence and no support for lesser forms of violence or other gray area events. As crime has been declining overall, we do not anticipate increases for these crime types so much as less steep drops in their trends. Analysis of crime trends from the NCVS does show less steep declines for domestic violence, lesser forms of sexual violence, and gray area events such as threats compared to more stereotypic crimes such as aggravated assault involving strangers. All forms of violence reported in the NCVS—both stereotypic crimes and the crimes of interest here—show increases in the proportion of crimes reported to the police over time, but the increases are greatest for rape and sexual assaults. This pattern is consistent with trends observed in police statistics where there were much smaller percentage declines in rape rates over time compared with other forms of violence. The cumulative evidence suggests that domestic violence has the greatest chance of having been the object of culturally based changes in definition and may have affected crime statistics by inflating these numbers.

I. Identifying Subclasses of Violence Susceptible to Changes in Definition

No continuous series of crime statistics span centuries, but the observations of historians and available data can be cobbled together to suggest a convergence of increased civility and a drop in behaviors previously viewed as violent. This pattern appears to produce a broader societal definition of violence (Pinker 2011; Eisner 2014). Criminological theory also provides a framework to support this evolution in the definition of violence. Durkheim's (1982) idea of homeostasis posits that as crime declines, the definition of crime will expand to maintain the balance between crime and punishment (Cohen 1974). While evidence and theory support the proposition that definitions of violence have expanded over long periods, less is known about whether and the extent to which this change occurs over shorter periods. It is unclear how the definition of violence may have changed, what the amount of this change is, and whether these changes affect crime statistics. To examine this issue, we focus on a few likely candidates that appear to have expanded the definition of violence in the near term and use these to identify possible effects on crime statistics.

Our present study takes a two-pronged approach to exploring whether certain subclasses of crime are susceptible to changing societal views of violence in the relative short term (or over the past few decades) in the United States. We first examine a set of specific crimes as identified through advocacy movements, particularly those movements seeking wholesale revisions in both the law and criminal justice system approaches to specific crimes. These movements focus on change not only via policy makers but also among the general public as they often include education components as a way to change how victims, potential victims, and the general public view specific acts. By changing perspectives to view these acts as crimes, the hope is to prompt reporting to police and accessing victim services.

Here we focus on advocacy surrounding two forms of violence against women: rape and sexual assault and domestic violence. Our emphasis on these crimes is not meant to suggest that these areas are the only ones in which advocacy has produced change in criminal laws, justice system processing, or public opinion. Other examples exist in areas such as hate crime, human trafficking, stalking, and bullying. We select these two as illustrative given the well-documented evidence of change as well as the long time series that arguably enables identification of the possible effect on crime statistics. Our second approach to identifying changes in definitions of crime focuses on overall popular perceptions of crime that may expand views of violence and that are not necessarily tied to specific advocacy movements or explicit changes in criminalizing particular behaviors. Here we use data from the NCVS to identify possible changes over time in response patterns for relatively minor forms of violence, which constitute what we referred to as gray area events.

A. Evidence of a Changing Definition of Violence: Advocacy

The status of women has increased in most developed nations, particularly in the United States, Canada, and western European countries. This change is reflected in strides and increases in women's educational attainment, participation in the workforce, and election to office and other political leadership positions (Spilsberry and Kidd 1997; Buchman and DiPrete 2006; Juhn and Potter 2006; Raley, Mattingly, and Bianci 2006; England et al. 2007; Havermann and Beresford 2012; Chu and

Posner 2013). A corollary has been efforts to redefine violence disproportionately affecting women and to consider violent behavior that was previously tolerated as no longer acceptable. The 1970s heralded a sea change as the women's movement not only promoted educational and economic opportunities but also focused on male violence against women especially in terms of rape, sexual assault, and domestic violence. Advocacy included mobilization to change laws to criminalize specific behaviors and to promote victim services, specialized police units, and more effective responses by the criminal justice system to acknowledge these crimes faster in order to assist victims better. As a result of these efforts, the general public began to identify violence against women—particularly in the areas of rape, sexual assault, and domestic violence—as a social problem and serious criminal behavior.

1. *Identifying Sexual Violence as a Crime.* Principal among crimes that disproportionately affect women are rape and sexual assault. Over the last 30 years intense efforts at legal reform have sought to expand the definition of rape and sexual assault in an effort to encourage reporting to police by victims and to facilitate convictions (Spohn and Horney 1992). Reform efforts sought to change the legal definition of rape to include a wider range of behavior, to ease the standards of evidence, and to increase the punishments imposed.

Advocates sought to expand the range of sexual offenses codified in criminal laws to allow associated gradation of punishment and permit less stringent standards of evidence to increase the likelihood of sanctioning. Ultimately reformers hoped that the greater likelihood of conviction would emphasize the criminal nature of all forms of sexual violence to encourage victims to report these crimes but also to discourage offenders in the first place. Examples of these changes include expanding behaviors included as illegal, broadening the victims covered by the criminal laws, increasing the degrees of severity, changing how the illegal behavior was labeled, and removing the requirements of proof of nonconsent, resistance, and corroboration of the victim's claims. Many states expanded the legal definition of rape beyond the traditional requirement of vaginal penetration with a penis to include anal and oral penetration, penetration with other body parts and objects, and acts that did not involve any penetration. Many states' laws began to protect nontraditional victims such as males, spouses and former intimates, and cohabitants. Another type of reform divided rape into a series of graded offenses with varying degrees of severity, based on circumstances such as the amount of coercion, the seriousness of the act (penetration vs. touching), the extent of injury inflicted on the victim, the age of the victim, and the incapacity of the victim. Some states eliminated use of the term "rape" and substituted terms such as "sexual assault" in order to emphasize the violent—rather than the sexual—aspect of the crime. In sum, no matter what the approach taken, the overall result was a broader definition of violence that was codified in state laws.

Advocates also demanded improvements for treatment of victims from their initial contact with police throughout their experience with the criminal justice system. Improving the initial interaction includes better training for police officers in general, specialized law enforcement units to address these crimes, and specially trained medical staff and nurses to facilitate evidence collection. Additional improvements have occurred throughout the criminal justice system. In prosecutors' offices, for example, adjustments include providing access to victim services and support for those going through the court system. The cumulative effect of these changes along with official statutory amendments likely affects public views of rape and sexual assault as criminal violence and an expanded view of violence in society (Loh 1981).

To match the new legal definitions of rape and sexual assault, advocates also worked to expand definitions of sexual violence for crime statistics (Loh 1981; Spohn and Horney 1992). In contrast to the victories obtained in legal and criminal justice reforms, advocates had mixed success in changing official crime statistics. Their efforts resulted in modest changes in the NCVS. The most significant one occurred during the 1992 redesign when screening questions and cues were added to ask specifically about rape and sexual assault. This revision reflected an important change as the initial iteration of the NCVS (the National Crime Survey) did not explicitly ask respondents about these crimes.[4]

While proponents emphasized changes to victimization surveys due to the underreporting of rape to police, the UCR was not immune to requests for change. In 2013, the UCR changed its definition of "forcible rape" to remove the requirement of force and include male and female victims (Tracy et al. 2012). Taken as a whole, these changes fall short of the requests for explicit and numerous survey questions by

[4] The National Crime Survey produced annual rape statistics for the United States but relied on victim responses to general questions about assault.

researchers and advocates in this area (Kilpatrick, Edmunds, and Seymour 1992; Koss 1993; Tjaden and Thoennes 2006).

Federal agencies like the Centers for Disease Control (CDC) have sponsored various national and local surveys examining rape and sexual assault as a public health issue that use this extensive and explicit questioning format. The National Intimate Partner and Sexual Violence Survey (NISVS) is the most recent example. The NISVS includes an expanded definition of sexual violence to include increasingly more minor forms of coercion such as repeated badgering for sex and treating sex when a victim is drinking alcohol as nonconsensual (Black et al. 2011). The CDC data provide an alternative measure of sexual violence but do not make up one of the official crime statistics published annually.

2. *Identifying Domestic Violence as a Crime.* Domestic violence is another subclass of violent crime that disproportionately affects women. In the United States, changes in societal views of domestic violence largely parallel the changes in views of sexual assault. Prior to the 1970s, behavior now classified as domestic violence was seen as a private matter that was largely condoned (Melody and Miller 2011). The women's movement and changing societal views prompted reforms across the criminal justice system as well as legislation and victim services. These changes and growing media attention reinforced views of domestic violence as criminal violence and not merely a private matter.

Reforms in the area of domestic violence since the 1970s have been profound to the point that researchers have labeled this period the "domestic violence revolution" (Buzawa, Buzawa, and Stark 2012, p. 2). Reforms have broadened the scope of behavior that is subject to criminal sanctions and promoted victim services. State and local laws and the federal Violence Against Women Act also provided increased awareness to domestic violence as a crime by funding victim services, hotlines, and public education programs (Buzawa and Buzawa 2003).

Changes also occurred in the criminal justice response to domestic violence, particularly the role of police. Prior to the 1960s, police officers had little training in domestic violence and responding to these calls (Belknap 1996). When victims did call police and police did respond, victims received little support. Arrests were infrequently made. While protective orders were encouraged, they were not vigorously enforced. This practice changed as a result of successful court cases against police departments and a series of prominent studies concerning mandatory arrest (Melody and Miller 2011). Although subsequent research suggested mixed effectiveness of mandatory arrest policies, its initial apparent success spawned a national change in policy (Buzawa and Buzawa 1996). In addition to mandatory arrest, policies were adopted to promote evidence collection and the like to assist in prosecution of these cases (Melody and Miller 2011). As noted by Kane (1999, p. 66), "it is clear—since at least the mid-1990s—that the police have been expected to forego the traditional arrest-avoidance posture in favor of an arrest-preferred or arrest-mandated approach to the handling of domestic violence events."

Other changes in the criminal justice system identified domestic violence as a serious social problem and supported reporting by victims and improved processing of these cases. In coordination with mandatory arrest policies, police departments created specialized family violence units and initiated training of all officers in best practices for handling domestic violence incidents (Buzawa and Buzawa 1990). Changes in prosecutors' offices also reflected taking these cases more seriously. For example, "no drop" policies were implemented that allowed the prosecutor's case to continue even without cooperation of the victim (Melody and Miller 2011). These changes combined with increased public awareness via focused campaigns and increased media attention likely changed societal views of domestic violence as a serious form of violence and a crime.

In summary, many changes occurred as a result of the elevation in the status of women in developed democracies over the past 30 years. For our purposes, the most significant have been organized efforts to criminalize classes of violence that disproportionately affect women, specifically sexual and domestic violence. Given the scope and persistence of advocacy in these areas and the push to change public views, we posit that to the extent a recent expansion in the definition of violence has occurred, it will be observed in these crime classes.

B. Evidence of a Changing Definition of Violence: Increased Public Identification of Violence

Overall societal changes are hypothesized to broaden the definition of violence. In addition to targeted advocacy campaigns designed to change views about particular behaviors, more subtle changes likely affect public perceptions about violence. Since these changes stem from ubiquitous causes, identifying how they affect—and expand—views of criminal violence is a challenge. In this second prong of our consideration of subclasses of crime susceptible to broader definitions of violence, we capitalize on the two-step screening-classification structure of the NCVS. In general, victimization surveys measure crime, including violent crime, by asking respondents whether they have been victimized in particular ways. As we elaborate on below, the NCVS does this by first asking a screening question to determine whether the respondent may have experienced a crime during the reference period. If a respondent gives a positive response to any of the screening questions, a more detailed incident form is used to gather information about the incident to classify it as a particular crime (or exclude it as behavior not covered by the NCVS).

The screener questionnaire is an essential component of the NCVS. If it fails to prompt respondent recall of victimization incidents, these crimes will be undercounted. Over time, survey methodologists have improved the manner in which these data are collected by refining the questions. Researchers have learned to avoid using legal terms such as "robbery" and "burglary" that may be misconstrued by laypersons (for a discussion, see Cantor and Lynch [2005]). In addition, researchers have learned that respondents need assistance in searching their memories to find and report all of the relevant crime events that may have happened to them in the past, even the very recent past (Biderman and Moore 1982; Martin et al. 1986). Not all respondents identify certain behaviors as crimes counted by the NCVS. For example, a respondent might consider only stranger-perpetrated events as crimes and not report an assault involving a family member. A respondent who works as a bouncer might not view assaults as "crimes" but rather "work-related" behaviors. To do its job, the screener questionnaire needs to prompt respondents to consider various locations, relationships, and situations in their recall of behaviors within the scope of the NCVS (Martin et al. 1986).

The overall recommendation for designing screening questions is that the more questions and cues that are used, the better respondents recall events, especially events that do not fit into paradigms of stranger-perpetrated crime in public places. On the basis of this conclusion, the NCVS screening questions were revised in 1992 to facilitate the cognitive task of searching memory for crime events (Cantor and Lynch 2005). A large number of cues were added to the screening interview, and special attention was given to those that clarify to the respondent that certain incidents were to be reported to the survey such as violence perpetrated by intimates, sexual assault, and workplace violence.

The NCVS screening cues are organized around attributes of crime events other than the criminal act itself (Biderman et al. 1985; Martin et al. 1986). The screening interview opens with a question about theft since these incidents are the most prevalent of the crimes covered by the NCVS. The interview then asks about assaultive crimes by first focusing on locations where the incident might have occurred. These cues help the respondent recall the incident on the basis of where they might have been and convey the idea that some gray area events are eligible for reporting in the survey. To illustrate this cuing strategy, two initial questions from the screening interview are presented below that concern theft and assaultive violence with a focus on location. The remaining questions appear in the appendix.

Question 36: (all respondents) (focus—item stolen)

I'm going to read some examples that will give you an idea of the kinds of crimes this study covers. As I go through them, tell me if any of these happened to you in the last 6 months, that is, since _____ ___, 20__.

Was something belonging to YOU stolen, such as—

(a) Things that you carry, like luggage, a wallet, purse, briefcase, book—
(b) Clothing, jewelry, or calculator—
(c) Bicycle or sports equipment—
(d) Things in your home—like a TV, stereo, or tools—
(e) Things outside your home such as a garden hose or lawn furniture—
(f) Things belonging to children in the household—
(g) Things from a vehicle, such as a package, groceries, camera, or cassette tapes—

OR

(h) Did anyone ATTEMPT to steal anything belonging to you?

MARK OR ASK—

Did any incidents of this type happen to you?

. . .

Question 40 (all respondents) (attack/item stolen—cue on place)

(Other than any incidents already mentioned), since _____ ___, 20__, were you attacked or threatened or did you have something stolen from you—

(a) At home including the porch or yard—

(b) At or near a friend's, relative's, or neighbor's home—
(c) At work or school—
(d) In places such as a storage shed or laundry room, a shopping mall, restaurant, bank, or airport—
(e) While riding in any vehicle—
(f) On the street or in a parking lot—
(g) At such places as a party, theater, gym, picnic area, bowling lanes, or while fishing or hunting—

OR

(h) Did anyone attempt to attack or attempt to steal anything belonging to you from any of these places?

MARK OR ASK—
Did any incidents of this type happen to you?

The NCVS interviewers are instructed to record the screening question that prompted mention of an event. The purpose is to facilitate asking the follow-up incident report questions. For our purposes, we can use these data to ascertain which questions are the most productive in generating recall of victimization events and variation over the years since the redesigned questions were implemented in 1992. This variation could indicate changes in the public's view of violence. Our hypothesis is that a trend toward a higher percentage of affirmative responses to the first screener questions would support a broadening definition of violence. As common views of violence broaden, fewer prompts should be needed to spark recall of a crime.

1. *Changes in Cuing Productivity for Greater and Lesser Forms of Violence.* To explore evidence from the screener questions about changing views of violence, we focus on three groups of crimes.[5] These include assaults in general and more particularly those involving female victims as we also consider violence against women (rape and sexual assault and domestic violence). We consider assaults in general as we believe that

[5] One point worth reiterating is that we are limited to crimes on which data are collected by the NCVS. To the extent that respondents are reporting a wider range of minor offenses not covered by the NCVS (such as stalking or bullying) or threats that are excluded by the survey's protocols, we do not have the ability to account for these changes. Our analyses assume that if we observe greater willingness to consider lesser violence as a crime within the scope of events in the NCVS, this is likely happening for crimes not captured in the survey.

these behaviors are susceptible to expanding views of violence particularly in minor assaultive behavior categories such as threats. We include these two forms of violence against women in a comparative effort to investigate the extent to which specific policy changes may be reflected in reporting behavior captured by the NCVS.

We identify the particular cuing question in the screening interview that prompted mention of the violent crimes of interest. For all three groups of crime, we separately examine the proportion of crimes mentioned in response to the initial screener questions and compare these patterns over time. To give these estimates greater stability, we aggregated the data into 6-year periods to create three groups, comparing estimates from 1992–98 with 1999–2005 and 2006–12.[6] To illustrate with an example, our hypothesis is that a higher proportion of simple assaults reported in response to the first cue over time would be evidence of an expanding definition of violence as respondents are increasingly seeing these acts as criminal with few prompts needed. While we focus on an expanding definition of violence being the motivation for changes we observe, other factors might be prompting reports of any crime earlier in the survey. To account for this possibility, we also examine cuing patterns for more stereotypic crimes such as aggravated assault by a stranger.

2. *Assaultive Violence.* The NCVS includes information on several forms of assaultive violence including completed, attempted, and threatened aggravated assaults and completed and threatened simple assaults. Aggravated assault includes completed and attempted assaults with a weapon as well as completed assaults in which serious injury results. Threatened aggravated assault concerns threats with a weapon. Simple assault does not include serious injury or a weapon. Threatened simple assaults are verbal threats in which no weapon is present. All of these types of crimes are separately identified in the NCVS via its "type of crime" coding. This disaggregation of crime types and identification of the screener question that prompted recall of the event allow us to focus on a subset of assaults that may be more affected by cultural changes in the definition of violence.

The proportion of simple assaults reported by respondents in response to the first violence cues in the screener (question 40 above)

[6] The NCVS employs a probability sample. Comparisons of the proportion reporting to the initial violence cues must be tested for statistical significance. The NCVS also uses a complex sampling design. Our analyses use a Taylor series linearization procedure to adjust for this design and obtain the corrected standard errors.

increased over time, from 45 percent in the period 1992–98 to 48 percent between 1999 and 2005 and ultimately to 50 percent between 2006 and 2012 (see table 1). The increases in 1999–2005 and 2006–12 are statistically significantly greater than in 1992–99. The proportion of completed aggravated assaults reported in response to the first violence cues showed a similar pattern, increasing from 47 percent to 49 percent to 53 percent. Here the only statistically significant difference observed is between 1992–99 and 2006–12. The similarity of these cuing patterns does not suggest that lesser forms of violence (i.e., assaults involving no injury and no weapon) were more readily recalled, which we would interpret to be indicia of an expanding view of criminal behavior. Both more and less serious violence were more likely to be reported in response to initial violence cues in the survey over time.

When threats are separately examined, the proportion of verbal threats reported in response to the first violence cues increases slightly more for verbal threats than for threats in which a weapon is present. The percentage of weapon-involved threats mentioned in response to the first screener cue remained essentially the same over the period 1992–2012 at about 35 percent. The percentage of verbal threats mentioned in response to the first screener cue increased from 48 percent to 53 percent. Here the only statistically significant difference is between the percentage reported in 1992–99 (48 percent) and that reported in 2006–12 (53 percent).

TABLE 1

Percentage of Crimes Reported in Response to Early and Generic Screener Cues by Crime, NCVS, 1992–2012

Type of Crime	1992–98 (1)	1999–2005 (2)	2006–12 (3)	Difference (1) − (2)	Difference (2) − (3)	Difference (1) − (3)
Aggravated assault	47.48	49.25	53.15	NS	S	S
Aggravated assault vs. stranger	43.0	41.0	44.0	NS	NS	NS
Simple assault	45.44	48.16	50.0	S	S	S
Weapons threats	35.19	35.8	36.6	NS	NS	NS
Verbal threats	48.0	50.7	53.4	NS	S	S
Rape and sexual assault	20.0	21.1	18.0	NS	NS	NS
Domestic violence	30.1	31.6	39.0	NS	S	S

NOTE.—S indicates a statistically significant difference at the .05 α level; NS indicates no statistically significant difference.

3. *Changes in Cuing Productivity for Rape and Sexual Assault.* In the case of rape and sexual assault, we see little change in responses to cues in the screening interview. Here we examine only rape and sexual assault incidents involving female victims, but the crimes include completed, attempted, and threatened rape and sexual assault. In the period 1992–98, 20 percent of incidents ultimately classified as NCVS rapes and sexual assaults were reported to the first cue (question 40). This percentage remained statistically the same in 1999–2005 (21 percent) and 2006–12 (18 percent). The same is true for the pattern of responses to cues specifically targeting rape and sexual assault (question 43, which appears in the appendix). Here the percentages of incidents were 34 percent in 1992–98, 34 percent in 1999–2005, and 39 percent in 2006–12. While the latter percentage is higher than the other two, it is not a statistically significant difference. If rape and sexual assault were becoming more central to the concept of violence, then on the basis of our hypothesis, we would have expected the percentages mentioned in response to cues designed to elicit sexual violence to have declined in the period 2006–12.

4. *Changes in Cuing Productivity for Domestic Violence.* In contrast with rape and sexual assault, the responses to screener cues for domestic violence, the other form of violence against women that we examined, show a pattern more consistent with increasing recognition of this behavior as a crime. Here we define domestic violence as incidents involving female victims; a solo offender who is a spouse, ex-spouse, or current or former boyfriend; and any form of completed, attempted, or threatened violent crime included in the NCVS.[7] The percentage of domestic violence incidents prompted by the initial attack cue (question 40) increased from 30 percent (1992–98) to 31 percent (1999–2005) to 39 percent (2006–12). The increases between 1992–98 and 2006–12 and 1999–2005 and 2006–12 are statistically significant. Similarly, the proportion of domestic violence incidents reported in response to other cues, including the cuing question (question 42 provided in the appendix) specifically designed to elicit domestic violence, decreased over the period 1992–2012, particularly when the periods 1992–98 and 2006–12 are compared. These findings suggest a reasonably consistent trend in respondents being increasingly willing to identify domestic violence inci-

[7] These violent crimes include rape and sexual assault, robbery, aggravated assault, and simple assault.

dents as crimes in responses to general violence cues as opposed to more extensive cuing and cues specifically designed to elicit domestic violence.

Despite our hypotheses, this observed relationship between reports to early cuing questions and the identification of domestic violence events may be attributable to factors not related to changes in the cultural definition of domestic violence as a crime. To get a purchase on the possible effects of these other factors, we compared changes in the domestic violence trends to changes in cuing patterns for completed, attempted, and threatened aggravated assault against male and female victims involving strangers during the same periods. We chose stranger aggravated assault because aggravated assault involves fairly serious violence. In addition, a stable consensus exists about aggravated assaults being a crime particularly when the offender is a stranger. We hypothesize that aggravated assault reporting would have greater stability over time than domestic violence. Over the period 1992–2012, no statistically significant changes are observed. Forty-three percent of these offenses were reported in response to question 40 in 1992–98, 41 percent in 1999–2005, and 44 percent in 2006–12. Over the same period, the proportion of domestic violence events mentioned in response to the first attack cue increased from 30 percent to 39 percent. We saw a similar pattern of more aggravated assault to be reported to earlier cues. This trend, though, is much more pronounced for domestic violence.

Our analysis of the screener questions does not indicate support for a dramatic expansion in the general concept of violence that would pass through the filters in crime statistics systems and influence crime rates. We did not find an increase in lesser forms of violence, such as verbal threats. Verbal threats ultimately classified as NCVS threatened assaults are not more likely to be mentioned in response to early and more general cues over time. In the case of rape and sexual assault, these crimes are within the scope of the major indicators of crime so that changes in the public definition of these crimes could pass the filters of these statistical series. Our analysis provides weak support for the assertion that rape and sexual assault have become more central to the concept of criminal violence over time. Domestic violence shows the strongest evidence of cultural change based on our screener analysis.

We offer a few explanations for these findings. One is that a change in societal views toward violence is not occurring; however, given the continued advocacy work and broadening definition of crime for behaviors such as stalking and bullying, we do not believe this is the case. Rather it may be that the procedural safeguards the NCVS uses are limiting and filtering out more minor offenses that respondents may be reporting. While advocates have lobbied to change laws and procedures to treat interpersonal behaviors involving minimal (if any) direct physical violence as a crime, many of these crime classes such as bullying and stalking are not included in the major statistical series measuring crime. In an associated research project of nonclassifying crimes (i.e., incidents reported to the crime survey but ultimately not classified as an NCVS crime type), common crimes involved incidents in which behaviors might appear threatening but no specific words of assault were mentioned (Addington 2012). With rape and sexual assault, these crimes may still be difficult to report in the survey as they include sexual behavior despite efforts to explicitly screen for these crimes. In addition, changes in rape policy may be occurring in waves, with initial substantial changes occurring in the 1970s and 1980s. More recently greater attention has been devoted at the college level to identifying and reporting sexual violence. Our work might not be sensitive enough or have enough early years of data and more recent years of data to identify these changes.

The evidence from our screener analysis for domestic violence is consistent with our hypothesis. A few reasons likely explain these findings. First, the crimes included as part of domestic violence are crimes within the scope of the NCVS (as compared with a broader view of threats). These incidents are less likely to be filtered out by the procedures meant to safeguard the statistical series. In addition, unlike threats or rape and sexual assault, domestic violence is often repeated, so this pattern permits more opportunities for reporting. It is unclear whether the first incident of domestic violence is reported (akin to a single sexual assault or single threat) or whether victims are more likely to report after subsequent incidents have occurred.

II. Comparisons of Trends in Recounting Events to the NCVS and Reporting to Police

We also looked at NCVS trends overall rather than only in conjunction with specific screening questions. We posit that changes in the definition of violence will affect trends in the NCVS largely from the greater willingness of survey respondents to identify their experience as a crime and to report that incident to the NCVS interviewer. The cuing analysis showed the largest and most consistent increases in the reporting of domestic violence in relation to the general assault cuing questions that appear early in the NCVS screening interview. These increases are greater than those observed for a clear paradigm of criminal violence: aggravated assault involving a stranger. In light of these findings, we would expect to see the greatest effect on crime trends for domestic violence. Given our finding of limited support for changes in reporting patterns for verbal threats and no support for changes in rape and sexual assault reporting, we expect to observe little change over time for these crimes. The NCVS trends will also be influenced by changes in the willingness of the survey to accept the crimes reported to interviewers as eligible crimes. Our time series of data begins after the major redesign in 1992. Since then, the procedures of the NCVS have remained relatively stable and should not affect observed changes in the trends observed.

In addition to considering an increased likelihood of recalling and reporting crimes to NCVS interviewers, we consider changes in reporting incidents to police. Here we anticipate that broader views of violence will prompt victims to report to police minor incidents or incidents not previously considered serious crimes at an increasing rate over time. We also posit that these patterns will be most pronounced for domestic violence and less so for verbal threats and rape and sexual assault. For rape and sexual assault, we can capitalize on data from the UCR. As with the NCVS, the UCR trends are affected in part by a greater willingness to report the incident to the police (Block and Block 1980; Baumer and Lauritsen 2010). While our ability to disaggregate UCR violence trends is limited, it is possible to compare rape trends to trends in other forms of violence. By so doing, we can ascertain if a crime that has been the focus of intense advocacy over time exhibits different patterns than other types of violence that have not received heightened attention.

One point to note concerns the trends we anticipate seeing. This expectation is affected by overall crime trends, which by all measures have been generally declining for the past 20 years. While the causes of this decline are in dispute (Blumstein and Wallman 2006; Zimring 2012), it is unlikely that changes in the definitions of violence will overcome the significant drop in crime and the variety of factors motivating this decline. If changes in the definition of crime are affecting crime trends, we should consistently observe smaller declines in trends for those crimes most likely to be affected by a broadened view of violence (such as with domestic violence) than those less likely to be affected (such as aggravated assault).

A. Comparisons of Crime Trends in the NCVS

In table 2, we compare various forms of assault to ascertain whether lesser forms of violence (simple assault and verbal threats) show a different pattern over time compared with more serious violence and incidents more likely to be considered violent over time (aggravated assaults and threats with a weapon). Contrary to our hypotheses, we find similar declines for both aggravated and simple assault rates. The rates for aggravated assault declined 57 percent between 1992–93 and 2011–12 and rates for simple assault by 58 percent. When threats are considered, we find support for our hypothesis of a smaller percentage decline for the "grayer" crime of verbal threats of assault than threats with a weapon. Rates of weapon threats declined 76 percent from 1992–93 to 2011–12, while rates of verbal threats fell only 59 percent.

The data on rape and sexual assault show similar comparative patterns. Rape rates, when considered separately from sexual assault, declined 71 percent from 1992–93 to 2011–12. This is comparable to the trends for more stereotypic crimes such as aggravated assaults by strangers,

TABLE 2

Percentage Change in Rates per 1,000 from 1992–93 to 2011–12 by Type of Crime, NCVS

Type of Crime	Rates 1992–93	Rates 2011–12	Percentage Change	Significance
Aggravated assault	3.07	1.28	−58.2	S
Simple assault	20.96	8.83	−57.8	S
Weapon threats	5.22	1.22	−76.55	S
Verbal threats	12.58	5.09	−59.52	S
Rape	1.48	.42	−71.17	S
Sexual assault	.57	.286	−49.76	S
Domestic violence:				S
Simple assault intimate	5.01	2.93	−41.38	S
Simple assault stranger	14.16	5.07	−64.16	S
Aggravated assault—intimate	1.32	.739	−42.46	S
Aggravated assault stranger	6.72	1.84	−72.38	S
Aggravated assault male victim	7.91	2.34	−70.36	S

NOTE.—S indicates a statistically significant difference at the .05 α level; NS indicates no statistically significant difference.

which also declined by about 71 percent. This suggests that rape may not be included in the broadening view of violence. This explanation is given additional support by our findings for sexual assault. Rates of sexual assault reported in the survey declined only 49 percent over the period 1992–2012. This pattern is more consistent with a broadening definition of more minor sexual violence.

As with our previous analyses, the trends for domestic violence are the most consistent with our hypothesis of a recent expanded view of violence. Simple assault rates for crimes involving strangers declined 64 percent from 1992 to 2012, while the rates for simple assault with intimate victims declined only 41 percent. The same pattern is observed for trends in more serious violence. Aggravated assaults with victims who are strangers fell 72 percent between 1992 and 2012 while aggravated assaults with intimate victims declined by only 42 percent during this same time period.

B. Trends in Reporting Violence to the Police

The act of reporting an incident to the police is an important indicator that the public views a particular behavior as criminal and rising to the level of severity to involve law enforcement.[8] Changes in patterns of reporting to the police provide another source of evidence that the definition of violence is broadening. The NCVS also allows exploration of these changes over time. While the NCVS measures criminal victimization, it specifically includes crimes whether or not the respondent reported the incident to the police. If tolerance for minor violence is decreasing, we would expect to see a greater proportion of more minor violence being reported to the police, while the proportion of more serious violence reported would stay constant. We would also expect that the reporting of crimes that have been the subject of intensive efforts at legal reform would also be reported to the police in greater proportions over time.

The proportion of violence reported to the police recorded in the NCVS has increased modestly over time (Baumer and Lauritsen 2010). This pattern is observed for all classes of violence and not just for crimes affected by a broadening view of violence that we discussed above with regard to violence against women and minor gray areas. As seen in table 3,

[8] An incident may be reported to the police for a variety of reasons (Xie et al. 2006). A common denominator is that the victim (or other person) believed the incident serious enough to bring to police attention.

TABLE 3

The Proportion of Crimes Reported to the Police by Type of Crime and Time, NCVS 1992–2012

Type of Crime	1992–98	2006–12	Significance
Aggravated assault	63	68	S
Simple assault	37	42	S
Weapons threat	50	54	NS
Verbal threat	32	37	S
Domestic violence:			
Aggravated assault on intimate	55	61	NS
Simple assault on intimate	50	56	S
Sexual assault	25	36	NS
Rape	31	43	NS

NOTE.—S indicates a statistically significant difference at the .05 α level; NS indicates no statistically significant difference.

the proportion of aggravated assaults reported to the police increased from 63 percent to approximately 68 percent from 1992 to 2012. Similarly, the proportion of simple assaults reported to the police increased from 37 percent to 42 percent. A similar pattern is observed for threats, the proportion of weapons threats reported to the police increasing from 50 percent to 54 percent over the period 1992–2012 and verbal threats from 32 percent to 37 percent. In comparison, the proportion of aggravated assaults with intimates as victims reported to the police rose from 55 percent to 61 percent between 1992 and 2012 while the proportion of simple assaults against intimates reported to the police increased from 50 percent to 56 percent. This pattern suggests that slightly more crimes were reported to the police over time regardless of the degree of violence or the victim-offender relationship.

With regard to rape and sexual assault, the proportion reported to the police increased modestly but about twice as much as for other forms of violence.[9] Here we parse out rapes reported to the police from sexual assaults. The proportion of sexual assaults reported to the police increased from 25 percent in 1992–98 to 36 percent in 2006–12 and the proportion of rapes reported to the police increased from 31 percent to 43 percent. While we did not find changes in reports of rape and

[9] These increases in reporting to the police are not statistically significant at the .05 level because of the extremely low base rates for rape and sexual assault that are less than 5 percent of the base rate for aggravated assault.

TABLE 4
Percentage Change in Crime Rates per 100,000 from the UCR, 1992–2006

Type of Crime	1992	2012	Percentage Change
Homicide	9.5	4.7	−51.0
Rape	41.1	26.9	−35.0
Robbery	256	113	−56.0
Aggravated assault	440.5	242.3	−45.0

NOTE.—Significance tests were not conducted for these trends since the UCR is a census and not a sample.

sexual assault to early cues in the screener questionnaire, this pattern of reporting to the police indicates that victims are increasingly willing to report rape and sexual assault to the police.

This finding lends support to a cultural change to broaden views of criminal violence.[10] This explanation of increased reporting by rape victims is further bolstered by trends observed in police administrative data during this same time period in which forcible rape declined substantially less than other forms of violence. During the period 1992–2012, homicide rates fell 51 percent, robbery 46 percent, and aggravated assault 45 percent (see table 4). In comparison, forcible rape rates declined only 35 percent. Using the UCR and NCVS in a complementary way suggests that the smaller decline in UCR rape rates relative to other forms of violence may be due to increased willingness of victims to report rapes to the police.

III. Conclusion

When a long view of history is taken, an expanding cultural definition of violence is readily apparent. Over time, society has deemed as criminal an increasing scope of behaviors. Less is known about the effect of these changes for a relatively shorter time period and, if these changes occur, the extent to which they affect our official crime statistics. Under-

[10] A variety of factors may be prompting increased reporting including improved victim services, better training for police and criminal justice personnel, and public relations campaigns to encourage victim reporting. All stem from advocacy efforts and, we believe, an underlying broadening of how violence is viewed by society.

standing this issue is important in order to get a better understanding of crime trends, especially to the extent that these patterns may be driven by changes in cultural definitions of violence rather than substantive changes in underlying behavior. To explore this issue, we considered two primary research questions: Has the popular definition of criminal violence expanded such that lesser violence not previously considered criminal now is? And to the extent that this change occurred, has it contributed to increases (or suppressed decreases) in trends in official crime statistics?

To consider the first question, we examined evidence from advocacy efforts to reform laws and criminal justice procedures in the area of violence against women and changes in public perceptions about grayer areas of crime as identified from responses to screener cues in the NCVS. On the basis of these analyses, we find support for a short-term expansion in the definition of criminal violence, with lesser forms of violence considered criminal that previously were not. We express these conclusions cautiously because our findings suggest that the change is less an across-the-board embracing of more civil behavior than increased moral intolerance for specific types of behavior in particular social contexts. Our findings are strongest for domestic violence. This pattern is likely due to advocacy efforts, and survey evidence is readily found as a result of procedural aspects of the NCVS itself. With regard to advocacy, domestic violence was one form of violence against women that had been the focus of efforts to define these acts as criminal, to raise public awareness, and to encourage reporting to the police. These efforts likely served to broaden the definition of violence to include domestic violence and to have the public see this behavior as clearly criminal in nature.

We also addressed the first question using data from the NCVS screening questions. These findings also provided support for this change. Our analysis of responses to cuing patterns in the NCVS screener suggests that advocacy efforts have not increased the public's willingness to define all these acts as criminal violence. For example, respondents in the NCVS were not more likely over time to mention rapes in response to earlier and more general violence cues in the screening interview, while responses for domestic violence showed more pronounced increases. Lesser forms of violence across the board did not show increases over time in the proportion of crimes mentioned in response to earlier and more general violence cues. This pattern might be explained by the filtering procedures the NCVS uses that may reject lesser forms of violence that are reported by respondents.

To examine the extent to which expanded views of violence may have affected official statistics, our analysis showed that lesser forms of violence such as verbal threats did not decline as much as more traditional and serious crime classes such as aggravated and even simple assault. The reductions in rape over time were comparable to those for aggravated assault, but the trends in sexual assault showed much smaller declines. All of these patterns are consistent with a more general expansion of the concept of violence. These lesser forms of violence are not declining as fast as rates of more serious violence presumably because more respondents are defining these acts as crimes. This explanation for these crime trends is not consistent with the screener cuing analysis that showed no differences in cuing patterns for verbal threats over time.

In contrast, the trends for domestic violence are more consistent with the hypothesis that expansions in the definition of domestic violence are affecting crime trends than those for grayer crimes such as threats. The cuing analysis shows that increasingly over time, domestic violence was reported in response to earlier and more general cues. The trends in rates of domestic violence show substantially smaller decreases over the period 1992–2012 than for aggravated or simple assault more generally.

Finally, trends in rape rates from the UCR are not declining as much as other types of violence. The NCVS data on rape indicate that the proportion of rapes reported to the police has increased more than any other violent crime. So the smaller declines in rape rates may be due to a greater willingness of victims to report events to the police rather than to expansions in the definition of rape.

Domestic violence provides the strongest evidence of a broadening definition of violence that has grown to include behavior that a few decades ago was considered private and almost sanctioned by society. Our findings suggest that this cultural change has affected trends in crime statistics. The evidence is not as consistent for rape and for lesser forms of violence more generally. These crimes show rate trends that are not declining as steeply as for other forms of violence, which may be explained by the evidence suggesting that changes have occurred in the popular definitions of these crimes that are not as strong as that for domestic violence.

These results suggest that domestic violence should be viewed separately when examining long-term trends in violence using statistical series, in order to avoid distortions that may come from changes in the definition of this crime over time. They also suggest that rape statistics based on police administrative data are becoming more inclusive because of increases in victims' willingness to report to the police. For this reason, rape should be distinguished from other violence when comparing long-term trends in police data.

Our analyses provide a useful place to start as no other work in the United States has explored the effects of societal changes in views of violence in a short-term period with possible effects on national statistical indicators like the NCVS.[11] Our study, though, has limitations that should temper any recommendations made. First, our methods for determining whether the cultural definition of violence has expanded to include lesser violence are indirect. The scope and persistence of advocacy efforts to criminalize behavior provide a good starting point for identifying forms of violence that may have changed, but effort is not always a measure of outcome. The cuing analysis is a more direct method of measuring definitional change, but it rests on certain assumptions about cognition, recall, and reporting. Our study also is limited to behaviors the NCVS includes in its definition of crime. We are interested in a broadening definition of violence. These same behaviors are likely the ones filtered out by the procedural safeguards in the NCVS.

Future work could seek more clearly to identify changes in views of criminal violence. One method for accomplishing this would be a survey specifically designed to examine changes in the definition of criminal violence. Such a survey, for example, could interview respondents and ask about a range of violent acts and whether they should be considered criminal. Another approach would be to combine survey data with incident-level police administrative data that would allow for distinguishing levels of violence within the large, heterogeneous crime classes used in the UCR. The UCR's National Incident Based Reporting System generates incident-level details necessary to conduct such work, but the time series of these data may be limited to certain jurisdictions and omit the largest police agencies. This approach would enable a wider range of trend analyses by distinguishing more from less violent offenses. A third future study could expand this work cross-nationally. We focused on the United States because we are most familiar with the sta-

[11] Few studies exist outside the United States. One notable exception is research by Kivivuori (2014) on threats and assaults in Finland.

tistical series here and the NCVS had unique features that contributed to this analysis. It would be useful to repeat at least the crime trends parts of this analysis in other nations to determine the generalizability of our US findings.

We approached the issue of the evolution in the definition of violent crime as a source of measurement error in crime statistics that should be identified and taken into account when assessing the long time series. The UCR and NCVS have procedures and safeguards in place to minimize the effect of societal changes and to provide reliable change measures. This consistency, though, is in stark contrast with other social indicators and is not without its own costs. The crimes included in the UCR's Part I offenses have changed little since the 1930s. During this same period, the International Classification of Diseases has changed 10 times to reflect changes in diseases and our knowledge of them. The Consumer Price Index is constantly updated to add new goods to the basket as consumer buying habits change. The NCVS is a bit more flexible, adding new types of crime such as identity theft or stalking in periodic supplements to the main survey, but these additions provide intermittent rather than annual estimates.

Insulating our crime indicators from change can impose its own set of costs. These relatively static measures may result in a definition of violence in particular and crime more broadly that no longer reflects the reality in which citizens negotiate their daily lives. They may yield data that do not generate a useful description of the nature of the crime problem. It is quite possible that if these "new" crimes—such as stalking or identity theft—were included in our social indicators, we would see an overall increase in crime and not a decline. These data also could provide a better perspective on risk and exposure. For example, if our crime indicators routinely reflected rates of identity theft, this information might limit panic after media reports of a corporate data breach. These data could provide a context for such breaches being relatively rare and not involving large losses. These observations are not intended to propose abandonment of traditional measures of violent crime or to discount the need to preserve series continuity, but rather to emphasize a balance that accurately describes the current crime problem. We must introduce new crimes into these systems in a manner that minimizes the disruption to the time series or certain parts of the time series.

Identifying a need for careful revisions to statistical systems is much easier than implementing it. The biggest impediment is the absence of a clear system of governance for crime statistics. We must have an orderly and routine way to make appropriate changes. No clear procedures are currently in place to do this. Both the UCR and NCVS have rather ad hoc systems that tend to take a piecemeal approach, especially in the absence of a significant redesign effort.

For the UCR, no change can be made unless it is approved through the Advisory Policy Board process.[12] This board is a series of committees staffed by persons responsible for assembling the UCR statistics in local police departments. Given the voluntary nature of participation in the UCR and a desire not to overburden police agencies, there is a strong self-interest to avoid making changes.

The NCVS has no governance process. Changes are made to the survey at the discretion of the director of the Bureau of Justice Statistics. Advice is usually sought from interested and knowledgeable parties, but this process is not part of a formal governance structure. Crime statistics should follow the example of statistical systems on health and the economy. Governing boards should be created that include all of the constituencies with an interest in crime and crime statistics and not only the persons charged with collecting the data. Assessments of the current system should be conducted at regular intervals, and new crimes should be added when they have become sufficiently prevalent or disruptive to warrant routine monitoring. Once identified, these crimes can be added in a manner that minimizes disruption to the time series.

APPENDIX

Question 41 (all respondents) (focus attack/threat—cue weapon)

(Other than any incidents already mentioned), has anyone attacked or threatened you in any of these ways?

EXCLUDE TELEPHONE THREATS

(a) With any weapon, for instance, a gun or knife—
(b) With anything like a baseball bat, frying pan, scissors, or stick—
(c) By something thrown, such as a rock or bottle—
(d) Include any grabbing, punching, or choking—

[12] Changes to the UCR governance structure may not be sufficient to provide the flexibility required of a statistical system. It may be necessary to move to a smaller, sample-based UCR that involves fewer agencies and requires less effort to incorporate changes than does the current census-based system.

(e) Any rape, attempted rape, or other type of sexual attack—
(f) Any face to face threats—

OR

(g) Any attack or threat or use of force by anyone at all? Please mention it even if you are not certain it was a crime.

MARK OR ASK—
Did any incidents of this type happen to you?
Question 42 (all respondents) (focus stolen item/attack/threat—cue someone you know)
People often don't think of incidents committed by someone they know. (Other than any incidents already mentioned), did you have something stolen from you or were you attacked or threatened by?
EXCLUDE TELEPHONE THREATS

(a) Someone at work or school—
(b) A neighbor or friend—
(c) A relative or family member—
(d) Any other person you've met or known?

MARK OR ASK—
Did any incidents of this type happen to you?
Question 43 (all respondents) (focus sexual assault)
Incidents involving forced or unwanted sexual acts are often difficult to talk about. (Other than any incidents already mentioned), have you been forced or coerced to engage in unwanted sexual activity by—

(a) Someone you didn't know before—
(b) A casual acquaintance—

OR

(c) Someone you know well?

MARK OR ASK—
Did any incidents of this type happen to you?
Question 44 (all respondents) (focus called police/thought was a crime)
Did you call the police during the last 6 months to report something (else) that happened to you which you thought was a crime? (Other than any incidents already mentioned.)
Question 45 (all respondents) (focus not call police/thought was a crime)
Did anything happen to you during the last 6 months which you thought was a crime, but did not report to the police? (Other than any incidents already mentioned.)

REFERENCES

Addington, Lynn A. 2012. *Examination of Unclassified NCVS Incidents*. Internal memorandum, Bureau of Justice Statistics. Washington, DC: US Department of Justice.

Baumer, Eric P., and Janet L. Lauritsen. 2010. "Reporting Crime to the Police, 1973–2005: A Multivariate Analysis of Long-Term Trends in the National Crime Survey (NCS) and National Crime Victimization Survey (NCVS)." *Criminology* 48:131–85.

Belknap, J. 1996. *The Invisible Woman: Gender, Crime and Justice*. Belmont, CA: Wadsworth.

Biderman, Albert, David Cantor, James P. Lynch, and Elizabeth Martin. 1985. *Final Report of the National Crime Survey Redesign*. Washington, DC: Bureau of Social Science Research.

Biderman, Albert, and Jeffery Moore. 1982. *Report on the Workshop on Cognitive Issues in Surveys of Retrospective Surveys*. Washington, DC: Bureau of Social Science Research and US Census Bureau.

Black, M. C., K. C. Basile, M. J. Breiding, S. G. Smith, M. L. Walters, M. T. Merrick, J. Chen, and M. R. Stevens. 2011. *The National Intimate Partner and Sexual Violence Survey (NISVS): 2010 Summary Report*. Atlanta: National Center for Injury Prevention and Control, Centers for Disease Control and Prevention.

Block, Richard, and Carolyn Rebecca Block. 1980. "Decisions and Data: The Transformation of Robbery Incidents into Robbery Statistics." *Journal of Criminal Law and Criminology* 71:636–62.

Blumstein, Alfred, and Joel Wallman. 2006. *The Crime Drop in America*. Rev. ed. New York: Cambridge University Press.

Buchmann, Claudia, and Thomas Diprete. 2006. "The Growing Female Advantage in College Completion: The Role of Family Background and Academic Achievement." *American Sociological Review* 71:515–41.

Buzawa, E. S., and C. G. Buzawa. 1990. *Domestic Violence: The Criminal Justice Response*. Newbury Park, CA: Sage.

———. 1996. *Domestic Violence: The Criminal Justice Response*. 2nd ed. Newbury Park, CA: Sage.

———. 2003. *Domestic Violence: The Criminal Justice Response*. 3rd ed. Newbury Park, CA: Sage.

Buzawa, E. S., C. G. Buzawa, and E. Stark. 2012. *Responding to Domestic Violence: The Integration of Criminal Justice and Human Services*. 4th ed. Los Angeles: Sage.

Cantor, David, and James P. Lynch. 2005. "Exploring the Effects of Changes in Design on the Analytical Uses of the NCVS Data." *Journal of Quantitative Criminology* 21:293–319.

Catalano, Shannan. 2012. *Stalking Victims in the United States*. Washington, DC: Bureau of Justice Statistics, US Department of Justice.

Chaplin, Rupert, John Farley, and Kevin Smith. 2011. *Crime in England and Wales, 2010/11*. Statistical Bulletin. London: Home Office.

Chu, Anne, and Charles Posner. 2013. *The State of Women in America: A Fifty State Analysis of How Women Are Faring across States*. Washington, DC: Center for American Progress.

Cohen, Albert K. 1974. *The Elasticity of Evil: Changes in the Social Definition of Deviance*. Oxford: Blackwell.

Durkheim, Emile. 1982. *Rules of the Sociological Method*. New York: Macmillan/Free Press.

Eisner, Manual. 2003. "Long-Term Historical Trends in Violent Crime." In *Crime and Justice: A Review of Research*, vol. 30, edited by Michael Tonry. Chicago: University of Chicago Press.

———. 2014. "From Swords to Words: Does Macro-Level Change in Self-Control Predict Long-Term Variation in Levels of Homicide?" In *Why Crime Rates Fall and Why They Don't*, edited by Michael Tonry. Vol. 43 of *Crime and Justice: A Review of Research*, edited by Michael Tonry. Chicago: University of Chicago Press.

England, Paula, Paul Allison, Su Li, Noah Mark, Jennifer Thompson, Michele Budig, and Han Sun. 2007. "Why Are Some Academic Fields Tipping toward Females? The Sex Composition of US Fields of Doctoral Degree Receipt, 1970–2002." *Sociology of Education* 80:23–42.

Faris, Robert, and Diane Felmlee. 2012. "Status Struggles: Network Centrality and Gender Segregation in Same- and Cross-Gender Aggression." *American Sociological Review* 76(1):48–73.

Havermann, Heather, and Lauren Beresford. 2012. "If You Are So Smart, Why Aren't You the Boss? Explaining the Persistent Vertical Gap in Management." *Annals of the American Academy of Social and Political Science* 639: 114–30.

Heimer, Karen, Janet L. Lauritsen, and James P. Lynch. 2009. "The National Crime Victimization Survey and the Gender Gap in Offending: Redux." *Criminology* 47(2):427–38.

Juhn, Chinhui, and Simon Potter. 2006. "Changes in Labor Force Participation in the United States." *Journal of Economic Perspectives* 20(3):27–46.

Kane, R. J. 1999. "Patterns of Arrest in Domestic Violence Encounters: Identifying a Police Decision-Making Model." *Journal of Criminal Justice* 27:65–79.

Kilpatrick, D. G., C. N. Edmunds, and A. Seymour. 1992. *Rape in America: A Report to the Nation*. Charleston: Medical School, University of South Carolina, National Victim Center, and Crime Victims Research and Treatment Center.

Kivivouri, Janne. 2014. "Understanding Trends in Personal Violence: Does Cultural Sensitivity Matter?" In *Why Crime Rates Fall and Why They Don't*, edited by Michael Tonry. Vol. 43 of *Crime and Justice: A Review of Research*, edited by Michael Tonry. Chicago: University of Chicago Press.

Koss, Mary. 1993. "Detecting the Scope of Rape: A Review of Prevalence Research Methods." *Journal of Interpersonal Violence* 8(2):198–220.

Kowalski, Robin M., Sue Limber, and Patricia W. Agatston. 2012. *Cyberbullying: Bullying in the Digital Age*. Malden, MA: Wiley and Blackwell.

Langton, Lynn, Michael Planty, and Jenna Truman. 2013. *Criminal Victimization in the United States*. Washington, DC: Bureau of Justice Statistics, US Department of Justice.

Lauritsen, Janet, Karen Heimer, and James P. Lynch. 2009. "Trends in the Gender Gap in Violent Offending: New Evidence from the National Crime Victimization Survey." *Criminology* 47(2):361–99.

Loh, Wallace. 1981. "What Has Rape Reform Legislation Wrought? A Truth in Criminal Labelling." *Journal of Social Issues* 37:28–52.

Lynch, James, and Lynn A. Addington. 2007 *Understanding Crime Incidence Statistics: Revisiting the Divergence of the UCR from the NCVS*. New York: Cambridge University Press.

Martin, E., R. M. Groves, J. Matlin, and C. Miller. 1986. *Report on the Development of Alternative Screening Procedures for the National Crime Survey*. Washington, DC: Bureau of Social Science Research.

Melody, M. L., and S. L. Miller. 2011. *The Victimization of Women: Law, Policies and Politics*. Oxford: Oxford University Press.

Pinker, Steven. 2011. *Better Angels of Our Nature: Why Violence Has Declined*. New York: Viking.

Poggio, Eugene, Stephen Kennedy, Jan Chaiken, and Kenneth Carlson. 1985. *Blueprint for the Future of the Uniform Crime Reporting Program*. Washington, DC: US Department of Justice.

Raley, Sarah, Marabeth Mattingly, and Suzanne Bianci. 2006. "How Dual Are Dual Income Families: Documenting Change from 1970 to 2001." *Journal of Marriage and Family* 68:1–28.

Robers, Simone, Jana Kemp, Amy Rathbun, Rachel Morgan, and Thomas Snyder. 2014. *Indicators of School Crime and Safety: 2013*. Washington, DC: Bureau of Justice Statistics and Department of Education.

Roe, Stephen, and Julie Ashe. 2008. *Young People and Crime: Findings from the Offending, Crime, and Justice Survey*. London: Home Office.

Spilsbury, Stephanie, and Michael P. Kidd. 1997. "The Gender Wage Gap: What Has Happened in Australia between 1973 and 1990?" *Australian Economic Papers* 36(December):205–23.

Spohn, Cassia, and Julie Horney. 1992. *Rape Law Reform: A Grassroots Revolution and Its Impact*. New York: Plenum.

Thornberry, Terence, and Marvin D. Krohn. 2011. "The Self-Report Method and the Development of Criminological Theory." In *Measuring Crime and Criminality*, edited by John MacDonald. Vol. 17 of *Advances in Criminological Theory*. New Brunswick, NJ: Transaction.

Tjaden, P., and N. Thoennes. 2006. *Extent, Nature, and Consequences of Rape Victimization: Findings from the National Violence Against Women Survey*. NCJ no. 210346. Washington, DC: US Department of Justice, National Institute of Justice.

Tonry, Michael. 2014. "Why Crime Rates Are Falling throughout the Western World." In *Why Crime Rates Fall and Why They Don't*, edited by Michael Tonry. Vol. 43 of *Crime and Justice: A Review of Research*, edited by Michael Tonry. Chicago: University of Chicago Press.

Tracy, Carol E., Terry L. Fromson, Jennifer Long, and Charlene Whitman. 2012. "Rape and Sexual Assault and the Legal System." Presentation at the National Academy of Science Panel on Measuring Rape and Sexual Assault in Household Surveys, Washington, DC, June 5.

van Dijk, Jan, John van Kesteren, and Paul Smit. 2007. *Criminal Victimisation in International Perspective: Key Findings from the 2004–2005 ICVS and EUICS.* The Hague: Netherlands Ministry of Justice.

Xie, Min, Greg Pogarsky, David McDowall, and James P. Lynch. 2006. "Prior Police Service and the Decision to Call the Police." *Justice Quarterly* 23 (4):481–501.

Zimring, Franklin. 2012. *The City That Became Safe: New York's Lessons for Urban Crime and Its Control.* New York: Oxford University Press.

John MacDonald

Community Design and Crime: The Impact of Housing and the Built Environment

ABSTRACT

Crime is influenced by the built environment. Broken windows, crime prevention through environmental design, situational crime prevention, and economic theories of the supply of and demand for criminal opportunities offer explanations. Zoning, designs of streets and housing, locations of public transit, and land uses shape the built environment in ways that can increase or reduce crime. Cross-sectional research shows that elements of the built environment are associated with crime rates in particular places. Quasi-experimental studies show that changes in zoning and street configurations, configuration and design of housing, and access to public transit can help manage crime. The mechanisms by which such changes influence crime are not well understood, though shifts in the supply of criminal opportunities most likely play a role. This evidence is promising. It suggests that the built environment can be modified to reduce both crime and reliance on criminal justice sanctions. Place-based experiments that manipulate features of the built environment will provide evidence for policy makers to use in designing cities in ways that reduce crime.

The idea that place matters in shaping social relations and crime has a long history. André-Michel Guerry and Adolphe Quetelet were among the

Electronically published July 30, 2015

John MacDonald is professor of criminology and sociology at the University of Pennsylvania. He is grateful for comments on earlier drafts from the editor, Michael Tonry, and

0192-3234/2015/0044-0011$10.00

first to connect crime and place empirically in their nineteenth-century analyses of statistical data in France. Work in England attempted to explain variations in crime rates between and within cities during the nineteenth century (Weisburd, Groff, and Yang 2012). Most of this work was descriptive and offered theories as to why crime rates varied from place to place but did not attempt to provide guidance on how to curb crime. By contrast, Snow's (1849) early work in England on the causes of cholera in contaminated drinking water during the nineteenth century noted the importance of the spatial environment in shaping human health and suggested the separation of sewers and drinking water wells to prevent waterborne diseases.

The focus on descriptive theory continued in the early twentieth century with the development of the Chicago school of human ecology, which argued that the urban form was important in shaping crime, mortality, and morbidity rates (Taylor 2001; Sampson 2012; Weisburd, Groff, and Yang 2012). Urban planners later largely discredited the ecological school for suggesting that cities grew in a natural evolutionary process and that there was "free competition for space among users" (Logan and Molotch 2007). Urban planners argued that places could be designed to affect human interactions and that cities did not grow in any natural way.

Since the 1960s a literature has developed that explains how the built environment affects crime. In urban planning, Jane Jacobs's *The Death and Life of Great American Cities* (1961) is the most influential work. She theorized that specific features of the built environment generate more or fewer "eyes upon the street" that in turn influence crime. She advocated mixed land uses that generate more foot traffic and building designs with closer setbacks from sidewalks to maximize sight lines to the street.[1] Urban planning scholar Schlomo Angel (1968) argued that commercial strips in Oakland, California, had higher crime rates than other commercial areas because of reduced foot traffic and increased vulnerability of would-be victims. Oscar Newman's *Defensible Space* (1972) also noted the importance of the physical design of places in relation to

---

anonymous reviewers, and for helpful discussions with James Anderson, Charles Branas, and Charles Loeffler on the topics covered in this essay.

[1] In an early effort, Fowler (1987) examined one of Jacobs's core ideas about land use diversity and reported crime. She examined 19 areas of two to three city blocks in Toronto in which she sought to maximize land use diversity differences. The sample was too small to generate meaningful *p*-values.

crime. Criminologists have developed these ideas in theories of crime prevention through environmental design (CPTED; Jeffery 1971) and situational crime prevention (Clarke 1995). More recently, public health scholars have paid increased attention to ways the design of communities affects crime, drawing on the literatures in urban planning and criminology (Mair and Mair 2003). Multiple fields now recognize that the built environment affects crime. A growing literature demonstrates that political decisions about how and where to invest public resources have fundamental influence on the urban form (Sampson 2012).

In this essay, I review literatures from criminology and urban planning to illustrate features of the built environment that are associated with crime. Extensive reviews on the criminology of place can be found elsewhere (Reiss and Tonry 1986; Kirk and Laub 2010; Sampson 2012; Weisburd, Groff, and Yang 2012). My goal is to connect theories of the criminality of place to understanding of how different features of the built environment affect crime. I build on an earlier *Crime and Justice* essay by Taylor and Gottfredson (1986), who provided a theoretical framework for explaining how offender cognition of neighborhood physical structures shapes crime in neighborhoods, street blocks, and specific sites. They also described cross-sectional evidence from the early 1980s on associations between features of the built environment and crime. I emphasize quasi-experimental studies.[2]

Policy guidance on design of the built environment to reduce crime has been based on case studies or cross-sectional evidence (Taylor and Harrell 1996; Zelinka and Brennan 2001; Cozens 2008; Cozens and Love 2009; Paulsen 2013). Case studies often examine changes in the built environment and crime in a single location, thereby providing little basis for examining whether changes could have occurred by chance. Cross-sectional studies provide statistical tests of chance differences but have the fundamental problem of being unidentified: multiple variables, both observed and unobserved, could explain the same distribution of crime. This is a problem with all observational studies and a primary reason for reliance in economics on quasi-experimental methods (Angrist and Pischke 2008). Quasi-experimental studies rely on plausible sources of random variation and attempt to approximate an experiment in which

[2] The best causal evidence would come from large-scale randomized controlled trials of changes in the built environment and subsequent changes in crime. I have not located any (see Welsh, Braga, and Bruinsma 2013).

groups are randomly assigned to receive treatment or control conditions.[3] Quasi-experimental studies provide stronger evidence.

There are myriad ways the built environment of places could be modified to reduce crime and reliance on criminal justice processes. First, evidence generated from structural changes to the built environment that are scalable and sustainable may be more amenable to policy interventions than are individual-based interventions that are difficult to implement en masse, expensive to maintain, and hard to replicate elsewhere (Branas and MacDonald 2014).

Second, changes to the built environment, such as adoption of new building or zoning codes, can be made through a regulatory framework without use of the criminal justice system. Current criminal justice policies are exceedingly expensive—about 7.9 percent of all local government spending (Kyckelhahn 2013). Trade-offs between expenditures on planning and on criminal justice should inform development of policies for shaping the built urban environment. Focusing on changing the built environment to reduce crime avoids the "causal fallacy" of thinking that crime can be reduced only by eliminating its root causes (Wilson 1983, p. 47).

A number of conclusions can be drawn. First, zoning of land to encourage mixing of residential and commercial uses reduces crime in commercial areas. Second, street configurations that reduce permeability of cars, such as cul-de-sacs, appear to reduce crime. Third, public transit is associated with crime in places, but research findings suggest that the opening of transit either has no effect on crime or reduces it by spurring economic development. Fourth, construction of public housing that concentrates poor people in segregated neighborhoods generates crime; low-income housing vouchers have little effect on crime. Fifth, mixed-income housing development may reduce crime compared with public housing development. Sixth, abandonment of housing due to economic distress appears to increase crime, but securing vacant housing appears to reduce it. Seventh, cleaning and greening vacant properties appear to reduce crime. Eighth, land uses related to alcohol, such as bars and alcohol outlets, may be associated with crime, but we lack strong evidence that they increase crime in areas over and above other existing risk factors. Ninth, although schools have been hypothesized to generate crime in places,

[3] In economics the term "exogenous variation" is used to refer to variation in variables of interest from outside of the model that are not correlated with confounding variables.

the evidence is weak. Quasi-experimental evidence suggests little relationship between crime in neighborhoods and the opening and closing of schools.

Quasi-experimental studies of the effects on crime of changes in the built environment have occurred only in a limited number of settings. Much more research should be done in different contexts to provide guidance to policy makers. Researchers should capitalize on natural experiments in which land is rezoned, housing is built or remediated, and public transit systems are developed or altered. Place-based experiments can be designed anywhere policy makers are considering changes in zoning or land use configuration.

Here is how this essay is organized. Section I examines data on the spatial concentration of crime and theories that attempt to explain how the built environment affects it. Sections II–V consider different features of the built environment that matter, including zoning, street design, public transit, housing design and configuration, and land use patterns. Section VI considers next steps for efforts to facilitate the design of safer cities.

I. Spatial Concentration

The severity and rates of crime vary greatly by time and location. In 2012, the 20 largest American cities' police agencies reported 3,110 murders, 21 percent of the 14,827 reported nationally. Only 10.79 percent of the population, however, lived in those cities.[4] Both official police data and victimization reports document higher crime rates in bigger cities (Glaeser and Sacerdote 1999). Within cities, crime is highly concentrated in specific neighborhoods and city blocks. Concentrations of street crime are greater in given blocks than among arrested individuals (Sherman 1995). Low-crime neighborhoods can become higher-crime neighborhoods (Schuerman and Kobrin 1986), sometimes reflecting patterns of gentrification of neighborhoods surrounded by poverty-stricken areas (Taylor and Covington 1988; Covington and Taylor 1989). Crime drops in cities occur mostly within a small fraction of city blocks (Weisburd, Groff, and Yang 2012). The hyperconcentration of crime in cities suggests that the criminality of place may be as important as the criminality of individuals in thinking about policy options to reduce crime.

[4] Author's calculations from Uniform Crime Report data (http://www.bjs.gov/ucrdata/Search/Crime/Crime.cfm; accessed February 17, 2014).

A. The Built Environment of Places and Crime

Crime is correlated with specific features of places. Areas plagued by crime tend also to have high rates of vacant or dilapidated housing, high residential turnover, unsupervised youths, poorly lit streets or poor visibility, highly permeable access to streets, and land uses such as liquor stores that generate crime (Skogan 1990; Weisburd, Groff, and Yang 2012).

Municipal codes governing building, occupancy rules, street design, and transit shape cities in ways that affect crime. Policy makers directly control municipal laws and rules and could, if they wished, use scientific knowledge to regulate the built environment to minimize crime. Extensive research shows associations between different aspects of the built environment and crime. This section summarizes classic cross-sectional and more recent quasi-experimental studies that show how changes in the built environment affect crime.

B. Different Mechanisms That Explain Why the Built Environment Matters

Why is crime concentrated in areas with specific features? Concentrated poverty is one reason. It is correlated with poor housing stock and land uses that attract crime. Poverty contributes to social and behavioral problems that make crime an intrinsic feature of poor areas. For example, poor individuals may be more consumed by worries, hunger, and stress that impair cognitive functioning (Mani et al. 2013). Poor families may be less able to engage in effective parenting practices that teach children to self-regulate. This is important because crime and other negative life outcomes are correlated with low self-control (Moffitt et al. 2011). Individuals living in poverty-stricken areas may be more likely than others to commit crimes because the expected benefit exceeds that from alternative legitimate wage-earning activities (Becker 1968). Endemic poverty may create or sustain cultural norms in which crime is seen as a legitimate method of economic gain and violence a socially appropriate response to insults or personal affronts (Anderson 1998). Poverty may lead to breakdowns in informal social controls that impede crime (Shaw and McKay 1942; Sampson 2012).

The poverty-crime explanation is plausible or persuasive to many people, but by itself it is too simple. Even in poor neighborhoods, crime is highly concentrated on specific blocks with specific features. More fundamentally, areas of relative wealth can have relatively high crime rates when features such as the presence of shopping and entertainment areas create attractive criminal opportunities (Brantingham and Brantingham

1995; Bernasco and Block 2011). Several prominent theories attempt to explain how the built environment affects crime.

1. *Broken Windows.* Wilson and Kelling's (1982, p. 29) broken windows theory explains that signs of blight and disorder in the built environment signal that an area is uncared for and thereby engenders crime. They observed, "Untended property becomes fair game for people out for fun or plunder. . . . Vandalism can occur anywhere once communal barriers—the sense of mutual regard and the obligations of civility—are lowered by actions that seem to signal that 'no one cares.'" Physical and social disorder neighborhoods tell motivated offenders that crime goes unabated.

Several studies suggest a connection between crime and disorder. Skogan's analysis of survey data from Atlanta, Chicago, Houston, and Newark showed that levels of disorder were more correlated than other social and economic variables with robbery victimization in neighborhoods (1990, p. 75). Taylor and colleagues found that reported crime in Baltimore and Philadelphia neighborhoods, and residents' fear of crime, were correlated with observable signs of blight and disorder on city blocks (Taylor, Shumaker, and Gottfredson 1985; Perkins and Taylor 1996).[5] Sampson and Raudenbush (1999) found that observed measures of physical disorder on street blocks in Chicago neighborhoods, such as garbage in the street, were correlated with self-reported violent victimization and crimes reported to the police.[6] However, when they controlled for measures of neighborhood collective efficacy, land use, concentrated poverty, and other factors, they found only an insignificant association between observed disorder and self-reported household victimization. Only

[5] Correlations between observed physical disorder and these outcomes were relatively weak and were strongest on blocks in moderate-income neighborhoods. This suggests that disorder and crime are linked to underlying poverty conditions. Perkins and Taylor's (1996) survey of low-rise housing residents in Baltimore neighborhoods at two times found a small but significant correlation between observed physical disorder ratings of randomly sampled households and reported fear of crime, controlling for perceived social and physical disorder by residents and basic demographics. These results suggest that residents on blocks with more blight have a higher fear of crime, even after taking into account individual differences in perceived disorder.

[6] They also include measures of social disorder calculated by adults loitering or congregating, drinking alcohol in public, peer groups with gangs present, public intoxication, adults fighting or arguing, selling drugs, or prostitutes on streets. With the exception of adults loitering or congregating (5 percent of blocks), the prevalence of observing social disorder was less than 1 percent of blocks observed (Sampson and Raudenbush 1999, p. 618), indicating that the scale mostly measured physical disorder.

police-reported robbery rates remained significantly associated with disorder after they controlled for collective efficacy and neighborhoods' prior crime rate. They suggest that disorder is correlated with crime, but neighborhood collective efficacy mediates its influence.

The fundamental problem with cross-sectional studies of disorder and crime is that measures are collected together and are endogenously related. Only a series of small-scale field experiments in the Netherlands has found strong evidence that physical disorder encourages other forms of disorder and minor offending (Keizer, Lindenberg, and Steg 2008).[7] Debate continues about the causal mechanisms by which disorder may lead to crime (Harcourt 2001; Harcourt and Ludwig 2006). Broken windows theory provides one candidate mechanism.

2. *Crime Prevention through Environmental Design.* The CPTED theory suggests that features of the built environment make places more or less attractive to would-be offenders (Jeffery 1971). Such features include poor visibility, unguarded opportunities, and permeable streets that make it easy to escape detection or apprehension. Densely populated buildings, for example, may be located on networks of short streets that are conducive to crime because they provide poor visibility. Thoroughfares between neighborhoods may provide relatively more permeable streets that allow easy access to and escape from crime. Features of places that make them more or less amenable to crime include the level of natural surveillance, access control, target hardening, and signs of territoriality (Cozens, Saville, and Hillier 2005).[8] Newman's (1972) work on defensible space makes similar points.[9] According to CPTED, the built environment influences crime in the ways it shapes criminal opportunities for motivated offenders.

[7] In one field experiment, adding graffiti to a wall next to a "no graffiti" sign where bicycles were parked doubled the prevalence of littering (throwing on the ground a flyer that had been placed on bicycles) compared with the control condition when no graffiti were present. In another experiment, graffiti were placed on a mailbox from which a clearly visible €5 bill protruded from an envelope; individuals were more likely to steal the letter when the mailbox bore graffiti. Another experiment found that bicycles illegally locked to a fence increased the likelihood that people would cut through an area marked "no trespassing."

[8] Key concepts and findings of CPTED are examined elsewhere (Cozens, Saville, and Hillier 2005).

[9] Newman makes clear that his ideas about defensible space architecture are more germane to poor areas in which families have fewer resources to hire doormen and take other protective measures than where there are more stay-at-home parents and people have other resources at their disposal.

3. *Situational Crime Prevention.* Situational crime prevention provides a theoretical framework for explaining how features of the built environment affect crime (Clarke 1995). Situational crime prevention is often linked to routine activities theory, which proposes that crime is a product of motivated offenders, suitable targets, and the absence of capable guardians (Cohen and Felson 1979). The built environment can influence crime by shifting the availability of suitable targets and capable guardians. Designs of areas that facilitate less anonymity and more ownership may enhance guardianship and persuade motivated offenders that an area is a less attractive target (Newman 1972). Similarly, situational crime prevention posits that crime rates depend on the ease with which motivated offenders recognize criminal opportunities. Hardening potential targets by use of security systems and other efforts will deter would-be offenders. Criminal behavior is influenced by "variations in opportunity and transitory pressures and inducements" (Clarke 1995, p. 95). The built environment shapes immediate or situational contingencies or opportunity structures that lead motivated offenders to decide whether to commit a crime.

This model provides a solid framework for thinking about how features of the built environment shape criminal opportunities. It suggests that structural changes can influence both choices of targets (e.g., convenience stores, banks) and facilitators of crime (e.g., drugs, alcohol; Clarke 1995, p. 103).

4. *The Supply of and Demand for Criminal Opportunities.* Cook (1977, 1986) links economic theory to situational crime prevention and CPTED by arguing that the supply of criminal opportunities affects crime. Situational crime prevention can easily be adapted to an economic framework by connecting changes in the physical environment to supplies of victims (e.g., strangers) and crime targets (Clarke 1995, p. 103). Cook uses a supply and demand model to show how changes in the supply of crime opportunities should result in additional effort to commit crimes. Shifts in the supply of attractive targets should also affect the demand for crime (Cook 1977, 1986). Figures 1*A* and 1*B* illustrate how shifts in the supply of criminal opportunities shape demand for crime. The crime rate is a product of the supply of opportunities and payoffs from crime. As the supply of potential victims decreases, there will be some updating from motivated offenders, so that the reduction in payoff from any given intervention will be offset by additional effort. Figure 1*A* shows a traditional supply and demand framework. The y-axis is the payoff (P) of committing an offense and the x-axis is the quantity of crime (Q). At one equilibrium there is a

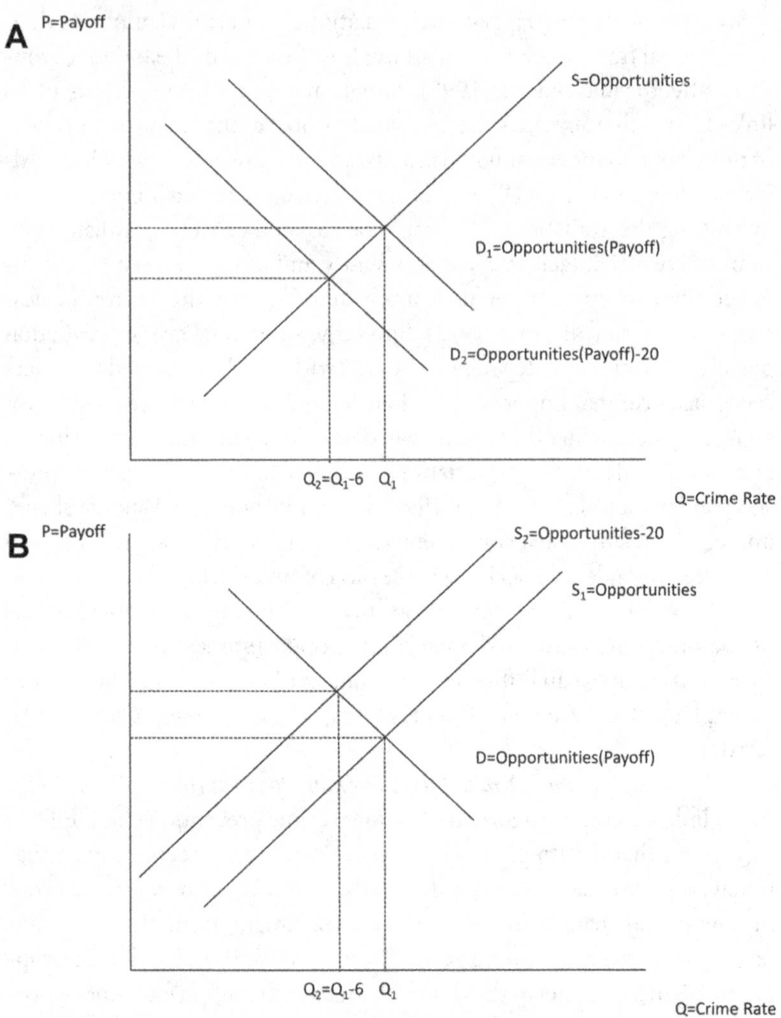

FIG. 1.—*A*, Elastic demand for crime: economic model. *B*, Inelastic demand for crime: situational crime prevention model.

given supply schedule for criminal opportunities (S). A shift in the built environment that makes crimes more difficult may cause the overall payoff from crime to move downward. This is shown in the leftward movement from D_1 to D_2.[10]

[10] I thank Emily Owens for helping me figure out how to express these ideas.

For illustration, imagine that a change in street parking rules, allowing only people with permits to park in a given neighborhood, causes a 20 percent downward shift in the payoff from breaking into cars. The parking regulation change may mean that fewer cars will be parked on the street. If people with a permit are more likely to live in the neighborhood and less likely to leave valuables in their cars, the average payoff from breaking into a car will go down. This means that the market price for breaking into a car will result in a lower overall rate of victimization reflected in the change from Q_1 to Q_2.

Some individuals, however, will still break into cars even if they expect a lower payoff. This means there is some elasticity to the demand for crime among motivated offenders. Therefore, a 20 percent decrease in the payoff will result in some lower threshold of crime reduction. A realistic benchmark might be a 6 percent reduction reflecting a demand elasticity of 0.3. The key insight is that shifting the supply of criminal opportunities also affects the demand for them, but this will not be reflected in a complete 20 percent reduction in theft from cars.

The installation of ignition immobilizers in recently manufactured automobiles provides another example (Cook and MacDonald 2011). The price of stealing a car will increase as cars become more difficult to steal; those without immobilizers will be older, less valuable models. As Cook's (1986) model envisions, individuals who want to keep stealing cars will have to take greater risks. This means that there will be some replacement and that the demand for crime will not fall in exact proportion to the increase in the difficulty of car theft. People who really want to steal a car will try harder: they will steal cars even with a lower expected payoff.

By contrast, proponents of other theoretical perspectives argue that demand is inelastic relative to the supply of criminal opportunities; motivated offenders will continue to seek opportunities and substitute other crimes. This is shown in figure 1*B*.

Assume that a change in the built environment of a place, such as a new building requirement for installation of improved window locks (Katyal 2002), makes it 20 percent more difficult to break into newer homes. Under this model, the overall supply of newer homes to burglarize will shift downward. The demand for crime will be the same, but burglars will have to work harder for the same payoff. This model is consistent with CPTED, which assumes that the supply of motivated offenders is constant and that only shifts in the supply of opportunities (S) determine the amount of crime (Q).

It is possible that shifts in supply through changes in the built environment could change the payoff from crime at every point of the demand for crime, but this does not seem plausible. Changes in criminal opportunities associated with changes in the built environment are unlikely to affect all crimes equally. It seems unlikely that criminals are completely inelastic, even if some individuals with extremely low impulse control may be less sensitive than others to changes in payoff prices.

Deciding which model is better is not my aim. The important point is that shifting the supply of criminal opportunities in places by changing the built environment can reduce crime overall without addressing underlying criminal propensities.

C. *Summary*

Crime is spatially concentrated. Physical features of places play some role in its generation. Broken windows, CPTED, situational crime prevention, and economic opportunity theories all propose mechanisms for explaining how changes in the built environment might affect crime. Changing the built environment to reduce crime does not necessarily imply that crime will fall absolutely; displacement to other targets and places is possible. Sensible changes can make crimes harder to commit for the marginally motivated offender. Less motivated offenders may stop committing certain crimes because opportunities are less available and payoffs are not as good. CPTED and situational crime prevention perspectives provide a basis for thinking about how the target richness of an area influences criminal offending. Broken windows theory suggests that changes in the built environment may reduce physical signs of disorder and thereby reduce enticing signals to motivated offenders. An economic model would argue that changes in the built environment may shift the equilibrium point at which the supply of criminal opportunities meets the demand for crime by motivated offenders. Truly motivated offenders will still commit crimes, but their average effort will produce less of a payoff. They will have to work harder to make the same buck, and the overall demand for crime may fall as a result.

These models provide plausible mechanisms for explaining how crime is influenced by built environments. So far these ideas have had only limited influence on crime prevention policy. A growing body of evidence, however, shows that changing aspects of the built environment can reduce crime.

II. Zoning and Street Design

The idea of drafting statutes to change the built environment to reduce crime is not new. King Edward I of England, for example, mandated in the *Statute of Winchester* (1285) that highways leading from "one market of town to another" be widened, woods and brush be cleared within 200 feet, and parks have walls constructed so that robbers would not have cover for their offending (Anderson et al. 2013).

A. Zoning

The built environment may affect crime through land use planning. Zoning changes that make criminal activity more difficult can be linked to prevention mechanisms articulated in CPTED, situational crime prevention, and economic opportunity theories. Nonresidential forms of land use may generate physical decay, which can be linked to broken windows theory.

1. *Cross-Sectional Studies.* A number of cross-sectional studies examine how land use varies with crime and other observable features of places. Taylor et al. (1995) found that Baltimore and Philadelphia blocks with more commercial uses had higher rates of vandalism, litter, abandoned property, and dilapidated buildings. Harrell and Roman (1994) found that higher rates of robbery occurred in Washington, DC, census tracts with higher percentages of lots zoned for commercial uses. Stucky and Ottensmann (2009) found that violent crime rates were higher in small geographic street grids in Indianapolis when areas were zoned for high-density residential units (eight or more per acre) and commercial land uses. High-density residential units, when concentrated in poor areas, were associated with higher violent crime rates. The opposite was true for commercial land use, suggesting that violent crime rates in areas of higher poverty are not particularly affected by commercial land uses. Thus, there appear to be some aspects of zoning that affect crime.

Browning et al. (2010) found that violent crime was associated with the density of commercial and residential buildings per census tract (n = 184) in Columbus, Ohio, controlling for poverty, residential stability, and other demographic factors. Homicide and assault followed a slightly curvilinear pattern. There was a slight increase in homicides and assaults in less densely settled areas, but they diminished after that, suggesting that more densely settled areas may be safer. The effects were relatively small: a 10 percent increase in the density of land translated into a 2–3 percent decrease in homicide and aggravated assault rates. By contrast, robberies tended to increase in blocks with greater density. These findings, they suggest, imply that robberies are more likely to be strategic and to occur around commercial areas. Homicides and assaults often arise from disputes that draw the attention of neighbors. Commercial areas also generate additional street traffic and population density during business hours.

A few studies have compared different land use designs of neighborhoods. Greenberg, Rohe, and Williams (1982) examined three pairs of neighborhoods in Atlanta that differed substantially in reported crime (high vs. low) but were contiguous and had similar income and racial composition characteristics (black middle income, black lower income, white middle income). Higher-crime neighborhoods (measured by crimes per block) were more likely to have commercial and other nonresidential uses, a lower percentage of blocks zoned solely for single-family homes, and large roadway arteries. It is important to note that these comparisons were only descriptive and did not involve statistical tests of differences.[11]

Greenberg and Rohe (1984) surveyed just over 500 residents in these neighborhoods to measure informal social controls, such as whether neighbors should "scold children," "keep an eye out for suspicious people," call the police when they observe vandalism, and intervene to help a neighbor being "mugged." They asked whether respondents had themselves ever taken direct actions (called the police or intervened for an observed disturbance) and the extent to which they had local ties in the community. There were few differences between higher- and lower-crime neighborhoods, suggesting that the crime-generating mechanisms had more to do with the design of the areas than with informal social controls.

Very few studies using large samples have examined whether variations in land use zoning within the same areas are correlated with differences in crime. Anderson et al. (2013) compared 205 blocks in eight Los Angeles neighborhoods selected because their crime rates were higher than the city average. Within each neighborhood, blocks were identified with different types of zoning (e.g., commercial single use, residential multiuse, and commercial multiuse) but similar demographic compositions. Block-to-block comparisons in the same neighborhoods reduce the risk that observed differences in crime result from systematic demographic differences. This design is similar to Greenberg, Rohe, and Williams's (1982)

[11] In a later analysis, many of these differences were statistically significant (Greenberg and Rohe 1984).

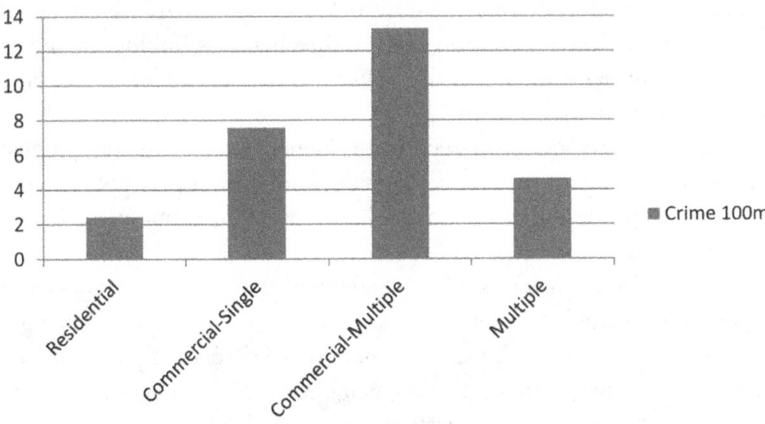

Fig. 2.—Estimated effect of zoning on crime counts 100 meters around blocks. Source: Anderson et al. (2013).

study in Atlanta but involves 205 blocks in eight neighborhoods as opposed to only six neighborhoods. Observational data on measures of disorder and land use were collected for each block. Blocks were selected without knowledge of their numbers of crime.

Blocks zoned for single-use residential had the lowest crime compared with blocks zoned for commercial or mixed use in the same neighborhoods. Multiple-use blocks that included multiple forms of residential and commercial uses had significantly lower crime than did commercially zoned areas (see fig. 2).

Blocks with single-use zones (whether residential, mixed, or commercial) had lower crime than other blocks. Mechanisms are unclear, but it is possible that single land use reduces street traffic in residential and commercial areas compared with multiple-use blocks.

Correlations were made between zoning differences between blocks and observed measures of the physical environment. Blocks zoned for residential-only uses had significantly lower scores on their general condition than did mixed-use blocks in the same areas. Blocks with residential-only uses were less likely to be next to crime attractors such as pawnshops, check-cashing stores, liquor stores, and convenience stores.[12] Conditional on zoning, being located near crime attractors was signifi-

[12] This is not surprising since single-residence-only use prohibits commercial establishments.

cantly associated with overall crime on blocks and with different types of crime. These findings suggest that the mechanisms linking zoning to crime may be associated with the ways in which zoning influences land uses in the built environment.

This study provides cross-sectional evidence from a large sample that mixed-use zoning may reduce crime. It does not, however, support a compelling causal inference. We do not know anything about crime before and after zoning changed.

2. *Quasi-Experimental Studies.* Anderson et al. (2013) conducted a quasi-experimental study of crime rates before and after zoning changes in Los Angeles neighborhoods (measured by 18 percent of police reporting districts) compared with other neighborhoods that had no zoning changes but had similar preexisting crime trends. The primary zoning change was to convert parcels to residential uses (e.g., condominiums). Adding residential parcels to neighborhoods was correlated with a 7 percent reduction in overall crime. The biggest effects involved thefts of and from automobiles, suggesting that adding residential uses reduces risks to cars. However, this analysis is limited because there were data only on changes in zoning and not in actual land use.

B. Street Configurations

Several studies examine relations between street configurations and crime. Street configurations can reasonably be linked to CPTED, situational crime prevention, and economic opportunity theories. Street configurations affect ease of access to areas, levels of guardianship, and the presence of potential victims and offenders. Signs of physical disorder may also be affected; thoroughfares generate more litter, graffiti, and debris and signal a low level of community control.

1. *Cross-Sectional Studies.* Hakim, Rengert, and Shachmurove (2001) surveyed Greenwich, Connecticut, residents. Residents of homes on dead-end streets and further away from a highway exit were significantly less likely to report being burglarized. Homes on corners of streets on the border of a wooded area or playground were significantly more likely to be burglarized. A street corner location was, after burglar alarms, the second-biggest predictor of burglary prevalence.[13] Yang (2006) found that bur-

[13] Clarke (1995) discusses a number of case studies of changes in street configuration that shifted different aspects of crime. This also connects to work on crime pattern theory and research that suggests that offenders are inhibited by inconveniences on their journeys to commit crimes (Bernasco 2014).

glaries in Gainesville, Florida, in parcels zoned for single-family living were significantly more likely in homes in close proximity to major roadway arteries, on longer-length blocks, and on street grids as opposed to other layouts (e.g., fragmented streets). Yang's analysis is suggestive of relationships between street design and crime, but the analysis consists mainly of bivariate tests of correlation. It is difficult to know to what extent poverty and other confounders explain the observed relationships.

Johnson and Bowers (2010) examined correlations between the structure of street segments in Merseyside (United Kingdom), home structures, and location-specific police burglary data over a 4-year period, controlling for basic demographic characteristics of areas measured by the census.[14] They characterized roads as major, minor, local, or private and whether they were segments off major roadways. Burglary rates per street segment were significantly lower when located on cul-de-sacs (both linear and sinuous) or on private roadways. Burglary rates per street segment were significantly greater on major roadways. This study controls for differences within census areas; identification of effects of permeability is largely due to within-area differences. These findings strongly suggest that street design influences burglary victimization within areas of similar housing stock and demographics. The sample size is sufficiently large to generate meaningful statistical variation.

2. *Quasi-Experimental Studies.* A quasi-experimental study examined what happened to crime on street segments before and after they were reconfigured as cul-de-sacs.[15] Lasley (1998) evaluated "Operation Cul-de-Sac" conducted by the Los Angeles Police Department to reduce drive-by shootings and other gang-on-gang motivated crimes in a 10-block area of South Central Los Angeles. Recognizing that 80–90 percent of drive-by shootings occur on street segments connected to major roadways, the LAPD installed traffic barriers (first temporary concrete barriers and then permanent metal gates that could be opened for emergency access) in

[14] These measures were taken from census output areas containing roughly 150 homes (Johnson and Bowers 2010, p. 102).

[15] The Asylum Hill neighborhood demonstration project in Hartford, CT, created different street designs. Major components included reducing the number of through streets and creating visual entrances to major streets entering the neighborhood. The evaluation design cannot be considered quasi-experimental as it involved only one neighborhood compared with the city as a whole using survey data taken at only four time points. Two published evaluations note statistically significant changes in outcomes (Fowler, McCalla, and Mangione 1979; Fowler and Mangione 1982). The number of time points used is too few to be confident that changes did not occur by chance.

February 1990. The LAPD assigned 15 officers working on foot, bicycle, and mounted patrol. In the aftermath of the 1992 Los Angeles riots, the barriers were in a state of disrepair. Most were removed by 1995. Homicides and assaults dropped significantly in the 2 years after installation of the barriers compared with the year before. A similar reduction was not observed in contiguous neighborhoods (Lasley 1996, table 2). More importantly, homicide and assault rates climbed back to pre-intervention levels after the barriers were broken and removed.

There were no discernible changes in property crime, suggesting that this cul-de-sac strategy was particular to the form of violence observed in Los Angeles and not to criminal offending generally. This study provides nice quasi-experimental evidence that street permeability may influence violent crime. The short duration and relatively small size of the intervention limit generalizations that can be offered.

III. Public Transit

The relationship between the built environment and crime has been explored in relation to public transit. Smith and Clarke (2000) reviewed research on crimes that occur on and near public transit and on design of transit systems to reduce crime. Transit may generate more individuals in places and lower guardianship, connecting to situational crime prevention and economic opportunity theories of crime. Transit may also attract transient populations who litter or graffiti, thus leading to physical signs of disorder. Transit may, however, also increase property values and spur economic development, thereby potentially reducing physical disorders and the attractiveness of an area for motivated offenders.

A. Cross-Sectional Studies

A number of cross-sectional studies conclude that bus and other public transit stops are hot spots for crime. Levine, Wachs, and Shirazi (1986) found that there was a high concentration of crime around bus stops in Los Angeles and that three had a disproportionate share of crime. Examination of these stops found drug dealing at one, a crowded sidewalk at another, and a high school at the third. Loukaitou-Sideris (1999) focused on the 10 highest-crime bus stops in LA. They accounted for 18 percent of all reported crime at more than 19,000 stops. The 10 were located in poor, high-crime neighborhoods and on busy intersections in commercial areas, often near vacant land or crowded sidewalks. The researchers compared four of the high-crime stops to four low-crime stops located in the same area of downtown LA and found a greater presence of graffiti and litter, alleys or midblock passageways, and vacant buildings.

Loukaitou-Sideris et al. (2001) studied crime at 60 intersections around bus stops that had relatively high ridership. They compared 40 stops with five or more crimes and 20 with lower crime counts over a 2-year period. A bivariate analysis found that crime was significantly higher ($p < .05$) at stops near an alley, a check-cashing store, or a liquor store; when graffiti or litter was moderate to high; and when the total number of "undesirable establishments" was high. Multivariate regression found that undesirable establishments were the only significant predictor of variation in crime between stops.

LaVigne (1997) used a similar approach to compare the built environment in Washington, DC, metro subway stops to census tracts around stations and found that average crime rates were significantly lower on the metro. She attributed that to a built environment of stations designed to minimize crime opportunities.

Block and Block (2000) conducted an ecological study to examine crime around transit stops in the northeast section of Chicago and the Bronx in New York City. Street robbery rates were correlated with distance from transit stops. In Chicago, transit stops were located in 10 of 11 robbery hot spots. In the Bronx, transit stops were located in or near 10 of 13 robbery hot spots. The transit stops were also located near bars and other businesses that may attract or generate crime. Analysis of robberies by distance suggested that areas just outside the transit stops were the most dangerous.

Kooi (2013) conducted a cross-sectional study that matched block groups in Lansing, Michigan, with bus stops ($n = 97$) and block groups without ($n = 17$), but with similar levels of poverty, population density, and immigrant households. The presence of a bus stop was not significantly associated with crime.

B. *Quasi-Experimental Studies*

A few quasi-experimental studies examine rail transit expansions. Poister (1996) examined crime changes within a 1–1.5-mile radius around two suburban Atlanta stations before and after they opened. In a comparison of monthly trends 42 months before and 15 months after opening with trends in the surrounding county as a whole, there was a small and inconsistent relationship between transit openings and crime. At one stop, there was a significant increase in larceny, auto theft, and robbery in the first month but a small, statistically significant reduction in burglary and disturbing the peace. In the other, there was a significant increase in burglary the first month. The 15-month trend for both stops relative to the county showed small reductions in assault, auto theft, and robbery and a slight increase in disturbing the peace, assault, and trespass. However, all effects estimated were small, suggesting little effect on suburban crime.

Liggett, Loukaitou-Sideris, and Iseki (2003) examined crime in LA neighborhoods after the opening of a rail transit system connecting poor inner-city neighborhoods and more affluent suburban neighborhoods. They compared the crime rates in a one-half-mile radius around each of 14 stations for 5 years before and after its opening relative to broader areas in which each was situated. Index crimes increased in six of 14 station areas relative to the comparison area. All six are in the city of Los Angeles. One suburban location showed a significant crime decrease.[16] In general, the evidence suggests that the new stations did not generate significant additional crime.

Ihlanfeldt (2003) examined expansion of transit locations and census tract crime over 4 years (1991–94) in Atlanta and found an increase in wealthy downtown areas and a decrease around suburban locations. The study used a target of one-fourth mile around stations; this is 4.3 percent (nine of 206) of all census tracts. A wider radius of one-half mile increased coverage to 9.7 percent of tracts. In either case, the effect observed was small relative to the share of transit in existence in Atlanta.

Jackson and Owens (2011) examined the effect of expanded public transit service hours on drinking-related crime.[17] They compared DC metro rail service on weekend nights before and after an expanded time of service relative to other days of the week when there was no extended service. They examined drinking-related crimes for areas with bars within walking distance. Disorderly conduct arrests increased with expanded service hours. Drinking and driving arrests went down.

Billings, Leland, and Swindell (2011) examined the effect of transit on crime more generally by comparing Charlotte, North Carolina, areas

[16] The effect sizes are not provided.

[17] Scholars of alcohol control have argued that expanding transit service to hours after bars close could reduce drinking and driving rates (Ross 1994).

where a light rail transit system opened with two areas of proposed future service. The two proposed areas were statistically similar to existing service areas in population, density, median income, transit usage, preexisting crime, and other demographic factors. The effect of rail on crime within one-half mile of each station was estimated using both announced and actual opening dates. The announced opening was associated with a significant decrease in property crimes. No effect on monthly crime was found for the actual opening. That rates did not change after the opening suggests that the announcement, not the opening, spurred changes.

C. Summary

There is often public worry that expanded public transit in cities will bring crime to neighborhoods (Poister 1996).[18] After all, public transit allows individuals who do not own cars to travel longer distances cheaply. Transit may increase ease of access to criminal opportunities and payoffs from crime. Expanding bus and rail routes may increase crime in relatively low-crime areas. However, most research has focused on the built environment around transit stops that make them more or less susceptible to crime, and not on whether the presence of transit itself produces crime. Studies with quasi-experimental designs provide little evidence that transit itself is a major generator of crime. Transit expansion may reduce crime by altering other features of the built environment.

IV. Housing

The type and conditions of housing available in cities are important features of the built environment that could shape opportunities for crime by shifting the supply of available targets. These mechanisms can be linked to situational crime prevention, CPTED, and economic opportunity theories. Neglected or vacant housing may signal criminals that an area is uncared for and spur crime through broken windows theory mechanisms.

A. Public Housing

Most empirical literature on housing and crime focuses on the location and design of public housing. Public housing might produce crime

[18] See http://www.theatlanticcities.com/commute/2012/01/transit-stations-may-actually-cut-down-crime/916/.

in diverse ways. Consistent with broken windows theory, if public housing is more likely than other forms of housing to be neglected and full of litter or graffiti, its presence may signal that properties are uncared for and crime is tolerated. Public housing design may decrease territoriality and guardianship by generating fewer areas of privately controlled space, mechanisms highlighted in CPTED and situational crime prevention theories. Public housing may increase the concentration of young, unmonitored adolescents who can be victims or offenders. Public housing may generate additional population, increase the supply of easy victims, and reduce the overall costs of committing crime.

1. *Classic Studies.* Oscar Newman's *Defensible Space* (1972) is widely credited for showing that variations in the design of public housing affect crime. He examined 1969 crime data collected by the New York City Housing Authority Police. The robbery rate was higher in high-rise buildings, although population density was often comparable in lower-rise developments. A reason for comparable population density was an architectural preference for open space between high-rise buildings—part of the "garden city" design (Jacobs 1961). Newman noted that 79 percent of crimes occurred inside the buildings, suggesting that the design of the buildings was more important than the surrounding grounds. Newman noted that natural surveillance was often impeded in lobbies and hallways of high-rise public housing complexes. Buildings of 13 stories and taller had a substantially greater share of crime in lobbies, elevators, and stairs than did three- to seven-story buildings.

Newman's primary statistical comparison was of the Brownsville and Van Dyke projects; they were nearly identical in residents and density but differed in design. Brownsville was designed with maximum six-story buildings. Lobbies were visible from the street, and there was a buffer zone from the parking lot to smaller segmented street walk-up stairways. All of this increased natural surveillance compared with the isolated corridors, stairs, and elevators of the high-rise buildings of the Van Dyke project. Brownsville had 34 percent fewer total crimes and 74 percent fewer inside robberies than Van Dyke. However, Newman's analysis was based on a sample of two housing complexes, and differences could have resulted from chance.

Newman and Franck (1982) examined the effects of building size on victimization rates in buildings and fear of crime for a larger sample of residents living in 63 federally assisted housing developments in three cities. Comparing high-rise, walk-up, and row house sites, they found only a modest association between building size and fear of crime and no association with personal crime. They examined the indirect relationship between building size and crime through its conditional association with managers' reports of rent collection, residents' reports of the use of space outside of apartments, social interactions among neighbors, and the perceived likelihood that residents would intervene in criminal or suspicious situations. Larger buildings were correlated with less perceived likelihood of residents intervening in criminal situations. This, in turn, was correlated with personal crime and fear of crime. However, building size may not independently generate these intervening variables; they might be endogenously related with crime and fear of crime. Reverse causality is also plausible; crime may shape beliefs that others will take action.

Using a nationally representative sample of public housing residents, Holzman, Kudrick, and Voytek (1996) conducted a cross-sectional analysis of associations between the number of apartments in a public housing development, fear of crime, and perceptions of crime and disorder. They found only a small association between building size and reported burglary or larceny victimization, problems with gunshots, fear of crime, and disorder problems associated with lighting and trash in yards. For large developments, building height was associated with few differences in outcomes. The study primarily describes associations; it does not report whether differences were statistically significant.

Newman (1996) suggests that creation of small multifamily public housing complexes in which a small number of residents share access and common space should heighten informal social controls and dissuade crime. Newman notes, "An important principle of defensible space design is that subdivisions allow residents to distinguish neighbor from intruder" (1972, p. 18). He provides examples of public housing units that were redesigned in multifamily style together with simple before and after comparisons of crime rates. There are no statistical tests because each is a case study with no comparison group.

Newman's work is noteworthy for being among the first to propose ways to design public housing to have lower crime rates, but his empirical analyses are not convincing by contemporary standards. There are no analyses of differences in crime before and after creation of housing complexes of different forms. The studies' samples are too small to generate meaningful tests for statistical inference. It is possible that public housing styles that generate less crime also attract less criminally involved residents or that housing projects with lower-rise designs were located near more affluent sections of cities.

2. *Matching Studies.* Kuo and Sullivan (2001) examined design differences in relation to public housing apartments and crime rates in Chicago. They suggest that crime was significantly lower in low-rise apartment buildings in the Ida B. Wells public housing development surrounded by trees and grass than around barren buildings in which pavement was used to reduce ground maintenance costs. The study relies on variations among 98 similar low-rise buildings in Ida B. Wells, excluding high-rise buildings and others that had an unusual location or structural design. The primary difference between facilities was the surrounding vegetation. The size of this sample and its comparability are improvements over Newman's work. Residents are similar in income, race, family size, and other factors. Crime differences between locations in theory can be attributed to the differences in the buildings' surroundings and designs.

Comparison of similar public housing complexes in close proximity makes the findings plausible, even though the study design was cross-sectional. However, it is possible that public housing complexes located in more barren surroundings attract or retain different kinds of tenants.

3. *Cross-Sectional Studies.* Cross-sectional research has examined associations between public housing and crime. Roncek, Bell, and Francik (1981) compared crime in 1970 in the 35 Cleveland blocks with public housing to the 3,958 blocks without it. Housing project size was correlated with more crimes per block, even after controlling for a host of factors (e.g., race and age distribution, percentage of female-headed households). Distance from public housing was more correlated with violent than with property crime, possibly because violent crime is more often spontaneous or situational. Distance from projects was not strongly predictive of crime after controlling for poverty-related variables. Suresh and Vito (2009) found that the location of public housing was correlated with spatial patterns in homicide in Louisville and Jefferson County, Kentucky, over a 19-year period. Griffiths and Tita (2009) found that the presence of public housing in South Los Angeles was associated with higher homicide.[19]

[19] Griffiths and Tita (2009) found that homicide victims in public housing census blocks were more likely to be killed near their homes and by someone who lives nearby than homicide victims in areas with no public housing.

Fagan and Davies (2000) analyzed violent crime rates in public housing projects and immediate surrounding areas in Bronx County, New York, and found that the rate of public housing in a census tract area was significantly correlated with rape, robbery, assault, and murder, controlling for basic demographic differences between areas. They compared variation in violent crime within 100 housing projects and found no consistent predictors, though the percentage of residents under age 21 predicted robbery rate differences. Haberman, Groff, and Taylor (2013) examined land use characteristics around 41 public housing complexes in Philadelphia. Complexes that were more highly concentrated and located closer to high schools, subway stations, and homeless shelters and to places that sell beer had significantly more street robberies.

It is unclear whether public housing is a generator of crime or whether higher concentrations of poor individuals create more opportunities for robbery and homicide. Recent research suggests that either features of residents of public housing or population concentrations make serious crime more likely. No clear evidence shows that the changes in public housing forms produce changes in crime.

Popkin et al. (2012) examined crime changes after demolition of public housing, focusing on Chicago and Atlanta, cities that experienced public housing transformations.[20] Crime declined significantly in places where public housing was demolished in both cities over multiple years, but the census tracts receiving public housing residents experienced significantly higher crime rates than did other census tracts. The combined reduction in census tracts where public housing was demolished and the increases in tracts receiving public housing residents, however, suggest small net declines in violent crime in both cities. This study suggests that the concentration of residents into high-density public housing creates greater crime rates. Crime rises in areas where residents are relocated suggest either that characteristics of individual families living in public housing or that consequences of a massive population shift generate crime in relocation areas.

B. Low-Income Housing

Public housing is only one form of subsidized housing. Other forms may produce changes in the built environment that affect crime. Low-income

[20] This study did not have a control group and accordingly should be considered a cross-sectional, time-series study.

housing, for example, may be high-density and have designs that reduce natural surveillance. Low-income housing may have smaller yards, which increases the number of individuals on the sidewalks and the supply of crime targets, consistent with situational crime prevention mechanisms. Low-income housing development may also reduce the overall level of target hardening of homes and personal effects, thereby increasing the ease of crime and reducing opportunity costs of offending. Low-income housing development may also increase neglect and blight in areas if residents are less able or likely to maintain subsidized properties, thereby signaling less community control of space.

1. *Cross-Sectional, Time-Series Studies.* Research on low-income housing is relatively recent, an outgrowth of the declining stock of public housing. Public provision of housing for the poor increasingly takes the form of rent and development subsidies to private markets. Ellen, Lens, and O'Regan (2012) examined the association of rent subsidies with crime in 10 large US cities between 1996 and 2008.[21] The number of subsidized housing voucher holders in a census tract had only a modest correlation with crime. When more extensive controls for area poverty were applied, the association between voucher holders and crime was weak. However, crime in one year predicted more voucher holders the following year, suggesting that voucher holders are more likely to move into areas where crime has been relatively high. Across all regression models, a change in public housing was positively correlated with a change in crime in affected census tracts, suggesting that public housing is associated with crime but low-income housing is not.

Lens (2013) examined changes in crime rates between 1997 and 2008 in 215 large US cities and changes in rates of subsidized housing.[22] He found little association, suggesting that changes in the public and subsidized housing stock had little impact on city-level crime rates. This need not imply that public housing has no effects on neighborhood crime rates. The net reduction in crime associated with demolition of high-rise public housing and the transition to scattered-site low-income housing

[21] The cities are Austin, TX; Chicago; Cleveland; Denver; Indianapolis; New York; Philadelphia; Portland, OR; Seattle; and Washington, DC. There are gaps in crime and housing data for all but two of these cities. The overall sample size of 30,016 census tract years is impressive.

[22] Subsidized housing was measured by Housing Choice Vouchers (section 8) issued, public housing units, Low-Income Housing Tax Credits, and HOPE IV grants.

markets may not produce enough of a city-level crime change to be detectable. The overall quality of housing produced through changes from public to subsidized housing markets may not be sufficiently different to generate crime changes in neighborhoods.

2. *Quasi-Experimental Studies.* Freedman and Owens (2011) conducted a quasi-experimental study of the effects of low-income housing stock on crime. They used variations in tax credits to real estate developers generated by changes in Department of Housing and Urban Development (HUD) program rules as an exogenous source of variation in low-income housing development (e.g., independent of county-level difference in crime rates). Increases in low-income housing were associated with greater reductions in robbery and assaults at the county level. By examining these patterns county by county, they avoid identification bias if affordable housing simply displaced crime to nearby areas.

This study suggests that public investment in private affordable housing can reduce crime, but the mechanisms by which this occurs are unclear. Tax credits may foster expansion of better mixed-income developments and less dense occupancy as Newman advocated (Newman 1972, 1995, 1996). Support from HUD grants was lucrative for developers and provided large subsidies to build affordable housing in residential developments but did not subsidize full-scale low-income housing.

A program that produces more mixed-income forms of housing appears to have some crime reduction benefits. It is unclear how much crime reduction results from shifts away from traditional public housing and how much it is an incidental benefit of additional economic development activities spurred by government housing grants that changed conditions under which poor individuals lived.

C. *Vacant Housing*

Vacant housing is often proposed as a risk factor for crime. There are multiple ways that could happen. Consistent with broken windows theory, vacant housing could send a signal of physical disorder and invite crime by communicating the sense that no one cares. Vacant housing offers unguarded crime targets that make situational aspects of crime more attractive. Consistent with CPTED and situational crime prevention theories, vacant houses may be less likely than others to have effective locks and other security measures. Vacant housing may reduce costs of crime by increasing the supply of easy theft and victimization opportunities. It is easier to avoid detection by stealing copper pipes from a vacant house than from an occupied one. Drug dens may proliferate in vacant houses.

1. *Cross-Sectional Studies.* Most of the literature on vacant or abandoned properties and crime is cross-sectional. Hannon (2005) found that the number of vacant houses in New York City per census tract was correlated with homicide differences in high- (n = 450) and extreme-poverty tracts (n = 227). Cohen et al. (2003) found that the rate of vacant houses per 1,000 properties in 105 cities was correlated with city-level differences in homicide, suicide, gonorrhea, cardiovascular disease mortality, cancer, and diabetes, even after controlling for poverty rates, education, family structure, percentage uninsured, and population changes over the prior decade. Hannon and Cuddy (2006) found that drug-dependency mortality was significantly higher in census tracts with a higher percentage of vacant houses.

Spelman (1993) used a matched cohort design to compare blocks in a neighborhood with a high prevalence of abandoned houses to blocks without abandoned residences but in a similarly poor part of Austin, Texas.[23] Blocks with abandoned property rated significantly higher on reported drug and property crimes. The difference overall was roughly three times compared with the control blocks. Physical inspections showed that abandoned buildings were being used for some form of criminal activity in 16 blocks. The crime rate on these 16 blocks was twice that of all other blocks. Illegal uses of buildings predicted crime rates on blocks; block location near commercial strips or other potential crime attractors, the number of vacant buildings, and demographics did not. Spelman (1993) argues for plausible causal identification in this cross-sectional study. The vacancies were caused by the real estate market crash and landlord abandonment of rental properties that was loosely clustered and somewhat random and was not a reaction to underlying crime conditions in neighborhoods. The plausibility of random selection of abandonment, however, seems less important than the finding that there was generally more crime on blocks where vacant buildings were used for criminal activity.

[23] The matched cohort approach from epidemiology attempts to rule out confounders by picking a control sample similar on observable factors to the disease sample. Spelman measured vacant property using data from the city housing agency on reported vacant properties, systematic observation of apparently abandoned properties, data on foreclosures, and data from the local utility company on electricity cutoff for 3 months or more.

Branas, Rubin, and Guo (2012) examined the association between vacant lots in neighborhoods and reported assaults in Philadelphia. From five years of annual counts of "dead" addresses from the US Postal Service (mail not collected for 90 days or more) at the census block level, vacancy rates were significantly associated with assaults, with and without guns, controlling for measures of population, residential properties, and demographic factors. The association between vacant properties and violence was stronger when alcohol outlets or parks and playgrounds were not present in census blocks. There was no difference between census tracts with and without alcohol outlets or with parks and playgrounds when they contained more than 21 vacant properties. The association of vacant lots and assaults apparently overrode the influence of parks or alcohol outlets once the vacancy level reaches a tipping point.

Raleigh and Galster (2014) used a repeat cross-sectional design to examine relations between crime and abandoned Detroit properties deemed ready for demolition. They assessed whether vacant properties in census blocks in the previous quarter predicted crime in the current quarter, controlling for housing stock, land uses (e.g., number of licensed liquor stores, on- and off-premise outlets, and schools), and demographic factors.[24] They found no temporal association between the proportion of vacant properties (lots or housing) and assaults, robberies, or overall violent crimes. For property crimes, vacant housing was correlated with higher burglary and drug arrests. Vacant lots were negatively correlated with burglaries, larceny, and overall property crimes. There apparently is little to steal on a vacant lot in Detroit.

2. *Quasi-Experimental Studies.* Branas et al. (2011) examined what happens when vacant lots are remediated. This study examines the effects of the Pennsylvania Horticultural Society (PHS) and Philadelphia Green's program to remediate vacant lots in the city. The lots largely had become garbage dumps. The program involves removing trash and debris, grading the land, planting grass and trees to create a park-like setting, and installing low wooden post-and-rail fences around abandoned properties that have had the structures removed. The cost of the land remediation and maintenance program is less than $2.00 per square foot. Between 1999 and 2008, PHS remediated 7.8 million square feet, about 8 percent of all vacant lots in the city. The study examined changes in crime around remediated lots

[24] They also include a spatial lag for crime in the adjacent area to account for the possibility that clustering of crime in particular areas of Detroit biased results.

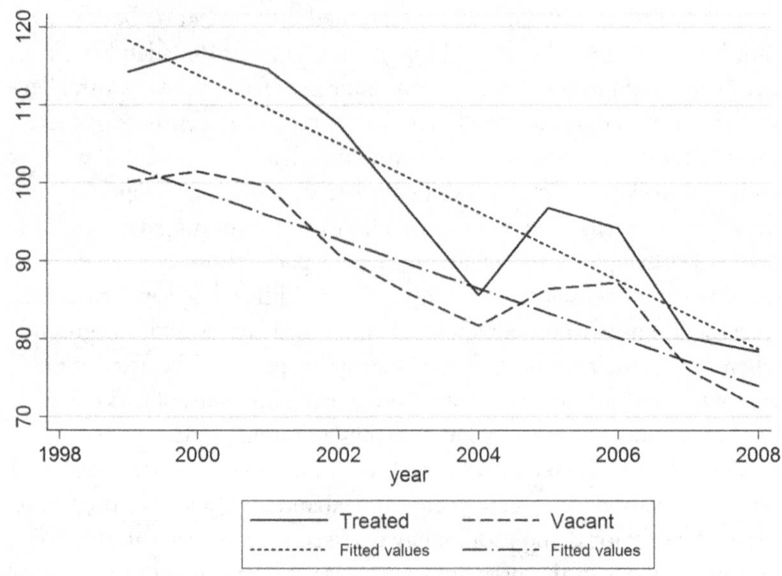

FIG. 3.—Philadelphia vacant lot remediation and changes in gun assault (1999–2008). Source: Author analysis based on data used in Branas et al. (2011).

compared with a sample of over 26,000 vacant lots that were matched in terms of city section, square footage, age of parcel, and unemployment.

Remediation of vacant lots was associated with reduced gun assaults and vandalism and improved health outcomes (less stress and more exercise) compared with similar lots that were not remediated. Gun assaults fell in all sections of the city by around 7 percent. This relatively greater decline in remediated lots is shown in figure 3. The results suggest some promise from efforts to reduce crime by remediating vacant properties. One limitation to this study is its focus on vacant lots. They may have a relationship with physical disorder different from that of vacant homes with relatively intact structures.

Vacant homes with intact structures may be a bigger source of concern than vacant lots in cities that continue to experience population decline and diminished quality of housing stock.[25] Cities are testing new

[25] According to housing inventory estimates from the 2010 census, there were 13.9 million vacant year-round homes in 2012 and 2013 (see http://www.census.gov/housing/hvs/files/qtr113/q113press.pdf, p. 4, table 3).

methods for addressing the abatement of abandoned properties. Philadelphia, for example, in 2011 enacted a Doors and Windows Ordinance requiring property owners to install operating doors and windows on all vacant properties. Noncompliance with the ordinance results in a court fine of $300 per day for each uncovered door and window (Department of Licenses and Inspections 2011). The ordinance requires owners to have buildings sealed by a licensed contractor (City of Philadelphia 2012). An evaluation found that 29 percent of cited properties complied (Kondo et al. 2015). There was a small but significant effect on crime around buildings in compliance compared with those not in compliance but in the same sections of Philadelphia. There were significant reductions in gun assaults, assaults, and nuisance crimes. Larger effects were apparent for houses that filed for renovation permits after being cited. No evidence was found of crime displacement to nearby areas.

D. *Housing Foreclosures*

The collapse of the housing market that started in 2005 and accelerated after 2008 spurred studies that examine the link between foreclosures and crime. Foreclosures provide a natural instrument for affecting the presence of abandoned or blighted properties. Numerous media reports describe foreclosed and abandoned properties as "magnets for criminals."[26] When properties go into foreclosure, residents will likely be less able or willing to maintain them. Home foreclosures may be a proxy for a broken windows theory link between disorder and crime. It is reasonable to assume that properties sold at auction or taken over by lenders are likely to be vacant, which may stimulate various criminogenic mechanisms.

1. *Cross-Sectional and Time-Series Studies.* Most studies of home foreclosures and crime are cross-sectional analyses at neighborhood, city, or county levels (Goodstein and Lee 2010; Jones and Pridemore 2012; Kirk and Hyra 2012; Katz, Wallace, and Hedberg 2013). Results are mixed. Some studies found that foreclosure rates were correlated with small but significant variations in crime rates (Goodstein and Lee 2010; Baumer, Wolff, and Arnio 2012; Katz, Wallace, and Hedberg 2013). Others found no relationship once underlying conditions of poverty and other stable differences between areas were held constant (Jones and Pridemore 2012;

[26] See, e.g., the *New York Times*: http://www.nytimes.com/2011/10/28/us/foreclosures-lead-to-crime-and-decay-in-abandoned-buildings.html?pagewanted=all.

Kirk and Hyra 2012). Studies with one data cross section typically compared differences in crime rates by controlling for a relatively recent prior period (Baumer, Wolff, and Arnio 2012; Katz, Wallace, and Hedberg 2013).

Kirk and Hyra (2012) controlled for stable between-neighborhood differences and found little relationship between changes in foreclosures and changes in neighborhood crime. Underlying conditions of concentrated poverty that were correlated with higher crime rates were also correlated with changes in foreclosure rates. However, the foreclosure crisis in poor Chicago neighborhoods may be so correlated with poverty that the two cannot be separated.

2. *Quasi-Experimental Studies.* A quasi-experimental study by Ellen, Lacoe, and Sharygin (2013) examines block-level change in New York City crime before and after a house on the block went into foreclosure in order to estimate the link between foreclosures and crime. Foreclosures were correlated with higher numbers of buildings per block and a greater vacancy rate, demonstrating that foreclosures and crime could be due to the same underlying conditions of concentrated poverty. To control for this possibility, the study team selected a control group of blocks in the same neighborhoods that did not have foreclosures. They also used foreclosures in the preceding quarter to predict crime in the current period as a guard against reverse causality. They found a small but significant change in public order offenses and violent crimes on blocks after a house goes into foreclosure. The effect was concentrated among blocks where three or more foreclosures reverted to lender-owned status or went to auction. This is important because properties that have reverted to banks or gone to auction are likely to be vacant. Future foreclosures were used as a covariate to control for underlying block-level propensities for properties to be foreclosed.

Ellen, Lacoe, and Sharygin (2013) is an almost ideal quasi-experimental study of home foreclosures and crime. It found intuitively plausible effects. Blocks with multiple vacant properties were more likely to display evidence of abandonment and physical decay. Foreclosures that reverted to lender-owned or were auctioned provide a stronger test of vacancy on crime than do other studies.

However, there are a few missing ingredients. First, there were no measures of observable vacancy. A necessary assumption is that blocks with foreclosures were visibly noticeable. Ideally, the longitudinal design should encompass observable changes in physical disorder. Second, the observed crime changes in New York City were statistically significant but small. Public order offenses and violent crimes rose by only around 1 percent on foreclosure blocks compared with control blocks. In any event, crime was dropping citywide during the study period, but not as fast on foreclosure blocks. This study suggests that foreclosures affected crime in the city, but the effects were highly concentrated and small.

E. Home Construction Rules

Few studies examine changes in crime before and after housing is built. Yet CPTED and situational crime prevention theories suggest that the quality of home construction should affect crime by influencing ease and access of crime targets. Comparing crime rates before and after building of different styles of homes could test some of these mechanisms.

Vollaard and van Ours (2011), in one of the few quasi-experimental studies of effects of housing types on crime, evaluated a change in building codes in the Netherlands requiring installation of "high-quality locks and burglary-proof windows and doors" (p. 486). They compared victimization data and address-level data on when houses were built; burglary risk fell 26 percent in newer homes, with no evidence of displacement to older homes. Car and bicycle theft among those living in newer homes did not rise.[27] The lack of displacement provides reassurance that Dutch burglars prevented from breaking into newer homes do not simply move to older homes or commit other property crimes.

This study, however, addresses only the effect of target hardening and not the more general built environment that may affect different forms of street crime. It has a convincing research design and shows that changing how houses are built can reduce crime. The lack of displacement found is consistent with evidence that many repeat burglars prefer to commit crimes in the same locations, often in areas with similar housing stock (Townsley, Homel, and Chaseling 2003; Short et al. 2009).

F. Summary

Consistent evidence across multiple contexts shows that large-scale public housing is correlated with higher neighborhood crime rates. Yet it is unclear whether this is a product of the concentration of poverty associated with public housing or the design and maintenance of public

[27] Most residential housing development in the Netherlands consists of "large-scale residential construction." The new standards applied to housing clustered in the same geographic areas.

housing. Many high-rise public housing complexes were developed in the 1950s and 1960s as garden city developments. This promoted open space and recreation in densely populated areas, at the cost of concentrating poor families in high-density apartments. Jacobs (1961) and Newman (1995) argued that these designs isolated individuals from casual neighborly interactions that can facilitate guardianship and lower crime. However, though there is some reasonable evidence that well-maintained vegetation may signal or cause lower crime, there is little quality evidence that public housing design itself is a strong predictor of crime. Public housing design may be less consequential for crime than for concentrating poor people in neighborhoods (Lens 2013).

Yet important policy margins for crime control might be gained from shifts in the public housing stock that afford greater opportunities for the co-ownership of public space (Newman 1996). Taylor, Gottfredson, and Brower (1984) examined residents' reports of fear of crime and police calls for service data. Measures of defensible space of households on 63 blocks were correlated with social ties and neighborhood identification, elements that research suggests may foster informal social controls (Sampson 2012).[28] However, with the exception of the building code changes in the Netherlands, only descriptive evidence is available on the influence of housing design on crime, despite Newman's long-standing advocacy of randomized experiments to test systematic changes in public housing complexes meant to enhance defensible space.[29] Large-scale public housing that concentrates poor people in isolated living environments feels like a recipe for more crime in a neighborhood. It is plausible to hypothesize and easy to imagine that crime will fester when building designs result in poorly lit hallways, isolated staircases, and convenient vantage points to see if police are coming. Quasi-experimental evidence suggests that development of low-income housing may lead to reductions in crime. Why that might be so remains unclear.

The evidence is strong that vacant properties increase crime in neighborhoods. Quasi-experimental studies of what happens after cleaning up

[28] To measure defensible space, this study used visible barriers around houses (e.g., restricted entry to alleys, controlled points of entry) and symbolic barriers to differentiate public from private space (e.g., boundary lines clearly demarcated).

[29] Newman (1972) showcases the Easer Hill Village in Richmond, CA, as one of eight public housing designs with reasonable defensive space and relatively low crime. This complex was later overrun by crime and was subject to HOPE IV redevelopment (http://www.mccormackbaron.com/component/sobi2/?sobi2Task=sobi2Details&catid=26&sobi2Id=50; retrieved February 18, 2014).

vacant lots or making aesthetic changes to vacant houses show meaningful effects on reducing crime. However, the effects are not huge and the programs are but one of the ways the built environment affects crime. No published studies document how social mechanisms in areas change when properties become vacant.

V. Land Use

The use of land is an important aspect of how the built environment affects crime. Land, especially commercially zoned land, gets used in myriad ways. Land use affects the composition of individuals in a place and the activities that go on there. Situational crime prevention, CPTED, broken windows, and economic opportunity theory offer explanations for how different land uses influence crime. I focus here on alcohol outlets and schools; both have been the subjects of considerable amounts of research.[30]

A. Alcohol Outlets

Alcohol outlets are major sources of crime. The mechanisms are numerous. An outlet may generate additional young males and increase the number of motivated offenders. Alcohol outlets produce drunken patrons, who are especially vulnerable to victimization and lower the overall costs of committing offenses. Alcohol outlets may draw disorder into neighborhoods and produce visible signs of decay.

1. *Cross-Sectional Studies.* Roncek has published several cross-sectional studies of the association between bars, taverns, lounges, and other liquor establishments and block-level variations in crime in Cleveland in the 1970s and early 1980s (e.g., Roncek and Pravatiner 1989). Roncek and Maier (1991, p. 733) examined associations between the average crime in surrounding areas and the locations of 654 taverns and 62 lounges in Cleveland, controlling for demographic, housing, area size, and residential population characteristics. Each additional outlet on a block was associated with an almost 40 percent increase in yearly crime (about 3.38 additional crimes per block)—a finding similar to an earlier finding (Roncek and Bell 1981). Taverns and lounges were not the only factor associated with

[30] Sherman, Gartin, and Buerger's (1989) seminal work found a higher prevalence of crime "hot spots" in areas with commercial establishments (department stores, discount stores, convenience stores, and bars).

higher-crime blocks, but they were present in 23 of the 110 highest-crime blocks in Cleveland.

Numerous studies show that the density of alcohol outlets is correlated with neighborhood differences in violent crime, even after controlling for other confounders. Scribner et al. (1999) found that a higher density of off-premise alcohol outlets in 155 census tracts in New Orleans was associated with higher homicide rates. Gorman et al. (2001) found that alcohol outlet density in each census tract in Camden, New Jersey, was associated with differences in violent crime, even after controlling for typical confounders. Zhu, Gorman, and Horel (2004) found that alcohol outlet density was associated with violent crime in San Antonio and Austin, Texas, after controlling for neighborhood housing, demographics, population differences, and spatial autocorrelation. Pridemore and Grubesic (2013) found that alcohol outlet density in Cincinnati was correlated with simple and aggravated assault rates over a 1-year period, controlling for population density, poverty, and demographic confounders. Off-premise establishments were more correlated with assaults than was the density of bars. Alcohol outlet types were more correlated with simple than with aggravated assault. Each additional off-premise outlet on a block group was associated with a 3 percent increase in the expected number of simple assaults.

2. *Quasi-Experimental Studies.* Teh (2008) examined changes in crime before and after the opening of alcohol outlets in Los Angeles. Using data from the alcohol licensing authority (the California Department of Alcoholic Beverage Control), Teh identified all businesses that sell alcohol for off-premise consumption and when they opened or closed operation.[31] She examined crime counts within one-half mile for 24 months before and after alcohol outlets opened or closed, compared with locations where alcohol outlets were always open. Because only off-premise outlets were being studied, this approach controls for unobserved selection effects concerning where alcohol outlets are located that may be related to crime differences in areas (e.g., poor neighborhoods may have less ability to block the approval of alcohol licenses).

The opening of alcohol outlets was correlated with increases in violent crime in the immediate block and property crime in the blocks one-quarter to one-half mile away. The addition of new outlets to areas that already had them increased property and violent crimes on blocks

[31] This includes liquor stores, gas stations, convenience stores, and grocery stores/supermarkets.

one-quarter to one-half mile away. The opening of alcohol outlets was also associated with property crime increasing on blocks in neighborhoods with a low socioeconomic status (SES); closing was associated with a decrease in property crime. The effects were inconsistent in high-SES areas.

The conclusion appears to be that alcohol outlets are bad for crime in poor neighborhoods, but the effect sizes observed are small and the size of the estimates diminishes substantially when models include neighborhood-specific trends. There appears to be some marginal effect of alcohol outlets on crime in Los Angeles. There are so many locations and types of off-premise alcohol distributors that the addition of a new outlet does not produce a large change in alcohol availability. This research should be replicated in poor neighborhoods in another city with tighter regulation on off-premise sales.

This study focused on retail off-premise sales of alcohol and not on bars or taverns. Crime well might drop when a tavern or bar in a poor neighborhood that attracts customers who are perpetrators or targets of crime closes. Teh's methodology might profitably be used to assess effects of opening or closing bars or taverns that sell alcohol for on-premises consumption.

B. Schools

Cook, Gottredson, and Na (2010) examined a considerable amount of research on school crime and its prevention. They concluded that schools are a major source of crime commission and victimization. They do not cover research on the effects of school locations on area crime. Situational crime prevention theory offers one explanation for why schools would generate more crime. They alter the overall numbers of potential offenders and victims as people travel to and from school. Schools may also generate physical signs of disorder in nearby areas if children are more likely to litter or graffiti near school grounds. The presence of a school may also increase the supply of potential victims for deviant youths or criminal adults who congregate nearby and reduce the opportunity costs of crime. Schools may also reduce crime in neighborhoods if the presence of school officials increases the number of responsible adults and guardians in an area who can curb criminal behavior.

1. *Cross-Sectional Studies.* Roncek and colleagues, in classic cross-sectional studies in Cleveland and San Diego, found higher crime rates in blocks located near public high schools compared with blocks further away, controlling for other forms of land use, housing characteristics,

and population composition (Roncek and Lobosco 1983; Roncek and Faggiani 1985). More recent similar studies have used more sophisticated regression specifications and found higher crime in neighborhoods with middle schools and high schools (Roman 2002; Wilcox et al. 2005; Murray and Swatt 2013; Willits, Broidy, and Denman 2013). Wilcox et al. (2005) found that robbery and assault rates in census tracts in Seattle over a 2-year period were significantly associated with having a school within three blocks, controlling for poverty, reported disorder, and involvement in neighborhood activities.

2. *Quasi-Experimental Studies.* Only a few quasi-experimental studies have examined the effects of school closings or openings. Closings of Catholic schools in Chicago neighborhoods were associated with crime rate increases in nearby neighborhoods compared with neighborhoods in which schools did not close (Brinig and Garnett 2009, 2012*a*, 2012*b*). The authors suggest that selection of schools to be closed was made largely by the parish priest, independent of structural features of neighborhoods. The presence of a charter school that replaces a closed Catholic school had no material effects on crime rates, suggesting that Catholic schools may have crime prevention benefits (Brinig and Garnett 2012*a*).

MacDonald and Nicosia (2013) examined schools as sources of neighborhood crime by capitalizing on Philadelphia's expansion of publicly funded charter schools. They enroll nearly one in five public school students. Changes in crime surrounding areas before and after the opening of 59 charter schools and 24 public schools were compared with changes in areas that retained existing schools. Comparison of crime counts around newly opened charter schools with those around ongoing public schools controlled for factors that may be correlated with crime, such as being near commercial or vacant land. The study cannot shed light on what might happen to crime in areas that are never likely to get a school.

Opening of a public or charter school was associated with fewer crimes within a square city block. Because only 60 school areas had crime in the relevant period, the estimates provide a basis only for estimating the effects of schools on crime in relatively high-crime areas. The analysis broadened to encompass areas within one-fourth mile. Significant reductions were found in analyses of estimates for 242 school areas.

Crime was generally going down in school areas during this period, suggesting that crime was not displaced from newly opened schools to existing public schools. However, when estimates were adjusted to take account of possibly different variations in crime around each school, no significant differences were associated with opening schools. There may be unique underlying propensities for crime in different areas where schools open. For example, taking over abandoned property may be more responsible for the crime decline than was the opening of schools. In either case, the presence of schools in Philadelphia was not causally associated with crime on blocks.

C. *Summary*

Crime is higher around land with uses related to alcohol and schools. It is unclear whether this results from the sorting of age groups that commit crimes at greater rates or from concentrations of people in particular places. Schools and alcohol outlets concentrate people in peak crime-prone years (15–25 years old). These studies provide bases for policy making if their results are accepted as prima facie evidence that alcohol outlets are criminogenic. It is much easier to regulate the number and location of alcohol outlets than to change the housing composition of settled neighborhoods (Roncek and Maier 1991).

Research on land use and crime is almost entirely descriptive and provides few strong empirical bases for ruling out the possibility that findings reflect the influence of confounding factors.[32] Land use is determined both by potential customers and by political decisions. Liquor stores may face fewer obstacles to receiving permits in high-poverty areas with higher crime rates (Maantay 2002). It is worth considering, however, whether land uses that attract or generate crime should be limited in areas of concentrated poverty.

VI. Where Now?

The built environment affects crime. Evidence from quasi experiments that examine effects of roadways, public transit, and housing stock and designs show changes in crime rates in relatively small geographic areas. Little is known about the mechanisms by which changes lead to changes in crime. Broken windows, CPTED, situational crime prevention, and economic opportunity theories propose candidate mechanisms. Economic

[32] Studies have examined correlations between the location of stripped cars and land use variation (Ley and Cybriwsky 1974), whether robberies are more prevalent in convenience stores located near specific land uses (Duffala 1976), and relations between street robberies and land uses (Smith, Frazee, and Davison 2000). All find land use and crime associations.

opportunity theory suggests that increasing the chance of detection of illegal behavior reduces crime because it raises costs (Cook 1986). Changes in the built environment can change the equilibrium between the supply of criminal opportunities and the demand for crime. There is little empirical evidence that crime mechanically moves next door when places become safer. This is consistent with defensible space, CPTED, and situational crime prevention theories that argue that modifications can impede criminal offending by increasing surveillance and making criminal opportunities in areas less attractive to criminals.

However, there is little empirical evidence on how offenders' decisions change when the built environment is changed. Several reasonably well-designed quasi experiments show changes in crime after features of the built environment are altered. We have a series of reduced-form estimates (Angrist and Pischke 2008). We do not have clear measurement of the theoretical mechanisms or empirical verification for a model of contexts in which altering the built environment reduces criminal behavior. Nor do we understand all the trade-offs. The roadblock barriers in Los Angeles meant to reduce drive-by shootings were criticized by the Christopher Commission as overreach by the Los Angeles Police Department that was inconsistent with community policing (Lasley 1996, p. 27).

However, we know more than we realize. Transit expansion is often subject to uninformed speculation about its effects on crime. Recent evidence finds that opening transit locations has no effect on crime or may reduce it, partly because the opening often spurs local economic development. The presence of high concentrations of poor residents in housing complexes with inadequate investment in building maintenance, tenant management, and public safety appears to increase crime. Mixed-income development appears to reduce it.

Policy makers should pay attention to trade-offs between housing development that concentrates poor people and developments with more mixed-income designs. We do not know whether enough poor can be accommodated in mixed-income developments and what longer-term occupancy rates will be. Cautious optimism is justified that places will be safer when they foster the deconcentration of households living in extreme poverty.

Regulating locations of certain activities and land uses can reduce crime. Zoning and street layouts can make places more or less attractive to crime. Cul-de-sacs can reduce burglaries or even drive-by shootings and assaults. However, context is important. Areas of highly concentrated poverty are not likely to experience growth in collective efficacy and reductions in home burglaries simply by shutting off road access. Reducing or remediating vacant housing and land use appears to reduce crime, as does limiting the density of off-premise alcohol retailers and taverns. However, we lack compelling evidence that school locations are by themselves a crime problem for neighborhoods. Places where adolescents congregate generate problems, but that does not mean that high schools are a good focus for place-based crime prevention planning.

Place-based efforts to restructure the built environment and reduce crime are malleable through sensible planning. They do not require wholesale investments in human capital to reduce income inequality. How housing is built, housing stock is rehabilitated, municipal codes are enforced, and the disadvantaged are "dispersed" can affect crime through direct policy changes (Sampson 1990, p. 531).

We lack good information on specific features of the built environment that facilitate crime reductions in different contexts. Context is important for understanding how changes in neighborhood environments facilitate changes in crime (Sampson 2013). We have few leads on precise mechanisms by which changes in the built environment can facilitate crime reductions. We do not know, for example, whether changing housing structure affects neighborhood engagement and collective efficacy. We do not know whether offending propensities decline when land uses change. A new housing development in a neighborhood that takes cars off the street and causes an old tavern to close down could change an active robber's offending because the price for a street robbery rises significantly. Zimring (2011) shows that parole cohorts in New York City reduced their offending after the city entered its era of safer streets without significant changes in underlying poverty conditions of neighborhoods.

There is opportunity to influence how policy makers think about design and regulation of the built environment of cities. The evidence does not exist to guide a specific architectural plan for crime control (Katyal 2002), but ambitious agendas of research partnerships can be laid out. Regulation can encourage sensible housing and build designs that minimize crime. Municipal codes can require securing of vacant buildings and use of burglary-resistant doors in new homes. Design changes are easier to accomplish than is organization of community crime prevention initiatives that require mobilization of people for collective action, especially in areas of concentrated poverty (Popkin et al. 1999). Redesigning places to be more habitable may be a first step toward increasing collective action. Remediating vacant land on a block and removing visible signs of blight and disorder may provide residents enough of a "nudge" to take collective actions to reduce crime on their streets.

More research should capitalize on natural experiments occurring in every city that changes municipal codes on zoning, land use, construction and occupancy, streets and sidewalks, and public transit access. Researchers can study pilot changes in particular places before they are adopted for an entire city.

Enough is known to move beyond natural experiments and undertake randomized place-based trials of changes to land use regulation in different contexts. A useful strategy would give priority to experiments that make "basic structural changes to places, are scalable to large populations, and have reasonable sustainability over time" (Branas and MacDonald 2014, p. 158). "Structural" refers to changes such as remediating property or changing building codes to require use of more secure doors. "Scalable" refers to changes that can be reproduced in other places to affect large populations. Successful changes can be scaled up. Changing street grids to cul-de-sacs in high-crime areas on a large scale, for example, could benefit many people. "Sustainability" refers to changes that can be reproduced "over time and ease of compliance by would-be beneficiaries" (p. 159). Building code changes concerning new home construction in specific areas, if proved beneficial for crime reduction, easily could be applied throughout the city.

REFERENCES

Anderson, Elijah. 1998. "The Social Ecology of Youth Violence." In *Youth Violence*, edited by Michael Tonry and Mark H. Moore. Chicago: University of Chicago Press.

Anderson, James, John MacDonald, Ricky Bluthenthal, and J. Scott Ashwood. 2013. "Reducing Crime by Shaping the Built Environment with Zoning: An Empirical Study of Los Angeles." *University of Pennsylvania Law Review* 161:699–756.

Angel, Schlomo. 1968. *Discouraging Crime through City Planning*. Berkeley, CA: Center for Planning and Development Research.

Angrist, Joshua D., and Jörn-Steffen Pischke. 2008. *Mostly Harmless Econometrics: An Empiricist's Companion*. Princeton, NJ: Princeton University Press.

Baumer, Eric P., Kevin T. Wolff, and Ashley N. Arnio. 2012. "A Multicity Neighborhood Analysis of Foreclosure and Crime." *Social Science Quarterly* 93 (3):577–601.

Becker, Gary S. 1968. "Crime and Punishment: An Economic Approach." *Journal of Political Economy* 76(2):169–217.

Bernasco, Wim. 2014. "Crime Journeys: Patterns of Offender Mobility." In *Oxford Handbooks Online in Criminology and Criminal Justice*, edited by Michael Tonry. Oxford: Oxford University Press.

Bernasco, Wim, and Richard Block. 2011. "Robberies in Chicago: A Block-Level Analysis of the Influence of Crime Generators, Crime Attractors, and Offender Anchor Points." *Journal of Research in Crime and Delinquency* 48 (1):33–57.

Billings, Stephen B., Suzanne Leland, and David Swindell. 2011. "The Effects of the Announcement and Opening of Light Rail Transit Stations on Neighborhood Crime." *Journal of Urban Affairs* 33(5):549–66.

Block, Richard, and Carolyn Rebecca Block. 2000. "The Bronx and Chicago: Street Robbery in the Environs of Rapid Transit Stations." In *Analyzing Crime Patterns: Frontiers of Practice*, edited by Victor Goldsmith, Philip G. McGuire, John H. Mollenkopf, and Timothy A. Ross. Thousand Oaks, CA: Sage.

Branas, Charles C., Rose A. Cheney, John M. MacDonald, Vicky W. Tam, Tara D. Jackson, and Thomas R. Ten Have. 2011. "A Difference-in-Differences Analysis of Health, Safety, and Greening Vacant Urban Space." *American Journal of Epidemiology* 174(11):1296–1306.

Branas, Charles C., and John M. MacDonald. 2014. "A Simple Strategy to Transform Health, All Over the Place." *Journal of Public Health Management and Practice* 20(2):157–59.

Branas, Charles C., David Rubin, and Wensheng Guo. 2012. "Vacant Properties and Violence in Neighborhoods." *ISRN Public Health* 2012:9.

Brantingham, Patricia, and Paul Brantingham. 1995. "Criminality of Place." *European Journal on Criminal Policy and Research* 3(3):5–26.

Brinig, Margaret F., and Nicole Stelle Garnett. 2009. "Catholic Schools, Urban Neighborhoods, and Education Reform." *Notre Dame Law Review* 85(3): 887–954.

———. 2012*a*. "Catholic Schools and Broken Windows." *Journal of Empirical Legal Studies* 9(2):347–67.

———. 2012*b*. "Catholic Schools, Charter Schools, and Urban Neighborhoods." *University of Chicago Law Review* 79(1):31–57.

Browning, Christopher R., Reginald A. Byron, Catherine A. Calder, Lauren J. Krivo, Mei-Po Kwan, Jae Yong Lee, and Ruth D. Peterson. 2010. "Commercial Density, Residential Concentration, and Crime: Land Use Patterns and Violence in Neighborhood Context." *Journal of Research in Crime and Delinquency* 47(3):329–57.

City of Philadelphia. 2012. "Department of License and Inspections' Vacant Property Management Strategy Named One of the Nation's Most Innovative Government Agencies." http://cityofphiladelphia.wordpress.com/2012/02/02/department-of-license-and-inspections-vacant-property-management-strategy-named-one-of-the-nations-most-innovative-government-agencies/.

Clarke, Ronald V. 1995. "Situational Crime Prevention." In *Building a Safe Society: Strategic Approaches to Crime Prevention*, edited by Michael Tonry and

David P. Farrington. Vol. 19 of *Crime and Justice: A Review of Research*, edited by Michael Tonry. Chicago: University of Chicago Press.
Cohen, Deborah A., Karen Mason, Ariane Bedimo, Richard Scribner, Victoria Basolo, and Thomas A. Farley. 2003. "Neighborhood Physical Conditions and Health." *American Journal of Public Health* 93(3):467–71.
Cohen, Lawrence E., and Marcus Felson. 1979. "Social Change and Crime Rate Trends: A Routine Activity Approach." *American Sociological Review* 44(4):588–608.
Cook, Philip J. 1977. "Punishment and Crime: A Critique of Current Findings Concerning the Preventive Effects of Punishment." *Law and Contemporary Problems* 41(1):164–204.
———. 1986. "The Demand and Supply of Criminal Opportunities." In *Crime and Justice: An Annual Review of Research*, vol. 7, edited by Michael Tonry and Norval Morris. Chicago: University of Chicago Press.
Cook, Philip J., Denise C. Gotfredson, and Chongmin Na. 2010. "School Crime Control and Prevention." In *Crime and Justice: A Review of Research*, vol. 39, edited by Michael Tonry. Chicago: University of Chicago Press.
Cook, Philip J., and John M. MacDonald. 2011. "The Role of Private Action in Controlling Crime." In *Controlling Crime: Strategies and Tradeoffs*, edited by Philip J. Cook, Jens Ludwig, and Justin McCrary. Chicago: University of Chicago Press.
Covington, Jeanette, and Ralph B. Taylor. 1989. "Gentrification and Crime: Robbery and Larceny Changes in Appreciating Baltimore Neighborhoods during the 1970s." *Urban Affairs Review* 25(1):142–72.
Cozens, Paul. 2008. "New Urbanism, Crime and the Suburbs: A Review of the Evidence." *Urban Policy and Research* 26(4):429–44.
Cozens, Paul, and Terence Love. 2009. "Manipulating Permeability as a Process for Controlling Crime: Balancing Security and Sustainability in Local Contexts." *Built Environment* 35(3):346–65.
Cozens, Paul, Greg Saville, and David Hillier. 2005. "Crime Prevention through Environmental Design (CPTED): A Review and Modern Bibliography." *Property Management* 23(5):328–56.
Duffala, Dennis C. 1976. "Convenience Stores, Armed Robbery, and Physical Environmental Features." *American Behavioral Scientist* 20(2):227–45.
Ellen, Ingrid Gould, Johanna Lacoe, and Claudia Ayanna Sharygin. 2013. "Do Foreclosures Cause Crime?" *Journal of Urban Economics* 74:59–70.
Ellen, Ingrid Gould, Michael C. Lens, and Katherine O'Regan. 2012. "American Murder Mystery Revisited: Do Housing Voucher Households Cause Crime?" *Housing Policy Debate* 22(4):551–72.
Fagan, Jeffrey, and Garth Davies. 2000. "Crime in Public Housing: Two-Way Diffusion Effects in Surrounding Neighborhoods." In *Analyzing Crime Patterns: Frontiers of Practice*, edited by Victor Goldsmith, Philip G. McGuire, John H. Mollenkopf, and Timothy A. Ross. Thousand Oaks, CA: Sage.
Fowler, E. P. 1987. "Street Management and City Design." *Social Forces* 66(2):365–89.

Fowler, F., Jr., and T. Mangione. 1982. *Neighborhood Crime, Fear, and Social Control: A Second Look at the Hartford Program*. Washington, DC: US National Institute of Law Enforcement and Criminal Justice.

Fowler, F., Jr., M. McCalla, and T. Mangione. 1979. *Reducing Residential Crime and Fear: The Hartford Neighborhood Crime Prevention Program*. Washington, DC: US Government Printing Office.

Freedman, Matthew, and Emily G. Owens. 2011. "Low-Income Housing Development and Crime." *Journal of Urban Economics* 70(2–3):115–31.

Glaeser, Edward L., and Bruce Sacerdote. 1999. "Why Is There More Crime in Cities?" *Journal of Political Economy* 107(6; suppl.):S225–S258.

Goodstein, Ryan M., and Yan Y. Lee. 2010. "Do Foreclosures Increase Crime?" Working Paper no. 2010-05. Washington, DC: Federal Deposit Insurance Corporation, Center for Financial Research.

Gorman, Dennis M., Paul W. Speer, Paul J. Gruenewald, and Erich W. Labouvie. 2001. "Spatial Dynamics of Alcohol Availability, Neighborhood Structure and Violent Crime." *Journal of Studies on Alcohol and Drugs* 62(5): 628–36.

Greenberg, Stephanie W., and William M. Rohe. 1984. "Neighborhood Design and Crime: A Test of Two Perspectives." *Journal of the American Planning Association* 50(1):48–61.

Greenberg, Stephanie W., William M. Rohe, and Jay R. Williams. 1982. "Safety in Urban Neighborhoods: A Comparison of Physical Characteristics and Informal Territorial Control in High and Low Crime Neighborhoods." *Population and Environment* 5(3):141–65.

Griffiths, Elizabeth, and George Tita. 2009. "Homicide In and Around Public Housing: Is Public Housing a Hotbed, a Magnet, or a Generator of Violence for the Surrounding Community?" *Social Problems* 56(3):474–93.

Haberman, Cory P., Elizabeth R. Groff, and Ralph B. Taylor. 2013. "The Variable Impacts of Public Housing Community Proximity on Nearby Street Robberies." *Journal of Research in Crime and Delinquency* 50(2):163–88.

Hakim, Simon, George F. Rengert, and Yochanan Shachmurove. 2001. "Target Search of Burglars: A Revised Economic Model." *Papers in Regional Science* 80(2):121–37.

Hannon, Lance E. 2005. "Extremely Poor Neighborhoods and Homicide." *Social Science Quarterly* 86(S1):1418–34.

Hannon, Lance E., and Monica M. Cuddy. 2006. "Neighborhood Ecology and Drug Dependence Mortality: An Analysis of New York City Census Tracts." *American Journal of Drug and Alcohol Abuse* 32(3):453–63.

Harcourt, Bernard E. 2001. *Illusion of Order: The False Promise of Broken-Windows Policing*. Cambridge, MA: Harvard University Press.

Harcourt, Bernard E., and Jens Ludwig. 2006. "Broken Windows: New Evidence from New York City and a Five-City Social Experiment." *University of Chicago Law Review* 73:271–320.

Harrell, Adele V., and Caterina Gouvis Roman. 1994. *Community Decay and Crime: Issues for Policy Research*. Washington, DC: Urban Institute.

Holzman, Harold R., Tari R. Kudrick, and Kenneth P. Voytek. 1996. "Revisiting the Relationship between Crime and Architectural Design: An Analysis of Data from HUD's 1994 Survey of Public Housing Residents." *Cityscape: A Journal of Policy Development and Research* 2:107–26.

Ihlanfeldt, Keith R. 2003. "Rail Transit and Neighborhood Crime: The Case of Atlanta, Georgia." *Southern Economic Journal* 70(2):273–94.

Jackson, C. Kirabo, and Emily Greene Owens. 2011. "One for the Road: Public Transportation, Alcohol Consumption, and Intoxicated Driving." *Journal of Public Economics* 95(1–2):106–21.

Jacobs, Jane. 1961. *The Death and Life of Great American Cities.* New York: Random House.

Jeffery, C. Ray. 1971. *Crime Prevention through Environmental Design.* Beverly Hills, CA: Sage.

Johnson, Shane D., and Kate J. Bowers. 2010. "Permeability and Burglary Risk: Are Cul-de-Sacs Safer?" *Journal of Quantitative Criminology* 26(1):89–111.

Jones, Roderick W., and William Alex Pridemore. 2012. "The Foreclosure Crisis and Crime: Is Housing-Mortgage Stress Associated with Violent and Property Crime in US Metropolitan Areas?" *Social Science Quarterly* 93(3):671–91.

Katyal, Neal Kumar. 2002. "Architecture as Crime Control." *Yale Law Journal* 111(5):1039–1139.

Katz, Charles M., Danielle Wallace, and E. C. Hedberg. 2013. "A Longitudinal Assessment of the Impact of Foreclosure on Neighborhood Crime." *Journal of Research in Crime and Delinquency* 50(3):359–89.

Keizer, Kees, Siegwart Lindenberg, and Linda Steg. 2008. "The Spreading of Disorder." *Science* 322(5908):1681–85.

Kirk, David S., and Derek S. Hyra. 2012. "Home Foreclosures and Community Crime: Causal or Spurious Association?" *Social Science Quarterly* 93(3):648–70.

Kirk, David S., and John H. Laub. 2010. "Neighborhood Change and Crime in the Modern Metropolis." In *Crime and Justice: A Review of Research*, vol. 39, edited by Michael Tonry. Chicago: University of Chicago Press.

Kondo, Michelle C., Danya Keene, Bernadette Hohl, John MacDonald, and Charles C. Branas. 2015. "A Difference-in-Differences Study of the Effects of a New Abandoned Building Remediation Strategy on Safety." *PLOS-One*, forthcoming.

Kooi, Brandon. 2013. "Assessing the Correlation between Bus Stop Densities and Residential Crime Typologies." *Crime Prevention and Community Safety* 15(2):81–105.

Kuo, Frances E., and William C. Sullivan. 2001. "Environment and Crime in the Inner City: Does Vegetation Reduce Crime?" *Environment and Behavior* 33(3):343–67.

Kyckelhahn, Tracey. 2013. *Local Government Corrections Expenditures, FY 2005–2011.* Washington, DC: Bureau of Justice Statistics, US Department of Justice.

Lasley, James. 1996. *Using Traffic Barriers to "Design Out" Crime: A Program Evaluation of LAPD's Operation Cul-de-Sac.* Washington, DC: National Institute of Justice, US Department of Justice.

———. 1998. *"Designing Out": Gang Homicides and Street Assaults*. Research in Brief. Washington, DC: US Department of Justice, National Institute of Justice.

LaVigne, Nancy G. 1997. *Visibility and Vigilance: Metro's Situational Approach to Preventing Subway Crime*. Research in Brief. Washington, DC: US Department of Justice, National Institute of Justice.

Lens, Michael C. 2013. "The Impact of Housing Vouchers on Crime in US Cities and Suburbs." http://pschousing.org/files/Lens%20-%20Impact%20of%20Housing%20Vouchers%20on%20Crime%20in%20US%20Cities%20%26%20Suburbs.pdf.

Levine, Ned, Martin Wachs, and Elham Shirazi. 1986. "Crime at Bus Stops: A Study of Environmental Factors." *Journal of Architectural and Planning Research* 4:339–61.

Ley, David, and Roman Cybriwsky. 1974. "The Spatial Ecology of Stripped Cars." *Environment and Behavior* 6:53–67.

Liggett, Robin, Anastasia Loukaitou-Sideris, and Hiroyuki Iseki. 2003. "Journey to Crime: Assessing the Effects of a Light Rail Line on Crime in the Neighborhoods." *Journal of Public Transportation* 6(3):85–115.

Logan, John, and Harvey Luskin Molotch. 2007. *Urban Fortunes: The Politcal Economy of Place*. Berkeley: University of California Press.

Loukaitou-Sideris, Anastasia. 1999. "Hot Spots of Bus Stop Crime." *Journal of the American Planning Association* 65(4):395–411.

Loukaitou-Sideris, Anastasia, R. Liggett, H. Iseki, and W. Thurlow. 2001. "Measuring the Effects of Built Environment on Bus Stop Crime." *Environment and Planning, B: Planning and Design* 28(2):255–80.

Maantay, Juliana. 2002. "Zoning Law, Health, and Environmental Justice: What's the Connection?" *Journal of Law, Medicine and Ethics* 30(4):572–93.

MacDonald, John M., and Nancy Nicosia. 2013. "Charter School Legislation and Crime Rates in Philadelphia Neighborhoods." Paper presented at the Association for Public Policy Analysis and Management meeting, Washington, DC, November 7.

Mair, Julie Samia, and Michael Mair. 2003. "Violence Prevention and Control through Environmental Modifications." *Annual Review of Public Health* 24: 209–25.

Mani, Anandi, Sendhil Mullainathan, Eldar Shafir, and Jiaying Zhao. 2013. "Poverty Impedes Cognitive Function." *Science* 341(6149):976–80.

Moffitt, Terrie E., Louise Arseneault, Daniel Belsky, Nigel Dickson, Robert J. Hancox, HonaLee Harrington, Renate Houts, Richie Poulton, Brent W. Roberts, Stephen Ross, Malcolm R. Sears, W. Murray Thomson, and Avshalom Caspi. 2011. "A Gradient of Childhood Self-Control Predicts Health, Wealth, and Public Safety." *Proceedings of the National Academy of Sciences* 108(7):2693–98.

Murray, Rebecca K., and Marc L. Swatt. 2013. "Disaggregating the Relationship between Schools and Crime: A Spatial Analysis." *Crime and Delinquency* 59(2):163–90.

Newman, Oscar. 1972. *Defensible Space: Crime Prevention through Urban Design*. New York: Macmillan.

———. 1995. "Defensible Space: A New Physical Planning Tool for Urban Revitalization." *Journal of the American Planning Association* 61(2):149–55.

———. 1996. *Creating Defensible Space*. Washington, DC: US Department of Housing and Urban Development, Office of Policy Development and Research.

Newman, Oscar, and Karen A. Franck. 1982. "The Effects of Building Size on Personal Crime and Fear of Crime." *Population and Environment* 5(4):203–20.

Paulsen, Derek J. 2013. *Crime and Planning: Building Socially Sustainable Communities*. New York: CRC Press.

Perkins, Douglas D., and Ralph B. Taylor. 1996. "Ecological Assessments of Community Disorder: Their Relationship to Fear of Crime and Theoretical Implications." *American Journal of Community Psychology* 24(1):63–107.

Poister, Theodore H. 1996. "Transit-Related Crime in Suburban Areas." *Journal of Urban Affairs* 18(1):63–75.

Popkin, Susan J., Victoria Gwiasda, Dennis Rosenbaum, Jean Amendolia, Wendell Johnson, and Lynn Olson. 1999. "Combating Crime in Public Housing: A Qualitative and Quantitative Longitudinal Analysis of the Chicago Housing Authority's Anti-drug Initiative." *Justice Quarterly* 16(3):519–57.

Popkin, Susan J., Michael J. Rich, Leah Hendey, Chris Hayes, Joe Parilla, and George Galster. 2012. "Public Housing Transformation and Crime: Making the Case for Responsible Relocation." *Cityscape* 14(3):137–60.

Pridemore, William Alex, and Tony H. Grubesic. 2013. "Alcohol Outlets and Community Levels of Interpersonal Violence: Spatial Density, Outlet Type, and Seriousness of Assault." *Journal of Research in Crime and Delinquency* 50(1):132–59.

Raleigh, Erica, and George Galster. 2014. "Neighborhood Disinvestment, Abandonment, and Crime Dynamics." *Journal of Urban Affairs*. http://www.neighborhoodindicators.org/sites/default/files/publications/raleigh_galster_uaa_032014.pdf.

Reiss, Albert J., and Michael Tonry, eds. 1986. *Communities and Crime*. Vol. 8 of *Crime and Justice: A Review of Research*, edited by Michael Tonry and Norval Morris. Chicago: University of Chicago Press.

Roman, Caterina Gouvis. 2002. "Schools as Generators of Crime: Routine Activities and the Sociology of Place." PhD dissertation, American University, Department of Sociology.

Roncek, Dennis W., and Ralph Bell. 1981. "Bars, Blocks, and Crimes." *Journal of Environmental Systems* 11(1):35–47.

Roncek, Dennis W., Ralph Bell, and Jeffrey M. A. Francik. 1981. "Housing Projects and Crime: Testing a Proximity Hypothesis." *Social Problems* 29(2):151–66.

Roncek, Dennis W., and Donald Faggiani. 1985. "High Schools and Crime: A Replication." *Sociological Quarterly* 26(4):491–505.

Roncek, Dennis W., and Antoinette Lobosco. 1983. "The Effect of High Schools on Crime in Their Neighborhoods." *Social Science Quarterly* 64(3):598–613.

Roncek, Dennis W., and Pamela A. Maier. 1991. "Bars, Blocks and Crimes Revisited: Linking the Theory of Routine Activities to the Empiricism of 'Hot Spots.'" *Criminology* 29(4):725–53.

Roncek, Dennis W., and M. A. Pravatiner. 1989. "Additional Evidence That Taverns Enhance Nearby Crime." *Sociology and Social Research* 73(4):185–88.

Ross, Hugh Laurence. 1994. *Confronting Drunk Driving*. New Haven, CT: Yale University Press.

Sampson, Robert J. 1990. "The Impact of Housing Policies on Community Social Disorganization and Crime." *Bulletin of the New York Academy of Medicine* 5:526–33.

———. 2012. *Great American City: Chicago and the Enduring Neighborhood Effect*. Chicago: University of Chicago Press.

———. 2013. "The Place of Context: A Theory and Strategy for Criminology's Hard Problems." *Criminology* 51(1):1–31.

Sampson, Robert J., and Stephen W. Raudenbush. 1999. "Systematic Social Observation of Public Spaces: A New Look at Disorder in Urban Neighborhoods." *American Journal of Sociology* 105(3):603–51.

Schuerman, Leo, and Solomon Kobrin. 1986. "Community Careers in Crime." In *Communities and Crime*, edited by Albert J. Reiss and Michael Tonry. Vol. 8 of *Crime and Justice: A Review of Research*, edited by Michael Tonry and Norval Morris. Chicago: University of Chicago Press.

Scribner, Richard, Deborah A. Cohen, Stephen Kaplan, and Susan H. Allen. 1999. "Alcohol Availability and Homicide in New Orleans: Conceptual Considerations for Small Area Analysis of the Effect of Alcohol Outlet Density." *Journal of Studies on Alcohol and Drugs* 60(3):310–16.

Shaw, Clifford R., and Henry D. McKay. 1942. *Juvenile Delinquency and Urban Areas*. Chicago: University of Chicago Press.

Sherman, Lawrence W. 1995. "Hot Spots of Crime and Criminal Careers of Places." In *Crime and Place*, edited by John E. Eck and David Weisburd. Monsey, NY: Criminal Justice Press.

Sherman, Lawrence W., Patrick R. Gartin, and Michael E. Buerger. 1989. "Hot Spots of Predatory Crime: Routine Activities and the Criminology of Place." *Criminology* 27(1):27–56.

Short, M. B., M. R. D'Orsogna, P. J. Brantingham, and G. E. Tita. 2009. "Measuring and Modeling Repeat and Near-Repeat Burglary Effects." *Journal of Quantitative Criminology* 25(3):325–39.

Skogan, Wesley G. 1990. *Disorder and Decline: Crime and the Spiral of Decay in American Neighborhoods*. Berkeley: University of California Press.

Smith, Martha J., and Ronald V. Clarke. 2000. "Crime and Public Transport." In *Crime and Justice: A Review of Research*, vol. 27, edited by Michael Tonry. Chicago: University of Chicago Press.

Smith, William R., Sharon Glave Frazee, and Elizabeth L. Davison. 2000. "Furthering the Integration of Routine Activity and Social Disorganization Theories: Small Units of Analysis and the Study of Street Robbery as a Diffusion Process." *Criminology* 38(2):489–524.

Snow, John. 1849. *On the Mode of Communication of Cholera*. London: John Churchill.

Spelman, William. 1993. "Abandoned Buildings: Magnets for Crime?" *Journal of Criminal Justice* 21(5):481–95.

Stucky, Thomas D., and John R. Ottensmann. 2009. "Land Use and Violent Crime." *Criminology* 47(4):1223–64.

Suresh, Geetha, and Gennaro F. Vito. 2009. "Homicide Patterns and Public Housing: The Case of Louisville, KY (1989–2007)." *Homicide Studies* 13(4):411–33.

Taylor, Ralph B. 2001. *Breaking Away from Broken Windows: Baltimore Neighborhoods and the Nationwide Fight against Crime, Grime, Fear and Decline*. Boulder, CO: Westview.

Taylor, Ralph B., and Jeanette Covington. 1988. "Neighborhood Changes in Ecology and Violence." *Criminology* 26(4):553–90.

Taylor, Ralph B., and Stephen D. Gottfredson. 1986. "Environmental Design, Crime, and Prevention: An Examination of Community Dynamics." In *Communities and Crime*, edited by Albert J. Reiss and Michael Tonry. Vol. 8 of *Crime and Justice: A Review of Research*, edited by Michael Tonry and Norval Morris. Chicago: University of Chicago Press.

Taylor, Ralph B., Stephen D. Gottfredson, and Sidney Brower. 1984. "Block Crime and Fear: Defensible Space, Local Social Ties, and Territorial Functioning." *Journal of Research in Crime and Delinquency* 21(4):303–31.

Taylor, Ralph B., and Addell Harrel. 1996. *Physical Environment and Crime*. Washington, DC: National Institute of Justice, US Department of Justice.

Taylor, Ralph B., Barbara A. Koons, Ellen M. Kurtz, Jack R. Greene, and Douglas D. Perkins. 1995. "Street Blocks with More Nonresidential Land Use Have More Physical Deterioration: Evidence from Baltimore and Philadelphia." *Urban Affairs Review* 31(1):120–36.

Taylor, Ralph B., Sally A. Shumaker, and Stephen D. Gottfredson. 1985. "Neighborhood-Level Links between Physical Features and Local Sentiments: Deterioration, Fear of Crime, and Confidence." *Journal of Architectural and Planning Research* 2(4):261–75.

Teh, Bing-Ru. 2008. "Essays on Crime and Urban Economics." PhD dissertation, University of California, Berkeley.

Townsley, Michael, Ross Homel, and Janet Chaseling. 2003. "Infectious Burglaries: A Test of the Near Repeat Hypothesis." *British Journal of Criminology* 43(3):615–33.

Vollaard, Ben, and Jan C. van Ours. 2011. "Does Regulation of Built-in Security Reduce Crime? Evidence from a Natural Experiment." *Economic Journal* 121(552):485–504.

Weisburd, David, Elizabeth Groff, and Sue-Ming Yang. 2012. *The Criminology of Place*. New York: Oxford University Press.

Welsh, Brandon C., Anthony A. Braga, and Gerben J. N. Bruinsma. 2013. *Experimental Criminology: Prospects for Advancing Science and Public Policy*. New York: Cambridge University Press.

Wilcox, Pamela, Michelle Campbell Augustine, Jon Paul Bryan, and Staci D. Roberts. 2005. "The 'Reality' of Middle-School Crime." *Journal of School Violence* 4(2):3–28.

Willits, Dale, Lisa Broidy, and Kristine Denman. 2013. "Schools, Neighborhood Risk Factors, and Crime." *Crime and Delinquency* 59(2):292–315.

Wilson, James Q. 1983. *Thinking about Crime*. New York: Vintage Books.

Wilson, James Q., and George L. Kelling. 1982. "Broken Windows: The Police and Neighborhood Safety." *Atlantic Monthly* 249(3):29–38.

Yang, Xiaowen. 2006. "Exploring the Influence of Environmental Features on Residential Burglary Using Spatial-Temporal Pattern Analysis." PhD dissertation, University of Florida, Gainesville.

Zelinka, Al, and Dean Brennan. 2001. *SafeScape: Creating Safer, More Livable Communities through Planning and Design*. Chicago: Planners Press, American Planning Association.

Zhu, L., Dennis M. Gorman, and S. Horel. 2004. "Alcohol Outlet Density and Violence: A Geospatial Analysis." *Alcohol and Alcoholism* 39(4):369–75.

Zimring, Franklin E. 2011. *The City That Became Safe: New York's Lessons for Urban Crime and Its Control*. New York: Oxford University Press.

Torbjørn Skardhamar, Jukka Savolainen, Kjersti N. Aase, and Torkild H. Lyngstad

Does Marriage Reduce Crime?

ABSTRACT

The "marriage effect" is one of the most widely studied topics of life course criminology. The contemporary consensus is that marriage promotes desistance from crime. Most of the 58 studies reviewed here find a negative longitudinal association between marriage and crime. The results are more consistent among men. Studies that attend to relationship quality, such as the level of marital attachment, tend to produce particularly strong associations. Critical scrutiny of the evidence regarding the causal nature of the reported associations suggests, however, that claims about the restraining influence of marriage are overstated. None of the studies demonstrates evidence of direct (counterfactual) causality; no study has served a causal estimate unbiased by selection processes. Moreover, only a few studies address time ordering, and some of those show that desistance precedes rather than follows marriage. Evidence in support of the theoretical mechanisms responsible for the marriage effect is also mixed and insufficient. The criminological literature has been insensitive to the reality that entering a marital union is increasingly unlikely to signify the point at which a committed, high-quality relationship is formed.

Some 25 years ago, criminologists engaged in a vigorous debate concerning the value of longitudinal research on criminal careers (Gottfredson and Hirschi 1987; Blumstein, Cohen, and Farrington 1988; Rowe, Osgood,

Electronically published July 30, 2015

Torbjørn Skardhamar is a senior researcher at Statistics Norway and an associate professor at the Department of Sociology and Human Geography at the University of Oslo. Jukka Savolainen is a research scientist at the Institute for Social Research, University of Michigan, where he serves as the director of the National Archive of Criminal Justice Data. Kjersti N. Aase is a former junior researcher at Statistics Norway and currently advisor for the Telemark county council. Torkild H. Lyngstad is a professor at the Department of Sociology and Human Geography at the University of Oslo.

0192-3234/2015/0044-0010$10.00

and Nicewander 1990; Greenberg 1991). Whichever our view of the analytical merits of the debate, it is clear that, as a matter of practical consequence, the position favoring the longitudinal approach has won the hearts and minds of academic criminologists. Today, the field known as *life course criminology* is stronger than ever. In 2012, the American Society of Criminology (ASC) established the Division of Developmental and Life Course Criminology. This is the most recent of the eight specialty areas formally recognized by the ASC. On a more international scale, a large number of the recipients of the Stockholm Prize in criminology can be classified as life course criminologists. Between 2006 (when the award was established) and 2014, a total of 16 individuals received the prize, and at least eight were awarded for work that relied on evidence from analysis of longitudinal life course data.[1]

The early work in life course criminology was focused on the onset of criminal careers. The basic goal was to address early childhood antecedents of serious criminality. Although this line of inquiry has remained central, it became less dominant following the publication of Sampson and Laub's *Crime in the Making* (1993), which brought the topic of desistance to the forefront. To illustrate, a Google Scholar search using the term "desistance crime" generated 219 results for the period 1980–90, compared with 5,390 in 2000–2010. Although much of this reflects the overall growth of academic criminology, the corresponding rate of increase for the search term "age of onset criminal" was only a fifth as large.

Life course criminology passed a turning point when, on the basis of a reanalysis of the Gluecks' rich longitudinal data tracking males born between 1924 and 1935, Sampson and Laub (1993) introduced their age-graded theory of informal social control. The main point of this work was to show that "life course matters," that the possibility of change, including desistance, is omnipresent in the human life course. The most influential take-home from the 1993 monograph was evidence suggesting that transitions to good marriages and stable employment can set in motion the process of desistance from crime. Although both marriage and work have received considerable attention in subsequent research (Siennick and Osgood 2008; Uggen and Wakefield 2008),

[1] Alfred Blumstein, David Farrington, Friedrich Lösel, John Laub, Terrie E. Moffitt, Daniel Nagin, David Olds, and Robert J. Sampson. John Hagan, who received the award in 2009 for his research on genocide, has also made significant contributions to life course criminology.

the marriage effect seems to have emerged as *primus inter pares*. The priority for marriage is subtle yet clear in Laub and Sampson's follow-up monograph *Shared Beginnings, Divergent Lives* (2003). The critically important chapter 6, "Why Some Offenders Stop," includes a separate section for "Marriage as Turning Point" but no equivalent subheading for employment. Instead, employment is discussed in fewer than two pages under "Unpacking the Desistance Process," where the marriage effect is discussed over six additional pages (Laub and Sampson 2003, pp. 134–41).[2] Judging from the program of the 2013 annual meeting of the ASC, the topic of marriage and crime is strong in the field at large. Nearly one-quarter of the papers in panels dedicated to life course criminology examined the association between marriage or romantic relationships and offending. By contrast, only two of the papers in these panels were focused on employment.[3]

We suspect that the appeal of the marriage hypothesis reflects its greater empirical success in the research literature. As we demonstrate, a number of high-profile studies report evidence of strong effects of marriage on desistance (e.g., Sampson, Laub, and Wimer 2006; King, Massoglia, and Macmillan 2007). By comparison, the track record for studies of employment is considerably weaker and more mixed (Bushway and Apel 2012; Skardhamar and Savolainen 2014). As observed in a recent article in *Criminology*, "[A] *consensus* has grown in the literature that marriage holds the potential to promote desistance from crime—commonly known as the 'marriage effect.' This relationship seems to be fairly robust and consistent across method, sample, gender, race, and socio-historical context. Whereas much of the *research has demonstrated that a marriage effect exists*, what is less clear is how marriage reduces one's criminal involvement" (Bersani and Doherty 2013, p. 400; our emphasis). Bersani and Doherty argue that the marriage effect has largely been established, and it is time to focus on explicating the mechanisms accounting for it. Similar claims can be found in other published studies, and a recent review concluded that there is evidence of "an overall protective effect of

[2] As an additional indication from *Shared Beginnings*, Laub and Sampson wrote that "our inferences are strongest for marriage" (2003, p. 272).

[3] If we include papers on parenthood, studies of family processes covered 43 percent of all the papers presented in these panels. These statistics are based on the records kept by one of the authors, who was the relevant area chair of the 2013 ASC meeting (available from authors).

marriage on subsequent criminal desistance" (Craig, Diamond, and Piquero 2014, p. 34).

Over the last few decades, there has been considerable progress both within life course criminology in general and in the marriage-crime literature in particular. One facet of this has to do with increasingly frequent collection and use of longitudinal data. Quite a few data sets allow for life course analyses of long-term change. The geographical coverage of high-quality data sources has increased beyond the United States and the United Kingdom. Another element of progress is the increasing sophistication of statistical methods that allow researchers to exploit longitudinal data. These include group-based trajectory models (Nagin 2005), which have been extremely important in criminal careers research, and the use of panel data models that allow controls for unobserved heterogeneity.

Despite these major leaps forward, there is room for improvement in the quality of research and the interpretation of the evidence. Our decision to write this essay was motivated, in part, by skepticism regarding the assumption that the causal effect of marriage on crime is as strong and robust as the criminological consensus suggests. The bar for making causal inferences in the social sciences has increased over the past decades (Morgan and Winship 2007). Central to this development is the increasing influence of the counterfactual model of causality, sometimes referred to as the "potential outcomes" framework (Rubin 2005), as an efficient analytical approach for specifying and estimating causal effects. Given that the marriage effect has emerged as one of the focal concerns of contemporary research in life course criminology, we think it is important to scrutinize the relevant evidence more carefully and critically than has been done in the past.

Although prior reviews of this literature have been informative and exceedingly helpful, our approach differs. First, we consider evidence of causal effects only if it holds up to contemporary methodological standards (see, e.g., Morgan and Winship 2007; Angrist and Pischke 2009; Berk 2010). Regardless of what any given study claims about causality, we do not consider an association causal unless the methodological approach provides a truly counterfactual causal estimate. We find consistent evidence of a negative association between marriage and crime, but this evidence does not rule out social selection. Second, as another aspect of causal inference, we pay close attention to evidence on time order in the association between transition to marriage and the onset of desistance. It is clear that marriage cannot be treated as a cause of desistance if it occurs after rather than before desistance. Most studies of marriage and crime have ignored this basic point. The few studies that have addressed the timing issue yield contradictory results. Third, we discuss the evidence in support of the hypothesized mechanisms in more detail than has been done in the past. We agree with Bersani and Doherty (2013) that there should be more focus on how marriage reduces involvement in crime. Once again, we identify major gaps in the literature: Many of the processes considered important as mediators of the marriage effect have received little or no attention. However, we do find consistent support for the expectations that high-quality romantic relationships are related to desistance more strongly than low-quality ones.

This essay is organized in five major sections. We begin by laying out the theoretical foundations of the marriage effect on crime in Section I. In Section II we describe the methods and criteria used to select the 58 studies on the relationship between marriage or cohabitation and crime, published between 1990 and 2014, that we reviewed. Section III offers a detailed discussion of the nature and extent of the evidence regarding the longitudinal association between romantic unions (marriage, cohabitation, and related states) and criminal offending. Section IV focuses on the quality of this evidence from the perspective of causal inference. Drawing on the prevailing standards of causal inference in the social sciences, we evaluate claims about causal effect presented in prior work. We also discuss the evidence regarding the timing issue and review the evidence regarding the mechanisms expected to produce the marriage effect on crime (peer processes, marital quality, etc.). We conclude in Section V with a general discussion of the literature on marriage and crime and suggest directions for the next generation of studies. The criminological literature has been insensitive to the reality that entering a marital union is increasingly unlikely to signify the point in which a committed, high-quality relationship is formed.

I. Theoretical Foundations

Given that Sampson and Laub were students of (early) Travis Hirschi, it is not surprising that their age-graded theory (AGT, henceforth) is rooted in social bonding theory (Hirschi 1969). In the original version of the AGT (Sampson and Laub 1993), the marriage effect is described in terms of attachment, that is, the strength of the emotional investment in the romantic partner. Subsequent analysts argued that Sampson and

Laub's study overplayed the role of bonding theory at the expense of processes more consistent with differential association and routine activities perspectives. Warr (1998) proposed (and found empirical support for the contention) that marriage limits offending by restructuring associations away from crime-prone peers. Following marriage, men are more likely to spend time in family settings (with relatives, other couples, friends with children) and less time with young, single men. These changes have the potential to disrupt routine activities in ways that reduce criminal temptations and opportunities.

The updated version of AGT articulated in *Shared Beginnings* (Laub and Sampson 2003), although still rooted in control theory, is considerably more pluralistic, embracing multiple pathways from marriage to criminal desistance. In addition to peer processes, routine activities, and emotional attachment, Laub and Sampson recognize the capacity of the spouse to serve as a situational agent of day-to-day social control. For example, the monograph describes a case in which the wife monitors the pace and timing of the husband's drinking and makes sure he gets up the next morning to go to work (p. 136). Drawing on such theorists as Maruna (2001) and Giordano, Cernkovich, and Rudolph (2002), Laub and Sampson incorporate changes in self-concept as an additional mechanism accounting for the influence of marital bonding on reduced criminal offending. These symbolic-interactionist perspectives argue that desistance from crime is not complete until the person has undergone a conversion process in which criminal identity has been replaced with that of a law-abiding family man.

Figure 1 is our attempt to summarize the key processes expected to contribute to the marriage effect on desistance. This model assigns priority

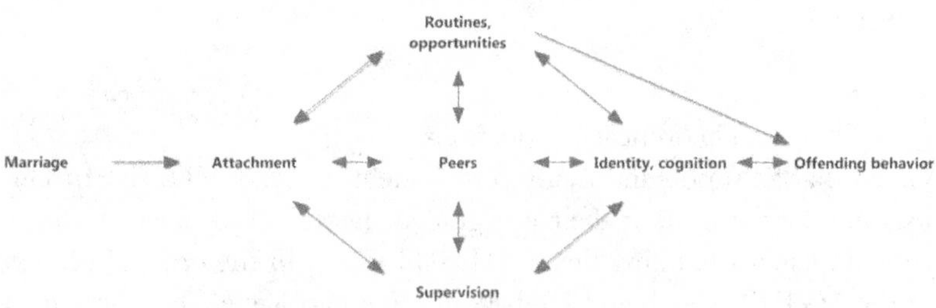

FIG. 1.—A causal model for the effect of marriage on desistance from crime

to attachment over the other intervening factors. This decision reflects our contention that any institutional bond, including marriage, is unlikely to exert restraining influence unless it is perceived as valuable by the actor. Although marriage without love is known to happen, in modern societies the very act of marriage is expected to signify emotional attachment to the partner: people are unlikely to marry without professing love for each other.[4] One might even argue that attachment is more likely to precede than to follow the transition to marriage. In that case, of course, we should not refer to the process as the *marriage* effect. Consistent with this insight, a number of studies have applied this theoretical framework to examine the effects of cohabitation and having a romantic partner on offending behavior. It should be obvious that the assumed mechanisms are not contingent on the legal status but on the strength of the relationship as perceived by the subject. We find it reasonable to assume that married couples, on average, are more committed than are cohabitants or other romantic couples (Rhule-Louie and McMahon 2007; Craig and Foster 2013, p. 33). From this perspective, the variable "marriage" in figure 1 could be understood as a formal marker of relationship quality rather than a causal agent in itself.

As denoted by the multiple reciprocal arrows, the model assumes spousal attachment to develop over time as a function of relationship dynamics (Laub, Nagin, and Sampson 1998). For example, emotional bonding is expected to influence partners' motivation to monitor and supervise spousal behavior, and this, in turn, affects the attachment between the two, either positively or negatively. Men who are attached to their wives and enjoy spending time with them are likely to modify their daily and weekly routines away from delinquent peers and criminal temptations. If these decisions are experienced as rewarding, they reinforce the attachment; but if the new lifestyle is "not working," the emotional bond is likely to diminish. Over time, if the day-to-day processes are conducive to change, a new (noncriminal) identity starts emerging

[4] We can imagine situations in which emotional attachment is not an important source of marital bonding. For example, a person facing economic hardship may be motivated to marry and stay in a relationship for financial reasons. However, we expect these situations to be rare in modern Western societies, and especially rare among the criminally active. Consistent with this idea, Laub and Sampson (2003, p. 137) recognize economic benefit as one additional bond that may help keep crime-prone men in check. They argue that most men in their sample "married up" and had more to lose from straying from the straight and narrow.

with enduring effects on desistance (Paternoster and Bushway 2009; Bersani and Doherty 2013).

Note that this account of the marriage effect includes both situational (contemporaneous) and developmental processes of influence. The model also recognizes that not any marriage is expected to contribute to desistance as the effect depends on what it "does" to the relationship and how it is perceived by the actors. Although we believe this to be a faithful characterization of the mechanisms behind the marriage effect, we acknowledge that this is our interpretation of the theoretical literature. To our knowledge, there is no authoritative organization of the various factors believed to underlie the marriage effect.[5] We hope figure 1 serves as a helpful starting point.

As important as it is to understand the mechanisms producing the effect, such discussions are predicated on the presence of a causal association. The literature on marriage and crime offers three distinct perspectives on causality. First, the AGT treats marriage as an exogenous "turning point" with the potential to trigger desistance. Laub and Sampson (2003, pp. 278–79) use the term *desistance by default* to describe this process: "Many men made a commitment to go straight without even realizing it. Before they knew it, they had invested so much time in a marriage or a job that they did not want to risk losing their investment."

Second, other theories, such as cognitive transformation (Giordano, Cernkovich, and Rudolph 2002) and the subjective-social model (LeBel et al. 2008), argue that changes in objective life circumstances are unlikely to facilitate change without a preexisting willingness to "go straight." From this perspective, desistance should already have started—at least psychologically if not behaviorally—before transitions to work, marriage, or parenthood can become influential. Marriage is understood as a potential "hook for change" (Giordano, Cernkovich, and Rudolph 2002) with the capacity to assist in the process of desistance, but it would be unrealistic to expect marriage to function as a triggering event. Third, it is possible for marriage to have no causal effect on offending. The negative association between marital bonding and criminal involvement may be a spurious function of maturation, that is, the age-variant but inevitable process of "aging out and settling down" (Mas-

[5] Bersani and Doherty's (2013) fig. 1 is a helpful way to distinguish between situational and developmental effects of marriage, but their graph is not intended as a causal model of marriage effect on desistance. Our fig. 1 is consistent with theirs.

soglia and Uggen 2010). According to the maturation perspective, if there is any causality in the association, it is expected to flow from desistance to marriage, as criminally active individuals are unlikely to make marital transitions; and to the extent that they are, they are unlikely to have partners with characteristics conducive to desistance (Hirschi and Gottfredson 1983; Morizot and Le Blanc 2007). This perspective expects substantial and sustained reductions in criminal offending as a precondition for marrying a person with the capacity to generate the kind of social capital described in figure 1.

Figure 2 offers a visual summary of the key differences between these three different accounts of the longitudinal association between marriage and desistance. Note that these graphs are ideal-typical representations of complex theoretical arguments. For example, we do not claim that the turning point hypothesis exhibits rigid stability prior to marriage or that the maturation perspective implies no change in offending following

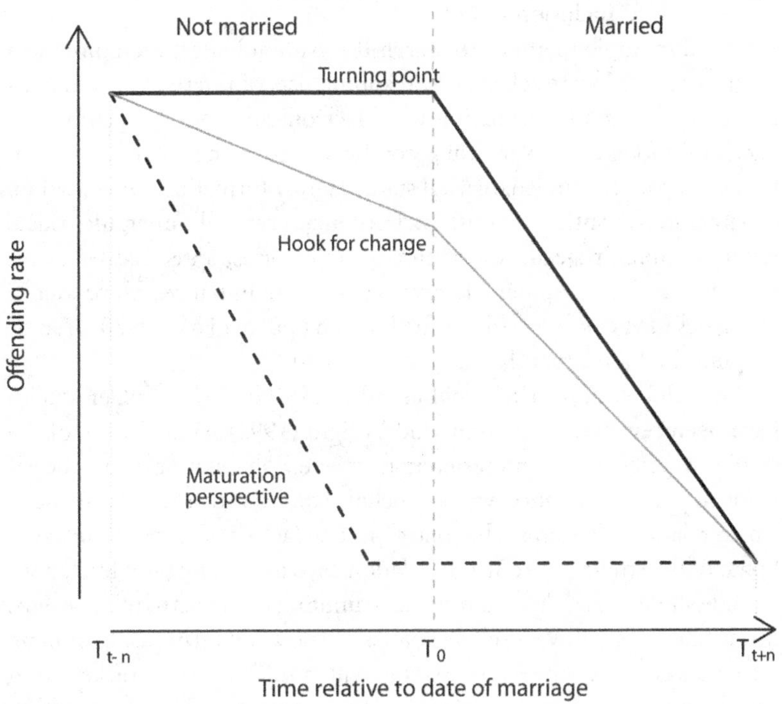

FIG. 2.—Three ideal-typical offending trajectories around the time of transition to marriage

marriage. The purpose of figure 2 is to highlight the difference between the maturation perspective and the two hypotheses that assume a causal effect of marriage on crime (turning point and hook for change). It is crucial to recognize that despite clear differences in etiological accounts, each of these three perspectives expects the average rates of offending to be lower during periods of marriage. The only difference has to do with the timing of change in the criminal trajectory vis-à-vis the transition to marriage. The maturation perspective expects desistance to precede marriage, the turning point hypothesis predicts the opposite pattern, and the hook for change hypothesis allows the onset of desistance to precede marital transition but expects additional reductions thereafter. Thus, as figure 2 shows, evidence of lower average offending rates during states of marriage is equally consistent with social selection and causation explanations of "the marriage effect."

II. Inclusion Criteria

We used multiple methods to search the criminological literature. The studies included were selected by scanning lists of references from published studies and by searching two electronic databases, Web of Science and Google Scholar, using combinations of the following search terms: marriage, married, marital status, family formation, cohabitation, cohabitant, romantic relationship, desistance, criminal career, life course crime, criminal trajectories, offending trajectories, antisocial behavior, deviance, and developmental criminology. The initial search produced 380 articles. We performed our final search update in March 2014; studies published after that date are not included.

We included only articles published in 1990 or later as older studies have been reviewed by Wright and Wright (1992). While many of the studies were primarily interested in marriage/cohabitation/romantic relationships and desistance, we also include studies with a broader scope in which relationship status is but one of several factors of empirical interest. Some of the studies on romantic relationships use young samples, but we exclude studies of adolescent romances, limiting our focus to relationships in adulthood. Thus, we exclude studies of romantic relationships among teenagers (19 or younger). In cases in which subjects were tracked from youth to adulthood, we included the study as long as the data extend to observations beyond age 20 years. We examine only studies featuring criminal or delinquent offending as the outcome variable. Some measured offending with official statistics, such as convictions or arrests; others used self-reported measures. We ignored studies of alcohol use but included studies of illicit drug use. Some included outcomes that were both within and outside the scope of this essay. In those cases we discuss the results pertaining to criminal or delinquent offending.

We included only individual-level studies, excluding studies based on aggregate data (e.g., Edlund et al. 2013). Unpublished studies, even if available as working papers, were not included (e.g., Andersen, Andersen, and Skov 2010). Working papers, by definition, are not the final versions, and results are likely to change following the peer-review process. We also excluded institutional or internal research reports because it is difficult to conduct a systematic search (e.g., Broidy and Cauffman 2006; Bersani and DiPietro 2013). Finally, we excluded theses and dissertations. Because we have read all the studies cited in this paragraph, however, they inform our perspective on the literature. Our decision to exclude a study does not mean we have ignored it.

Most of the studies that turned up in our literature searches are quantitative. This speaks to the nature of the literature and does not reflect our selection criteria. To make sure we did not miss important qualitative studies, we considered all relevant studies covered by Veysey, Martines, and Christian's (2014) review of qualitative research on desistance. We benefited from two recent book chapters evaluating the evidence on the marriage effect on crime. Focused on evidence from the Netherlands, Bersani and van Schellen (2014) reviewed nine studies. Craig, Diamond, and Piquero's (2014) review was not limited by geography and covered 31 studies.

Table 1 lists and describes the studies included in our analysis: 58 publications met our selection criteria. In addition, we came across a couple of relevant additional studies (Bersani and DiPietro 2014; Siennick et al. 2014). Because they are too recent to have appeared in our systematic search, we do not include them among the 58 studies. Studies not yet in print but made available online (e.g., Craig 2015) are included.

III. Empirical Evidence

To our knowledge, the first ever review of the marriage-crime literature was authored by Wright and Wright (1992). The majority of studies included were cross-sectional; only six were longitudinal (West 1982; Gibbens 1984; Shavit and Rattner 1988; Caspi, Bem, and Elder 1989;

TABLE 1

Overview of Studies of the Marriage Effect

Study	Country	Data Source	Gender	Analytic Sample Size	Methods	Findings on the Marriage Effect	Citations according to Google Scholar, March 2014
Barnes and Beaver (2012)	United States	Add Health (waves 1–3)	Men and women	4,568	Logistic regression, sibling differences	Beneficial	11
Barnes et al. (2014)	United States	Add Health (waves 1–4)	Men and women	~13,000	Crossed-lagged model (Granger causality test) and reciprocal model	Endogenous relationship between marriage and criminal behavior	3
Beaver et al. (2008)	United States	Add Health (waves 1–3)	Men and women	1,994	Logistic regression, sibling differences	Beneficial	52
Beijers, Bijlevel, and van Poppel (2012)	Netherlands		Men only	971	Fixed- and random-effect Poisson regression analysis	Beneficial if married after 1970	4
Bersani and Doherty (2013)	United States	NLSY97	Men and women	2,838	Hierarchical linear modeling	Beneficial	4
Bersani, Laub, and Nieuwbeerta (2009)	Netherlands	CCLC	Men and women	4,615	Hierarchical linear modeling	Beneficial	79
Blokland and Nieuwbeerta (2005)	Netherlands	(A) CCLC; (B) Dutch National Crime Survey	Men and women	(A) 4,615 (B) 2,951	Semiparametric group-based trajectory modeling	Beneficial	167

Burt et al. (2010)	United States	Minnesota Twin Family Study	Men only	289 twin pairs	Multilevel regression modeling (twin design)	Beneficial	16
Capaldi, Kim, and Owen (2008)	United States	OYS and the Couples Study	Men only	110	Zero-inflated Poisson modeling	Beneficial (only for relationship stability among men with prior arrests)	42
Craig (2015)	United States	Add Health (waves 1–4)	Men and women	3,327	OLS regression	Marriage is found to lead to changes in levels of offending among whites and Hispanics but not blacks	0
Craig and Foster (2013)	United States	Add Health (waves 1–3)	Men and women	3,082	Survey-adjusted OLS regression	Beneficial for both men and women	4
Doherty and Ensminger (2013)	United States	Woodlawn Project	Men and women	965	Hierarchical linear modeling	Beneficial (at least for men)	7
Duncan, Wilkerson, and England (2006)	United States	NLSY79	Men and women	1,997–3,959 individuals, depending on outcome	Logistic OLS and Tobit regression	Beneficial (but only for married men and marijuana use)	124
Farrington and West (1995)	United Kingdom	Cambridge Study	Men only	378 (73 for within-individual analyses)	OLS and logistic regression	Beneficial	168

TABLE 1 (*Continued*)

Study	Country	Data Source	Gender	Analytic Sample Size	Methods	Findings on the Marriage Effect	Citations according to Google Scholar, March 2014
Forrest and Hay (2011)	United States	NLSY79	Men and women	2,325	Logistic regression	Beneficial for marriage, not significant for cohabitation; not significant estimate for married when controlling for self-control.	12
Giordano, Cernkovich, and Rudolph (2002)	United States	Ohio Life-Course Study	Men and women	197	Regression analysis	No association between spousal attachment and criminal involvement	503
Giordano et al. (2011)	United States	TARS	Men and women	1,066	Hierarchical linear modeling	No significant associations	9
Godfrey, Cox, and Farrall (2007)	United Kingdom	Historical (end of 19th century) data from Crewe, United Kingdom	Men and women	101		No significant difference in conviction rates between married and unmarried; convictions went up after marriage	26

Herrera, Wiersma, and Cleveland (2011)	United States	Add Health	Men and women	1,267 romantic partners pairs		Positive impact of relationship quality and relationship length	5
Horney, Osgood, and Marshall (1995)	United States	Survey of offenders sentenced to Nebraska Dept. of Corrections	Men only	617	Hierarchical linear modeling	Living with girlfriend: significantly more likely to commit any crime or drug crime; living with wife: significantly less likely to commit an assault; otherwise not significant	598
Jaffee, Lombardi, and Coley (2013)	United States	Add Health (waves 1–4)	Men only	4,149	Four different: logistic regression, propensity score matching models, fixed-effects models, and random-effects models of sibling differences.	Beneficial	1
Kerr et al. (2011)	United States	OYS	Men only	206	Multilevel modeling	Beneficial for marriage, not significant for cohabitation	11

TABLE 1 (*Continued*)

Study	Country	Data Source	Gender	Analytic Sample Size	Methods	Findings on the Marriage Effect	Citations according to Google Scholar, March 2014
King, Massoglia, and Macmillan (2007)	United States	NYS, 1976	Men and women	1,725	Propensity score matching	Beneficial (only for men [all] and women [with moderate propensity to marry])	149
Kreager, Matsueda, and Erosheva (2010)	United States	Denver Youth Survey	Women only	567	Fixed-effect logistic models	No significant associations between marriage and delinquency; negative association between marriage and drug use	37
Kruttschnitt, Uggen, and Shelton (2000)	United States	Minnesota community-based sex offender program evaluation project	Men and women	556	Cox regression	No significant assocation between married/cohabiting at sentencing and reoffense or union dissolution and reoffense	144

Laub and Sampson (2003)	United States	Glueck and Glueck's study on delinquent boys	Men only	52 (ages 17–70) and 419 (ages 17–32)	Hierarchical overdispersed Poisson model, qualitative interviews	Beneficial	1,310
Laub, Nagin, and Sampson (1998)	United States	Glueck and Glueck's study on delinquent boys	Men only	480	Semiparametric Poisson mixture model and hierarchical linear modeling	Beneficial	659
Leverentz (2006)	United States	Women in halfway house in Chicago	Women only	49	Qualitative interviews		68
Lyngstad and Skardhamar (2013)	Norway	Norwegian register data	Men only	90,919	Logistic regression	Beneficial only in the years before marriage	3
Massoglia and Uggen (2007)	United States	Youth Development Survey	Men and women	1,000	Logistic regression	Relationship quality beneficial for all four outcomes	40
Maume, Ousey, and Beaver (2005)	United States	NYS (waves 5 and 6)	Men and women	593	Logistic and bivariate probit model	Beneficial, but only for those with high marital attachment	69
McGloin et al. (2011)	Netherlands	CCLC	Men and women	4,612	Random- and fixed effect models	Beneficial	7
McGloin et al. (2007)	United States	Survey of offenders sentenced to Nebraska Dept. of Corrections	Men only	658	Hierarchical linear modeling		72

TABLE 1 (*Continued*)

Study	Country	Data Source	Gender	Analytic Sample Size	Methods	Findings on the Marriage Effect	Citations according to Google Scholar, March 2014
Mercer, Zoutewelle-Terovan, and van der Geest (2013)	Netherlands	17Up	Men and women	540	Trend vector model	Beneficial	0
Monahan, Dimitrieva, and Cauffman (2014)	United States	Pathways to Desistance Study	Men and women	354	Conditional growth models	No impact of current romantic relationship; relationship length beneficial only for boys, opposite for girls	1
O'Connell (2003)	United States	Ongoing studies project for those at risk for drug use	Men and women	576	Structural equation modeling (SEM)	Marriage not significant	31
Oudekerk, Burgers, and Reppucci (2014)	United States	GAP	Women only	114	Regression	Negative association between relationship length and violent offending; no significant association between other outcomes	1

Petras, Nieuwbeerta, and Piquero (2010)	Netherlands	CCLC	Men and women	5,000	Two-part latent growth curve	Beneficial on both prevalence and frequency	13
Piquero, MacDonald, and Parker (2002)	United States	California Youth Authority (serious convicted offenders)	Men only	524	Negative-binomial model with random disturbance term	Marriage beneficial for total arrests and nonviolent arrests; when stratified by race: significantly more violent arrests among whites after they marry	60
Ragan and Beaver (2010)	United States	Add Health (waves 1–3)	Men and women	1,884	Logistic regression	Beneficial	11
Salvatore and Taniguchi (2012)	United States	Add Health (wave 3)	Men and women	4,880	Negative binomial regression	Beneficial	1
Sampson, Laub, and Wimer (2006)	United States	Glueck and Glueck's study on delinquent boys	Men only	440 to age 32, 52 to age 70	Inverse probability of treatment weighting and hierarchical Poisson modeling	Beneficial (both marriage and cohabitation)	291
Sampson and Laub (1993)	United States	Glueck and Glueck's study on delinquent boys	Men only	622 at the most	Regression analysis, event history analysis	Significant negative associations between marital attachment and all measures of crime and deviance	3,474

TABLE 1 (*Continued*)

Study	Country	Data Source	Gender	Analytic Sample Size	Methods	Findings on the Marriage Effect	Citations according to Google Scholar, March 2014
Sampson and Laub (1990)	United States	Glueck and Glueck's study on delinquent boys	Men only	622 at the most	Regression analysis	Significant negative associations between marital attachment and all measures of crime and deviance	707
Savolainen (2009)	Finland	National Recidivism Study (register data)	Men only	1,325	Negative binomial regression	Beneficial (cohabitation); not significant (marriage)	92
Schroeder, Giordano, and Cernkovich (2007)	United States	Ohio Life-Course Study	Men and women	152	Regression analysis	No significant associations between marital/initmate partner happiness and desistance or persistance in full models	60
Simons et al. (2002)	United States	Iowa Youth and Families Project	Men and women	236 and their romantic partners	SEM and logistic regression	Positive association between having antisocial romantic partner and criminal behavior; quality of romantic relationship significant only for females	138

Simons and Barr (2012)	United States	FACHS	Men and women	589		Negative binomial regression	No significant association between having a romantic partner and criminal behavior, but significantly less crime for those having a high-quality relationship (although not significant when controlling for criminogenic structure)	4
Skardhamar, Monsbakken, and Lyngstad (2014)	Norway	Norwegian register data	Men only	80,064		Generalized additive modeling	Beneficial in the years before marriage, but potentially also for those who marry a criminal woman	0
Theobald and Farrington (2013)	United Kingdom	Cambridge Study	Men only	319		Propensity score matching and logistic regression	Separated men who formed a new relationship (cohabitation or remarriage) had a smaller increase in offending than those who remained separated	2

TABLE 1 (*Continued*)

Study	Country	Data Source	Gender	Analytic Sample Size	Methods	Findings on the Marriage Effect	Citations according to Google Scholar, March 2014
Theobald and Farrington (2011)	United Kingdom	Cambridge Study	Men only	111	Propensity score matching and analysis of covariance	Beneficial only if married before age 25	19
Theobald and Farrington (2009)	United Kingdom	Cambridge Study in Delinquent Development	Men only	140	Propensity score matching	Beneficial only if married before age 25	42
Thompson and Petrovic (2009)	United States	NYS (waves 5–7)	Men and women	1,496	Logistic panel models with fixed effects	Marriage beneficial (only men); relationship strength beneficial for women; increasing drug use for men	21
Uggen and Kruttschnitt (1998)	United States	National Supported Work Demonstration Project	Men and women	Illegal earnings: 2,667; arrests: 3,020	Cox proportional hazard model	No significant associations between living with spouse and outcome variables	155

van Schellen, Apel, and Nieuwbeerta (2012)	Netherlands	CCLC	Men and women	4,615	Fixed-effect Poisson regression	For men: beneficial only if married to nonconvicted spouse; for women: beneficial	5
Warr (1998)	United States	NYS (waves 5 and 6)	Men and women	1,725	Logistic regression	Beneficial, but not significant associations when controlling for having delinquent friends and time spent with friends	501
Zoutewelle-Terovan et al. (2012)	Netherlands	17Up	Men and women	540	Fixed and random-effect models	Beneficial (significant only for men); No significant association between marriage duration and offending	6
Zoutewelle-Terovan et al. (2013)	Netherlands	17Up	Men and women	93 couples	Cox regression		0

Farrington 1989; Sampson and Laub 1990). None of the six suggested that marriage per se contributed to significant reductions in crime. For example, West (1982) found no significant difference in self-reported delinquency between married and unmarried men but observed that delinquents were more likely to marry delinquent women. Farrington (1989) found convicted men to be less likely to get along with their spouses. Gibbens (1984) found the association to be causally ambiguous because the men were more likely to marry as their lives were becoming more stable. Sampson and Laub (1990) found that marriage was not associated with reduced offending but presented evidence suggesting that marital attachment reduced offending.

Wright and Wright (1992, p. 54) concluded that "no clearly confirming set of findings has emerged from research to date that demonstrates that getting married and having children reduces the likelihood of criminal offense." This is no longer the dominant impression (see fig. 3). There has been a tremendous growth in availability of longitudinal data

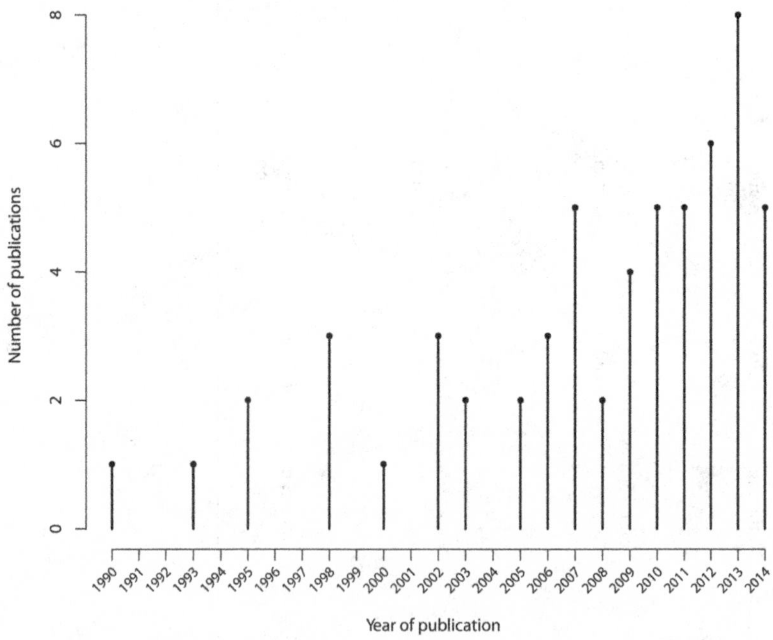

FIG. 3.—Number of studies published by year. The figure for 2014 is for the first three months of the year.

sets and increased methodological sophistication since the early literature on marriage and crime. The contemporary opinion is much more confident about the capacity of marriage to exert restraining influence on crime (Craig, Diamond, and Piquero 2014). This confidence is understandable given that of the 58 publications that met our selection criteria, 36 found marriage (or related states) to be associated with desistance from crime. Nine additional studies found mixed evidence. Thus, as many as 45 (78 percent) studies reported at least some support for the expectation that marriage is associated with reduced offending.

Because much of this literature is based on a relatively small number of longitudinal data sets (see fig. 4), we grouped the 58 studies under headings indicating the data source used. The length of the bar in figure 4 shows the number of publications generated by the data set. The number next to the bars provides the combined citation count from all the reviewed studies using these data. In terms of citations, the Glueck study resurrected by Sampson and Laub (1993) is in a league of its own. With 6,441 citations, it is more influential than the rest of the studies combined.[6] In terms of publication count, the National Longitudinal Study of Adolescent Health (Add Health) leads the way with nine articles, followed by the Dutch Criminal Career and Life Course study (CCLC) and the Glueck study. It is notable, however, that two of the publications from the Glueck data are book-length monographs. The Cambridge Study, the National Youth Study (NYS), and the National Longitudinal Studies (1979 and 1997) of Youth (NLSY) are also prominent. The Ohio Life-Course Study and the Nebraska Inmate Sample are influential in terms of citation counts.

A. *Glueck Sample*

Sampson and Laub's seminal research program is grounded on reanalysis and reconstruction of longitudinal data collected by Sheldon and Eleanor Glueck (1940) when the boys were 14 years of age and additional waves at ages 25 and 32. The Gluecks sampled 500 boys born between 1924 and 1935 from a correctional school in Boston and matched them with same-aged boys from a "normal" population sample. The first article by Sampson and Laub (1990) examined the association

[6] Citation count should be treated as only a rough indicator of influence. The monographs by Sampson and Laub are general treatises that cover multiple topics of life course criminology, while many of the other studies are more narrowly focused.

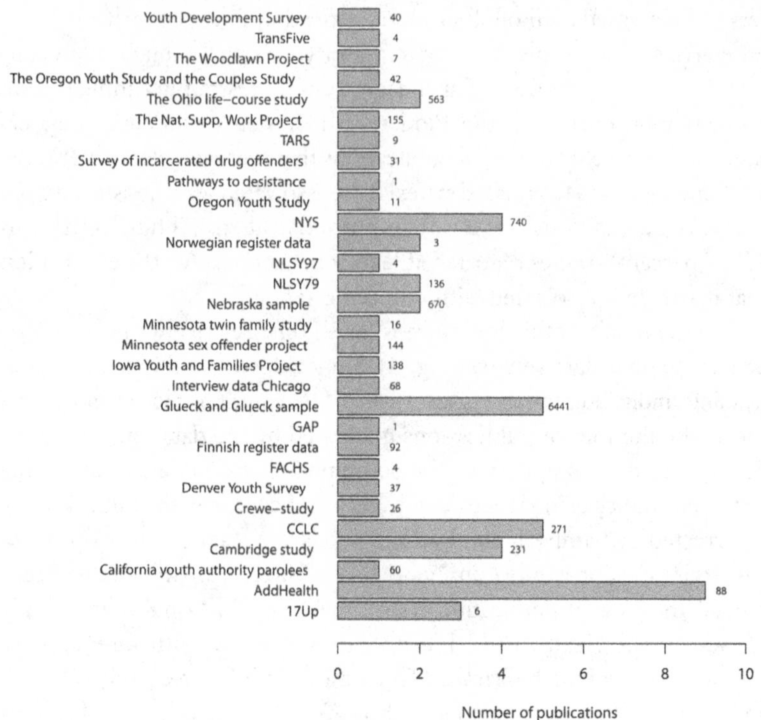

FIG. 4.—Number of publications by data set. Sums of citations according to Google Scholar are to the right of each bar. The figures for CCLC include one study also including the Dutch national crime survey (Blokland and Nieuwbeerta 2005).

between spousal attachment and rates of crime and deviant behavior at ages 17–25 and 25–32, controlling for confounding factors measured in childhood and early adulthood. In analysis of the full sample, they found no association between marriage and offending as measured by both self-reported delinquency and official arrests. However, they found a negative association between marital attachment and crime in the analysis limited to ever-married men. Sampson and Laub's *Crime in the Making* (1993) largely replicated the results from the 1990 article with some adjustments and elaborations. For example, some of the analyses were extended to ages 32–45. Their main conclusion was that "childhood and adult social bonds in the form of job stability and marital attachment independently explain significant variations in adult crime" (1993, p. 178).

In a subsequent article, Laub, Nagin, and Sampson (1998) analyzed the Glueck sample from ages 14 to 32. Their theoretical argument was focused on the quality of marital bonding and the incremental nature of this effect. Importantly, this study attended to the possibility of a "courtship effect," that is, the potential effect of romantic bonding prior to entering marriage. They found no evidence of a courtship effect. However, among those with strong marital attachment, the estimates showed evidence of an incremental decrease in offending in each annual time point during the postmarriage period. Consistent with the hypothesis, no such effect was observed among men with weak spousal attachment.

In order to extend the original data to later points in the life course, Laub and Sampson (2003) made an effort to track the men from the Glueck study. They were able to interview 52 individuals and to update their conviction records up to age 70. On the basis of retrospective data from life history narratives, the quantitative analyses estimated annual changes in the number of convictions. The results showed reduced rates of offending during states of marriage. Importantly, these models ignored variation in the quality of marital bonding; the results were generalized to marital unions of any kind. Evidence from qualitative interviews provided additional evidence in support of marriage as a major turning point. One of the men stated that his wife straightened him out (p. 121) and that marriage probably even saved his life (p. 134). The key message of the 2003 monograph was "that marriage may lead to desistance because of direct social control effects by spouses" (p. 136) but also that in-laws provided additional support (p. 137). The latter is related to the assumption that these men usually "married up" and gained access to additional resources through the extended family of the wife. Overall, the qualitative evidence was consistent with processes of informal social control, change in routine activities, identity shift, and social capital formation through the extended family.

From the perspective of causal inference, Sampson, Laub, and Wimer (2006) offer the most stringent test of the marriage effect on desistance. They used inverse probability of treatment weighting as the methodological approach to imitate an experimental design.[7] The idea is to approximate a comparison—within the limits of observational data—between in-

[7] We discuss this method further in the next section as we evaluate the evidence on causality.

dividuals who are otherwise as similar as possible with the exception of marital status. They concluded that marriage is associated with a 35 percent average reduction in crime (p. 496). Moreover, this reduction was greater among those reporting high marital attachment. In an additional analysis, they report evidence suggesting that a similar association applies to cohabiting couples. Thus, having a stable partner may promote desistance regardless of union type according to this study.

B. National Youth Study

The NYS is a panel study of 1,725 males and females selected to be representative of the US population. The study started in 1976 when the participants were between 11 and 17 years of age, and they have been followed up so far to ages 39–45. The study is now called the National Youth Survey and Family Study.[8]

Warr (1998) used the NYS data waves 5 and 6 to examine the relationship between marriage and desistance. His theoretical goal was to illuminate the mechanisms responsible for the marriage effect. He advanced the argument emphasizing the salience of differential association processes as an alternative to the social bonding explanation offered by Sampson and Laub (1993). He argued that marriage is influential because it restructures activities away from (delinquent) male peers and toward increased time with the spouse and in the family setting. This study documented a significant negative association between marital status and three indicators of self-reported delinquency—petty theft, vandalism, and marijuana use—all measured at wave 6. Consistent with the hypothesis, this association disappeared when controlling for differences in exposure to delinquent friends. Owing to data limitations, the more compelling analysis, based on change scores between waves 5 and 6, was possible only for marijuana use as the outcome variable. This test was consistent with the findings from the more comprehensive cross-sectional analysis. Warr concluded that marriage reduced delinquency because of its effect on peer associations.

Maume, Ousey, and Beaver (2005) used the NYS to reexamine Warr's hypothesis but focusing on marital attachment rather than mere marital status as the measure of romantic bonding. Consistent with the AGT, high levels of marital attachment were related to desistance, and the

[8] For more information, see http://www.colorado.edu/ibs/NYSFS/index.html.

effect persisted even controlling for the influence of delinquent peer associations. This analysis suggests that marital attachment has a direct effect on desistance, with "only a small portion being due to delinquent peers" (p. 48).

Ignoring the question of mechanisms, King, Massoglia, and Macmillan (2007) used NYS data to estimate the causal effect of marriage on desistance. They employed propensity score matching on data from NYS wave 7, when the average age of the participants was 24 years. Marital status was measured as being married the year before, and a large number of covariates from previous waves were used to estimate the propensity to marry. Their main finding was that marriage reduced crime among men but not significantly among women. Moreover, they stratified the sample on the propensity score, interpretable as the probability of marrying. This analysis suggests that, although the effect of marriage on crime applies to all men, it is the strongest among those least likely to marry.

Thompson and Petrovic (2009) found that marriage reduced drug use among men and women. In addition, they included an index of relationship strength, which covered married as well as nonmarried couples. Controlling for marital status, relationship strength was associated with further declines in female drug use but, surprisingly, an increase among men.

C. *The Ohio Life-Course Study and the Toledo Adolescent Relationship Study*

The sample for the Ohio Life-Course Study was drawn in 1982 from inmates in state-run institutions for delinquent girls (N = 127) and boys (N = 127). The participants were contacted again in 1995 and 2003. The data were analyzed using quantitative as well as qualitative methods.

Focusing on the two first waves, Giordano, Cernkovich, and Rudolph (2002) found no significant association among males or females between attachment to spouse and criminal involvement. They proposed that it is the combination of marriage and stable jobs that provides sufficient bonding and social control to assist in desistance. They refer to this combination as a "respectability package." They found that individuals with a high-quality package (i.e., marital happiness and stable earnings) were more likely to desist. Evidence from qualitative interviews highlighted the importance of initial willingness to change as well as structural constraints limiting opportunities to achieve life goals consistent with the motivation to go straight.

Giordano, Cernkovich, and Holland (2003) elaborated on these findings with a special focus on understanding dynamics in romantic relationships. They argued that marital (or romantic) attachment is unlikely to reduce crime unless the spouse truly wishes and makes an effort to limit behaviors and habits conducive to criminal involvement. They argued that "a decision to align with a relatively more conforming partner generally represents an affirmative, agentic move away from a criminal lifestyle. And the spouse's respectability is often a critical component of the actor's own continuing identity transformation project" (p. 306). They also suggested that an intimate partner can be used to invoke a kind of "cover" for not participating in criminal opportunities as now being a "family man" (p. 305). Under this framework, marriage may help redirect lives away from crime, but this pathway is preceded by a subjective desire to change. The relationship quality is not something that "happens" but reflects a choice to gravitate toward a partner with these characteristics (p. 321).

Using all three waves of the Ohio Life-Course Study, Schroeder, Giordano, and Cernkovich (2007) investigated the role of drug use in the desistance process. This study was informed by Laub and Sampson's (2003) conjecture that involvement in substance misuse sustained criminality because this lifestyle made it difficult to establish bonds to marriage and work (p. 212). Schroeder, Giordano, and Cernkovich (2007) did not find an association between marriage and crime, and the association between drug use and crime was not mediated by marital quality.

The Toledo Adolescent Relationships Study (TARS) is based on a stratified random sample of 1,066 students in seventh, ninth, and eleventh grades across 62 schools in seven school districts, followed until age 21 on average. Marital status was included as a covariate with a primary focus on parenthood. Giordano et al. (2011) found no significant association between cohabitation/marriage and offending. However, parents (mothers and fathers) who resided with the other biological parent were found to experience "marginally significant reductions in criminal activity" (p. 9). Evidence from qualitative interviews suggested that many of the romantic partners "would be unlikely to provide a solid prosocial anchor" (p. 9).

In sum, the work of Giordano and colleagues challenges the idea that marriage or even marital attachment promotes desistance from crime. Rather, marriage (to a conventional partner) in combination with stable income is more likely to reflect the individual's decision to change and ability to capitalize on opportunities to do so. Importantly, the results indicate that a large number of individuals in their sample were afflicted with disadvantages that made it very difficult for them to realize their motivation to change.

D. Criminal Career and Life Course Study

Several important studies of marriage and crime have been based on the Dutch CCLC study, which is a random 4 percent sample of all persons convicted in the Netherlands in 1977 (N = 4,164). The CCLC contains information about the entire conviction history up to 1977 and all subsequent convictions through 2002. In the first publication using these data, Blokland and Nieuwbeerta (2005) found that marriage was associated with a within-individual reduction in crime among offenders of low to moderate frequency, but not for sporadic offenders.

The CCLC is not a birth cohort study but follows a random cross section of convicted offenders who vary in age and who married at different periods of time. The oldest members of the sample were born in 1907 and the youngest in 1965. Sensitive to this issue, Bersani, Laub, and Nieuwbeerta (2009) stratified the sample into three groups based on age in 1977: those aged 32 and up (born before 1945), those aged 22–31 (born 1946–55), and those aged 12–21 (1956–65).[9] They found that marriage was associated with a reduction in crime across each cohort, but more strongly among males and among the more recent cohorts.

McGloin et al. (2011) used the CCLC to examine the effect of marriage on versatility of criminal offending. They found marriage to be associated with a decline in versatility, and this was not fully explained by reductions in the frequency of offending. Moreover, they report evidence suggesting that the declining trend in offending started before the year of marriage (p. 370). Petras, Nieuwbeerta, and Piquero (2010) found marriage to be associated with a decline in both the prevalence and frequency of offending. Another study investigated whether the marriage-crime association depends on the criminal history of the spouse (van Schellen, Apel, and Nieuwbeerta 2012). The results showed that those who married a criminal spouse did not experience any decline in offending. Additional nuances are suggested by van Schellen, Poortman, and Nieuwbeerta

[9] In a footnote, the authors discuss the concern that the sample is selected on being convicted in 1977, making some by definition adult offenders (or serious offenders).

(2012), who found that convictions, and particularly recent convictions, lowered the chances of getting married and increased the chances of marrying a criminal partner, and for these reasons, offenders are less likely to experience protective effects of marriage.

E. National Longitudinal Studies of Youth

There are three studies included in our review based on the National Longitudinal Studies of Youth (NLSY79 or NLSY97). These are panel surveys of nationally representative samples of men and women born in the years 1957–64 and 1980–84, respectively. In each survey, the respondents were 12–17 years of age at the time of the first interview.[10] Both studies include a main sample and two supplementary samples. In the first supplementary sample, Hispanics or Latinos, blacks, and economically disadvantaged, nonblack/non-Hispanics were oversampled. The second supplementary sample consists of persons serving in the military. The total sample sizes of the NLSY79 and NLSY97 are 12,686 and 8,984, respectively.

Duncan, Wilkerson, and England (2006) examined changes in marijuana use across 11 waves from the NLSY79. The authors selected a subsample of everyone married for the first time and operationalized the "marriage period" as the 5 years before and after the year of entering marriage, so that each person contributed up to 11 person-years to the analysis. To isolate the potential marriage effect from other dynamic factors, they specified a piecewise linear spline distinguishing the periods before marriage (periods −5 through −2), surrounding marriage (periods −1 through 1), and after marriage (periods +1 through +5). Under this design, the difference between the first and second splines constitutes the marriage effect (pp. 695–96). They applied the same approach to cohabitation. The findings showed that marriage but not cohabitation reduced marijuana use among men, but neither union type had any effect among women.

Forrest and Hay (2011) proposed that objective life course transitions, such as marriage, may influence levels of self-control and that this may be a mechanism that contributes to the effect of marriage on desistance. Drawing on NLSY79 waves 1996–2004, Forrest and Hay examined this hypothesis focusing on changes in marijuana use. The models included a dummy predictor representing the state of marriage and another

[10] For more information, see https://www.nlsinfo.org/content/cohorts/NLSY79; for NLSY97, see https://www.nlsinfo.org/content/cohorts/nlsy97.

dummy for cohabitation. These effects were estimated controlling for a wide range of potentially confounding variables. Both marriage and cohabitation were found to be associated with increased levels of self-control, and marriage (but not cohabitation) was associated with reduced levels of marijuana use, even controlling for differences in self-control. They concluded that changes in self-control mediate some of the relationship between marriage and desistance.

Using 13 waves from the NLSY97, Bersani and Doherty (2013) examined whether there was a longitudinal association between marriage and the risk of arrest, and what happens to this association when marriage dissolves. In an attempt to devise a crucial test between two theories, they argued that if identity transformation is the key mechanism of influence, there should be little or no change following divorce; but if social bonding and changes in routine activities are the driving force, we should expect an increase (or relapse) following divorce. They first established the presence of a negative association between state of marriage and risk of arrest. To estimate the effect of divorce, the next step of the analysis was limited to those who got married and, thus, were at risk of divorce. The results showed strong increases in offending among those who divorced.

F. National Longitudinal Study of Adolescent Health

Add Health is a nationally representative study of US adolescents sampled initially during 1994–95. So far, there have been four waves of data collection up to ages 24–32. A total of 20,745 students were interviewed in the first wave. Add Health includes a wide range of health-related information, including biomarkers, such as saliva samples for genotyping. Participants in the genetic subsample ($N = 2{,}574$) had a twin or sibling participating in the Add Health study.

Focusing on the genetic subsample, Beaver et al. (2008) selected one sibling from each twin pair ($N = 1{,}994$) to examine genetic and environmental correlates of desistance. They found that married persons were more likely to desist from crime. The serotonin transporter gene was associated with desistance for females, and there were significant interaction effects between marriage and the transporter genes DRD2 and DRD4 and monoamine oxidase A (MAOA). They concluded that the effect of marriage is heterogeneous as a function of genetic differences.

Barnes and Beaver (2012) used a sibling and twin design to shed light on to what extent genetic confounders account for the frequently observed marriage effect. The study capitalized on information about the zygosity of twins, relatedness of siblings (half vs. full siblings), and even cousin relationships. This information was used to decompose the variances reflecting genetic similarities and thereby isolating the influence of genetic factors on desistance from crime. The findings showed a notable genetic component to the association between marriage and desistance: the association was reduced by more than 50 percent once cleaned from the influence of genetic relatedness.

Jaffee, Lombardi, and Coley (2013) used four complementary methods of analysis to assess the effect of marriage on crime: lagged multivariate regression models, propensity score matching, fixed-effects models, and sibling analysis. Each methodological approach found marriage to be associated with reduced levels of delinquent offending, suggesting that the finding is robust.

Another study based on Add Health found that marriage was associated with a reduction in crime among both males and females. Focusing on racial differences, Craig (2015) found support for the marriage effect among Caucasians and Hispanics, but not among African Americans. Salvatore and Taniguchi (2012) estimated the effects of several indicators of social bonding and turning points on criminal offending, finding that marriage was associated with reduced offending. Ragan and Beaver (2010) found marriage to be associated with desistance from marijuana use between waves 1 and 2 of Add Health data.

Barnes et al. (2014) noted that prior studies of the marriage effect have failed to address the possibility that the association between marriage and crime may be reciprocal, that is, that crime may affect marriage. They estimated cross-lagged structural equation models between marital status and criminal behavior in waves 3 and 4 of Add Health. They found that being married was associated with reductions in crime but also that crime was negatively related to the probability of marriage. When accounting for reciprocal effects, the direct effect of marriage on crime was no longer statistically significant. This study suggests that ignoring reciprocal pathways in the association results in overstated estimates of the marriage effect.

G. *The Cambridge Study in Delinquent Development*

The Cambridge Study is one of the most cited in the criminal careers literature. The data include 411 boys from a working-class neighborhood in South London, first interviewed in 1961–62 at the ages of 8 and 9. The sample includes all boys in this age group who lived in that area at the time. The data collection consists of nine waves, the last of which occurred when the sample participants were age 48.

Farrington and West (1995) estimated a set of regression models predicting convictions between ages 21 and 32, convictions in the 5 years before the interview at age 32, and self-reported offending in the last 5 years up to age 32. They found stable marriage to be negatively associated with crime. They also conducted a within-individual analysis comparing the number of convictions in the 5 years before marriage and the 5 years after marriage and by matching each married man with an unmarried man on the basis of the number of convictions in the 5 years before marriage. The results showed that men who married accrued significantly fewer convictions after marriage.

Two recent studies focused on a subsample of 162 convicted men from the Cambridge Study, excluding those whose marriages lasted less than 5 years (Theobald and Farrington 2009, 2011). These men got married at different ages and were matched using propensity score methods to those not (yet) married at the same age. Theobald and Farrington (2009) concluded that early marriage (18–24 years of age) was associated with reduced offending, but they did not observe a similar pattern among those who married later (25+ years of age). In a later study, they explored the characteristics of those who married early versus late (Theobald and Farrington 2011) and found that those who married late were different from those who married early. They were more likely to have grown up in a broken home, to be more nervous, and to have married a woman older than themselves (p. 153).

H. Nebraska Inmate Sample

Horney, Osgood, and Marshall (1995) interviewed a sample of 658 newly convicted men sentenced to prison in Nebraska in 1989–90. The inmates were interviewed using a life history calendar covering 25–36 months leading up to the arrest leading to imprisonment. The instrument recorded monthly changes in offending behavior and "local life circumstances," such as marriage and employment. Using a hierarchical linear model (HLM) with covariates centered at individuals' mean values, the study estimated within-individual changes in rates of offending in response to changes in life circumstances. They found that living with a wife was negatively associated with offending, while cohabitation increased the risk of crime. In a reanalysis of the same data,

McGloin et al. (2007) showed that marriage was also negatively associated with offending versatility.

I. Studies Based on Nordic Administrative Register Data

Desistance scholars in Finland and Norway have taken advantage of the systems for administrative records and official statistics available in the Nordic countries. These data sets typically cover the total population, with longitudinal, individual-level information on marital events, crime, and a wide range of other characteristics, such as educational attainment and socioeconomic background. The sources have been used widely in demography and public health but remain relatively untapped in criminology (Lyngstad and Skardhamar 2011).

Savolainen (2009) examined a national sample of felony offenders from Finland. They were convicted in 1996 and tracked through 2001 using data from interlinked population registries. The study focused on a subsample of high-rate offenders who were unemployed, single (neither married nor cohabiting), and childless at the start of the tracking for new offenses (beginning of 1996). The study sought to examine whether changes in offending were related to transitions to adult social roles (work and family). With respect to marriage, Savolainen found that living in a romantic union (i.e., marriage or cohabitation) was associated with significant reductions in the rate of offending. However, when this association was disaggregated by marital status, it turned out that this "effect" was generated by changes among men who were cohabiting; the marriage effect was no longer statistically significant. As a possible explanation of the unexpected findings, he proposed that, in Finland, marriage is typically preceded by several years of cohabitation. In this normative context, women who are relatively quick to marry a man with an intense criminal history may be more approving of the criminal lifestyle than women who delay marriage. In other words, in this situation, men in the cohabitation category may be more likely to live with a prosocial partner.

Lyngstad and Skardhamar (2013) used Norwegian data on all men who got married between 1997 and 2001 and examined their annual rates of officially recorded offending 5 years before and after the year of marriage. The results demonstrated a declining trend in offending during the period leading up to marriage but no additional decline after marriage. As in Finland, the suggested explanation was that marriage is typically preceded by several years of cohabitation and that entering marriage may be a poor proxy for when the potential effects of romantic bonding take place. Skardhamar, Monsbakken, and Lyngstad (2014) used a similar design to investigate whether results varied by the criminal history of the wife. Unsurprisingly, men who married a criminal woman were more involved in crime themselves. However, these men also experienced the greatest declines in offending, and some of that occurred after marriage.

J. 17Up

Another Dutch study, 17Up, sampled 270 males and 270 females released from a juvenile treatment center in the Netherlands. Recorded crimes were collected from age 12 onward and linked to information on marital status and other demographic variables available from the Municipal Population Registration database. The data file also contains information gleaned from the treatment files of the juvenile institution. Studies using these data show that marriage was associated with reduced offending in property crime among males and females but with an increase in violent crime among men (and a decrease among women). No significant association between marriage and drug crimes was observed for either gender (Mercer, Zoutewelle-Terovan, and van der Geest 2013). The duration of marriage had no additional effect over and above marital status (Zoutewelle-Terovan et al. 2012), but having a deviant spouse was shown to support a criminal lifestyle (Zoutewelle-Terovan et al. 2013).

K. Additional Studies

Some data sources were associated with only one relevant publication. The Youth Development Study features a sample of 1,000 students from public schools in St. Paul, Minnesota. Massoglia and Uggen (2007) showed that relationship quality was consistently associated with desistance across multiple measures of offending. The Denver Youth Study is a probability sample of households from disadvantaged neighborhoods in Denver, Colorado. Using a subsample of 567 women, Kreager, Matsueda, and Erosheva (2010) found no association between marriage and delinquency, with the exception of reduced marijuana use. In a sample of 965 first-grade children from the nine public and three parochial schools located in a disadvantaged Chicago neighborhood, marriage was a consistent correlate of desistance among men, but the results varied by type of offending among women (Doherty and Ensminger 2013).

O'Connell (2003), studying recidivism in a sample of persons with serious drug problems serving a prison sentence in Delaware ($N = 576$), found marriage to be unrelated to either rearrest or drug use. Uggen and Kruttschnitt (1998) used a sample consisting of participants in a supported employment experiment to explore factors related to desistance. Living with a spouse was not a statistically significant correlate. In a study of 206 men from a medium-sized metropolitan area, marriage was associated with reductions in self-reported crime, fewer arrests, and reduced marijuana use, while cohabitation was not statistically significantly related to these outcomes (Kerr et al. 2011). In a 7-year follow-up of 524 parolees from California, Piquero, MacDonald, and Parker (2002) found that marriage was negatively associated with nonviolent arrests for both whites and nonwhites but not for violent arrests. Common-law marriages were associated with increased offending among nonwhites but not among whites.

A number of studies have focused on attachment or other aspects of relationship quality. Using data from the Oregon Youth Study (OYS), a community sample of 206 high-risk men, Capaldi, Kim, and Owen (2008) identified relationship stability as a key predictor of desistance, while attachment to a partner was not influential. Simons and Barr (2012) used data from the Family and Community Health Study (FACHS), consisting of 100 African Americans living in Iowa or Georgia. The results showed that a nonmarital relationship in early adulthood was associated with desistance only if it was warm and supportive and that change in peer associations explained a marginal proportion of the association. Simons et al. (2002) used a sample of 236 persons across eight counties in Iowa interviewed in ninth grade and then again 6 years later. Having a conventional romantic partner and a high-quality relationship were associated with a reduction in adult crime. Among males, this association was insignificant once exposure to delinquent friends was taken into account.

Several studies have focused on the effect of partner characteristics, especially the criminality of the spouse. On the basis of a sample drawn from juvenile courts in two US metropolitan areas, Monahan, Dmitrieva, and Cauffman (2014) found evidence suggesting that having a prosocial partner was associated with a decrease in antisocial behavior. The Gender and Aggression Project (GAP) sampled 141 girls from a juvenile correction facility and followed them up to 20–23 years of age (Oudekerk, Burgers, and Reppucci 2014). This research suggests that living in a stable romantic relationship tempers offending only among those with a noncriminal partner. Leverentz (2006) conducted qualitative interviews of 14 women living in a halfway house after release from prison. Many had an antisocial partner unlikely to curb drug use and offending. In some cases the couple sought treatment together, providing mutual support for recovery.

Some of the studies stand out because of the unique character of the data or the research design. Burt et al. (2010) analyzed 289 male twin pairs from the Minnesota Twin Family Study and found that the within-pair association between marriage and crime was significant for monozygotic twins, suggesting an association independent of a clear selection effect into marriage. Kruttschnitt, Uggen, and Shelton (2000) studied a sample of sex offenders placed on probation in Minnesota in 1992 ($N = 556$). In a 5-year follow-up, they found that marital status exerted almost no effect on recidivism. Focusing on a cohort of men who were criminally active in late nineteenth- and early twentieth-century England, Godfrey, Cox, and Farrall (2007) found no evidence of desistance following transition to marriage. They suggest that wives were economically too dependent during this period to exercise effective social control. Finally, Beijers, Bijleveld, and van Poppel (2012) examined an intergenerational sample consisting of descendants of males placed in a Dutch reform school between 1911 and 1914. They found that the restraining effect of marriage was limited to cohorts entering marriage after 1970.

L. *Overview of Patterns*

We conclude with a brief summary of main patterns. One important theme has to do with the salience of marriage versus cohabitation, inasmuch as cohabitation has become increasingly common in recent decades. Whether marriage affects both women and men has been discussed frequently. So has the universality or specificity of the marriage effect across historical periods and cultural contexts.

1. *Cohabitation.* Some scholars have suggested that marriage may be qualitatively different from other romantic relationships: "taking the conscious step to get married demonstrates some non-negligible commitment, being married appears to be more protective of future offending than cohabiting" (Craig, Diamond, and Piquero 2014, p. 33). Although we find this assumption plausible, it is worth emphasizing that it underscores systematic selection into marriage as an important mechanism of influence. Perhaps marriage is associated more strongly with desistance

than cohabitation because "tying the knot" is more likely to occur after sustained behavioral change.

Some studies find no significant association between cohabitation and crime (Duncan, Wilkerson, and England 2006; Schroeder, Giordano, and Cernkovich 2007; Forrest and Hay 2011; Giordano et al. 2011; Kerr et al. 2011), and two studies found that living with a girlfriend increased offending (Horney, Osgood, and Marshall 1995; Piquero, MacDonald, and Parker 2002). Contrary to these, other studies have found cohabitation to have effects similar to those of marriage (Sampson, Laub, and Wimer 2006) or even more important than marriage (Savolainen 2009). One recent study found cohabitation to be associated with a reduction in substance abuse, but the association was not statistically significant for criminal offending (Siennick et al. 2014). Irrespective of the formal status of the union, the evidence on relationship quality is fairly consistent. Virtually all the studies that include measures of "good" marriage or cohabitation report significant effects in the expected direction (Simons et al. 2002; Massoglia and Uggen 2007; Capaldi, Kim, and Owen 2008; Simons and Barr 2012; Oudekerk, Burgers, and Reppucci 2014).

2. *Gender Differences.* The literature has been dominated by studies of male-only samples. The question has been raised whether the association holds for women. Women have lower crime rates than men, and their role in the family remains different. If Laub and Sampson (2003) are correct that many male offenders "marry up" in terms of resources as well as criminal propensity, it follows that women marry "down." Whether this is true for offenders has not been empirically established, as none of the studies investigated the spouse's socioeconomic characteristics. Evidence from the demographic literature suggests that it is women, not men, who "marry up" (Birkelund and Heldal 2003).

A number of studies have found the marriage effect to be stronger for, or even limited to, men (e.g., Duncan, Wilkerson, and England 2006; King, Massoglia, and Macmillan 2007; Beaver et al. 2008; Bersani, Laub, and Nieuwbeerta 2009; Zoutewelle-Terovan et al. 2012; Doherty and Ensminger 2013; Mercer, Zoutewelle-Terovan, and van der Geest 2013). Others found no gender difference in the association between marriage or marital attachment and crime (Giordano, Cernkovich, and Rudolph 2002; Simons et al. 2002). Van Schellen, Apel, and Nieuwbeerta (2012) found greater reductions in crime among females following marriage (see also Giordano et al. 2011). Thompson and Petrovic (2009) found no gender difference in the association between state of marriage and illicit drug use, but the strength of marital attachment reduced drug use among women and increased it among men.

3. *National Context.* Bersani, Laub, and Nieuwbeerta (2009) argued that the association between marriage and crime is universal and robust across sociohistorical context, but other studies have provided evidence to the contrary (e.g., Godfrey, Cox, and Farrall 2007; Savolainen 2009; Lyngstad and Skardhamar 2013). The meaning of marriage may vary among the United States, southern and northern Europe, and especially the Nordic countries, where cohabitation is widespread and in many ways comparable to marriage. As shown in figure 5, the vast majority of the studies on marriage and crime are based on data from the United States. The 17 publications from outside the United States represent a relatively narrow selection of nations: the Netherlands, England, Finland, and Norway. It is premature to make strong conclusions about the universality of the association between marriage and crime.

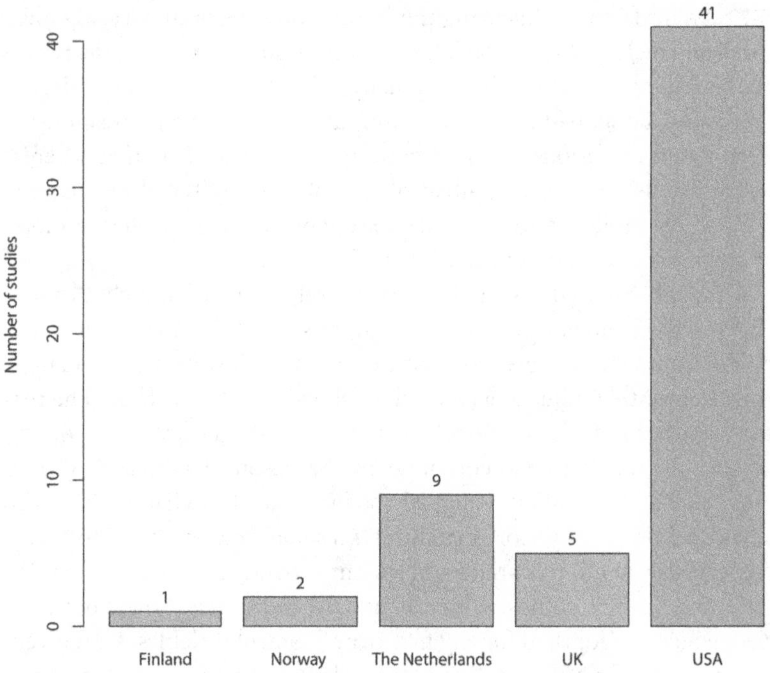

FIG. 5.—Number of publications by the country from which the data are collected

IV. So, Is There a "Marriage Effect"?

Belief in the marriage effect is strong in the criminological literature. Most of the studies we examined frame their empirical findings as consistent with theories predicting a causal effect of marriage on crime. Much of this evidence, however, is equally consistent with noncausal theories, such as the maturation perspective. In order to demonstrate causality, the evidence should rule out social selection as the alternative account of the negative association between marriage and crime. The social selection hypothesis posits that marriage is associated with desistance because individuals who have "cleaned up their acts," that is, matured out of crime, are more likely to marry than those who persist in crime. Evidence that fails to rule out this interpretation does not demonstrate causality.

Most research on the marriage-crime relationship relies on some technique of multivariate regression to control for the influence of observed confounders. It is increasingly well understood that this method can establish causality only under the highly unrealistic assumption that all the relevant factors influencing the association have been perfectly measured and included in the model. If this assumption is not met, the results are biased by unobserved heterogeneity: "To the extent that marriage is influenced by individual self-selection, the marriage-crime relationship is potentially spurious. … The bottom line seems to be that whereas causal claims are frequent, albeit often ambiguously stated or rendered implicit, the strategies that are used to support them often fall well short" (Sampson, Laub, and Wimer 2006, p. 70).

Although fixed-effects models (and closely related hierarchical models) of within-individual change are more sophisticated than the traditional approach of regression with covariate adjustment, this analytic approach is still limited as a method for showing a causal effect. The reason is that fixed-effects models cannot rule out the influence of unobservable time-varying confounders (Sampson, Laub, and Wimer 2006, p. 71; Bjerk 2009). King, Massoglia, and Macmillan (2007), who advocated propensity score matching as a superior alternative, observed, "As typically used, [covariate adjustment models] give mean offending differences between those who are married and those who are not married, which are adjusted for any number of control variables. Under very specific conditions, such as when respondents are randomly assigned to a particular status, the results generated from regression models may represent the actual treatment effect of marriage on crime. As marriage is not a randomly occurring event, we use propensity score matching estimators to assess the treatment effect of marriage on adult offending" (p. 43). In this section, we critically examine the evidence in support of the causal interpretation of the marriage-crime association. First, we discuss two influential studies aiming at direct causal estimates. Next, we discuss two kinds of evidence that speak to the causal interpretation, albeit more indirectly: evidence on the timing of change and evidence on proposed theoretical mechanisms.

A. Evidence of Counterfactual Causal Effects

A counterfactual causal effect is defined as the difference in the outcome under treatment condition Y_1 and the outcome without treatment Y_0. Under random assignment, any pretreatment characteristics that vary across the individuals, X, are unrelated to the treatment, D. Thus, if we could study the marriage effect experimentally, those in the control group would allow us to observe the counterfactual, that is, what would have happened to the treatment group had they not been "exposed" to marriage. Formally, the average treatment effect can be expressed as

$$E(Y_1 - Y_0) = E(Y|D = 1, X) - E(Y|D = 0, X).$$

For events that are not randomly allocated, D depends on X, and therefore, any difference between the two groups reflects systematic differences in who receives the "treatment" as opposed to the treatment effect. This is a formal definition of selection effect.

Propensity score matching (henceforth PSM) has sometimes been described as a method that overcomes this problem in observational (nonexperimental) data. There are two particularly influential publications in the marriage-crime literature that rely on this approach, and both make causal claims. King, Massoglia, and Macmillan (2007) employ PSM as the main analytical technique. Sampson, Laub, and Wimer (2006) exploit a more advanced method of inverse probability of treatment weighting (IPTW), which involves the use of propensity scoring as an element of HLM of within-person change.

King, Massoglia, and Macmillan (2007) use a nearest-neighbor PSM to mimic an experimental design. This procedure involves estimating the probability of marrying to construct a comparison group of nonmarried people by matching each married person to a nonmarried person.

Exact matching on a large number of variables is impossible in practice, but as shown by Rosenbaum and Rubin (1985), matching on the propensity score can achieve balance on all covariates. The propensity score is the probability of treatment, D. This quantity has to be estimated, typically with a logistic regression model predicting the treatment outcome, such as marriage. Each married person is then matched with a nonmarried person with a similar propensity score. Using this approach, a quasi control group is created, and the treatment effect can be estimated by calculating the difference in the observed outcomes between the treatment and the quasi control groups, $Y_1 - Y_0$.

The goal of PSM is to achieve balance on all covariates, so that all variables included in X are identically distributed in the treatment and the control groups. In other words, the goal is to make the two groups equal on all pretreatment characteristics. It is critical to understand that matching on the set of observable characteristics X does not necessarily provide balance on unobserved characteristics. Thus, not unlike traditional regression analysis, propensity score methods yield causal effect estimates insofar as all the relevant variables are observed, measured, and included in the matching model—and assuming these variables are balanced after matching.[11] Thus, the problem of omitted variable bias is omnipresent. We have a truly causal estimate only if we assume the absence of omitted variable bias—an assumption that can never be fully evaluated. As Heckman and Pinto (2013, p. 10) put it, "The literature on matching ... solves the problem of confounders by *assumption*. It postulates that a set of observed pre-program variables, say $\mathbf{X}$, spans the space generated by unobserved variables $\mathbf{V}$ although it offers no guidance on how to select this set" (our emphasis). Although there are several kinds of matching methods, they all rest on this basic assumption for making causal inferences. It should be noted that matching methods have useful justifications beyond the estimation of causal effects (Morgan and Winship 2007, p. 142).

[11] The balance criterion must be further checked as balance is a necessary (but not sufficient) condition for causal interpretation. While balance ideally is assessed by comparing the joint empirical distribution of all covariates X between the matched and control groups, this becomes infeasible with high-dimensional X (Imai, King, and Stuart 2008, p. 495). In practice, many studies do what King, Massoglia, and Macmillan (2007) did, comparing the average values of each covariate, reporting statistics such as t-tests and standardized bias. This is less than thorough. Other balance checks that compare the distribution of each variable should be considered (see, e.g., Diamond and Sekhon 2013).

Sampson, Laub, and Wimer (2006) used the related IPTW approach based on propensity scores. The basic procedure is as follows. First, the probability of being married is estimated for each time point in the longitudinal data set. Using this propensity score, a weight variable is constructed for each individual at each point in time, which represents the inverse of the probability of being in the state (married or unmarried) that the individual is in at that point in time (for details, see Sampson, Laub, and Wimer [2006, p. 73]). In the next stage, the observations are weighted by the weight variable in subsequent regression models.

This approach does not yield unbiased and consistent estimates of causal effects unless important assumptions are met, such as the "assumption of sequential ignorability, which states that the treatment assignment of unit *i* at time *j* is exogenous given treatment and covariate history of the same unit up to that point in time" (Imai and Ratkovic, forthcoming, p. 2). In other words, it assumes no time-varying unmeasured confounders. If time-varying confounders are missing from the propensity score model, the results may be biased.

The problem of confounders is well understood in the literature and acknowledged by both Sampson, Laub, and Wimer (2006) and King, Massoglia, and Macmillan (2007). Indeed, the key argument by Sampson, Laub, and Wimer against omitted variable bias is precisely that they have included a large number of relevant variables in the propensity score model, so that any effect of an omitted variable would be "implausibly large" (p. 499). However, increasing the number of covariates is hardly a persuasive approach to ruling out potentially important confounders, as it is unlikely that one can adequately measure all such confounders

These studies fail to demonstrate a causal effect of marriage on crime as defined by prevailing methodological standards. Given the nature of the research question—the effect of marriage on crime—the absence of studies demonstrating counterfactual causality is not surprising. While it is possible to experiment with some life course transitions—such as employment (see, e.g., Uggen 2000; Bushway and Apel 2012)—a randomized study of the effect of marriage on crime is implausible. Neither are methodological substitutes such as instrumental variables likely to work very well, as Sampson, Laub, and Wimer (2006) have noted: "In practice, however, finding plausible instruments that can pass the necessary identifying restrictions has proven very difficult. . . . We are not aware of any plausible instrument for identifying causal effect of marriage on crime in the literature to date" (p. 473).

We recognize that the criticism we have laid against these sophisticated studies may seem unreasonable to scholars accustomed to evaluating causal hypotheses with observational data. If it is implausible to conduct randomized experiments and unrealistic to identify valid instrumental variables, why should we not pursue the next-best approach? We believe that research interested in the real thing should not settle for an imitation. If the true interest is the causal effect of marriage on crime, these methodological realities should not be ignored. We should not relax our criteria of causality simply because our data do not allow demonstration of causal effects.

It is possible to learn about causal mechanisms without estimating causal effects (Berk et al. 2015), but we should avoid overstating our conclusions. Instead, we should be clear on what we can and what we cannot learn from the data. We believe that one source of confusion about causal effects in the social sciences is the pervasive use of words such as "effect" and "impact" when these are not warranted by the data and methods used. In most cases, authors are quite aware of the limitations but use these terms as loose alternatives to "coefficient" and "association." By being more precise and explicit, one could avoid some of this confusion.

B. Time Order: Does Desistance Happen Before or After Marriage?

On a more optimistic note, a direct test of causality is not the only way to evaluate causal claims empirically. According to one classic definition, causality is a function of three components: the presence of an association, the absence of spuriousness (confounders), and correct time order. Much of the discussion thus far has been concerned with evidence of the (negative) association between marriage and crime and methods of eliminating spuriousness (selection effect). We now turn to the third component, namely, the timing issue, which has been largely ignored in this literature. In order for marriage to qualify as a causal factor in desistance, reductions in offending should occur after marriage, not before. If desistance occurs before marriage, marriage should be understood either as a consequence of desistance or as a downstream effect of whatever is causing desistance, such as cognitive transformation or maturation (see fig. 2). The majority of studies compare average offending rates in each state, but this approach does not capture changes occurring within each state.

A widely cited study by Laub, Nagin, and Sampson (1998) addressed the timing issue with the Glueck data up to age 32. In the first analytic step, they estimated group-based trajectories (Nagin and Land 1993) for the entire observational period from age 7 to 32 and then assigned each person to a group on the basis of posterior probabilities. In the second stage, they regressed the number of arrests in each 2-year interval from age 17 to 32 on changes in marital status and quality, controlling for group membership and other characteristics. In addition, they conducted separate regression analyses by trajectory group membership. The results showed that, among those whose unions progressed into "good marriages" (measured at the last wave), arrest rates were stable during the courtship period (the two periods preceding marriage), followed by a gradual decline in offending during the state of marriage. They found no evidence of a courtship effect and thus concluded that good marriages reduce crime gradually after marriage. We are somewhat hesitant to endorse this conclusion for methodological reasons. Because the trajectories were estimated over the entire period—including the marital period—controlling for group membership implies controlling for postmarriage offending outcomes as well. We expect this aspect of the analytic strategy to bias the results, but further efforts are needed to assess the substantive implications of this methodological approach.

Duncan, Wilkerson, and England (2006) used a fine methodological approach to examine the timing of change in substance misuse with respect to marriage. Focusing on only those who got married, they used data covering 5 years before and 5 years after the year of marriage, thus creating a panel structure with 11 observations per person. Using a piecewise linear spline, they separated the changes in the premarriage period, around the time of marriage, and the period following the transition to marriage. They found a pattern that resembles the "hook for change" trajectory described in figure 2: a slight declining trend during the premarriage period followed by accelerated decline during the period of marriage.

While Duncan, Wilkerson, and England (2006) used piecewise splines, Lyngstad and Skardhamar (2013) used a similar approach to estimate parameters for single-year dummy variables—one for each time point. The main advantage of this approach is that it avoids imposing parametric restrictions (e.g., linearity) on the curve, permitting a more accurate analysis of the timing of change in offending relative to the timing of marriage. (As a potential downside for most data sets, this method requires a large number of data points.) The results showed that the decline in offending began long before the transition to marriage, and the period after marriage was associated with an increase (a "rebound") in offending rather than further declines. This pattern contradicts the expected marriage effect. Lyngstad and Skardhamar acknowledge that romantic bonding, including cohabitation, preceding the marital transition may be responsible for some of this pattern.

Finally, there are two Dutch studies that provide information about the timing of change as a by-product of the main analysis. McGloin et al. (2011) employed a set of dummies representing each year before and after marriage, with nonmarried as the reference category. The marriage coefficients changed from −.01 2 years before marriage to −.02 at the time of marriage and the year after and then back to −.01 the second year after marriage. Each of these effects is significant with respect to the reference category, but the authors do not report whether these coefficients were different from each other, that is, if the changes in the marriage effects were significant. The study by Beijers, Bijleveld, and van Poppel (2012), which found evidence of historical contingency in the marriage effect, includes a descriptive trend chart showing levels of criminal offending in the 10 years preceding and following the year of marriage (fig. 3, p. 435). In this study the negative association between marriage and crime is limited to those born after 1970; there was no significant association among the older cohorts. Focusing on those born after 1970, it is clear that offending started to decline sharply about 3 years before the year of marriage. The overall level of crime continues to drop following marriage, but at a slower rate with occasional periods of increase.

In conclusion, the evidence on timing of desistance relative to marriage is addressed by only a handful of publications. Although the results are mixed, and to some extent difficult to compare because of methodological variation, the evidence suggests that marriage is more likely to occur as a consequence of desistance in northern Europe. The results from American studies are mixed. The most certain conclusion one can draw is that there is no clear evidence showing time order consistent with the turning point hypothesis as described in figure 2. The available evidence is more consistent with the maturation or hook for change perspectives.

C. Evidence on Causal Mechanisms

Theories of the marriage effect assume specific causal mechanisms, such as informal social control, to produce the effect. In this section, we evaluate the empirical evidence pertaining to the mechanisms or processes suggested by theories of the marriage effect.

Laub and Sampson's account involves a number of theoretical mechanisms. The primary process of influence is social control through stakes in conformity. Attachment to the spouse is expected to restrain crime-prone individuals from offending. In addition, romantic partners have the capacity to serve as effective monitors and guardians. In relation to these processes, marriage is expected to change routine activities in ways that increase time spent in prosocial settings and reduce time spent with antisocial peers. These environmental effects are expected to facilitate psychological change in self-concept to a point at which personal identity becomes inconsistent with criminal behavior. Finally, Laub and Sampson (2003, p. 137) observe that some of the men in their sample gained concrete economic benefits by marrying women with some wealth and income or women from families that were able to offer financial security.

In this section we discuss direct empirical evidence pertaining to these mechanisms. We focus on research that has attempted to measure one or more of the processes explicated in the theoretical model.

1. *Marital Quality and Spousal Attachment.* Sampson and Laub's key argument is that marriage assists in desistance because of the social bonds it creates. Accordingly, we should expect the marriage effect to materialize in the presence of strong attachment. Despite this clear assumption, many studies ignore the quality of marriage, probably because the data do not permit appropriate measures. We found 17 publications that feature direct measures of attachment to a spouse or a romantic partner. The operationalization of this concept varies from psychological indicators of attachment to the mere length of marriage. The most prominent support for the bonding process is documented in research testing Sampson and Laub's age-graded theory of informal social control (Sampson and Laub 1990, 1993; Laub, Nagin, and Sampson 1998; Laub and Sampson 2003). All these studies find evidence that marital attachment is negatively related to criminal offending. This pattern has been replicated in other studies (Massoglia and Uggen 2007; Capaldi, Kim, and Owen 2008; Herrera, Wiersma, and Cleveland 2011).

Some studies have found mixed support for the hypothesized association. For example, marital attachment may be important for some types of offending or only for males (or females) (Simons et al. 2002; Oudekerk, Burgers, and Reppucci 2014). Other studies have failed to find any evidence in support of the attachment/bonding process (Giordano, Cernkovich, and Rudolph 2002; Schroeder, Giordano, and Cernkovich 2007; Simons and Barr 2012). It has been observed that if the romantic partner is antisocial, that is, does not disapprove of a criminal lifestyle, attachment, however strong, is unlikely to assist in desistance (Giordano, Cernkovich, and Holland 2003). We would add that a measure of relationship quality (stability, warmth, attachment) may be related to the individual characteristics of the partner. For example, unions with an antisocial partner should be more "stormy" than unions with a prosocial partner. It is possible that the evidence consistent with the marital quality hypothesis reflects the normative orientation of the romantic partner.

A number of studies find marriage to be associated with desistance without paying attention to the quality of the union. Among the 41 studies with no measures of marriage quality, 31 found marriage to be associated with desistance for at least one outcome measure. In sum, there is some evidence that "good marriages" are associated with reduced offending, but there is also ample evidence from studies that ignore the qualitative aspects of the relationships. Perhaps most marriages are so "good" (or good enough) that the average association tends to be statistically significant.

2. *Direct Social Control by Spouse.* Although the idea that a prosocial spouse may act as a guardian of crime-prone adults is frequently discussed, we were unable to find a single study testing this hypothesis using direct measures of relevant behavior. One way spouses may exert social control is by limiting time spent with peers and by modifying routine activities. However, as these are not direct measures of spousal control, we discuss evidence on routines and peer association in a separate section below.

The idea of spousal control is based on an assumption that the spouse disapproves of antisocial behavior. Owing to assortative mating by antisocial behavior (Krueger et al. 1998), this assumption is questionable. If crime-prone men are likely to marry antisocial women, the processes of social control are less likely to emerge (Knight 2011; van Schellen, Poortman, and Nieuwbeerta 2012). As a special case of the peer effect, antisocial partners may even encourage or at least enable criminal behavior. A broader review of research on romantic relationships and problem behaviors suggests that the nature of the influence depends on the characteristics of the romantic partner (Rhule-Louie and McMahon 2007, p. 91).

We found 13 studies attending to the criminality of the partner. The majority support the assumption that having an antisocial partner promotes rather than curbs antisocial behavior (Simons et al. 2002; Schroeder, Giordano, and Cernkovich 2007; Herrera, Wiersma, and Cleveland 2011; Simons and Barr 2012; Monahan, Dmitrieva, and Cauffman 2014; Oudekerk, Burgers, and Reppucci 2014). Maume, Ousey, and Beaver (2005) and Sampson, Laub, and Wimer (2006) found that the restraining effect of marriage was attenuated but remained statistically significant, controlling for spousal criminality. Farrington and West (1995, p. 275) found that reductions in crime were similar among men who married women with and without a criminal record, noting the caveat that there were very few convicted wives. Although individuals who marry someone with a criminal record tend to be more criminal themselves, Skardhamar, Monsbakken, and Lyngstad (2014) found more substantial declines in offending among those individuals compared with those who married a noncriminal. Leverentz (2006) observed that deviant couples may provide support for each other if both are oriented toward desistance.

3. *Acquiring Social Capital through Spouse and Extended Family.* Laub and Sampson (2003) report that the partnership helped the men in their sample "in organizing and managing their affairs as adults" and that marrying a socioeconomically stable partner generated "many concrete benefits such as housing, employment, and other material goods" (p. 137). Outside the qualitative observations from the Glueck men, we did not find any other studies that systematically investigated these processes.

4. *Routine Activities and Peer Associations.* We found six studies focusing on peer associations and routine activities as potential mediators. In a seminal article, Warr (1998) presented differential association mechanisms as an alternative to the social bonding account of the marriage effect. He found support for the hypothesis that changes in time spent with peers were responsible for reduced offending associated with marriage. Similarly, Simons et al. (2002) found that having a prosocial romantic partner was unrelated to adult crime once associating with deviant peers was held constant—regardless of the quality of romantic bonding. However, using the same data source as Warr (1998), Maume, Ousey, and Beaver (2005) found that changes in peer association explained very little of the strong negative association between marital attachment and crime. Similar conclusions were reached in two additional studies using different data sets (Capaldi, Kim, and Owen 2008; Simons and Barr 2012).

Differential association theory is sometimes presented as a competing explanation to social control theory, but we do not think they should be treated as inconsistent. Changes in peer context may be a direct result of social bonding with the spouse (spending more time with her or him limits time spent with peers), or it may reflect deliberate acts of social control by the spouse (he or she demands that less time be spent with peers).

Either way, showing that peer associations mediate the marriage effect is not inconsistent with the social bonding process.

5. *Changes in Identity or Cognitions.* Quantitative research on desistance features few attempts to capture changes in motivations, identity, and other subjective states. These processes have mostly been studied in qualitative research. Some of these studies extend to the realm of marriage (Giordano, Cernkovich, and Rudolph 2002; Giordano, Cernkovich, and Holland 2003; Laub and Sampson 2003; Godfrey, Cox, and Farrall 2007).

Laub and Sampson's qualitative analysis of life history narratives includes an example in which the respondent "took his marital responsibilities very seriously" (2003, p. 121) and another one in which "marriage was part of 'being a man' that required becoming 'serious and responsible'" (p. 134). The men engaged in forging a new identity as "a family man, hard worker, and good provider" (p. 146). It is difficult to ascertain whether such changes in identity follow from marriage (or other relationships) or whether marriage is merely a downstream effect of a process that started earlier. Giordano and colleagues (Giordano, Cernkovich, and Rudolph 2002; Giordano, Cernkovich, and Holland 2003; Giordano et al. 2011) suggest that marriage to a prosocial spouse is an expression of a willful effort to change. More in line with Laub and Sampson, Simons and Barr (2012) in a quantitative study found changes in "criminogenic knowledge structure" to mediate the longitudinal association between romantic bonding and desistance.

V. Conclusion

Understanding desistance from crime has been a focal concern of criminological inquiry in the past 20 years. Sampson and Laub (1993) offer arguably the most influential perspective in this literature. The effect of marriage on desistance is their most celebrated finding. Given the appeal of the marriage effect in the criminological literature, our aim is to provide a critical appraisal of the relevant research. We identified 58 studies addressing the longitudinal association between marriage (and other adult romantic partnerships) and criminal or delinquent offending. A descriptive survey of results sustains the widely held view that levels of offending tend to be lower among those who are married. The association is stronger and more consistent across studies that attend to the influence of marital quality (attachment or stability). Importantly, this also holds for other romantic relationships, such as cohabitation. The direction of the association depends on the objective characteristics of the partner. Involvement with an antisocial partner is unlikely to promote desistance.

These findings are consistent with predictions from the age-graded theory that a "good" marriage can serve as a turning point in the criminal trajectory (Sampson and Laub 1993; Laub and Sampson 2003). However, the observed patterns are equally consistent with a number of alternative explanations, such as the theory of cognitive transformation (Giordano, Cernkovich, and Rudolph 2002). Importantly, limited to comparisons of average offending rates between married and unmarried individuals (or states of marriage as is the case in models of intra-individual change), these findings are also consistent with noncausal explanations, such as the maturation perspective. In other words, the existing evidence base is unable to rule out the possibility that desistance "triggers" marriage rather than vice versa. We think it realistic to treat sustained desistance as a precondition for entering stable marriage with a prosocial partner, and we encourage future research to continue to investigate the timing issue more closely. One major conclusion we draw is that the literature has failed to establish the correct time order in the longitudinal association between marriage and crime.

Efforts to isolate causality from selection processes have received growing attention across the social sciences over the last decade or so. In the evaluative part of this essay, we concluded that there is no direct evidence of a counterfactual causal effect of marriage on crime. This is not surprising given the difficulty of establishing such effects with observational data (Morgan and Winship 2007). We believe that the literature on marriage and crime has a lot to gain from quasi-experimental methodologies, such as instrumental variable estimation, that take a more strict perspective on causality (e.g., Bushway and Apel 2010). An example of a study exploiting quasi-random variation is provided by a recent aggregate-level study from China in which variation in sex ratios was used as an instrument for the proportion of men who will never get married (Edlund et al. 2013). However, we agree with Sampson, Laub, and Wimer (2006, p. 471), who think it is very difficult to find credible instruments for marriage, especially at the individual level of analysis.

Research using nonexperimental (i.e., observational) data should focus on more productive ways to examine the proposed hypotheses. The research on timing is illustrative. Those studies are purely descriptive in the sense that they do not estimate the "effect" of marriage on crime but evaluate the plausibility of the conjecture that marriage causes desistance. Timing of change is a critical component of this conjecture. Descriptive evidence like this should not be underappreciated as it provides valuable insights into the processes of interest (Berk 2010). If it can be established that stable and "good" marriages rarely occur until after a period of sustained desistance, there is little reason to invest in research on the unlikely "marriage effect."

Another productive area is for observational research to focus on the mechanisms thought responsible for the marriage effect. Many more studies address potential mediators (and, to a lesser extent, moderators) of the association between marriage and crime than investigate timing. However, this literature could be more comprehensive and systematic. It could cover mechanisms that have received limited attention so far. For example, there are no quantitative studies of desistance that describe the dynamics of social control by spouses. Given how frequently this process is invoked in the theoretical literature, we should know more about whether the wives of crime-prone men actually behave as agents of social control. This argument is plausible only if the wife disapproves of crime and is willing and able to monitor and punish such behavior. If the evidence shows that these conditions are present, the mechanisms articulated in theory would appear more plausible. Additionally, we should know how crime-prone men respond to their wives' efforts to control their behavior: does it work or does it perhaps create conflict and thereby increase crime in the form of domestic violence? Our general suggestion is to investigate the conditions under which marriage is expected to have an effect. To make this more systematic, we favor increased use of the tools of mechanism-oriented social research—sometimes referred to as analytical sociology (Hedström 2005; Manzo 2010).

Our final point concerns changes in union formation in Western societies. The trend toward increased cohabitation is well known, although it remains poorly incorporated in the criminological literature. It is important to understand that the term cohabitation covers a diverse class of unions. Some cohabiting couples are comparable to married couples in terms of commitment, duration, and even the presence of children. Stable "marriage-like" cohabitation is particularly common in the Nordic countries, but it is becoming more prevalent elsewhere.

Other cohabiting unions are more casual and short-lived. Romantic relationships are often more similar to (serious) dating than to marriage. These include situations in which a couple share a rental apartment partly because it is economically sensible. It is difficult to interpret the effects of cohabitation versus marriage given the amount of heterogeneity in the former category.

It has become increasingly common for adults to have multiple cohabiting relationships before marrying. It is typical for married couples to have cohabited for a while before getting married. Thus, cohabiting is in many cases a stepping-stone toward marriage. It is accordingly less and less plausible to expect marriage, that is, the formal act of "tying the knot," to emerge as a life event of major influence. Future research would benefit from redirecting attention from marriage per se to the sequences of union formation as they occur in the population. There is more reason than ever to treat marriage as a developmental outcome than as a behavioral turning point.

REFERENCES

Andersen, Lars Højsgaard, Signe Hald Andersen, and Peer Skov. 2010. "Partners in Crime? On the Causal Effect of Marrying a Delinquent vs. a Law-Abiding Spouse." In *International Sociological Association World Congress*. Gothenburg, Sweden: International Sociological Association.

Angrist, Joshua D., and Jörn-Steffen Pischke. 2009. *Mostly Harmless Econometrics: An Empiricist's Companion*. Princeton, NJ: Princeton University Press.

Barnes, J. C., and Kevin M. Beaver. 2012. "Marriage and Desistance from Crime: A Consideration of Gene-Environment Correlation." *Journal of Marriage and Family* 74:19–33.

Barnes, J. C., K. Golden, C. Mancini, B. B. Boutwell, K. Beaver, and B. Diamond. 2014. "Marriage and Involvement in Crime: A Consideration of Reciprocal Effects in a Nationally Representative Sample." *Justice Quarterly* 31(2):229–56.

Beaver, K. M., J. P. Wright, M. DeLisi, and M. G. Vaughn. 2008. "Desistance from Delinquency: The Marriage Effect Revisited and Extended." *Social Science Research* 37:736–52.

Beijers, Joris, Catrien Bijleveld, and Frans van Poppel. 2012. "Man's Best Possession: Period Effects in the Association between Marriage and Offending." *European Journal of Criminology* 9(4):425–41.

Berk, Richard A. 2010. "What You Can and Can't Properly Do with Regression." *Journal of Quantitative Criminology* 27(4):481–87.

Berk, Richard A., Lawrence Brown, Edward George, Emil Pitkin, Mikhail Traskin, Kai Zhang, and Linda Zhao. 2015. "What You Can Learn from Wrong Causal Models." In *Handbook of Causal Analysis for Social Research*, edited by Stephen L. Morgan. New York: Springer.

Bersani, Bianca E., and Stephanie M. DiPietro. 2013. *An Examination of the "Marriage Effect" on Desistance from Crime among US Immigrants*. Washington, DC: National Institute of Justice.

———. 2014. "Examining the Salience of Marriage to Offending for Black and Hispanic Men." *Justice Quarterly* 31(2):1–28.

Bersani, Bianca E., and Elaine Eggleston Doherty. 2013. "When the Ties That Bind Unwind: Examining the Enduring and Situational Processes of Change behind the Marriage Effect." *Criminology* 51(2):399–433.

Bersani, Bianca E., John H. Laub, and Paul Nieuwbeerta. 2009. "Marriage and Desistance from Crime in the Netherlands: Do Gender and Socio-historical Context Matter?" *Journal of Quantitative Criminology* 25(1):3–24.

Bersani, Bianca E., and Marieke van Schellen. 2014. "The Effectiveness of Marriage as an 'Intervention' in the Life Course: Evidence from the Netherlands." In *Effective Interventions in the Lives of Criminal Offenders*, edited by J. A. Humphrey and P. Cordella. New York: Springer.

Birkelund, Gunn Elisabeth, and Johan Heldal. 2003. "Who Marries Whom? Educational Homogamy in Norway." *Demographic Research* 8(1):1–30.

Bjerk, David. 2009. "How Much Can We Trust Causal Interpretations of Fixed-Effects Estimators in the Context of Criminality?" *Journal of Quantitative Criminology* 25(4):391–417.

Blokland, A. A. J., and Paul Nieuwbeerta. 2005. "The Effects of Life Circumstances on Longitudinal Trajectories of Offending." *Criminology* 43(4):1203–40.

Blumstein, Alfred, Jacqueline Cohen, and David P. Farrington. 1988. "Criminal Career Research: Its Value for Criminology." *Criminology* 26(1):1–35.

Broidy, Lisa M., and Elizabeth E. Cauffman. 2006. *Understanding the Female Offender*. Report Award no. 2001-IJ-CX-0034. Washington, DC: US Department of Justice.

Burt, Alexandra S., Brent Donnellan, Mikhila N. Humbad, Brian M. Hicks, Matt McGue, and William G. Iacono. 2010. "Does Marriage Inhibit Antisocial Behavior? An Examination of Selection vs Causation via a Longitudinal Twin Design." *Archives of General Psychiatry* 67(12):1309–15.

Bushway, Shawn D., and Robert J. Apel. 2010. "Instrumental Variables in Criminology and Criminal Justice." In *Handbook of Quantitative Criminology*, edited by Alex Piquero and David Weisburd. New York: Springer.

———. 2012. "A Signaling Perspective on Employment-Based Reentry Programming." *Criminology and Public Policy* 11(1):21–50.

Capaldi, Deborah M., Hyoun K. Kim, and Lee D. Owen. 2008. "Romantic Partners' Influence on Men's Likelihood of Arrest in Early Adulthood." *Criminology* 46(2):267–99.

Caspi, A., D. J. Bem, and Glen H. Elder. 1989. "Continuities and Consequences of Interactional Styles across the Life Course." *Journal of Personality* 57(2):375–403.

Craig, Jessica M. 2015. "The Effects of Marriage and Parenthood on Offending Levels over Time among Juvenile Offenders across Race and Ethnicity." *Journal of Crime and Justice* 38(2):163–82.

Craig, Jessica M., Brie Diamond, and Alex R. Piquero. 2014. "Marriage as an Intervention in the Lives of Criminal Offenders." In *Effective Interventions in the Lives of Criminal Offenders*, edited by J. A. Humphrey and P. Cordella. New York: Springer.

Craig, Jessica M., and Holly Foster. 2013. "Desistance in the Transition to Adulthood: The Roles of Marriage, Military, and Gender." *Deviant Behavior* 34(3):208–23.

Diamond, Alexis, and Jasjeet S. Sekhon. 2013. "Genetic Matching for Estimating Causal Effects: A General Multivariate Matching Method for Achieving Balance in Observational Studies." *Review of Economics and Statistics* 95(3):932–45.

Doherty, Elaine Eggleston, and Margaret E. Ensminger. 2013. "Marriage and Offending among a Cohort of Disadvantaged African Americans." *Journal of Research in Crime and Delinquency* 50:104–31.

Duncan, Greg J., Bessie Wilkerson, and Paula England. 2006. "Cleaning Up Their Act: The Effect of Marriage and Cohabitation on Licit and Illicit Drug Use." *Demography* 43(4):691–710.

Edlund, Lena, Hongbin Li, Junjian Yi, and Junsen Zhang. 2013. "Sex Ratios and Crime: Evidence from China." *Review of Economics and Statistics* 95(5):1520–34.

Farrington, David P. 1989. "Later Life Outcomes of Offenders and Nonoffenders." In *Children at Risk: Assessment, Longitudinal Research and Intervention*, edited by M. Brambring, F. Losel, and H. Skowronek. New York: de Gruyter.

Farrington, David P., and Donald J. West. 1995. "Effects of Marriage, Separation, and Children on Offending by Adult Status." In *Delinquency and Disrepute in the Life Course*, edited by Z. S. Blau and J. Hagan. Greenwich, CT: JAI.

Forrest, Walter, and Carter Hay. 2011. "Life-Course Transitions, Self-Control and Desistance from Crime." *Criminology and Criminal Justice* 11(5):487–512.

Gibbens, T. C. N. 1984. "Borstal Boys after 25 Years." *British Journal of Criminology* 24(1): 49–62.

Giordano, Peggy C., Stephen A. Cernkovich, and Donna D. Holland. 2003. "Changes in Friendship Relations over the Life Course: Implications for Desistance from Crime." *Criminology* 41(2):293–337.

Giordano, Peggy C., Stephen A. Cernkovich, and J. L. Rudolph. 2002. "Gender, Crime, and Desistance: Toward a Theory of Cognitive Transformation." *American Journal of Sociology* 107(4):990–1064.

Giordano, Peggy C., P. M. Seffrin, W. D. Manning, and M. A. Longmore. 2011. "Parenthood and Crime: The Role of Wantedness, Relationships with Partners, and SES." *Journal of Criminal Justice* 39(5):405–16.

Glueck, Sheldon, and Eleanor Glueck. 1940. *Juvenile Delinquents Grown Up*. New York: Commonwealth Fund.

Godfrey, Barry S., David J. Cox, and Stephen D. Farrall. 2007. *Criminal Lives, Family Life, Employment and Offending*. New York: Oxford University Press.

Gottfredson, Michael R., and Travis Hirschi. 1987. "The Methodological Adequacy of Longitudinal Research on Crime." *Criminology* 25(3):581–614.

Greenberg, David F. 1991. "Modeling Criminal Careers." *Criminology* 29(1):17–46.

Heckman, James J., and Rodrigo Pinto. 2013. "Econometric Mediation Analysis: Identifying the Sources of Treatment Effects from Experimentally Estimated Production Technologies with Unmeasured and Mismeasured Inputs."

NBER Working Paper no. 19314. Cambridge, MA: National Bureau of Economic Research.

Hedström, Peter. 2005. *Dissecting the Social.* Cambridge: Cambridge University Press.

Herrera, Veronica M., Jacquelyn D. Wiersma, and H. Harrington Cleveland. 2011. "Romantic Partners' Contribution to the Continuity of Male and Female Delinquent and Violent Behavior." *Journal of Research on Adolescence* 21 (3):608–18.

Hirschi, Travis. 1969. *Causes of Delinquency.* Berkeley: University of California Press.

Hirschi, Travis, and Michael Gottfredson. 1983. "Age and the Explanation of Crime." *American Journal of Sociology* 89(3):552–84.

Horney, Julie, D. Wayne Osgood, and Ineke Haen Marshall. 1995. "Criminal Careers in the Short-Term: Intra-individual Variability in Crime and Its Relation to Local Life Circumstances." *American Sociological Review* 60(5): 655–73.

Imai, Kosuke, Gary King, and Elizabeth A. Stuart. 2008. "Misunderstandings between Experimentalists and Observationalists about Causal Inference." *Journal of the Royal Statistical Society*, series A, 171(2):481–502.

Imai, Kosuke, and Marc Ratkovic. Forthcoming. "Robust Estimation of Inverse Probability Weights for Marginal Structural Models." *Journal of the American Statistical Association.*

Jaffee, Sara R., Caitlin McPherran Lombardi, and Rebekah Levine Coley. 2013. "Using Complementary Methods to Test Whether Marriage Limits Men's Antisocial Behavior." *Development and Psychopathology* 25:65–77.

Kerr, David C. R., Deborah M. Capaldi, Lee D. Owen, Margit Wiesner, and Katherine C. Pears. 2011. "Changes in At-Risk American Men's Crime and Substance Use Trajectories Following Fatherhood." *Journal of Marriage and Family* 73:1101–16.

King, Ryan D., Michael Massoglia, and Ross Macmillan. 2007. "The Context of Marriage and Crime: Gender, the Propensity to Marry, and Offending in Early Adulthood." *Criminology* 45(1):33–65.

Knight, Kelly E. 2011. "Assortative Mating and Partner Influence on Antisocial Behavior across the Life Course." *Journal of Family Theory and Review* 3(3):198–219.

Kreager, Derek A., Ross L. Matsueda, and Elena A. Erosheva. 2010. "Motherhood and Criminal Desistance in Disadvantaged Neighborhoods." *Criminology* 48(1):221–58.

Krueger, Robert F., Terrie E. Moffitt, Avshalom Caspi, April Bleske, and Phil A. Silva. 1998. "Assortative Mating for Antisocial Behavior: Developmental and Methodological Implications." *Behavior Genetics* 28(3):173–86.

Kruttschnitt, Candace, Christopher Uggen, and Kelly Shelton. 2000. "Predictors of Desistance among Sex Offenders: The Interaction of Formal and Informal Social Controls." *Justice Quarterly* 17(1):61–87.

Laub, John H., Daniel S. Nagin, and Robert J. Sampson. 1998. "Trajectories of Change in Criminal Offending: Good Marriages and the Desistance Process." *American Sociological Review* 63(2):225–39.

Laub, John H., and Robert J. Sampson. 2003. *Shared Beginnings, Divergent Lives: Delinquent Boys to Age 70*. Cambridge, MA: Harvard University Press.

LeBel, Thomas P., Ros Burnett, Shadd Maruna, and Shawn Bushway. 2008. "The 'Chicken and Egg' of Subjective and Social Factors in Desistance from Crime." *European Journal of Criminology* 5(2):131–59.

Leverentz, Andrea M. 2006. "The Love of a Good Man? Romantic Relationships as a Source of Support or Hindrance for Female Ex-Offenders." *Journal of Research in Crime and Delinquency* 43(4):459–88.

Lyngstad, Torkild Hovde, and Torbjørn Skardhamar. 2011. "Nordic Register Data and Their Untapped Potential for Criminological Knowledge." In *Crime and Justice in Scandinavia*, edited by Michael Tonry and Tappio Lappi-Seppälä. Vol. 40 of *Crime and Justice: A Review of Research*, edited by Michael Tonry. Chicago: University of Chicago Press.

———. 2013. "Changes in Criminal Offending around the Time of Marriage." *Journal of Research in Crime and Delinquency* 50(4):608–15.

Manzo, G. 2010. "Analytical Sociology and Its Critics." *European Journal of Sociology* 51(1):129–70.

Maruna, Shadd. 2001. *Making Good: How Ex-Convicts Reform and Rebuild Their Lives*. Washington, DC: American Psychological Association.

Massoglia, Michael, and Christopher Uggen. 2007. "Subjective Desistance and Transition to Adulthood." *Journal of Contemporary Criminal Justice* 23:90–103.

———. 2010. "Settling Down and Aging Out: Toward an Interactionist Theory of Desistance and the Transition to Adulthood." *American Journal of Sociology* 116(2):543–82.

Maume, Michael O., Graham C. Ousey, and Kevin Beaver. 2005. "Cutting the Grass: A Reexamination of the Link between Marital Attachment, Delinquent Peers and Desistance from Marijuana Use." *Journal of Quantitative Criminology* 21(1):27–53.

McGloin, Jean Marie, Christopher J. Sullivan, Alex R. Piquero, Arjan Blokland, and Paul Nieuwbeerta. 2011. "Marriage and Offending Specialization: Expanding the Impact of Turning Points and the Process of Desistance." *European Journal of Criminology* 8(5):361–76.

McGloin, Jean Marie, Christopher J. Sullivan, Alex R. Piquero, and Travis C. Pratt. 2007. "Local Life Circumstances and Offending Specialization/Versatility Comparing Opportunity and Propensity Models." *Journal of Research in Crime and Delinquency* 44(3):321–46.

Mercer, Natalie, Maria Vasilica Zoutewelle-Terovan, and Victor van der Geest. 2013. "Marriage and Transitions between Types of Serious Offending for High-Risk Men and Women." *European Journal of Criminology* 10(5):534–54.

Monahan, Kathryn C., Julia Dmitrieva, and Elizabeth E. Cauffman. 2014. "Bad Romance: Sex Differences in the Longitudinal Association between Romantic Relationships and Deviant Behavior." *Journal of Research on Adolescence* 24(1):12–26.

Morgan, Stephen L., and Christopher Winship. 2007. *Counterfactuals and Causal Inference: Methods and Principles for Social Research*. Analytical Methods for Social Research. New York: Cambridge University Press.

Morizot, Julien, and Marc Le Blanc. 2007. "Behavioral, Self, and Social Control Predictors of Desistance from Crime: A Test of Launch and Contemporaneous Effect Models." *Journal of Contemporary Criminal Justice* 23(1):50–71.

Nagin, Daniel S. 2005. *Group-Based Modeling of Development*. Cambridge, MA: Harvard University Press.

Nagin, Daniel S., and Kenneth C. Land. 1993. "Age, Criminal Careers, and Population Heterogeneity: Specification and Estimation of a Nonparametric, Mixed Poisson Model." *Criminology* 31(3):327–62.

O'Connell, Daniel J. 2003. "Investigating Latent Trait and Life Course Theories as Predictors of Recidivism among an Offender Sample." *Journal of Criminal Justice* 31:455–67.

Oudekerk, Barbara A., Darcy E. Burgers, and N. Dickon Reppucci. 2014. "Romantic Partner Deviance and the Continuity of Violence from Adolescence to Adulthood among Offending Girls." *Journal of Research on Adolescence* 24(1):27–39.

Paternoster, Ray, and Shawn Bushway. 2009. "Desistance and the Feared Self: Toward an Identity Theory of Criminal Desistance." *Journal of Criminal Law and Criminology* 99(4):1103–56.

Petras, Hanno, Paul Nieuwbeerta, and Alex R. Piquero. 2010. "Participation and Frequency during Criminal Careers across the Life Span." *Criminology* 48 (2):607–37.

Piquero, Alex R., John M. MacDonald, and Karen F. Parker. 2002. "Race, Local Life Circumstances and Criminal Activity." *Social Science Quarterly* 83(3): 654–70.

Ragan, Daniel T., and Kevin M. Beaver. 2010. "Chronic Offenders: A Life-Course Analysis of Marijuana Users." *Youth and Society* 42(2):174–98.

Rhule-Louie, Dana M., and Robert J. McMahon. 2007. "Problem Behavior and Romantic Relationships: Assortative Mating, Behavior Contagion, and Desistance." *Clinical Child and Family Psychology Review* 10(1):53–100.

Rosenbaum, Paul R., and Donald B. Rubin. 1985. "Constructing a Control Group Using Multivariate Matched Sampling Methods That Incorporate the Propensity Score." *American Statistician* 39(1):33–38.

Rowe, David R., D. Wayne Osgood, and W. Alan Nicewander. 1990. "A Latent Trait Approach to Unifying Criminal Careers." *Criminology* 28(2):237–70.

Rubin, D. 2005. "Causal Inference Using Potential Outcomes." *Journal of the American Statistical Association* 91(434):444–55.

Salvatore, Christopher, and Travis A. Taniguchi. 2012. "Do Social Bonds Make for Emerging Adults?" *Deviant Behavior* 33(9):738–56.

Sampson, Robert J., and John H. Laub. 1990. "Crime and Deviance over the Life Course: The Salience of Adult Social Bonds." *American Sociological Review* 55:609–27.

———. 1993. *Crime in the Making: Pathways and Turning Points through Life*. Cambridge, MA: Harvard University Press.

Sampson, Robert J., John H. Laub, and Christopher Wimer. 2006. "Does Marriage Reduce Crime? A Counterfactual Approach to Within-Individual Causal Effects." *Criminology* 44(3):465–508.

Savolainen, Jukka. 2009. "Work, Family, and Criminal Desistance: Adult Social Bonds in a Nordic Welfare State." *British Journal of Criminology* 49:285–304.

Schroeder, Ryan D., Peggy C. Giordano, and Stephen A. Cernkovich. 2007. "Drug Use and Desistance Processes." *Criminology* 45(1):191–222.

Shavit, Y., and Arye Rattner. 1988. "Age, Crime, and the Early Life Course." *American Journal of Sociology* 93(6):1457–71.

Siennick, Sonja E., and D. Wayne Osgood. 2008. "A Review of Research on the Impact on Crime of Transitions to Adult Roles." In *The Long View of Crime: A Synthesis of Longitudinal Research*, edited by A. M. Liberman. Washington, DC: Springer.

Siennick, Sonja E., Jeremy Staff, D. Wayne Osgood, John E. Schulenberg, Jerald G. Bachman, and Matthew Van Eseltine. 2014. "Partnership Transitions and Antisocial Behavior in Young Adulthood: A Within-Person, Multi-cohort Analysis." *Journal of Research in Crime and Delinquency* 51(6):735–58.

Simons, Ronald L., and Ashley B. Barr. 2012. "Shifting Perspectives: Cognitive Changes and the Impact of Romantic Relationships on Desistance from Crime." *Justice Quarterly* 29(2):1–29.

Simons, Ronald L., Eric Stewart, Leslie C. Gordon, Rand D. Conger, and Glen H. Elder Jr. 2002. "A Test of Life-Course Explanations for Stability and Change in Antisocal Behavior from Adolescence to Young Adulthood." *Criminology* 40(2):401–34.

Skardhamar, Torbjørn, Christian W. Monsbakken, and Torkild Hovde Lyngstad. 2014. "Crime and the Transition to Marriage: The Role of the Spouse's Criminal Involvement." *British Journal of Criminology* 54(3):411–27.

Skardhamar, Torbjørn, and Jukka Savolainen. 2014. "Changes in Offending around the Time of Job Entry: A Study of Employment and Desistance." *Criminology* 52(2):263–91.

Theobald, Delphine, and David P. Farrington. 2009. "Effects of Getting Married on Offending: Results from a Prospective Longitudinal Survey of Males." *European Journal of Criminology* 6:496–516.

———. 2011. "Why Do the Crime-Reducing Effects of Marriage Vary with Age?" *British Journal of Criminology* 51:136–58.

———. 2013. "The Effects of Marital Breakdown on Offending: Results from a Prospective Longitudinal Survey of Males." *Psychology, Crime, and Law* 19(4): 391–408.

Thompson, Melissa, and Milena Petrovic. 2009. "Gendered Transitions: Within-Person Changes in Employment, Family, and Illicit Drug Use." *Journal of Research in Crime and Delinquency* 46:377–408.

Uggen, Christopher. 2000. "Work as a Turning Point in the Life Course of Criminals: A Duration Model of Age, Employment, and Recidivism." *American Sociological Review* 65:529–46.

Uggen, Christopher, and Candace Kruttschnitt. 1998. "Crime in the Breaking: Gender Differences in Desistance." *Law and Society Review* 32(2):339–66.

Uggen, Christopher, and Sara Wakefield. 2008. "What Have We Learned from Longitudinal Studies of Work and Crime?" In *The Long View of Crime*, edited by A. M. Liberman. New York: Springer.

van Schellen, Marieke, Robert Apel, and Paul Nieuwbeerta. 2012. "Because You're Mine, I Walk the Line? Marriage, Spousal Criminality, and Criminal Offending over the Life Course." *Journal of Quantitative Criminology* 28:701–23.

van Schellen, Marieke, Anne-Rigt Poortman, and Paul Nieuwbeerta. 2012. "Partners in Crime? Criminal Offending, Marriage Formation, and Partner Selection." *Journal of Research in Crime and Delinquency* 49(4):545–71.

Veysey, Bonita M., Damian J. Martines, and Johnna Christian. 2014. "Getting Out: A Summary of Qualitative Research on Desistance across the Life Course." In *Handbook of Life-Course Criminology*, edited by C. L. Gibson and M. D. Krohn. New York: Springer.

Warr, Mark. 1998. "Life-Course Transitions and Desistance from Crime." *Criminology* 36(2):183–216.

West, Donald. 1982. *Delinquency, Its Roots, Careers, and Prospects*. Cambridge, MA: Harvard University Press.

Wright, Kevin N., and Karen E. Wright. 1992. "Does Getting Married Reduce the Likelihood of Criminality? A Review of the Literature." *Federal Probation* 56(3):50–56.

Zoutewelle-Terovan, Maria Vasilica, Victor van der Geest, Catrien Bijleveld, and Aart C. Liefbroer. 2013. "Associations in Criminal Behavior for Married Males and Females at High Risk of Offending." *European Journal of Criminology* 11(3): 340–60.

Zoutewelle-Terovan, Maria Vasilica, Victor van der Geest, Aart C. Liefbroer, and Catrien Bijleveld. 2012. "Criminality and Family Formation: Effects of Marriage and Parenthood on Criminal Behavior for Men and Women." *Crime and Delinquency* 60(8): 1209–34.

Brandon C. Welsh, David P. Farrington, and B. Raffan Gowar

Benefit-Cost Analysis of Crime Prevention Programs

ABSTRACT

The number of high-quality benefit-cost analyses of crime prevention programs has grown from 12 to 23 since 2000, and numerous benefit-cost ratios have been calculated by the Washington State Institute for Public Policy. Benefits are often estimated conservatively, whereas costs are usually estimated in full. Benefits nonetheless exceed costs for most programs, especially for preschool and cognitive-behavioral programs, target hardening and improved lighting, Communities That Care programs, and Business Improvement Districts. However, benefits and costs are not estimated comparably in different studies; few analyses are strongly comparable. There is great need for the establishment and use of a standard list of benefits and costs. Better research designs are needed, especially including randomized controlled trials. It is more cost-beneficial to invest in prevention than in imprisonment. The time is ripe for major investment to improve the lives of disadvantaged children.

The first detailed review of benefit-cost analyses of crime prevention programs was published 15 years ago in *Crime and Justice* (Welsh and Farrington 2000*b*). Benefit-cost studies of crime prevention were then

Electronically published July 30, 2015

Brandon C. Welsh is professor in the School of Criminology and Criminal Justice at Northeastern University and Royal Netherlands Academy of Arts and Sciences Visiting Professor and senior research fellow at the Netherlands Institute for the Study of Crime and Law Enforcement in Amsterdam. David P. Farrington is Emeritus Professor of Psychological Criminology and Leverhulme Trust Emeritus Fellow, and B. Raffan Gowar is a graduate research assistant, both in the Institute of Criminology at Cambridge University. We are grateful to Michael Tonry for especially helpful comments.

0192-3234/2015/0044-0009$10.00

exceedingly rare, an underused research tool. The evidence, however, suggested that monetary benefits usually outweighed monetary costs. This was at least partly because benefit-cost analyses were mainly conducted on effective programs; it was not clear how many analyses were planned prospectively. We found that developmental prevention provided important monetary benefits beyond crimes reduced and that benefits of situational prevention appeared to be confined largely to crime reduction. Two final points concerned methodological issues. One was that benefit-cost analyses needed to be methodologically rigorous and comprehensive in scope. The other was that the value of a benefit-cost analysis (or any type of economic analysis) is limited by the quality of the research design; greater use of experimental and high-quality quasi-experimental designs was needed.

This essay updates that earlier one. Its main aim is to investigate what advances have been made and what challenges still exist. This time we set a higher screening standard of methodological quality; only studies with experimental or high-quality quasi-experimental designs are included. In the earlier essay, we also included less rigorous studies that did not employ control groups and could be categorized as one-group pre-post designs. We lamented this, but the small number of available analyses required it. During the intervening years, there has been considerable interest and growth in research on the economics of crime and crime prevention. Some of our other past works discuss it (e.g., Welsh and Farrington 1999, 2000*a*, 2009*a*, 2009*b*, 2011*a*; Farrington, Petrosino, and Welsh 2001; Welsh 2001, 2003; Welsh, Farrington, and Sherman 2001; Farrington and Welsh 2007). Recent reviews of benefit-cost analyses have been completed by Swaray, Bowles, and Pradiptyo (2005) and McDougall et al. (2008), a recent book was published by Roman, Dunworth, and Marsh (2010), and recent expositions of benefit-cost analysis in criminology were completed by Dossetor (2011) in Australia and McIntosh and Li (2012) in Canada.

We offer several main conclusions, some of which mirror our conclusions 15 years ago. First, despite the considerable interest and growth in the subject, benefit-cost analysis continues to be underused in the study of crime prevention. Only 23 studies meeting our current increased methodological quality criteria were identified: 11 on developmental prevention, eight on situational prevention, and four on community prevention. In addition, many benefit-cost analyses have been carried out by Aos and his colleagues at the Washington State Institute for Public Policy (Lee et al. 2012). This compares with 12 high-quality studies in the earlier essay.[1] We expected to find many more. Second, monetary benefits usually outweigh monetary costs for all three strategies.

Third, developmental prevention and, to a lesser extent, community prevention provide important monetary benefits beyond crimes reduced, while the benefits of situational prevention continue to appear to be confined largely to crime reduction. It is important to investigate to what extent monetary benefits persist over time.

Fourth, benefit-cost analyses need to be comprehensive in their coverage of costs and benefits and conducted as part of the highest-quality research designs to evaluate program effects. There is a great need for a standard list of costs and benefits and for more randomized controlled trials. The strong implication is that better, more complete benefit-cost models would yield even stronger evidence of the comparative benefits of crime prevention measures that take place outside of the criminal justice system. The analyses should be planned in advance as part of evaluations of crime prevention programs; there are a number of advantages of prospective designs.

Fifth, it is high time that economic analysis research, especially benefit-cost analysis, is given even more consideration in the debate on crime prevention versus imprisonment. Washington State is a leading example of the dividends that can accrue for taxpayers, government, and potential crime victims by ensuring that the highest-quality scientific research is at center stage in the policy-making process. We recommend that resources be transferred from imprisonment to crime prevention.

This essay is organized as follows. Section I reports on new developments in economic analysis research. Section II covers key issues in the economic analysis of crime prevention programs, including the main techniques, the methodological framework for conducting economic analyses, and the different measures of economic efficiency. Sections III, IV, and V review, respectively, the monetary costs and benefits of developmental prevention, situational prevention, and community prevention. Each reviews the theoretical bases of the respective strategy, summarizes key features of the studies and the main findings pertaining to monetary costs and benefits, and reviews in detail one important study.

[1] The breakdown then was six on developmental prevention, five on situational prevention, and one on community prevention.

Section VI brings together the main conclusions and identifies gaps in knowledge and priorities for research.

I. New Developments in Economic Analysis Research

In our first *Crime and Justice* essay, we reported that there had been a steady growth of economic analysis of crime prevention. This growth has continued unabated and can be characterized as highly impressive. This has to do not just with the number of studies that have been conducted but also with their methodological rigor. Benefit-cost studies, our focus, are but one of the many approaches that have been used to assess the independent and comparative economic efficiency of different prevention programs and policies. Moreover, economic analyses have continued to focus on the crucial question whether prevention or punishment provides the best economic return for society and have probed issues central to this debate (see Welsh and Farrington 2011*a*).

A. Washington State Institute for Public Policy

Perhaps the most important body of new research in this area is the Washington State Institute for Public Policy's comparative benefit-cost model. We reported on the initial stage of this work in the earlier essay. In 1997, the Washington state legislature commissioned the institute, the nonpartisan research arm of the legislature, to assess the effectiveness and economic efficiency of a range of crime prevention and criminal justice programs with the aim to "identify interventions that reduce crime and lower total costs to taxpayers and crime victims" (Aos, Barnoski, and Lieb 1998, p. 1). The institute developed a comprehensive benefit-cost model along the lines of a "bottom line" financial analysis, which it envisioned to parallel the approach used by investors who study rates of return on financial investments (Drake, Aos, and Miller 2009). This model and its results are highly cited, highly influential, and well regarded in both academic and policy communities (Greenwood and Welsh 2012). Aos et al. (2004) concluded that 37 out of 60 youth prevention programs had benefits that exceeded their costs. There is now a national effort to aid other states to develop similar tools (Aos and Drake 2010; Pew Center on the States 2012). In the United Kingdom, the Youth Justice Board has funded the Dartington Social Research Unit to replicate these analyses for the United Kingdom (see http://investinginchildren.eu/cost-benefit).

The institute's research began with a systematic review of experimental and high-quality quasi-experimental studies, carried out in conjunction with the University of Washington's Social Development Research Group. A five-step analytical model is then used to describe each program's economic contribution. The first step of the model involves estimating each program's effectiveness, and meta-analytic techniques are used. Effect sizes are converted into numbers of crimes saved. Step 2 looks at whether previously measured program results can be replicated in Washington State. Step 3 involves an assessment of program costs, estimated on the basis of what it would cost the Washington state government to implement a similar program (if the program was not already operating in the state). Step 4 involves monetizing each program's effects on crime. Savings to the justice system and crime victims are estimated. The final step involves calculating the economic contribution of the program, which is expressed as a benefit-cost ratio and in net present value. On the basis of this, programs can be judged on their independent and comparative economic efficiency.

What started out as a highly rigorous yet fairly modest policy research initiative soon turned into the most comprehensive approach to develop evidence-based crime policy in the United States (Greenwood 2006). Following the institute's first set of reports, the legislature authorized a number of system-level randomized controlled trials of the most effective and cost-beneficial juvenile and adult intervention programs. The results of these trials helped to refine local practice and service delivery. By 2006, the institute had systematically reviewed and analyzed almost 600 of the highest-quality evaluations of crime prevention and criminal justice programs, estimated the costs and benefits of effective programs, and "projected the degree to which alternative 'portfolios' of these programs could affect future prison construction needs, criminal justice costs, and crime rates in Washington" (Aos, Miller, and Drake 2006, p. 1). This work was commissioned by the legislature to address the projected need for two new state prisons by 2020 and possibly a third by 2030, based on predicted crime rates.

On the basis of a moderate-to-aggressive portfolio of evidence-based programs (i.e., \$63–\$171 million expenditure in the first year), it was found that a significant proportion of future prison construction costs could be avoided—about \$2 billion saved by taxpayers—and crime rates lowered slightly (Aos, Miller, and Drake 2006, p. 16). A year later, the state legislature abandoned plans to build one of the two prisons and in its place approved a sizable spending package ($48 million) on evidence-based crime prevention and intervention programs (Drake, Aos, and Miller 2009). This research showed that other strategies were more effective than prison and would generate substantial financial savings to the state government and taxpayers.

The latest report, by Lee et al. (2012), gives benefit-cost ratios for a number of developmental and community prevention programs. In most cases, these ratios are substantial. For example, in the area of child welfare, the ratio for the Triple P positive parenting program was 6.06, for Parent Child Interaction Therapy it was 4.62, and for the Nurse-Family Partnership program it was 2.37.[2] In the area of children's mental health, the ratio was 7.11 for Cognitive Behavioral Therapy with depressed adolescents, 6.08 for Brief Strategic Family Therapy, 5.63 for Triple P in a group, and 2.53 for Parent Child Interaction Therapy, but it was only 1.14 for Multisystemic Therapy and 1.14 for the Incredible Years Parent and Child Training. In the area of general prevention programs, the ratio was 31.19 for the Good Behavior Game and 2.92 for Guiding Good Choices, but only 1.74 for youth mentoring programs and 0.17 (a loss) for Promoting Alternative Thinking Strategies (PATHS). In the area of education, the ratio was 2.99 for early childhood education, but only 0.22 for early Head Start. Lee et al. (2012) also reviewed juvenile and criminal justice programs but not situational prevention.

B. *Comparing Imprisonment and Early Prevention*

Closely related to the research of the Washington State Institute for Public Policy, a number of new benefit-cost analyses of standard prison and other sentencing alternatives conclude that prisons are not economically efficient (Marsh and Fox 2008; Bierie 2009; see also McDougall et al. 2006). It is only when prisons are reserved for the most serious and violent offenders that their benefits begin to offset their operating costs (Marsh, Fox, and Hedderman 2009).

Other economic analyses have demonstrated the value of early prevention and other alternatives compared to imprisonment. While our previous essay reported on the earlier research, it seems worthwhile to revisit two landmark studies. The first was conducted by Greenwood

[2] Information about all the programs, all the results, and all the calculations can be obtained in Lee et al. (2012); see also http://www.wsipp.wa.gov/benefitcost.

et al. (1996). This study assessed the cost-effectiveness (i.e., serious crimes prevented per $1 million spent, using 1993 dollars) of California's new three-strikes law compared with four prevention and intervention programs with demonstrated efficacy in reducing crime: a combination of home visits and day care, parent training, graduation incentives, and supervising delinquent youth. A mathematical model of "criminal populations in prison and on the street, as affected by criminal career initiation, arrest and sentencing, release, and desistance from criminal activity" was used to compute each program's effects on crime and criminal justice system costs (Greenwood et al. 1996, p. 17).

Parent training and graduation incentives were the most cost-effective of the five programs. The number of serious crimes prevented per $1 million expended was estimated at 258 for graduation incentives, 157 for parent training, 72 for delinquent supervision, 60 for the three-strikes law, and 11 for home visiting/day care.[3] It is important to comment briefly on the poor showing of the home visiting/day care program. The small number of crimes prevented per $1 million is attributable to two key factors (a third is discussed below): first, the long-term delay in achieving an effect on crime and, second, the high cost of delivering the services, particularly the day care component, which was estimated at $6,000 per child per year over 4 years.

Donohue and Siegelman (1998) carried out an equally rigorous thought experiment, which has some similarities to the Washington state institute's comparative benefit-cost model. The authors set out to investigate "whether the social resources that will be expended a decade or more from now on incarcerating today's youngsters could instead generate roughly comparable levels of crime *prevention* if they were spent today on the most promising social programs" (p. 31). These included a range of early prevention programs and a national vocational program, and most of the estimates were based on well-known experiments or quasi-experiments with small to large sample sizes.

On the basis of a 50 percent increase in the US prison population over 15 years, assumed from the level in December 1993 and trends at the time, it was estimated that this policy would cost between $5.6 and $8 billion (in 1993 dollars) and result in a 5–15 percent reduction

[3] Crimes prevented were not calculated on a per annum basis. Instead they represent the predicted total effect produced by each program on each California cohort (an estimated 150,000 at-risk children born in California every year).

in crime. From the selected prevention programs, it was found that comparable reductions in crime could be achieved if they were allocated the upper bound amount that would have been spent on prisons.

Nagin (2001*a*, 2001*b*) reanalyzed these two studies and drew attention to the need to consider the full potential benefits of early prevention programs. By its very nature, developmental crime prevention is designed to improve individual functioning across multiple domains. But Greenwood et al. (1996) and Donohue and Siegelman (1998) only considered the benefits from lower rates of delinquency and criminal activity. Education, employment, family, health, and other important benefits were not taken into account, which had the effect of greatly underestimating the true economic return to society. A more recent benefit-cost analysis by Donohue (2009) embraces this view; he concludes that "there is reason to believe that alternatives to incarceration might well be more socially attractive than our current reliance on incarceration as the predominant crime-fighting strategy" (p. 308).

The potential savings in incarceration costs was the focus of a simulation model, by Ebel et al. (2011), that estimated the extent to which the US homicide rate might be reduced by implementing a number of developmental and community crime prevention programs. They especially focused on the Nurse-Family Partnership program (Eckenrode et al. 2010), the Perry Preschool program (Schweinhart et al. 2005), and Multisystemic Therapy (Sawyer and Borduin 2011). They estimated the effects of these programs on arrests for violence, combined this information with data from the Pittsburgh Youth Study on the probability of an arrest for violence being followed by a homicide conviction, and scaled up to national US homicide figures. The effectiveness of the programs was scaled down by half to allow for attenuation of effects from demonstration projects to national implementation (see Welsh, Sullivan, and Olds 2010).

On the basis of 2002 figures, it was estimated that these three prevention programs, implemented nationally and consecutively, could prevent one-third of all homicides in the United States. The programs might save 4,200 lives and nearly 80,000 years of potential life lost. Furthermore, they might save almost 225,000 person-years of incarceration, accounting for over $5 billion per year savings in incarceration costs.

Recent studies on the costs of crime are also making important contributions to assessing the benefits and costs of early prevention compared to prison. But it is important to note that high crime costs do not in themselves suggest a policy solution.[4] For this we need to carry out an economic analysis, preferably a benefit-cost analysis. What these cost studies do is provide information on the unit costs of crime as well as the order of magnitude of the problem. Cohen and Piquero (2009) estimated that the typical criminal career over the juvenile and adult years costs society between $2.7 and $4.8 million (in 2007 dollars). They also estimated the dollar costs of the associated problem behaviors of heavy drug use and dropping out of high school, bringing the total societal cost of a high-risk youth to $3.2–$5.8 million.

In a follow-on study that looked at the costs of crime across offender trajectories for a real-life cohort in Philadelphia, Cohen, Piquero, and Jennings (2010) found that the 200 high-rate chronic offenders cost society more than $200 million (in 2007 dollars). On the basis of another real-life cohort of 500 Pittsburgh boys, Welsh et al. (2008) conservatively estimated that this group caused a substantial burden of harm to society in the form of victimization costs, ranging from $89 to $110 million (in 2000 dollars). From an early age the cohort was responsible for substantial crime victim losses, with these losses mounting in the adolescent years. Similar results have been obtained in other countries. For example, Raffan Gowar and Farrington (2013) estimated that the 400 males in the Cambridge Study in Delinquent Development cost £6 million in officially recorded offending and £44 million according to self-reported offending over 13 years.

Since the cost of offending is very high, programs do not need to be very effective to save money. For example, if a program cost $1,000 per participant, and 1,000 persons received the program, $1 million would have been spent. On the basis of Cohen and Piquero's (2009) estimates, if only one person were saved from a life of crime, between $3.2 million and $5.8 million would be saved. Therefore, the benefits could outweigh the costs even if the program was only effective with one in 1,000 participants. Of course, most programs are much more effective than this, and some programs cost more than $1,000 per participant. On any reasonable assumptions about program costs in relation to the cost of a life of crime, programs do not need to be very effective.

[4] This point is often lost on critics of these studies, as well as on those who use the cost estimates to advance their partisan political goals.

II. Economic Analysis of Crime Prevention Programs

Economic analysis is a tool that allows choices to be made between alternative uses of resources or alternative distributions of services (Knapp 1997, p. 11). Many criteria are used in economic analyses. The most common is efficiency, which is the focus throughout this essay. Efficiency is about achieving maximum outcomes from minimum inputs. One measurement of efficiency involves "aggregating all the gains and losses from a program in such a way that the net gain from one program can be compared to that of an alternative" (Barnett and Escobar 1987, p. 389). From this, the most economically efficient program can be identified. What cannot be concluded from an economic analysis, however, is the fairness or equity in the distribution of the services available (e.g., Are those individuals or families most in need of the services receiving them?). This decision, as noted by Barnett and Escobar (1990), must be left to the value choices of policy makers.

Discussions of the economic efficiency of crime prevention programs can be very persuasive and have gained wide appeal in political, policy, and, academic settings. In many ways, the interest in attaching dollar values to crime prevention programs can be seen as an outgrowth of the focus on "what works" in preventing crime and is a key component of evidence-based crime policy (Mears 2007, 2010; Welsh and Farrington 2011*b*). Efficiency, performance measures, and targeting resources (among other terms) have become the common currency of crime prevention. However, compared to the number of outcome evaluation studies of crime prevention programs, there is a dearth of economic analysis evaluation studies.

A. Techniques of Economic Analysis

Benefit-cost (or cost-benefit) analysis and cost-effectiveness analysis are the two most widely used techniques of economic analysis. These terms have technical meanings. Barnett and Escobar (1987, 1990) describe cost-effectiveness analysis as an incomplete benefit-cost analysis. The incompleteness in cost-effectiveness analysis is because no attempt is made to estimate the monetary value of effects produced (benefits), only of program resources used (costs). Benefit-cost analysis, by contrast, monetizes both costs and benefits and compares them. Cost-effectiveness analysis does, however, provide a point of comparison between program inputs or costs and outcomes (e.g., *X* dollars produced *Y* crimes prevented), therefore permitting an assessment of which program represents the most desirable investment. Another way to think about how benefit-cost and cost-effectiveness analysis differ is that "cost-effectiveness analysis may help one decide among competing program models, but it cannot show that the total effect was worth the cost of the program" (Weinrott, Jones, and Howard 1982, p. 179), unlike benefit-cost analysis. We use the term "cost-beneficial" to refer to programs whose benefits outweigh their costs.

By way of a simple illustration, a benefit-cost analysis of a Head Start program would first attempt to monetize all program effects on the children and parents (such as reduced crime) and resources used by the program and then divide total monetary benefits by total monetary costs. This gives a "bottom line" statistic that shows whether the effects produced by the program exceed the resources spent on the program. A cost-effectiveness analysis of the same program would first need to be compared to one or more alternative prevention programs (e.g., Head Start without a parent training component), taking into account the need for like-with-like comparisons (Knapp and Netten 1997). For each program, all resources used are monetized and one program effect (such as crime) is selected, so that for each program there are total costs (resources used) and total crimes reduced. By using these similar metrics, a determination of the most cost-effective program can then be made: the program with the lowest cost per crime reduced is the most cost-effective.

Cost analysis also deserves brief mention here because of its wide application to crime prevention programs. In economic terms, cost analysis is not an economic analysis technique; there is no quantified relationship between program costs and effects, as in the case of cost-effectiveness and benefit-cost analysis. Similar to cost-effectiveness analysis, cost analysis assigns monetary values to all program inputs (or resources used) but does not value program outcomes. In the example of the Head Start program, a cost analysis would estimate the monetary value of the total resources used by the program but would not assess the absolute or comparative economic efficiency of the program. Having information on program costs could, nonetheless, be useful to funders and could serve as the basis of a cost-effectiveness analysis once costs are compared with outcomes.[5]

[5] See Knapp, Robertson, and McIvor (1992) for an excellent cost study of alternative criminal justice sanctions in Scotland.

B. Doing an Economic Analysis

An economic analysis is a step-by-step process that follows a standard set of procedures. The six steps are as follows: (i) define the scope of the analysis, (ii) obtain estimates of program effects, (iii) estimate the monetary value of costs and benefits, (iv) calculate present value and assess profitability, (v) describe the distribution of costs and benefits (an assessment of who gains and who loses, e.g., program participants, government/taxpayers, crime victims), and (vi) conduct sensitivity analyses (Barnett 1993, pp. 143–48). It is beyond the scope of this essay to discuss each methodological step, but interested readers should consult the excellent reviews and applications of this methodology in the context of early child intervention programs by Barnett and Escobar (1987, 1990) and Barnett (1993, 1996). In the case of benefit-cost analysis, all of the six steps are carried out; for cost-effectiveness analysis, the estimation of the monetary value of benefits in step iii is omitted, and step v is consequently omitted.

In practical terms, an economic analysis of the efficiency of a program is an extension of an outcome evaluation (Barnett and Escobar 1990) and is only as defensible as the evaluation on which it is based. Weimer and Friedman (1979, p. 264) recommend that benefit-cost analyses be limited to programs that have been evaluated with an "experimental or strong quasi-experimental design." The most convincing method of evaluating crime prevention programs is the randomized experiment (Farrington 1983, 2013; Farrington and Welsh 2005, 2006). The key feature of randomized experiments is that the experimental and control groups are equated before the experimental intervention on all possible extraneous variables (within the limits of statistical fluctuation). Therefore, any subsequent differences between them must be attributable to the intervention.

The randomized experiment, however, is only the most convincing method of evaluation if a sufficiently large number of units are randomly assigned to ensure that the program group is equivalent to the control group on all possible extraneous variables. As a rule of thumb, at least 50 in both categories are needed (Farrington 1997; for a contrasting view, see Gill and Weisburd [2013]). This number is relatively easy to achieve with individuals but very difficult to achieve with larger units such as schools or areas. For larger units, the best and most feasible design usually involves before-and-after measures in experimental and control areas, together with statistical control of extraneous variables.

Nonrandomized experiments and before-after designs without a control group are less convincing methods of evaluating crime prevention programs.

C. Measures of Economic Efficiency

The benefit-cost ratio is an expression of the ratio of monetary benefits to costs and is, ultimately, a measure of economic efficiency. In this essay, we have used the benefit-cost ratio to measure the economic efficiency of programs rather than net value (benefits minus costs) for three principal reasons: it controls for differences in national currencies, it controls for the different time periods of programs (e.g., the benefit-cost ratio of a program that used 1992 US dollars can reasonably be compared with the benefit-cost ratio of a program that used 1996 British pounds), and it provides a single measurement of the benefits of a program that are gained from a one monetary unit of investment or expenditure. Arguments such as for every dollar spent, seven dollars were saved in the long run (Schweinhart, Barnes, and Weikart 1993) have proved to be very powerful. The decision to use the benefit-cost ratio is particularly important because, in many cases, it is a direct measurement of the value that the taxpaying public receives for its investment. It could be argued that expressing the value of publicly funded programs in this understandable form is concordant with the movement by governments toward a greater degree of transparency and accountability.

The "public" (government/taxpayer and crime victim) and "society" (government/taxpayer, crime victim, and program participant) perspectives are most commonly used in the economic analysis of crime prevention programs. The decision about which perspective to take has important implications for evaluating the program, particularly if it is being funded by public money. That is, if conclusions are to be drawn about the monetary value of a program to the public, the benefits and costs must be those that the public will either receive or incur. More important, the perspective that one takes can have important implications for the program's monetary value. For instance, adopting the society perspective for a marginally successful program, and therefore increasing the number of parties to which benefits may accrue, will likely increase the chances that the program will produce a return rather than a loss on investment. However, if the same program is the subject of a benefit-cost analysis that takes only the government or taxpayer perspective, the chances of producing a return rather than a loss on investment will likely decrease. In this essay, we have taken the middle-of-the-road approach, by reporting on, as far as possible, the public (government/taxpayer and crime victim) perspective in calculating benefits and costs. For some of the studies reviewed here, it was not possible to disaggregate the published benefits and costs in accordance with our desired perspective.

D. *Other Key Issues in Economic Analysis*

Although this is not the place for an exhaustive discussion of the technical issues to be addressed in benefit-cost studies, several fundamental issues warrant introduction and brief discussion.

1. *Marginal versus Average Costs.* In the context of program resources used, "marginal costs describe how the total cost of an operation changes as the unit of activity changes by a small amount," while "average costs are derived by simply dividing total costs by total workload in a given period of time" (Aos 1998, p. 13). The main limitation of average costs, as noted by Aos (p. 13), is that "some of those costs . . . are fixed and do not change when workload changes." By using marginal cost estimates for a preschool program, for example, only the direct costs of an additional student (e.g., food, supplies) would be readily taken into account, while a more expensive operating budget item—personnel costs—would be excluded up to the point where the number of additional students required additional staff coverage.

In the context of costs to victims of crime, Cohen (1998, p. 8) notes that using marginal cost estimates excludes "such important costs as fear of crime, private security expenditures, and 'averting' behavior such as taking cabs instead of walking or changing one's lifestyle due to the risk of victimization." These costs are excluded because they are not affected by the actions of any one criminal (p. 8). It would, however, be important to assess these costs if a prevention program operated on a scale large enough (e.g., citywide) to have a potential impact on them. In the majority of the benefit-cost studies reviewed here, and in almost all of the situational crime prevention studies, average costs were used.

2. *Operating versus Capital Costs.* Program resources used (costs) can be divided into two main categories: operating costs (e.g., staff salaries and benefits, overhead) and capital costs (e.g., constructing facilities). Both a detailed description of the program and the resources it used are needed in calculating operating and capital costs. A related issue to capital costs is the borrowing of money to pay for a program. This often

occurs in situational crime prevention programs, which undertake large-scale, capital-intensive projects (e.g., installation of technical hardware, such as closed-circuit television [CCTV] cameras). A key question is how best to account for the payments on the capital expenditure and debt charges on the loan in calculating the costs of the program. In assessing the economic efficiency of a program that lasts for only a short period of time, it might be unreasonable to include the total capital expenditure, which might dwarf any benefits accrued over this time period. The Safe Neighbourhoods Unit (1993, p. 145) recommends spreading the payments and the debt charges over the life expectancy of the program, but not beyond the loan repayment period, and using this "period as the basis for estimating a more realistic annual capital costs figure." This is by no means arbitrary; it is standard practice in benefit-cost analysis. The majority of the studies reviewed here included both operating and capital costs in their benefit-cost calculations; however, few involved or provided information on large-scale capital expenditures.

3. *Present Value.* Present value is concerned with making all monetary costs and benefits of a program comparable over time. The time value of money is best understood as follows: "A dollar today is worth more than a dollar next year because today's dollar can be invested to yield a dollar plus interest next year" (Barnett and Escobar 1987, p. 390). If a program's costs and benefits are confined to 1 year, then the calculation of present value is unnecessary.

Two separate steps must be carried out to adjust for differences in the value of money over time. First, the effect of inflation is removed by "translating nominal dollars from each year into dollars of equal purchasing power, or *real dollars*" (Barnett 1993, p. 146). This is achieved by the application of a price index to the nominal monetary units, which more or less cancels out the effect of inflation. Second, the time value of money is taken into account "by calculating the *present value* of real dollars from each year" (p. 146). For this to be achieved, real monetary units from different years must be discounted using an inflation-adjusted discount rate (between 2 and 7 percent in the United States) to their "common value at the beginning of a program (or earliest program if two are compared)" (Barnett and Escobar 1987, p. 390). About two-thirds of the studies that had costs and benefits lasting for more than 1 year calculated present value.

4. *Victimization Costs.* Monetary costs to victims of crime can be divided into two main categories: tangible or out of pocket (e.g., property

loss, medical expenses, lost wages) and intangible (e.g., impaired quality of life, pain, suffering, fear). For violent crimes, intangible victim costs far outweigh tangible victim costs, whereas for property crimes the reverse is true. In the case of robbery, for example, intangible costs are almost 2.5 times tangible costs ($6,700 vs. $2,700 in 1997 dollars; Cohen 1998). For the property crime of burglary, tangible costs are $1,300 and intangible costs are $350. The reason why violent crimes have higher intangible victim costs than property crimes is that there is a greater likelihood of injury from violent crimes, and it is this harm that contributes to the costly effects of pain, suffering, and reduced quality of life. Some crimes also carry a risk of death. In the case of robbery, for example, adding the risk of death to the tangible and intangible victim costs increases the total victim costs of a typical robbery by two-thirds, from $9,400 to $15,600.[6] This approach can be critiqued because risk of death is a probabilistic outcome of injury.

The estimation of intangible victimization costs and their use in different contexts, including in benefit-cost analyses of crime prevention programs, is controversial (see Zimring and Hawkins 1995, chap. 7). This is at least in part because of the large estimates that have been produced for victim costs (see Cohen 1988, 1998; Miller, Cohen, and Rossman 1993; Cohen, Miller, and Rossman 1994; Miller, Cohen, and Wiersema 1996; Cohen and Piquero 2009) but especially because of the methodology used. Victim costs of pain, suffering, and lost quality of life are typically estimated on the basis of what a civil court would pay crime victims (jury compensation method) or what the public would willingly pay for additional safety (willingness-to-pay or contingent valuation method).[7] Methods of estimating the costs of crime on the basis of the costs of different components (e.g., victim costs, criminal justice costs, lost productivity) are often referred to as the "bottom-up" approach. This is contrasted with the "top-down" approach of contingent valuation or willingness to pay, which is considered by many to be the more accurate method (see Cook and Ludwig 2000; Cohen and Piquero

[6] This is calculated by multiplying the risk of death for an average robbery by the "value of a statistical life" (Cohen 1998, p. 11). Cohen (1998) uses a value of a statistical life of $3.4 million (in 1997 dollars). See Miller, Cohen, and Wiersema (1996, pp. 21–22) for an overview of the published estimates of the cost of a statistical life.

[7] See Rajkumar and French (1997) for an overview of different methods for estimating both tangible and intangible victim costs.

2009). Several of the benefit-cost studies reviewed in this essay included intangible costs to crime victims.

Zimring and Hawkins (1995, p. 139) are critical of the jury compensation method, contending that "pain and suffering damages for personal injury in Anglo-American law are notorious for both their arbitrariness and their inflated size." Perhaps the more pressing problem facing this method is its unrepresentativeness. Very few crimes have sufficiently sympathetic victims and sufficiently deep-pocketed defendants to entice contingent-fee plaintiff's lawyers to take cases.

The contingent valuation method is based on asking people what they would pay for a desirable outcome, either for themselves or society at-large, when "observable market prices are not available" (Cook and Ludwig 2000, p. 97). For example, in a large-scale study of public preferences for responses to juvenile offending in the Commonwealth of Pennsylvania, Nagin et al. (2006) found that the public values early prevention and offender treatment significantly more than increased incarceration. Households were willing to pay an average of $126 in additional taxes on nurse home visitation programs to prevent delinquency compared to $81 on longer sentences. Households were also willing to pay more in taxes for treatment than for longer sentences: $98 versus $81. At the state-level, public support for the prevention option translated into $601 million that hypothetically could be used to prevent delinquency compared to $387 million for longer sentences for juvenile offenders.

In another contingent valuation study to gauge the public's preferences for a range of alternative responses to crime, Cohen, Rust, and Steen (2006) found that the public overwhelmingly supported the increased spending of tax dollars on youth prevention programs compared to building more prisons. Public support for spending more taxes on drug treatment for nonviolent offenders as well as on police also ranked higher than support for building more prisons but not as high as support for youth prevention programs. Other contingent valuation studies show public support for allocating money to early prevention rather than to building more prisons (see Cullen et al. 2007; Roberts and Hastings 2012).

5. *Standard Variables.* The most crucial issue involved in carrying out benefit-cost studies in crime prevention or other areas is how to decide which program resources used (costs) and effects produced (benefits) should have dollar figures attached. No prescribed formula exists

for what to include (or exclude). Prest and Turvey (1965, p. 683) note that benefit-cost analysis "implies the enumeration and evaluation of all the relevant costs and benefits." Estimating the monetary value of program benefits requires a great deal of ingenuity on the part of the evaluator. Unlike program costs, program benefits are disparate and involve a number of assumptions in order to arrive at reasonable estimates of monetary value.[8] In some ways, estimating the monetary value of the benefits of crime prevention programs is limited (beyond the limits imposed by the quality of the outcome evaluation) only by the ingenuity of the evaluator and the resources available to the evaluator. A standard list of costs and benefits that should be measured, and how they should be monetized, might overcome some of the difficulties that face researchers in conducting benefit-cost analyses of crime prevention programs and would greatly facilitate comparisons of the benefit-cost findings of different crime prevention programs and with prevention programs in other domains (Karoly 2012; Crowley et al. 2014; Institute of Medicine and National Research Council 2014). It is beyond the scope of this essay to attempt the development of such a comprehensive list of costs and benefits that should be measured in all studies, but it is useful to sketch an outline of what a standard list might comprise.

Key outcome variables that should be measured in crime prevention programs include crime and delinquency, substance abuse, education, employment, health, and family factors. Table 1 provides a summary of the relevant (potential) benefits on these outcome variables as well as some of the key program costs. For crime, an assessment of benefits should focus on affected agencies within the criminal justice system (e.g., police, courts, probation, corrections) and crime victims and their families. Tangible and intangible crime-victim costs should be assessed in accordance with a theoretically sound and standardized methodology. Where relevant, it is also important to include tangible and intangible costs avoided by offenders from being incarcerated (e.g., family disruption, impediments to future employment). Many of the same benefits assessed for crime can also be examined in relation to substance abuse.

[8] Some disagree with this view. Levin (as cited in Institute of Medicine and National Research Council [2014, p. 21]) states, "Benefit-cost analyses tend to use calipers to measure effects and witching rods to measure costs." He goes on to say that "a budget is not necessarily a full or accurate metric for determining costs."

TABLE 1

Summary of Program Costs and Benefits to Be Measured

Program Costs	Program Benefits
Operating: Staff salaries and benefits, overhead, supplies Capital: Constructing facilities, loan repayment charges	Delinquency/crime: Savings to criminal justice system (e.g., police, courts, probation, corrections); tangible and intangible costs avoided by crime victims (e.g., medical care, damaged and lost property, lost wages, lost quality of life, pain, suffering); tangible and intangible costs avoided by family members of crime victims (e.g., funeral expenses, lost wages, lost quality of life); tangible and intangible costs avoided by offenders (e.g., incarceration costs, family disruption, loss of employment) Substance abuse: Savings to criminal justice system, improved health Education: Improved educational output (e.g., high school completion, enrollment in college or university), reduced schooling costs (e.g., remedial classes, support services) Employment: Increased wages (tax revenue for government), decreased use of welfare and unemployment services Health: Decreased use of public health care (e.g., fewer visits to hospital and clinic), improved mental health Family factors: Fewer childbirths to at-risk women; more parental time spent with children; less parental discord, divorce, and separation; effects on next generation

For education, benefits should be assessed for educational output (e.g., high school completion, enrollment in college or university) and schooling expenses (e.g., remedial classes, support services). Increased wages (tax revenue for governments) and decreased use of welfare services are two of the potential benefits that should be examined in relation to employment. For health, benefits should be assessed for use of public health care (e.g., visits to hospitals or clinics) and mental health. For family issues, a number of potential benefits should be assessed, including fewer child births to at-risk women, increased parental time spent with children, and lower rates of divorce and separation. This short list of some of the most relevant benefits of crime prevention programs demonstrates the potential scope needed in benefit-cost studies in this area, a scope that will not always be feasible or affordable. At a minimum, benefit-cost studies should measure the most salient program costs and benefits.

A simple way for researchers to estimate the monetary benefits of crime prevention programs is to use the cost-of-crime estimates published by government agencies. For example, in a Home Office report, Brand and Price (2000) estimated the average costs of different types of crimes in England and Wales, at 1999 prices. Their estimates took account of property stolen and damaged, emotional and physical impact on victims, lost output, health costs, victim services, criminal justice system costs, and insurance costs. The average residential burglary, for example, was estimated to cost £2,300 (or about $3,700). A simple estimate of the monetary benefits of a crime prevention program can be obtained by multiplying the number of each type of crime prevented by the average cost of each type of crime.

As an example, Painter and Farrington (2001) estimated that improved street lighting in Dudley, England, prevented 65 residential burglaries in their experimental area in 1993 (see below for a description of this project). They also estimated that the average cost of a residential burglary in 1993 was £1,941, since the retail price index increased by 18.5 percent between 1993 and 1999 (£2,300 divided by 1.185 = £1,941). Therefore, the cost savings from fewer burglaries were estimated to be £126,165 (65 × £1,941), and the net cost savings in the experimental area (compared with the control area) were estimated to be £339,186. Since the improved lighting program cost £54,815, the benefit-cost ratio was 6.19. The Home Office has since updated their cost-of-crime estimates twice (Dubourg, Hamed, and Thorns 2005; Home Office 2011).

In estimating numbers of crimes saved from numbers of convictions saved, it is essential to take account of co-offending. For example, if 500 convictions are saved, this is really a savings of 500 offender-offense combinations. If the average offense is committed by two offenders, then only 250 offenses will be saved. As an example, Farrington and Koegl (2015) evaluated a cognitive-behavioral program in Toronto. They estimated that it saved 17.1–31.4 burglary convictions per 100 boys between ages 12 and 20. However, since Canadian burglaries are committed by 1.91 offenders on average up to age 20, these numbers corresponded to 9.0–16.4 burglaries per 100 boys.

III. Developmental Crime Prevention

In this essay, we focus on three of the four main crime prevention strategies, as articulated in the typology advanced by Tonry and Farrington (1995): developmental, situational, and community; criminal justice prevention is not included. Important in our decision to focus exclusively on these three strategies is their shared emphasis on addressing the underlying causes or motivations that lead to a criminal event or a life of crime. Also, each strategy operates outside of the confines of the criminal justice system, representing an alternative, perhaps even a socially progressive, way to reduce crime (Welsh and Farrington 2012; Welsh and Pfeffer 2013).

In keeping with our past review, we searched criminological, psychological, health, and economic literatures throughout the Western world for published studies on the prevention of crime that had carried out an economic analysis and had either calculated or permitted the calculation of a benefit-cost ratio for the purpose of assessing the program's economic efficiency. In addition, we searched for references that cited studies in our earlier essay and new reports that we discovered. Studies that did not perform an economic analysis were included if they presented sufficient cost and benefit data to enable an assessment of economic efficiency. Studies have been included only if there was a measure of personal crime, in which the primary victim was a person or household, and if they were "real-life" programs—that is, program outcomes were neither assessed using statistical modeling techniques alone nor hypothesized on the basis of case study data, but rather research designs were employed with the capacity to control for threats to internal validity (i.e., experimental and rigorous quasi-experimental designs).

We have used the scientific methods scale first developed by Sherman et al. (1997) and updated by Farrington et al. (2006), which is extremely helpful in assessing the methodological quality of intervention studies. This is as follows, with level 1 being the lowest and level 5 the highest:

Level 1.—Correlational evidence: low offending correlates with the program.

Level 2.—Nonequivalent control group or one-group pre-post design: program group compared with nonequivalent control group; program group measured before and after the intervention (with no control group).

Level 3.—Equivalent control group design: program group compared with comparable control group, including pre-post and experimental-control comparisons. This was considered to be the minimum interpretable design by Cook and Campbell (1979) and is the minimum design for inclusion of studies in the current essay.

Level 4.—Control of extraneous variables: program group compared with control group, with control of extraneous influences on the outcome (e.g., by matching, prediction or propensity scores, or statistical controls).

Level 5.—Randomized experiment: units assigned at random to program and control groups.

Developmental prevention aims to influence the scientifically identified risk factors or "root causes" of juvenile delinquency and later criminal offending (Farrington and Welsh 2007). It is informed generally by motivational or human development theories on criminal behavior and specifically by longitudinal studies that follow samples of young persons from their early childhood experiences to the peak of their involvement with crime in their teens and 20s (e.g., Farrington 1995). The developmental perspective postulates that criminal offending in adolescence and adulthood is influenced by "behavioral and attitudinal patterns that have been learned during an individual's development" (Tremblay and Craig 1995, p. 151). Detailed reviews of the theoretical bases of developmental prevention have been presented elsewhere (e.g., Farrington 2010; Cullen, Benson, and Makarios 2012).

Eleven developmental crime prevention studies were found that met the criteria for inclusion. Table 2 provides a brief overview of the 11 studies. (Table A1 provides a more detailed summary of the key features of the studies.) The most prominent of these studies, and one of the studies with an especially high-quality benefit-cost analysis—the Perry Preschool program (Schweinhart et al. 2005)—is reviewed in detail. Benefit-cost analyses of correctional programs that include a developmental component (e.g., therapeutic counseling; Klietz, Borduin, and Schaeffer 2010) are not included.

The studies in table 2 have been organized in chronological order. Ten of the studies were conducted in the United States; the other, by Farrington and Koegl (2015), was conducted in Canada. At the start of the intervention, subjects ranged in age from prebirth to 19 years, with six of the projects commencing before the formal school years. The studies manipulated a variety of different risk factors, including parenting, education, cognitive development, and behavioral problems. There was a great deal of variability in the duration of the interventions, ranging from 10 weeks to 6 years. Seven of the studies had very long follow-up periods to assess outcomes, ranging from 7 to 36 years. This is a sharp contrast to our first *Crime and Justice* essay (Welsh and Farrington 2000*b*) and is, in part, a function of some of these studies employing a longitudinal-experimental design (Farrington and Welsh 2013).

The methodological rigor of the 11 studies was extremely high, with six employing random assignment to experimental and control conditions. All interventions reported desirable effects for all or some outcomes. For example, in the latest follow-up of the Abecedarian enriched early childhood program—when participants were in their midthirties—program group members showed significant improvements in health (e.g., a lower prevalence of risk factors for cardiovascular and metabolic diseases) relative to their control counterparts (Campbell et al. 2014).[9] Ten of the 11 studies performed a benefit-cost analysis, while the one study that did not (Earle 1995) provided sufficient cost and benefit data to permit an estimation of its economic efficiency.

Two high-quality developmental prevention studies that have measured delinquency and childhood aggression and presented data on the monetary value of the programs—the Syracuse University Family Development Research Project (Lally, Mangione, and Honig 1988) and the Yale Child Welfare Research Program (Seitz, Rosenbaum, and Apfel 1985)—are not included here. This is because the published data were insufficient to calculate benefit-cost ratios to assess the economic efficiency of the programs. The Syracuse program began prenatally, providing program mothers with a range of educational and health services. After birth, trained paraprofessionals visited the homes weekly to assist mothers (and other family members) with issues of child rearing, family relations, employment, and community functioning. Children were provided with 4.5 continuous years of enriched child care (50 weeks a year), commencing with 5 half days a week at 6–15 months and, thereafter,

[9] This follow-up is not reported in table 2 because a benefit-cost analysis has not yet been carried out.

TABLE 2

Overview of Developmental Crime Prevention Studies

Main Source	Program Name and Short Description	Sample Size	Benefit-Cost Ratio*
Lipsey, Cordray, and Berger (1981)	Los Angeles County Delinquency Prevention Program: Family counseling, academic tutoring, employment training	7,637 youths	1.4
Long, Mallar, and Thornton (1981)	Job Corps: Vocational training, education, health care	5,100 youths	1.45
Hahn (1994)	Quantum Opportunities Program: Education, skills development	250 youths	3.68
Earle (1995)	Hawaii Healthy Start: Parent education, parent support, family planning, community support	2,706 families	.38
Schweinhart et al. (2005)	Perry Preschool Program: Preschool intellectual enrichment, parent education	123 children	12.9
Schochet, Burghardt, and McConnell (2006)	Job Corps: Vocational training, education, health care, socialization activities	11,313 youths	Full sample: .25; age group 20–24: 2.3
Barnett and Masse (2007)	Abecedarian Program: Preschool intellectual enrichment	111 children	2.5
DuMont et al. (2010)	Healthy Families New York: Parent education, parenting skills, parent support, parental and child health care, home visits	1,173 families	Full sample: .15; HPO subgroup: .25; RRO subgroup: 3.16

Reynolds, Temple, White, et al. (2011)	Child-Parent Center Early Education Program: Education, family support, parent involvement, parent support, health care, continuity between preschool and early elementary school	1,539 children	Preschool program: 7.2; school-age program: 2.11; preschool plus school-age: 5.21
Miller (2013)	Nurse-Family Partnership: Parent education, parent support, community support, family planning, nurse home visits	371 families	2.9
Farrington and Koegl (2015)	Stop Now and Plan—Under 12 Outreach Project (SNAP-ORP): Skills training, cognitive problem solving, self-control and anger management, cognitive self-instruction, family management training, and parent management training	376 boys	2.05–3.75 (17.33–31.77 scaled up to self-reports)

NOTE.—HPO = high prevention opportunity; RRO = recurrence reduction opportunity.

* Expressed as a ratio of benefits to costs in monetary units (national currencies).

with 5 full days a week until age 60 months. Lally, Mangione, and Honig (1988) did not provide data on the resources used (costs), only on the cost savings to the criminal justice system.

The Yale program also began prenatally. It involved four main interventions administered up to 30 months postpartum. First, professional home visits were provided to assist with short-term (e.g., reducing physical danger) and long-term (e.g., reaching career goals) family problems and link families to community services. Second, pediatric care services were provided to the mother and child, decreasing in intensity from birth to infancy. Children received from 13 to 17 examinations. Emphasis was placed on educating parents in observing their child's health. Third, each child attended an enriched day care program that focused on the child's emotional and social development for, on average, 13.2 months. Fourth, regular developmental examinations were carried out with the child, with the parent present, using standardized instruments. Seitz, Rosenbaum, and Apfel (1985) provided information on program resources used and benefits, but this was insufficient to provide a fair assessment of program efficiency.

A. Summary of Economic Analysis Findings

The types of benefits measured by the 11 developmental prevention studies were wide-ranging, including criminal justice system, education, health care, social services, employment (from tax revenue on earnings), and savings to crime victims. Eight of the 11 studies yielded a favorable benefit-cost ratio for all parties; another two studies (Schochet, Burghardt, and McConnell 2006; DuMont et al. 2010) reported mixed results. For the 10 studies that reported at least one favorable benefit-cost ratio, the economic return on a $1 investment ranged from a low of $1.40 (in the Los Angeles County Delinquency Prevention Program; Lipsey 1984) to a high of $12.90 (in the Perry program). The one study that did not show a favorable benefit-cost ratio (Earle 1995) was the one for which we carried out a simple benefit-cost analysis.

A favorable benefit-cost ratio was found for each of the eight studies in which the intervention commenced after birth. The one exception was the evaluation of Job Corps by Schochet, Burghardt, and McConnell (2006), which also reported an unfavorable benefit-cost ratio for the full sample. By comparison, two of the three studies that began prenatally (Earle 1995; DuMont et al. 2010) reported mixed results. The

Hawaii Healthy Start and the full sample of Healthy Families New York showed unfavorable ratios of 0.38 and 0.15, respectively, while the higher risk sample for Healthy Families New York showed a favorable return of 3.16. In the case of Hawaii Healthy Start, a limited range of program effects—only program effects on child abuse and neglect could be monetized—contributed to its poor economic showing. In contrast, Miller's (2013) multistudy benefit-cost analysis of the Nurse-Family Partnership program, which begins in the final trimester of pregnancy, showed a favorable return of $2.90 for every dollar spent on the program.

For five of the 10 studies that reported at least one favorable benefit-cost ratio (Long, Mallar, and Thornton 1981; Schweinhart et al. 2005; Reynolds, Temple, White, et al. 2011; Miller 2013; Farrington and Koegl 2015), savings from reduced delinquency and later offending (as measured by less involvement with the justice system, fewer victims of crime, or both) accounted for a substantial proportion of the measured benefits.[10] Reduced offending in the Perry program at age 40 accounted for almost nine-tenths (87.7 percent) of the total economic benefits, or $11.31 of $12.90. In the case of the preschool component of the Chicago Child-Parent Center program, reduced criminal activity at age 26 accounted for almost seven-tenths (69.3 percent) of the total benefits, or $4.99 of $7.19 (Reynolds, Temple, White, et al. 2011; see also Reynolds, Temple, Ou, et al. 2011). Some of the other benefits produced by these programs included reduced reliance on welfare, increased economic output of the program participants that generated increased tax revenue for the government, and increased educational achievement, which, in some cases, meant less use of remedial school services. Overall, developmental prevention appears to be a highly promising strategy in reducing the monetary costs associated with delinquency and later criminal offending and improving the life-course development of at-risk children and their families.

B. The Perry Preschool Program

Perry Preschool started in 1962 in Ypsilanti, Michigan. The Perry study is perhaps the best known longitudinal study in the Western world that has rigorously charted the effects of an early childhood intervention program. The principal hypothesis of Perry was that "good preschool

[10] This was the only type of benefits measured by Farrington and Koegl (2015).

programs can help children in poverty make a better start in their transition from home to community and thereby set more of them on paths to becoming economically self-sufficient, socially responsible adults" (Schweinhart, Barnes, and Weikart 1993, p. 3).

1. *Design and Method.* Before the start of the program, 123 children age 3–4 years were randomly assigned to either a program group that received the preschool program (n = 58) or a control group that did not (n = 65). The sample consisted of 72 boys and 51 girls. Families were recruited if they had low socioeconomic status and their children showed low intellectual performance. Some of the characteristics of the sample families at the time of recruitment included 40 percent unemployment, 49 percent receiving welfare assistance, 47 percent single-parent households, and low high school completion rates (11 percent for men; 21 percent for women).

The main intervention strategy involved high-quality, active learning preschool programming administered by professional teachers for 2 years. Preschool sessions were 1 half day long and were provided 5 days a week for the duration of the 30-week school year. The educational approach focused on supporting the development of the children's cognitive and social skills through individualized teaching and learning. Each day, the children planned what they were going to do, did it, and then reviewed what they had done. Weekly home visits were also carried out by the teachers to provide parents with educational information and to encourage parents to take an active role in their child's early education.

The sample was most recently assessed at age 40, or 36 years post-intervention. Data sources included personal interviews; school, police, court, and social service records; and a standardized survey to test general literacy. The sample attrition was exceedingly low at this follow-up stage (only 8.9 percent). Earlier assessments were carried out annually from age 3–11, at 14–15 (hereafter referred to as age 15), at 19, and at 27 years.

2. *Results.* At age 40, the program continued to make an important difference in the lives of the participants (Schweinhart et al. 2005). In commenting on this latest follow-up, Kirp (2004, p. 34) noted, "By almost any measure we might care about—education, income, crime, family stability—the contrast with those who didn't attend Perry is striking." Compared to the control group, program group members had significantly fewer lifetime arrests for violent crimes (32 vs. 48 percent), prop-

erty crimes (36 vs. 58 percent), and drug crimes (14 vs. 34 percent) and were significantly less likely to be arrested five or more times (36 vs. 55 percent). Improvements were also recorded in many other important life-course outcomes. For example, significantly higher levels of schooling (77 vs. 60 percent graduating from high school), better records of employment (76 vs. 62 percent), and higher annual incomes were reported by the program group compared to the control.

3. *Economic Analysis.* A comprehensive benefit-cost analysis of the Perry program (Barnett, Belfield, and Nores 2005; see also Belfield et al. 2006) found that the program's effects translated into substantial savings for both the program group participants and the public. In the benefit-cost analysis, which adjusted all figures to 2000 dollars, the program's measured effects through age 40 and the program's projected effects beyond age 40 (41–65) were both included. Although the projected effects may be somewhat controversial, this combined measure is what is reported throughout the literature and is used here. Monetary benefits through age 40 accounted for nine-tenths (or 90.2 percent) of total program benefits per program group participant ($176,434 out of $195,621).[11] Also, we report on program benefits accruing to the public (taxpayers and crime victims); benefits received by individual participants are not included in the benefit-cost calculations.

The total costs of the program were estimated at $15,166 per program group participant. Program costs were derived from two categories: basic operating costs, which included instruction, administration and support staff, overhead, supplies, and psychological screening, and capital costs, which took into account the school district classrooms and other facilities used by the program (Barnett 1993, 1996). The total program benefits were estimated at $195,621 per program group participant. As noted above, the greatest benefits—almost nine-tenths (or 87.7 percent)—were from combined savings to the justice system and crime victims ($171,473).

Participants' arrest and incarceration histories were used to estimate savings to the main components of the criminal justice system: police, prosecutors, court, prison, and probation. Savings to crime victims were estimated in a two-step process. First, participants' arrest histories were linked with national data on the ratio of arrests to crimes committed,

[11] For the benefit-cost analysis at age 27 (Barnett 1993, 1996), which also used projected effects, monetary benefits of the measured effects (excluding the projected effects) accounted for 70.1 percent of total program benefits per program group participant.

which provided an estimate, by age, of the number and type of crimes actually committed by program group participants. Second, these crime estimates were then combined with previously developed estimates of crime-specific costs to victims (e.g., Cohen 1998), which produced estimates of victim costs from crimes committed by program group participants at each age. Costs to crime victims were not limited to tangible or out-of-pocket monetary losses (e.g., lost property, wages, medical expenses), as is usually the case in such calculations. Also taken into account, where applicable, were the intangible costs of reduced quality of life, pain, and suffering, as well as the risk of death (Barnett, Belfield, and Nores 2005).

The other monetary benefits received by the public, expressed as per preschool participant, included higher educational output and reduced schooling costs, $7,303; revenue generated from taxes on increased earnings, $14,078; and reduced reliance on welfare, $2,768. Dividing total benefits per participant ($195,621) by total costs per participant ($15,166) produced a highly desirable benefit-cost ratio of 12.90. In other words, for every dollar spent on the program, $12.90 was returned to the public, making the Perry program a very sound investment of public resources (Schweinhart et al. 2011).

Three earlier benefit-cost analyses of the Perry program, when participants were age 15, 19, and 27, also showed that the program was a sound investment of taxpayer dollars. At age 15, a benefit-cost ratio of 2.48 was reported (Weber, Foster, and Weikart 1978; Schweinhart and Weikart 1980); at age 19, a benefit-cost ratio of 3.00 was reported (Berrueta-Clement et al. 1984); and at age 27, a benefit-cost ratio of 7.16 was reported (Barnett 1993, 1996). The differences among these three ratios, as well as the age 40 ratio of 12.90, stem largely from the continued improvements of the program group compared to the control group and from benefits being calculated cumulatively. Another reason for the change in benefit-cost findings over time, particularly between the second and third assessments (ages 19 and 27), has to do with the inclusion of intangible crime victim costs in the later analysis.

The benefit-cost analysis, performed by Barnett, Belfield, and Nores (2005), was methodologically rigorous, not to mention comprehensive in its coverage of costs and benefits, and the estimates of lifetime effects and benefit-cost findings in the Perry project are among the most defensible in the field. Support for these views come from a reanalysis of Perry's benefit-cost findings by Heckman and his colleagues (2010*a*,

2010*b*), which found a slightly lower but still very high return of the order of $7 of benefit per dollar of cost.

IV. Situational Crime Prevention

Situational crime prevention is defined as "a preventive approach that relies, not upon improving society or its institutions, but simply upon reducing opportunities for crime" (Clarke 1992, p. 3). Reducing opportunities for crime is achieved through some modification or manipulation of the environment. The origins of situational crime prevention are based in the larger body of opportunity theory that sees the offender "as heavily influenced by environmental inducements and opportunities and as being highly adaptable to changes in the situation" (Clarke 1995*a*, p. 57). Generally, situational crime prevention is based on rational choice theory (Clarke and Cornish 1985) and routine activity theory (Cohen and Felson 1979). An elaboration of the theoretical bases and principles of situational prevention is beyond the scope of this essay; however, excellent reviews of these areas have been provided by Clarke (1995*b*, 2008), Eck (2006), and Smith and Clarke (2012). Specific situational interventions have also been reviewed, including CCTV (Welsh and Farrington 2009*b*), improved street lighting (Farrington and Welsh 2002), and neighborhood watch (Bennett, Holloway, and Farrington 2009).

Cornish and Clarke (2003) classified situational crime prevention into 25 techniques divided into five main approaches: (i) increasing perceived effort (target hardening, access control, deflecting offenders, and controlling tools and weapons), (ii) increasing perceived risks (increasing guardianship, reducing anonymity, formal surveillance, surveillance by employees, and natural surveillance), (iii) reducing anticipated rewards (concealing or removing targets, identifying property, disrupting markets, and denying benefits), (iv) reducing provocations (reducing frustration, avoiding disputes, reducing peer pressure, reducing arousal, and discouraging imitation), and (v) removing excuses (setting rules, posting instructions, alerting consciences, assisting compliance, and controlling drugs and alcohol).

Eight situational crime prevention studies were identified that met our inclusion criteria. Table 3 provides a brief overview of these studies, two of which were reported by Painter and Farrington (2001). (Table A2 provides a more detailed summary of the key features of the studies.)

TABLE 3

Overview of Situational Crime Prevention Studies

Main Source	Program Name/Type and Short Description	Sample Size	Benefit-Cost Ratio*
Cirel et al. (1977)	Block Watch: Natural surveillance targeted on residential burglary	1,474 homes	.4
Skilton (1988)	Concierges: Employee surveillance targeted on vandalism in public housing	305 homes (in two high-rises)	1.44
Ekblom, Law, and Sutton (1996)	Safer Cities Programme: Target hardening (locks, alarms, entry systems) focused on residential burglary	7,500 homes	High risk: 3.0; average risk: .9
Ayres and Levitt (1998)	Lojack: Formal surveillance targeted on auto theft	6 cities with populations over 250,000	15
Painter and Farrington (2001), Dudley	Improved street lighting: Natural surveillance targeted on property and personal crime	879 homes	6.2–121
Painter and Farrington (2001), Stoke-on-Trent	Improved street lighting: Natural surveillance targeted on property and personal crime	540 homes	5.4–54
Bowers, Johnson, and Hirschfield (2004)	Alley gates: Target hardening focused on residential burglary	106 housing blocks	6 months: 1.01; 12 months: 1.86
Gill and Spriggs (2005)	CCTV: Formal surveillance targeted on property and personal crime	7 projects	City outskirts: 1.24; Hawkeye: .67; other five: 0

* Expressed as a ratio of benefits to costs in monetary units (national currencies).

Several were conducted in multiple sites, and the largest of these multisite studies—the CCTV evaluation by Gill and Spriggs (2005)—is reviewed in detail later. As mentioned, we have only included studies that reach level 3 or above on the scientific methods scale. There are, however, a number of benefit-cost analyses of situational crime prevention programs that reach only level 2 because they are based on before-and-after comparisons with no control condition. For completeness, these are reviewed later but not in great detail.

As before, the studies in table 3 have been organized in chronological order. Six were conducted in the United Kingdom and two in the United States. Five were targeted on only one crime, namely, burglary, vandalism, or vehicle theft. Seven of the studies (all except Ayres and Levitt 1998) had very short follow-up periods. The interventions were based on natural surveillance (Block Watch and improved lighting), employee surveillance, formal surveillance (CCTV and Lojack), and target hardening (alley gates and better physical security). All of the studies except Gill and Spriggs (discussed below) found that the intervention was successful in causing a reduction in crime.

A. Summary of Economic Analysis Findings

Six of the studies (all except Cirel et al. [1977] and Gill and Spriggs [2005]) found that the monetary benefits exceeded the monetary costs of the intervention. Ayres and Levitt (1998) reported a high benefit-cost ratio of 15 in their evaluation of the Lojack stolen car retrieval system. They studied a time series of vehicle thefts in six cities in which Lojack had been introduced, 5 years before and 5 years after the introduction, and compared the results with vehicle thefts in all other US cities during the same time period. They found that Lojack caused an increase in stolen vehicle recovery rates from 60 to 95 percent. They estimated that the monetary benefits were approximately $1,500 per year per vehicle compared with the cost of Lojack over the life of a vehicle of about $100 per year. No other benefits were studied. The results were largely driven by findings in the high-crime central cities.

Painter and Farrington (1997, 1999) carried out two evaluations of the effects of improved street lighting, in Dudley and Stoke-on-Trent, England. In Dudley, street lighting was improved in an experimental area, and the results were compared with a control area in which lighting was not improved. Victimization surveys were carried out in both areas before and after the improved lighting in the experimental area, to assess the number of crimes in the year before and the year after. Both areas were local authority housing estates that had been built at approximately the same time (mid-1930s), had similar numbers of dwellings (about 1,200–1,300 each), and had similar types of housing. The Stoke-on-Trent project had a very similar design but had both adjacent and non-adjacent control areas in order to investigate displacement and diffusion of benefits (see Clarke and Weisburd 1994; Johnson, Guerette, and Bowers 2012).

The benefit-cost analyses were based on the numbers of different types of crimes prevented and the average cost of each crime according to the Home Office (Brand and Price 2000). For example, in Dudley, it was estimated that 641 crimes were saved in the experimental area of 1,200 houses in 1 year, saving £558,415. However, crime also decreased in the control area, so that the net savings were £339,186. The improved lighting cost £55,000, but it was £185 per year cheaper to run. Comparing the net 1-year benefits of £339,186 with the 1-year costs of £54,815, the benefit-cost ratio was 6.19. (The corresponding ratio in Stoke-on-Trent was 5.40.)

The new streetlights, however, were expected to last 20 years. Assuming that the capital cost of the lights in Dudley was paid off over 20 years at an interest rate of 6 percent, annual payments at the end of each year of £4,796 would clear the debt. Therefore, it would be reasonable to translate the cost of the improved street lighting into an annual cost of £4,611 (£4,796 − £185). Comparing the net 1-year benefits of £339,186 with the 1-year cost of £4,611 produces a very high benefit-cost ratio of 121. (The corresponding figure for Stoke-on-Trent was 54.)

Situational prevention techniques are usually implemented, and are believed to be more effective, in high-crime areas. This was demonstrated in the multisite evaluation by Ekblom, Law, and Sutton (1996) of the large-scale Safer Cities Programme. Many cost and benefit figures are presented in this report, making it difficult to know which is the most appropriate. However, in their conclusions (on pp. 60–61), separate figures are given for high-risk and average areas and for victimization surveys compared with police data. On the basis of victimization surveys, a burglary cost £400 to prevent in high-risk areas and £1,400 to prevent in average areas. Comparing these figures with the average estimated victimization cost of a burglary of £1,200 yielded benefit-cost ratios of 3.0 in high-risk areas and 0.9 in average areas. On the basis of police data, a burglary cost £550 to prevent in high-risk areas and £1,000 to prevent in average areas. Comparing these figures with the average estimated police cost of a burglary of £1,100 yielded benefit-cost ratios of 2.0 in high-risk areas and 1.1 in average areas.

There was some evidence of a dose-response relationship in the evaluation by Bowers, Johnson, and Hirschfield (2004) of installing lockable alley gates in the central city of Liverpool, England. These gates, installed at the rear of properties, restricted access to residents who had keys. Bowers and her colleagues carried out their benefit-cost analysis by comparing the cost of the gates (£659 each) with the cost of burglaries prevented, using the Home Office estimate of the average cost of each burglary of £2,300 (Brand and Price 2000). Experimental and control areas were compared. They concluded that the benefit-cost ratio was 1.86, where gates had been installed for at least 12 months, but only 1.01 where gates had been installed for at least 6 months.

Most situational crime prevention evaluations have had short follow-up periods. It is important to investigate the extent to which effects persist or wear off. Benefit-cost ratios often increase over time (e.g., Jolliffe, Farrington, and Howard 2013). Also, some of these evaluations greatly underestimated the benefits of programs. For example, Cirel et al. (1977) reported a 61 percent decrease in burglaries. However, they only took account of the tangible losses in a burglary and found that the benefits from reduced burglaries ($1,832 per 100 households) were only 40 percent of the costs of the program ($4,614 per 100 households). If they had taken account of the other costs of a burglary (e.g., criminal justice costs, pain and suffering of victims), or other benefits of their program, their benefit-cost ratio would have been higher and more realistic.

B. The National UK Multisite CCTV Evaluation

The effects of CCTV on crime have been assessed most rigorously in a large-scale English national quasi-experimental, multisite evaluation (Gill and Spriggs 2005; Farrington, Gill, et al. 2007).[12]

1. *Design and Method.* Fourteen CCTV projects were evaluated: eight in housing areas, four in city centers, one in a hospital, and the final one (Hawkeye) in 57 train station parking lots. The aim was to compare each experimental area with a comparable nonadjacent control area, an adjacent buffer area (to investigate displacement and diffusion of ben-

[12] We have counted this as one project, but it could have been counted as several evaluations.

efits), and the rest of the police division containing the experimental area. Ideally, police and victimization survey data were collected, but it was not possible to collect all the data in all the sites.

2. *Results.* The results were generally disappointing, although in concordance with the previous systematic review of the effectiveness of CCTV by Welsh and Farrington (2003). Basically, CCTV was effective in reducing vehicle crimes in car parks but hardly anywhere else. CCTV was effective in only one of the 12 evaluations in housing areas and city centers (in City Outskirts), and there were some signs that it was effective in the hospital, although not significantly so. In all three cases where CCTV appeared to be effective, it was combined with other security improvements, especially with improved lighting. Farrington, Gill et al. (2007) found a significant correlation between the effectiveness of the CCTV project and the degree of coverage of the cameras, which was 95–100 percent in the station car parks. They concluded: "CCTV was only effective in car parks, where crimes were committed in public view, where a large fraction of the area could be covered by the cameras, where there was controlled access, where the vehicle crimes probably involved rational decision-making, where it seems likely that potential offenders were deterred by the risk of detection, and where CCTV was combined with other interventions" (p. 34).

3. *Economic Analysis.* The benefit-cost analysis was carried out by Gill and Spriggs (2005, chap. 5). They studied Hawkeye and six other areas and concluded that the benefit-cost ratio was substantial only in City Outskirts (1.24) and in high-risk car parks (1.27). The benefit-cost ratio was only 0.67 for Hawkeye overall, because thefts from vehicles and damage to vehicles were relatively inexpensive crimes.[13] While Gill and Spriggs (2005) concluded that CCTV provided the best value for money in City Outskirts, they also pointed out that the desirable effects in City Outskirts could have been caused by confounding factors other than CCTV, such as improved lighting. Overall, CCTV did not seem to be a cost-beneficial intervention.

C. Excluded Evaluations of Situational Crime Prevention

Table 4 provides a brief overview of 10 benefit-cost analyses of situational crime prevention projects that were excluded from our current

[13] They also used the Home Office figures for costs of different crimes (Brand and Price 2000).

TABLE 4

Overview of Excluded Situational Crime Prevention Studies

Main Source	Program Name/Type and Short Description	Sample Size	Benefit-Cost Ratio*
Schnelle et al. (1979)	Silent alarms: Formal surveillance targeted on armed robbery	48 stores	.36
Laycock (1986)	Property marking: Identifying property targeted on residential burglary	2,234 homes	.78
van Andel (1989)	Special transport officials: Formal surveillance targeted on vandalism, toll fraud, and assault	Metro, bus, and tram in three cities	.32
Clarke and McGrath (1990)	Time-locks, cash limits: Target hardening focused on robbery	429 betting shops (average)	1.71
Forrester et al. (1990)	Kirkholt Burglary Prevention Project: Removal of coin meters	2,280 homes on public housing estate	5.04
Poyner (1992)	CCTV: Employee surveillance targeted on vandalism	80 buses	2.35
Davidson and Farr (1994)	CCTV: Employee surveillance targeted on vandalism and residential burglary	5 public housing blocks	.47
Knight (1994)	Security guards: Formal surveillance targeted on vandalism and residential burglary	1,767 homes on public housing estate	1.31
van Ours and Vollaard (2011)	Electronic engine immobilizer: Target hardening focused on auto theft	All new cars sold since 1998	England and Wales: 29; The Netherlands: 7
Vollaard and van Ours (2011)	Certified burglary-proof locks and window and door frames: Target hardening focused on residential burglary	All new built homes since 1999—approximately 70,000 houses annually	1.07

* Expressed as a ratio of benefits to costs in monetary units (national currencies).

review because they had a before-after design with no control condition. (Table A3 provides a more detailed summary of the key features of the studies.) This design is seriously flawed. For example, crime in many different countries started to decrease around the mid-1990s, so that any evaluation after this time period would likely find a decrease in crime that was not necessarily caused by the intervention. A control condition is essential to estimate what would have happened in the absence of the intervention and therefore to disentangle the effects of the intervention from the effects of many other changing factors.

These 10 evaluations produced mixed results. The most successful interventions were the Kirkholt project, which was fully described in our previous *Crime and Justice* essay, and the evaluation of electronic engine immobilizers for cars by van Ours and Vollaard (2011). The evaluation of CCTV in buses by Poyner (1992) also yielded a substantial benefit-cost ratio. However, the other benefit-cost ratios were either below 1.0 (in four cases) or between 1.0 and 2.0 (in three cases).

V. Community Crime Prevention

Community crime prevention has been defined as "actions intended to change the social conditions that are believed to sustain crime in residential communities" (Hope 1995, p. 21). There are basically two types of community crime prevention. In the first type, community resources are mobilized to promote social cohesion and guardianship and to tackle neighborhood disorder and deterioration. Community mobilization programs often include community-based mentoring, after-school sport and recreation, and gang prevention and often provide residents with opportunities for involvement in desirable activities. Community programs targeting disorder and deterioration sometimes overlap with situational crime prevention. In the second type of community prevention, the community is the setting within which other types of programs, typically targeted on individuals and families, are delivered. These types of programs sometimes overlap with developmental crime prevention. Therefore, the boundaries between community prevention and situational or developmental prevention are sometimes blurred.

Building on Bennett (1998), Welsh and Hoshi (2006) reviewed the theories on which the first type of community crime prevention is based. Community disorganization theory suggests that offending is caused by a breakdown in the social organization that is maintained by social institutions such as the family, school, church, and community centers. A later development of this theory focuses on the role of the "collective efficacy" of neighborhoods in intervening to prevent offending (Sampson, Raudenbush, and Earls 1997). Community disorder theory, based on the Broken Windows hypothesis of Wilson and Kelling (1982), suggests that physical deterioration and decline influences public disorder and crime and that minor crime (e.g., graffiti) needs to be tackled so that it does not escalate into more serious street crime. Finally, community regeneration theory emphasizes the need for investment in the community, commercial interest in the area, and improvement in the housing stock, in order to reduce crime and disorder (Bennett 1998, p. 376).

For the second type of community prevention, where the community acts largely as the context, the key theories are largely the same as for developmental crime prevention. Typically, the aim is to reduce risk factors for offending and to enhance protective factors. Table 5 provides a brief overview of four community crime prevention projects that met our inclusion criteria. (Table A4 provides a more detailed summary of the key features of the studies.) Three are mainly developmental in nature, and one is mainly situational. Three are discussed in the next section, and then the fourth project—Communities That Care—is described in more detail.

A. *Summary of Economic Analysis Findings*

The only community crime prevention program that was reviewed in our previous *Crime and Justice* essay was the Participate and Learn Skills (PALS) program of Jones and Offord (1989). This was implemented in a public housing complex in Ottawa, Canada, and aimed to improve nonschool skills (e.g., sport and cultural activities, such as swimming, ice hockey, music, and art). An experimental housing complex was compared with a control housing complex, and crime and disorder were measured before, during, and after the program. The program was successful, since arrests of juveniles were 80 percent lower in the experimental site than in the control site.

The benefit-cost analysis was quite limited and clearly underestimates the monetary benefits of this program. However, this was very much a pioneering economic evaluation. Most of the monetary benefits accrued to the city housing authority, because of the reduced demand for private security in the experimental complex. The next largest portion of the benefits was caused by fewer calls to the city fire department.

TABLE 5

Overview of Community Crime Prevention Studies

Main Source	Program Name and Short Description	Sample Size	Benefit-Cost Ratio*
Jones and Offord (1989)	Participate and Learn Skills: Nonschool, skill development program	905 children and teens	2.55
Cook and MacDonald (2011)	Business Improvement Districts: CCTV, development planning, improved policing, and other city services, security guards	1,072 areas of city	18.8–21.3
Kuklinski et al. (2012)	Communities That Care: Implementation of needs-based, tested, and effective prevention programs	4,407 children and youths in 24 communities	5.3–10.23
Heller et al. (2013)	Becoming a Man: In-school and after-school programs, cognitive behavioral therapy	2,740 boys (grades 7–10)	2.3–33

* Expressed as a ratio of benefits to costs in monetary units (national currencies).

The monetary benefits accruing to the youth liaison section of the city police were small, but the researchers did not take account of realistic crime costs (including victim costs). Overall, the benefit-cost ratio was reported to be 2.55.

The community program evaluated by Cook and MacDonald (2011) was largely based on situational crime prevention. They evaluated the impact of Business Improvement Districts (BIDs) in Los Angeles. A BID is funded by a tax on all property owners in a district and is run by a nonprofit organization that aims to make the area clean and safe. Typically, money is spent on private security services, CCTV, combating disorder, repairing vandalized property, removing graffiti, and improving sanitation services and trash removal.

Cook and MacDonald (2011) studied recorded crimes and arrests in 30 BID and 1,042 non-BID areas from 1994 to 2005, a time span that encompassed the creation of all the BIDs. Their figure 1 seems to show that crime declined similarly during this period in BID and non-BID areas. (The BID areas had higher crime rates throughout.) However, their regression analyses concluded that there was a significant desirable effect of BIDs on crimes and arrests (robbery, assault, burglary, and vehicle theft), with no displacement. They used two estimates of the costs of crimes, based on jury awards and willingness to pay. They found that 28 fewer serious crimes in each BID translated into a savings of between $183,000 and $208,000, compared with the cost of each BID of $10,000. Adding in savings of $5,000 from fewer arrests produced a benefit-cost ratio between 18.8 and 21.3.

Heller et al. (2013) evaluated a program called Becoming a Man that was targeted on high-crime Chicago neighborhoods and implemented by two nonprofit organizations. The program consisted of mentoring (interactions with a prosocial adult), after-school programming including sports (to occupy youth during the risk hours after school), and cognitive-behavioral therapy in school. The youths were all either black or Hispanic, and their average age was 15. In total, 2,740 males were randomly assigned to receive the program or to be in a control group, and half of those who were assigned actually participated in the program.

The main result was that there was a 44 percent decrease in arrests for violence during the program year, a 36 percent decrease in other arrests, and improvements in educational outcomes. The costs of crimes were estimated using jury awards and willingness to pay. The program cost $1,100 per youth, and the crime benefits were estimated to be between

$5,300 and $33,000 per youth. However, the benefits were largely driven by decreases in homicide, which is a very costly crime. Excluding homicide, the crime benefits were estimated to be between $2,300 and $12,000 per youth. Therefore, the benefit-cost ratio based on fewer arrests was between 2.3 and 33. Heller et al. (2013) also estimated that the likely benefits from increases in graduation rates were between $38,000 and $84,000 per youth, but these estimates were based on rather contentious assumptions about the link between observed changes in grade point averages and later changes in graduation rates. After-school recreation activities were also found to be cost-beneficial in a randomized experiment by Ott et al. (2006), but this did not measure crime outcomes.

B. *Communities That Care*

Perhaps more than any other program, Communities That Care (CTC) is evidence based and systematic: the choice of interventions depends on empirical evidence about what are the important risk and protective factors in a particular community and on empirical evidence about "what works" (Sherman et al. 2006). CTC was developed in the United States but has been implemented widely in many other countries, including the United Kingdom.

1. *Design and Method.* CTC was developed as a risk-focused prevention strategy by Hawkins and Catalano (1992), and it soon became a core component of the US Office of Juvenile Justice and Delinquency Prevention's Comprehensive Strategy for Serious, Violent, and Chronic Juvenile Offenders (Wilson and Howell 1993). CTC is based on a theory (the social development model) that organizes risk and protective factors. The intervention techniques are tailored to the needs of each particular community. The "community" could be a city, a county, a small town, or even a neighborhood or a public housing community. This program aims to reduce delinquency and drug use by implementing particular prevention strategies that have demonstrated effectiveness in reducing risk factors or enhancing protective factors. It is modeled on large-scale community-wide public health programs designed to reduce illnesses such as coronary heart disease by tackling key risk factors. There is great emphasis in CTC on enhancing protective factors and building on strengths, partly because this is more attractive to communities than tackling risk factors.

CTC programs begin with community mobilization. Key community leaders (e.g., elected representatives, education officials, police chiefs, business leaders) are brought together, with the aim of getting them to agree on the goals of the prevention program and to implement CTC. The key leaders then set up a community board that is accountable to them, consisting of neighborhood residents and representatives from various agencies (e.g., school, police, social services, probation, health, parents, youth groups, business, church, media). The community board takes charge of prevention on behalf of the community.

The community board then carries out a risk and protective factor assessment, identifying key risk factors in that particular community that need addressing and key protective factors that need enhancing. This risk assessment might involve the use of police, school, social, or census records or local neighborhood or school surveys. After identifying key risk and protective factors, the community board assesses existing resources and develops a plan of intervention strategies. With specialist technical assistance and guidance, they choose programs from a menu of strategies that have been shown to be effective in well-designed evaluation research.

The menu of strategies listed by Hawkins and Catalano (1992) includes prenatal and postnatal home visiting programs, preschool intellectual enrichment programs, parent training, school organization and curriculum development, teacher training, and media campaigns. Other strategies include child skills training, antibullying programs in schools, situational prevention, and policing strategies. The choice of prevention strategies is based on empirical evidence about effective methods of tackling each particular risk factor, but it also depends on what are identified as the biggest problems in the community. While this approach is not without its challenges and complexities (e.g., cost, implementation, establishing partnerships among diverse agencies), an evidence-based approach that brings together the most effective prevention programs across multiple domains perhaps offers the greatest promise for reducing crime and building safer communities.

2. *Results.* Hawkins et al. (2009, 2012) evaluated the effectiveness of CTC in an ambitious large-scale randomized experiment (the Community Youth Development Study). Twenty-four communities across the United States (in seven states) were placed into 12 matched pairs, and one community in each pair was chosen at random to receive CTC. Participating communities were small to moderate-sized incorporated towns. Communities were asked to focus their prevention plans on youth age 10–14 and their families and schools. The effectiveness of CTC was

evaluated using repeated annual surveys of over 4,000 students from grade 5 (age 10–11) to grade 8 (age 13–14). The results showed that CTC caused a reduction in delinquency, alcohol use, and cigarette use but not in marijuana use.

3. *Economic Analysis.* The benefit-cost analysis by Kuklinski et al. (2012) was based only on the reductions in smoking and delinquency. CTC reduced the onset of smoking by grade 8 by 38 percent and the onset of delinquency by grade 8 by 21 percent. Benefits were projected over the lifetime of participants (up to age 74). The benefits of reducing the onset of smoking were estimated on the basis of known links between early smoking, adult smoking, health, and mortality. All benefits were discounted by 3 percent per year to 2004 prices (the year that CTC was first implemented). The smoking benefits were estimated to be $812 per youth. The benefits of reducing the onset of delinquency were based on the tangible and intangible costs of crime and criminal justice as estimated by Miller, Cohen, and Wiersema (1996), Aos et al. (2004), and McCollister, French, and Fang (2010). The savings from reduced crime were estimated to be $4,438 per youth. Therefore, the total savings came to $5,250 per youth.

The costs of CTC arose from the community coalition, the intervention programs, training, technical assistance, implementation monitoring, and other costs (e.g., in-kind contributions such as the cost of substitutes during teacher training periods). The average cost per youth was $991. However, the three smallest communities, each with fewer than 500 youth age 10–14, incurred very high costs per youth, skewing the average cost. Therefore, the median cost per youth was studied, and this came to $513. It was considered that this figure better reflected the cost per youth in most communities in the sample. On the basis of these figures, the benefit-cost ratio was estimated to be between 5.30 and 10.23.

VI. Discussion and Conclusions

On the basis of benefit-cost ratios, the most cost-beneficial developmental crime prevention programs include preschool intellectual enrichment programs and cognitive-behavioral treatment. The most cost-beneficial situational programs involve target hardening and improved lighting. CCTV is not a cost-beneficial way of reducing crime (although it may have other benefits such as increasing the probability that offenders will plead guilty). The most cost-beneficial community programs include CTC and BIDs. On the basis of the reviews of the Washington State Institute for Public Policy, parent training programs are also cost-beneficial. Generally, programs targeted on the highest risk areas or people have the highest benefit-cost ratios. However, it must be admitted that benefit-cost analyses are often only conducted after a program has been shown to be effective in reducing crime.

Our focus is on crime prevention benefits. However, developmental prevention in particular has important monetary benefits beyond reduced crime. These can take the form of, for example, increased tax revenues from higher earnings, savings from reduced usage of social services, and savings from lower health care use. The benefits of situational prevention, by contrast, appear largely to be confined to reductions in crime and often to reductions in specific types of crime. This may be because only crime benefits were measured in situational evaluations. Nevertheless, developmental prevention has a potentially wider range of benefits than situational prevention. Also, the benefits of developmental prevention may persist longer than the benefits of situational prevention, although little is known about the long-term effects of situational prevention.

Our analysis has several important limitations. First, it is necessarily based on a small number of studies. Second, costs and benefits were not estimated comparably in all studies. Some used a rigorous economic analysis methodology to assess costs and benefits, while others used a less adequate design, focusing mainly on savings from reduced crimes. Also, program benefits tended to be estimated conservatively, while program costs were often taken into account in full. Third, different perspectives (e.g., the public or society) were used in the economic analyses, so that the parties who were the recipients of the economic benefits or losses were not always comparable. For many of the studies it was not possible to disaggregate the benefit-cost findings from a consistent perspective across the studies. As far as possible, we used the perspective of the public (government/taxpayers and crime victims).

Another problem is that benefit-cost ratios are greatly affected by different assumptions made in the analysis, which is why a sensitivity analysis is essential. For example, according to the Institute of Medicine and National Research Council (2014), the benefit-cost ratio for CTC could vary from 3.58 to 14.70, depending on different assumptions. Confidence intervals around benefit-cost ratios are often large. Some aspects of benefit-cost analyses, such as the projection of benefits up to age 65 or 74, are contentious.

In order to learn more about benefit-cost ratios, a number of key issues need to be addressed. First, policy makers and researchers should play a greater role in ensuring that prevention programs include, as part of the original research design, provision for an economic analysis, preferably a benefit-cost analysis. Prospective economic analyses have many advantages over retrospective ones. Ideally, independent analyses should be carried out by researchers who were not involved in devising the program (Eisner 2009). However, it would also be desirable, as part of a program of research, to carry out a number of retrospective economic evaluations of crime prevention programs, particularly for programs that have been shown to work in reducing delinquency and crime. Programs could be selected according to criteria that would increase confidence in the benefit-cost findings, including high-quality research designs, preferably randomized experimental designs, large samples, and long-term follow-ups with low sample attrition. Second, researchers must ensure that economic analyses are not only methodologically rigorous but also comprehensive: all resources used (costs) and all relevant program effects (benefits) need to be monetized.

Third, there is the need for a standard list of costs and benefits that should be measured in all studies. This is an important issue that raises key questions about the inclusion of certain types of costs and benefits, in particular, the intangible costs to crime victims of pain, suffering, and lost quality of life. In Section II, we outlined the key outcome variables that should be measured in crime prevention programs (e.g., crime and delinquency, substance abuse, education, employment, health) and some of the relevant benefits that need to be assessed in those areas. A standard list of costs and benefits would greatly facilitate comparisons of the benefit-cost findings of different programs (Karoly 2012; Crowley et al. 2014; Institute of Medicine and National Research Council 2014).

Fourth, greater use of experimental research designs, particularly randomized experiments, is needed. For programs based on large units such as communities, experimental-control designs with before and after measures are usually the most appropriate and feasible. However, the CTC evaluation used a randomized trial in which the unit of assignment was the community. As an economic analysis is only as strong as the evaluation on which it is based, the stronger the research design of the outcome evaluation, the more confidence that can be placed in the findings of the economic analysis.

Fifth, funding bodies must be prepared to finance economic evaluation research. Government agencies with responsibility for the prevention of crime should commit a percentage of their research budgets to support economic evaluations of new and existing prevention programs. Government agencies, foundations, private sector organizations, and other groups that fund crime prevention schemes need to make future funding conditional on a built-in evaluation component that includes an assessment of monetary costs and benefits.

Two important methodological issues concern scaling-up and taking to scale. Most evaluations of crime prevention programs measure recorded crime, arrests, or convictions. However, these only capture the tip of the iceberg of crimes committed. In order to derive a more realistic estimate of the number of crimes prevented, and therefore of the benefit-cost ratio, it is important to estimate the true number of crimes committed. On the basis of analyses in Seattle and Pittsburgh, Farrington et al. (2003) and Farrington, Jolliffe, et al. (2007) estimated that the scaling-up factor from court appearances to self-reported offenses was of the order of 20–30. The second issue is that effects achieved in a small-scale demonstration project are often lower in a large-scale routine implementation. It is important to estimate the likely effects of taking programs to scale (Welsh, Sullivan, and Olds 2010).

While we have not explicitly compared early prevention and imprisonment in this essay, we believe that there is much evidence that it is more cost-beneficial to invest in early prevention than in imprisonment (Welsh and Farrington 2011*a*). Many other researchers have advocated that the time is ripe for a major investment to improve the lives of disadvantaged children (e.g., Heckman 2006; Knudsen et al. 2006; Kilburn and Karoly 2008; Doyle et al. 2009). The research of the Washington State Institute for Public Policy, and its effects in Washington state, on increasing investment in effective prevention programs and reducing investment in imprisonment is a model for the world. We recommend that more research should be conducted on the most cost-beneficial programs in different settings. This should lead to more responsible expenditure on crime prevention and to increased public safety. That would be in everyone's interest.

APPENDIX

TABLE A1
Developmental Crime Prevention Studies

Authors and Location	Age at Intervention	Risk Factors Manipulated	Context of Intervention	Duration and Type of Intervention	Sample Size	Scientific Methods Score	Follow-Up and Results*	Benefits Measured	Benefit-Cost Ratio†
Lipsey, Cordray, and Berger (1981), Lipsey (1984), Los Angeles County Delinquency Prevention Program	<15 years (average)	Behavioral problems	Community-based center	10 weeks; family counselling, academic tutoring, employment training	7,637 youths (all in program): T = NA, C = NA	3 (before-after, experimental control)	10 weeks: police arrests+	Criminal justice system	1.4
Long, Mallar, and Thornton (1981), Job Corps, United States	18 years (average)	Education, employment	Residential-based center	NA; vocational training, education, health care	5,100 youths: T = NA, C = NA	4 (before-after, experimental control with matching)	18 months (average): police arrests+, substance abuse+, school achievement+, employment+, wages+	Crime victim expenses (direct), criminal justice system, employment earnings, social service use	1.45
Hahn (1994), Quantum Opportunities Program, United States	15 years (average)	Education	Community-based agency, home	4 years; education, skills development	250 youths: T = 125, C = 125	5 (randomized experiment)	4.5 years: police arrests+, school achievement+, social services use+	Educational output, fewer children	3.68

Earle (1995), Hawaii Healthy Start	Prenatal and birth	Parenting, family planning	Home	4 years; parent education, parent support, family planning, community support	2,706 families: T = 1,353, C = 1,353	3 (before-after, experimental control)	4 years: child abuse and neglect+	Child protective services	.38
Schweinhart et al. (2005), Perry Preschool Program, Ypsilanti, Michigan	3–4 years	Cognitive development	Preschool, home	1–2 years; preschool intellectual enrichment, parent education	123 children (72 boys, 51 girls): T = 58, C = 65	5 (randomized experiment—stratified assignment)	36 years: educational achievement+, employment+, family stability+, police arrests+, school achievement+, substance abuse+, wages+, social services use0	Crime victim expenses (direct and indirect), criminal justice system, employment earnings, remedial education, social services use	12.9
Schochet, Burghardt, and McConnell (2006), Job Corps, United States	19.1 years (average)	Education, employment	Residential-based center	8 months (average); vocational training, education, health care, socialization activities	11,313 youths: T = 6,828, C = 4,485	5 (randomized experiment)	9 years: educational achievement+, police arrests+, school achievement+, family stability0, fertility0, social services use0, substance abuse0; full sample: wages0; age group 20–24: wages+	Criminal justice system, employment earnings, remedial education expenses, social services use	Full sample: .25; age group 20–24: 2.3
Barnett and Masse (2007), Abecedarian Program, North Carolina	12 weeks–5 years	Social, emotional, and cognitive areas of development—particular emphasis given to language	Center-based preschool	4–5 years; full-time, high-quality education	111 children: T = 57, C = 54	5 (randomized experiment)	21 years: educational achievement+, school achievement+, criminal behavior0, tobacco use0	Educational output, employment earnings (mother), public health care, social services use	2.5

TABLE A1 (*Continued*)

Authors and Location	Age at Intervention	Risk Factors Manipulated	Context of Intervention	Duration and Type of Intervention	Sample Size	Scientific Methods Score	Follow-Up and Results*	Benefits Measured	Benefit-Cost Ratio†
DuMont et al. (2010), Healthy Families New York, New York	Prenatal and birth	Parenting, family planning	Home	1.7 years (average); parent education, parenting skills, parent support, prenatal and child health care, home visits	1,173 families: T = 579, C = 594 (942 mothers and 800 children interviewed at 7 year follow-up)	5 (randomized experiment)	7 years: mothers, full sample: social services use+, child abuse and neglect0, discipline0; HPO and RRO subgroups: child abuse and neglect+, discipline+; children: school achievement+, problem behavior0, socioemotional development0	Child protective services, public health care, social services use	Full sample: .15; HPO subgroup: .25; RRO subgroup: 3.16
Reynolds, Temple, White et al. (2011), Child-Parent Center Early Education Program, Chicago	3 years	Behavior problems, child abuse and neglect, cognitive development/ school performance, physical health	Center-based preschool, home	1–6 years; education, family support, parent involvement, parent support, health care, continuity between preschool and early elementary school	1,539 children: T = 989, C = 550	4 (before-after, experimental control with matching)	24 years: child abuse and neglect+, depression+, educational achievement+, police arrests+, school achievement+, substance abuse+, tobacco use+	Child protective services, crime victim costs (tangible and intangible), criminal justice system, employment earnings, public health care, remedial education expenses	Preschool program: 7.2; school-age program: 2.11; preschool plus school-age: 5.21

Miller (2013), Nurse-Family Partnership, Denver (CO), Elmira (NY), Louisiana, Memphis (TN), Orange County (CA)	Prenatal, postnatal	Parenting, family planning	Home	1.5 years (average); parent education, parent support, community support, family planning, nurse home visits	371 families (average): T = 149 (average), C = 222 (average)	5–3 (randomized experiment—before-after, experimental control)	19 years (Elmira): child abuse and neglect+, child mortality+, health+, police arrests+, school achievement+, social services use+, substance abuse+	Child protective services, criminal justice system, public health care, remedial education expenses, social services use	2.9
Farrington and Koegl (2015), Stop Now and Plan—Under 12 Outreach Project (SNAP-ORP), Toronto, Canada	9.6 years (average)	Cognitive-behavioral self-control and problem solving	Community-based center	12 weeks; skills training, cognitive problem solving, self-control and anger management, cognitive self-instruction, family management training, and parent management training	376 boys; T = NA, C = NA	4 (before-after, experimental control with matching), based on independent evaluations	9 years: criminal behavior+	Convictions	2.05–3.75 (17.33–31.77 scaled up to self-reports)

NOTE.—T = treatment group; C = control group; HPO = high prevention opportunity; RRO = recurrence reduction opportunity; NA = not available.

* 0 = null effects; + = significant desirable effects; − = significant undesirable effects.

† Expressed as a ratio of benefits to costs in monetary units (national currencies).

TABLE A2
Situational Crime Prevention Studies

Authors and Location	Crimes Targeted	Context of Intervention	Duration and Primary Technique of Intervention	Sample Size	Scientific Methods Score	Follow-Up and Results*	Benefits Measured	Benefit-Cost Ratio†
Cirel et al. (1977), Seattle, WA	Burglary	Home	1 year; natural surveillance (Block Watch)	1,474 homes	3 (before-after, experimental control)	1 year: burglary+	Crime victim expenses (person, direct)	.4
Skilton (1988), South Kilburn Estate, London Borough of Brent	Vandalism	Public housing estate	1 year; employee surveillance (concierges)	305 homes (in two high rises)	3 (before-after, experimental control)	1 year: vandalism+	Crime victim expenses (public sector, direct), public housing	1.44
Ekblom, Law, and Sutton (1996), Safer Cities Programme, England and Wales	Burglary	Home	1–2 years; target hardening (locks, alarms, entry systems)	7,500 households	4 (before-after, experimental control and statistical analyses)	1–2 years: burglary+	Crime victim expenses (person, direct), criminal justice system (police)	3.0 (high risk), .9 (average risk)
Ayres and Levitt (1998), Boston (MA), Chicago (IL), Long Beach (CA), Los Angeles (CA), Miami (FL), Newark (NJ)	Auto theft	Vehicles	5 years; formal surveillance (remotely activated location transmitter)	6 cities with populations over 250,000	3 (before-after, experimental control)	5 years: vehicle theft+	Crime victim expenses (person and private sector, direct)	15

Painter and Farrington (2001), Dudley, England	Property and personal crime in general	Residential streets	1 year; natural surveillance (street lighting)	T = 431 homes, C = 448 homes	4 (before-after, experimental control and statistical analyses)	1 year: burglary+, personal crime+, theft+, vandalism+, vehicle theft+	Crime victim expenses (person, direct), criminal justice system, damaged/stolen property, increased security, lost output	6.2–121
Painter and Farrington (2001), Stoke-on-Trent, England	Property and personal crime in general	Residential streets and footpaths	1 year; natural surveillance (street lighting)	T = 317 homes, C = 223 homes	4 (before-after, experimental control and statistical analyses)	1 year: burglary+, personal crime+, theft+, vandalism+, vehicle theft+	Crime victim expenses (person, direct), criminal justice system, damaged/stolen property, increased security, lost output	5.4–54
Bowers, Johnson, and Hirschfield (2004), Liverpool, England	Burglary	Residential areas	0–12 months; target hardening (alley gates)	106 housing blocks	3 (before-after, experimental control)	1 year: burglary+	Crime victim expenses (person, direct), criminal justice system, damaged/stolen property, increased security, lost output	6 months: 1.01; 12 months: 1.86
Gill and Spriggs (2005), England and Wales	Property and personal crime in general	Car parks, hospitals, residential areas, town and city centers	4–24 months; remote surveillance (CCTV)	7 CCTV projects	3 (before-after, experimental control)	1 year: police recorded crime0, vehicle crime+	Crime victim expenses (person, direct), criminal justice system, damaged/stolen property, increased security, lost output	City Outskirts: 1.24; Hawkeye: .67; other five: 0

NOTE.—T = treatment group; C = control group.

* 0 = null effects; + = significant desirable effects; − = significant undesirable effects.

† Expressed as a ratio of benefits to costs in monetary units (national currencies).

TABLE A3

Excluded Situational Crime Prevention Studies

Authors and Location	Crimes Targeted	Context of Intervention	Duration and Primary Technique of Intervention	Sample Size	Scientific Methods Score	Follow-Up and Results*	Benefits Measured	Benefit-Cost Ratio[†]
Schnelle et al. (1979), Nashville, TN	Armed robbery	Store	6 and 11 months; formal surveillance (silent alarms)	48 stores	2 (before-after)	5 and 15 months: armed robbery0	Crime victim expenses (private sector, direct)	.36
Laycock (1986), Caerphilly, Wales	Burglary	Home	1 year; identifying property (property marking)	2,234 homes	2 (before-after)	1 year: burglary+	Criminal justice system (police)	.78
van Andel (1989), VICs, The Netherlands	Vandalism, toll fraud, assault	Public transport system	3 and 4 years; formal surveillance (special transport officials)	Metro, bus, and tram in three cities	2 (before-after)	3 and 4 years: vandalism+, toll fraud+, assault+	Crime victim expenses (public sector, direct), toll revenue	.32
Clarke and McGrath (1990), Victoria, Australia	Robbery	Betting shop	1–8 years; target hardening (time-locks, cash limits)	429 betting shops (average)	2 (before-after, some control)	1–8 years: robbery+	Crime victim expenses (public sector, direct)	1.71
Forrester et al. (1990), Kirkholt Burglary Prevention Project, Rochdale, England	Burglary	Public housing estate	3 years; target removal (removal of coin meters)	2,280 homes	2 (before-after, some control)	3 years: burglary+	Crime victim expenses (person, direct), criminal justice system, public housing	5.04

Poyner (1992), North Shields, England	Vandalism	Public transport system	9 months; employee surveillance (CCTV)	80 buses	2 (before-after)	9 months: vandalism+	Crime victim expenses (public sector, direct)	2.35
Davidson and Farr (1994), Mitchellhill Estate, Glasgow	Vandalism, burglary	Public housing estate	15 months; employee surveillance (CCTV)	5 housing blocks	2 (before-after)	15 months: vandalism+, burglary+	Crime victim expenses (public sector, direct), rental income	.47
Knight (1994), Possil Park Estate, Glasgow	Vandalism, burglary	Public housing estate	1 year; formal surveillance (security guards)	1,767 homes	2 (before-after)	1 year: vandalism+, burglary+	Crime victim expenses (person and private sector, direct)	1.31
van Ours and Vollaard (2011), England and Wales and The Netherlands	Auto theft	Vehicles	7–10 years; target hardening (electronic engine immobilizer)	All new cars sold since 1998	2 (before-after)	7–10 years: vehicle crime+	Crime victim expenses (person, direct), criminal justice system, damaged/stolen property, increased security, lost output	England and Wales: 29; The Netherlands: 7
Vollaard and van Ours (2011), The Netherlands	Burglary	Home	5 years; target hardening (certified burglary-proof locks and window and door frames)	All new-built homes since 1999—approximately 70,000 houses annually	2 (before-after)	5 years: burglary+	Crime victim expenses (person, direct), criminal justice system, damaged/stolen property, increased security, lost output	1.07

* 0 = null effects; + = significant desirable effects; − = significant undesirable effects.

† Expressed as a ratio of benefits to costs in monetary units (national currencies).

TABLE A4
Community Crime Prevention Studies

Authors and Location	Crimes Targeted	Context of Intervention	Duration and Primary Technique of Intervention	Sample Size	Scientific Methods Score	Follow-Up and Results*	Benefits Measured	Benefit-Cost Ratio†
Jones and Offord (1989), Participate and Learn Skills, Ottawa, Canada	Risk and protective factors	Communities	32 months; developmental crime prevention (nonschool, skill development programs)	905 children, 5–15 years old (average): T = 417, C = 488	3 (before-after, experimental control)	2 years: criminal behavior+, integration into their communities+	Reduced use of publicly funded agencies (police, housing agency, community center, fire department)	2.55
Cook and MacDonald (2011), Business Improvement Districts, Los Angeles, CA	Property and personal crime in general	Neighborhoods	2 years; privately funded situational crime prevention (CCTV, development planning, improved policing and other city services, security guards)	30 BID areas, 1,042 non-BID areas	4 (before-after, experimental control and statistical analyses)	2 years: assault+, burglary+, robbery+, vehicle crime0	Crime victim expenses (person, direct), criminal justice system	18.8–21.3

Kuklinski et al. (2012), Communities That Care, Colorado, Illinois, Kansas, Maine, Oregon, Utah, and Washington state	Risk and protective factors	Communities	3 years; developmental crime prevention (implementation of needs-based, tested, and effective prevention programs)	4,407 10–14-year-olds across 24 communities: T = 12 communities, C = 12 communities	5 (randomized experiment)	3 years: criminal behavior+, tobacco use+	Crime victim expenses (public sector, direct), criminal justice system, health, mortality	5.3–10.23
Heller et al. (2013), Becoming a Man, Chicago	Risk and protective factors	School	1 year; developmental crime prevention (in-school and after-school programs, cognitive behavioral therapy)	2,740 males grade 7–10: T = NA, C = NA	5 (randomized experiment)	2 years: criminal behavior+, educational achievement+; 1 year: criminal behavior0, educational achievement+	Crime victim expenses (person, direct), criminal justice system	2.3–33

NOTE.—T = treatment group; C = control group; BID = Business Improvement Districts; NA = not available.

* 0 = null effects; + = significant desirable effects; − = significant undesirable effects.

† Expressed as a ratio of benefits to costs in monetary units (national currencies).

REFERENCES

Aos, Steve. 1998. "Costs and Benefits: Estimating the 'Bottom Line' for Crime Prevention and Intervention Programs; A Description of the Cost-Benefit Model, Version 2.0." Unpublished manuscript. Olympia: Washington State Institute for Public Policy.

Aos, Steve, Robert Barnoski, and Roxanne Lieb. 1998. "Preventive Programs for Young Offenders: Effective and Cost-Effective." *Overcrowded Times* 9 (2):1, 7–11.

Aos, Steve, and Elizabeth K. Drake. 2010. *Fight Crime and Save Money*. Olympia: Washington State Institute for Public Policy.

Aos, Steve, Roxanne Lieb, Jim Mayfield, Maria Miller, and Annie Pennucci. 2004. *Benefits and Costs of Prevention and Early Intervention Programs for Youth*. Olympia: Washington State Institute for Public Policy.

Aos, Steve, Marna G. Miller, and Elizabeth K. Drake. 2006. *Evidence-Based Public Policy Options to Reduce Future Prison Construction, Criminal Justice Costs, and Crime Rates*. Olympia: Washington State Institute for Public Policy.

Ayres, Ian, and Steven D. Levitt. 1998. "Measuring Positive Externalities from Unobservable Victim Precaution: An Empirical Analysis of Lojack." *Quarterly Journal of Economics* 113:43–77.

Barnett, W. Steven. 1993. "Cost-Benefit Analysis." In *Significant Benefits: The High/Scope Perry Preschool Study through Age 27*, by Lawrence J. Schweinhart, Helen V. Barnes, and David P. Weikart with W. Steven Barnett and Ann S. Epstein. Ypsilanti, MI: High/Scope Press.

———. 1996. *Lives in the Balance: Age-27 Benefit-Cost Analysis of the High/Scope Perry Preschool Program*. Ypsilanti, MI: High/Scope Press.

Barnett, W. Steven, Clive R. Belfield, and Milagros Nores. 2005. "Lifetime Cost-Benefit Analysis." In *Lifetime Effects: The High/Scope Perry Preschool Study through Age 40*, edited by Lawrence J. Schweinhart, Jeanne Montie, Zongping Xiang, W. Steven Barnett, Clive R. Belfield, and Milagros Nores. Ypsilanti, MI: High/Scope Press.

Barnett, W. Steven, and Colette M. Escobar. 1987. "The Economics of Early Educational Intervention: A Review." *Review of Educational Research* 57:387–414.

———. 1990. "Economic Costs and Benefits of Early Intervention." In *Handbook of Early Childhood Intervention*, edited by Samuel J. Meisels and Jack P. Shonkoff. Cambridge: Cambridge University Press.

Barnett, W. Steven, and Leonard N. Masse. 2007. "Comparative Benefit-Cost Analysis of the Abecedarian Program and Its Policy Implications." *Economics of Education Review* 26:113–25.

Belfield, Clive R., Milagros Nores, W. Steven Barnett, and Lawrence J. Schweinhart. 2006. "The High/Scope Perry Preschool Program: Cost-Benefit Analysis Using Data from the Age-40 Follow-Up." *Journal of Human Resources* 41:162–90.

Bennett, Trevor H. 1998. "Crime Prevention." In *The Handbook of Crime and Punishment*, edited by Michael H. Tonry. New York: Oxford University Press.

Bennett, Trevor H., Katy Holloway, and David P. Farrington. 2009. "A Review of the Effectiveness of Neighborhood Watch." *Security Journal* 22:143–55.
Berrueta-Clement, John R., Lawrence J. Schweinhart, W. Steven Barnett, Ann S. Epstein, and David P. Weikart. 1984. *Changed Lives: The Effects of the Perry Preschool Program on Youths through Age 19*. Ypsilanti, MI: High/Scope Press.
Bierie, David. 2009. "Cost Matters: A Randomized Experiment Comparing Recidivism between Two Styles of Prisons." *Journal of Experimental Criminology* 5:371–97.
Bowers, Kate J., Shane D. Johnson, and Alex F. G. Hirschfield. 2004. "Closing Off Opportunities for Crime: An Evaluation of Alley-Gating." *European Journal on Criminal Policy and Research* 10:285–308.
Brand, Sam, and Richard Price. 2000. *The Economic and Social Costs of Crime*. Home Office Research Study no. 217. London: Home Office.
Campbell, Frances, Gabriella Conti, James J. Heckman, Seong Hyeok Moon, Rodrigo Pinto, Elizabeth Pungello, and Yi Pan. 2014. "Early Childhood Investments Substantially Boost Adult Health." *Science* 343:1478–85.
Cirel, Paul, Patricia Evans, Daniel McGillis, and Debra Whitcomb. 1977. *An Exemplary Project: Community Crime Prevention*. Washington, DC: National Criminal Justice Reference Service.
Clarke, Ronald V. 1992. "Introduction." In *Situational Crime Prevention: Successful Case Studies*, edited by Ronald V. Clarke. Albany, NY: Harrow & Heston.
———. 1995*a*. "Opportunity-Reducing Crime Prevention Strategies and the Role of Motivation." In *Integrating Crime Prevention Strategies: Propensity and Opportunity*, edited by Per-Olof H. Wikström, Ronald V. Clarke, and Joan McCord. Stockholm: National Council for Crime Prevention.
———. 1995*b*. "Situational Crime Prevention." In *Building a Safer Society: Strategic Approaches to Crime Prevention*, edited by Michael Tonry and David P. Farrington. Vol. 19 of *Crime and Justice: A Review of Research*, edited by Michael Tonry. Chicago: University of Chicago Press.
———. 2008. "Situational Crime Prevention." In *Environmental Criminology and Crime Analysis*, edited by Richard Wortley and Lorraine Mazerolle. Cullompton, UK: Willan.
Clarke, Ronald V., and Derek B. Cornish. 1985. "Modeling Offenders' Decisions: A Framework for Research and Policy." In *Crime and Justice: An Annual Review of Research*, vol. 6, edited by Michael Tonry and Norval Morris. Chicago: University of Chicago Press.
Clarke, Ronald V., and Gerry McGrath. 1990. "Cash Reduction and Robbery Prevention in Australian Betting Shops." *Security Journal* 1:160–63.
Clarke, Ronald V., and David Weisburd. 1994. "Diffusion of Crime Control Benefits: Observations on the Reverse of Displacement." In *Crime Prevention Studies*, vol. 2, edited by Ronald V. Clarke. Monsey, NY: Criminal Justice.
Cohen, Lawrence E., and Marcus Felson. 1979. "Social Change and Crime Rate Trends: A Routine Activity Approach." *American Sociological Review* 44:588–608.
Cohen, Mark A. 1988. "Pain, Suffering, and Jury Awards: A Study of the Cost of Crime to Victims." *Law and Society Review* 22:537–55.

———. 1998. "The Monetary Value of Saving a High-Risk Youth." *Journal of Quantitative Criminology* 14:5–33.

Cohen, Mark A., Ted R. Miller, and Shelli B. Rossman. 1994. "The Costs and Consequences of Violent Behavior in the United States." In *Understanding and Preventing Violence*, vol. 4, *Consequences and Control*, edited by Albert J. Reiss Jr. and Jeffrey A. Roth. Washington, DC: National Academy Press.

Cohen, Mark A., and Alex R. Piquero. 2009. "New Evidence on the Monetary Value of Saving a High Risk Youth." *Journal of Quantitative Criminology* 25:25–49.

Cohen, Mark A., Alex R. Piquero, and Wesley G. Jennings. 2010. "Studying the Costs of Crime across Offender Trajectories." *Criminology and Public Policy* 9:279–305.

Cohen, Mark A., Roland T. Rust, and Sara Steen. 2006. "Prevention, Crime Control or Cash? Public Preferences toward Criminal Justice Spending Priorities." *Justice Quarterly* 3:317–35.

Cook, Philip J., and Jens Ludwig. 2000. *Gun Violence: The Real Costs*. New York: Oxford University Press.

Cook, Philip J., and John M. MacDonald. 2011. "Public Safety through Private Action: An Economic Assessment of BIDS." *Economic Journal* 121:445–62.

Cook, Thomas D., and Donald T. Campbell. 1979. *Quasi-Experimentation: Design and Analysis Issues for Field Settings*. Chicago: Rand McNally.

Cornish, Derek B., and Ronald V. Clarke. 2003. "Opportunities, Precipitators and Criminal Decisions: A Reply to Wortley's Critique of Situational Crime Prevention." In *Theory for Practice in Situational Crime Prevention*, edited by Martha J. Smith and Derek B. Cornish. Crime Prevention Studies 16. Monsey, NY: Criminal Justice.

Crowley, D. Max, Laura Griner Hill, Margaret R. Kuklinski, and Damon E. Jones. 2014. "Research Priorities for Economic Analyses of Prevention: Current Issues and Future Directions." *Prevention Science* 15:789–98.

Cullen, Francis T., Michael L. Benson, and Matthew D. Makarios. 2012. "Developmental and Life-Course Theories of Offending." In *The Oxford Handbook of Crime Prevention*, edited by Brandon C. Welsh and David P. Farrington. New York: Oxford University Press.

Cullen, Francis T., Brenda A. Vose, Cheryl N. L. Jonson, and James D. Unnever. 2007. "Public Support for Early Intervention: Is Child Saving a 'Habit of the Heart'?" *Victims and Offenders* 2:109–24.

Davidson, Jo, and John Farr. 1994. "Mitchellhill Estate: Estate Based Management Initiative." In *Housing Safe Communities: An Evaluation of Recent Initiatives*, edited by Steve Osborn. London: Safe Neighbourhoods Unit.

Donohue, John J. 2009. "Assessing the Relative Benefits of Incarceration: Overall Changes and the Benefits on the Margin." In *Do Prisons Make Us Safer? The Benefits and Costs of the Prison Boom*, edited by Steven Raphael and Michael A. Stoll. New York: Russell Sage.

Donohue, John J., and Peter Siegelman. 1998. "Allocating Resources among Prisons and Social Programs in the Battle against Crime." *Journal of Legal Studies* 27:1–43.

Dossetor, Kym. 2011. *Cost-Benefit Analysis and Its Application to Crime Prevention and Criminal Justice Research*. Technical and Background Paper no. 42. Canberra: Australian Institute of Criminology.

Doyle, Orla, Colm P. Harmon, James J. Heckman, and Richard E. Tremblay. 2009. "Investing in Early Human Development: Timing and Economic Efficiency." *Economics and Human Biology* 7:1–6.

Drake, Elizabeth K., Steve Aos, and Marna G. Miller. 2009. "Evidence-Based Public Policy Options to Reduce Crime and Criminal Justice Costs: Implications in Washington State." *Victims and Offenders* 4:170–96.

Dubourg, Richard, Joe Hamed, and Jamie Thorns. 2005. *The Economic and Social Costs of Crime against Individuals and Households 2003/04*. London: Home Office.

DuMont, Kimberly, Kristen Kirkland, Susan Mitchell-Herzfeld, Susan Ehrhard-Dietzel, Monica L. Rodriguez, Eunju Lee, China Layne, and Rose Greene. 2010. *A Randomized Trial of Healthy Families New York (HFNY): Does Home Visiting Prevent Child Maltreatment?* Final Report. New York: New York State Office of Children and Family Services.

Earle, Ralph B. 1995. *Helping to Prevent Child Abuse—and Future Consequences: Hawaii Healthy Start*. Washington, DC: National Institute of Justice, US Department of Justice.

Ebel, Beth E., Frederick P. Rivara, Rolf Loeber, and Dustin A. Pardini. 2011. "Modeling the Impact of Preventive Interventions on the National Homicide Rate." In *Young Homicide Offenders and Victims: Risk Factors, Prediction, and Prevention from Childhood*, by Rolf Loeber and David P. Farrington with contributions by Robert B. Cotter et al. New York: Springer.

Eck, John E. 2006. "Preventing Crime at Places." In *Evidence-Based Crime Prevention*, rev. ed., edited by Lawrence W. Sherman, David P. Farrington, Brandon C. Welsh, and Doris Layton MacKenzie. New York: Routledge.

Eckenrode, John, Mary Campa, Dennis W. Luckey, Charles R. Henderson, Robert Cole, Harriet Kitzman, Elizabeth Anson, Kimberly Sidora-Arcoleo, Jane Powers, and David L. Olds. 2010. "Long-Term Effects of Prenatal and Infancy Nurse Home Visitation on the Life Course of Youths: 19-Year Follow-Up of a Randomized Trial." *Archives of Pediatrics and Adolescent Medicine* 164:9–15.

Eisner, Manuel. 2009. "No Effects in Independent Prevention Trials: Can We Reject the Cynical View?" *Journal of Experimental Criminology* 5:163–83.

Ekblom, Paul, Ho Law, and Mike Sutton. 1996. *Safer Cities and Domestic Burglary*. Home Office Research Study no. 164. London: Home Office.

Farrington, David P. 1983. "Randomized Experiments on Crime and Justice." In *Crime and Justice: An Annual Review of Research*, vol. 4, edited by Michael Tonry and Norval Morris. Chicago: University of Chicago Press.

———. 1995. "The Development of Offending and Antisocial Behaviour from Childhood: Key Findings from the Cambridge Study in Delinquent Development." *Journal of Child Psychology and Psychiatry* 36:929–64.

———. 1997. "Evaluating a Community Crime Prevention Program." *Evaluation* 3:157–73.

———. 2010. "The Developmental Evidence Base: Prevention." In *Forensic Psychology*, edited by Graham J. Towl and David A. Crighton. Oxford: Blackwell.

———. 2013. "Longitudinal and Experimental Research in Criminology." In *Crime and Justice, 1975–2025*, edited by Michael Tonry. Vol. 42 of *Crime and Justice: A Review of Research*, edited by Michael Tonry. Chicago: University of Chicago Press.

Farrington, David P., Martin Gill, Sam Waples, and Javier Argomaniz. 2007. "The Effects of Closed-Circuit Television on Crime: Meta-analysis of an English National Quasi-Experimental Multi-site Evaluation." *Journal of Experimental Criminology* 3:21–38.

Farrington, David P., Denise C. Gottfredson, Lawrence W. Sherman, and Brandon C. Welsh. 2006. "The Maryland Scientific Methods Scale." In *Evidence-Based Crime Prevention*, rev. ed., edited by Lawrence W. Sherman, David P. Farrington, Brandon C. Welsh, and Doris Layton MacKenzie. New York: Routledge.

Farrington, David P., Darrick Jolliffe, J. David Hawkins, Richard F. Catalano, Karl Hill, and Rick Kosterman. 2003. "Comparing Delinquency Careers in Court Records and Self-Reports." *Criminology* 41:933–58.

Farrington, David P., Darrick Jolliffe, Rolf Loeber, and D. Lynn Homish. 2007. "How Many Offenses Are Really Committed per Juvenile Court Offender?" *Victims and Offenders* 2:227–49.

Farrington, David P., and Christopher J. Koegl. 2015. "Monetary Benefits and Costs of the Stop Now and Plan Program for Boys Aged 6–11, Based on the Prevention of Later Offending." *Journal of Quantitative Criminology* 31:263–87.

Farrington, David P., Anthony A. Petrosino, and Brandon C. Welsh. 2001. "Systematic Reviews and Cost-Benefit Analyses of Correctional Interventions." *Prison Journal* 81:339–59.

Farrington, David P., and Brandon C. Welsh. 2002. "Improved Street Lighting and Crime Prevention." *Justice Quarterly* 19:313–42.

———. 2005. "Randomized Experiments in Criminology: What Have We Learned in the Last Two Decades?" *Journal of Experimental Criminology* 1: 9–38.

———. 2006. "A Half Century of Randomized Experiments on Crime and Justice." In *Crime and Justice: A Review of Research*, vol. 34, edited by Michael Tonry. Chicago: University of Chicago Press.

———. 2007. *Saving Children from a Life of Crime: Early Risk Factors and Effective Interventions*. New York: Oxford University Press.

———. 2013. "Randomized Experiments in Criminology: What Has Been Learned from Long-Term Follow-Ups?" In *Experimental Criminology: Prospects for Advancing Science and Public Policy*, edited by Brandon C. Welsh, Anthony A. Braga, and Gerben J. N. Bruinsma. New York: Cambridge University Press.

Forrester, David, Samantha Frenz, Martin O'Connell, and Ken Pease. 1990. *The Kirkholt Burglary Prevention Project: Phase II*. Crime Prevention Unit Paper no. 23. London: Home Office.

Gill, Charlotte E., and David Weisburd. 2013. "Increasing Equivalence in Small-Sample Place-Based Experiments: Taking Advantage of Block Randomization Methods." In *Experimental Criminology: Prospects for Advancing Science and Public Policy*, edited by Brandon C. Welsh, Anthony A. Braga, and Gerben J. N. Bruinsma. New York: Cambridge University Press.

Gill, Martin, and Angela Spriggs. 2005. *Assessing the Impact of CCTV*. Research Study no. 292. London: Home Office.

Greenwood, Peter W. 2006. *Changing Lives: Delinquency Prevention as Crime-Control Policy*. Chicago: University of Chicago Press.

Greenwood, Peter W., Karyn E. Model, C. Peter Rydell, and James Chiesa. 1996. *Diverting Children from a Life of Crime: Measuring Costs and Benefits*. Santa Monica, CA: Rand.

Greenwood, Peter W., and Brandon C. Welsh. 2012. "Promoting Evidence-Based Practice in Delinquency Prevention at the State Level: Principles, Progress, and Policy Directions." *Criminology and Public Policy* 11:493–513.

Hahn, Andrew. 1994. *Evaluation of the Quantum Opportunities Program (QOP): Did the Program Work?* Waltham, MA: Center for Human Resources, Heller Graduate School, Brandeis University.

Hawkins, J. David, and Richard F. Catalano. 1992. *Communities That Care: Action for Drug Abuse Prevention*. San Francisco: Jossey-Bass.

Hawkins, J. David, Sabrina Oesterle, Eric D. Brown, Michael W. Arthur, Robert D. Abbott, Abigail A. Fagan, and Richard F. Catalano. 2009. "Results of a Type 2 Translational Research Trial to Prevent Adolescent Drug Use and Delinquency: A Test of Communities That Care." *Archives of Pediatrics and Adolescent Medicine* 163:789–98.

Hawkins, J. David, Sabrina Oesterle, Eric D. Brown, Kathryn C. Monahan, Robert D. Abbott, Michael W. Arthur, and Richard F. Catalano. 2012. "Sustained Decreases in Risk Exposure and Youth Problem Behaviors after Installation of the Communities That Care Prevention System in a Randomized Trial." *Archives of Pediatrics and Adolescent Medicine* 166:141–48.

Heckman, James J. 2006. "Skill Formation and the Economics of Investing in Disadvantaged Children." *Science* 312:1900–1902.

Heckman, James J., Seong Hyeok Moon, Rodrigo Pinto, Peter Savelyev, and Adam Yavitz. 2010*a*. "Analyzing Social Experiments as Implemented: A Reexamination of the Evidence from the HighScope Perry Preschool Program." *Quantitative Economics* 1:1–46.

———. 2010*b*. "The Rate of Return to the HighScope Perry Preschool Program." *Journal of Public Economics* 94:114–28.

Heller, Sara, Harold A. Pollack, Roseanna Ander, and Jens Ludwig. 2013. "Preventing Youth Violence and Dropout: A Randomized Field Experiment." Working Paper 19014. Cambridge, MA: National Bureau of Economic Research.

Home Office. 2011. *Revisions Made to the Multipliers and Unit Costs of Crime Used in the Integrated Offender Management Value for Money Toolkit*. London: Home Office.

Hope, Tim. 1995. "Community Crime Prevention." In *Building a Safer Society: Strategic Approaches to Crime Prevention*, edited by Michael Tonry and David P. Farrington. Vol. 19 of *Crime and Justice: A Review of Research*, edited by Michael Tonry. Chicago: University of Chicago Press.

Institute of Medicine and National Research Council. 2014. *Considerations in Applying Benefit-Cost Analysis to Preventive Interventions for Children, Youth, and Families: Workshop Summary*. Washington, DC: National Academies Press.

Johnson, Shane D., Rob T. Guerette, and Kate J. Bowers. 2012. "Crime Displacement and Diffusion of Benefits." In *The Oxford Handbook of Crime Prevention*, edited by Brandon C. Welsh and David P. Farrington. New York: Oxford University Press.

Jolliffe, Darrick, David P. Farrington, and Philip Howard. 2013. "How Long Did It Last? A 10-Year Reconviction Follow-Up Study of High Intensity Training for Young Offenders." *Journal of Experimental Criminology* 9:515–31.

Jones, Marshall B., and David R. Offord. 1989. "Reduction of Antisocial Behaviour in Poor Children by Nonschool Skill-Development." *Journal of Child Psychology and Psychiatry* 30:737–50.

Karoly, Lynn A. 2012. "Toward Standardization of Benefit-Cost Analysis of Early Childhood Interventions." *Journal of Benefit-Cost Analysis* 3:1–43.

Kilburn, M. Rebecca, and Lynn A. Karoly. 2008. *The Economics of Early Childhood Policy: What the Dismal Science Has to Say about Investing in Children*. Santa Monica, CA: Rand.

Kirp, David. 2004. "Life Way after Head Start." *New York Times Magazine*, November 21.

Klietz, Stephanie J., Charles M. Borduin, and Cindy M. Schaeffer. 2010. "Cost-Benefit Analysis of Multisystemic Therapy with Serious and Violent Juvenile Offenders." *Journal of Family Therapy* 24:657–66.

Knapp, Martin. 1997. "Economic Evaluations and Interventions for Children and Adolescents with Mental Health Problems." *Journal of Child Psychology and Psychiatry* 38:3–25.

Knapp, Martin, and Ann Netten. 1997. "The Cost and Cost Effectiveness of Community Penalties: Principles, Tools and Examples." In *Evaluating the Effectiveness of Community Penalties*, edited by George Mair. Aldershot, UK: Avebury.

Knapp, Martin, Eileen Robertson, and Gill McIvor. 1992. "The Comparative Costs of Community Service and Custody in Scotland." *Howard Journal of Criminal Justice* 31:8–30.

Knight, Barry. 1994. "Possil Park Estate: Security Scheme." In *Housing Safe Communities: An Evaluation of Recent Initiatives*, edited by Steve Osborn. London: Safe Neighbourhoods Unit.

Knudsen, Eric I., James J. Heckman, Judy L. Cameron, and Jack P. Shonkoff. 2006. "Economic, Neurobiological, and Behavior Perspectives on Building America's Future Workforce." *Proceedings of the National Academy of Sciences* 103:10155–62.

Kuklinski, Margaret R., John S. Briney, J. David Hawkins, and Richard F. Catalano. 2012. "Cost-Benefit Analysis of Communities That Care Outcomes at Eighth Grade." *Prevention Science* 13:150–61.

Lally, J. Ronald, Peter L. Mangione, and Alice S. Honig. 1988. "The Syracuse University Family Development Research Program: Long-Range Impact of an Early Intervention with Low-Income Children and Their Families." In *Parent Education as Early Childhood Intervention: Emerging Directions in Theory, Research and Practice*, edited by D. R. Powell. Norwood, NJ: Ablex.

Laycock, Gloria. 1986. "Property Marking as a Deterrent to Domestic Burglary." In *Situational Crime Prevention: From Theory into Practice*, edited by Kevin Heal and Gloria Laycock. London: H.M. Stationery Office.

Lee, Stephanie, Steve Aos, Elizabeth K. Drake, Anne Pennucci, Marna G. Miller, and Laurie Anderson. 2012. *Return on Investment: Evidence-Based Options to Improve Statewide Outcomes*. Olympia: Washington State Institute for Public Policy.

Lipsey, Mark W. 1984. "Is Delinquency Prevention a Cost-Effective Strategy? A California Perspective." *Journal of Research in Crime and Delinquency* 21:279–302.

Lipsey, Mark W., David S. Cordray, and Dale E. Berger. 1981. "Evaluation of a Juvenile Diversion Program: Using Multiple Lines of Evidence." *Evaluation Review* 5:283–306.

Long, David A., Charles D. Mallar, and Craig V. D. Thornton. 1981. "Evaluating the Benefits and Costs of the Job Corps." *Journal of Policy Analysis and Management* 1:55–76.

Marsh, Kevin, and Chris Fox. 2008. "The Benefit and Cost of Prison in the UK: The Results of a Model of Lifetime Re-offending." *Journal of Experimental Criminology* 4:403–23.

Marsh, Kevin, Chris Fox, and Carol Hedderman. 2009. "Do You Get What You Pay For? Assessing the Use of Prison from an Economic Perspective." *Howard Journal of Criminal Justice* 48:144–57.

McCollister, Kathryn E., Michael T. French, and Hai Fang. 2010. "The Cost of Crime to Society: New Crime Specific Estimates for Policy and Program Evaluation." *Drug and Alcohol Dependence* 108:98–109.

McDougall, Cynthia, Mark A. Cohen, Amanda Perry, and Raymond Swaray. 2006. "Costs and Benefits of Sentencing." In *Preventing Crime: What Works for Children, Offenders, Victims, and Places*, edited by Brandon C. Welsh and David P. Farrington. New York: Springer.

McDougall, Cynthia, Mark A. Cohen, Raymond B. Swaray, and Amanda Perry. 2008. "Benefit-Cost Analyses of Sentencing." *Campbell Systematic Reviews* 2008:10.

McIntosh, Cameron, and Jobina Li. 2012. *An Introduction to Economic Analysis in Crime Prevention: The Why, How and So What*. Research Report 2012-5. Ottawa: Department of Justice Canada.

Mears, Daniel P. 2007. "Towards Rational and Evidence-Based Crime Policy." *Journal of Criminal Justice* 35:667–82.

———. 2010. *American Criminal Justice Policy: An Evaluation Approach to Increasing Accountability and Effectiveness*. New York: Cambridge University Press.

Miller, Ted R. 2013. *Nurse-Family Partnership Home Visitation: Costs, Outcomes, and Return on Investment*. Beltsville, MA: H.B.S.A.

Miller, Ted R., Mark A. Cohen, and Shelli B. Rossman. 1993. "Victim Costs of Violent Crime and Resulting Injuries." *Health Affairs* 12:186–97.

Miller, Ted R., Mark A. Cohen, and Brian Wiersema. 1996. *Victim Costs and Consequences: A New Look*. Washington, DC: National Institute of Justice, US Department of Justice.

Nagin, Daniel S. 2001*a*. "Measuring Economic Benefits of Developmental Prevention Programs." In *Costs and Benefits of Preventing Crime*, edited by Brandon C. Welsh, David P. Farrington, and Lawrence W. Sherman. Boulder, CO: Westview.

———. 2001*b*. "Measuring the Economic Benefits of Developmental Prevention Programs." In *Crime and Justice: A Review of Research*, vol. 28, edited by Michael Tonry. Chicago: University of Chicago Press.

Nagin, Daniel S., Alex R. Piquero, Elizabeth S. Scott, and Laurence Steinberg. 2006. "Public Preferences for Rehabilitation versus Incarceration of Juvenile Offenders: Evidence from a Contingent Valuation Survey." *Criminology and Public Policy* 5:627–52.

Ott, Marilyn, Gina Browne, Carolyn Byrne, Jacqueline Roberts, Amiram Gafni, and Amanda H. Bateman. 2006. "Recreation for Children on Social Assistance, 4–17 Years Old, Pays for Itself the Same Year." *Journal of Public Health* 28:203–8.

Painter, Kate A., and David P. Farrington. 1997. "The Crime Reducing Effect of Improved Street Lighting: The Dudley Project." In *Situational Crime Prevention: Successful Case Studies*, 2nd ed., edited by Ronald V. Clarke. Guilderland, NY: Harrow & Heston.

———. 1999. "Street Lighting and Crime: Diffusion of Benefits in the Stoke-on-Trent Project." In *Crime Prevention Studies*, vol. 10, edited by Kate A. Painter and Nick Tilley. Monsey, NY: Criminal Justice.

———. 2001. "The Financial Benefits of Improved Street Lighting, Based on Crime Reduction." *Lighting Research and Technology* 33:3–12.

Pew Center on the States. 2012. "Results First: Helping States Assess the Costs and Benefits of Policy Options and Use That Data to Make Decisions Based on Results." Pew Charitable Trusts. http://www.pewcenteronthestates.org.

Poyner, Barry. 1992. "Video Cameras and Bus Vandalism." In *Situational Crime Prevention: Successful Case Studies*, edited by Ronald V. Clarke. Albany, NY: Harrow & Heston.

Prest, A. R., and Ralph Turvey. 1965. "Cost-Benefit Analysis: A Survey." *Economic Journal* 75:683–735.

Raffan Gowar, B., and David P. Farrington. 2013. "The Monetary Cost of Criminal Careers." In *Kriminologie, Kriminalpolitik, Strafrecht: Festschrift für Hans-Jürgen Kerner zum 70. Geburtstag*, edited by Klaus Boers, Thomas Feltes, Joerg Kinzig, Lawrence W. Sherman, Franz Streng, and Gerson Trueg. Tubingen: Mohr Siebeck.

Rajkumar, Andrew S., and Michael T. French. 1997. "Drug Abuse, Crime Costs, and the Economic Benefits of Treatment." *Journal of Quantitative Criminology* 13:291–323.

Reynolds, Arthur J., Judy A. Temple, Suh Ruu Ou, Irma A. Arteaga, and Barry A. B. White. 2011. "School-Based Early Childhood Education and Age-28 Well-Being: Effects by Timing, Dosage, and Subgroups." *Science* 333:360–64.

Reynolds, Arthur J., Judy A. Temple, Barry A. B. White, Suh Ruu Ou, and Dylan L. Robertson. 2011. "Age 26 Cost-Benefit Analysis of the Child-Parent Center Early Education Program." *Child Development* 82:379–404.

Roberts, Julian V., and Ross Hastings. 2012. "Public Opinion and Crime Prevention: A Review of International Trends." In *The Oxford Handbook of Crime Prevention*, edited by Brandon C. Welsh and David P. Farrington. New York: Oxford University Press.

Roman, John K., Terence Dunworth, and Kevin Marsh. 2010. *Cost-Benefit Analysis and Crime Control*. Washington, DC: Urban Institute.

Safe Neighbourhoods Unit. 1993. *Crime Prevention on Council Estates*. London: H.M. Stationery Office.

Sampson, Robert J., Stephen W. Raudenbush, and Felton Earls. 1997. "Neighborhoods and Violent Crime: A Multilevel Study of Collective Efficacy." *Science* 277:918–24.

Sawyer, Aaron M., and Charles M. Borduin. 2011. "Effects of Multisystemic Therapy through Midlife: A 21.9-Year Follow-Up to a Randomized Clinical Trial with Serious and Violent Juvenile Offenders." *Journal of Consulting and Clinical Psychology* 79:643–52.

Schnelle, John F., Robert E. Kirchner, Frank Galbaugh, Michelle Domash, Adam Carr, and Lynn Larson. 1979. "Program Evaluation Research: An Experimental Cost-Effectiveness Analysis of an Armed Robbery Intervention Program." *Journal of Applied Behavior Analysis* 12:615–23.

Schochet, Peter Z., John Burghardt, and Sheena McConnell. 2006. *National Job Corps Study and Longer-Term Follow-Up Study: Impact and Benefit-Cost Findings Using Survey and Summary Earnings Records Data*. Final Report. Princeton, NJ: Mathematica Policy Research.

Schweinhart, Lawrence J., Helen V. Barnes, and David P. Weikart, eds. 1993. *Significant Benefits: The High/Scope Perry Preschool Study through Age 27*. Ypsilanti, MI: High/Scope Press.

Schweinhart, Lawrence J., Jeanne Montie, Zongping Xiang, W. Steven Barnett, Clive R. Belfield, and Milagros Nores, eds. 2005. *Lifetime Effects: The High/Scope Perry Preschool Study through Age 40*. Ypsilanti, MI: High/Scope Press.

———. 2011. *The High/Scope Perry Preschool Study through Age 40: Summary, Conclusions, and Frequently Asked Questions*. Ypsilanti, MI: High/Scope Press.

Schweinhart, Lawrence J., and David P. Weikart. 1980. *Young Children Grow Up: The Effects of the Perry Preschool Program on Youths through Age 15*. Ypsilanti, MI: High/Scope Press.

Seitz, Victoria, Laurie K. Rosenbaum, and Nancy H. Apfel. 1985. "Effects of Family Support Intervention: A Ten-Year Follow-Up." *Child Development* 56:376–91.

Sherman, Lawrence W., David P. Farrington, Brandon C. Welsh, and Doris Layton MacKenzie, eds. 2006. *Evidence-Based Crime Prevention*, rev. ed. New York: Routledge.

Sherman, Lawrence W., Denise C. Gottfredson, Doris L. MacKenzie, John E. Eck, Peter Reuter, and Shawn D. Bushway. 1997. *Preventing Crime: What Works, What Doesn't, What's Promising*. Washington, DC: National Institute of Justice, US Department of Justice.

Skilton, Mike. 1988. *A Better Reception: The Development of Concierge Schemes*. London: Estate Action and Department of the Environment.

Smith, Martha J., and Ronald V. Clarke. 2012. "Situational Crime Prevention: Classifying Techniques Using 'Good Enough' Theory." In *The Oxford Handbook of Crime Prevention*, edited by Brandon C. Welsh and David P. Farrington. New York: Oxford University Press.

Swaray, Raymond B., Roger Bowles, and Rimawan Pradiptyo. 2005. "The Application of Economic Analysis to Criminal Justice Interventions: A Review of the Literature." *Criminal Justice Policy Review* 16:141–63.

Tonry, Michael, and David P. Farrington. 1995. "Strategic Approaches to Crime Prevention." In *Building a Safer Society: Strategic Approaches to Crime Prevention*, edited by Michael Tonry and David P. Farrington. Vol. 19 of *Crime and Justice: A Review of Research*, edited by Michael Tonry. Chicago: University of Chicago Press.

Tremblay, Richard E., and Wendy M. Craig. 1995. "Developmental Crime Prevention." In *Building a Safer Society: Strategic Approaches to Crime Prevention*, edited by Michael Tonry and David P. Farrington. Vol. 19 of *Crime and Justice: A Review of Research*, edited by Michael Tonry. Chicago: University of Chicago Press.

van Andel, Henk. 1989. "Crime Prevention That Works: The Care of Public Transport in the Netherlands." *British Journal of Criminology* 29:47–56.

van Ours, Jan C., and Ben Vollaard. 2011. "Lessons from the Economics of Crime: What Works in Reducing Offending? The Engine Immobilizer: A Non-starter for Car Thieves." Munich: Ifo Institute of Economic Research and the Centre for Economic Studies, Ludwig-Maximilians University.

Vollaard, Ben, and Jan C. van Ours. 2011. "Does Regulation of Built-In Security Reduce Crime? Evidence from a Natural Experiment." *Economic Journal* 121:485–504.

Weber, Carol U., Phillips W. Foster, and David P. Weikart. 1978. *An Economic Analysis of the Ypsilanti Perry Preschool Project*. Ypsilanti, MI: High/Scope Press.

Weimer, David L., and Lee S. Friedman. 1979. "Efficiency Considerations in Criminal Rehabilitation Research: Costs and Consequences." In *The Rehabilitation of Criminal Offenders: Problems and Prospects*, edited by Lee Sechrest, Susan O. White, and Elizabeth D. Brown. Washington, DC: National Academy of Sciences.

Weinrott, Mark R., Richard R. Jones, and James R. Howard. 1982. "Cost-Effectiveness of Teaching Family Programs for Delinquents: Results of a National Evaluation." *Evaluation Review* 6:173–201.

Welsh, Brandon C. 2001. "Economic Costs and Benefits of Early Developmental Prevention." In *Child Delinquents: Development, Intervention, and Service Needs*, edited by Rolf Loeber and David P. Farrington. Thousand Oaks, CA: Sage.

———. 2003. "Economic Costs and Benefits of Primary Prevention of Delinquency and Later Offending: A Review of the Research." In *Early Prevention of Adult Antisocial Behaviour*, edited by David P. Farrington and Jeremy W. Coid. New York: Cambridge University Press.

Welsh, Brandon C., and David P. Farrington. 1999. "Value for Money? A Review of the Costs and Benefits of Situational Crime Prevention." *British Journal of Criminology* 39:345–68.

———. 2000*a*. "Correctional Intervention Programs and Cost-Benefit Analysis." *Criminal Justice and Behavior* 27:115–33.

———. 2000*b*. "Monetary Costs and Benefits of Crime Prevention Programs." In *Crime and Justice: A Review of Research*, vol. 27, edited by Michael Tonry. Chicago: University of Chicago Press.

———. 2003. "Effects of CCTV on Crime." *Annals of the American Academy of Political and Social Science* 587:110–35.

———. 2009*a*. *Making Public Places Safer: Surveillance and Crime Prevention*. New York: Oxford University Press.

———. 2009*b*. "Public Area CCTV and Crime Prevention: An Updated Systematic Review and Meta-analysis." *Justice Quarterly* 26:716–45.

———. 2011*a*. "The Benefits and Costs of Early Prevention Compared with Imprisonment: Toward a New Crime Policy." *Prison Journal* 91(3):120–37.

———. 2011*b*. "Evidence-Based Crime Policy." In *The Oxford Handbook of Crime and Criminal Justice*, edited by Michael Tonry. New York: Oxford University Press.

———. 2012. "Crime Prevention and Public Policy." In *The Oxford Handbook of Crime Prevention*, edited by Brandon C. Welsh and David P. Farrington. New York: Oxford University Press.

Welsh, Brandon C., David P. Farrington, and Lawrence W. Sherman, eds. 2001. *Costs and Benefits of Preventing Crime*. Boulder, CO: Westview.

Welsh, Brandon C., and Akemi Hoshi. 2006. "Communities and Crime Prevention." In *Evidence-Based Crime Prevention*, rev. ed., edited by Lawrence W. Sherman, David P. Farrington, Brandon C. Welsh, and Doris Layton MacKenzie. New York: Routledge.

Welsh, Brandon C., Rolf Loeber, Bradley R. Stevens, Magda Stouthamer-Loeber, Mark A. Cohen, and David P. Farrington. 2008. "Costs of Juvenile Crime in Urban Areas: A Longitudinal Perspective." *Youth Violence and Juvenile Justice* 6:3–27.

Welsh, Brandon C., and Rebecca D. Pfeffer. 2013. "Reclaiming Crime Prevention in an Age of Punishment: An American History." *Punishment and Society* 15:534–53.

Welsh, Brandon C., Christopher J. Sullivan, and David L. Olds. 2010. "When Early Crime Prevention Goes to Scale: A New Look at the Evidence." *Prevention Science* 10:115–25.

Wilson, James Q., and George L. Kelling. 1982. "Broken Windows: The Police and Neighborhood Safety." *Atlantic Monthly* 11:29–38.

Wilson, John J., and James C. Howell. 1993. *A Comprehensive Strategy for Serious, Violent, and Chronic Juvenile Offenders*. Washington, DC: Office of Juvenile Justice and Delinquency Prevention, US Department of Justice.

Zimring, Franklin E., and Gordon Hawkins. 1995. *Incapacitation: Penal Confinement and the Restraint of Crime*. New York: Oxford University Press.

Cheryl Lero Jonson and Francis T. Cullen

Prisoner Reentry Programs

ABSTRACT

Only in the past decade has prisoner reentry been "discovered" and become a central policy concern in the United States. This is due in part to the sheer number of released inmates (more than 600,000 annually) and in part to a movement that has defined the issue as "reentry." A growing number of programs have been created in prisons and the community. Implementing them effectively, however, poses substantial challenges. A wide diversity of programs fall under the rubric and only a limited number of rigorous evaluations have been conducted. Research suggests that, overall, reentry services reduce recidivism, but program effects are heterogeneous and at times criminogenic. Effective programs tend to be consistent with the risk-need-responsivity model. A sustained effort to evaluate carefully designed programs rigorously is needed and may require development of a "criminology of reentry." More needs to be understood about why recidivism rates are high in the first year after reentry, why some offenders have late-onset failure, whether who comes home matters, and how stigma and other collateral consequences of conviction can be managed.

> I cannot fully describe the feelings that I had as I stepped out of the House of Corruption. . . . The prison clerk had given me seven cents for carfare. Walking along the street to the streetcar line, I studied the seven cents in my hand, and cynically and silently sneered at the city's benevolent generosity toward its forsaken wards. After a year of idleness and monotony in that stagnant cesspool I was now supposed to make

Electronically published July 31, 2015

Cheryl Lero Jonson is assistant professor of criminal justice at Xavier University. Francis T. Cullen is Distinguished Research Professor Emeritus of Criminal Justice and senior research associate at the University of Cincinnati.

0192-3234/2015/0044-0007$10.00

> good on seven cents. A fine start, I'll say, with not one word of advice from anyone. They just kick you out of the place, and to hell with you. (Stanley, "The Jack-Roller," in Shaw [(1930) 1966], p. 167)

> Let us not forget for one moment that ninety-seven out of every (one) hundred of the men and women we send to prison must some day come out of prison again. . . . More than one-half of the persons in prison today have had to be locked up at least once before for a violation of the law. Yes, we might was well admit it. Taking it by and large, we have bungled in the manner and the method of their release.
>
> After the necessarily strict routine of prison life we know that it is difficult for a discharged prisoner to stand on his own feet in the swift-running currents of a free man's world. Often, if he has been in prison very long, he will have lost the habit of making his own decisions. He usually faces tremendous difficulties finding a job. In many cases his prison record cuts him off from the friendship of law-abiding people. These circumstances tend to push a man back to a life of crime unless we make it our business to help him overcome them. . . . That is the reason (why) I have long been of the opinion that this problem of parole is the most promising method of terminating a prison sentence. (President Franklin D. Roosevelt 1939, pp. 11–12)

Stanley and Franklin D. Roosevelt came from opposite social worlds. Born into an immigrant family of Polish immigrants in the "jungle" of inner-city Chicago, Stanley entered crime early in life and would be imprisoned several times, including in the city's House of Corrections (Shaw [1930] 1966; Snodgrass 1982). Franklin Roosevelt was born into wealth and ascended to the White House. But if they shared little else, both Stanley and Franklin could see that imprisonment created a fundamental challenge: the vast majority of inmates eventually return to the community. Writing in the 1930s—a time not long after Progressive Era reforms had legitimized the rehabilitative ideal (Rothman 1980)—they agreed that the challenge of prisoner reentry was not being met successfully. For Stanley, he was failed in two ways—inside prison where idleness and corruption prevailed and outside prison where his release was of little concern to anyone. For FDR, statistics confirmed his commonsense observations: released offenders faced a number of barriers that, if left unaddressed, made recidivism probable.

For the remainder of the century, however, Stanley's plea for support and FDR's admonition that dire circumstances will "tend to push a man back to a life of crime unless we make it our business to help him overcome them" were largely ignored. Corrections officials and scholars understood these issues, of course, and often urged that they be given more attention. Still, inmates' return to society never quite seemed to rise to the level of being an urgent policy concern. Instead, the task of ensuring community reintegration was allocated to parole (Rothman 1980).

As Simon (1993) documents, the parole enterprise over time has been guided by different organizing models. Although these models were never fully hegemonic and when superseded never fully vanished, different ways of thinking were preeminent during particular periods. Before World War II and especially afterward, "disciplinary" or "industrial" parole was normative. Building on the cultural belief that the discipline of routine work instills moral fiber, states required parolees to have a job to secure release and to keep a job to avoid reincarceration. Fluctuations in the economy and high unemployment among minority offenders increasingly made the work requirement less tenable. According to Simon (1993), beginning in the 1950s, a "clinical" model arose in which parole agents were tasked with normalizing offenders by building close relationships and delivering treatment services. In the 1960s, the treatment approach encouraged the implementation of halfway houses and of efforts at "community reintegration" (Latessa and Smith 2011). Concern for parolees' welfare increased but would soon be severely curtailed.

By the mid-1970s, a coalition of liberals and conservatives attacked the rehabilitative ideal (Cullen 2013; Cullen and Gilbert 2013). They took special aim at the indeterminate sentence and parole release—and had little confidence in the value of delivering treatment during parole supervision. For liberals, parole boards lacked the expertise and political insulation to make legitimate decisions on who should, or should not, be released from prison. Their discretion was seen as unfettered, inequitable, and an invitation for racial and class bias. For conservatives, parole boards were a source of unwarranted leniency, allowing dangerous offenders serving long sentences to "con" board members into returning them to the community prematurely. This revolving door of justice was said to rob the legal system of its deterrent powers, by teaching that crime pays, and of its capacity to incapacitate, by allowing predators to roam free on neighborhood streets (Tonry 1996; Cullen and Gilbert 2013).

In response, more than 20 states moved to some form of determinate sentencing and abolished parole release, although Colorado, Connecticut, and Mississippi later restored it (Petersilia 1999; Caplan and Kinnevy 2010; Rhine 2011). Even in states that retained parole, certain types of crimes (e.g., violent and multiple felonies) often rendered offenders ineligible for release, leading Rhine to conclude that "regardless of sentencing structures... parole boards have experienced a pronounced contraction in their releasing authority" (2011, p. 612). Eventually, all states constrained sentencing discretion by passing laws stipulating mandatory minimum sentences, truth in sentencing, and life or lengthy sentences for those convicted of "third strikes" (Tonry 1996, 2013; Johnson 2011). The result was what Tonry (2013, p. 141) has called a "crazy quilt" of sentencing policies that mix, across and often within states, elements of determinacy and indeterminacy (Reitz 2011). One consequence is that as of 2012, one in five inmates "maxes" out (serves a full sentence) and is subject to no postrelease supervision (Pew Charitable Trusts 2014*a*). In states lacking parole, offenders are typically given some period of postrelease supervision (e.g., 1–3 years).

Taken together, these various changes helped to usher in a new model of supervision—what Simon (1993) terms "managerial parole." As the label implies, this model emphasized the close surveillance of offenders to curtail their potential misconduct. This could involve risk assessment to know whom to supervise intensively, drug testing, electronic monitoring, and revocation for the noncompliant. Simon (1993) uses the metaphor of "waste management" to describe the purpose of this parole model and argues that this is not simply a "polemical label." Rather, the term is simply an "acknowledgment that many of the young men who encounter the criminal justice system will likely become lifetime clients." As in any waste management system, "it follows that methods must be deployed to allow this population"—this waste—"to be maintained securely at the lowest possible cost." Importantly, this parole model legitimated the denial of attempts to invest in or enrich the lives of offenders; in short, it attenuated the rationale for the delivery of treatment services. The use of such "expensive techniques," notes Simon, is "not warranted if the basic assumption is that there is no realistic potential to alter the offenders' status as toxic waste" (p. 259).

Then, rather unexpectedly, things changed. First, the attack on parole lost steam. Since 2000, observes Rhine, "No parole board was abolished or lost a significant amount of authority relative to its discretionary release decision making. In fact, one state (Mississippi) recently restored the parole granting function" (2011, p. 632). Second, and more significantly, the term *reentry* entered the correctional and public policy lexicon. Although Franklin Roosevelt had the same insight in 1939—as have others repeatedly since—there was an emerging acceptance of what Jeremy Travis called "the iron law of imprisonment: they all come back" (2005, p. xxi). It suddenly seemed indefensible to ignore the stubborn reality that 95 percent of the prison population—more than 600,000 ex-inmates annually—were reentering society, many of whom would recidivate and be reincarcerated. The waste management system was failing. It became "obvious" that mere surveillance was not sufficient to allow offenders to negotiate the barriers and burdens of reentry. Programs would have to be developed to help offenders make the difficult transition between prison and citizenship.

In fact, Rhine and Thompson (2011) document the rise over the past decade of "the reentry movement in corrections" (see also Petersilia 2009; Garland and Wodahl 2014). Social scientists disagree on what qualifies a reform as a "social movement," but prisoner reentry meets three of the most important criteria (Staggenborn 2005). First, resource mobilization theory highlights the importance of organizations, often in loosely coupled networks, supporting the reform. Reentry has been embraced and supported by federal government agencies, state and local governments, correctional and legal professional associations, and faith-based groups (Frazier 2011; Rhine and Thompson 2011). Second, political process theory emphasizes that movements are not possible without political opportunities. In part due to President George W. Bush's support of the Second Chance Act, reentry has enjoyed strong bipartisan support from Democrats and Republicans (Listwan et al. 2008). The salience of reentry was heightened by the deep recession starting in 2008 that made the cost of mass imprisonment seem unsustainable and thus focused attention on ways to keep offenders from returning to prison. Third, culture theory emphasizes the role in generating movements of collective identity and of "*collective action frames* [which] are ways of presenting issues that identify injustices, attribute blame, suggest solutions, and inspire collective action" (Staggenborn 2005, p. 755; emphasis in original). Academics have been particularly important in constructing reentry as a social problem, providing solutions, and calling for a concerted effort to transform the back end of the correctional system (see, e.g., Petersilia 2003; Travis 2005).

A key feature of the reentry movement is its focus on developing programs to facilitate the successful return of prisoners to the community. This emphasis is important because it ties reentry to the rehabilitative ideal. Implicit in the very idea of programming—whether conducted inside or outside the prison—is that offenders face personal and situational risks that, if left unaddressed, will likely lead them back into crime. Reentering prisoners are thus seen as being at risk for recidivating—but not destined to this fate. The challenge is thus to develop programs that work—which are effective and evidence based.

Conceptually, the term reentry can also be employed to describe the process of an inmate's movement from custody into society. In a sense, this usage is amorphous because it potentially includes almost any experience that offenders have had during and after their incarceration. Other than describing the obvious—that prisoners become nonprisoners—it is not clear what the term adds substantively. Perhaps its one advantage, however, is that it reminds us that reentry covers not only inmates who are paroled but also those released without supervision. In any event, we use the term reentry generally to describe the process of inmates "coming home" but focus specifically on the nature and effectiveness of programs established to reduce postprison recidivism.

To provide context, Section I describes the reentry problem. We first discuss why reentry is an objective problem and then examine how it became socially constructed as a problem worthy of special attention. We conclude that reentry is likely to persist as a permanent feature of the correctional enterprise, in part because the idea of offender reentry is becoming organizationally institutionalized and is supported by the public. Section II examines challenges in delivering effective reentry programs. Many programs are based on no credible scientific theory and are not implemented with fidelity to treatment integrity. The diversity of programs falling under the category of reentry has resulted in even the best programs typically being evaluated by a single study. Overall, reentry services tend to reduce recidivism, but there is wide heterogeneity in program effects. On the basis of admittedly limited evidence, it appears possible to identify the likely components of effective interventions: high treatment fidelity, use of therapeutic communities during imprisonment, continuity of care from the prison into the community, and targeting of high-risk offenders and their risk factors for change. We conclude in Section III with a call to create a "criminology of reentry."

Knowledge gaps restrict the capacity to develop effective reentry programs. Beyond the need to conduct more high-quality evaluations, it is essential to understand more about why recidivism is pronounced in the period immediately after release, why some offenders avoid arrest for several years before experiencing late-onset failure, and how stigma and other collateral consequences of conviction inhibit reentry success.

I. The Reentry Problem

Social problems have two features: first, that the issue is by objective standards a problem and, second, that an objective problem is recognized or "socially constructed" as a "problem" (Specter and Kitsuse 1977). In this section we initially discuss why prisoner reentry is objectively a pressing public policy concern. Then, we argue that a confluence of events in the first part of the current century have worked to define reentry as a social problem. This social construction has been instrumental in elevating reentry from neglect into a central correctional issue.

A. Nature of the Problem

In his address to the National Parole Conference at the White House, Franklin D. Roosevelt articulated the rationale for expanded and effective parole: in 1939, 97 percent of inmates returned to the community, many of whom recidivated. Although other law enforcement, court, and prison reforms had been made, observed the president, "it seems to me that we have made the least progress in the very important matter of getting people from prison back . . . to society" (Roosevelt 1939, p. 11). To FDR, the magnitude of the problem merited special mention: "Between 60,000 and 70,000 persons are released from Federal and state prisons and reformatories back into the communities of the country every single year" (p. 11). The stunning fact is that 75 years later, the challenges identified by President Roosevelt still exist—except that the reentering prisoner population has grown tenfold.

The problem of reentry is inextricably tied to the problem of mass imprisonment. The numbers are stated with numbing regularity: on any given day in the United States, more than 1.5 million offenders are incarcerated in state and federal prisons, with the count exceeding 2.2 million when jail inmates are included (Glaze and Herberman 2013). As state and federal prison populations rose intractably—from around

200,000 in the early 1970s to over 1.6 million in 2008—the "iron law" of incarceration that "they all come back" remained in effect (Travis 2005). Growing prison inputs produced growing prison outputs.

As table 1 shows, by 1978, the number of offenders released each year from state and federal prisons had "only" doubled since FDR's address four decades earlier, standing at 142,033 inmates. Scarcely a decade later in 1990, however, the impact of mass incarceration could be seen: the number of prison releases had more than doubled again to more than 400,000. By the turn of the century, the count had jumped by another 230,000 annually. Five years later in 2005, releases broke the 700,000 barrier. They fell below 700,000 in 2011 and more steeply the following year. In 2013, prison releases stood at 623,337 (Carson and Golinelli 2013; Carson 2014).

These figures do not include offenders cycled through local jails. After reaching a high of 13.6 million admitted to a jail during 2008, the yearly population of admissions has stabilized since 2011 at about 11.7 million.

TABLE 1

Number of Prisoners Released from State and Federal Prisons, 1978–2013

Year	Inmates Released	Year	Inmates Released
1978	142,033	1996	488,748
1979	154,277	1997	514,322
1980	157,604	1998	546,616
1981	162.294	1999	574,624
1982	174,808	2000	635,094
1983	212,302	2001	628,626
1984	208,608	2002	633,947
1985	219,310	2003	656,574
1986	247,619	2004	672,202
1987	288,781	2005	701,632
1988	318,889	2006	709,874
1989	367,388	2007	721,161
1990	404,000	2008	734,144
1991	420,000	2009	729,749
1992	428,300	2010	708,877
1993	434,082	2011	691,072
1994	434,766	2012	637,411
1995	474,296	2013	623,337

NOTE.—Adapted from table 2 in Carson and Golinelli (2013), p. 4. Data for 2013 from Carson (2014), p. 10.

This is about 16 times larger than the average daily jail population of about 730,000 (Minton and Golinelli 2014). Even considering the jailed inmates awaiting trial who later will be sent to state prisons, it is likely that jails release upward of 10 million offenders annually. Further, 38 percent of the jail population was serving sentences due to a conviction, meaning that when released these offenders experience many of the same reentry challenges as those returning from prison (Minton and Golinelli 2014). This issue is likely to become increasingly significant in California, where downsizing of the state's prison population mandated by the US Supreme Court is leading to a rise in offenders serving sentences in local jails. California jails now house over 80,000 inmates, up from 69,404 in June 2011 (Minton and Golinelli 2014; Petersilia and Cullen 2015).

Prisons do not seem to reduce the criminality of inmates, making offenders' return to the community problematic. Mounting evidence exists that the effect of imprisonment on reoffending is likely null or criminogenic (Nagin, Cullen, and Jonson 2009; Cullen, Jonson, and Nagin 2011; see also Mears, Cochran, and Cullen, forthcoming). In fact, recidivism rates remain at high levels. In their classic study of the recidivism of released prisoners, Langan and Levin (2002) traced 272,111 discharged inmates in 15 states. They comprised two-thirds of the reentering offenders that year. Within 3 years, 67.5 percent of the sample had been rearrested for a new offense, 46 percent had been reconvicted, and 25.4 percent had been resentenced to prison. Including technical violations, over half (51.8 percent) had been returned to prison. They had been charged with 744,480 new offenses, including more than 100,000 violent crimes and 2,871 homicides. Notably, failure after reentering society was pronounced in the first 6 months to a year. The cumulative rate of rearrest was 29.9 percent for 6 months and 44.1 percent for 1 year; the percentage then climbed more slowly to 59.2 percent for 2 years and 67.5 percent for 3 years.

More recent research by Durose, Cooper, and Snyder (2014) presents similar data. They examined the experiences of 404,638 prisoners released in 30 states from 2005 to 2010. The percentage of former inmates arrested for a new crime in 3 years—67.8—was nearly identical to the 67.5 percent figure found by Langan and Levin. The 5-year statistic for arrests was more than three-fourths of the sample (76.6 percent). For those age 24 or younger, the figure was 84.1 percent. Again, failure was highest in the time shortly after release, with about one-third (36.8 percent) arrested within 6 months and more than half (56.7 percent) by the end of the first year. Data on 23 states revealed that about half (49.7 percent) were returned to prison in 3 years and 55.1 percent in 5 years.

These two studies reveal that inmate reentry is marked by widespread failure. High proportions of released offenders have contact with the law, often soon after reentry, and about half are reincarcerated. For those concerned with public safety and inmate welfare, the current system of reentry is difficult to justify. A problem exists that warrants a solution.

Reentry is hampered by a lack of treatment services available to prisoners before release. A particularly stark example is California, a state that turned decidedly away from rehabilitation with the passage of determinate sentencing in 1976 (Cullen and Gilbert 2013; see also Kruttschnitt and Garner 2005; Page 2011). Petersilia reports that on the basis of 1997 data, only 2.5 percent of the state's inmates in "high need of drug treatment received professionally run treatment" (2008, p. 236). For California offenders released in 2006, almost half sat idle during their entire prison sentence, participating in no work or treatment program. The negative consequence of this lack of services is palpable. "They return to communities unprepared for reentry," observes Petersilia, "and two-thirds are returned to prison within 3 years, nearly twice the national rate" (p. 211).

National statistics reveal a similarly bleak picture. On the basis of 1997 data, Lynch and Sabol (2001) found that the proportion of soon-to-be-released inmates who had participated in treatment was only 27 percent for vocational programs, 35 percent for educational programs, and 13 percent for prerelease programs. More recently, Taxman, Pattavina, and Caudy (2014) have shown that the prevalence of treatment services in prisons is high, but the proportion of inmates participating in such programs is low (see also Taxman, Perdoni, and Harrison 2007). Drawing on the National Criminal Justice Treatment Practices survey, Taxman, Pattavina, and Caudy (2014, p. 56, table 2) report that 74 percent of prisons have outpatient substance abuse programs available. However, only 13.3 percent of inmates participate in the programs during their incarceration, and only 4.7 percent of offenders with a specific need for such treatment can gain access to appropriate services. The pattern of high prevalence (many prisons have an array of programs) but low inmate usage appears to occur for a variety of treatment services. According to Taxman, Perdoni, and Harrison (2007, p. 246), "access is an issue with correctional programs in that few inmates are involved with any program." For example, most prisons offer educational/GED and vocational training/job readiness programs. But on any given day, only 7–8 percent of the adult inmate population is involved in such treatment. The implications of these findings are clear: "In other words, a routine regime of treatment and programming is more likely to produce positive outcomes than programming that is rare or offered to few individuals within a prison or correctional setting. Essentially, what happens inside prison will affect what happens in the community; the result being that mass incarceration will have a long-term impact on offenders, their families, and communities" (Taxman, Pattavina, and Caudy 2014, p. 51).

A final component of the reentry problem consists of the array of barriers that prisoners face upon release that parole authorities and state policy makers are ill-prepared to address. Many offenders likely share the sentiment of Stanley, "The Jack-Roller," who upon reentering society stated, "They just kick you out of the place, and to hell with you" (Shaw [1930] 1966, p. 167). Other than funds accumulated in personal accounts, most states release prisoners with little concern for their material welfare. Inmates are typically given $20–$100 in gate money, a bus ticket to an in-state location, the single set of clothes worn on their backs, and prescription medicine that will expire in 1 week to 60 days (Community Corrections Research Team 2011; Rukus and Lane 2014). Prisoners must depend on family members or other relatives or friends to house them with no compensation from the government. An unknown number—one study in New York State placed the 2-year rate at 11.4 percent—will become homeless (Travis 2005). Those with a criminal record can be barred under federal law from public housing (Travis 2005; Alexander 2010). Private rental housing, often in short supply in the impoverished communities to which prisoners return, may request and check criminal record information on rental applications. A 2006 survey found that 60 percent of state parole supervising agencies had no housing assistance programs (Bonczar 2008).

With limited vocational training, literacy capacity, and educational degrees, securing living-wage employment can be challenging, especially in a recession-period labor market with declining use for unskilled workers (Bushway, Stoll, and Weiman 2007). Many offenders lack a stable work history before incarceration to fall back on, with one-third unemployed at the time of their most recent arrest (Petersilia 2011).

Other barriers exist as well. A major collateral consequence of a criminal conviction is being barred from work in the "fields of child care, education, security, nursing, and home health care—exactly the types of jobs that are expanding" (Petersilia 2011, p. 940). Occupations requiring licensure either automatically exclude or limit those with criminal records. As Alexander (2010, p. 146) notes, this can even include self-employment as a "barber, manicurist, gardener, or counselor," even if the offenders' crimes "have nothing at all to do with their ability to perform well in their chosen profession."

Beyond legally mandated exclusions, employers are reluctant to hire released inmates. In 2001, Holzer, Raphael, and Stoll (2007, p. 120) polled 619 establishments in Los Angeles about their willingness to "accept an applicant with a criminal record for the last non-college job filled." More than 40 percent answered "probably not" (24.1 percent) or "definitely not" (18.5 percent); another 36.4 percent stated that it "depends on the crime" (2007, p. 124). A 2011 survey of 69 of the largest employers in the Pensacola, Florida, standard metropolitan statistical area produced comparable results, with 40.6 percent of the respondents stating that their company does not "hire people who are formerly convicted felons" (Swanson, Schnippert, and Tryling 2014, p. 213). Experimental studies have probed this issue by submitting employment applications from matched pairs identical except for the admission of a criminal record and seeing whether the fictitious job seekers receive a call back for an interview. In a study of newspaper-advertised openings for entry-level jobs located within a 25-mile radius of Milwaukee, Pager (2007) discovered that whites with a criminal record were half as likely to receive a call back as those with no criminal record (17 vs. 34 percent). For blacks, the callback ratio was about one in three (5 vs. 14 percent). Pager (2007, p. 146) notes that the low probability of African Americans with a criminal record receiving a call back suggests a case of "a 'two strikes and you're out' mentality among employers, who appear to view the combination of blackness and criminal record as an indicator of serious trouble" (see also Pager, Western, and Bonikowski 2009). Similar findings have been reported from a 2011–12 study in Phoenix, Arizona, that included the submission of both online and in-person job applications (Decker et al. 2014).

The difficulty of inmate reentry is further exacerbated by offenders' limited access to appropriate rehabilitation services while under parole supervision. For example, among all those in community corrections (probation and parole), Taxman, Perdoni, and Caudy (2013, p. 82) report that seven in 10 have "some type of substance abuse disorder." On any given day, however, only 5 percent receive appropriate clinical treatment services. Most of them complete only "low intensity" treatment, such as "infrequent counseling and some type of pharmacological medications" (Taxman, Perdoni, and Harrison 2007, p. 78). Similarly, a study of 17 state agencies found that only 9 percent of parolees "were enrolled in a mental health treatment program operated by a formally trained mental health professional" (Bonczar 2008, p. 6). By contrast, it is estimated that 16 percent of those under correctional supervision in the United States have a serious mental disorder, such as major depression, bipolar disorder, or schizophrenia (Manchak and Cullen 2014).

B. Discovery of the Problem

These considerations suggest that prisoner reentry has been a long and growing problem. Each year, more than 600,000 inmates are released who are at a high risk of arrest and reincarceration. Most do not receive treatment services appropriate to their criminogenic needs either during or after imprisonment (see Andrews and Bonta 2010). Instead, they face substantial barriers to assuming social roles—particularly employment—that are at the core of citizenship and integral to desistance from crime (Sampson and Laub 1993; see also Porporino 2010).

An objective disquieting condition does not become a social problem, however, unless it is "discovered." As labeling theorists have pointed out, even harmful conditions—such as child abuse or corporal violence—can exist with little public awareness or intervention for lengthy periods (Pfohl 1985; Cullen, Maakestad, and Cavender 1987). As Spector and Kitsuse (1977) pointed out, social problems are "constructed" through a definitional process. This process of persuading others that a problem exists involves "claims-making" activities in which the negative consequences are highlighted and ameliorative steps requested. But the other part of this process involves attaching a specific label to the condition, which is pregnant with meaning and policy implications. For example, calling erratic emotional conduct "mental illness" implies that troubled people should be seen as patients suffering from a disease that merits clinical treatment by professional experts in either an office visit or a psychiatric hospital (Szasz 1970). Similarly, the construct of "juvenile delinquency" suggests that childhood is a distinct developmental stage and that the state, through the juvenile court, should have wide discretionary powers to regulate not only youths' violation of criminal law but also risky conduct (e.g., status offenses) seemingly predictive of the onset of a criminal career (Platt 1969; Empey 1982).

In this context, the challenges posed by offenders returning to society after their incarceration had existed since the invention of prisons and, as the address by President Roosevelt (1939) indicates, had long been an objective problem. Until the beginning years of the current century, however, this condition had not been defined or "framed" in a way that made it a "social problem" salient to policy makers and thus central to the correctional enterprise. The issue of released inmates was subsumed under the umbrella of parole, which was criticized by liberals as being inequitable and by conservatives as being overly lenient. At times, the issue was seen as a matter of offender reintegration, which was part of the rehabilitative model embraced by the Left but not the Right. Perhaps because they were enmeshed in ideological debates, "parole" and "reintegration" failed to emerge as labels capable of inspiring concrete actions to address the problem of prisoners released into society. Even when the number of released inmates surpassed the 600,000 mark in 2000, discussions of reentry were just beginning, and no movement was yet on the horizon to address this objective problem.

Soon thereafter, however, the term "reentry" galvanized attention. It entered the correctional lexicon as the now-accepted way of defining the inmate release process. This concept had two distinct advantages. First, it had no apparent ideological preference. Unlike parole, reentry was not attached to any existing correctional practice or organization that had been the object of political dispute. Unlike reintegration, it did not mandate any particular practices. It was not a construct of the Left or the Right but a description of an empirical phenomenon. Second, use of the term reentry thus had a sobering quality to it. Reentry was an "iron law"—they all come home (Travis 2005). To ignore this stubborn reality was manifestly irrational and, from a correctional policy standpoint, irresponsible. In short, framing the issue as a problem of reentry made it easier for claims-makers to argue that action should be taken.

Despite its useful qualities, there is nothing inherent in the word reentry that, in and of itself, would have inspired a policy movement. Might not "return" have sufficed just as well? Rather, it was the use of the term "reentry" in two influential books that gave the term currency and encouraged its embrace in academic, policy-making, and practitioner circles. These books had similar titles and both linked the inescapability of prisoners "coming home or back" to the term "reentry." In 2003, Joan Petersilia published *When Prisoners Come Home: Parole and Prisoner Reentry*. Two years later, Jeremy Travis's *But They All Come Back: Facing the Challenges of Prisoner Reentry* appeared.

There was nothing inevitable in their use of the term reentry. Historical contingency, not unavoidable discovery, led each independently to adopt it (see also Cullen 2005). According to Petersilia (2009), she was originally scheduled to write an essay entitled "Parole in the United States" to appear in a prisons volume in *Crime and Justice* that she was coediting with Michael Tonry (Tonry and Petersilia 1999). Here is where a turning point in correctional history occurred: "[Tonry] changed the title to read, "Parole and *Prisoner Reentry* in the United States," observing that my chapter described not only the parole system but also the individual-level experiences of prisoners returning home—what we now think of as prisoner reentry. Writing that chapter was the starting point for what became my professional absorption and ultimately resulted in this book, *When Prisoners Come Home: Parole and Prisoner Reentry*" (Petersilia 2009, p. 249; emphasis in original). Petersilia sought to use the book "to gain attention for what I believed was one of the most significant *social problems* of our time: the challenges posed by the more than 600,000 adults who leave prison and return home each year" (pp. 249–50; emphasis added). Her goal as a prominent claims-maker was "to deliver a national prisoner reentry 'wake-up call,' spurring progressive prison reform" (p. 250).

Jeremy Travis's interest in reentry was perhaps more serendipitous. While serving as the director of the National Institute of Justice (NIJ) in 1999, he was asked by then–US Attorney General Janet Reno, "What are we doing about all the people coming out of prison?" (Travis 2005, p. xi). The answer was almost nothing, which prompted Travis, with the assistance of Laurie Robinson, to delve into the issue in more detail. Because many inmates were being released unsupervised, Travis and Robinson decided that they could not focus only on parole. At this point, Travis made a crucial contribution: "I suggested we use the word 'reentry' to capture the experience of being released from custody, and the word quickly became a convenient shorthand for our inquiry. An examination of 'prisoner reentry,' we hoped, would allow us to set aside debates over sentencing policy and avoid the pitfalls of defending or critiquing parole. We hoped that the topic of 'prisoner reentry' would be broad enough to allow conservatives and liberals, pro- and antiprison advocates to come together with pragmatic answers to Janet Reno's question" (2005, p. xii).

It would be an exaggeration to suggest that the celebrated use of the word reentry was in and of itself transformative. Importantly, in his position as NIJ director, Travis took steps to translate the concept into reality. He sponsored funding for eight communities to develop "reentry courts" and for "the first Reentry Partnerships in another five sites, bringing together police, corrections agencies, and community leaders to improve reentry planning" (Travis 2005, p. xii). When he moved in 2000 to the Urban Institute as a senior fellow, he established a diverse study group, the Reentry Roundtable, and published an NIJ Research in Brief entitled *But They All Come Back: Rethinking Prisoner Reentry* (2000). He was invited by the Urban Institute to write the book carrying the similar title, *But They All Come Back: Facing the Challenges of Prisoner Reentry*. Together, Travis's and Petersilia's books provided a thorough account of the objective nature of the problem and made a persuasive claim for a series of policy reforms.

Still, what might have occurred if they had not employed the term reentry? Assessing this counterfactual situation is speculative, but consider, for example, if Petersilia had subtitled her book *The Problem of Parole* and had not used reentry as her organizing concept. In all likelihood, *When Prisoners Come Home* would have been seen as a valuable critique of parole but not much more. And if Travis's book had not used the term reentry—or if he had never been asked by Janet Reno to think about the issue —his role in defining mass prisoner release as a problem of "reentry" would not have taken place.

In short, just as constructs such as mental illness and juvenile delinquency were "invented," so too was prisoner "reentry." Petersilia and Travis defined prisoner release as reentry, and as claims-makers they argued that this was a social problem in need of attention. It helped, of course, that their claims were true. There was a constituency ready to join a reentry movement. Every correctional leader and academic analyst knew that the existing system of prisoner release was designed to fail and in need of reform.

C. A Decade Later

A decade after its "invention," reentry shows few signs of being a fad that will soon vanish. "Interest in prisoner re-entry over the last decade," notes Petersilia, "has fueled the development of hundreds of programs across the United States" (2011, p. 945). Although this movement was boosted by a number of developments, two events were especially important. First, in 2003, the federal government allocated more than $110 million to fund the Serious and Violent Offender Reentry Initiative (SVORI). Located in all 50 states, 69 agencies received between $500,000 and $2 million over a 3-year period. In all, 89 programs were implemented that focused on reducing recidivism and improving "employment, health (including substance use and mental health), and housing outcomes" (Lattimore and Visher 2009, p. ES-1).

Second, on January 20, 2004, George Bush delivered a critical State of the Union address. Citing the September 11 attacks, he noted that "our greatest responsibility is the active defense of the American people" (Bush 2004, p. 1). On the domestic front, he touted tax relief, the No Child Left Behind Act, policies advancing free and fair trade, defense of traditional marriage against "activist judges," and support for immigration reform. Toward the end, however, he turned his attention to the nation's imprisoned population. Echoing President Roosevelt's themes 65 years earlier, he asked Americans to give a "second chance" to prisoners reentering society:

> In the past, we've worked together to bring mentors to the children of prisoners and provide treatment for the addicted and help for the homeless. Tonight I ask you to consider another group of Americans in need of help.
>
> This year, some 600,000 inmates will be released from prison back into society. We know from long experience that if they can't find work or a home or help, they are much more likely to commit crime and return to prison.
>
> So tonight, I propose a four-year, $300 million Prisoner Re-Entry Initiative to expand job training and placement services, to provide transitional housing and to help newly released prisoners get mentoring, including from faith-based groups. (Applause)
>
> America is the land of second chance, and when the gates of the prison open, the path ahead should lead to a better life. (Applause) (Bush 2004, pp. 9–10)

President Bush's support eventually led to the passage of the 2008 Second Chance Act and to millions of dollars in annual funding for reentry services. Perhaps more important, his remarks were a clear departure from the punitive rhetoric that had long characterized crime-related commentary among conservative political elites (Simon 2007; Hagan 2010). At least to a degree, they signaled that prisoner reentry was potentially open to bipartisan support.

Four factors are likely to sustain reentry as a permanent feature of the correctional landscape. First, the genie is out of the bottle. Now that prisoner release has been socially constructed as a problem and given an identifiable name—reentry—it is difficult to imagine how ignoring the annual return of hundreds of thousands of offenders to society could be justified. As Petersilia (2009, p. 255) notes, reentry may have "staying power" because it "makes good sense, plain and simple."

Second, reentry is being institutionalized as a standard practice in state correctional and parole agencies. Wacquant cautions that reentry remains largely a ceremonial reform that is "but a minor bureaucratic adaptation to the glaring contradictions of the punitive regulation of poverty" (2010, p. 614). He points out that funding provided by the Second Chance Act "provides the princely sum of $20 monthly per new convict released, enough to buy them a sandwich each week" (p. 614). Of course, reentry funding is for the creation of programs and not for income redistribution on a per inmate basis, but Wacquant is right to warn that advocates should avoid unwarranted hubris about what has been achieved. Nonetheless, it is difficult to find a state correctional agency that has not institutionalized some form of reentry. A survey of 42 correctional systems in the United States (eight did not respond) found that all but three offered inmates planned release programs. In 14 states, these were mandatory (Community Corrections Research Team 2011). Numerous reentry programs now exist in states, counties, and communities across the nation. Further, as Rhine and Thompson observe, a "sizable cluster" of states have actively participated in reentry initiatives (e.g., Transition to Community Initiative, Prisoner Reentry Policy Academy). In fact, "state departments of corrections are found exercising leadership across these initiatives, deploying high level executive staff to stimulate and engage in such efforts" (2011, pp. 203–4).

"Reentry" is now an accepted part of the lexicon of American corrections. Books with reentry in the title are appearing with regularity (see, e.g., Gideon and Sung 2011; Gunnison and Helfgott 2013; Crow and Smykla 2014; Mears and Cochran 2015). Panels on reentry are commonplace at national criminology meetings. A number of websites exist to promote reentry, including the National Reentry Resource Center's What Works in Reentry Clearinghouse and Reentry Central News Headlines (for a full list, see Mears and Cochran [2015, p. 234]). A Google search for "reentry" leads to an array of sites offering resources to those wishing to learn more about current practices. With the assistance of Krisina Zuniga, we used Google Ngram Viewer to graph how often the phrase "prisoner reentry" was used in English language books between 1990 and 2008. The first use did not appear until 1998. After 2000, the curve on the graph showed a dramatic and steady growth upward.

Third, the call for a movement to address the problem of reentry came at a propitious time: when the get-tough era of mass imprisonment is winding down. A June 2014 Gallup poll revealed that when asked about the "most important problem facing the country today," Americans register scant concern about crime; only 3 percent identified "crime/violence" as a concern (Gallup 2014). Crime rates—especially in many major cities—have declined precipitously and stabilized at low levels (Zimring 2007, 2012). "Law and order" has receded as a contentious political issue, playing almost no role in recent political campaigns. Instead, a growing consensus exists on the left and right that mass imprisonment is no longer sustainable financially and that downsizing the nation's inmate population is necessary (Petersilia and Cullen 2015). Importantly, effective reentry is consistent with this bipartisan interest in returning more offenders to the community while not jeopardizing public safety. For example, the deep red state of Mississippi enacted reform legislation in 2014 intended to stave off prison growth and save $266 million. Part of the package was the implementation of "comprehensive reentry planning for all offenders returning to the community" (Pew Charitable Trusts 2014*b*, p. 9).

Fourth, the public strongly favors prisoner reentry programs. This sentiment is part of a broader, long-standing support of rehabilitation by the American citizenry (Cullen, Fisher, and Applegate 2000; Jonson, Cullen, and Lux 2013). For example, in a 2001 national survey, Cullen, Eck, and Lowenkamp (2002, p. 137) found that 92 percent of the respondents agreed that "it is a good idea to provide treatment for offenders who are in prison." Similarly, 88 percent supported providing "treatment for offenders who are supervised by the court and live in the community." What follows are recent findings specifically about prisoner reentry:

- A 2006 national poll reported that from 53 to 81 percent of respondents indicated that it was "very important" to provide "people reentering society after being incarcerated" housing, mentoring, family support, mental health services, drug treatment, and job training. Over nine in 10 believed that "planning for an incarcerated person's reentry" should occur during incarceration, including 44 percent favoring beginning such planning at the time of sentencing. Further, 79 percent expressed support for the Second Chance Act (Krisberg 2006).
- In a 2007–8 survey of New York, New Jersey, and Connecticut residents, approximately 85 percent stated that they were "concerned" about "the fact that about 700,000 prisoners will be released from prison to their home communities." Similarly, 83 percent expressed support for the Second Chance Act (Gideon and Loveland 2011, pp. 28–29).
- A 2008 study of Missouri residents showed that 88.7 percent agreed that "it is a good idea to help people who are coming out of prison readjust to life in society," and 77.8 percent agreed that "people coming home from prison can benefit from well-run services and programs in their community." More than nine in 10 respondents favored substance abuse and mental health treatment for ex-offenders (Garland, Wodahl, and Schuhmann 2013, pp. 37–39).
- A 2010 poll of Oregon residents found that a high percentage supported providing reentry support to offenders such as mental health services (81 percent), housing help (89 percent), drug treatment (91 percent), education (91 percent), and job training (93 percent) (Sundt et al. 2012).
- A 2012 national poll revealed that 87 percent of the respondents agreed that "ninety-five percent of people in prison will be released. If we are serious about public safety, we must increase access to treatment and job training programs so they can become productive citizens once they are back in the community" (Public Opinion Strategies and the Mellman Group 2012, p. 4).

These findings show that there is considerable ideological space for policy makers to implement prisoner reentry initiatives (Jonson, Cullen, and Lux 2013). Citizens understand that investing in offenders' transition from prison to the community is rational governance aimed at improving both public safety and ex-inmates' lives. However, this global support should not be seen as a blank check. Thus, in their Missouri survey, Garland, Wodahl, and Schuhmann (2013) found that support for reentry programs diminished when the respondents were asked to raise taxes to pay for them or to give ex-offenders preference for services over nonoffenders. These data should not be taken as evidence that the public's endorsement of reentry is soft. However, as with any policy issue, correctional policy attitudes change depending on the factors that the public is asked to consider (Cullen, Fisher, and Applegate 2000). Raising taxes or proposing to give benefits to those (offenders) generally considered to be less eligible for them would understandably dampen enthusiasm for reentry policies. Alternatively, support for reentry programs would likely rise if the respondents could be shown that such services facilitate prison downsizing by quickening inmate release, are cost effective, and reduce recidivism. The quality of reentry programs thus can play an integral role in sustaining support among the American public.

II. The Challenge of Effectiveness

As in fields such as medicine and education, the idea that practice should be evidence based has gained increasing legitimacy in corrections (MacKenzie 2006; Cullen, Myer, and Latessa 2009; Cullen and Jonson 2012). Demonstrably ineffective interventions can erode public confidence, cause offenders to become further entrenched in criminal careers, and irresponsibly endanger public safety. The difficulty, however, is that unlike the marketing of drugs by the pharmaceutical industry, correctional "treatments" can be delivered with no prior testing or proven effectiveness. The absence of appropriate governmental regulation or civil liability is exacerbated by a lack of internal occupational regulation. Because corrections has not been fully professionalized, service providers are not required to possess up-to-date scientific expertise on treatment efficacy or to comply with a code of ethics, enforced by sanctions, that forbids harmful practices (Latessa, Cullen, and Gendreau 2002; Cullen 2011). Perhaps not surprisingly, corrections has been susceptible to the creation of plausible but ultimately ineffective programs, such as Scared Straight (Finckenauer 1982), intensive offender supervision (Petersilia and Turner 1993), boot camps (Cullen et al. 2005), and probation based on the Project HOPE model (Duriez, Cullen, and Manchak 2014).

The challenge for the reentry movement is to avoid the trap of developing programs that ultimately prove to be ineffective. In fact, the movement's creation of numerous programs is far outstripping knowledge about "what works" in reentry. Given their human services orientation, it is likely that many programs are providing prisoners needed social support before and after release. However, little evidence exists that reentry programs have lasting effects and, in particular, are capable of reducing offender recidivism. In this section, we first identify four barriers to reentry effectiveness: diversity of programs, lack of programs based on a credible theory of recidivism, lack of treatment fidelity in the implementations of programs, and the inability of the major reentry evaluation study to date (SVORI) to produce a clear blueprint for how best to deal with released offenders. We then review beginning efforts to construct knowledge about how to deliver reentry more efficaciously.

A. Barriers to Effectiveness

The main strategy has been to develop evidence-based websites that list programs found to "work." Because this advice is based on limited evaluation data, it must be followed with caution. A recent meta-analysis by Ndrecka (2014) offers the most systematic assessment of the components of reentry effectiveness. For the most part, her findings are consistent with what is currently known about treatment effectiveness more generally (see Andrews and Bonta 2010).

1. *Diversity of Programs.* Deciding "what works" is difficult enough when studies evaluate a single treatment modality, such as boot camps or cognitive-behavioral therapy. But assessing how best to facilitate prisoner reentry is especially daunting because of the heterogeneity of interventions that fall under this category (Gunnison and Helfgott 2013; Mears and Cochran 2015). Reentry programs vary along several dimensions: existing rehabilitation programs relabeled as "reentry" versus programs created specifically to facilitate reentry; the setting of the program (in prison, in the community, in between, or across all three phrases of reentry); programs that are multimodal versus those that focus on specific criminogenic or life needs, such as deficits in behavioral and cognitive behavioral skills, mental health, substance abuse, and problems surrounding housing, employment, family bonds, and physical health; and formal programs administered by correctional agencies versus programs staffed by volunteers and run by nonprofit organizations, faith-based groups, or ex-offenders.

Given that most programs are not evaluated (Mears and Cochran 2015), it is difficult to build a large body of studies that assesses each variant of reentry programming. As we discuss below, this means that reentry programs—including those that appear promising—are rarely evaluated by more than one or two studies. With this level of empirical support, it is unclear whether such programs should be touted as evidence-based models to be implemented in other contexts. The other option to constructing knowledge on effectiveness is to analyze programs across treatment modalities—either through a qualitative assessment of effective programs or quantitatively through a meta-analysis—so as to try to discern components that most effective programs seem to possess (more generally, see Lipsey 2009).

2. *Lack of Credible Theory Informing Programs.* As Mears and Cochran observe, most "reentry efforts . . . rest on little to no coherent or credible theoretical foundation" (2015, p. 209). Most often, program inventors do not rely on scientific criminology when implementing an intervention. Instead, most programs are developed to address the readily observable problems that offenders face. If offenders are mentally ill or addicted to drugs, does it not make sense to address these needs? If offenders lack job skills and are unemployed, are homeless, or have lost ties to family members, does it not make sense to address these needs? To improve offenders' quality of life—if not on sheer humanitarian grounds—the answer is yes. But what is not clear is whether such programs, if not rooted in a credible treatment theory, have any chance of reducing recidivism.

Sometimes, the theory underlying a reentry program is attractive because it resonates with common sense. The Parallel Universe program—used in Missouri and then later in Arizona—is one example (Schriro 2000, 2009; Schriro and Clements 2001). The word "parallel" is used because the program attempted to make life inside prison approximate life outside of prison. Inmates worked or went to school during the day; participated in community service, religious programming, or recreation in off hours; were encouraged to participate in prison governance by serving on councils and committees; and were held accountable for their decisions, with positive incentives offered for responsible conduct. The underlying theory is plausible: living a structured prosocial life inside prison will lead offenders to live the same way upon release. Still, the theory's appeal rests more on common sense than on an empirically validated criminological theory linking compliant behavior inside institutions to law-abiding behavior in the community. An evaluation based on limited qualitative observations and nonexperimental quantitative data suggested that Arizona's Parallel Universe program (called Getting Ready) improved the quality of institutional life but, at best, had a small effect on recidivism (Gaes 2009). Although a well-known reentry program, it is thus not clear that creating a "parallel universe" in prison is the best option for producing meaningful savings in recidivism.

The alternative approach is to develop reentry programs based on a scientifically validated correctional theory such as the risk-need-responsivity (RNR) model pioneered by Andrews, Bonta, Gendreau, and other Canadian scholars (Cullen 2013). Programs that adhere to the components of the RNR model tend to be more effective, even if not based explicitly on the principles of effective interventions (Petersilia 2011; Turner and Petersilia 2012; Mears and Cochran 2015). The RNR model, which is the leading treatment approach in corrections, has been explained elsewhere in detail (Andrews 1995; Gendreau 1996; Andrews and Bonta 2010; Cullen 2013). Briefly, however, it posits that rehabilitative interventions, including reentry programs, will be most effective if they do as follows: focus on high-risk offenders (the risk principle); target for change predictors of recidivism that can change, such as antisocial attitudes and low self-control (the need principle); and use treatment modalities that are "responsive to" and thus capable of reducing the risk factors that lead to reoffending, such as cognitive-behavioral therapy (the responsivity principle).

The value of following the RNR model is demonstrated by Lowenkamp and Latessa's (2002) now-classic study of the effects of halfway houses on recidivism. Using a 2-year follow up, they compared rearrests and reincarcerations for 3,737 offenders released in 1999 from 37 halfway houses with those of a comparison group of 3,058 offenders. The analysis revealed considerable heterogeneity in effects, with some halfway houses reducing recidivism by more than 30 percent and others increasing it by more than 35 percent. Using the RNR model as their guide, Lowenkamp and Latessa discovered that this heterogeneity was explained by the risk principle. According to Andrews and Bonta (2010, p. 47, emphasis in original), "the risk principle involves the idea of *matching levels of treatment services to the risk level of the offender*." Specifically, to reduce their recidivism, "higher-risk offenders need more intensive and extensive services"; by contrast, for "low-risk offenders, minimal or even no intervention is sufficient" (p. 48). Consistent with this principle, halfway houses serving low-risk offenders were associated with increased rearrest and reincarceration, whereas programs targeting high-risk offenders resulted in lower recidivism rates. A follow-up evaluation largely replicated the earlier study (Lowenkamp, Latessa, and Smith 2006). Lowenkamp and Latessa concluded that failure to comply with the risk principle can have criminogenic effects, especially for low-risk offenders (see also Andrews et al. 1990).

3. *Lack of Integrity in Program Implementation.* Rhine, Mawhorr, and Parks (2006, p. 347) argue that implementation problems are "the bane of correctional programs." Andrews and Bonta (2010, p. 395) argue that correctional programs that fail to adhere to the "principles of RNR clinical practice, staffing and management, core practices and program integrity" are ineffective, if not criminogenic. Such failure, however, is commonplace, especially in real world programs as opposed to demonstration projects designed by researchers. Given that most reentry programs fall into the former category, their effectiveness is likely circumscribed.

The challenge of implementation is illuminated by Project Greenlight, "an institution-based transitional services demonstration program that was piloted in New York State's Queensboro correctional facility" (Wilson et al. 2005, p. 8; see also Wilson and Davis 2006; Wilson 2007). Developed and largely run by the Vera Institute of Justice, the program was based on the "what works" literature and employed a form of cognitive-behavioral treatment (Reasoning and Rehabilitation; see Ross and Fabiano 1985; Ross 1995). During the 60-day intervention, a variety of risk factors were targeted, including substance abuse, short- and long-term housing, employment, family counseling, practical life skills (e.g., managing bank accounts, using public transportation), and antisocial behavior and thinking. Offenders also received reentry plans to follow upon release. Evaluation results, however, were disappointing, with the recidivism rates of Project Greenlight participants exceeding those of two control groups (Wilson et al. 2005; Wilson and Davis 2006).

Implementation problems likely account for the program's ineffectiveness. Thus, the dosage (60 days) may have been too brief for high-risk offenders, the treatment groups were at least twice as large as is recommended by the inventors of Reasoning and Rehabilitation, and offenders received no systematic aftercare once released (Wilson and Davis 2006). Commenting on the program, Andrews and Bonta (2010, p. 399) note that "even programs that were designed with reference to 'what works' are often not well implemented." As they observed:

> A few points are striking. The inmates, without any discussion or consent, were taken abruptly from their prison and transferred to the program site. Many "clients" experienced program participation as the equivalent of being mistreated by the system. No reference is made to the employment of risk/need assessment instruments. Indeed, participation in the substance abuse program was mandatory, even for inmates who did not have a substance abuse problem. The selection of program staff explicitly did to follow the recommendations of the creators of the program. The negative outcomes associated with two of the four workers totally accounted for the program failure. (P. 399)

4. *Inability of SVORI to Guide Program Development.* Implemented in 2003, the Serious and Violent Offender Reentry Initiative (SVORI) was a collaborative effort by the US Departments of Justice, Labor, Education, Housing and Urban Development, and Health and Human Services. These agencies awarded $100 million in federal funds to 89 adult and juvenile programs that attempted to increase successful offender reentry in five areas: criminal justice, housing, health, employment, and education (National Institute of Justice 2011). Given its scope, SVORI had the potential to establish a clear blueprint for effective reentry programming. Lattimore and her colleagues undertook a systematic evaluation of the initiative (Lattimore, Steffey, and Visher 2009; Lattimore and Visher 2009; Lindquist et al. 2009; Lattimore et al. 2012). The evaluation included 1,618 adult males, 348 adult females, and 337 juvenile males drawn from 12 adult and four juvenile programs "diverse in approach and geographically distributed" (Lattimore et al. 2012, p. 7; for a list of programs, see Lattimore and Visher [2009, p. 23]). Because random assignment was not possible for all programs, propensity-score matching and multivariate analysis were used to compare SVORI participants and nonparticipants.

Even though the 16 programs were selected from among SVORI grantees because they were "deemed most promising as impact candidates" (Lattimore et al. 2012, p. 7), the effect of SVORI participation on recidivism and other life outcomes was inconsistent. In a 2009 "summary and synthesis" of the "multi-site evaluation," Lattimore and Visher reported that as the follow-up progressed, SVORI participation had no effect on juvenile self-reported crime. Among adults, SVORI women, but not men, had lower arrests than the comparison group. However, by 24 months, both male and female SVORI participants had higher reincarceration rates. Similarly, an analysis of rearrest and nine other self-reported outcomes (e.g., housing, employment, job pay and benefits, drug use, committed any crime) at 15 months showed that SVORI participation had mostly "beneficial but non-significant" effects (Lattimore et al. 2012, p. ES-10). In a subsequent follow-up at 56 months or more for adults and 22 months for juveniles, more promising findings were reported (Lattimore et al. 2012). All groups were found to have a longer time to arrest and fewer arrests after release. Adult males also had a longer time to reincarceration and fewer reincarcerations (but this latter effect was not statistically significant). No statistically significant findings on reincarceration were reported for adult females or juvenile males.

Unpacking the results further was difficult because a process evaluation was not part of the evaluation design, and thus there was no "detailed information on the nature and implementation of the SVORI programs," including program quality, specific services provided, and dosages of treatment delivered (Lattimore et al. 2012, p. ES-14). Through surveys with study participants, the researchers did develop self-reported measures of services received (e.g., a reentry plan, help with life skills, access to mental health treatment). But these services tended to be unrelated to recidivism measures and, in some cases, had criminogenic effects.

In the end, the federal government spent $100 million to fund 89 programs and sponsored a long-term, careful evaluation by respected researchers. But the stubborn reality is that the investment did not yield a clear blueprint for how to conduct an effective reentry program. Participation in SVORI had only "limited effects . . . on intermediate outcomes" (such as housing and employment) and, over the long term, seemed to reduce arrests but had mixed effects on reincarceration (Lattimore et al. 2012, p. 148). Unfortunately, it is not clear why SVORI had these effects or which specific SVORI programs should serve as evidence-based models for future program development. Perhaps the best that can be said is that a well-intentioned reentry program that seems promising on the surface generally is better than doing nothing, but its impact is likely to be mixed and modest.

B. Knowledge Construction

Efforts have been made to construct knowledge about best practices in prisoner reentry. Government agencies have developed websites that seek to accumulate and give ready access to evaluation research on program effectiveness. These efforts are part of a broader agenda to sponsor what John Laub (2011, p. 3), then director of the NIJ, called "translational criminology," which involves the "dissemination of scientific knowledge" so as to enhance practice and "to reduce crime, improve public safety, and promote justice." An alternative approach to knowledge construction is to undertake reviews of the evaluation literature to identify program components that contribute to effectiveness. This approach has been used to analyze the broader treatment literature with success (see, e.g., Lipsey 2009; Andrews and Bonta 2010).

1. *Reentry Program Websites.* The NIJ (CrimeSolutions.gov) and the Council of State Governments Justice Center (What Works in Reentry Clearinghouse) have each created a well-known website that catalogs effective reentry programs. Because they share similar features, we discuss only the NIJ site. Introduced in July 2011, CrimeSolutions.gov uses available research to identify "what works" to improve outcomes in criminal justice; "reentry/release" is one of its topical areas. To assess effectiveness, a rigorous protocol is followed. Two reviewers, selected for their substantive and scientific expertise, use a detailed Program Evidence Rating Instrument to assess studies used to evaluate a nominated program. On the basis of the methodological quality of the evaluation and the findings, programs are rated as "effective," "promising," or "no effects."

Accordingly, CrimeSolutions.gov is an important effort to construct and disseminate knowledge. By visiting a single website, it is possible to learn which reentry programs have been evaluated and vetted by experts. Detailed descriptions of the program are provided, including the intervention's goals, target population, and services provided. The studies used to evaluate any given program are listed, and full citations are provided. Twenty-seven programs are now listed and rated. The website also is dynamic, with the possibility of adding new evaluated reentry programs in the future.

Despite its advantages, CrimeSolutions.gov also illuminates why it remains a daunting task to discern "what works" in reentry and to answer with confidence the following simple question: If policy makers and practitioners wished to improve prisoner reentry in their jurisdiction, what should they do? Developed from information provided by Crime Solutions.gov, table 2 provides an analysis of the programs included on the website. It omits seven programs rated as having "no effects"—including SVORI (Lattimore and Visher 2009) and Project Greenlight

(Wilson et al. 2005). Of the 20 studies included, only one—Project BUILD—was judged to be "effective" (on the basis of a single study by Lurigio et al. [2000]). The other 19 programs were rated as "promising." This rating is defined by CrimeSolutions.gov as follows: "Programs have some evidence to indicate they achieved their intended outcome" (2015, p. 15). At least one study must exist that "demonstrates promising (perhaps inconsistent) evidence in favor of the program when evaluated with a design of high quality (quasi-experimental)" (p. 14). Then the key warning is provided: "More extensive research is required" (p. 14).

Three points merit attention. First, it is not possible to take the one "effective" program and use it widely. Project BUILD is targeted for a limited population, as its description on the website shows: "A violence prevention curriculum designed to assist youths in detention overcome obstacles such as gangs, violence, crime, and substance abuse." Second, although CrimeSolutions.gov is an exercise in evidence-based corrections, the evidence available to be listed is slim. Due to limitations in the quality of study design or consistency of results, the standard program rating is only "promising." In practical terms, this means that such interventions are not proven and can be relied on as models for program implementation only with caution. Further, it is instructive that few programs were subjected to multiple evaluations. Of the 20 programs, 17 were rated on the basis of a single evaluation study (see table 2). In the other three instances, the multiple evaluations were not conducted by a different group of independent researchers. Rather, a research team that included one or more of the original authors returned to reevaluate the program using a longer follow-up period. Third, the sheer diversity of programs—varying by treatment targets, offender population, phases, and location (prison, community, both)—makes it hard to generalize about the core components of reentry effectiveness. Table 2, however, contains some hints as to what such components might be. Our analysis of program types revealed that four promising reentry initiatives conducted at least partially in prison placed offenders in a therapeutic community (TC).[1] Further, nine of the 19 promising programs were not

[1] Where possible in table 2, we categorized programs by "type." In a few cases, the program did not fall under any common treatment modality and thus no categorization was possible. In a few other cases, we noted that the initiative was "not really" a reentry program either because of the population served (i.e., probationers) or because no rehabilitative human services were provided (e.g., electronic monitoring in Florida).

TABLE 2

Effective and Promising Reentry/Release Programs Reported by CrimeSolutions.gov

Program Name	Type	Targets	Population	Number of Phases	Research Design	Location	Number of Studies
Project BUILD (effective)	. . .	Self-esteem, communication, problem solving, goal setting, and decision making	Juvenile males and females	One	Quasi-experimental: random sample compared to matched random sample	Detention center	One
Amity in-Prison Therapeutic Community	TC	Substance Abuse	Adult males	Three	Experimental: random assignment	Prison (offered to continue community aftercare TC for 1 year)	Three
Auglaize County Transition Program	. . .	Medical and mental health, employment, substance abuse, education, MRT, church, anger management, life skills	Adult males and females	Two	Quasi-experimental: matched control group	Jail and community	One
Boston Reentry Initiative	. . .	Identification/drivers licenses, health insurance, shelter, transportation, interim job, substance abuse, mental health, education, employment, permanent housing, mentoring	Adult males 18–32	Two	Quasi-experimental: equivalent control group (nonrandomized)	Jail and community	One

Community and Law Enforcement Resources Together (ComALERT)	. . .	Substance abuse, employment, housing, financial, life skills	Adult males and females	One	Quasi-experimental: matched control group (propensity scores)	Community	One
Delaware KEY/Crest Substance Abuse Program	TC	Substance abuse	Adult males and females	Three	Quasi-experimental	Prison and community	Three
Electronic Monitoring	Not really reentry		Adults 14 and older	One	Mixed methods: propensity score matching	Community	One
Forever Free	Multimodal	Substance abuse, self-esteem, anger management, assertiveness training, PTSD, codependency, parenting, sex and health, education, vocation, CBT	Adult women	Two	Control variables	Prison and community (voluntary)	One
InnerChange Freedom Initiative	Faith based	RNR, substance abuse, victim-impact awareness, life-skills development, cognitive skill development, moral development, education, vocational, religion, mentor	Adult males	Three	Quasi-experimental: matched comparison	Prison and community	One

TABLE 2 (*Continued*)

Program Name	Type	Targets	Population	Number of Phases	Research Design	Location	Number of Studies
Minnesota Prison-Based Sex Offender Treatment Program	TC	Sex treatment, victim awareness, substance abuse, family education, CBT, emotional regulation, moral	Adult males	Two	Quasi-experimental: matched comparison (retrospective)	Prison	One
Modified Therapeutic Community for Offenders with Mental Illness and Chemical Abuse (MICA) Disorders	TC	Mental health, substance abuse, CBT, medication	Adult males	Four	Experimental: random assignment	Prison and community	One
Naltrexone for Federal Probationers	Not really reentry	Substance abuse	Adult males and females	One	Experimental: volunteers randomly assigned at a ratio of 2:1	Community	One
New Jersey Community Resource Center	Day reporting center	Education, vocational, employment, substance abuse, family, life skills	Adult males and females	One	Control variables	Community	One
New Jersey Halfway Back Program	Halfway house	Education, substance abuse, conflict resolution, family, gang prevention, vocational, employment, motivational interviewing	Adult males and females	One	Control variables	Community	One

Operation New Hope	Reality therapy	Life skills, decision making, substance abuse, CBT, conflict resolution, leadership, mentoring, family	Males and females 16–22	One	Quasi-experimental: nonrandomized treatment and comparison group	Community	One
Preventing Parolee Crime Program (PPCP)	Parolee program	Substance abuse, education, employment, housing	Adult males and females	One	Quasi-experimental	Community	One
Prison-Initiated Methadone Maintenance Treatment	Medication	Substance abuse	Adult males 35–45	Two	Experimental: three-group randomized controlled trial	Prison and community (voluntary)	Two
Strategic Training Initiative in Community Supervision (STICS)	Job training program for probation officers to apply RNR—not really reentry	Training probation officers in RNR	Adult males and females	One	Experimental randomized	Community	One
Thinking for a Change	CBT—not really reentry	Cognitive self-change, social skills, problem-solving skills	Adult males and females	One	Quasi-experimental	Community	One
West Midlands (England) High-Crime Causing Users (HCCU)	Inpatient/outpatient—not really reentry	Access to medication, psychosocial support, housing, training and education, detoxification, substance abuse treatment and prevention	Individuals arrested and tested positive at arrest for heroin or cocaine at least three times in past 12 months	One	Quasi-experimental	Community	One

NOTE.—TC = therapeutic community; MRT = moral reconation therapy; PTSD = posttraumatic stress disorder; CBT = cognitive behavioral therapy; RNR = risk-need-responsivity.

limited to a single setting (prison or community) but were conducted in "phases" in which treatment was initially provided to prison inmates and then continued after release into the community. In short, continuity of care may increase the likelihood of reentry program effectiveness.

Recently, CrimeSolutions.gov has added a new category called "practices." Unlike programs, practices are general categories of programs—or treatment modalities—that share similar procedures and strategies. These practices are rated on the basis of one or more meta-analyses that have been assessed by reviewers for methodological quality (see Wilson, Gallagher, and MacKenzie 2000; Chappell 2004; Aos, Miller, and Drake 2006; Davis et al. 2013). CrimeSolutions.gov has identified one practice as having "no effects" (noncustodial employment programs) and four practices as "promising" (correctional work industries, corrections-based adult basic and secondary education, corrections-based vocational training, postsecondary correctional education). This approach suggests that education and building work experience and skills may reduce recidivism. Again, however, the evidence must be viewed with caution because of the limitations of the available evaluation research.

The study by Wilson, Gallagher, and MacKenzie (2000) assessed multiple practices and thus was identified as part of the "evidence base" for the four promising modalities. In the original article that assessed a "collection of 33 comparison group evaluations of corrections-based education, vocation, and work programs," Wilson and colleagues reported that "assuming a 50 percent recidivism rate for nonparticipants, participants recidivate, on average, at a rate of 39 percent" (p. 361). For two reasons, however, they warned that the evidence may be "insufficient" to conclude that these programs diminish reoffending. First, the typical study in their meta-analysis used a quasi-experimental design that did not control fully for potential differences in criminal propensity between the treatment and control groups. As a result, selection effects could not be ruled out. Second, they discovered "large heterogeneity across studies within program types," suggesting that "some programs may be highly effective, whereas others, may have no effects, or at least a minimal effect, on future offending behaviors" (p. 361). In practical terms, this means that although the work or education practice or modality may tend to reduce recidivism, no guarantee can be given that any specific program will be effective.

2. *Research Reviews.* Two major comprehensive reviews have been conducted to help determine what is effective in prisoner reentry. First,

Seiter and Kadela (2003) used the five-point Maryland Scale of Scientific Methods (MSSM) created by Sherman et al. (1998) to evaluate reentry programs that were grouped into six categories. The MSSM measured scientific rigor from a low score of 1 (correlation with recidivism, typically with no control group) to a high score of 5 (the "gold standard" of random assignment into control and treatment groups; Sherman et al. 1998). For an intervention to be categorized as "what works," two studies with a score of at least 3 had to show statistically significant, positive findings. On the basis of an assessment of 32 studies, Seiter and Kadela (2003) concluded that four program categories—vocation and work programs, drug rehabilitation, halfway houses, and prerelease programs—were effective in reducing postrelease offending. Sexual and violent offender programming were judged as promising but in need of further research to demonstrate their effectiveness. Although educational programs had a positive impact on achievement scores, they were rated as having no effect on recidivism.

Second, Ndrecka (2014) conducted a meta-analysis to synthesize the findings from 53 studies. Overall, reentry programs were found to reduce recidivism by 6 percent (i.e., 47 vs. 53 percent). However, considerable heterogeneity in effects was found, with some programs increasing recidivism by as much as 17 percent while others reduced recidivism 62 percent. Importantly, the value of the meta-analytic technique is that it is possible to unpack these effects by empirically exploring program characteristics—"moderators"—that affect program outcomes.

Ndrecka (2014, p. 143) concluded that program success was related to adherence "to the risk, need, responsivity, and fidelity principles" of the RNR model. Furthermore, programs had a larger effect on recidivism when they lasted long enough (13 weeks or more) and provided continuity of care (had multiple phases, beginning in the institution and extending into the community upon release). Finally, therapeutic communities, programs targeted to mentally ill offenders with addiction issues, and programs that mix a variety of treatments also produced a reduction in recidivism. Halfway house programs were found to be iatrogenic.

C. *Taking Stock of Effectiveness*

The capacity to develop reentry programs informed by evidence-based corrections is limited. Existing evaluations are spread across a diversity of programs, rarely use high-quality experimental designs, and at times yield inconsistent results. Systematic reviews, including meta-analyses, suggest that, overall, reentry services tend to reduce recidivism, but program effects are heterogeneous and at times criminogenic. Promising programs have been identified and could be modeled for specific correctional populations (e.g., offenders with substance abuse problems, violence prevention among high-risk juvenile detainees). Doing so must be undertaken with caution because of the risk that positive findings might not replicate across different contexts. Finally, several conclusions from the evaluation literature, mostly consistent with the RNR model, can be drawn that might inform reentry program development:

- Programs that provided a continuity of care, beginning in the prison and continuing once prisoners were released into the community, were found to be more effective.
- Programs lacking treatment fidelity often showed no appreciable effects on recidivism.
- Programs targeting high-risk offenders and their criminogenic needs were found to be more effective.
- Programs that employed therapeutic communities were found to be effective.

III. Closing the Knowledge Gap

The reentry movement is now in its second decade. Reentry is increasingly an integral component of the correctional enterprise and likely will remain so for the foreseeable future. But name recognition and institutionalization do not ensure that reentry will "work." Intervening successfully with offenders is a daunting challenge. The history of corrections instructs that most treatment programs fail, not only because they are poorly implemented but also because they were poorly conceived in the first place (Lipton, Martinson, and Wilks 1975; Latessa, Cullen, and Gendreau 2002; Andrews and Bonta 2010). Many reentry initiatives have never been evaluated. Those that have been assessed reveal mixed results, with even some carefully designed programs producing disappointing or detrimental outcomes. Enough promising findings exist, however, to allow for cautious optimism that reentry programming can diminish offender recidivism. Available information may allow a beginning effort to identify characteristics of effective programs. It is clear, however, that far more must be known and done to "make reentry work" consistently.

Other commentators have provided good advice on how prisoner reentry might be improved further (Petersilia 2003; Taxman, Young, and Byrne 2004; Travis 2005; Listwan, Cullen, and Latessa 2006; Turner and Petersilia 2012; Gunnison and Helfgott 2013; Wright and Cesar 2013; Mears and Cochran 2015). Our approach is complementary to these recommendations, as we attempt to identify core issues that reentry programs and reforms should address. In particular, we suggest that further advancement in constructing effective reentry programs will need to address a "knowledge gap." Beyond the general advice that more rigorous evaluations of high-quality programs are needed, we identify five tasks that if addressed seriously could make reentry work more effectively: create a criminology of reentry, take coming home seriously, prevent late-onset recidivism, focus on whether the diversity of "who comes home" matters, and confront the collateral consequences effect.

A. A Criminology of Reentry

In correctional rehabilitation, individualized treatment is intended to mirror the medical model (Rothman 1980). Similar to the diagnosis of a patient's illness, wayward offenders are assessed to determine which factors are leading them into crime. These risk factors are then targeted for treatment. If the correct intervention or "medicine" is used—if the treatment is "responsive" to the underlying causal condition—then the risk factors will be changed and the offender cured.

It is difficult to imagine what other model could be followed. It makes logical sense to identify what is causing an offender to break the law, to target these criminogenic factors for change, and to use proven treatment modalities to accomplish this task. In fact, this approach is used by virtually every acclaimed model program that deals with antisocial or criminal problems, whether among younger or older offenders. For example, in his nurse home visitation program (now called the Nurse-Family Partnership), program inventor David Olds (2007, p. 200) begins by laying out a causal model that identifies the prenatal factors (poor health behavior by mother, such as smoking or taking drugs) and postnatal factors (child abuse and neglect) that lead to poor "birth outcomes," "child neurodevelopmental impairment," and eventually to compromised "child/adolescent functioning" (e.g., "antisocial behavior, substance abuse, psychopathology"). The goal of the intervention is to focus on these "modifiable risks" (p. 211). Nurses were chosen to visit young, pregnant mothers so as to help improve their prenatal health practices, parental care after birth, and subsequent decision making related to future pregnancies and reaching educational and employment goals. To ensure that risks would be appropriately targeted, nurses "followed detailed visit-by-visit guidelines whose content reflects the challenges parents are likely to confront during specific stages of pregnancy and the first two years of the child's life. Specific assessments were made of maternal, child, and family functioning that correspond to those stages, and specific activities were recommended based upon problems and strengths identified through the assessments" (p. 212). Similar approaches are taken by the inventors of other model programs such as multisystemic therapy (Henggeler 1998) and the Seattle Social Development Project (Hawkins et al. 2007). In each case, they first identify empirically established "targeted risk and protective factors" (Henggeler 1998, p. 11) and then specify how their intervention will "reduce specific risk factors and increase protective factors" (Hawkins et al. 2007, p. 167). Importantly, they clearly demarcate the protocols and treatment modalities to be used.

Those more familiar with corrections will be aware that this same intervention paradigm is employed by the RNR model invented by Andrews, Bonta, Gendreau, and fellow Canadian scholars (Cullen and Jonson 2012). Andrews and his colleagues start with the premise that it is essential to identify those deficits ("criminogenic needs") that increase the likelihood that offenders will recidivate. They focus only on those causes of recidivism that can be changed, which they call "dynamic risk factors." They have now compiled eight separate meta-analyses to show empirically which factors are the strongest predictors of recidivism and thus should be targeted in treatment for change (Andrews and Bonta 2010, p. 65).

They call these the "Central Eight," which consists of the "Big Four" and the "Moderate Four" (Andrews and Bonta 2010, pp. 58–60). The Big Four include a history of antisocial behavior, antisocial personality patterns (weak self-control, anger management, and problem solving skills), antisocial cognition (attitudes, rationalizations, identity favorable to crime), and antisocial associates (interaction mainly with pro-criminal others). Antisocial history is included despite appearing to be a static risk factor, because even though a "history cannot be changed," it is possible to focus on "appropriate intermediate targets of change" including "building up new noncriminal behaviors in high-risk situations and building self-efficacy beliefs supporting reform ('I know what to do to avoid criminal activity and I know that I can do what is required')" (p. 58). The Moderate Four are family/marital circumstances, school/work, leisure/recreation, and substance abuse (pp. 59–60). Andrews and his colleagues use these dynamic risk factors in their assessment instrument (the Level of Service Inventory) and in their selection of modalities to address these factors (e.g., cognitive-behavioral treatment).

It is striking how few reentry programs use anything approximating this intervention paradigm (Turner and Petersilia 2012; Mears and Cochran 2015). We hasten to say that we are not referring specifically to the RNR model per se; other factors, not identified by this model, might be involved in reentry success, such as hope about the future and self-identification as a "family man" rather than as a criminal (Maruna 2001; LeBel et al. 2008). Rather, we use the term "paradigm" more as an approach to undertaking intervention that involves carefully demarcating the risk (and protective) factors held to underlie recidivism, the treatment being proposed that can change (be responsive to) these risk factors, and the specific protocols and activities that will be used when delivering the intervention.

Instead, reentry programs often are marked by a lack of a clear theoretical model and by a failure to specify which risk factors are being targeted and whether they are empirically established predictors of recidivism (Mears and Cochran 2015). In many instances, program advocates seem to rely on liberal common sense that doing something for offenders—such as helping them to secure a job or a place to reside—will improve their lives and enable them to escape a life in crime. This intuition may not be fully incorrect, but it ignores the reality that interventions will likely fail or have only modest results when targeting weak predictors of recidivism or targeting them in the wrong way (Listwan, Cullen, and Latessa 2006).

Employment is a useful example, because it is difficult to imagine any person—offender or not—having a structured, prosocial, fulfilling life without having a job. Still, employment reentry programs may have, at best, a modest impact on recidivism for three reasons. First, Andrews and Bonta (2010) identify work (and school) as a risk factor meriting intervention. However, employment is a moderate risk factor and seven other risk factors comprise the Central Eight. If these other factors are not addressed in the intervention, they may continue to exert a criminogenic influence on offenders. Second, merely having a job may not be enough to go straight upon release. It may be that recidivism is reduced only if quality employment is secured, a point made by Sampson and Laub (1993). Similarly, Andrews and Bonta (2010) emphasize that work or school are conduits for diminishing criminal propensity mainly because they provide "quality interpersonal relationships." These activities can be used as "intermediate targets for change" if steps are taken to "enhance performance, involvement, and rewards and satisfactions" (p. 59).

Third, recent research by Skardhamar and Savolainen (2014, pp. 270–71) studied a sample of Norwegian "crime-prone offenders" (at least five felonies) with an "unstable work history who managed to get stable jobs." They found that employment fostered desistance but only for less than 2 percent of the sample. For most offenders, the causal ordering was reversed, with stable employment following rather than preceding desistance. This finding suggests that for offenders to take advantage of employment—sometimes called a "hook for change"—it might first be necessary to evoke a cognitive transformation that reduces their criminal propensity and allows them to take advantage of a new life chance (see Maruna 2001; Giordano, Cernkovich, and Rudolph 2002). In concluding her comprehensive book *What Works in Corrections*, MacKenzie (2006, p. 335) makes this same point:

> When I compared the effective programs to the ineffective programs I noticed an interesting difference. Almost all of the effective programs focused on individual-level change. In contrast, the ineffective programs frequently focused on developing opportunities. For example, the cognitive skills programs emphasize individual-level changes in thinking, reasoning, empathy, and problem solving. In contrast, life skills and work programs, examples of ineffective programs, focus on giving offenders opportunities in the community. Based on these observations, I propose that effective programs must focus on changing the individual. This change is required before the person will be able to take advantage of opportunities in the environment.

This discussion implies that a pressing need exists for a more sophisticated—theoretically informed and empirically based—criminology of reentry (see also the call for a "science of punishment" by Mears and Cochran [2015, p. 243]). It may be possible, of course, to use existing treatment models, such as the RNR model or multisystemic therapy, as a basis for reentry programming (see Turner and Petersilia 2012). However, grafting treatment models onto reentry does not provide a systematic knowledge base for understanding how interventions should be delivered at each stage. For one thing, there is a glaring lack of knowledge about how the prison experience affects postincarceration recidivism and how potentially criminogenic sanction effects can be lessened (Nagin, Cullen, and Jonson 2009; Mears, Cochran, and Cullen, forthcoming). Systematic knowledge also is needed about how offenders adapt once released into the community. Four issues, which are related to this task, occupy the remainder of our attention.

B. *Take Coming Home Seriously*

Much of the failure experienced by reentering offenders occurs in the first 6 months to a year after their release. More than two in five (just under 45 percent) are arrested by the end of their first year, with that percentage climbing only to two-thirds in 3 years (Langan and Levin 2002; Durose, Cooper, and Snyder 2014). It is critical that the period in which offenders first "come home" be taken seriously. Not surprisingly, a common recommendation is to concentrate services during this time period rather than spread them evenly across all offenders under supervision (Turner and Petersilia 2012). As Petersilia notes, the recidivism data "suggest that the most intensive services and surveillance should begin immediately upon release and be front-loaded in the first six months to the first year" (2003, p. 153).

But here is where basic knowledge about reentry is lacking. Why does failure occur so soon after release? The most obvious answer is that the strain and difficulty of adjusting to society after life in a total institution, combined with joblessness and unstable living arrangements, undermine integration into prosocial roles. Research also indicates that return to a neighborhood where criminogenic influences are ubiquitous and quality treatment providers are limited can increase the chances of recidivating (Wright and Cesar 2013). This explanation might be called an "adjustment model." But two other explanations, which may be complementary or mutually exclusive, can be set forth.

One, which might called the "propensity model," is that rapid failure is a propensity effect—that is, simply a matter of moderate-risk to high-risk offenders returning to crime as soon as the opportunity presents itself upon release. This thesis is consistent with research showing that imprisonment's effect on reoffending is null or even slightly criminogenic (Cullen, Jonson, and Nagin 2011). Inmates do not improve while incarcerated; instead, they are "put on ice" in "behavioral deep freeze" (Gendreau and Goggin 2014). Thus, they return to society unchanged—just as criminal, if not more so, as when they first entered the institution. Although prisoners' criminogenic propensities are blocked during their incarceration, they reappear as soon as they are back on the streets. High rates of immediate recidivism are the result.

Another possibility, which might be called the "supervision model," is that offenders recidivate due to inadequate supervision upon release. This can occur either because returning inmates are not placed on parole and thus receive no supervision or because parole involves methods, such as control-oriented intensive supervision, that do not reduce recidivism (Petersilia and Turner 1993; MacKenzie 2006; Schaefer, Cullen, and Eck 2014). Alternative supervision approaches have been proposed for parole (and probation), ranging from officers imposing greater deterrence through the use of graduated sanctions in a swift-and-certain way (Hawken 2010; for a critique, see Duriez, Cullen, and Manchak [2014]), to using RNR principles and core correctional practices in office meetings with parolees (Andrews and Bonta 2010; Smith et al. 2012; Lowenkamp, Alexander, and Robinson 2014) and relying on crime-science principles to limit parolees' access to routines, places, and associates where opportunities to offend are available (Cullen, Eck, and Lowenkamp 2002; Schaefer, Cullen, and Eck 2014).

As this discussion shows, the sources of early reentry failure remain largely unknown, with understanding remaining at a prescientific level of informed speculation. Closing this knowledge gap has obvious important implications. Although front-loading services appears imperative, it is difficult to know what is causing prisoners' high rates of recidivism upon release and thus which services should be given priority. At present, reentry programs tend to take a "shotgun" approach, spraying services in hopes that something will hit the appropriate mark. This may produce some promising results, but it will likely be of limited value until we understand better the factors producing early failure.

C. Prevent Late-Onset Recidivism

Although reentry failure is concentrated soon after release, other offenders become enmeshed with the law much later. In Durose, Cooper, and Snyder's (2014) study of released prisoners between 2005 and

2010, 43.4 percent were arrested in the first year, a figure that climbed to nearly 59.5 percent by the second year and to 67.8 percent by the third year. In the next 2 years, however, released prisoners continued to fail, with another 10 percent being arrested. The 5-year recidivism rate thus rose to 76.6 percent—or more than three-fourths of the returning offenders.

These statistics prompt a salient question: What causes such late-onset recidivism? A first challenge is to define what is meant by "late onset." It could be limited only to those who reoffend after 3 years, or it could be used more expansively to include any released prisoner who fails after the first year where the risk of recidivism is most pronounced. Regardless, the point is that an appropriate concern with the first stages of reentry where the risk of being arrested is highest should not divert attention fully from later-onset recidivism. Front-loading services, which is a sensible policy, does contain the danger that released prisoners in good standing will not receive the support needed to sustain their prosocial life course.

Another knowledge gap, however, exists. Why does late-onset recidivism occur? Again, three alternative explanations can be proposed. The first, what might be called the "social bond" model, would argue that otherwise prosocial offenders return to crime because they experience a loss of conventional social bonds (Sampson and Laub 1993). In this model, social bonds—and the informal social controls, social supports, and structured lives they promote—facilitate desistance when they are acquired but evoke crime onset when they are lost. This approach thus would predict that the risk of late-onset offending is increased when released prisoners lose employment, marriage, or other connections to the conventional order.

A second explanation, which might be called the "social problems model," is that late-onset recidivism arises from accumulation of risk factors that become too burdensome to cope with. In research based on the Oxford Study of the Dynamics of Recidivism, LeBel and his colleagues (2008, p. 143) examined the effect on reoffending of "social problems" experienced in multiple areas: "housing, employment, finances, relationships (partner/spouse and family), alcohol and drug." Over a 10-year period, they discovered that the number of problems during reentry had "a large and significant impact on the probability of both reconviction and re-imprisonment" (p. 149). "Each additional social problem," they observed, "increased the odds of reconviction by 110 percent and increased the odds of re-imprisonment by 38 percent Therefore, someone reporting six problems has odds of reconviction over the 10-year follow-up 330 percent higher than someone reporting three problems"; the comparable odds for reimprisonment were 114 percent (p. 149). Notably, the number of reentry social problems was measured only 4–6 months after release. Even so, the long-term effect of problems would suggest that their accumulation would have consequences at any point after release. These problems are dynamic, not static, and could rise (or fall) in number across the life course. Late-onset recidivism would be expected when, several years after release, problems increased to the point at which the risk of recidivism was commensurately heightened.

A third possible explanation might be called the "propensity-detection model." This would suggest that late-onset recidivism is produced by offenders with a high criminal propensity who managed to escape the detection of their offending until this time period. In a study of four waves of the National Longitudinal Study of Adolescent Health (respondents age 24–34 at wave 4), Barnes (2014) examined the likelihood that persistent offenders—those who self-reported criminal acts during each wave (6.64 percent of the sample)—would be arrested and sanctioned by the criminal justice system. He discovered that the wrongdoing of a clear majority of persistent, self-reported offenders was eventually detected, with 63 percent being arrested. This finding also suggests, however, that about one-third of this group offended with impunity, breaking the law and never being caught. The implications for late-onset recidivism are clear: the timing of arrest a year or more after release may reflect not a sudden return to crime but offenders' misfortune of finally having their persistent criminality detected. The corresponding policy implications are clear as well: front-load services to diminish as much propensity as possible and, thereafter, continue to identify through assessment and treat high-risk offenders who have yet officially to run afoul of the law.

D. *Discover Whether Who Comes Home Matters*

For heuristic reasons, discussions of reentry, including this one, refer to "prisoners" who reenter society. But the word "prisoners" suggests a degree of homogeneity that does not exist; heterogeneity among prison inmates is the stubborn reality that must be addressed. As Mears and

Cochran (2015, pp. 179–80) detail, "inmates vary greatly along many dimensions. . . . Diversity aptly characterizes the ex-prisoner population" (see also Gunnison and Helfgott 2013). Such differences might involve age, racial and ethnic status, and sex. It might involve offenders whose institutional stays have varied from a year to decades, who have coped well or poorly with imprisonment, who have been victimized and traumatized or not, who have been housed in a supermax prison or in a minimum-security facility. It might involve offenders who improved their lives behind bars and others who return with persistent mental health or substance abuse problems. "Some of these differences," observe Mears and Cochran (2015, p. 179), "may be inconsequential for understanding the behavior of individuals during and after reentry. Others, however, may be quite consequential." Part of a criminology of reentry will be studying whether and how these heterogeneous factors affect recidivism.

This diversity of offenders suggests that reentry programs must be equally diverse—if not individualized then at least divided by salient demographic (e.g., gender) or problem (e.g., homeless, unemployed) characteristics. The RNR model, however, would take a different position. This perspective recommends submerging such diversity and instead using assessments such as the Level of Service Inventory, sorting offenders into one of three risk levels (low, moderate, high). Offender characteristics unrelated to risk fall under the category of "specific responsivity" (this is in contrast to "general responsivity," which refers to using a treatment modality, such as cognitive-behavioral/social learning therapies, capable of inducing change among all offenders).

According to Andrews and Bonta (2010, p. 46), the principle of specific responsivity requires that providers "adapt the style and mode of service according to the setting of services and to relevant characteristics of individual offenders, such as their strengths, motivations, preferences, personality, age, gender, ethnicity, cultural identification, and other factors." Phrased differently, individual differences are relevant in shaping how a treatment is delivered (e.g., do not use confrontational techniques with highly anxious offenders, ensure that treatment is communicated in an age- or developmentally appropriate way; Andrews and Bonta 2010, p. 508). As for "noncriminogenic needs," these would be targeted only "for purposes of enhancing motivation, the reduction of distracting factors, and for reasons having to do with humanitarian and entitlement issues" (p. 46).

The advantage of the RNR model's perspective on offender diversity is that it is part of a coherent theoretical framework that is rooted in a wealth of empirical evidence (Cullen 2012). Still, the principle of specific responsivity may be the weakest component of this model because, as Andrews and Bonta (2010, p. 507) admit, "it remains underexplored."

Other treatment approaches might see factors relegated to specific responsivity or to secondary status in the RNR model as central to successful reentry. For example, models based on desistance research would emphasize the need to build human and social capital (e.g., positive identity, sense of self-efficacy, job acquisition, quality interpersonal relationships) to reduce recidivism (Maruna and Immarigeon 2004; Raynor and Robinson 2009; Brayford, Cowe, and Deering 2010). Research thus is needed to untangle how offender diversity affects reentry and how these factors should be incorporated into programs designed for returning offenders.

Part of this research agenda also might involve drawing on offender interviews, surveys, and ethnographies that seek to capture the lived reality of offenders, especially those who cycle between the inner-city neighborhoods and prison (see, e.g., Maruna 2001; Leverentz 2010; Rios 2011; Gunnison and Helfgott 2013; Lerman and Weaver 2014). This research is useful in documenting the perceived needs of offenders, both at the prerelease and later reentry stages, and of needs in the areas of employment, education, housing, and health care (Lattimore, Steffey, and Visher 2009). Some evidence exists that these deficits are higher for female than for male offenders (Lindquist et al. 2009). At times, this research documents how offenders exercise human agency and positive narratives to overcome barriers to reentry (Maruna 2001; Leverentz 2010). At other times, offender accounts highlight feelings of alienation, desperation, and hopelessness, including a sense of being "custodial citizens" who remain under the watchful eye of the state whether in prison or on neighborhood streets (Lerman and Weaver 2014, p. 8). They often link desistance from crime and reentry success to social supports received from caring individuals or from programs that address material and social deprivation. It is difficult to know how much credence to invest in these insights, given that offenders tend to externalize blame and not identify in themselves deficits that are criminogenic (e.g., low self-control, antisocial thinking errors). Nonetheless, the ways offenders interpret their lives comprise potentially important cognitions that must be addressed when helping them to construct prosocial futures.

E. Confront the Collateral Consequences Effect

One of the more disquieting policy developments in corrections has been the steady expansion of the collateral consequences attached to a criminal conviction (Alexander 2010). These legislated mandates deprive ex-offenders of an array of employment, housing, government, family, and civil rights. The courts have defined these consequences not for what they clearly are—added on punishments—but as a matter of behavior regulation (Chin 2012). However, it has now become apparent that even if these statutory limitations satisfy legal requirements of having a rational basis, many are gratuitous and have little plausible relationship to public safety. In many ways, those on the political left and right—such as Senators Cory Booker and Rand Paul in their recently proposed "Redeem Act" (Terkel 2014)—see collateral consequences as a matter of overregulation. Indeed, if subjected to the same cost-benefit analyses as are made of other government regulations, it is unclear how many of these statutes would withstand scrutiny. Efforts are being made to bring more standardization and fairness to this area, such as through the Uniform Collateral Consequences of Convictions Act proposed by the National Conference of Commissioners on Uniform State Laws (2010). We believe all statutes imposing collateral consequences should be "sunset laws" that expire within a specified period (e.g., 5 years) unless reinstated by legislative vote. This would ensure that only collateral consequences that have an enduring rationale would remain operative. At present, collateral consequences instituted over many years accumulate, leading to "literally hundreds of collateral sanctions and disqualifications on the books" (National Conference of Commissioners on Uniform State Laws 2010, p. 3).

What remains to be determined, however, is whether collateral consequences are related to offender recidivism. With the exception of deportation, such consequences—since they are not legally punishments—do not have to be conveyed to offenders during a plea negotiation or at the time of sentencing (Chin 2012). It is not clear that most of those working with offenders are informed about such consequences and communicate these potential disabilities to their offender clients (Burton et al. 2014). How to secure an expungement of a criminal record also is not discussed or planned for (since applying to have a record cleansed might occur 3–5 years later). In terms of reentry, there is a knowledge gap about offenders' awareness of collateral consequences and how such legal discrimination hinders successful reintegration.

More generally, there is a lack of research on the stigma faced by reentering offenders. This is in marked contrast to research on mental patients where theory and research is extensive and where stigma has been shown to have deleterious effects (see, e.g., Link et al. 1989; Link and Phelan 2001). Studies show variation in offenders' hope and optimism about their future prospects (Maruna 2001; LeBel et al. 2008; Benson et al. 2011). There is also evidence consistent with the view that stigma from official labels leads offenders to lose conventional bonds and be exposed to criminal influences, thus increasing the risk of recidivism (Krohn, Lopes, and Ward 2014; Raphael 2014). However, given the social stigma and legal consequences associated with being an "ex-offender," a clear need exists for sustained analysis of how these factors affect reentry prospects.

F. Making Reentry Work

One inevitable consequence of mass imprisonment has been—and will remain—the problem of mass reentry. Since the 1930s, as the remarks of President Roosevelt and of Stanley, the Jack-Roller, show, the challenges facing released prisoners have been apparent. But mere awareness of a social issue, including reentry, does not mean that that concern has risen to the point at which it is clearly conceptualized as a social problem and becomes the object of policy intervention. In this context, an important advance since the early 2000s has been the clear definition of mass prisoner release as a problem of "reentry" and the concomitant call for system changes and program implementation to facilitate inmates' return to society.

The risk in addressing reentry, however, is that good intentions may have disappointing results. Changing inmate behavior, especially in the context of a transition from a total institution into a community where offenders face an array of barriers, is a daunting prospect. Part of taking this challenge more seriously is recognizing its difficulty and the need to use science to direct rehabilitative efforts (Cullen 2012). Doing so—and making reentry work more effectively—will involve two steps.

First, those inventing and implementing reentry programs need to consult existing knowledge about treatment. Relying on common sense—liberal or otherwise—is no longer justified (Latessa, Cullen, and Gendreau 2002). Second, a criminology of reentry is sorely needed to produce the kind of detailed scientific insights required to direct program development. Although meaningful advances in the science of offender treatment have been made (see, in particular, Andrews and Bonta [2010]), serious knowledge gaps exist. Basic facts about the reentry experience and how they affect postprison adjustment remain to be identified and systematically studied. The criminology of reentry is in its beginning stages. Given the hundreds of thousands of inmates who will be released annually, this is an area of theory, research, and practice that warrants concentrated and sustained attention.

REFERENCES

Alexander, Michelle. 2010. *The New Jim Crow: Mass Incarceration in the Age of Colorblindness*. New York: New Press.

Andrews, Donald A. 1995. "The Psychology of Criminal Conduct and Effective Treatment." In *What Works: Reducing Reoffending; Guidelines from Research and Practice*, edited by James McGuire. New York: Wiley.

Andrews, Donald A., and James Bonta. 2010. *The Psychology of Criminal Conduct*. 5th ed. New Providence, NJ: Anderson.

Andrews, Donald A., Ivan Zinger, Robert D. Hoge, James Bonta, Paul Gendreau, and Francis T. Cullen. 1990. "Does Correctional Treatment Work? A Clinically-Relevant and Psychologically Informed Meta-analysis." *Criminology* 28:369–404.

Aos, Steve, Marna Miller, and Elizabeth K. Drake. 2006. *Evidence-Based Adult Corrections Programs: What Works and What Does Not*. Olympia: Washington State Institute for Public Policy.

Barnes, J. C. 2014. "Catching the Really Bad Guys: An Assessment of the Efficacy of the U.S. Criminal Justice System." *Journal of Criminal Justice* 42:338–46.

Benson, Michael L., Leanne Fiftal Alarid, Velmer S. Burton, and Francis T. Cullen. 2011. "Reintegration or Stigmatization: Offenders' Expectations of Community Re-entry." *Journal of Criminal Justice* 39:385–93.

Bonczar, Thomas P. 2008. *Characteristics of State Parole Supervising Agencies, 2006*. Washington, DC: Bureau of Justice Statistics, US Department of Justice.

Brayford, Jo, Francis Cowe, and John Deering, eds. 2010. *What Else Works? Creative Work with Offenders*. Cullompton, UK: Willan.

Burton, Velmer S., Jr., Colleen Fisher, Cheryl Lero Jonson, and Francis T. Cullen. 2014. "Confronting the Collateral Consequences of a Criminal Conviction: A Special Challenge for Social Work with Offenders." *Journal of Forensic Social Work* 4:80–103.

Bush, George W. 2004. Text of President Bush's 2004 State of the Union Address. *Washington Post*, January 20. http://www.washingtonpost.com/wp-srv/politics/transcripts/bushtext_012004.html.

Bushway, Shawn, Michael A. Stoll, and David F. Weiman, eds. 2007. *Barriers to Reentry? The Labor Market for Released Prisoners in Post-industrial America*. New York: Russell Sage.

Caplan, Joel M., and Susan C. Kinnevy. 2010. "National Surveys of State Paroling Authorities: Models of Service Delivery." *Federal Probation* 74(1):34–42.

Carson, E. Ann. 2014. *Prisoners in 2013*. Washington, DC: Bureau of Justice Statistics, US Department of Justice.

Carson, E. Ann, and Daniela Golinelli. 2013. *Prisons in 2012: Trends in Admissions and Releases, 1991–2012*. Washington, DC: Bureau of Justice Statistics, US Department of Justice.

Chappell, Cathryn A. 2004. "Postsecondary Correctional Education and Recidivism: A Meta-analysis of Research Conducted 1990–99." *Journal of Correctional Education* 55:148–69.

Chin, Gabriel J. 2012. "The New Civil Death: Rethinking Punishment in the Era of Mass Conviction." *University of Pennsylvania Law Review* 160: 1789–1833.

Community Corrections Research Team. 2011. "Reentry: Survey Summary." *Corrections Compendium* 36(4):12–32.

CrimeSolutions.gov. 2015. "Program Evidence Rating Instrument—Part 2." Development Services Group, Bethesda, MD. https://www.crimesolutions.gov/pdfs/ratinginstrument_part2.pdf.

Crow, Matthew S., and John Ortiz Smykla, eds. 2014. *Offender Reentry: Rethinking Criminology and Criminal Justice*. Burlington, MA: Jones & Bartlett Learning.

Cullen, Francis T. 2005. "The Twelve People Who Saved Rehabilitation: How the Science of Criminology Made a Difference; The American Society of Criminology 2004 Presidential Address." *Criminology* 43:1–42.

———. 2011. "Making Corrections Work: It's Time for a New Penology." *Journal of Community Corrections* 21(Fall):5–6, 15–18.

———. 2012. "Taking Rehabilitation Seriously: Creativity, Science, and the Challenge of Offender Change." *Punishment and Society* 14:94–114.

———. 2013. "Rehabilitation: Beyond Nothing Works." In *Crime and Justice in America, 1975–2025*, edited by Michael Tonry. Vol. 42 of *Crime and Justice: A Review of Research*, edited by Michael Tonry. Chicago: University of Chicago Press.

Cullen, Francis T., Kristie R. Blevins, Jennifer S. Trager, and Paul Gendreau. 2005. "The Rise and Fall of Boot Camps: A Case Study in Common-Sense Corrections." *Journal of Offender Rehabilitation* 40(3–4):53–70.

Cullen, Francis T., John E. Eck, and Christopher T. Lowenkamp. 2002. "Environmental Corrections: A New Paradigm for Effective Probation and Parole Supervision." *Federal Probation* 66(2):28–37.

Cullen, Francis T., Bonnie S. Fisher, and Brandon K. Applegate. 2000. "Public Opinion about Punishment and Corrections." In *Crime and Justice: A Review of Research*, vol. 14, edited by Michael Tonry. Chicago: University of Chicago Press.

Cullen, Francis T., and Karen E. Gilbert. 2013. *Reaffirming Rehabilitation*. 2nd ed. Waltham, MA: Anderson.

Cullen, Francis T., and Cheryl Lero Jonson. 2012. *Correctional Theory: Context and Consequences*. Thousand Oaks, CA: Sage.

Cullen, Francis T., Cheryl Lero Jonson, and Daniel S. Nagin. 2011. "Prisons Do Not Reduce Recidivism: The High Cost of Ignoring Science." *Prison Journal* 91:S48–S65.

Cullen, Francis T., William J. Maakestad, and Gray Cavender. 1987. *Corporate Crime under Attack: The Ford Pinto Case and Beyond*. Cincinnati: Anderson.

Cullen, Francis T., Andrew J. Myer, and Edward J. Latessa. 2009. "Eight Lessons Learned from *Moneyball*: The High Cost of Ignoring Evidence-Based Corrections." *Victims and Offenders* 4:197–213.

Davis, Lois M., Robert Bozick, Jennifer L. Steele, Jessica Saunders, and Jeremy N. V. Miles. 2013. *Evaluating the Effectiveness of Correctional Education: A Meta-analysis of Programs That Provide Education to Incarcerated Adults*. Washington, DC: Bureau of Justice Assistance, US Department of Justice, Office of Justice Programs.

Decker, Scott H., Cassia Spohn, Natalie R. Ortiz, and Eric Hedberg. 2014. *Criminal Stigma, Race, Gender and Employment: An Expanded Assessment of the Consequences of Imprisonment for Employment*. Report Submitted to the US Department of Justice. Phoenix: Arizona State University, School of Criminology and Criminal Justice.

Duriez, Stephanie A., Francis T. Cullen, and Sarah M. Manchak. 2014. "Is Project HOPE Creating a False Sense of Hope? A Case Study in Correctional Popularity." *Federal Probation* 78(2):57–70.

Durose, Matthew R., Alexia D. Cooper, and Howard N. Snyder. 2014. *Recidivism of Prisoners Released in 30 States in 2005: Patterns from 2005 to 2010*. Washington, DC: Bureau of Justice Statistics, US Department of Justice.

Empey, LaMar T. 1982. *American Delinquency: Its Meaning and Construction*. Rev. ed. Homewood, IL: Dorsey.

Finckenauer, James O. 1982. *Scared Straight! and the Panacea Phenomenon*. Englewood Cliffs, NJ: Prentice-Hall.

Frazier, Beverly D. 2011. "Faith-Based Prisoner Reentry." In *Rethinking Corrections: Rehabilitation, Reentry, and Reintegration*, edited by Lior Gideon and Hung-En Sung. Thousand Oaks, CA: Sage.

Gaes, Gerald. 2009. "Evaluation of Getting Ready." *NIJ Journal* 263:1, 9.

Gallup. 2014. "Most Important Problem." Gallup. http://www.gallup.com/poll/1675/most-important-problem.aspx.

Garland, Brett, and Eric Wodahl. 2014. "Coming to a Crossroads: A Critical Look at the Sustainability of the Prisoner Reentry Movement." In *Offender Reentry: Rethinking Criminology and Criminal Justice*, edited by Matthew S. Crow and John Ortiz Smykla. Burlington, MA: Jones & Bartlett Learning.

Garland, Brett, Eric Wodahl, and Robert Schuhmann. 2013. "Value Conflict and Public Opinion toward Prisoner Reentry Initiatives." *Criminal Justice Policy Review* 24:27–48.

Gendreau, Paul. 1996. "The Principles of Effective Intervention with Offenders." In *Choosing Correctional Interventions That Work: Defining the Demand and Evaluating the Supply*, edited by Alan T. Harland. Newbury Park, CA: Sage.

Gendreau, Paul, and Claire Goggin. 2014. "Practicing Psychology in Correctional Settings." In *The Handbook of Forensic Psychology*, 4th ed., edited by Irving B. Weiner and Randy K. Otto. Hoboken, NJ: Wiley.

Gideon, Lior, and Natalie Loveland. 2011. "Public Attitudes toward Rehabilitation and Reintegration: How Supportive Are People of Getting-Tough-on-Crime Policies and the Second Chance Act?" In *Rethinking Corrections: Rehabilitation, Reentry, and Reintegration*, edited by Lior Gideon and Hung-En Sung. Thousand Oaks, CA: Sage.

Gideon, Lior, and Hung-En Sung, eds. 2011. *Rethinking Corrections: Rehabilitation, Reentry, and Reintegration*. Thousand Oaks, CA: Sage.

Giordano, Peggy C., Stephen A. Cernkovich, and Jennifer L. Rudolph. 2002. "Gender, Crime, and Desistance: Towards a Theory of Cognitive Transformation." *American Journal of Sociology* 107:990–1064.

Glaze, Lauren F., and Erinn J. Herberman. 2013. *Correctional Populations in the United States, 2012*. Washington, DC: Bureau of Justice Statistics, US Department of Justice.

Gunnison, Elaine, and Jacqueline B. Helfgott. 2013. *Offender Reentry: Beyond Crime and Punishment*. Boulder, CO: Rienner.

Hagan, John. 2010. *Who Are the Criminals? The Politics of Crime Policy from the Age of Roosevelt to the Age of Reagan*. Princeton, NJ: Princeton University Press.

Hawken, Angela. 2010. "The Message from Hawaii: HOPE for Probation." *Perspectives* 34(3):36–49.

Hawkins, J. David, Bruce H. Smith, Karl G. Hill, Rick Kosterman, and Richard F. Catalano. 2007. "Promoting Social Development and Preventing Health and Behavior Problems during the Elementary Grades: Results from the Seattle Social Development Project." *Victims and Offenders* 2:161–81.

Henggeler, Scott W. 1998. *Blueprints for Violence Prevention: Multisystemic Therapy*. Boulder: Institute of Behavioral Science, University of Colorado.

Holzer, Harry J., Steven Raphael, and Michael A. Stoll. 2007. "The Effect of an Applicant's Criminal History on Employer Hiring Decisions and Screening Practices: Evidence from Los Angeles." In *Barriers to Reentry? The Labor Market for Released Prisoners in Post-industrial America*, edited by Shawn Bushway, Michael A. Stoll, and David F. Weiman. New York: Russell Sage.

Johnson, Brian D. 2011. "Sentencing." In *The Oxford Handbook of Crime and Criminal Justice*, edited by Michael Tonry. New York: Oxford University Press.

Jonson, Cheryl Lero, Francis T. Cullen, and Jennifer L. Lux. 2013. "Creating Ideological Space: Why Public Support for Rehabilitation Matters." In *What Works in Offender Rehabilitation: An Evidence-Based Approach to Assessment and Treatment*, edited by Leam Craig, Louise Dixon, and Theresa Gannon. London: Wiley-Blackwell.

Krisberg, Barry. 2006. *Focus: Attitudes of U.S. Voters toward Prisoner Rehabilitation and Reentry Programs*. Oakland, CA: National Council on Crime and Delinquency.

Krohn, Marvin D., Gina Lopes, and Jeffrey T. Ward. 2014. "Effects of Official Intervention on Later Offending in the Rochester Youth Development Study." In *Labeling Theory: Empirical Tests*, edited by David P. Farrington and Joseph Murray. Advances in Criminological Theory 18. New Brunswick, NJ: Transaction.

Kruttschnitt, Candace, and Rosemary Gartner. 2005. *Marking Time in the Golden State: Women's Imprisonment in California*. New York: Cambridge University Press.

Langan, Patrick A., and David J. Levin. 2002. *Recidivism of Prisoners Released in 1994*. Washington, DC: Bureau of Justice Statistics, US Department of Justice.

Latessa, Edward J., Francis T. Cullen, and Paul Gendreau. 2002. "Beyond Correctional Quackery: Professionalism and the Possibility of Effective Treatment." *Federal Probation* 66(2):43–49.

Latessa, Edward J., and Paula Smith. 2011. *Corrections in the Community*. 5th ed. Burlington, MA: Anderson.

Lattimore, Pamela K., Kelle Barrick, Alexander Cowell, Debbie Dawes, Danielle Steffey, Stephen Tueller, and Christy A. Visher. 2012. *Prisoner Reentry Services: What Worked for SVORI Evaluation Participants?* Final Report. Washington, DC: National Institute of Justice.

Lattimore, Pamela K., Danielle M. Steffey, and Christy A. Visher. 2009. *Prisoner Reentry Experiences of Adult Males: Characteristics, Service Receipts, and Outcomes of Participants in the SVORI Multi-site Evaluation*. Research Triangle Park, NC: RTI International.

Lattimore, Pamela K., and Christy A. Visher. 2009. *The Multi-site Evaluation of SVORI: Summary and Synthesis*. Research Triangle Park, NC: RTI International.

Laub, John H. 2011. "Moving the National Institute of Justice Forward." *Criminologist* 36(2):1, 3–5.

LeBel, Thomas P., Ros Burnett, Shadd Maruna, and Shawn Bushway. 2008. "The 'Chicken and the Egg' of Subjective and Social Factors in Desistance from Crime." *European Journal of Criminology* 5:131–59.

Lerman, Amy E., and Vesla M. Weaver. 2014. *Arresting Citizenship: The Democratic Consequences of American Crime Control*. Chicago: University of Chicago Press.

Leverentz, Andrea. 2010. "People, Places, and Things: How Female Ex-Prisoners Negotiate Their Neighborhood Context." *Journal of Ethnography* 39:646–81.

Lindquist, Christine H., Pamela K. Lattimore, Kelle Barrick, and Christy A. Visher. 2009. *Prisoner Reentry Experiences of Adult Females: Characteristics, Service Receipt, and Outcomes of Participants in the SVORI Multi-site Evaluation*. Research Triangle Park, NC: RTI International.

Link, Bruce G., Francis T. Cullen, Elmer Struening, Patrick E. Shrout, and Bruce G. Dohrenwend. 1989. "A Modified Labeling Theory Approach to Mental Disorders: An Empirical Assessment." *American Sociological Review* 54:400–423.

Link, Bruce G., and Jo C. Phelan. 2001. "Conceptualizing Stigma." In *Annual Review of Sociology*, vol. 27, edited by Karen S. Cook and John Hagan. Palo Alto, CA: Annual Reviews.

Lipsey, Mark W. 2009. "The Primary Factors That Characterize Effective Interventions with Juvenile Offenders: A Meta-analytic Overview." *Victims and Offenders* 4:124–47.

Lipton, Douglas, Robert Martinson, and Judith Wilks. 1975. *The Effectiveness of Correctional Treatment: A Survey of Treatment Evaluation Studies.* New York: Praeger.

Listwan, Shelley Johnson, Francis T. Cullen, and Edward J. Latessa. 2006. "How to Prevent Prisoner Re-entry Programs from Failing: Insights from Evidence-Based Corrections." *Federal Probation* 70(3):19–25.

Listwan, Shelley Johnson, Cheryl Lero Jonson, Francis T. Cullen, and Edward J. Latessa. 2008. "Cracks in the Penal Harm Movement: Evidence from the Field." *Criminology and Public Policy* 7:423–65.

Lowenkamp, Christopher T., Melissa Alexander, and Charles Robinson. 2014. "Using 20 Minutes Wisely: Community Supervision Officers as Agents of Change." In *Offender Reentry: Rethinking Criminology and Criminal Justice*, edited by Matthew S. Crow and John Ortiz Smykla. Burlington, MA: Jones & Bartlett Learning.

Lowenkamp, Christopher T., and Edward J. Latessa. 2002. *Evaluation of Ohio's Community Based Correctional Facilities and Halfway House Programs.* Technical Report. Cincinnati: Center for Criminal Justice Research, University of Cincinnati.

Lowenkamp, Christopher T., Edward J. Latessa, and Paula Smith. 2006. "Does Correctional Program Quality Really Matter? The Impact of Adhering to the Principles of Effective Intervention." *Criminology and Public Policy* 5:201–20.

Lurigio, Arthur, Gad Bensinger, S. Rae Thompson, Kristin Elling, Donna Poucis, Jill Selvaggio, and Melissa Spooner. 2000. "A Process and Outcome Evaluation of Project BUILD: Years 5 and 6." Unpublished report. Chicago: Loyola University.

Lynch, James P., and William J. Sabol. 2001. *Prisoner Reentry in Perspective.* Washington, DC: Urban Institute.

MacKenzie, Doris Layton. 2006. *What Works in Corrections: Reducing the Criminal Activities of Offenders and Delinquents.* New York: Cambridge University Press.

Manchak, Sarah M., and Francis T. Cullen. 2014. "When Troubled Offenders Come Home: Removing Barriers to Reentry for Offenders with Mental Illness." In *Offender Reentry: Rethinking Criminology and Criminal Justice*, edited by Matthew S. Crow and John Ortiz Smykla. Burlington, MA: Jones & Bartlett Learning.

Maruna, Shadd. 2001. *Making Good: How Ex-Convicts Reform and Rebuild Their Lives*. Washington, DC: American Psychological Association.

Maruna, Shadd, and Russ Immarigeon, eds. 2004. *After Crime and Punishment: Pathways to Offender Reintegration*. Cullompton, UK: Willan.

Mears, Daniel P., and Joshua C. Cochran. 2015. *Prisoner Reentry in the Era of Mass Incarceration*. Thousand Oaks, CA: Sage.

Mears, Daniel P., Joshua C. Cochran, and Francis T. Cullen. Forthcoming. "Incarceration Heterogeneity and Its Implications for Assessing the Effectiveness of Imprisonment on Recidivism." *Criminal Justice Policy Review*. doi:10.1177/0887403414528950.

Minton, Todd D., and Daniela Golinelli. 2014. *Jail Inmates at Midyear 2013: Statistical Tables*. Washington, DC: Bureau of Justice Statistics, US Department of Justice.

Nagin, Daniel S., Francis T. Cullen, and Cheryl Lero Jonson. 2009. "Imprisonment and Reoffending." In *Crime and Justice: A Review of Research*, vol. 38, edited by Michael Tonry. Chicago: University of Chicago Press.

National Conference of Commissioners on Uniform State Laws. 2010. *Uniform Collateral Consequences of Conviction Act*. Chicago: National Conference of Commissioners on Uniform State Laws.

National Institute of Justice. 2011. *About the Serious and Violent Offender Reentry*. Washington, DC: National Institute of Justice.

Ndrecka, Mirlinda. 2014. "The Impact of Reentry Programs on Recidivism: A Meta-analysis." PhD dissertation, University of Cincinnati, School of Criminal Justice.

Olds, David L. 2007. "Preventing Crime with Prenatal and Infancy Support of Parents: The Nurse-Family Partnership." *Victims and Offenders* 2:205–25.

Page, Joshua. 2011. *The Toughest Beat: Politics, Punishment, and the Prison Officers in California*. New York: Oxford University Press.

Pager, Devah. 2007. *Marked: Race, Crime, and Finding Work in an Era of Mass Incarceration*. Chicago: University of Chicago Press.

Pager, Devah, Bruce Western, and Bart Bonikowski. 2009. "Discrimination in a Low-Wage Labor Market: A Field Experiment." *American Sociological Review* 74:777–99.

Petersilia, Joan. 1999. "Parole and Prisoner Reentry in the United States." In *Prisons*, edited by Michael Tonry and Joan Petersilia. Vol. 26 of *Crime and Justice: A Review of Research*, edited by Michael Tonry. Chicago: University of Chicago Press.

———. 2003. *When Prisoners Come Home: Parole and Prisoner Reentry*. New York: Oxford University Press.

———. 2008. "California's Correctional Paradox of Excess and Deprivation." In *Crime and Justice: A Review of Research*, vol. 37, edited by Michael Tonry. Chicago: University of Chicago Press.

———. 2009. "Transformation in Prisoner Reentry: What a Difference a Decade Makes." In *When Prisoners Come Home: Parole and Prisoner Reentry*, rev. ed. New York: Oxford University Press.

———. 2011. "Parole and Prisoner Re-entry." In *The Oxford Handbook of Crime and Criminal Justice*, edited by Michael Tonry. New York: Oxford University Press.

Petersilia, Joan, and Francis T. Cullen. 2015. "Liberal but Not Stupid: Meeting the Promise of Downsizing Prisons." *Stanford Journal of Criminal Law and Policy* 2:1–43.

Petersilia, Joan, and Susan Turner. 1993. "Intensive Probation and Parole." In *Crime and Justice: A Review of Research*, vol. 17, edited by Michael Tonry. Chicago: University of Chicago Press.

Pew Charitable Trusts. 2014*a*. *Max Out: The Rise in Prison Inmates Released without Supervision*. Washington, DC: Pew Charitable Trusts.

———. 2014*b*. *Mississippi's 2014 Corrections and Criminal Justice Reform*. Washington, DC: Pew Charitable Trusts.

Pfohl, Stephen. 1985. *Images of Deviance and Social Control: A Sociological History*. New York: McGraw-Hill.

Platt, Anthony M. 1969. *The Child Savers: The Invention of Delinquency*. Chicago: University of Chicago Press.

Porporino, Frank J. 2010. "Bringing Sense and Sensitivity to Corrections: From Programmes to 'Fix' Offenders to Services to Support Desistance." In *What Else Works? Creative Work with Offenders*, edited by Jo Brayford, Francis Cowe, and John Deering. Cullompton, UK: Willan.

Public Opinion Strategies and the Mellman Group. 2012. *Public Opinion on Sentencing and Corrections Policy in America*. Washington, DC: Pew Center on the States.

Raphael, Steven. 2014. "The Effects of Conviction and Incarceration on Future Employment Outcomes." In *Labeling Theory: Empirical Tests*, edited by David P. Farrington and Joseph Murray. Advances in Criminological Theory 18. New Brunswick, NJ: Transaction.

Raynor, Peter, and Gwen Robinson. 2009. *Rehabilitation, Crime and Justice*. Rev. ed. Hampshire, UK: Macmillan.

Reitz, Kevin R. 2011. "Sentencing." In *Crime and Public Policy*, edited by James Q. Wilson and Joan Petersilia. New York: Oxford University Press.

Rhine, Edward E. 2011. "The Present Status and Future Prospects of Parole Boards and Parole Supervision." In *The Oxford Handbook of Sentencing and Corrections*, edited by Joan Petersilia and Kevin R. Reitz. New York: Oxford University Press.

Rhine, Edward E., Tina L. Mawhorr, and Evalyn C. Parks. 2006. "Implementation: The Bane of Effective Correctional Programs." *Criminology and Public Policy* 5:347–58.

Rhine, Edward E., and Anthony C. Thompson. 2011. "The Reentry Movement in Corrections: Resiliency, Fragility, and Prospects." *Criminal Law Bulletin* 47:177–209.

Rios, Victor M. 2011. *Punished: Policing the Lives of Black and Latino Boys*. New York: New York University Press.

Roosevelt, Franklin D. 1939. "Address of the President to the National Parole Conference in the White House, 4/17/1939." Speeches of the President. National Archives Catalog, Washington, DC. https://catalog.archives.gov/#/id/197862.

Ross, Robert R. 1995. "The Reasoning and Rehabilitation Program for High-Risk Probationers and Prisoners." In *Going Straight: Effective Delinquency Prevention and Offender Rehabilitation*, edited by Robert R. Ross, Daniel H. Antonowicz, and Gurmeet K. Dhaliwal. Ottawa: Air Training and Publications.

Ross, Robert R., and Elizabeth A. Fabiano. 1985. *Time to Think: A Cognitive Model of Delinquency Prevention and Offender Rehabilitation*. Johnson City, TN: Institute of Social Sciences and Arts.

Rothman, David J. 1980. *Conscience and Convenience: The Asylum and Its Alternatives in Progressive America*. Boston: Little, Brown.

Rukus, Joseph, and Jodi Lane. 2014. "Unmet Need: A Survey of State Resources at the Moment of Reentry." In *Offender Reentry: Rethinking Criminology and Criminal Justice*, edited by Matthew S. Crow and John Ortiz Smykla. Burlington, MA: Jones & Bartlett Learning.

Sampson, Robert J., and John H. Laub. 1993. *Crime in the Making: Pathways and Turning Points through Life*. Cambridge, MA: Harvard University Press.

Schaefer, Lacey, Francis T. Cullen, and John E. Eck. 2014. "Environmental Corrections: Reinventing Probation and Parole Supervision." Unpublished manuscript. University of Queensland.

Schriro, Dora. 2000. *Correcting Corrections: Missouri's Parallel Universe*. Sentencing and Corrections 8. Washington, DC: Office of Justice Programs, US Department of Justice.

———. 2009. "Getting Ready: How Arizona Has Created a 'Parallel Universe' for Inmates." *NIJ Journal* 263:1–9.

Schriro, Dora, and Tom Clements. 2001. "Missouri's Parallel Universe: A Blueprint for Effective Prison Management." *Corrections Today* 63(2):140–43, 152.

Seiter, Richard P., and Karen R. Kadela. 2003. "Prisoner Reentry: What Works, What Does Not, and What Is Promising." *Crime and Delinquency* 49:360–88.

Shaw, Clifford R. 1966. *The Jack-Roller: A Delinquent Boy's Own Story*. Chicago: University of Chicago Press. (Originally published 1930.)

Sherman, Lawrence W., Denise C. Gottfredson, Doris Layton MacKenzie, John Eck, Peter Reuter, and Shawn D. Bushway. 1998. *Preventing Crime: What Works, What Doesn't, What's Promising*. Research in Brief. Washington, DC: National Institute of Justice, US Department of Justice.

Simon, Jonathan. 1993. *Poor Discipline: Parole and the Social Control of the Underclass, 1890–1990*. Chicago: University of Chicago Press.

———. 2007. *Governing through Crime: How the War on Crime Transformed American Democracy and Created a Culture of Fear*. New York: Oxford University Press.

Skardhamar, Torjørn, and Jukka Savolainen. 2014. "Changes in Criminal Offending around the Time of Job Entry: A Study of Employment and Desistance." *Criminology* 52:263–91.

Smith, Paula, Myrinda Schweitzer, Ryan M. Lebreque, and Edward J. Latessa. 2012. "Improving Probation Officers' Supervision Skills: An Evaluation of the EPIC's Model." *Journal of Crime and Justice* 35:189–99.

Snodgrass, Jon. 1982. *The Jack-Roller at Seventy*. Lexington, MA: Lexington Books.

Spector, Malcolm, and John I. Kitsuse. 1977. *Constructing Social Problems*. Menlo Park, CA: Cummings.

Staggenborn, Suzanne. 2005. "Social Movement Theory." In *Encyclopedia of Social Theory*, edited by George Ritzer. Thousand Oaks, CA: Sage.

Sundt, Jody, Renee Vanderhoff, Laura Shaver, and Sarah Lazzeroni. 2012. *Oregonians Nearly Unanimous in Support of Reentry Services for Former Prisoners*. Research in Brief. Portland, OR: Criminal Justice Policy Research Institute, Portland State University.

Swanson, Cheryl C., Courtney W. Schnippert, and Amanda L. Tryling. 2014. "Reentry and Employment: Employees' Willingness to Hire Formerly Convicted Felons in Northwest Florida." In *Offender Reentry: Rethinking Criminology and Criminal Justice*, edited by Matthew S. Crow and John Ortiz Smykla. Burlington, MA: Jones & Bartlett Learning.

Szasz, Thomas S. 1970. *The Manufacture of Madness*. New York: Dell.

Taxman, Faye S., April Pattavina, and Michael Caudy. 2014. "Justice Reinvestment in the United States: An Empirical Assessment of the Potential Impact of Increased Correctional Programming on Recidivism." *Victims and Offenders* 9:50–75.

Taxman, Faye S., Matthew L. Perdoni, and Michael Caudy. 2013. "The Plight of Providing Appropriate Substance Abuse Treatment Services to Offenders: Modeling the Gaps in Service Delivery." *Victims and Offenders* 8:70–93.

Taxman, Faye S., Matthew L. Perdoni, and Laura D. Harrison. 2007. "Drug Treatment Services for Adult Offenders: The State of the State." *Journal of Substance Abuse Treatment* 32:239–54.

Taxman, Faye S., Douglas Young, and James M. Byrne. 2004. "With Eyes Wide Open: Formalizing Community and Social Control Intervention in Offender Reintegration Programmes." In *After Crime and Punishment: Pathways to Offender Reintegration*, edited by Shadd Maruna and Russ Immarigeon. Cullompton, UK: Willan.

Terkel, Amanda. 2014. "Cory Booker and Rand Paul Team Up on Criminal Justice Reform." *Huffington Post*, August 7. http://www.huffingtonpost.com/2014/07/08/cory-booker-rand-paul_n_5566800.htlm.

Tonry, Michael. 1996. *Sentencing Matters*. New York: Oxford University Press.

———. 2013. "Sentencing in America, 1975–2025." In *Crime and Justice in America, 1975–2025*, edited by Michael Tonry. Vol. 42 of *Crime and Justice: A Review of Research*, edited by Michael Tonry. Chicago: University of Chicago Press.

Tonry, Michael, and Joan Petersilia, eds. 1999. *Prisons*. Vol. 26 of *Crime and Justice: A Review of Research*, edited by Michael Tonry. Chicago: University of Chicago Press.

Travis, Jeremy. 2000. "But They All Come Back: Rethinking Prisoner Reentry." Research in Brief. Washington, DC: National Institute of Justice.

———. 2005. *But They All Come Back: Facing the Challenges of Prisoner Reentry*. Washington, DC: Urban Institute.

Turner, Susan, and Joan Petersilia. 2012. "Putting Science to Work: How the Principles of Risk, Need, and Responsibility Apply to Reentry." In *Using Social Science to Reduce Violent Offending*, edited by Joel A. Dvoskin, Jennifer L. Skeem, Raymond W. Novaco, and Kevin S. Douglas. New York: Oxford University Press.

Wacquant, Loïc. 2010. "Prisoner Reentry as Myth and Ceremony." *Dialectical Anthropology* 34:605–20.

Wilson, David B., Catherine A. Gallagher, and Doris L. MacKenzie. 2000. "A Meta-analysis of Corrections-Based Education, Vocation, and Work Programs, for Adult Offenders." *Journal of Research in Crime and Delinquency* 37:347–68.

Wilson, James A. 2007. "Habilitation or Harm: Project Greenlight and the Potential Consequences for Correctional Programming." *National Institute of Justice Journal* 257:2–7.

Wilson, James A., Yury Cheryachukin, Robert C. Dabis, Jean Dauphinee, Robert Hope, and Kajal Gehi. 2005. *Smoothing the Path from Prison to Home: An Evaluation of the Project Greenlight Transitional Service Demonstration Program*. New York: Vera Institute.

Wilson, James A., and Robert C. Davis. 2006. "Good Intentions Meet Hard Realities: An Evaluation of the Project Greenlight Reentry Program." *Criminology and Public Policy* 5:303–38.

Wright, Kevin A., and Gabriel T. Cesar. 2013. "Toward a More Complete Model of Offender Reintegration: Linking the Individual-, Community-, and System-Level Components of Recidivism." *Victims and Offenders* 8:373–98.

Zimring, Franklin E. 2007. *The Great American Crime Decline*. New York: Oxford University Press.

———. 2012. *The City That Became Safe: New York's Lessons for Urban Crime and Its Control*. New York: Oxford University Press.

Kathryn Monahan, Laurence Steinberg, and Alex R. Piquero

Juvenile Justice Policy and Practice: A Developmental Perspective

ABSTRACT

Responses to juvenile offending have swung between rehabilitative and punishment approaches since the 1960s. A shift back toward rehabilitation has been influenced by recent research on adolescence, adolescent decision making, and adolescent brain development. US Supreme Court decisions on juvenile sentencing have been influenced by them. Major changes from adolescence into early adulthood have been demonstrated in the frontal lobe and especially the prefrontal cortex, which helps govern executive functions such as self-control and planning. Compared with adults, adolescents are more impulsive, short-sighted, and responsive to immediate rewards and less likely to consider long-term consequences. Adolescents are thus less blameworthy than adults. Responses to juvenile offending should take account of malleable aspects of psychosocial functioning in a developmentally informed manner.

The early juvenile court viewed and treated juveniles as distinct from adults, with a greater focus on rehabilitation as opposed to punishment for youthful criminal behavior (Mack 1909; Tanenhaus 2005, 2012).

Electronically published July 28, 2015

Kathryn Monahan is assistant professor of psychology at the University of Pittsburgh. Laurence Steinberg is Distinguished University Professor and Laura H. Carnell Professor of Psychology at Temple University. Alex R. Piquero is Ashbel Smith Professor of Criminology at the University of Texas at Dallas. This essay draws heavily on Steinberg (2009, 2012, 2013). We thank Barry Feld, Francesca Filbey, Michael Tonry, and an anonymous reviewer for useful comments and suggestions.

0192-3234/2015/0044-0006$10.00

Since then, the relative orientation toward punishment or rehabilitation has shifted back and forth. The mid-twentieth century witnessed intense evolution of juvenile justice policy (before *Kent* and *Gault* were decided and the proceduralism shift in the 1970s with *McKeiver*).[1] Changes in crime rates, political culture, public perceptions, and public policies in the late twentieth century resulted in a more punitive approach. Since the turn of the twenty-first century, the pendulum has swung back toward more rehabilitative approaches. The shift results from multiple causes, including historic declines in crime rates beginning in the 1990s, increased public support for rehabilitation and prevention (see, e.g., Nagin et al. 2006; Cullen et al. 2007; Applegate, Davis, and Cullen 2009; Piquero et al. 2010; Piquero and Steinberg 2010), and burgeoning evidence on adolescence from developmental psychology and developmental neuroscience. We focus in this essay on how the science of adolescent development has informed understanding of juvenile offending and juvenile punishment.

Since the mid to late 1990s, scientific research has provided consistent evidence that adolescents are developmentally different from adults in ways that have implications for the treatment of young people in the justice system.[2] Adolescents demonstrate unique decision-making processes compared with adults, there are continued changes and growth in brain functioning and maturation from mid adolescence to the mid-20s, and most criminal offending ceases as youths move from adoles-

[1] In *In re Gault*, 387 U.S. 1 (1967), the US Supreme Court decided that juveniles in delinquency proceedings are constitutionally guaranteed a right to counsel and to confront witnesses. In *Kent v. United States*, 383 U.S. 541 (1966), the Court decided that juveniles are entitled to hearings that "measure up to due process" and to specified procedural protections when waiver to adult court jurisdiction is considered. In *McKeiver v. Pennsylvania*, 403 U.S. 528 (1971), the Court held that trial by jury is not constitutionally required in juvenile delinquency proceedings.

[2] It is difficult to pinpoint an exact age range for the adolescence period. Developmental psychologists tend to recognize the period between 12 and 17 years as crucial. Steinberg and Schwartz (2000) note that this period is characterized by rapid and dramatic changes in physical, mental, emotional, and social capabilities; greater susceptibility to external influences from family and peer groups, and formation of developmental trajectories despite characteristic malleability; and tremendous variability within and between individuals. Others have expanded the traditional conception of adolescence. Casey (2015, p. 295) considers adolescence as the "transition from childhood to adulthood that begins around the onset of puberty and ends with relative independence from the parent." Arnett (2000) posits a new phase of the life course, emerging adulthood, spanning the age range between 18 and 25 that bridges adolescence and adulthood.

cence into adulthood. Evidence from each of these areas of research has helped spur a reconsideration of the assumptions underlying the nature and patterning of juvenile offending and the appropriate justice system responses to it (Steinberg 2007, 2008). These lines of research explicitly informed the US Supreme Court's thinking about juvenile punishment. A series of landmark decisions at the beginning of the twenty-first century—*Roper v. Simmons*, 543 U.S. 551 (2005); *Graham v. Florida*, 130 S. Ct. 2011 (2010); *Miller v. Alabama*, 132 S. Ct. 2455 (2012); and *Jackson v. Hobbs*, 132 S. Ct. 1733 (2012)—recognized this emerging developmental science and used it, in part, fundamentally to alter conceptions of adolescent offenders and the nature of juvenile punishment (Steinberg 2013).[3]

Two recent National Academy of Sciences panels have highlighted the importance of using research on adolescent development to guide juvenile justice decision making under a developmentally oriented model. One panel summarized the burgeoning knowledge base on adolescent development and its implications for juvenile justice policy (National Research Council 2013). The other used those insights to develop an implementation plan that adheres to the developmental framework for guiding juvenile justice policy within the Office of Juvenile Justice and Delinquency Prevention (National Research Council 2014).[4]

[3] The United States is unique in how it responds to adolescent offenders. Other Western nations deal with adolescent offenders in a more treatment-focused fashion (Loeber and Farrington 2012). In late 2014, the Dutch government passed legislation for special treatment for 16–23-year-olds. For this age group, judges can consider delinquents as adolescents and apply juvenile justice rules (personal communication from R. Loeber, December 8, 2014). Very little research has been conducted on whether particular sanctions are more or less effective for different adolescent age groups; for an important exception, see Mears et al. (2014).

[4] Recognizing that the goals of the juvenile justice system are to hold youths accountable, provide fair processes and treatment, and prevent reoffending, the 2013 report articulated a "developmental approach" to be carried throughout all of the stages of the juvenile justice process and, in particular, that knowledge about adolescent development and research related to juvenile justice interventions be used in all aspects of decision making. The 2014 report identified seven hallmarks of a developmental approach to juvenile justice: accountability without criminalization, alternatives to justice system involvement, individualized responses based on assessment of needs and risks; confinement only when necessary for public safety; a genuine commitment to fairness; sensitivity to disparate treatment; and family engagement. The panel recommended that they be incorporated into the policies and practices of the Office of Juvenile Justice and Delinquency Prevention and

Our aim in this essay is to examine the behavioral and neuroscience evidence that supports developmental immaturity of youthful offenders. We summarize findings from research over the past 20 years regarding brain, cognitive, and psychosocial development in adolescence. The main conclusions support the view that adolescence is a distinct period of development and that juvenile offenders deserve differential treatment and have much to gain from a less punitive orientation than at present. This recent developmental science is used to consider three issues in juvenile justice policy: the criminal culpability of adolescents, adolescents' competence to stand trial, and the effects of punitive sanctions on adolescents' development and behavior.[5]

This essay has four sections. In Section I, we discuss the literature that characterizes adolescence as a distinct developmental period, highlighting research from developmental neuroscience and at the intersection of developmental neuroscience and behavioral science. Section II discusses the implications of developmental neuroscience for juvenile offending and juvenile processing. We outline implications of developmental science for judgments about juvenile culpability and competence and its implications for juvenile placement and punishment. In Section III, we highlight the influence of brain science on changes in juvenile justice policy over the past quarter century. Section IV outlines desirable next steps with respect to research and policy. Collectively, these sections document a story about the development—and accumulation—of knowledge and its current significant and prospectively substantial influences on conventional understanding of juvenile offending, juvenile justice practices, and juvenile justice policy.

I. Adolescence as a Developmental Period

In the past 25 years, evidence has converged to indicate that criminal behavior—and risk taking more broadly—follows a distinct developmental trajectory. There is more than ample evidence that most forms of risky behavior follow an inverted U-shaped curve, rising during early adolescence and peaking in mid to late adolescence, and declining in early

---

local, state, and tribal jurisdictions to achieve the goals of a juvenile justice system based on a developmentally oriented model.

[5] Procedural competence involves a wider range of issues in addition to competence to stand trial.

adulthood and, especially dramatically, through the 20s (Sweeten, Piquero, and Steinberg 2013). This pattern is observed in a variety of behaviors, including crime, age of onset of illicit drug abuse or dependence, unwanted pregnancies, and driver deaths. Similar patterns characterize nonfatal self-inflicted injuries and unintentional drownings (Steinberg 2013, p. 516). Regardless of the outcome variable examined, what many criminologists refer to as the "age-crime curve" may actually be better characterized as an "age-recklessness curve." Crime is just one instance of a more general age-related risky behavior pattern (cf. Gottfredson and Hirschi 1990).

That criminal behavior is one indicator of a larger syndrome of teenage recklessness is important because it suggests that there are many neurobiological and psychosocial similarities between adolescents who break the law and those who express their risk-taking propensities in other ways. Juvenile offenders may simply be different in how this maturational balance is expressed. The universal nature of these behaviors raises some interesting questions (National Research Council 2011). Why are these trends replicable across behaviors? Do these acts have something in common? Is there something potentially different in being an adolescent compared with being an adult?

Our view, supported by a wealth of empirical research, is that increases in criminal and other behavior problems during adolescence are due, in great part, to the neurological and psychosocial immaturity that mark this developmental period. Across adolescence, there are distinct changes in brain development and developmental change in psychosocial processes that appear to make youths susceptible to becoming involved in criminal behavior and reckless behavior more generally. In this section, we highlight key developmental changes in brain structure and function and psychosocial processes that mark adolescence.

A. The Developmental Neuroscience of Adolescence

In general, developmental neuroscience on the adolescent brain can be divided into two areas. In the first, neuroscientists have documented age-related changes in the basic structure of the brain and circuit-based changes within the brain. In the second, neuroscientists have documented age-related changes in how the brain functions.[6]

[6] Feld, Casey, and Hurd (2013) provide additional details regarding the foundations of developmental neuroscience and its implications for juvenile justice.

1. *Brain Structure.* Four structural changes in the brain during adolescence are noteworthy. First, there is a decrease in gray matter in prefrontal regions of the brain, reflective of synaptic pruning, the process through which unused connections between neurons are eliminated (De Bellis et al. 2001; Sowell et al. 2002). This occurs mainly during preadolescence and early adolescence, the periods when major improvements in basic cognitive abilities and logical reasoning are seen. Those improvements are in part due to these anatomical changes (Steinberg 2012). In other words, synaptic pruning during early adolescence increases the efficiency of the brain in ways that promote cognitive abilities and decision making.

Second, there are important changes around the onset of puberty in activity involving the neurotransmitter dopamine (Steinberg 2010). There are substantial changes in the density and distribution of dopamine receptors in pathways that connect the limbic system, where emotions are processed and rewards and punishments experienced, and the prefrontal cortex, which is the brain's chief executive officer. Because dopamine plays a critical role in our experience of pleasure, these changes have important implications for sensation seeking (Gjedde et al. 2010; Norbury et al. 2013; Petit et al. 2013).

A third change in brain structure during adolescence (that continues into the early 20s) is an increase in white matter in the prefrontal cortex (Giedd 2004). This is the result of myelination, the process through which nerve fibers become sheathed in myelin, a white, fatty substance that improves the signal transmission efficiency of brain circuits. Unlike the synaptic pruning of the prefrontal areas, which is mainly finished by mid adolescence, myelination continues well into the 30s. More efficient neural connections within the prefrontal cortex are important for facilitating higher-order cognitive functions regulated by multiple prefrontal areas working in concert—functions such as planning ahead, weighing risks and rewards, and making complicated decisions. In essence, then, across adolescence and into early adulthood, individuals demonstrate increasing higher-order cognitive functioning ability. Giedd's (2004) work with a sample of adolescent youths who were given magnetic resonance imaging (MRI) scans and neuropsychological testing is particularly informative with respect to the development of the adolescent brain. His brain imaging results show that the region charged with controlling impulses (the dorsolateral prefrontal cortex) is one of the last parts of the brain regions to mature.

The fourth change in brain structure during adolescence is an increase in the strength of connections between the prefrontal cortex and other brain regions (Brenhouse, Sonntag, and Andersen 2008; Steinberg 2012). Improved connectivity between the prefrontal cortex and the limbic system is especially important for emotion regulation, which is facilitated by increased cross-talk between regions important in the processing of emotional information and those important in self-control. Like myelination, these changes in the teenage brain continue well into late adolescence. If one were to compare a young teenager's brain with that of a young adult, a much more extensive network of cables connecting brain regions would be observed in the adult.[7]

2. *Brain Function.* Beyond being an important period for changes in the brain's structure, adolescence is also an important time of change in how the brain functions. There are three major changes. First, over the course of adolescence and into early adulthood, there is a strengthening of activity in brain systems involving self-regulation (Steinberg 2014). For example, during tasks that require a great deal of self-control, adults employ a wider network of brain regions than do adolescents, which may make self-control easier, by distributing the work across multiple areas rather than overtaxing a smaller number of regions. Brain systems important for self-control continue to become more effective into the early 20s. For example, recent functional MRI- (fMRI-) based studies show that "areas underlying emotion regulation and reward sensitivity are in a state of heightened connectivity in the absence of any goal-directed behavior in RT [risk-taking] adolescents compared with NRT [non-risk-taking] adolescents" (DeWitt, Aslan, and Filbey 2014, p. 162).[8] In other words, the teenage brain appears to become increasingly efficient

[7] There are significant changes during adolescence in three brain areas and their interconnections and circuitry that support self-control: the amygdala, prefrontal cortex, and ventral striatum (Casey 2015). Casey's recent overview of circuit-based accounts of adolescent behavior nicely summarizes these changes and their effects on behavior: "The ability to suppress inappropriate emotions, desires, and actions in favor of alternative appropriate ones is diminished in the presence of salient environmental cues. An apparent sensitivity to environmental cues—positive and negative—leads to heightened reactivity both behaviorally and neurally in adolescents relative to both children and adults along with limited capacity to regulate these responses. In parallel, emotional contexts, especially threatening contexts, yield little behavioral response during this time. These dynamic changes in behavior are paralleled by regional changes in the strength of connections within limbic circuitry across development" (p. 300).

[8] Functional MRI studies use MRI technology to measure brain activity by detecting changes in blood flow (Huettel, Song, and McCarthy 2009).

in self-regulation during adolescence and into early adulthood, particularly in ways that affect regulation of risky behaviors.

Second, around the time of puberty, there are important changes related to hormonal changes that alter the way the brain responds to rewards (Spear 2010). Brain scans during a task in which individuals are shown rewarding stimuli, such as piles of coins or pictures of happy faces, show that adolescents' reward centers "light up" more than do children's or adults' when they expect something pleasurable to happen. Heightened sensitivity to rewards motivates adolescents to engage in acts, even risky acts, when the potential for pleasure is high.

A third change in brain function over the course of adolescence involves increases in the simultaneous involvement of multiple brain regions in response to arousing stimuli, such as pictures of angry or fearful faces. The ability to regulate these feelings improves as regions that govern emotional processing and self-control become more interconnected. This is one reason why susceptibility to peer pressure declines as adolescents mature into adulthood; they are better able to put the brakes on an impulse aroused by friends (Steinberg and Monahan 2007). Not surprisingly, the association between peer and individual delinquency wanes as youths move into adulthood (Monahan, Steinberg, and Cauffman 2009). Co-offending tends to decrease as early adulthood ensues (Reiss and Farrington 1991; Piquero, Farrington, and Blumstein 2007; Zimring and Laqueur 2015).

The emergence of a scientific knowledge base with respect to brain structure and brain functioning is a recent phenomenon, in large part as a result of the advent of the technology (MRI and fMRI) to carry out imaging analyses. This knowledge base is limited by its reliance on small, selective samples (largely because of cost), but the accumulated evidence is consistent with respect to assessing adolescent motivation, especially regarding reward sensitivity, and differences between adolescents and adults in information processing (and decision making) regarding risks and rewards (see, e.g., Smith et al. 2011). We highlight two of the most recent and important scientific studies on brain functioning, structure, and differences across age.

In a study of 53 persons between ages 10 and 23, Van Leijenhorst et al. (2010) examined "developmental differences in neural activation that was related to different phases of reward processing" (p. 62). Using fMRI data in concert with a slot machine task, their analytic focus on the brain regions implicated in reward processing and uncertainty showed that, overall, "middle adolescence is characterized by overactive incentive-related neurocircuitry, [an effect that was] most pronounced during the phase of reward receipt [and thus] favors the hypothesis that overactive reward-related circuitry and immature PFC circuitry potentially bias adolescents toward taking risks [see also Ernst, Pine, and Hardin 2006; Galvan et al. 2006; Casey, Getz, and Galvan 2008]" (p. 66).

Second, in a notably rare longitudinal study on brain functioning, Ordaz et al. (2013, p. 18109) analyzed longitudinal fMRI data from 123 subjects aged 9–26. They identified distinct developmental trajectories for brain regions and functioning with respect to inhibitory control that supports a "hierarchical pattern of maturation of brain activation that supports the gradual emergence of adult-like inhibitory control."[9] Across these studies, evidence is converging to suggest that the brains of young teens are undergoing changes in structure and function that will ultimately allow for more regulated behavior in early adulthood.

3. *Developmental Timing of Changes in Brain Structure and Function.* The structural and functional changes just described do not all occur along one uniform timetable. Differences in timing raise two important points relevant to the influence of neuroscience on public policy. First, there is no simple answer to the question of when an adolescent brain becomes an adult brain. Brain systems implicated in basic cognitive processes reach adult levels of maturity by mid adolescence, when synaptic pruning of the prefrontal cortex is complete. Cognitive processes important for things like impulse control do not mature, however, until late adolescence or even early adulthood. In other words, adolescents mature intellectually before they mature socially or emotionally (Steinberg, Cauffman, et al. 2009).

Beyond this developmental asynchrony between brain structure and function during adolescence, there are likely to be broad individual differences in these developmental processes, linked at least in part to individual differences in the age of puberty. These individual differences are not well understood. Taken cumulatively, it becomes very difficult to draw a bright line about the age at which an adolescent brain is like

[9] We do not wish to leave readers with the impression that adolescents continually seek risk and engage in antisocial behavior. As is well known, although many adolescents engage in antisocial behavior, many do not necessarily suffer from brain immaturity. In some cases, adolescents may perform better than adults on some cognitive and socio-emotional tasks (Crone and Dahl 2012).

an adult brain, because the answer depends on the individual and the aspect of functioning in question (cf. Casey 2015).

B. The Intersection of Developmental Neuroscience and Behavioral Science

Neuroscientific evidence is mainly important because it can provide additional validation for behavioral evidence when the neuroscience and the behavioral science are conceptually and theoretically aligned. Scientific evidence of any sort is always more compelling when it has been shown to be valid. When neuroscientific findings about adolescent brain development are consistent with findings from behavioral research, the neuroscience provides added confidence in the behavioral findings. But neuroscientific evidence should not be privileged over behavioral evidence (or vice versa); they should be considered in concert (see, more generally, Morse 2006, 2012; Maroney 2009, 2011*a*, 2011*b*, 2014).[10]

One reason why the neuroscience of adolescent development is compelling is that it parallels what we have learned from behavioral science over the past quarter century. For instance, longitudinal studies have illustrated that sensation seeking tends to increase during puberty and decline in the early 20s, while impulse control is low during childhood and adolescence but generally improves in late adolescence and into early adulthood.[11] This developmental pattern has been observed even in samples of known juvenile offenders, providing evidence that this phe-

[10] A somewhat related cautionary lesson can be drawn from an examination of judges' sentencing decisions. Aspinwall, Brown, and Tabery (2012) conducted an experiment in which a sample of US state trial judges were randomly assigned to presenting party (prosecution/defense) and biomechanism (absent/present) and asked to indicate their sentencing preferences in a hypothetical case. Regarding the biomechanism condition, "Participants in the biomechanism-absent condition received only expert testimony concerning the diagnosis of psychopathy. Participants in the biomechanism-present condition received identical expert testimony concerning the diagnosis of psychopathy plus expert testimony from a neurobiologist who presented an explanation of the biomechanism contributing to the development of psychopathy (here, low MAOA activity, atypical amygdala function, and other neurodevelopmental factors)" (p. 846). A key finding is that "the addition of a biomechanism for psychopathy significantly reduced the degree to which psychopathy was rated as aggravating" (p. 847). The expert testimony concerning a biomechanism for psychopathy increased the number of judges invoking mitigating factors.

[11] According to Skeem, Scott, and Mulvey (2014, p. 730), "neurobehavioral research indicates that the onset of puberty marks the beginning of dramatic changes in reward processing, processing of emotional stimuli, and social-cognitive reasoning. Biological changes during this period sensitize youths to their social world and create tendencies to explore and engage" (see also Crone and Dahl 2012).

nomenon may be a general feature of adolescence (Monahan et al. 2013). During adolescence, sensation seeking is at a high point while impulse control is at a low point. Multiple neurological models of adolescence posit that differences in the development of brain systems and connectivity between them influence adolescent risk taking and psychopathology (Nelson et al. 2005; Steinberg 2008; Ernst and Fudge 2009). Relative to adults, adolescents are more impulsive, more likely to focus on potential rewards in lieu of potential costs of a risky situation, and more likely to be short-sighted in their decision making (Steinberg and Scott 2003)—especially "in the heat of the moment, under potential threat, and in the presence of peers thereby increasing the likelihood of reckless behavior" (Cohen and Casey 2014, p. 65).

The relevance and role of peers occupy a much more central place in decision making in adolescence than during adulthood. For example, Gardner and Steinberg (2005) showed that the presence of peers increased risky decision making in a sample of adolescents, assessed with a video game called "Chicken," but not in a sample of older individuals. Further, using fMRI to measure the brain activity of adolescents, young adults, and adults during a simulated driving task, Chein et al. (2011) found that adolescents evinced greater activation in reward-related brain regions, which was related to subsequent risk taking, thereby indicating that the presence of peers activates the reward regions of the brain, which, in turn, increases risk taking. These findings parallel evidence that ability to resist peer influence increases across adolescence (Steinberg and Monahan 2007), that delinquent peer association is a weaker predictor of crime in later adolescence than earlier (Monahan, Steinberg, and Cauffman 2009), and that co-offending declines during the transition to adulthood (see Reiss and Farrington 1991; Piquero, Farrington, and Blumstein 2007; Zimring and Laqueur 2015). In general, these normative developmental increases in psychosocial capacities parallel changes in structure and function of the adolescent brain.

In sum, the brain science, in and of itself, should not carry the day, but when it is taken in concert with the evidence from the behavioral sciences, it suggests that developmentally normative phenomena that mark the lives of many adolescents are a critical (but not the only) piece of the puzzle for understanding antisocial and criminal behavior.[12]

[12] Monahan et al. (forthcoming) review how developmental neuroscience contributes to delinquency and psychopathology more broadly during adolescence.

II. Implications for Juvenile Offenders and Juvenile Processing

Cohen and Casey (2014) considered the intersection of developmental neuroscience and legal policy by focusing on the most recent advances in cognitive and neuropsychological and neurobiological research. They highlight something long known but until recently not backed by scientific evidence: "adolescents are more reactive in emotionally charged and social situations than adults due to changes in refinement of competing brain circuitry" (p. 63). Particularly in emotionally charged situations that involve similar-aged peers, emotional regulation is compromised, resulting in a failure of self-control and a higher probability of poor decision making and involvement in risky behavior. The probability of risky decision making is most notably increased when heightened activity in the reward- or emotion-related region of the brain is met with the presence of peers: "teenagers are attracted to novel and risky activities, including criminal activity, particularly with peers, at a time when they lack the judgment to exercise self-control and to consider the future consequences of their behavior" (Bonnie and Scott 2013, p. 159).[13]

This is a compelling explanation of the increase in criminal behavior observed during adolescence, but this imbalance is not fixed. It is transient. As most adolescents age and enter young adulthood, the prefrontal cognitive control region matures and begins to overpower the limbic (emotion-related) region. There is little denying that "adoption of a developmental perspective holds out substantial promise" (Mulvey 2014, p. 2) for understanding juvenile offending and juvenile punishment. In this section, we consider the implications of developmental neuroscience for culpability and competence and the implications of juvenile placement and punishment for adolescent development.

A. Implications of Developmental Neuroscience for Juvenile Culpability and Competence

The increase in the past quarter century in the number of juveniles tried as adults (or eligible to be) has raised two broad categories of questions about developmental differences between adolescents and adults. One concerns juveniles' *adjudicative and procedural competence*, a phrase

[13] Dahl (2001, p. 69) describes this gap between the limbic system and development of executive control functions as "starting the engines with an unskilled driver."

that refers to their competence to stand trial in adult court and to make legal decisions about such matters as whether to submit to an interrogation by a law enforcement agent, testify in their own defense, or accept a proposed plea agreement.[14] A second concerns juveniles' *criminal culpability*, which refers to the extent to which they should be held to the same standards as adults.

Both sets of questions concern differences between adolescents and adults with respect to their psychological abilities and capacities, but discussions of juveniles' competence and culpability are not the same. Questions about adjudicative and procedural competence ask whether adolescents and adults differ in abilities necessary to make informed decisions and, if so, whether these differences warrant providing juveniles with added or special protections. In this sense, questions about adjudicative competence share much in common with questions about other aspects of juveniles' competence, such as their competence to consent to a medical procedure or provide informed consent in a research setting. In contrast, questions about adolescents' criminal culpability pertain to the extent to which juveniles are legally responsible for criminal behavior and should be punished for it.

Questions about culpability concern the juvenile's mental state at the time of an offense. Questions about competence concern the juvenile's ability to make legal decisions after an offense has occurred or been alleged. Some psychological capacities are relevant to both competence and culpability, but others are not. For instance, the ability to foresee the future consequences of one's actions might influence an adolescent's decision to participate in an activity that might endanger another person (and is therefore relevant to judgments about the juvenile's culpability for any harm that may have occurred as a result). It might also influence how a juvenile responds to a police interrogation (and is therefore relevant to decisions about whether a juvenile who decided to confess to a crime was competent to understand the ramifications of this decision) (cf. Feld 2013).[15]

[14] These are only one portion of broader issues of competence that implicate juveniles' waivers of *Miranda* rights during interrogation (see Feld 2013) and waivers of the right to counsel (Feld 1993; Feld and Schaefer 2010).

[15] We appreciate insights gained from Barry Feld, who observed, "For legal purposes, the decision to waive Miranda does not require an understanding of the ramifications of the decisions—i.e. collateral consequences, impact on plea bargaining, or even nature of the offense itself. It requires only a cognitive understanding of the words of the warn-

By contrast, whether a juvenile defendant who has committed a crime understands the difference between the goals of a prosecutor and a judge is relevant to his or her competence to stand trial but has nothing to do with responsibility for the offense. It is possible, therefore, for an adolescent to be fully responsible for a criminal act but incompetent to be tried in a criminal proceeding or less than fully responsible for a criminal act but competent to stand trial.

1. *Culpability.* Criminal responsibility concerns the extent to which an individual is responsible for his or her actions. In order for something to diminish criminal responsibility, it has to be something outside the person's control. A person with an untreatable tumor on her frontal lobe that makes her unable to control aggressive outbursts is less than fully responsible for her aggressive behavior. This, if believed by the jury or judge, would be viewed as an excusing factor in a trial for a violent crime or as a mitigating factor at sentencing. However, if a person with no neurobiological deficit goes into a bar, drinks himself into a state of rage, and commits a violent crime as a result, that he was drunk does not diminish his responsibility. It does not matter whether the mitigating factor is biological, psychological, or environmental. The issue is whether the diminished responsibility is in some meaningful sense the person's fault and whether the individual could have compensated for whatever it is that was uncontrollable. This is the crux of the argument for why neuroscience of adolescent development is important for understanding criminal culpability: it points to something outside an adolescent's control that affects criminal behavior.

Studies of psychosocial development indicate continued maturation beyond mid adolescence in capacities such as impulse control (Steinberg 2008), risk aversion (Steinberg 2009), resistance to peer pressure (Steinberg and Monahan 2007), sensitivity to costs as well as rewards (Cauffman et al. 2010), and future orientation (Steinberg, Graham, et al. 2009). Steinberg, Cauffman, et al. (2009) argue that developmental immaturity of these processes is relevant to assessments of criminal responsibility. To the extent that neuroscience supports these developmental trends as likely to be the result of universal developmental difference in brain structure and function, adolescents' brain functioning may have implications for criminal responsibility. This developmental immaturity

ing. Even with respect to basic understanding, the developmental psych is that kids 15 and younger just don't get it" (personal communication, July 31, 2014; see also Feld 2013).

may make a youthful offender somewhat less culpable for his or her behavior.

2. *Competence.* A criminal proceeding satisfies constitutional due process requirements only when the defendant is competent to stand trial, which includes capacities to assist counsel and to understand the nature of the proceeding sufficiently to participate in it and make decisions about it (*Dusky v. U.S.*, 362 U.S. 402 [1960]; *Godinez v. Moran*, 509 U.S. 389 [1993]). The conventional standard for competence to stand trial focuses on mental illness and disability, but there has been growing recognition that some youths without mental illness or disability may be legally incompetent because of developmental immaturity (Grisso et al. 2003).

Analyses of legal competence have outlined specific functional abilities with which the law is concerned (Grisso 2002); these are often referred to as the "*Dusky* criteria." They include basic comprehension of the purpose and nature of the trial process, capacity to provide relevant information to counsel, ability to reason about this information in a logical fashion, and ability to apply information to one's own situation in a manner that is neither distorted nor irrational.[16] In addition to defendants' basic understanding and reasoning abilities, their "decisional competence" may be significant in cases in which defendants must make important decisions about the waiver of constitutional rights (Bonnie 1992, 1993). Adolescents' competence to stand trial is clearly important in discussions of whether and under what circumstances they might be tried as adults (since the *Dusky* criteria apply to all criminal defendants, regardless of age), but they are also important considerations involving juvenile court proceedings that over time have created a more adversarial climate in the juvenile justice system. There is disagreement whether the competence standards in juvenile courts should be identical to or less stringent than those in criminal courts (Redding and Frost 2002; see also Scott and Grisso 2004). The majority of states have agreed that, given the potentially serious outcomes of a delinquency adjudication (including, perhaps, a long period of confinement in a prison-like facility), some minimum standard of competence should apply to juvenile court proceedings (Woolard, Fried, and Reppucci 2013).

[16] Issues of competence generally arise in the context of mental illness or retardation. Recognition of age per se as an entirely disabling condition, which we do not favor, should not be adopted.

There are two obvious ways in which adolescents and adults differ in their basic cognitive abilities (e.g., ability to recall specific pieces of information) and life experiences (e.g., familiarity with the roles of the various participants in a trial). A less frequently considered but potentially important difference between adolescents and adults involves aspects of psychosocial maturation that include progress toward greater future orientation, better risk perception, and less susceptibility to peer influence (Scott et al. 1995; Cauffman and Steinberg 2000).

Several authors have hypothesized that these developmental factors could result in differences between adolescents' and adults' decision making about important rights in the adjudicative process, including—assuming that juveniles have defense counsel—whether to submit to an interrogation (and, if so, how to respond to questions); whether to provide information to one's defense counsel (and, if so, how completely and honestly to disclose important facts); whether to testify in one's defense; and whether to accept a proposed plea agreement (Grisso et al. 2003). Although it might be assumed that adolescents who are less than fully competent can rely on the advice of adults when making these decisions, adults are not always present (e.g., when an adolescent is picked up for questioning) and are not always wise about legal matters (i.e., not all adults are competent). They also do not always have the same interests as those of the adolescent (e.g., a mother who is angry at her adolescent for having gotten into trouble in the past may encourage him or her to confess to a crime not committed; see Woolard et al. 2008).

Several studies of age differences in various capacities relevant to adjudicative and procedural competence have been conducted (for a review, see Grisso [2005]). In general, these studies indicate that individuals 15 and younger may be less likely than those 16 and older to possess the skills and capacities likely to render them competent to stand trial or to make important legal decisions. These include decisions that arise during interrogations (e.g., whether to waive *Miranda* rights) and trial proceedings (e.g., whether to waive a right to a jury trial) and whether to accept a proffered plea agreement.

Steinberg, Graham, et al. (2009) have noted that these age differences concerning adjudicative and procedural competence parallel age differences in other domains of competence (e.g., granting informed consent) and in basic information-processing and logical reasoning abilities. The psychosocial immaturity that marks adolescence compared with adulthood (i.e., diminished impulse control, resistance to peer pressure, etc.) may not necessarily result in age differences in competence to stand trial, perhaps because these social and emotional deficiencies are less likely to impair adolescents' judgment under the conditions in which legal decisions are made.[17]

Competence to stand trial is only one aspect of legal competence, which also includes competence to make legal decisions outside the courtroom. The most frequently studied aspect of noncourtroom legal decision making concerns adolescents' responses to interrogations by law enforcement officials (Kassin et al. 2010; Feld 2013). Researchers have studied age differences in individuals' comprehension of *Miranda* warnings (Grisso 1980), in decisions whether to confess to a crime they have committed (Grisso et al. 2003), and in susceptibility to making false confessions (Kassin 2008; Malloy, Shulman, and Cauffman 2014). Generally speaking, these studies show that adolescents, especially those younger than 16, are less likely than adults to understand their rights, more likely to comply with authority, and less likely to make decisions that reflect their best interests (e.g., remaining silent rather than confessing, giving a false confession in order to please an interrogator). Results of these studies have prompted many to call for greater protections for juveniles during interrogations, including mandatory videotaping or the presence of an adult (Kassin et al. 2010; Feld 2013).

B. *Effects of Juvenile Placement and Punishment on Adolescent Development*

Classical deterrence theory assumes that punishments, including incarceration, reduce offending, with most research being focused on adults. The contemporary consensus is that there is little to no convincing evidence supporting the deterrence assumption (Piquero and Blumstein 2007; Nagin, Cullen, and Jonson 2009; Nagin 2013). This is particularly important concerning juvenile crime because only a small fraction of offenders will continue to offend in adulthood (Piquero, Farrington, and Blumstein 2003). It is exceptionally difficult to identify this subset of youths prospectivêly, but deterring juveniles from continued offending is a central policy question (Schneider 1990).

Only a handful of studies have examined the effects of juvenile justice involvement on subsequent criminal careers. The limited evidence avail-

[17] Differences between cognitive competence and judgment require a more nuanced appreciation of long-term consequences.

able is due in part to methodological issues of differential selection that determines the likelihood of youth incarceration and in part to challenges in obtaining the data to investigate the effect of juvenile placement on recidivism. Here, we highlight a few of the most relevant studies of the effects of juvenile court and punishment experiences on subsequent offending.[18] We divide these studies into two groups: those that focus on the effects of incarceration and those that focus on the effects of waiver to the adult court. They suggest that neither incarceration (especially lengthy) nor waiver to adult court results in reduced offending among those juveniles affected.

1. *Incarceration.* One key study used 20 years of data from the Montreal Longitudinal and Experimental Study, a sample of over 1,000 boys who attended kindergarten classes in disadvantaged areas of Montreal in 1984 (Gatti, Tremblay, and Vitaro 2009). The goal was to assess the effects of juvenile justice system interventions compared with less restrictive interventions. Juvenile justice intervention was strongly predictive of adult crime, by almost a factor of seven, even after controlling for risk and protective variables collected during adolescence such as self-reported delinquency, verbal ability, deviant peers, impulsivity, family income, and parental supervision. When studying effects of specific forms of juvenile justice interventions (without supervision, with supervision, and with placement), Gatti, Tremblay, and Vitaro found that supervision and placement were significantly and strongly related to adult crime. Placement interventions increased the risk of adult crime by a factor of almost 38.

In an important, methodologically sophisticated extension of work on the same sample of Montreal boys, Petitclerc et al. (2013) assessed longer-term iatrogenic effects of juvenile court exposure and adult crime between ages 18 and 25. They used propensity score matching methods, which help account for potential differences between those exposed and not exposed to juvenile court so as to better isolate a causal relationship.

[18] In this section, we are concerned only with the effects of juvenile justice involvement and not the effects of arrest on subsequent offending (see Bernburg and Krohn 2003; Bernburg, Krohn, and Rivera 2006; Morris and Piquero 2013; Ward, Krohn, and Gibson 2014). Our focus on the effects of placement on subsequent behavior is limited to juveniles and not within samples of adults. Nagin, Cullen, and Jonson (2009) provide an in-depth overview of the literature surrounding imprisonment and reoffending more generally. A few other studies examine the effects of incarceration on subsequent offending in samples that combine adolescent and adult offenders (Sweeten and Apel 2007; Wermink et al. 2013). We focus on juvenile justice placements.

They found that "male adolescents processed in juvenile court . . . had three times the odds of being convicted of an adult criminal offence by age 25, and committed close to twice as many violent and nonviolent adult offences, compared with matched peers who were arrested by the police, but not sent to court" (p. 295). Taken together, these findings provide strong evidence of an iatrogenic effect of court involvement on subsequent criminality.

Two additional studies focus on effects of juvenile justice intervention on youth outcomes: one on criminal behavior (Loughran et al. 2009) and the other on psychosocial outcomes (Dmitrieva et al. 2012). Both used data from the Pathways to Desistance project, a longitudinal study of 1,354 serious adolescent offenders from Philadelphia and Phoenix who were followed from mid adolescence to early adulthood.

Loughran et al. (2009) sought to answer two questions: what is the causal effect of institutional placement compared with probation on subsequent rearrest rates, and what is the marginal effect of longer stays in placement on subsequent offending (i.e., a dose-response analysis)? Using four years of follow-up data subsequent to sanctioning decisions, no deterrent effect of institutional placement on future offending was detected, measured either with official records or with self-reports of offending. There was little benefit (in terms of less offending) from longer lengths of stays among those who were institutionalized. Careful attention was paid to possible selection bias concerning those incarcerated: the authors ruled out 66 potential confounding variables that spanned individual, situational, and familial domains. Like the Montreal studies, this one provides strong evidence against a deterrence effect of placement on subsequent criminal activity.

Dmitrieva et al. (2012) examined the long-term (7-year) effects of different types of incarceration on different components of psychosocial maturity, including temperance, perspective, and responsibility. The study also investigated how youths' ages and facility characteristics moderated the effects of incarceration on subsequent psychosocial maturity. Those who spent more time in secure facilities during the 7-year follow-up period had lower psychosocial maturity at the start of the study; however, more time incarcerated in secure settings was not related to global psychosocial maturity (pp. 1080–81).

The effects for placement in residential treatment facilities, however, were slightly different. Males who spent more time in residential treatment had higher global psychosocial maturity at the outset of the study, but more time spent in such facilities over the 7-year follow-up was related to slower increases in psychosocial maturity. By the end of the study (age ~25), global psychosocial maturity among males with either low amounts of secure confinement or low amounts of residential treatment facility placement was virtually identical and remained higher (i.e., better psychosocial maturity) than that of males with high secure confinement or high residential treatment exposure. The two groups with high confinement experiences had virtually identical global psychosocial maturity scores at the study's end. Findings regarding potential moderating effects of age and facility quality were mixed, with no clear pattern of results, or null, indicating very few differences.[19]

2. *Waiver to Adult Court.* Researchers have devoted significant attention to understanding the effects of juvenile waiver on subsequent offending. We briefly highlight this line of research. Full reviews are available elsewhere (Fagan 2008; Redding 2008; Feld and Bishop 2012*a*, 2012*b*).

Many of the early studies showed that transferred youths were more likely to recidivate than those who were retained in the juvenile system. That finding was observed in a number of states and using different methodologies, different measures of recidivism, and large samples (see, e.g., Bishop and Frazier 2000; Fagan and Zimring 2000; Kupchik 2003; Lanza-Kaduce et al. 2005). In the late 2000s, the Office of Juvenile Justice and Delinquency Prevention concluded that transfer to adult criminal court "does not engender community protection by reducing recidivism [and in fact] substantially increases recidivism" (Redding 2008, p. 6). With some notable exceptions (Smith and Paternoster 1990; Fagan 1995; Winner et al. 1997; Myers 2003), much of the early work did not adequately address potential selection bias.[20]

[19] Other studies have examined effects of official intervention on subsequent criminal behavior and non-crime-related outcomes such as employment, drug use, and life chances. In general, they show that official intervention increases the likelihood of worse outcomes (Bernburg and Krohn 2003; Bernburg, Krohn, and Rivera 2006; Lopes et al. 2012; Morris and Piquero 2013; Ward, Krohn, and Gibson 2014). Murray et al. (2014, p. 226) examined the long-term effects of conviction and incarceration on males in the Cambridge Study in Delinquent Development, a longitudinal study of South London males followed into late middle adulthood. Results showed that "all adult outcomes [self-reported crime, antisocial personality, poor life success] were worse for men who were first incarcerated between ages fifteen and twenty-six, compared with matched men who were convicted between ages fifteen and twenty-six but not incarcerated up to age twenty-six."

[20] The issue here is that some covariates may simultaneously affect both the likelihood that a youth is transferred and the likelihood of subsequent recidivism. A complete depic-

A recent study using data from the Pathways to Desistance project addressed the issue. After using propensity score matching to reduce potential selection bias for 59 covariates, Loughran et al. (2010) estimated the effects of transfer on 4-year rearrests for 128 youths. They found a null effect on rearrest but differential effects depending on adolescents' offending histories. The sample was divided in two ways, by type of charge (property vs. person) and by the number of prior petitions (zero to one vs. two or more), to assess possible differences in the effects of transfer. The small sample size limited the investigation, but results showed that the rearrest rate was lower among transferred person offenders compared with transferred property offenders. There was no interaction effect between priors and transfer to adult court. There was a main effect for the number of priors: persons with fewer priors had a lower rate of rearrest regardless of juvenile or adult court processing. These findings suggest that it may be worthwhile to examine heterogeneity among youths transferred to adult court in order to draw more accurate conclusions about recidivism outcomes.

Coupled with evidence that transfer policies have no deterrent effects on youthful offenders (McGowen et al. 2007),[21] the weight of the evidence suggests that involvement with the juvenile justice system does more harm than good, with negative effects magnified as punishments become harsher (Petrosino, Turpin-Petrosino, and Guckenburg 2010; Mears et al. 2011). This does not imply that the system cannot be effective, especially if meaningful services are provided to the youths, but that current justice system practices do not appear to deter criminal activity.

In light of the neuroscientific evidence on developmental immaturity, it is a distinct possibility that punitive settings disrupt adolescent development in ways that increase the likelihood of subsequent crime. If adolescence is a critical time for the development of capacities that underlie good adult decision making, it stands to reason that experiences that disrupt that development—such as incarceration—should be minimized. Greater understanding of the neurological and psychosocial effects of these experiences is needed.

---

tion of the relationship between transfer and subsequent offending must consider the confounding of these potential covariates. Jordan (2014), using data from a sample of Pennsylvania violent youths, provides a good example.

[21] Zimring and Rushin (2013) examined whether state law changes in juvenile justice systems in the 1990s contributed to declines in juvenile homicide rates through 2009. They found little confirmatory evidence.

III. The Influence of Brain Science on Changes in Juvenile Justice Policy

Four recent US Supreme Court cases have addressed changing views on the culpability, competence, and effects of punishment on youthful offenders. The Court increasingly over time took account of neuroscientific and behavioral evidence. We briefly review these cases and show how developmental psychology informed the Court's views of these cases.

Roper v. Simmons (2005) considered whether juveniles who commit capital crimes before age 18 may be sentenced to death. A 5–4 decision declared it unconstitutional to impose capital punishment for crimes committed under the age of 18. *Roper* overturned the laws of the 25 states with lower minimum ages. Five years later in *Graham v. Florida*, the Court decided that juvenile offenders may not constitutionally be sentenced to life imprisonment without the possibility of parole for cases not involving homicide. In *Miller v. Alabama* and *Jackson v. Hobbs* (usually referred to jointly as *Miller*), the court extended the reasoning in *Graham* to homicide and declared mandatory sentences for juvenile offenders to life imprisonment without the possibility of parole (LWOP) for murder to be unconstitutional.

Before the 2005 *Roper* decision, brain science research documenting differences between adolescents and adults was not acknowledged in Supreme Court juvenile justice decisions, largely because there were few empirical studies of adolescent brain development (Steinberg 2013). By the time *Miller* was decided, however, there had been significant growth in behavioral science research on adolescent brain development and decision making, and in comparison with adults.

The opinion in *Miller* devoted significant attention to this work, discussing issues related to adolescent immaturity in higher-order executive functioning. The Court cited amicus briefs, including one filed by the American Psychological Association (APA), that summarized the relevant literature and related it to the issues facing the Court (Steinberg 2013, p. 4).[22]

The successive briefs that the APA filed in these cases demonstrate the growing influence of adolescent brain science. It was discussed cau-

[22] All APA amicus briefs for these cases can be found at http://www.apa.org/about/offices/ogc/amicus/.

tiously in the *Roper* (2005) brief but with increasing confidence concerning *Graham* (2010) and *Miller* (2012). Collectively, the APA briefs argued against severe sentences for juvenile offenders primarily because juveniles' immaturity, vulnerability, and changeability make them less culpable than adults and accordingly that, as a result of their lower responsibility and ability to change, they should be deemed less responsible and thus less punishable. The APA reviewed evidence showing that adolescents are inherently more impulsive, short-sighted, and susceptible to peer influence.[23]

Scott (2013*b*) observed that the Court has shown its willingness to consider research from developmental science regarding the immaturity that characterizes adolescents' criminal and other risk-taking behavior and to take it into account in forbidding imposition of some harsh punishments on young offenders.[24] She suggests that the Court has embraced a developmental model of crime policy for adolescent offenders that is attuned to the science underlying juvenile decision making and neurobiological and structural brain differences between juveniles and adults. Bonnie and Scott (2013, p. 160) similarly observe that the decisions acknowledged differences in parts of the brain that govern emotional and behavioral control among adolescents and that developmental science can guide and inform juvenile crime policy.[25]

The Court's willingness to use psychological and neuroscientific evidence can be seen in the progression of opinions in the three cases. In *Roper*, writing for the majority, Justice Anthony Kennedy pointed to three differences between adolescents and adults that made it difficult to classify juveniles "among the worst of offenders": their immaturity

[23] Zimring (1998, pp. 76–78) noted that three characteristics of adolescent immaturity explain why juveniles are less culpable than adults. Adolescents lack fully developed cognitive abilities, which inhibit their ability to apply legal and moral rules to social situations. They have a limited capacity to control their impulsiveness. They do not have complete ability to resist peer influence and pressure. This suggests that adolescents process, prioritize, and use information differently than adults (Steinberg and Cauffman 1999, p. 52). With age, children become more adept at processing information, better able to exercise restraint and resist pressure, and better able make more reasoned decisions (see Scott and Grisso 1997).

[24] The cases concern capital punishment and LWOP sentences. Juveniles remain vulnerable to mandatory decades-long and discretionary life sentences.

[25] This does not mean that juveniles cannot be punished, especially for serious offenses. The Court suggested that subjecting juveniles to adult prosecution and punishment "should be 'unusual' and individualized," and sanctions applied to juveniles should "focus on maximizing young offenders' potential for reform" (Scott 2013*a*, p. 71).

and an underdeveloped sense of responsibility, which compromised their decision-making ability (noting that this was the very reason that states limited many juveniles' rights); their heightened susceptibility to external influence, including peer pressure, which gave them less control over their environment; and their still-developing character. The first two differences make adolescents less responsible than adults for their behavior and, accordingly, less culpable for their crimes. The third difference diminishes their culpability but also makes them better candidates for rehabilitation. Kennedy noted that the characteristics that make juveniles less culpable also make them less likely to be deterred by capital punishment, thereby undercutting the deterrence claims of death penalty proponents.

The dissenting justices in *Roper* questioned the need for a categorical exclusion of adolescents from death penalty eligibility instead of case-by-case decision making by judges or juries. They acknowledged that there could be instances in which a juvenile's immaturity mitigated his or her criminal responsibility but raised concerns about cases in which the crime was an especially heinous one committed by an older adolescent who demonstrated adult-like premeditation. The relevant developmental evidence concerned the difficulty of reliably predicting the future behavior of a juvenile offender.

Developmental scientists argued that, even for especially heinous crimes, it is impossible to distinguish between juveniles who are and are not incorrigible. The Court majority agreed, noting, "If trained psychiatrists with the advantage of clinical testing and observation refrain, despite diagnostic expertise, from assessing any juvenile under 18 as having antisocial personality disorder, we conclude that States should refrain from asking jurors to issue a far graver condemnation that a juvenile offender merits the death penalty" (at 19).

Roper was important for three reasons. First, the Court widened the prohibition against capital punishment to a wider age range (*Thompson v. Oklahoma*, 487 U.S. 815 [1988], prohibited capital punishment for youths younger than 16, but almost no murders are committed by people younger than this age). Second, developmental science showing differences between adolescents and adults was mentioned numerous times during oral arguments and in the Court's decision. In previous rulings on juveniles' criminal culpability, differences between adolescents and adults were presented mainly as a matter of common sense. Finally, research on adolescent brain development was introduced as evidence in support of the contention that adolescents were inherently less mature than adults.

Neuroscience was not mentioned in the Court's opinion but was discussed at oral argument. An exchange between an attorney and Justice Breyer suggested just how influential neuroscience may have been:

> Justice Breyer: Now, I thought that the—the scientific evidence simply corroborated something that every parent already knows, and if it's more than that, I would like to know what more.
>
> Mr. Waxman: Well, it's—I think it's—it's more than that in a couple of respects. It—it explains, corroborates, and validates what we sort of intuitively know, not just as parents but in adults that—that—who live in a world filled with adolescents. And—and the very fact that science—and I'm not just talking about social science here, but the important neurobiological science that has now shown that these adolescents are—their character is not hard-wired. (US Supreme Court 2004, p. 40)

Five years after *Roper*, the Court in *Graham v. Florida* (2010) extended the logic of its abolition of the juvenile death penalty to mandatory LWOP sentences for juveniles convicted of crimes other than homicide. The majority explicitly observed that "no recent data provide reason to reconsider the Court's observations in *Roper* about the nature of juveniles. As petitioner's *amici* point out, developments in psychology and brain science continue to show fundamental differences between juvenile and adult minds. For example, parts of the brain involved in behavior control continue to mature through late adolescence. See Brief for American Medical Association et al. as *Amici Curiae* 16–24; Brief for American Psychological Association et al. as *Amici Curiae* 22–27" (*Graham v. Florida*, No. 08-7412, slip. op. at 17). As in *Roper*, the dissenting justices once again asked why the prohibition of LWOPs for juveniles convicted of nonhomicides needed to be categorical.

The LWOP decision was noteworthy in at least two other respects (Maroney 2011*a*). First, *Graham* was the first case in which developmental neuroscience findings were explicitly mentioned in the opinion ("For example, parts of the brain involved in behavior control continue to mature through late adolescence"; at 17). Developmental differences in behavior remain more important for debates about adolescent culpability than about developmental differences in brain structure or function (Steinberg 2012), but the Court's acceptance of neurobiological immaturity as a part of a more general developmental immaturity signaled a shift in thinking that encouraged lower courts to look to brain science to justify differential treatment of adolescents.

Second, moving beyond the realm of capital punishment opened the door for developmental immaturity arguments more generally. If adolescents' relative immaturity made the use of LWOP unfair, why, then, could this argument not be applied to any sentencing decision?

Historically, many of the arguments employed to limit the use of the death penalty relied on the notion that "death is different," which justifies special scrutiny of circumstances under which capital punishment is applied (*California v. Ramos*, 463 U.S. 992 [1983]). In *Graham*, the Court majority argued that, for adolescents, LWOPs were different too, noting that a juvenile sentenced to life would spend more years and proportionately more of his or her life in prison than an adult. This paved the way for subsequent rulings in state courts that limited the use of excessively long sentences for juveniles, even if they were not life sentences.[26]

Graham applied only to instances in which an individual had been convicted of a nonhomicide offense. Its practical implications were limited; nearly all individuals serving LWOP sentences for crimes committed as juveniles had been convicted of homicide. In 2012, the Court revisited juvenile LWOPs in *Miller* and *Jackson*. Each involved a 14-year-old convicted of homicide and sentenced to LWOP. When these cases were argued, nearly 2,500 people were serving life sentences for crimes committed as juveniles.

Just as *Graham* built on *Roper*, *Miller* built on *Graham*, with the Court majority again concluding that adolescents' developmental immaturity limited their criminal culpability. The opinion noted that the science had become stronger since *Roper* and *Graham*, pointed out that the earlier conclusions in the earlier cases continued to be strengthened by neuroscience, and went into greater detail about research findings. For example, the opinion mentioned immaturity in adolescence of higher-order executive functions such as impulse control (which had

[26] In California, e.g., the State Supreme Court ruled that a sentence in which the date of parole eligibility exceeded a juvenile's natural life expectancy violated the portion of the *Graham* ruling that requires that juveniles convicted of nonhomicides be given a meaningful opportunity to demonstrate their rehabilitation. The issue of retroactivity with respect to *Graham* has been decided both ways by appellate courts and at the time of writing is on the Supreme Court's calendar for argument and decision.

been highlighted in *Graham*) and deficiencies in planning ahead and risk avoidance.

The *Miller* ruling differed from *Roper* and *Graham* in one significant way. The earlier cases placed categorical bans on the use of punishments for juveniles. *Miller* left LWOP as an option, prohibiting states only from mandating LWOPs for juvenile murderers, on the grounds that such mandates do not permit courts to take into account the juvenile's developmental immaturity. Justice Elena Kagan in the Court's opinion noted, "But given all we have said in *Roper*, *Graham*, and this decision about children's diminished culpability and heightened capacity for change, we think appropriate occasions for sentencing juveniles to this harshest possible penalty will be uncommon" (*Miller v. Alabama*, No. 10-9646, slip op. at 17, 2012). It is not yet clear whether this prediction will hold true.

IV. What's Next for Research and Policy with Respect to Adolescent Development and Juvenile Justice?

In this essay, we set out to provide a broad overview of the empirical, legal, and policy issues at the intersection of adolescent development and juvenile justice. An authoritative treatment of all the key issues is well beyond the scope of any single article. Our intention has been to give readers a deeper appreciation of the complexity of the issues, the significant research developments made in the past quarter century, how developmental science research has entered into the policy discussion and especially legal decision making at the highest levels, and how advances in the research have influenced government agencies in altering how they carry out their missions.

Starting in the mid-1990s, in large part with support of the MacArthur Foundation and its Research Network on Adolescent Development and Juvenile Justice, research on adolescent development, adolescent decision making, and adolescent brain science began to be linked to debates about juvenile justice policy and practice. In general, findings from brain imaging and neuropsychological research documented that there is great change and continued development from adolescence into early adulthood in the frontal lobe and, especially, the prefrontal cortex, which helps to govern executive functions such as self-control and planning. At the same time, findings from the behavioral and decision making research showed that, compared to adults, adolescents are impulsive, short-sighted, exceptionally sensitive to the prospect of immediate rewards, and less likely to consider the long-term consequences of their actions—a pattern that is even more pronounced in the context of similar-aged peers. As a result, arguments were made that adolescents are less culpable (or less blameworthy) than adults. In due course, *Roper*, *Graham*, and *Miller* acknowledged the brain and behavioral research on age differences in decision making.

Still, there are a wide range of research questions and policy issues that need attention. In this closing section, we highlight a few of the ones we believe most worth considering.

A. Next Steps in Science

Behavioral and neuropsychological research has provided important evidence regarding adolescent decision making and brain development. With respect to behavioral research, there is a need to undertake studies of high-risk and offender samples as they represent the policy group of interest regarding persistence and desistance from crime (Laub and Sampson 2001; Mulvey et al. 2004). Such studies should consider the full range of developmental and life course issues (e.g., factors associated with the onset of antisocial behavior, its escalation into more severe crimes for some, and the transition away from most adult offending for the majority), including recent findings that bear on legal issues raised in *Roper*, *Graham*, and *Miller* (cf. Piquero 2013).

Second, several studies have shown that individual differences in adolescent psychosocial maturity are moderated by the presence of peers. Consideration of other types of contexts such as family and neighborhood environments should be better understood in concert with adolescent psychosocial maturity. Owing to data constraints, there is little empirical research on "how individual risk factors for criminal involvement interact with different contexts, and even less about how these may differ over the course of adolescent development" (Mulvey 2014, p. 7). More research aimed at understanding the contexts in which individual differences more or less influence antisocial behavior is needed (Cohen and Casey 2014, p. 65).

Third, for several reasons, some related to data and some linked to researchers' reluctance or nervousness about these issues, there is a need to study whether and, if so, how aspects of adolescent development relate differently across ethnicity and gender to risky decision making and serious criminal behavior. Males and minorities are overrepresented in serious criminal activity. Understanding the reasons for these patterns has received little research attention but remains critically important (Piquero 2008). Research is needed on at least the following questions: Are differences that have emerged from adolescent behavioral and brain research race or gender specific? Do males experience an earlier emotion-driven system while females' executive functioning develops faster and earlier in the life course? Do minorities evince more of the risk factors than nonminorities with respect to crime? Does social context magnify these potential individual differences across race and ethnicity? Do juvenile justice personnel weigh and consider the behavior—and the reasons underlying it—differently depending on the juvenile's race, ethnicity, or gender (e.g., Bridges and Steen 1998; Bechtold et al., forthcoming)?

Fourth, it is clear that adolescence is a distinct period of the life course, one marked by immature decision-making capacities, low impulse control, and lessened ability to resist peer influences (Steinberg and Cauffman 1999). There may be other individual differences among adolescents worthy of investigation. As seen in insights borrowed from general strain theory (Agnew 1997, pp. 112–13), adolescents compared with adults may have more negative relations with others, may interpret such relations as aversive, and may be more likely to cope with adversity through antisocial behavior. But as adolescents move into adulthood, they may come to have more control over their life and learn to react to adverse situations in a more prosocial manner.

With respect to neuroscientific research, several specific issues would be especially helpful to future discussions of adolescents' criminal responsibility and appropriate responses to juvenile crime. First, very few studies have linked changes in brain structure or function between adolescence and adulthood to changes in legally relevant behaviors, especially as they occur outside of controlled laboratory investigations, in order to investigate what other sources, aside from brain structure functioning, influence adolescent offending (Pfeifer and Allen 2012). Research is needed that directly links age differences in brain structure and function to age differences in legally relevant capacities and capabilities, especially within a longitudinal context (see Ordaz et al. 2013). Research is also needed on how social contexts influence the development and functioning of the brain across the adolescence-adult transitional period in an effort to understand how decision making may change, especially around pubertal maturity (e.g., Crone and Dahl 2012). There also remains a need for longitudinal research on brain functioning and structure to assess both normal developmental changes and changes related to trauma, injury, and substance use and abuse.

Second, almost all research on age-related changes in brain structure and function has been carried out with youths not involved in the justice system. Very few studies involve high-risk samples of young people. Although it has been crucial for purposes of legal policy to draw on studies of brain development in general population samples, it is important to know whether resulting conclusions generalize to populations of adolescents more likely to come into contact with the justice system. These include juveniles subjected to trauma and abuse, exposed to high levels of alcohol and illicit drugs, diagnosed with attention deficit and hyperactivity disorder and conduct disorders, and raised in dire poverty.

Third, although it is often assumed that adolescents are more amenable to rehabilitation than adults, little neurobiological research has examined this proposition. Work is needed on the nature, correlates, and causes of adolescent neuroplasticity, especially in connection with conditions of confinement in juvenile correctional facilities. We have good reason to suspect that harsh conditions such as solitary confinement impair brain development during a time of heightened susceptibility to the environment, but research on this proposition has yet to be conducted.

Finally, there is growing interest in whether neurobiological data, alone or with other types of data, can improve prediction of future behavior at the individual level with respect to recidivism or responses to intervention. Studies have compared juvenile offenders' brain structures or functions with those of nonoffenders, but using neuroscience to predict individuals' future behavior is different and more difficult. It is critically important to assess the accuracy of such predictions, especially when persons do not follow expected paths (i.e., persons without structural deficits who offend and vice versa). Research on these and related issues is necessary to move beyond the science of the laboratory and into real-world decision making and behaviors, so as not to minimize brain processing and behavior as "being defined by a battle between reason/regulation . . . versus the emotions" (Pfeifer and Allen 2012, p. 326).

Developmental science can play an important role in informing the legal response to youth crime (Scott 2013*a*, p. 103). Research on adolescence and adolescent risk taking provides some guidance for formulating crime policies that are fair to young offenders and may be effective in reducing offending.

B. Next Steps in Policy and Law

Informed policy making necessitates that actors in the juvenile justice system be knowledgeable about developmental changes during childhood and adolescence and about capabilities and characteristics that are relevant to competence, culpability, and likely responses to treatment (Steinberg 2009, p. 465; National Research Council 2014). For example, police officers need to deal with young persons in a developmentally appropriate manner. Training for police on this already exists, particularly with minority youths, in the police academy curriculum of the Philadelphia Police Department and the Chicago Police Department's training course on Procedural Justice and Police Legitimacy. Scientific information is important for judges' decisions about what to do with a juvenile offender, prioritizing the need to make fair and just decisions. Attorneys need information from developmental science to practice law more effectively and to better assess juveniles' understanding of court processes. Such information is pertinent to mental health professionals who make recommendations about adolescents' adjudicative competence (Grisso 2005). Legislators and other policy makers need this information to create laws and policies that are developmentally appropriate and scientifically reasonable. In short, knowledge about adolescents and adolescent development is needed to improve every component of the juvenile justice system.

The US Supreme Court left open the possibility of LWOPs for juveniles convicted of homicide. This raises two problems. First, it is unclear what criteria should be used to differentiate adolescents who warrant this sentence from those who do not. The majority of juvenile offenders do not become adult offenders, but social scientists are not infallible at predicting which juvenile offenders will become adult criminals (Piquero, Jennings, and Barnes 2012). Only a small proportion of juvenile offenders persist into adulthood, but it is very difficult to predict who they are, even with more, and better, information than any court will ever have (see Laub and Sampson 2003; Mulvey et al. 2010).

Factors that have nothing to do with risks of future violence may unconsciously influence sentencing decisions. Because race is likely to continue to be one of these, concern remains that LWOPs will disproportionately be imposed on black and Latino youths. There is some evidence that subjective perceptions by officials of youthful immaturity vary as a function of the race of the young person, with black adolescents being perceived as more mature and therefore more responsible for their criminal behavior (Graham and Lowery 2004). More work in this area, especially in the policing and prosecutorial decision-making context, is needed.

States are grappling with implications of *Miller* in at least two respects.[27] First, if not LWOP, then what? Life sentences with the possibility of parole remain available, but individuals convicted of first-degree or capital murder are seldom granted parole. Very long sentences for juveniles without possibility of parole will function much like life sentences. The California Supreme Court, for example, recently held a sentence of 110 years on a juvenile unconstitutional because his eligibility for parole would fall outside his natural life expectancy. But what about less draconian measures? For a 16-year-old, a 50-year sentence, well within his life expectancy, might as well be a life sentence.

A second concern involves retroactivity: Are individuals sentenced to LWOPs as juveniles before *Miller* was decided entitled to resentencing? States disagree. Moreover, it is not clear what an appropriate revised sentence is or the criteria to be used to determine it. Should the focus be the circumstances of the original offense, the behavior of the inmate during his incarceration, the likelihood of rehabilitation, or some combination of the three? And within each of these categories, what factors are relevant? Recently, and in part motivated by prison overcrowding, California Governor Jerry Brown signed into law a bill that provides for review of sentences of juveniles who were convicted as adults and served at least 15 years of their original sentence. This provision will apply retroactively. The review is to take into account the age of the offender at the time of the crime and his or her prospects for rehabilitation.

Two states have applied the logic of *Miller* to discretionary juvenile LWOPs concerning which the youth's age was not fully considered

[27] States are divided on whether *Miller* has retroactive application and on criteria to use in resentencing affected prisoners. They are also grappling with whether *Graham* applies to specific term-of-year sentences, even if very lengthy (see Liles and Moak 2015). Moriearty (2015) addresses retroactivity by considering whether *Miller* articulates a "substantive" rule of constitutional law, in which case it would be retroactive, or is "procedural," in which case it would not. She argues that *Miller* creates a substantive side and should be applied retroactively. The Court was going to consider the question in 2015 (*Toca v. Louisiana*), but a negotiated agreement was reached between Toca and the district attorney. In March 2015, however, the US Supreme Court granted review in *Montgomery v. Louisiana* (USSC No. 14-280, cert. granted March 23, 2015) to address the question of whether *Miller* applies retroactively to individuals serving mandatory juvenile LWOP sentences (Juvenile Law Center 2015).

(South Carolina Supreme Court: *Aiken v. Byars*, 765 S.E.2d 572 [S.C. 2014]; Ohio Supreme Court: *State v. Long*, 8 N.E.3d 890 [Ohio 2014]). *Aiken* held that *Miller* refers retroactively to all individuals serving LWOPs for crimes committed as juveniles and provides for review of cases in which a juvenile's youthful attributes were not considered during sentencing.

Third, the juvenile justice system more than the adult system is likely to offer intensive risk reduction programs and ranges of educational and other services that respond to the developmental needs of adolescents (Bishop and Frazier 2000; Scott and Steinberg 2008; Mulvey and Schubert 2012). Such efforts should be fully funded and supported by policy officials. Several evidence-based programs exist for juvenile offenders (Washington State Institute for Public Policy 2007; Greenwood 2008), and the Office of Juvenile Justice and Delinquency Prevention identifies effective strategies for adolescent offenders on its Model Programs Guide website (http://www.ojjdp.gov/MPG).

Guidelines for correctional interventions among high-risk youths have been outlined and are summarized by Skeem, Scott, and Mulvey (2014, p. 733) to include the following:

1. interventions should be structured to respond to the developmental needs of adolescents;
2. programs should target risk factors for recidivism in individual youths;
3. correctional interventions should be in the community (unless the juvenile poses serious threats): it is important and easier to involve families in community-based treatment, and it is better to equip youths with tools to deal with criminogenic influences in their community (National Research Council 2013);
4. developmentally responsive risk reduction programs should be an integral part of facility-based dispositions; and
5. evidence-based programming should continue during reentry into the community.

In short, and unlike much twentieth-century juvenile offender programming, there should be consideration of the malleable aspects of psychosocial functioning in a developmentally informed manner. Programs need to be modeled after the lessons learned from developmental science in order to intervene most effectively and as early in the life course as possible (e.g., Piquero et al. 2009). At the same time, there needs to be resistance to any use of such information "on an individual basis for legal purposes" (Bonnie and Scott 2013, p. 158). We anticipate continued research into the areas noted above as well as deeper penetration of this knowledge base into both public discourse and policy-making efforts and decisions surrounding adolescent offenders.

REFERENCES

Agnew, R. 1997. "Stability and Change in Crime over the Life Course: A Strain Theory Explanation." In *Developmental Theories of Crime and Delinquency*, edited by T. P. Thornberry. Vol. 7 of *Advances in Criminological Theory*. New Brunswick, NJ: Transaction.

Applegate, Brian K., R. K. Davis, and Frank T. Cullen. 2009. "Reconsidering Child Saving: The Extent and Correlates of Public Support for Excluding Youths from the Juvenile Court." *Crime and Delinquency* 55:51–77.

Arnett, J. J. 2000. "Emerging Adulthood: A Theory of Development from the Late Teens through the Twenties." *American Psychologist* 55:469–80.

Aspinwall, L. G., T. R. Brown, and J. Tabery. 2012. "The Double-Edged Sword: Does Biomechanism Increase or Decrease Judges' Sentencing of Psychopaths?" *Science* 337:846–49.

Bechtold, J., K. C. Monahan, S. Wakefield, and E. Cauffman. Forthcoming. "The Deep End of the System: Racial Disparity in Response to Juvenile Probation Violations." *Psychology, Public Policy, and Law*.

Bernburg, J. G., and M. D. Krohn. 2003. "Labeling, Life Chances, and Adult Crime: The Direct and Indirect Effects of Official Intervention in Adolescence on Crime in Early Adulthood." *Criminology* 41:1287–1318.

Bernburg, J. G., M. D. Krohn, and C. J. Rivera. 2006. "Official Labeling, Criminal Embeddedness, and Subsequent Delinquency: A Longitudinal Test of Labeling Theory." *Journal of Research in Crime and Delinquency* 43:67–88.

Bishop, D. M., and C. E. Frazier. 2000. "Consequences of Transfer." In *The Changing Borders of Juvenile Justice: Transfer of Adolescents to the Criminal Court*, edited by Jeffrey Fagan and Franklin Zimring. Chicago: University of Chicago Press.

Bonnie, R. J. 1992. "The Competence of Criminal Defendants: A Theoretical Reformulation." *Behavioral Sciences and the Law* 10:291–316.

———. 1993. "The Competence of Criminal Defendants: Beyond *Dusky* and *Drope*." *University of Miami Law Review* 47:539–601.

Bonnie, R. J., and E. S. Scott. 2013. "The Teenage Brain: Adolescent Brain Research and the Law." *Current Directions in Psychological Science* 22:158–61.

Brenhouse, H. C., K. C. Sonntag, and S. L. Andersen. 2008. "Transient D1 Dopamine Receptor Expression on Prefrontal Cortex Projection Neurons: Relationship to Enhanced Motivational Salience of Drug Cues in Adolescence." *Journal of Neuroscience* 28(10):2375–82.

Bridges, G. S., and S. Steen. 1998. "Racial Disparities in Official Assessments of Juvenile Offenders: Attributional Stereotypes as Mediating Mechanisms." *American Sociological Review* 63:554–70.

Casey, B. J. 2015. "Beyond Simple Models of Self-Control to Circuit-Based Accounts of Adolescent Behavior." *Annual Review of Psychology* 66:295–315.

Casey, B. J., S. Getz, and A. Galvan. 2008. "The Adolescent Brain." *Developmental Review* 28:62–77.

Cauffman, E., E. P. Schulman, L. Steinberg, E. Claus, M. T. Banich, S. Graham, and J. Woolard. 2010. "Age Differences in Affective Decision Making as Indexed by Performance on the Iowa Gambling Task." *Developmental Psychology* 46:193–207.

Cauffman, E., and L. Steinberg. 2000. "(Im)maturity of Judgment in Adolescence: Why Adolescents May Be Less Culpable than Adults." *Behavioral Sciences and the Law* 18:741–60.

Chein, J., D. Albert, L. O'Brien, K. Uckert, and L. Steinberg. 2011. "Peers Increase Adolescent Risk Taking by Enhancing Activity in the Brain's Reward Circuitry." *Developmental Science* 14:F1–F20.

Cohen, A. O., and B. J. Casey. 2014. "Rewiring Juvenile Justice: The Intersection of Developmental Neuroscience and Legal Policy." *Trends in Cognitive Sciences* 18:63–65.

Crone, E. A., and R. E. Dahl. 2012. "Understanding Adolescence as a Period of Social-Affective Engagement and Goal Flexibility." *Nature Reviews Neuroscience* 13:636–50.

Cullen, F. T., B. A. Vose, C. L. Jonson, and J. D. Unnever. 2007. "Public Support for Early Intervention: Is Child Saving a 'Habit of the Heart'?" *Victims and Offenders* 2:109–24.

Dahl, R. 2001. "Affect Regulation, Brain Development and Behavioral/Emotional Health in Adolescence." *CNS Spectrums* 6:60–72.

De Bellis, M. D., M. S. Keshavan, S. R. Beers, J. Hall, K. Frustaci, A. Masalehdan, and A. M. Boring. 2001. "Sex Differences in Brain Maturation during Childhood and Adolescence." *Cerebral Cortex* 11(6):552–57.

DeWitt, Samuel J., Sina Aslan, and Francesca M. Filbey. 2014. "Adolescent Risk-Taking and Resting State Functional Connectivity." *Psychiatry Research: Neuroimaging* 222:157–64.

Dmitrieva, J., K. C. Monahan, E. Cauffman, and L. Steinberg. 2012. "Arrested Development: The Effects of Incarceration on the Development of Psychosocial Maturity." *Development and Psychopathology* 24:1073–90.

Ernst, M., and J. L. Fudge. 2009. "A Developmental Neurobiological Model of Motivated Behavior: Anatomy, Connectivity and Ontogeny of the Triadic Nodes." *Neuroscience and Biobehavioral Reviews* 33(3):367–82.

Ernst, M., D. S. Pine, and M. Hardin. 2006. "Triadic Model of the Neurobiology of Motivated Behavior in Adolescence." *Psychological Medicine* 36:299–312.

Fagan, Jeffery. 1995. "Separating the Men from the Boys: The Comparative Advantage of Juvenile versus Criminal Court Sanctions on Recidivism among

Adolescent Felony Offenders." In *Serious, Violent, and Chronic Juvenile Offenders*, edited by J. Howell, B. Krisberg, J. D. Hawkins, and J. Wilson. Thousand Oaks, CA: Sage.

———. 2008. "Juvenile Crime and Criminal Justice: Resolving Border Disputes." *Future of Children* 18:81–118.

Fagan, Jeffery, and Franklin Zimring. 2000. *The Changing Borders of Juvenile Justice*. Chicago: University of Chicago Press.

Feld, Barry C. 1993. "The Politics of Race and Juvenile Justice: The 'Due Process Revolution' and the Conservative Reaction." *Justice Quarterly* 20:765–800.

———. 2013. *Kids, Cops, and Confessions: Inside the Interrogation Room*. New York: New York University Press.

Feld, Barry C., and Donna M. Bishop, eds. 2012*a*. *The Oxford Handbook of Juvenile Crime and Juvenile Justice*. New York: Oxford University Press.

———. 2012*b*. "Transfer of Juveniles to Criminal Court." In *The Oxford Handbook of Juvenile Crime and Juvenile Justice*, edited by Barry C. Feld and Donna M. Bishop. New York: Oxford University Press.

Feld, Barry C., B. J. Casey, and Y. L. Hurd. 2013. "Adolescent Competence and Culpability: Implications of Neuroscience for Juvenile Justice Administration." In *A Primer on Criminal Law and Neuroscience*, edited by F. J. Morse and A. J. Roskies. New York: Oxford University Press.

Feld, Barry C., and S. Schaefer. 2010. "The Right to Counsel in Juvenile Court." *Criminology and Public Policy* 9:327–56.

Galvan, A., T. A. Hare, C. E. Parra, J. Penn, H. Voss, G. Glover, and B. J. Casey. 2006. "Earlier Development of the Accumbens Relative to Orbitofrontal Cortex Might Underlie Risk-Taking Behavior in Adolescents." *Journal of Neuroscience* 26:6885–92.

Gardner, M., and L. Steinberg. 2005. "Peer Influence on Risk Taking, Risk Preference, and Risky Decision Making in Adolescence and Adulthood: An Experimental Study." *Developmental Psychology* 41:625–35.

Gatti, U., R. E. Tremblay, and F. Vitaro. 2009. "Iatrogenic Effect of Juvenile Justice." *Journal of Child Psychology and Psychiatry* 50:991–98.

Giedd, J. N. 2004. "Structural Magnetic Resonance Imaging of the Adolescent Brain." *Annals of the New York Academy of Science* 1021:77–85.

Gjedde, A., Y. Kumakura, P. Cumming, J. Linnet, and A. Møller. 2010. "Inverted-U-Shaped Correlation between Dopamine Receptor Availability in Striatum and Sensation Seeking." *Proceedings of the National Academy of Sciences* 107(8):3870–75.

Gottfredson, M. R., and T. Hirschi. 1990. *A General Theory of Crime*. Stanford, CA: Stanford University Press.

Graham, S., and B. S. Lowery. 2004. "Priming Unconscious Racial Stereotypes about Adolescent Offenders." *Law and Human Behavior* 28:483–504.

Greenwood, P. 2008. "Prevention and Intervention Programs for Juvenile Offenders." *Future of Children* 18:185–210.

Grisso, T. 1980. "Juveniles' Capacities to Waive Miranda Rights: An Empirical Analysis." *California Law Review* 68:1134–66.

———. 2002. *Evaluating Competencies: Forensic Assessments and Instruments*. 2nd ed. New York: Kluwer/Plenum.

———. 2005. *Evaluating Juveniles' Adjudicative Competence: A Guide for Clinical Practice*. Sarasota, FL: Professional Resource Press/Professional Resource Exchange.

Grisso, T., L. Steinberg, J. Woolard, E. Cauffman, E. Scott, S. Graham, F. Lexcen, N. Reppucci, and R. Schwartz. 2003. "Juveniles' Competence to Stand Trial: A Comparison of Adolescents' and Adults' Capacities as Trial Defendants." *Law and Human Behavior* 27:333–63.

Huettel, S. A., A. W. Song, and G. McCarthy. 2009. *Functional Magnetic Resonance Imaging*. 2nd ed. Sunderland, MA: Sinauer.

Jordan, K. L. 2014. "Juvenile Transfer and Recidivism: A Propensity Score Matching Approach." *Youth Violence and Juvenile Justice* 12:315–31.

Juvenile Law Center. 2015. "U.S. Supreme Court to Address Question of Miller Retroactivity" (April 2). http://jlc.org/blog/us-supreme-court-address-question-miller-retroactivity.

Kassin, S. M. 2008. "The Psychology of Confessions." *Annual Review of Law and Social Science* 4:193–217.

Kassin, S. M., S. A. Drizin, T. Grisso, G. H. Gudjonsson, R. A. Leo, and A. D. Redlich. 2010. "Police-Induced Confessions: Risk Factors and Recommendations." *Law and Human Behavior* 34:3–38.

Kupchik, A. 2003. "Prosecuting Adolescents in Criminal Court: Criminal or Juvenile Justice?" *Social Problems* 50:439–60.

Lanza-Kaduce, L., J. Lane, Donna M. Bishop, and C. E. Frazier. 2005. "Juvenile Offenders and Adult Felony Recidivism: The Impact of Transfer." *Journal of Crime and Justice* 28:59–77.

Laub, John H., and R. J. Sampson. 2001. "Understanding Desistance from Crime." In *Crime and Justice: A Review of Research*, vol. 28, edited by Michael Tonry. Chicago: University of Chicago Press.

———. 2003. *Shared Beginnings, Divergent Lives: Delinquent Boys to Age 70*. Cambridge, MA: Harvard University Press.

Liles, A., and S. C. Moak. 2015. "Changing Juvenile Justice Policy in Response to the US Supreme Court: Implementing Miller v. Alabama." *Youth Justice* 15:79–62.

Loeber, R., and David P. Farrington, eds. 2012. *From Juvenile Delinquency to Adult Crime: Criminal Careers, Justice Policy, and Prevention*. New York: Oxford University Press.

Lopes, G., M. D. Krohn, A. J. Lizotte, N. Schmidt, B. E. Vasquez, and J. G. Bernburg. 2012. "Labeling and Cumulative Disadvantage: The Impact of Official Intervention on Life Chances and Crime in Emerging Adulthood." *Crime and Delinquency* 58:456–88.

Loughran, T. A., E. P. Mulvey, C. A. Schubert, L. A. Chassin, L. Steinberg, A. R. Piquero, J. Fagan, S. Cota-Robles, E. Cauffman, and S. Losoya. 2010. "Differential Effects of Adult Court Transfer on Juvenile Offender Recidivism." *Law and Human Behavior* 34:476–88.

Loughran, T. A., E. P. Mulvey, C. A. Schubert, Jeffery Fagan, A. R. Piquero, and S. H. Losoya. 2009. "Estimating a Dose-Response Relationship between

Length of Stay and Future Recidivism in Serious Juvenile Offenders." *Criminology* 47:699–740.

Mack, J. W. 1909. "The Juvenile Court." *Harvard Law Review* 23:104–22.

Malloy, L. C., E. P. Shulman, and E. Cauffman. 2014. "Interrogations, Confessions, and Guilty Pleas among Serious Adolescent Offenders." *Law and Human Behavior* 38:181–93.

Maroney, T. A. 2009. "The False Promise of Adolescent Brain Science in Juvenile Justice." *Notre Dame Law Review* 85:89–176.

———. 2011*a*. "Adolescent Brain Science after Graham v. Florida." *Notre Dame Law Review* 86:765–94.

———. 2011*b*. "Persistent Cultural Script of Judicial Dispassion." *California Law Review* 99:629–82.

———. 2014. "The Once and Future Juvenile Brain." In *Choosing the Future for American Juvenile Justice*, edited by Franklin E. Zimring and D. S. Tanenhaus. New York: New York University Press.

McGowen, A., R. Hahn, A. Liberman, A. Crosby, M. Fullilove, R. Johnson, E. Moscicki, L. Price, S. Snyder, F. Tuma, J. Lowy, P. Briss, S. Cory, G. Stone, and Task Force on Community Preventive Science. 2007. "Effects on Violence of Laws and Policies Facilitating the Transfer of Juveniles from the Juvenile Justice System to the Adult Justice System: A Systematic Review." *American Journal of Preventative Medicine* 32(4S):S7–S28.

Mears, D. P., J. C. Cochran, S. J. Greenman, A. S. Bhati, and M. A. Greenwald. 2011. "Evidence on the Effectiveness of Juvenile Court Sanctions." *Journal of Criminal Justice* 39:509–20.

Mears, D. P., J. C. Cochran, B. J. Stults, S. J. Greenman, A. S. Bhati, and M. A. Greenwald. 2014. "The 'True' Juvenile Offender: Age Effects and Juvenile Court Sanctioning." *Criminology* 52:169–94.

Monahan, K. C., A. Guyer, J. Silk, T. Fitzwater, and L. Steinberg. Forthcoming. "Integration of Developmental Neuroscience and Contextual Approaches to the Study of Adolescent Psychopathology." *Developmental Psychopathology*.

Monahan, K. C., L. Steinberg, and E. Cauffman. 2009. "Affiliation with Antisocial Peers, Susceptibility to Peer Influence, and Desistance from Antisocial Behavior during the Transition to Adulthood." *Developmental Psychology* 45:1520–30.

Monahan, K. C., L. Steinberg, E. Cauffman, and E. Mulvey. 2013. "Psychosocial (Im)maturity from Adolescence to Early Adulthood: Distinguishing between Adolescence-Limited and Persisting Antisocial Behavior." *Development and Psychopathology* 25:1093–1105.

Moriearty, P. L. 2015. "*Miller v. Alabama* and the Retroactivity of Proportionality Rules." *University of Pennsylvania Law Review* 17:929–90.

Morris, R. G., and A. R. Piquero. 2013. "For Whom Do Sanctions Deter and Label?" *Justice Quarterly* 30:837–68.

Morse, S. J. 2006. "Brain Overclaim Syndrome and Criminal Responsibility: A Diagnostic Note." *Ohio State Journal of Criminal Law* 3:397–412.

———. 2012. "Brain Overclaim Redux." *Law and Inequality* 31:509–34.

Mulvey, E. P. 2014. "Using Developmental Science to Reorient Our Thinking about Criminal Offending in Adolescence." *Journal of Research in Crime and Delinquency* 51:467–79.

Mulvey, E. P., and C. A. Schubert. 2012. "Some Initial Policy Implications from the Pathways to Desistance Study." *Victims and Offenders* 7(4):407–27.

Mulvey, E. P., L. Steinberg, J. Fagan, E. Cauffman, A. R. Piquero, L. Chassin, and S. H. Losoya. 2004. "Theory and Research on Desistance from Antisocial Activity among Serious Adolescent Offenders." *Youth Violence and Juvenile Justice* 2:213–36.

Mulvey, E. P., L. Steinberg, A. R. Piquero, M. Besana, J. Fagan, C. Shubert, and E. Cauffman. 2010. "Trajectories of Desistance and Continuity in Antisocial Behavior Following Court Adjudication among Serious Adolescent Offenders." *Development and Psychopathology* 22:453–75.

Murray, J., A. Blokland, D. P. Farrington, and D. Theobald. 2014. "Long-Term Effects of Conviction and Incarceration on Men in the Cambridge Study in Delinquent Development." In *Labeling Theory: Empirical Tests*, edited by D. P. Farrington and J. Murray. Vol. 18 of *Advances in Criminological Theory*. New Brunswick, NJ: Transaction.

Myers, D. L. 2003. "The Recidivism of Violent Youths in Juvenile and Adult Court: A Consideration of Selection Bias." *Youth Violence and Juvenile Justice* 1:79–101.

Nagin, Daniel S. 2013. "Deterrence in the Twenty-First Century." In *Crime and Justice in America, 1975–2015*, edited by Michael Tonry. Vol. 42 of *Crime and Justice: A Review of Research*, edited by Michael Tonry. Chicago: University of Chicago Press.

Nagin, Daniel S., Frank T. Cullen, and C. L. Jonson. 2009. "Imprisonment and Reoffending." In *Crime and Justice: A Review of Research*, vol. 38, edited by Michael Tonry. Chicago: University of Chicago Press.

Nagin, Daniel S., A. R. Piquero, E. S. Scott, and L. Steinberg. 2006. "Public Preferences for Rehabilitation versus Incarceration for Juvenile Offenders: Evidence from a Contingent Valuation Survey." *Criminology and Public Policy* 5(4):627–51.

National Research Council. 2011. *The Science of Adolescent Risk-Taking: Workshop Report*. Washington, DC: National Academies Press.

———. 2013. *Reforming Juvenile Justice: A Developmental Approach*. Committee on Assessing Juvenile Justice Reform, Committee on Law and Justice, Division of Behavioral and Social Sciences and Education. Washington, DC: National Academies Press.

———. 2014. *Implementing Juvenile Justice Reform: The Federal Role*. Committee on a Prioritized Plan to Implement a Developmental Approach in Juvenile Justice Reform, Committee on Law and Justice, Division of Behavioral and Social Sciences and Education. Washington, DC: National Academies Press.

Nelson, E. E., E. Leibenluft, E. McClure, and D. S. Pine. 2005. "The Social Reorientation of Adolescence: A Neuroscience Perspective on the Process and Its Relation to Psychopathology." *Psychological Medicine* 35:163–74.

Norbury, A., S. Manohar, R. D. Rogers, and M. Husain. 2013. "Dopamine Modulates Risk-Taking as a Function of Baseline Sensation-Seeking Trait." *Journal of Neuroscience* 33:12982–86.

Ordaz, S. J., W. Foran, K. Velenova, and B. Luna. 2013. "Longitudinal Growth Curves of Brain Function Underlying Inhibitory Control through Adolescence." *Journal of Neuroscience* 33:18109–24.

Petit, G., C. Kornreich, P. Verbanck, A. Cimochowska, and S. Campanella. 2013. "Why Is Adolescence a Key Period of Alcohol Initiation and Who Is Prone to Develop Long-Term Problem Use? A Review of Current Available Data." *Socioaffective Neuroscience and Psychology* 3:21890.

Petitclerc, A., U. Gatti, F. Vitaro, and R. E. Tremblay. 2013. "Effects of Juvenile Court Exposure on Crime in Young Adulthood." *Journal of Child Psychology and Psychiatry* 54:291–97.

Petrosino, A., C. Turpin-Petrosino, and S. Guckenburg. 2010. "Formal System Processing of Juveniles: Effects on Delinquency." *Campbell Systematic Reviews* 1:88.

Pfeifer, J. H., and N. B. Allen. 2012. "Arrested Development? Reconsidering Dual-Systems Models of Brain Function in Adolescence and Divisions." *Trends in Cognitive Science* 15:322–29.

Piquero, A. R. 2008. "Disproportionate Minority Contact." *Future of Children* 18:59–79.

———. 2013. "Youth Matters: The Meaning of Miller for Theory, Research, and Policy Regarding Developmental/Life-Course Criminology." *New England Journal on Criminal and Civil Confinement* 39:347–61.

Piquero, A. R., and A. Blumstein. 2007. "Does Incapacitation Reduce Crime?" *Journal of Quantitative Criminology* 23:267–85.

Piquero, Alex R., Frank T. Cullen, James D. Uneever, N. L. Piquero, and J. A. Gordon. 2010. "Never Too Late: Public Optimism about Juvenile Rehabilitation." *Punishment and Society* 12:187–207.

Piquero, Alex R., David P. Farrington, and A. Blumstein. 2003. "The Criminal Career Paradigm: Background and Recent Developments." In *Crime and Justice: A Review of Research*, vol. 30, edited by Michael Tonry. Chicago: University of Chicago Press.

———. 2007. *Key Issues in Criminal Career Research: New Analyses of the Cambridge Study in Delinquent Development*. Cambridge: Cambridge University Press.

Piquero, Alex R., David P. Farrington, Brian C. Welsh, R. Tremblay, and W. Jennings. 2009. "Effects of Early Family/Parent Training Programs on Antisocial Behavior and Delinquency." *Journal of Experimental Criminology* 5 (2):83–120.

Piquero, Alex R., W. G. Jennings, and J. C. Barnes. 2012. "Violence in Criminal Careers: A Review of the Literature from a Developmental Life-Course Perspective." *Aggression and Violent Behavior* 17:171–79.

Piquero, Alex R., and L. Steinberg. 2010. "Public Preferences for Rehabilitation versus Incarceration of Juvenile Offenders." *Journal of Criminal Justice* 38:1–6.

Redding, R. E. 2008. "Juvenile Transfer Laws: An Effective Deterrent to Delinquency?" Juvenile Justice Bulletin 2. Washington, DC: Office of Juvenile Justice and Delinquency Prevention.

Redding, R. E., and L. E. Frost. 2002. "Adjudicative Competence in the Modern Juvenile Court." *Virginia Journal of Social Policy and the Law* 9:353–410.

Reiss, Albert J., Jr., and David P. Farrington. 1991. "Advancing Knowledge about Co-offending: Results from a Prospective Longitudinal Survey of London Males." *Journal of Criminal Law and Criminology* 82:360–95.

Schneider, A. L. 1990. *Deterrence and Juvenile Crime: Results from a National Policy Experiment*. New York: Springer.

Scott, E. S. 2013*a*. "Children Are Different: Constitutional Values and Justice Policy." *Ohio State Journal of Criminal Law* 11:71–105.

———. 2013*b*. "Miller v. Alabama and the (Past and) Future of Juvenile Crime Policy." *Minnesota Journal of Law and Inequality* 31:535–58.

Scott, E. S., and T. Grisso. 1997. "The Evolution of Adolescence: A Developmental Perspective on Juvenile Justice Reform." *Journal of Criminal Law and Criminology* 137:154–67.

———. 2004. "Developmental Incompetence, Due Process, and Juvenile Justice Policy." *North Carolina Law Review* 83:793–845.

Scott, E. S., N. Reppucci, N. Dickon, and J. L. Woolard. 1995. "Evaluating Adolescent Decision Making in Legal Contexts." *Law and Human Behavior* 19:221–44.

Scott, E. S., and L. D. Steinberg. 2008. *Rethinking Juvenile Justice*. Cambridge, MA: Harvard University Press.

Skeem, J. L., E. Scott, and E. P. Mulvey. 2014. "Justice Policy Reform for High-Risk Youth: Using Science to Achieve Large-Scale Crime Reduction." *Annual Review of Clinical Psychology* 10:709–39.

Smith, A. B., R. Halari, V. Giampetro, M. Brammer, and K. Rubia. 2011. "Developmental Effects of Reward on Sustained Attention Networks." *Neuroimage* 56:1693–1704.

Smith, D. A., and R. Paternoster. 1990. "Formal Processing and Future Delinquency: Deviance Amplification as Selection Artifact." *Law and Society Review* 24:1109–32.

Sowell, E. R., D. A. Trauner, A. Gamst, and T. L. Jernigan. 2002. "Development of Cortical and Subcortical Brain Structures in Childhood and Adolescence: A Structural MRI Study." *Developmental Medicine and Child Neurology* 44(1):4–16.

Spear, L. P. 2010. *The Behavioral Neuroscience of Adolescence*. New York: Norton.

Steinberg, L. 2007. "Risk Taking in Adolescence: New Perspectives from Brain and Behavioral Science." *Current Directions in Psychological Science* 16:55–59.

———. 2008. "A Social Neuroscience Perspective on Adolescent Risk Taking." *Developmental Review* 28:78–106.

———. 2009. "Adolescent Development and Juvenile Justice." *Annual Review of Clinical Psychology* 5:459–85.

———. 2010. "A Dual Systems Model of Adolescent Risk-Taking." *Developmental Psychobiology* 52:216–24.

———. 2012. "Should the Science of Adolescent Brain Development Inform Public Policy?" *Issues in Science and Technology* 28(Spring):67–78.

———. 2013. "The Influence of Neuroscience on US Supreme Court Decisions about Adolescents' Criminal Culpability." *Nature Reviews: Neuroscience* 14:513–18.

———. 2014. *Age of Opportunity: Lessons from the New Science of Adolescence*. New York: Houghton Mifflin Harcourt.

Steinberg, L., and E. Cauffman. 1999. "A Developmental Perspective on Serious Juvenile Crime: When Should Juveniles Be Treated as Adults?" *Federal Probation* 63:52–57.

Steinberg, L., E. Cauffman, J. Woolard, S. Graham, and M. Banich. 2009. "Are Adolescents Less Mature than Adults? Minors' Access to Abortion, the Juvenile Death Penalty, and the Alleged APA 'Flip Flop.'" *American Psychologist* 64:583–94.

Steinberg, L., S. Graham, L. O'Brien, J. Woolard, E. Cauffman, and M. Banich. 2009. "Age Differences in Future Orientation and Delay Discounting." *Child Development* 80:28–44.

Steinberg, L., and K. C. Monahan. 2007. "Age Differences in Resistance to Peer Influence." *Developmental Psychology* 43:1531–43.

Steinberg, L., and R. G. Schwartz. 2000. "Developmental Psychology Goes to Court." In *Youth on Trial*, edited by Thomas Grisso and Robert G. Schwartz. Chicago: University of Chicago Press.

Steinberg, L., and E. Scott. 2003. "Less Guilty by Reason of Adolescence: Developmental Immaturity, Diminished Responsibility, and the Juvenile Death Penalty." *American Psychologist* 58:1009–18.

Sweeten, G., and R. Apel. 2007. "Incapacitation: Revisiting an Old Question with a New Method and New Data." *Journal of Quantitative Criminology* 23:303–26.

Sweeten, G., A. R. Piquero, and L. Steinberg. 2013. "Age and the Explanation of Crime, Revisited." *Journal of Youth and Adolescence* 42:921–38.

Tanenhaus, D. S. 2005. *Juvenile Justice in the Making*. New York: Oxford University Press.

———. 2012. "The Elusive Juvenile Court: Its Origins, Practices, and Reinventions." In *The Oxford Handbook of Juvenile Crime and Juvenile Justice*, edited by Barry C. Feld and Donna M. Bishop. New York: Oxford University Press.

US Supreme Court. 2004. Transcript of oral argument in *Roper v Simmons*, No. 03-633, October 13. http://www.supremecourt.gov/oral_arguments/argument_transcripts/03-633.pdf.

Van Leijenhorst, L., K. Zanolie, C. S. Van Meel, P. M. Westenberg, S. A. R. B. Rombouts, and E. A. Crone. 2010. "What Motivates the Adolescent? Brain Regions Mediating Reward Sensitivity across Adolescence." *Cerebral Cortex* 20:61–69.

Ward, J., M. D. Krohn, and C. L. Gibson. 2014. "The Effects of Police Contact on Developmental Trajectories of Violence: A Group-Based, Propensity Score Matching Analysis." *Journal of Interpersonal Violence* 29:440–75.

Washington State Institute for Public Policy. 2007. *Evidence-Based Juvenile Offender Programs: Program Description, Quality Assurance, and Cost*. Olympia: Washington State Institute for Public Policy.

Wermink, H., R. Apel, P. Nieuwbeerta, and A. A. J. Blokland. 2013. "The Incapacitation Effect of First-Time Imprisonment: A Matched Samples Comparison." *Journal of Quantitative Criminology* 29:579–600.

Winner, L., L. Lanza-Kaduce, D. M. Bishop, and C. E. Frazier. 1997. "The Transfer of Juveniles to Criminal Court: Re-examining Recidivism over the Long Term." *Crime and Delinquency* 43:548–63.

Woolard, J. L., H. M. Cleary, S. A. Harvell, and R. Chen. 2008. "Examining Adolescents' and Their Parents' Conceptual and Practical Knowledge of Police Interrogation: A Family Dyad Approach." *Journal of Youth and Adolescence* 37(6):685–98.

Woolard, J. L., C. S. Fried, and N. D. Reppucci. 2013. "Toward an Expanded Definition of Adolescent Competence in Legal Contexts." In *Psychology in the Courts: International Advances in Knowledge*, edited by R. Roesch, R. Corrado, and R. Dempster. London: Routledge.

Zimring, Franklin E. 1998. *American Youth Violence*. New York: Oxford University Press.

Zimring, Franklin E., and H. Laqueur. 2015. "Kids, Groups, and Crime: In Defense of Conventional Wisdom." *Journal of Research in Crime and Delinquency* 52:403–13.

Zimring, Franklin E., and S. Rushin. 2013. "Did Changes in Juvenile Sanctions Reduce Juvenile Crime Rates? A Natural Experiment." *Ohio State Journal of Criminal Law* 11:57–69.